A History and Criticism

of

American Public Address

VOLUME I

A History and Criticism

of

American Public Address

PREPARED UNDER THE AUSPICES OF

The Speech Association of America

VOLUME I

WILLIAM NORWOOD BRIGANCE

Editor

New York

RUSSELL & RUSSELL

Editorial Board

v

Preface

This work deals with the influence of American public address on the flow of history.

Not only is history written with words. It is made with words. Most of the mighty movements affecting the destiny of the American nation have gathered strength in obscure places from the talk of nameless men, and gained final momentum from leaders who could state in common words the needs and hopes of common people. Great movements, in fact, are usually led by men of action who are also men of words, who use words as instruments of power, who voice their aims in words of historic simplicity:

> *. . . that government of the people, by the people, and for the people, shall not perish from the earth.*
> *. . . to make the world safe for democracy.*
> *I have nothing to offer but blood, toil, tears, and sweat.*

Literature in times of crisis becomes the words of men of action, of men who understand the power of words as weapons of warfare. The poets come afterwards. We are here concerned with men who have used words to direct the course of American history.

The preparation of these volumes was begun early in 1934. It was made possible by Henry L. Ewbank, then president of the National Association of Teachers of Speech, who appointed an editorial board and charged it with the responsibility of preparation and publication. He was not to escape so easily, however, for after his presidential term had ended he was drafted by the editorial board for active service.

The fact that more than nine years have been consumed in preparation is not to be taken as a sign of lassitude on the part of editors or authors. It is rather an index of the attempt at thoroughness in both planning and writing, for in both there have been difficulties.

To begin with, no adequate history of public address in America has yet been written, and the general national histories have given no systematic account of its influence. This we have attempted to do in the historical chapters; but the amount of research required was vast, and the space that could be devoted to these chapters was less than we desired.

Likewise, in these historical chapters, the pattern of approach was vexing. None of the preliminary patterns proved suitable; so as their weaknesses became apparent, each was in turn discarded, and a new pattern was evolved to fit each historical period. For that reason every such chapter presents a difference in pattern of approach. The process was laborious, but the results justified the labor.

The emergence of women on the American platform was so distinctive a phase of history that it seemed best to give it fitting emphasis in a separate chapter. Likewise, the teaching of rhetoric in American colleges, which was highly significant throughout the classical period of higher education, could not properly be divided into Colonial, early national, and later national periods; so it, too, was given separate treatment.

The standard of literary criticism also had to be determined. Historically, the distinction between the criticism of poetry and public address has often been confused, poetry at times being defended by giving it the practical usefulness of public address, and public address at times being viewed by the absolute standard of a timeless world, with critics trying to measure it in terms of permanence and aesthetic excellence. Neither of these standards has been accepted in this work. That public address may have permanence and aesthetic excellence is not denied, nor is it ignored; but final judgment is here based on effect instead of beauty, on influence instead of appeal to the imagination.

For this reason it was not easy to determine which speakers, among the many influential ones in American history, should be selected for special study. To include only the traditional names, those commonly listed in the histories of "oratory," would have been to continue the confusion between those who spoke "eloquently" and those who spoke effectively, for not always did the same persons do both. Conversely, to designate a group of speakers as *the* most influential in American history would call for a degree of presumption that we ought not to exhibit and would undertake to fix historical values in a world wherein values ought frequently to be reassessed. Consequently we have not attempted to offer a definitive list of *the* most influential speakers but have chosen twenty-eight men of high competence in public address, drawn in part from certain professions in which leadership and public address are inherently related and in part from historical movements that have produced spokesmen as their leaders.

Nevertheless, we have not chosen these names without careful consideration. In making the selection, we consulted the following historians who had demonstrated an understanding of public address as a force in American life; who, taken together, were authorities on the various movements in American history; and who also, as a group, had had long and continued access to the major historical research centers in all parts of the nation: E. C. Barker, University of Texas; Harry J. Carman, Columbia

University; E. Merton Coulter, University of Georgia; William E. Dodd, University of Chicago; Theodore G. Gronert, Wabash College; John D. Hicks, University of Wisconsin; Allan Nevins, Columbia University; Roy F. Nichols, University of Pennsylvania; Frederic L. Paxson, University of California; Theodore C. Pease, University of Illinois; Charles W. Ramsdell, University of Texas; W. T. Root, State University of Iowa; and A. M. Schlesinger, Harvard University. To them we designated certain fields of American thought: statecraft, religion, reform, law, education, etc., without insisting that these fields all be included and without excluding other fields that might be deemed important. We further consulted the following authorities in religious history: Bishop G. Bromley Oxnam, formerly professor of homiletics in Boston University; and W. W. Sweet, professor of religious history in the University of Chicago. Finally we consulted the following authorities on legal biography: William Draper Lewis, American Law Institute; Francis S. Philbrick, University of Pennsylvania; James G. Rogers, Yale University; and John H. Wigmore, Northwestern University. Our consultation with these men was prolonged and thorough. To them we are indebted for their judgment, but we do not hold them responsible for our final decisions.

We recognize that objections can be raised both against speakers who are included and against the omission of others who might have been included. It might be asked, for example, if fields like religion and law are included, why not also include business, finance, and perhaps scientific thought? It is likewise obvious that our standard of choosing lawyers on the basis of their influence on the course of history almost automatically excluded such brilliant pleaders as Seargent S. Prentiss, David Paul Brown, and Charles O'Conor in favor of practitioners before the United States Supreme Court.

We are also aware that the four spokesmen in religion are Protestant churchmen of a certain austerity, that no Catholic spokesman is represented, that Brigham Young—leader of one of the greatest treks of modern times—and Dwight L. Moody, the great evangelist, are not included. We confess to have excluded George Whitefield on the arbitrary ground that he was an Englishman, not an American.

Finally, we recognize that the spokesmen of some political movements have been omitted. It might be asked if Patrick Henry is included as the spokesman for American independence, why not Alexander Hamilton as spokesman for Constitutional union? If John C. Calhoun represents nullification, why not L. Q. C. Lamar, the Confederacy? If Henry Clay represents compromise and the American system, why not Thomas Hart Benton, expansion and manifest destiny?

Preface

These are representative questions that have been considered. But a work of this size is necessarily limited, and limitations require severity of selection and balance. We have plowed here only the opening furrows. A great part of the field is left for those who follow.

In making the selections, we have considered the various areas—such as statecraft, law, and education—in which public address has influenced thought; and we have attempted to maintain a reasonable balance among them. This resulted in our giving greater weight perhaps to these areas, as such, than we wanted. It was obviously impossible to consider Theodore Parker, a religious leader, alongside Thomas Corwin, a political leader; nor could we consider Edwin A. Alderman, an educator, beside Seargent S. Prentiss, a lawyer. In the end we had to weigh Parker with other religious leaders and to inquire whether Alderman's influence in rebuilding higher education in the South after the Civil War entitled him to be a representative spokesman in education.

In spite of this, however, we do not imply that these areas of thought are to be taken as positive and separate units or that a speaker who is listed under one of them might not also belong to another. Webster too obviously belongs to the law as well as to statecraft, Beecher's influence was in statecraft and reform as well as in religion, and Booker T. Washington could almost as fittingly be assigned to education as to reform. Nevertheless, the consideration of these areas helped to guide us in the final selection.

In the critical studies, as in the historical studies, the reader will find a wide diversity in patterns of treatment. To those who would prefer that one standardized pattern of rhetorical criticism be followed, we answer that it would have been neither possible nor, in our opinion, desirable. It would not have been possible because the best scholars are not all adherents of the same philosophy of criticism. Some prefer the pure Aristotelian pattern. Some prefer their Aristotelianism diluted. Others abjure it altogether. Among such vigorous dissenters no collation would have been possible.

Nor do we think it would have been desirable. Uniformity in so large a number of studies would inevitably have led to sterility. The speakers to be appraised lived in different periods and labored in different fields, moved against different backgrounds of history, aimed at different goals, and were influenced by different currents. "Monism is the natural disease of philosophers, who hunger and thirst not (as they think) for truth, but for unity. . . . The formula may become a sort of number-worship." Monism, at least, will not be found in these volumes. The student of critical techniques will find as much interest perhaps, and possibly as much value, in the variety of techniques here used as in the subjects to which they are applied.

It may not be out of place for the editor to add a word here on the valuable aid given by members of the Editorial Board. To them fell the heavy task of reading the manuscripts, of recommending revisions, of helping to bring the various chapters, written by authors living far apart, into a single focus. Normally, five members of the board read each chapter during its various stages of development. Their work was heavy, so heavy, in fact, that some who originally had planned to write chapters were forced to give up the writing in order to meet their editorial obligations. Their influence is important, although their names do not appear at the beginning of chapters.

As for the authors, the individual chapters speak for themselves; but it ought to be added that when forty-one authors work on thirty-four fronts, coordination is not easy. For liaison they had to depend on the Editorial Board, and the work was thus made harder than if each had been engaged in an individual enterprise.

WILLIAM NORWOOD BRIGANCE.

WABASH COLLEGE,
June, 1943.

Acknowledgments

The Editorial Board is indebted to the following men for assistance in editorial details: Bower Aly, University of Missouri; Theodore S. Cox, College of William and Mary; Orville A. Hitchcock, University of Akron; Ray K. Immel, University of Southern California; James H. McBurney, Northwestern University; Edwin W. Schoenberger, Lawrence College; and Andrew T. Weaver, University of Wisconsin.

Contents

I. THE HISTORICAL BACKGROUND OF AMERICAN PUBLIC ADDRESS

II. LEADERS IN AMERICAN PUBLIC ADDRESS

IN RELIGION

Contents

Contents

I

The Historical Background of American Public Address

1

The Colonial Period

by GEORGE V. BOHMAN

Background for Speaking

The Colonial period in American history, from the first settlements along the Atlantic seaboard to the formation of the present Constitution in 1787, is chiefly significant today for the story of the development and adaptation of Old World society, primarily that of the British Isles, to the special requirements of the New World. What institutions and customs were transferred with slight change to the American frontier communities? What new or greatly modified customs arose in the new environment? This theme affords a fertile field for investigation when it is applied to Colonial public address, or public speaking, because nearly every colonist directly participated in the activities of public speaking, as either speaker or audience member, and because this means of social communication and expression was more readily available throughout this period, or at least until the years of the Revolution, than the various written means of communication.

Books and pamphlets making up small, but intensely read, private libraries arrived with the first settlers, and importations from England continued to be even greater than apparent monetary surpluses might have justified, but Colonial printing did not begin in Massachusetts until 1639 and began only in Virginia, Pennsylvania, Maryland, and New York before the end of the seventeenth century. About a thousand publications comprised the total output of the presses before 1700, the bulk of which consisted of religious treatises, sermons, and official documents such as proclamations, laws, and governors' speeches. Because of limited resources and generally careful official supervision of the presses, no newspapers and very few controversial nonreligious books and pamphlets were published in seventeenth century America. In contrast to the limited opportunities for written expression in the colonies during this period, public speaking at religious, legislative, academic, and popular meetings was plentiful. Speaking occasions afforded much of the public entertainment, major facilities for exchanging information, and almost the only opportunities, aside from

3

private conversation, for the discussion of current problems and the control of public opinion.[1]

In the eighteenth century, printed sources of information became increasingly plentiful. From 1709 to 1763 printing presses were established in Connecticut (1709), New Jersey (1723), Rhode Island (1727), South Carolina (1731), North Carolina (1749), New Hampshire (1756), Delaware (1761), and Georgia (1763). Censorship and strict supervision of the press gave way to limited freedom. The first Colonial newspapers published little more than documents, colorless bits of news that were as often foreign as colonial, and simple advertisements. There were no editorials, no letters to the editors, no reporters' comments, although a few political advertisements soon began to appear, to be followed slowly by mild criticisms of the government. Attempts to control such criticisms in the *New England Courant* failed, as did the prosecution of John Peter Zenger in New York a decade later. Interpretations of libel continued to vary from case to case. However, licensing clauses finally disappeared from royal instructions to colonial governors, and the press became more and more powerful as a means of influencing public opinion.[2]

Although the legal basis for freedom of the press was not yet clear, the quantity of printing continued to increase rapidly. In 1763 the number of newspapers was 21, and on the eve of the Revolution in 1775 there were 42 newspapers, of which 15 were in New England, 13 in the Middle colonies, and 14 in the Southern colonies. Circulation averaged no more than 300 copies for the weeklies, although the *Boston Gazette* claimed a circulation of 2,000 and the *New York Gazetteer*, 3,600 copies.[3] In addition to newspapers and imported books, eight or nine thousand books, pamphlets, and broadsides were published in the colonies between 1700 and 1760 and another ten or twelve thousand items from 1760 to 1787. The effect of this greater mass of available printed matter and its wide circulation among the colonists was to decrease the relative importance of public address as a source of general information and news and to set up a strong medium to compete with public address for the control of public opinion and for entertainment.[4] After 1760 this rivalry was intensified on the one hand by the development of the controversial pamphlet and newspaper article, and

[1] Thomas G. Wright, *Literary Culture in Early New England*, 1620–1730 (New Haven, 1920).

[2] C. A. Duniway, *The Development of Freedom of the Press in Massachusetts* (Harvard Historical Studies, 12, New York, 1906).

[3] Philip Davidson, *Propaganda and the American Revolution* 1763–1783 (Chapel Hill, 1941), pp. 225–226.

[4] *Cf.* Wright, *op. cit.* Franklin founded the Library Company of Philadelphia in 1731. See also Michael Kraus, *Intercolonial Aspects of American Culture on the Eve of the Revolution* (New York, 1928), for a discussion of reprinting of news and the circulation of printed matter.

by the increased use of speeches at popular meetings on the other. At the same time, both printed books and occasional speeches were being freed from the predominant religious control and authorship that characterized them in the seventeenth and early eighteenth centuries. But speeches also met with further competition within the field of oral communication from formal dialogues and dramatic presentations that gained the attention of those desiring entertainment and were mildly effective as propaganda.[1]

Of course, many speeches also circulated as printed documents. During the Colonial period more than 2,000 sermons and 300 secular speeches came from the presses. About 130, or more than two-thirds, of the secular speeches printed before 1760 were delivered by the governors to Colonial assemblies. But from 1761 to 1787, 68 popular speeches, 33 academic speeches, and six legislative speeches, as against only 20 by the governors, were printed. Altogether, the number of printed speeches of all kinds remained very small in comparison with the total number delivered. Among various types of speeches, sermons, especially occasional sermons, clearly had the greatest opportunities to wield influence upon the reading audience, even when the frequent reprinting of governors' speeches in mid-eighteenth century newspapers is considered.

The degree to which the colonists had attained recognition of the right to free speech determined the extent and influence of oral communication, much as the recognition of freedom of the press did for written communication. Recognition of the right of free speech came slowly and with varying success from colony to colony and from year to year. In general, the earliest governments of Massachusetts Bay and Virginia made little distinction between criticism of the government, its officers, and its laws or the church and its officials and acts on the one hand, and treason or heresy on the other. In effect, then, prosecutions of those who differed either with the church or state greatly limited freedom of discussion in all colonies except Pennsylvania and Rhode Island during the seventeenth century.[2] Within the groups supporting established institutions, considerable freedom existed. The Colonial assemblies demanded for their lower houses the freedom of debate claimed by the House of Commons. After 1679 in Virginia and from

---

[1] For a general analysis of the relative effectiveness of various means of communication for propaganda purposes, see Davidson, *op. cit.*, Chap. 3 and Chaps. 10 to 13; M. C. Tyler, *The History of American Literature* (2 vols., New York, 1879), and *The Literary History of the American Revolution* (2 vols., New York, 1897).

[2] *Cf.* S. M. Ames, *Studies of the Virginia Eastern Shore in the Seventeenth Century* (Richmond, 1940), p. 195, Daniel Cugley cases. Religious intolerance resulted in the exile of Anne Hutchinson, Roger Williams, and others, the enforced resignation of President Henry Dunster, of Harvard, during the Anabaptist controversy, and the law of 1656. See also "Shaftesbury Papers," *South Carolina Historical Collections*, 5: 114.

1691 generally, the council or upper house enjoyed freedom of debate by royal instruction.[1]

In seventeenth century America, the attainment of free speech was discouraged and delayed by (1) the prevalent intense religious intolerance, (2) constant fear of attack by near-by Frenchmen, Spaniards, Indians, and pirates, which seemed to demand unity at the expense of liberty, (3) the limitations upon freedom of speech still in force in Europe and England, and (4) the severe punishments meted out to individual offenders. Signs of improvement could be noted, however, in (1) the wide reading of English tracts such as the *Areopagitica*, (2) the assertion of freedom in assembly debates, (3) the preservation of free debate in New England town meetings, and (4) legally supported tolerance in Pennsylvania and Rhode Island.

In the eighteenth century, (1) the arrival of thousands of Europeans with varied religious and cultural backgrounds, (2) the regularization of legislative and judicial procedures, and (3) the impact of the Great Awakening and English and French doctrines of freedom and individual rights tended to increase freedom of speech. For the most part, prosecutions for oral expressions were limited to cases of slander, the law of which needed as much clarification as did the libel law. Before the Revolution, radical groups made full use of freedom of expression both in speech and in print, despite the doubts of conservatives that such unrestrained freedom was legal.[2] At the same time, through the use of mob rule, threats, and intimidation, the radicals denied to the Tories similar freedom of expression. Once the war began, the test of loyalty to the Whig cause was applied to the few Tories who endeavored to speak or write against the Revolution. Not until the adoption of bills of rights in various state constitutions and finally the Federal Constitution did Americans achieve positive legal guarantees of freedom of speech and assembly.[3] Expanding freedom of speech tended to broaden the usable topics for discussion and debate and probably indirectly encouraged more and more men otherwise inhibited by fear of prosecution to participate in public discussion along with professional speakers such as the lawyers and the clergy.

The geographical distribution of the people in the colonies, their everyday life and interests, ideas, education, and social stratification further determined the nature of public address in respect to both audiences and speakers.

[1] L. W. Larabee, *Royal Instructions to British Colonial Governors* 1670–1776 (New York, 1935), I, 47, Sec. 83.

[2] *Cf.* Davidson, *op. cit.*, p. 226. Through control of assemblies, town-meetings, county governments, and many of the courts, the Whigs talked freely with little fear of prosecution.—P. 48.

[3] *Cf.* John Trumbull's poem "*M'Fingal*" for a vivid, reliable picture of the hounding of outspoken Tories.

The total population of the thirteen colonies did not reach one million until about 1750. Despite continued rapid immigration from Europe, the total population at the beginning of the Revolution was only about two and a half millions, of which upwards of a half million were Negroes.[1] The earliest settlers remained in villages, of which there were hundreds by the mid-eighteenth century. In the Middle and Southern colonies, later settlers pushed westward to individual farms or extremely scattered settlements. Before the Revolution, only five cities, Boston, Philadelphia, New York, Newport, and Charleston, had developed, and less than 10 per cent of the population was urban.[2]

The slowness and hardship of travel for even a few miles severely limited the number and size of audiences on the frontier and in the villages and towns. On the frontier even religious services were irregularly held in cabins or outdoors; courts were distant or occasional; and local government, outside New England, consisted of court days or elections, with a little stump speaking. In villages and towns, meetings of religious congregations, town meetings, and sessions of the courts afforded speakers increased opportunities. Distinctly urban problems, such as highways and streets, fire and police protection, pauperism, community health and education, stimulated meetings of special groups as well as local government in the cities and larger towns.[3]

[1] For detailed estimates of Colonial populations, see E. B. Greene and V. D. Harrington, *American Populations before the Federal Census of* 1790 (New York, 1932). The total for 1783 was estimated at 3,300,000, including 520,000 Negroes, and the 1790 census found 3,893,635, including 694,280 slaves.

[2] *Cf.* C. P. Nettels, *Roots of American Civilization* (New York, 1938), pp. 226, 227, 335, 394, 395, 397, 539, 693, a series of eight maps by H. R. Friis showing the distribution of population 1650–1780. Carl Bridenbaugh, *Cities in the Wilderness* (New York, 1938), pp. 6, 143, 303n., estimated the population of the five cities at 9 per cent of the whole Colonial population in 1690, 8 per cent in 1720, and 5.4 per cent in 1742. Bridenbaugh estimates the populations of the five cities as follows:

	New Amsterdam	Boston	Newport	Philadelphia	Charleston
1650	1,000	2,000	300		
1680–1685	3,200	4,500	2,500	2,500	900
1700	5,000	6,700	2,600	5,000	2,000
1720	7,000	12,000	3,800	10,000	3,500
1742	11,000	16,258	6,200	13,000	6,800
1774[1]	25,000–30,000	20,000	12,000	40,000	*ca.* 9,000–12,000
1790[2]	33,131	18,038	6,716	42,444	16,359

[1] 1774 data, except Charleston, from Nettels, *op. cit.*, p. 457.

[2] Federal Census of 1790, from *A Century of Population Growth from the First Census of the United States to the Twelfth*, 1790–1900 (Bureau of Census, 1909), p. 11.

[3] Bridenbaugh, *op. cit.*, pp. 468ff.

In all but the four or five cities, the largest audiences were numbered in hundreds. The ordinary church auditorium held but two to five hundred people, and in the absence of larger halls, occasional mass meetings during religious revivals of the Great Awakening and prerevolutionary agitation were held outdoors. Faneuil Hall, with a capacity of about twelve hundred, was packed for a few sensational trials; Old South Church, holding about two thousand, was filled for a few town meetings and body meetings in Boston; a large auditorium was constructed for Whitefield in Philadelphia; college commencements often filled churches to overflowing. But these were exceptional occasions, in contrast to small attendance at the average town meeting, unfilled pews even in the smaller churches, small courtrooms, and legislative chambers, which were mostly without galleries until the mid-eighteenth century.

Almost all the settlers had fled some kind of economic, political, or religious oppression in their homelands, yet there were wide differences in their economic and social status. The earliest colonists lived under quite similar conditions of pioneer life, which necessitated hard work, thrift, and the ability to withstand privation. This continued to be true of life for freehold farmers and life on the frontier; but in the towns and cities and on Southern plantations an improved labor supply of slaves and servants permitted the growth of a leisure class of large plantation owners and merchants as well as the clergy and small numbers of lawyers, doctors, and artisans. By the mid-eighteenth century, these economic interests and differences were clearly outlined in dress, culture, and behavior, although the bulk of the population belonged to the middle and lower middle class groups made up of freeholders on small plantations and farms, smaller merchants and shopkeepers, and free laborers, in addition to professional men and artisans. Characteristic of the middle class was a spirit of individual self-reliance coupled with a willingness for community cooperation, industry, a stern moral code, a religious tradition, and a desire to improve its own lot materially and culturally. The lower middle class lacked rights of suffrage and office holding but was not bound to service, as was the large lower class, in which, however, were thousands of indentured servants who later took advantage of cheap land to become freeholders when their service was over.

Religious interests were extremely prominent in Colonial life, despite the scattered settlements, considerable degeneration of the Anglican clergy, and a lack of emphasis upon educational pursuits for large numbers of Southern colonists. Two factors were responsible for the prominence of religious interests. In the earlier and more populous colonies, either religious purposes largely motivated the settlement or the Anglican Church, as in the South, zealously guarded its legal dominance. The masses in the South-

8

ern colonies, however, were relatively unaffected by religion until the Great Awakening and the subsequent development of strong Baptist and Methodist churches.

Anglicans and some Baptists were to be found in every colony. In New England the Congregationalists maintained their hold upon the religious life until long after the Revolution, and in the Middle colonies, groups of Presbyterians, Friends, German Lutherans, German and Dutch Reformed, Moravians, and a few Roman Catholics and Jews were close neighbors. After the Revolution, the newly formed Methodist societies grew rapidly. Baird estimates that all these denominations possessed in 1775 some 1,400 clergy and 1,850 churches or societies.[1]

The settlers brought with them varying backgrounds of British and European social status and culture, and it was characteristic of them to transplant as much as possible of this background in the New World. They succeeded in developing wealth enough to enjoy many material comforts of the homeland. They brought with them their clergy, laws, books, and their interest in education and the arts, to be passed on, insofar as wealth and time permitted, to their children.[2]

Chief among the cultural viewpoints brought with the settlers was Puritanism, whose dominant influence in seventeenth century New England constituted a continuant major force in Colonial thought, education, religion, government, and everyday social behavior. Puritanism was, first of all, a piety, but it was more. A recent study traced four principal sources of Puritan intellectualism: (1) European Protestantism, essentially Calvinism and anti-Papism in general, (2) systematization and adaptation of Calvinism by seventeenth century writers, (3) the rise of humanism and the absorption into Protestantism of much classical and scientific literature, and (4) medieval scholasticism, which, despite Puritan denials, "supplied content for every department of Puritan thought."[3]

An avid curiosity about natural phenomena, profound admiration for skill in logic and the use of the learned languages of Greek, Hebrew, Chaldee, and Latin, concern over the rights of man and his duty to God, all—superimposed upon an economy of freeholders and merchants—combined to create a virile, self-reliant society in New England, albeit with disadvantages in the emphasis upon religious intolerance, piety, the sternness of the moral code, and a degree of self-righteousness. From the time of Winthrop to Jonathan Edwards, Puritanism met objection from tolerant liberals like Roger Williams, the Quakers, and various political and religious forces to

[1] Robert Baird, *Religion in the United States of America* (Glasgow, Edinburgh, 1844).
[2] Wright, *op. cit.*, p. 75.
[3] Perry G. Miller, *New England Mind in the Seventeenth Century* (New York, 1939), p. 105; this summary of Puritan ideas, pp. 92ff.

which it appeared antagonistic; yet its spirit dominated New England leaders like Sam Adams throughout the period.

In the Southern colonies no such distinctive or intensive cultural pattern was produced, but the small, powerful upper class depended directly upon Britain for its clergy, its printing, and the education of its sons and looked to British nobility for its counterpart well into the eighteenth century. Then it gained much from the Middle colony colleges and the general interchange in Colonial culture. The secularization of life and interests that became general in the colonies prior to the Revolution was stronger from the first in both the Southern and the Middle colonies. Quaker tolerance, the Dutch heritage in New York, New Jersey, and Delaware, together with tremendous eighteenth century immigration and a geographical position at the crossroads of the seaboard likewise resulted in a cosmopolitan culture in the Middle colonies.

To the Puritan emphasis upon the natural rights of man, with opportunities for self-government, common education, and freeholds of land, the Great Awakening and the infiltration of French philosophy added doctrines of social justice, encouraging the equalization of opportunities, the relief of debtors, the disestablishment of religion, and the removal of restrictions upon the suffrage—all of which tended to give new dignity to the lower middle class, that had been largely overlooked in Puritan applications of the theories of English Independency and laissez-faire economics. The result was a society more democratic but quite diverse in its interests and viewpoints. Individuals could move culturally and materially from one class to another easily enough, so that the only significant cleavage seemed to be between the debtor and creditor economic groups.[1]

With the spread of more liberal social theories, the increased immigration of the mid-eighteenth century, the development of urban interests, and the establishment of presses, libraries, and colleges came demands for educational reform to provide increased opportunity for functional courses suited for the everyday living of masses of colonists.

The first settlers varied greatly in their education. The clergy and some others attended English universities and schools, but the majority lacked formal training. In the New World, educational opportunities were every-

---

[1] V. L. Parrington, *The Colonial Mind* (New York, 1927), Introduction, pp. lv–lvi, and *passim*; Miller, *op. cit.*; H. W. Schneider, *The Puritan Mind* (New York, 1930).

Upon the democratic social influences of the Great Awakening, consult W. M. Gewehr, *The Great Awakening in Virginia*, 1740–1790 (Durham, N. C., 1930); C. H. Maxson, *The Great Awakening in the Middle Colonies* (Chicago, 1920); and upon deism and materialism, H. M. Morais, *Deism in Eighteenth Century America* (New York, 1934); Kraus, *op. cit.*; Bernard Faÿ, *Franklin, the Apostle of Modern Times* (Boston, 1929); and M-M. H. Barr, *Voltaire in America*, 1744–1800 (Baltimore, 1941).

where limited by time and money, although in New England the children of the clergy and the well to do might receive a strictly classical and Calvinistic grammar schooling in preparation for college, and in the Southern and Middle colonies, children similarly fortunate received tutoring, attended a few private schools, and sometimes went to Scottish or English preparatory schools and universities. Elementary education was nowhere universal and was rarely publicly supported outside New England until late in the Colonial period.

In higher education, the classical pattern of the English and European universities was repeated at Harvard (1636) and eight later Colonial colleges. In seventeenth century Harvard, the students spoke and were taught in Latin a curriculum of Greek and Semitic languages, mathematics, history, logic, ethics, and rhetoric, intended primarily for prospective ministers, the career of a majority of Harvard's 430 graduates before 1700. Although Latin ceased to be the medium of collegiate communication in the eighteenth century, its study, along with that of Greek and Hebrew, continued to be intense, and the structure of the curriculum, except for the greater use and reading of English, remained.[1]

During the mid-eighteenth century the classical curriculum received severe criticism from Quakers interested in education of a "practical sort," which would fit every individual to "earn a livelihood," increasing secular interests even among college students, demands for broader educational opportunity, the special problems raised by European immigrants, and some interest in publicly supported education on the part of British officialdom.[2] "English schools" were especially urged by Benjamin Franklin and similar liberals and by the Quakers, who thought little of classical ministerial education. For the masses of children, the emphasis was placed upon training for everyday living to supplement the classical schools already training the few who would attend college.[3] Along with the doctrine of functionalism came an interest in eighteenth century English literature and scientific investigations, as reflected in the organization of the American Philosophical Society. Religious interests also continued to motivate the

---

[1] C. Meriwether, *Our Colonial Curriculum* 1607–1776 (Washington, D.C., 1907), p. 11. Also see the various college histories.

[2] Larabee, *op. cit.*, II, 504, Sec. 729; Kraus, *op. cit.*, p. 204; Thomas Woody, *Early Quaker Education in Pennsylvania* (New York, 1920), p. 268. The proportion of college graduates who became ministers declined during the eighteenth century from more than half to less than one-third, while the number of lawyers, doctors, merchant-landowners, and politicians increased. The total number of graduates of Harvard, to 1787, was 2,950; of Yale, 1,860; of King's College, 1758–1776, about 110; of the College of New Jersey, 455.

[3] Benjamin Franklin, "Idea of an English School," *Writings* (A. H. Smyth, ed., New York, 1905–1907), III, 21–29 (written about 1750–1751).

general development of intellectual and educational activities, especially through the common acceptance of the idea of man's indefinite perfectibility through education, a doctrine whose full force was to be felt in education during the national period.[1]

Variations in Colonial speech and language partially determined what pronunciation and language individual speakers used and in some degree the intelligibility and persuasiveness of speeches to Colonial audiences.

The early settlers of New England and the Southern Tidewater, nearly nine-tenths of whom came from England and a large majority from southern and eastern counties, brought with them "those characteristics of Southern English speech that are still marked today." These stocks were affected but slightly by eighteenth century immigration.[2]

After 1680 the Middle colonies of New York, Pennsylvania, the Jerseys, and western New England were settled by people from northern England, where the Quakers had a strong hold, and from the Lowlands of Scotland, both of which areas "spoke a quite different dialect. . . . "[3]

In a fanwise spread along the frontiers of the Appalachian valleys into the Piedmont regions of Virginia and the Carolinas, and westward from Tennessee and New York, the northern English dialect was acquired by Scots, Ulsterites, Irish, and German immigrants, producing the virile "General American" dialect of the nineteenth and twentieth centuries.[4] Despite these two major dialectal areas and despite other variations to be discussed later the opinions of British and Colonial travelers during the later eighteenth century more often than not emphasized the comparative uniformity and "purity" of American pronunciation.[5] The best American critic of speech, John Witherspoon, agreed that "The vulgar in America speak much better than the vulgar in Great-Britain, for the very obvious reason, viz. that being much more unsettled, and moving frequently from

[1] A. O. Hansen, *Liberalism and American Education in the Eighteenth Century* (New York 1926), Chap. I.

[2] H. L. Mencken, *American Language* (4th ed., New York, 1936), p. 357; Hans Kurath, "The Origins of the Dialectal Differences in Spoken American English," *Modern Philology*, 25 (May, 1928): 391ff.; P. J. Hall, *Immigration* (2d ed., New York, 1913), p. 4; Nettels, *op. cit.*, pp. 392–394. Benjamin Franklin, in 1751, estimated the one million population of New England to have been produced from an original immigration of 80,000.

[3] Kurath, *op. cit.*, p. 392.

[4] Mencken, *op. cit.*, p. 357; Kurath, *op. cit.*, p. 391.

[5] Mencken, *op. cit.*, p. 354; Nicholas Cresswell, *Journal*, 1774–1777 (New York, 1924), p. 271; Jonathan Boucher, "Letters," *Maryland Historical Magazine*, 10 (March, 1915): 30; *Boucher's Glossary of Archaic and Provincial Words: A Supplement to the Dictionaries of the English Language*, (Joseph Hunter and Joseph Stevenson, eds., London, 1832, written ca. 1800); and *Reminiscences of an American Loyalist* (Boston, 1925), p. 61; W. Eddis, *Letters from America* 1769–1777 (London, 1792), pp. 59–60; John Harriott, *Struggles Through Life* (3d ed., London, 1815), II, 117.

place to place, they are not so liable to local peculiarities, either in accent or phraseology."[1]

From the limited evidence offered today, it appears that the Colonial speaker's vowel system included [i], [ɪ], [e], [ɛ], [æ], probably [ɒ], [ɔ], [o], [ʊ], [u], and [ʌ], with confusion still apparent in the low vowel group, the probable absence of the Italian *a* until the 1780's, and numerous interchanges such as [ɪ-i], [ɛ-e], [e-i], [i-e], [ɛ-æ], [ɪ-ɛ], and [ɛ-ɪ].[2] Diphthongs were also affected by confusion in the low vowel group: such as [ʌɪ] for [ɑɪ] in *divine* and *rising;* and failure in colloquial and possibly most Colonial speech to distinguish [ɔɪ] and [ɑɪ] in many words. The use of diphthongized vowels in *new, few, kind, cow,* and even *power* was not uncommon.[3]

In most respects consonantal usage was similar to modern American. Final consonants were frequently weakened or dropped; [v], [w], and [ʍ] were not clearly distinguished; and in New England and the Southern Tidewater, the earliest settlers "probably pronounced a weak [r] before consonants and, finally, the later ones not at all." By the end of the eighteenth century the fall of the final [r] had occurred, but neither the intruded [r] between vowels nor the unstressed final [ə] in *better* had yet developed. In the Middle Colonies, the [r] continued strong in all positions, the "Scotch . . . probably reduc[ing] their trilled [r] to the fricative [ɹ] in contact with the Quakers. The German element eventually adopted the resulting local pronunciation."[4]

Coupled with the changes in vowels and consonants, of course, were variations in intonation and rhythms on which evidence is too poor to draw conclusions.

Numerous observers noted a peculiar "twang," "a whining cadence,"[5] implying nasality or denasality or both in New England speech, and refer-

---

[1] John Witherspoon, "The Druid," *Works* (2d ed., revised and corrected, Philadelphia, 1802), IV, 458. Also *cf.* John Pickering's "Essay" (June, 1816), reprinted in M. M. Mathews, *The Beginnings of American English* (Chicago, 1931), p. 67.

See also Benjamin Franklin, "A Scheme for a New Alphabet and a Reformed Mode of Spelling . . . " (1768), *Writings* (Smyth, ed.), V, 169–178; William Angus, "Poor Richards' Alphabet and His Pronunciation," *Speech Monographs,* II (1935), 60–70; *cf.* Orbeck, *op. cit.,* and various studies utilizing early New England town records.

See also Boucher's "Glossary"; A. W. Read, "Boucher's Linguistic Pastoral of Colonial Maryland," *Dialect Notes,* VI (1933), Part VII, 353–360; David Humphreys, *The Yankey in England* (1815), "Glossary"; various writings of Noah Webster, Dearborn, Isaiah Thomas, and S. Willard.

[2] See Franklin, *op. cit.,* V, 169–178; C. H. Grandgent, "Fashion and the Broad A," *Old and New* (Cambridge, 1920), pp. 25–30; Kurath, *op. cit.,* p. 390.

[3] Grandgent, "New England Pronunciation," *op. cit.,* pp. 121–149. *Sody* for *soda* may have antedated the fall of the final *r.*

[4] Kurath, *op. cit.,* pp. 391, 393; Mencken, *op. cit.,* p. 357; Grandgent, *op. cit.,* pp. 133ff.

[5] Thomas Anburey, *Travels Through the Interior Parts of America* (reprinted, Boston,

ences to "country dialect" indicated considerable variations in pronuncia-tion between rural and urban, frontier and seaboard areas.[1]

Further recognizable geographical variations in pronunciation were ascribed by travelers to Jerseymen, Pennsylvanians, and Virginians.[2]

Non-English immigration created new speech problems in America. Added to the small groups of Dutch and Swedish settlers who came in the seventeenth century were thousands of French, German, Irish, Scottish, and Ulsterite immigrants as well as African slaves. By 1760 approximately one-third of the population was foreign born and largely European in origin.[3]

An analysis of the surnames in the Census of 1790 indicated 60.9 per cent English; 18 per cent Irish, Scot, and Ulsterite; 8.7 per cent German; 3.4 per cent Dutch; 1.7 per cent French; 0.7 per cent Swedish; and 6.6 per cent unassigned names in the population of the original states, Vermont, and Kentucky-Tennessee. New England remained preponderantly English (average 69.5 per cent) and the colonies of Delaware, Maryland, Virginia, North and South Carolina, principally English (57.4 to 68.5 per cent); but in the three Middle colonies of New York, New Jersey, and Pennsylvania, the force of European immigration showed its cosmopolitan influence. Pennsylvania had only 35.3 per cent English names, as compared with 23 per cent Irish-Scot-Ulsterite and 33.3 per cent German. In addition to educational, political, and social problems, the immigrants developed hybrid dialects of English and their native languages that raised barriers against comprehension and persuasion for speakers who did not belong to those particular national groups. And conversely, when speakers from these groups used their hybrid dialects or brogues in public meetings, legislatures, and the courts, they were subject to ridicule.[4] The Germans of

---

1923), II, 32; Patrick Campbell, *Travels in the Interior Parts of Inhabited North America* (Edin-burgh, 1793), p. 181; Cresswell, *op. cit.*, p. 271; J. F. D. Smyth, *A Tour of the United States of America* (London, 1784), II, 363.

[1] See various sources cited in A. W. Read, "British Recognition of American Speech," *Dialect Notes*, Vol. VI; *American Museum* 1 (February, 1787): 152; Mencken, *op. cit.*, pp. 364–365, regarding vulgar New England dialect in American literature.

[2] John Davis, *Travels of Four Years and a Half in the United States of America* (London, 1803), p. 367; Mathews, *op. cit.*, pp. 33–34; Read, *op. cit.*, p. 327. Contrary to earlier opinions, it now appears that Negro slaves "learned the accent of their masters. There is literally no pronunciation common among Negroes, with possible exceptions in Gullah, that does not occur generally in vulgar, or old-fashioned American speech."—W. C. Greet, "Southern Speech," *Culture in the South* (W. T. Couch, ed., Chapel Hill, 1934), p. 612, and Cleanth Brooks, Jr., *Relation of the Alabama-Georgia Dialect to the Provincial Dialects of Great Britain* (Baton Rouge, 1935).

[3] Nettels, *op. cit.*, p. 383.

[4] Alexander Hamilton, *Itinerarium* (A. B. Hart, ed., St. Louis, 1907), pp. 47 and 50. For satirical purposes, a supposed speech of a member of the New York Assembly in the "Debates

Pennsylvania and New Jersey kept their own language through their own newspapers, books, and schools. When the men learned enough English to carry on trade and politics, they developed the so-called "Pennsylvania Dutch" dialect, whose characteristics have persisted for two centuries.[1]

References to speakers with speech defects are rare. James Iredell, the jurist, and Cotton Mather had impediments in their speech, but both men gained reputations for speaking. Stuttering, slowness, vocal defects such as hoarseness, coarseness, denasality and nasality, lisping, and weak articulation, as well as the foreign dialects, were identifying marks for many individuals.[2]

From the beginning, the American language differed chiefly from the standard English of Britain in (1) innovations and adaptations to the new environment through Indian, French, Dutch, Spanish, and German loan words and changed meanings given to common English words; and (2) a tendency to cling to words and usage brought by the early settlers from the dialects of eastern and southern England, but since become archaic.[3] The rise of a native aristocracy, the difficulties of communication with England, the tenacity with which Puritan education held to the King James Bible, and the emphasis upon Latin, Greek, and Hebrew to the neglect of modern English as represented by Shakespeare and later literary works encouraged the retention of archaisms in American.

According to the observations of Boucher, Parkinson, Chastellux, and Hamilton, American usage showed a "passion for innovating," was "flaccid and inaccurate," and was given to "grandiloquence," errors in grammar, and vulgarisms, which, common in lower class speech, were, as in England, subject to ridicule and witticism.[4] Even before the end of the Colonial

---

on Dividing Orange County" was published in Dutch dialect. Enemies of Witherspoon and other Scotch-Irish divines and of German legislators in Pennsylvania noted their dialects. *Cf.* Mencken, *op. cit.*, Appendix I*b*. Boucher's "Supplement," quoted by Mencken, *op. cit.*, p. 354; Philip Padelford, *Honyman's Journal '75* (San Marino, 1939), p. 62, Apr. 2, 1775; and Hamilton's *Itinerarium*, p. 134, July 22, 1744. See also Sylvester Primer, "The Huguenot Element in Charleston's Pronunciation," *Publications of the Modern Language Association*, 4: 214–244.

[1] Benjamin Franklin, *Complete Works* (J. Bigelow. ed., New York, 1887–1888), II, 297–299; Benjamin Rush, "An Account of the Manners of the German Inhabitants of Pennsylvania," *Proceedings and Addresses of the Pennsylvania-German Society* (reprinted, 1789), XIX, 104; P. Padelford, *Honyman's Journal*, p. 20; Mencken, *op. cit.*, Appendix I*a*; Joseph Johnson, *Traditions and Reminiscences* (Charleston, 1851), p. 450*n*.

[2] Barrett Wendell, *Cotton Mather* (Cambridge, 1926), p. 48; G. J. McRee, *Life and Correspondence of James Iredell* (New York, 1857), I, 76; A. W. Read, "Speech Defects and Mannerisms among Slaves and Servants in Colonial America," *Quarterly Journal of Speech*, 24 (1938): 397–401.

[3] Mencken, *op. cit.*, pp. 104ff.; Mathews, *op. cit.*, pp. 1–9.

[4] Witherspoon, *op. cit.*, IV, 459.

15

era, leading men hoped to improve the quality and "purity" of American English. John Adams, Benjamin Rush, and others projected an American academy or university for "correcting, improving, and ascertaining the English language," but such plans came to naught.[1]

On the whole, variations in speech and language among those of English ancestry created few barriers to the general intelligibility of speakers from the most distant colonies. However, positive persuasive values could be gained by those who spoke what was considered socially acceptable English without obvious provincialism or vulgarity.[2]

The foreign dialects of Dutch and German and, to an extent, of Scotch and Irish did vary sufficiently to make some speakers using these dialects before English audiences difficult to understand. After the first few years of contact with English-speaking people, the immigrant audiences probably had little trouble understanding English speakers. But the theory that persuasion is better effected by speakers of the audiences' own dialect and culture led committees of safety just before the Revolution to utilize Scotch-Irish and German clergymen to help conduct campaigns for support in the back-country settlements.[3]

Travel habits tended to minimize the problems of speech and language. In the seventeenth century travel was so slight that speakers belonged almost entirely to the colony in which they worked or to which they had migrated. But in the eighteenth century migration from seaboard to frontier and increased travel for mercantile, military, religious, and social reasons often brought together audiences and speakers from different colonies. The Great Awakening, the French wars, and finally the Revolution broadened the geographical area of influence of preachers, lawyers, and politicians, with the apparent result that both speakers and listeners became fairly accustomed to what differences there were in speech and language. Inter-colonial communication of all kinds in the eighteenth century was exerting a strong force for uniformity, to which itinerant speakers and listeners contributed and from which they benefited.[4]

---

[1] Governor Wentworth to the Secretary of State, Apr. 24, 1774, quoted in Mathews, *op. cit.*, p. 40; Benjamin Franklin to David Hume, Sept. 27, 1760, Benjamin Franklin, *Writings* (Smyth, ed.), IV, 84; John Adams, *Works*, VII, 249ff.; Benjamin Rush, "Plan for a Federal University," *American Museum* 4 (1788): 442–444.

[2] For example, see William Wirt, *Sketches of the Life and Character of Patrick Henry* (Hartford, 1854), p. 53 and 53n.

[3] *South Carolina Historical Collections*, 2: 31, 57, 64; John Drayton, *Memoirs of the American Revolution* (Charleston, 1821), I, 324; Davidson, *op. cit.*, p. 199. Similarly, in Pennsylvania and New Jersey, the prominent ministerial family of the Mühlenbergs worked among the Germans to promote the Whig cause.

[4] Kraus, *op. cit.*; Seymour Dunbar, *History of Travel in America* (Indianapolis, 1915), Vol. I; Maxson, *op. cit.*; and among the diaries, those of John Adams and Ezra Stiles.

By the end of the eighteenth century the love of speaking and attending speeches seems to characterize Americans of all classes, despite the increasing number of diversions for entertainment and better written means of communication. Jonathan Boucher thought "Americans, in general, . . . eminently endowed with a knack of talking; they seem to be born orators."[1] Ability to speak well gained prestige for men not only in the professions but in village and rural frontier areas, where young men like John Marshall practiced stump speaking for the sheer pleasure of it.[2] Intrinsic in the love of speaking was an almost universal enjoyment of argument over questions of politics, law, and religion. Burke said in the famous speech on conciliation with America that all people in government there were lawyers or "smatterers in law" and continued: "This study renders men acute, inquisitive, dexterous, prompt in attack, ready in defense, full of resources. [There] they anticipate the evil, and judge of the pressure of a grievance by the badness of the principle. They augur misgovernment at a distance, and snuff the approach of tyranny in every tainted breeze."[3]

Yet prior to the Great Awakening and the Revolutionary movement, opportunities for speaking had been largely limited to professional speakers: the clergy, judges, lawyers, teachers, and legislators. Only in New England did town and congregational meetings give ample time to all who cared to speak.[4] Women did not usually speak in public, except in the case of itinerant Quaker preachers and a few women like Anne Hutchinson and leaders of similar Methodist and Baptist home prayer circles during the eighteenth century revivals.[5]

The Great Awakening and its accompanying equalitarian ideas encouraged public speaking by untrained men who became lay preachers, gave testimony in public, and took fresh interest in political activities. The agitation against British rule offered further occasions at which to speak, and both movements increased the attendance of lower middle class people at speeches. In addition, religious revivals brought the hitherto absent servants and slaves to meetings. After the Revolution, broader suffrage, constitutional guarantees of free speech and the toleration of religions, and the numerous institutions of state and local government made possible the

---

[1] Jonathan Boucher, *Reminiscences of an American Loyalist*, p. 61.

[2] A. J. Beveridge, *Life of John Marshall* (Boston, 1916–1919), I, 72–73.

[3] Edmund Burke, *Works* (Pinney, ed., Boston, 1871), II, 125.

[4] The Plymouth Church Records, June 17, 1688, indicated the importance attached by early New Englanders to oral testimony as a condition of church membership. *Publications Colonial Society Massachusetts*, 22: 163.

[5] The only recorded public speech by a woman other than in religious activities is Mrs. Bernard Elliott's fifty words of July 1, 1776, presenting colors to Major Elliott's regiment at Charleston.—Text of speech, "Barnard Elliott's Diary," *City of Charleston Yearbook*, 1889, p. 221; see also Drayton, *op. cit.*, II, 306.

realization of much of John Adams' hope that "eloquence will become the instrument for recommending men to their fellow-citizens, and the principal means of advancement through the various ranks and offices of society."[1]

Until the mid-eighteenth century, most Colonial speaking was done by men trained in the American or English colleges and schools. Such were the clergy except for a few Quakers and Baptists, most of the governors, lawyers, and judges, and some legislators, as well as all the academic speakers. After the mid-eighteenth century, it is true that many of the Methodist and Baptist clergy, who were added by the Great Awakening, and many popular speakers lacked college training, yet the majority of speakers continued to represent both the general education and the special rhetorical training of the colleges.

The pattern of rhetorical training, transferred to Harvard College with few changes from the English and European systems, consisted of declamations, disputations, orations, and commonplacing in the learned languages, together with lectures and readings in rhetoric and logic. In preparation for college, students learned to speak and read Latin and delivered short, formal declamations. English was little used in academic speaking.[2]

The Harvard laws of 1655 required bimonthly public declamations, disputations in which bachelors participated fortnightly and undergraduates twice weekly, repeating of sermons publicly in courses by undergraduates, and commonplacing by bachelors. The whole college attended lectures on rhetoric Friday mornings and spent the day studying rhetoric from the limited number of classical works, manuals of rhetoric, and model orations that were available.[3]

Although the pattern of rhetorical training remained almost constant for more than a century at Harvard and later at William and Mary and Yale, the content and viewpoint were more quickly modified. Harvard teachers followed Petrus Ramus, Omer Talon, and Dugard in dividing the classical field of rhetoric into logic and a limited "rhetoric" consisting of *elocutio* and *pronunciatio*. As a result students were prone to overlook the

---

[1] John Adams, *Works*, VII, 249–250. John Witherspoon found the "evident tautology" "fellow countrymen" in common use by 1781.—*Op. cit.*, IV, 462.

[2] Harvard Laws of 1642–1646, Art. 13, "Harvard College Records," *Publications Colonial Society Massachusetts*, 15: 26; Laws of 1655, *ibid.*, 31: 333; S. E. Morison, *Harvard College in the Seventeenth Century* (Cambridge, 1936), I, 169ff.

[3] Morison, *op. cit.*, I, 179ff., discussion of the declamation. The commonplace was essentially a short sermon, required of upper classmen as a declamation. *Cf.* Meriwether, *op. cit.*, pp. 276ff., and on commonplacing, pp. 226ff.; Morison, *op. cit.*, I, 143ff.; "Harvard College Records," *Publications Colonial Society Massachusetts*, 31: 288, relation between English university customs and Harvard under Dunster. Morison, *op. cit.*, I, 141ff.; the fines, or mulcts, are listed in the Laws of 1655. See S. E. Morison, *Harvard College in the Seventeenth Century*, I, 141ff., for a table of the weekly schedule of the college.

persuasive purpose of speaking in the processes of *inventio* and *dispositio* because these were viewed from the standpoint of formal logic and the syllogistic rather than the forensic disputation. *Elocutio* and *pronunciatio* became skills more sought after for their ornamental than their functional persuasive values. Neither Quintilian nor Aristotle seems to have been read directly by seventeenth century Harvard students. In logic, there was an "interplay of three distinct systems: . . . the Aristotelian, Ramean, and Cartesian."[1]

In the early eighteenth century, rhetoric in the broad classical sense of the term gained adherence through direct reading of Quintilian, Aristotle, and Cicero and indirectly, through more comprehensive contemporary texts such as the *Art of Speaking* and John Ward's *System of Oratory*.[2]

Thus, during the first decades of the eighteenth century, with the passing of the Puritan leaders, rhetoric in America "gradually . . . recovered vitality and richness," and by regaining the classical viewpoint prepared the way for its part in mid-eighteenth century educational reform.[3]

Closely related to the movement for functionalizing Colonial education supported by the liberal thinking of the latter half of the eighteenth century were reforms in the pattern of rhetorical exercises and methods of teaching public speaking.

Benjamin Franklin's *Proposals Relating to the Education of Youth in Pennsylvania* (1744) was among the earliest attacks upon classical formalism in American education. Franklin demanded the training of youth in the English tongue, for, "Thus instructed, Youth will come out of this School fitted for learning any Business, Calling or Profession, except wherein Languages are required; and tho' unacquainted with any antient or foreign Tongue, they will be masters of their own, which is of more immediate and general Use; . . . . "[4]

Both in the *Proposals* and the *Idea of the English School* (*ca.* 1751), he outlined courses that emphasized speaking and reading skills. He wanted

---

[1] Morison, *op. cit.*, I, 177–178, 193. A list of manuals, orations, etc., that were studied included Omer Talon's *Rhetorica*, Dugard, Farnaby's *Index rhetoricus*, Aldus's *Phrases Linguae Latinae*, the *Colloquies* of Erasmus, Johannes Buchler's *Thesaurus*, and some collections of speeches.

[2] The catalogues of Harvard College Library for 1723 and 1725 also list the orations of Isocrates, Porcensis, and Demosthenes; some later rhetorics; Glenvil's *Collection of Sundry Trials;* Napir's collection of Latin orations; and a volume entitled *Parliamentary Speeches.*

[3] For general surveys of rhetoric in colonial America, see Morison, *op. cit.*, I, 172; Miller, *op. cit.*, chapters on Rhetoric and The Plain Style; and Warren A. Guthrie, The Development of Rhetorical Theory in America, 1635–1850, unpublished Ph.D. thesis, Northwestern University. See also Chapter 5 in this volume by Ota Thomas on The Teaching of Rhetoric in the United States during the Classical Period of Education.

[4] Benjamin Franklin, "Idea of the English School," *Writings* (Smyth, ed.), III, 29.

youth to develop clarity and conciseness, to pronounce distinctly, and "to form their own Stiles. . . . " In his plans, he did not overlook the study of model speeches, the elements of rhetoric and logic, translations of classics, and the latest British literature of Milton, Locke, Addison, Pope, and Swift or the use of the dictionary; for, he wrote, "it is impossible a Reader should give the due Modulation to his Voice, and pronounce properly, unless his understanding goes before his Tongue." Further, "Declamations, repeating Speeches, delivering Orations, ... [and] Publick Disputes warm the Imagination, whet the Industry, and strengthen the Natural Abilities."[1]

Franklin's theories seem to have grown out of his wide acquaintance with contemporary English and French writers, his deism, and his emphasis upon the good-works doctrine, which certainly gave an incentive to a more utilitarian education. To such cosmopolitanism were added the dialect problems that were alarming the Middle colonies and the newly stimulated interest in public speaking among untrained, nonprofessional men, which came out of the Great Awakening and the succeeding prerevolutionary political agitation.[2]

Coincidental with these social pressures and the active support of such representative Americans as Franklin, college students themselves attempted to make up for the lack of adequate English speaking exercises by the organization of literary and debating societies, which encouraged debating, oratory, and parliamentary procedure.[3]

Educators reluctantly modified the classical pattern of exercises in speaking. Franklin and many others urged upon Yale, King's, and the College of Philadelphia revised rules that emphasized English speaking as well as Latin.[4] By 1770 every one of the established colleges had included more forensic disputes, orations, and declamations in English in their

---

[1] Benjamin Franklin, "Proposals Relating to the Education of Youth in Pennsylvania," *Writings* (Smyth, ed.), II, 386–396. The principles that Franklin advocated were applied in the English School of the Academy of Philadelphia. Franklin's "Observations" (1789), *ibid.*, X, 9–31, contains an account of the varying success with which the plan was administered, despite the author's persisting faith in it.

[2] Benjamin Franklin, *Writings* (Smyth, ed.), III, 24.

[3] See the various college histories and G. A. Koch, *Republican Religion* (New York, 1933), p. 20; F. B. Dexter, *Literary Diary of Ezra Stiles* (New Haven, 1901), II, Apr. 4, 1781; H. D. Berkley, "A Maryland Medical Student and His Friends," *Maryland Historical Magazine*, 24: 23–30; "Original Records of Phi Beta Kappa Society," *William and Mary Quarterly*, 4: 213–260; Alexander Graydon, *Memoirs of a Life Chiefly Passed in Pennsylvania* (Edinburgh, 1822), p. 87; J. N. Beam, *The American Whig Society* (Princeton, 1933). The Linonia Literary and Debating Society was reputedly founded at Yale on Sept. 12, 1753.

[4] Benjamin Franklin, *Works* (J. Sparks, ed., Chicago, 1882), VII, 55. The reformers met strong opposition, however, from the classicists, and even at Philadelphia, Franklin's absence gave the classical school an opportunity to regain its supremacy. Ebenezer Baldwin, *Annals*

rhetorical exercises. Dramatic dialogues were introduced into commencement programs. At Princeton, President Witherspoon held prize contests in reading English, reading and speaking Latin, and "pronouncing English orations."[1] Latin ceased to be a living language for students, and the syllogistic disputation lost ground to forensic disputations arranged in the style of modern debating.[2]

Not only were the rhetorical exercises modified but the abandonment of the class-tutor system for specialized tutors and professors in various subjects tended to intensify the teaching of rhetorical theory. Ebenezer Kinnersley, at the College of Philadelphia (1753–1778), William Small, at William and Mary before 1762, and John Witherspoon, at the College of New Jersey, gave lectures and did special teaching in public speaking.[3]

In 1766, the Overseers of Harvard College, in connection with the new tutorial system, ordered "that on Friday and Saturday mornings each class shall be instructed by a distinct Tutor, in Elocution, Composition in English, Rhetoric, and other parts of Belles-Lettres."[4] On October 23, 1776, Yale granted permission to the senior class for "instruction in Rhetoric, History, and Belles Lettres."[5]

The rhetorical theory taught students during the latter half of the eighteenth century showed a still stronger emphasis upon the principal classical sources, including Quintilian's *Institutes*, Aristotle's *Rhetoric* and *Poetic*, Cicero's *De oratore*, the critical epistles of Horace and Longinus. Too late for influencing Colonial speakers, Hugh Blair's *Lectures on Rhetoric and Belles Lettres* was being adopted as a textbook. Both classic and English speeches and sermons continued to be read and studied, and in the lower

---

of Yale College (New Haven, 1831), p. 98: "So far as prudence would admit, the Tutors encouraged the study of the English language, composition and oratory."

Cf. "An Account of the College of New Jersey . . . " (Woodbridge, 1764), in John Maclean, *History of the College of New Jersey* (Philadelphia, 1877), I, 259; Herbert and Carol Schneider, *Samuel Johnson . . . His Career and Writings* (New York, 1929); T. H. Montgomery, *A History of the University of Pennsylvania . . .* (Philadelphia, 1900), pp. 239ff.; *American Magazine*, October, 1758, pp. 630ff.

[1] Maclean, *op. cit.*, I, 312: "All present were permitted to vote who were graduates of this or any other College." *Cf. Pennsylvania Gazette*, Oct. 13, 1773.

[2] *Cf.* Josiah Quincy, *History of Harvard University* (Cambridge, 1840), II, 124, for an account of attempts of the Overseers to stimulate English speaking, October, 1754; Laws of Harvard College, 1767, "Harvard College Record," *Publications Colonial Society Massachusetts*, 21: 352.

[3] See Montgomery, *op. cit.*, I, 170ff.; 229ff., accounts of Kinnersley; Maclean, *op. cit.*, I, 387, account of Witherspoon's lecturing; Thomas Jefferson, *Writings* (H. A. Washington, ed., Washington, D. C., 1853), I, 2–3, regarding William Small.

[4] Quincy, *op. cit.*, II, Appendix XIV, text of tutorial arrangement.

[5] *Historical Register of Yale University*, 1701–1937 (New Haven, 1929), p. 14.

classes often memorized and declaimed as well, as companions to the readings and lectures in theory.

The critical Tory Jonathan Boucher considered the reformed curriculum and exercises at Philadelphia and Princeton frivolous and superficial, "but their chief and peculiar merit was thought to be in Rhetoric and the 'belles lettres,' a term not easily defined nor understood. Hence in no country were there so many orators, or so many smatterers."[1]

It seems clear that during the eighteenth century American college men received extensive training in the theory and practice of public speaking that was increasingly well adapted to popular participation in speaking, through (1) broadening the scope of speaking activities for students and (2) providing a richer background of textual materials.

The schools were doing much to utilize and foster the love of speaking that so many observers called an American characteristic.[2]

Types of Speech Occasion

An analysis of the institutions and customs of public address reveals five principal types of speaking occasion: (1) religious, (2) legislative, (3) legal, (4) academic, and (5) popular. Each will be studied in some detail, but it should be kept in mind that the types of occasion are often difficult to distinguish and that in some instances any classification is arbitrary. As the first portion of this study has pointed out, religious speaking was plentiful from the first settlements of the colonies. Legislative, legal, and academic speaking soon began to show the outlines of customs transferred and adapted to the colonies. Outside the New England town meeting, institutions of popular speaking developed slowly and did not come into effective use until the prerevolutionary period.

1. RELIGIOUS SPEAKING. The ordinary exercises of New England churches and of the Reformed faiths generally consisted of a morning and afternoon service on the Sabbath, the Wednesday or Thursday afternoon "lecture," and occasional meetings, such as the Fast Day in the spring, the annual Thanksgiving in the fall, ordinations of the clergy, funerals, and election-day services. Each occasion had its sermon or "lecture."

On the Sabbath, each service usually lasted from two to three hours, depending largely upon the length of the sermon. There were a prayer; the reading and, in the earlier years, the expounding of Scripture; singing; and

[1] Jonathan Boucher, *Reminiscences of an American Loyalist*, pp. 101–102.

[2] Blair's *Lectures* was adopted at Yale in 1785. On May 21, 1786, John Quincy Adams requested a copy of Blair's *Lectures* in octavo.—*Writings* (W. C. Ford, ed., New York, 1913), I, 25. Guthrie, *op. cit.*, considered 1785 as the beginning of the third period of American rhetorical history, dominated by Blair's, Campbell's, and Whately's rhetorics but including the appearance of the American lectures of John Witherspoon and John Quincy Adams.

a sermon. The congregation stood for prayer and, in some churches, for the reading. Usually the sermon took an hourglass or a little less, but Mather Byles occasioned no surprise when he said, "Now we will take a second glass." On these occasions, the deacons and the tithingman with his fur-tipped rod were ever vigilant to preserve quiet, dignity, solemnity, reverence, and wakefulness. Breaches of discipline no greater than laughing, sleeping, conversing, or suspected scoffing brought such severe punishments as suspension or excommunication, which were voted after long and solemn church trials. The extreme winter cold in the Northern colonies, the uncomfortable seats, and the length of the services diminished even the social values of the Sabbath meeting.

In the seventeenth century, probably almost all the sermons had been prepared with great care, written down, and then either read or repeated from memory, but in the eighteenth century, the evangelical preachers practiced extemporaneous and even impromptu speaking. Among the extempore speakers who sometimes spoke without any notes or outlines were George Whitefield, Gilbert Tennent (to 1743), Devereaux Jarratt, Samuel Johnson of King's College, Ezra Stiles (after 1770), Aaron Burr, and George Duffield.

Such notable preachers as Jonathan Edwards, Samuel Finley, and Jonathan Dickinson used written sermons. Samuel Davies read from his manuscript, but John Witherspoon, Eleazer Wheelock, Increase Mather, and Cotton Mather memorized most of theirs.

Contemporary writers commend the clear, strong, and pleasing voices of Byles, Davies, Wheelock, and Whitefield. Others, like Witherspoon, however, could be heard only with difficulty in their comparatively small auditoriums.

Probably a great number of preachers either seemed to their listeners as those who "'in one lazy tone, through the long, heavy, painful page,' drawled on" or justified such contemporary criticism as "florid elocution," "acrimonious expression," "facetious & addicted to laughing & Humor," "a very indifferent Figure in the pulpit," and "Calvinistic, practical & very solemn," or "His motions with his head, body, and hands are a little stiff and affected."[1]

We might conclude from the fact that so many sermons were written carefully before delivery that compactness, accuracy of statement, and clear, logical development would characterize them. However, such a conclusion would be far from true. The artificial, highly ornate, but often loose and rambling style that was popular in the seventeenth century often prevented plainness and clarity, and since the style was usually coupled

---

[1] The last statement is John Adams's, in criticism of the famous Dr. Samuel Cooper, in Adams, *Works*, I, 305.

with a declamatory delivery, it pleased neither discriminating listeners nor later readers. Cotton Mather represents the extreme absurdity in this kind of sermon, so much that even as mild a critic as Samuel Sewall was disgusted with such expressions as "sweetscented hands of Christ," "Lord High Treasurer of Aethiopia," and "Ribband of Humility" (sermon, January 26, 1686). Classical allusions and quotations of every kind fill the pages. Many later sermons, moreover, were hardly less objectionable as eclectic productions thrown together from the writings of English theologians, philosophers, and sermon writers. On the other hand, sermons such as that which the haughty and vain William Vesey (1674–1746) preached at the funeral of Governor Lovelace are as simple, direct, and clearly outlined as could be wished.[1] In the eighteenth century, Boston liberals, orthodox Presbyterians, and most of the Anglicans attained considerable skill in closeness of organization and a logical order of development in their doctrinal sermons.

Although lacking in these skills of composition, the evangelical preachers, especially in the revivals, learned the value of direct appeals through the frequent use of such devices as the use of personal pronouns, hortatory verbs, and vivid, dramatic pictures through which they aroused extreme enthusiasm and terror.

Too often the preachers threatened, condemned, scolded, or displayed irritable temperaments and uncompromising attitudes, especially in conditioning religion upon rigid standards of daily living. Southerners in the eighteenth century were exposed to reproach for gambling, drinking, and "partying" with a vigor hardly less discomfiting than the austere moral teachings of the elder Puritan divines of the seventeenth.

Despite the absence of adequate contemporary evaluations and despite the glamour that has surrounded the names of many preacher-statesmen of early New England, a few of these men seem to deserve a place in the front rank of speakers: Thomas Shepard (1605–1649), Thomas Hooker (1586?–1647), Charles Chauncy (1592–1671/2), and John Cotton (1585–1652). John Norton (1606–1663), Jonathan Mitchell (1624–1668), and Richard Mather (1596–1669) were also good speakers, but the reputations of such men as Roger Williams seem to have been based on abilities other than preaching.

At the turn of the century and for a period of some fifty years, Increase Mather (1639–1723) was preeminent among New England preachers. His contemporaries agreed that he worked exceedingly hard at the preparation of his sermons and pamphlets and that he read as widely if not as critically as any New Englander of his day. He was the leading politician, the best

---

[1] William Vesey, sermon, May 12, 1709, reprinted, *New York Historical Society Collections*, 13: 323–338.

diplomat, for a time the president of Harvard, and a man of highly respected character.

As a writer, he fell short of the "heights of universal beauty in style and never recaptured in his own work the genius of the translators of the English Bible," yet he wrote much and well.[1] As a preacher, his laboriously written and memorized sermons were characterized by a simple, clear, yet heavy and sometimes loosely constructed style. He tried, however, to avoid the quaintness and artificiality that other preachers, including his famous son Cotton (1662/3–1727/8), cultivated. Increase Mather delivered his sermons with a variety of voice and action ranging from a "Grave and Wise Deliberation" to such a "*Tonitrous Cogency* that Hearers would be struck with *Awe*, like what would be Produced on the fall of Thunderbolts."[2] As another critic wrote, Mather used "great plainness of speech, with much light and heat, force and power." His sermon subjects were as varied as his interests and his reading—theological, sociological, political, and scientific—as he tried, sometimes more bravely than clearly, to relate natural phenomena and current problems to his quite conservative religious beliefs.[3]

Increase Mather exerted a greater influence than any New England preacher of his era, yet he will be remembered best not for brilliance or succinctness or eloquence but for an avid interest in what was new, a degree of tolerance not common among his fellows, and, above all, a plainness of speaking.

The other two notable preachers of the Colonial era, George Whitefield (1714–1770) and Jonathan Edwards (1703–1758), led the first wave of religious enthusiasm that swept the Atlantic seaboard and the back-country settlements. This Great Awakening began almost simultaneously (1726–1739) (1) among the Dutch Reformed and Presbyterian churches, (2) in Northampton, Massachusetts, where Edwards was preaching, and (3) in the Southern colonies, upon Whitefield's arrival from England.

By 1740, Whitefield had made a triumphal journey to New England, preaching to crowds that were estimated at more than ten thousand.[4] Everywhere he created either enthusiasm or bitter controversy with those who opposed extreme forms of evangelism. Francis Alison, Charles Chauncy, Jonathan Mayhew, Timothy Cutler, and Devereaux Jarratt condemned such emotional preaching and the "protracted meetings." With the support, however, of such leaders as the Tennents, Theodorus Frelinghuysen,

[1] K. B. Murdock, *Increase Mather* (Cambridge, 1925), p. 395.

[2] Cotton Mather, *Parentator* (Boston, 1724), p. 210.

[3] Benjamin Colman, in W. B. Sprague, *Annals of the American Pulpit* (New York, 1866), I, 158.

[4] An excellent account is found in Franklin's *Autobiography* (J. Bigelow, ed., Philadelphia, 1884, 1905), I, 265ff.

Samuel Blair, Samuel Davies, and a host of lay preachers and exhorters, Whitefield continued for three decades, until his death at Newburyport in 1770, to be the most popular and effective preacher in America.[1] He preached several times a day, for two or more hours at a time, to tremendous audiences, which often met outdoors. Yet he seemed to retain a personal hold upon his listeners by means of directness, fluency of language, strong gestures, vividness, and a remarkable ability to dramatize himself.[2]

Jonathan Edwards preached quite differently from Whitefield, but nevertheless with great effectiveness. A stern, austere personality, he evinced a vivid imagination and a capable intellect in sermons that made real and personal the horrors of eternal hell-fire for members of congregations whose religious faith had badly degenerated since the days when Cotton, Hooker, and, more recently, the Mathers ruled their flocks by Old Testament law. Edwards, too, succeeded in throwing off the floundering and artificial style of Cotton Mather, but he was surprised and for a time puzzled at the fervor that he and his associates in the revival aroused in their audiences.

After selecting Increase Mather, Edwards, and Whitefield from the hundreds of Colonial clergy who achieved favorable reputations, it is difficult to list, with discrimination, the others who deserve praise for their preaching abilities. Probably the next group should include: Francis Alison (1705–1779), Jonathan Mayhew (1720–1766), Mather Byles (1706/7–1788), and Devereaux Jarratt (1733–1801), all of whom were noted for many effective sermons. To these we can readily add another dozen names of importance: Benjamin Colman (1673–1747), Samuel Cooper (1725–1783), Thomas Coombe (1747–1822), Jacob Duché (1737–1798), George Duffield (1732–1790), John Ewing (1732–1802), Samuel Finley (1715–1766), Peter Mühlenberg (1746–1807), Ezra Stiles (1727–1795), Gilbert Tennent (1703–1764), Eleazer Wheelock (1711–1779), John Witherspoon (1723–1794), and John Joachim Zubly (1724–1781).[3]

---

[1] Whitefield spent about eleven years of the period 1739–1770 in the colonies.

[2] For contemporary accounts of Whitefield's preaching, see J. Gillies, *Memoirs of George Whitefield* (rev. ed., Middletown, 1836); the "Stephens Journal," *Georgia Historical Society Collections;* Hermon Husband, "Some Remarks on Religion" (1761 pamphlet), reprinted in *North Carolina Historical Commission Publications,* "Some Eighteenth Century tracts . . . " (W. K. Boyd, ed., Raleigh, 1927), pp. 193–246.

[3] There is still a third group of those who received some degree of popularity as preachers and whose names are often listed by religious historians: Charles Beatty, Jeremy Belknap, Joseph Bellamy, Samuel Blair, Hugh Henry Brackenridge, Jonathan Boucher, Aaron Burr, Archbishop Carroll, Samuel Davies, Jonathan Dickinson, Timothy Dwight, Andrew Eliot, Theodorus Frelinghuysen, Jacob Green, Samuel Locke, Alexander McWhorter, Thomas Rankin, John Rogers, George Shadford, Samuel Stillman, Nathaniel Whitaker, and Captain Webb. Many of these came into prominence during and after the Revolution.

We have noted that the clergy held a commanding position in Colonial life. They were well educated. They gave a general impetus to the printing of books, newspapers, and pamphlets and to the education of laymen.

In their sermons, the clergy continued to preach religious orthodoxy and a stern personal morality. Many non-Anglicans, however, introduced significantly liberal political doctrines obtained from the works of Locke, Milton, and the French philosophers, as well as from the classics of Greece and Rome. For some years before the struggles with the Crown became critical, these political teachings had an especially profound effect upon the parishioners.[1]

What the ministers said in their sermons exerted a peculiarly strong influence upon both the immediate congregations and public opinion generally, because (1) as a source of information upon current problems the clergy were quite reliable and (2) they spoke with authority as pastors who "ruled" their flocks, represented God in their communities, and maintained high social and political prestige long after direct theocratic government had disintegrated. Until shortly before the Revolution, sermons and weekday lectures overshadowed newspapers, pamphlets, town meetings, and assemblies in molding public opinion.

In a quite different way, the Great Awakening profoundly affected American life. The successive waves of revivals ultimately brought religion to the lower classes, the back-country settlements, and the Negroes. The new dissenting churches taught men the doctrine of the equality of souls, increased their social activities, and furnished them with common emotional and intellectual interests that led to the emergence of the first intercolonial leaders and brought support for the first intercolonial activities. In these respects, the influence of the revivalist preachers in laying a foundation for American union equaled that of the Congregationalist, Reformed, and Presbyterian clergy in preaching the intellectual doctrines of resistance and liberty.

2. LEGISLATIVE SPEAKING. The characteristics of legislative speaking will be considered in three phases: (*a*) Colonial assembly debates, (*b*) governors' speeches to the assemblies, (*c*) congressional debates, 1774–1787.

In the Colonial legislative assemblies, elected representatives of the people engaged in free discussions that varied from extreme informality in committee meetings and much of the time on the floor of the house to carefully prepared, read or memorized speeches in formal debate.[2]

---

[1] Excellent discussions of the sources of liberal political views in America may be read in Alice Baldwin, *New England Clergy and the Revolution* (Durham, N. C., 1931); Parrington, *op. cit.;* and G. A. Koch, *Republican Religion* (New York, 1933).

[2] The rules of Colonial assemblies were largely patterned after those of the English House of Commons.—R. V. Harlow, *The History of Legislative Methods in the Period before 1825* (New Haven, 1917); E. I. Miller, *The Legislature of the Province of Virginia* (New York, 1907).

Except in the Colonies of Massachusetts and Virginia, the earlier assemblies were composed of fifty members or less and met in small rooms in churches, meetinghouses, town houses, or capitols, in which prepared speeches, formality, and loud speaking were discouraged.[1] In capitols, chairs at small tables or wall benches replaced pews as seats, with tables in the forepart of the room for the secretary and his clerks and a large chair for the speaker on a small daïs at the front, facing the main entrance doors.[2]

Josiah Quincy, Jr., described the rather ornate but otherwise typical customs of the South Carolina Assembly:

The first thing done at the meeting of the house is to bring the mace . . . , lay it on the table before the speaker. . . .

The next thing is for the Clerk to read over in a vary [*sic*] audible voice, the doings of the preceding day. The Speaker is robed in black and has a very large wig of State, when he goes to attend the Chair (with the Mace borne before him) on delivery of speeches, etc. . . . The members of the house all sit with their hats on, and uncover when they rise to speak: they are not confined (at least they did not confine themselves) to any one place to speak in. The members conversed, lolled, and chatted very much like a friendly jovial society, when nothing of importance was before the house. . . . The speaker put the questions sitting, and conversed with the House sitting: the members gave their votes by rising from their seats, the dissentients did not rise.[3]

Prior to 1761 the Colonial assembly journals indicate prolonged, bitter debates over such matters as the governor's salary, trade policies, appropriations for defense, the Indians, land banks, the encouragement of manufactures, and powers of the assembly. In the absence of satisfactory methods of reporting, these speeches were lost. Moreover, when skill in shorthand developed before the Revolution, the reluctance of legislators agitating against the Crown to have their speeches in print was quite as effective in preventing detailed reports. When Benjamin Franklin quit the clerkship to become a member of the Pennsylvania Assembly, he wrote: "I was at length tired with sitting there to hear debates, . . . which were often so unentertaining that I was induc'd to amuse myself with making magic squares or circles, or anything to avoid weariness."[4] After he had listened

[1] Harlow, *op. cit.*, p. 63n., table of sizes of lower houses before 1776.

[2] For full descriptions of capitols, see *The Old State House Memorial* (Boston, v.d.); F. M. Etting, *Historical Account of the Old State House of Pennsylvania, Now Known as the Hall of Independence* (Boston, 1876, 1891, etc.); David Ridgely, *Annals of Annapolis* (Baltimore, 1841), p. 146; *The Handbook for the Exhibition Buildings of Colonial Williamsburg* (v.d.).

[3] "Journal," *Massachusetts Historical Society Proceedings*, 49: 451ff., Mar. 19, 1773.

[4] *Autobiography*, I, 293. See Eddis, *Letters*, Feb. 17, 1772, for a favorable estimate of the Maryland Assembly.

to Patrick Henry's "high-flown and bold delivery," which seemed to deal "more in words than in reasons," Johann Schoepf concluded:

Men of this stamp, either naturally eloquent or become so through their occupation, as, e. g. lawyers, invariably take the most active and influential part in these Assemblies: the other members, for the most part farmers without clear and refined ideas, with little education or knowledge of the world, are merely there to give their votes, which are sought, whenever the House is divided into parties, by the insinuations of agreeable manners and in other ways.[1]

Generally, contemporary evidence recorded outstanding emotional appeals, unusually fiery invective, or elegant delivery in the legislatures.[2] During the height of the agitation against British policies, Patrick Henry (1736–1799) "blazed out with violent" speeches, and such men as James Otis (1725–1783), Samuel Adams (1722–1803), Thomas McKean (1734–1817), John Witherspoon (1723–1794), Christopher Gadsden (1724–1805), and William Henry Drayton (1742–1779), capable of "a copious stream of irony and sarcasm," bitter name calling, and abuse, hotly denounced Tory officials and raised the cry that liberty was endangered by tyranny.[3]

Despite the small chambers and memberships of most assemblies and the extemporaneous or impromptu nature of most debating, a few texts of prepared speeches before 1775 were printed.[4]

[1] Johann D. Schoepf, *Travels in the Confederation* (A. J. Morrison, ed., Philadelphia, 1911), II, 56.

[2] Exceptions: Drayton, *op. cit.*, II, 173, Feb. 10, 1776; Peter Force, *Tracts*, I, No. 8, p. 14, the clichés of an old Virginia assemblyman, Mr. Presley; and Thomas Hutchinson, *History of Massachusetts Bay* (L. S. Mayo, ed., Boston, 1936), II, 220, description of the "aged Senator," Mr. Sewall, who spoke "with great gravity and simplicity, in primitive stile."

[3] Thomas Jefferson, *Autobiography*, I, 4; *American Historical Review*, 26: 726–747; 27: 70–89, for witness accounts of Henry in 1765. J. M. Miller, *Sam Adams, Pioneer in Propaganda* (Boston, 1936), pp. 120–131, for a discussion of Otis' violent speeches and Adams' strategy in the Massachusetts assembly.

When Governor William Franklin "refused to answer questions . . . denouncing the [New Jersey legislature] as lawless, ignorant and vulgar," Witherspoon replied, "reflecting upon the Governor's want of proper early training in liberal knowledge and alluding to an infirmity in his pedigree."—G. G. Hill, "Princeton to the Close of the Revolutionary War," *Americana*, 27 (1932): 28–39. See also Drayton, *op. cit.*, I, 211.

[4] Samuel Mulford's *Speech to the Assembly at New York, April the Second, 1714* (New York, 1714), in which the conclusion reads: "Although We are compared to a Peevish child, that Cried for Salt Beef for its Own Hurt; yet I hope you will have the Sense of the Burn't Child, which Dreads the Fire: and not be like Persons Non Compos Mentus, to Wilfully Run into the Same"; *The Speech of John Dickinson, Esq.* . . . *May 24, 1764* (Philadelphia, 1764); *The Speech of Joseph Galloway, Esq.* . . . *May 24, 1764* . . . (Philadelphia, 1764); *Speech of Mr. Justice Livingston* . . . *25th of January* [1771] (New York, 1771); *A Speech Said to Have Been Delivered Some Time before the Close of the Last Sessions, by a Member Dissenting from the Church* [Archibald Kennedy?] (New York, 1755; now reproduced as *Massachusetts Historical Society Photostat Americana*, 2d series, No. 70).

In the conventions of 1775 to form state governments, two speeches are worthy of study: (1) Patrick Henry's famous appeal of March 23, 1775, in the Virginia Convention and (2) James Wilson's (1742–1798) "speech in Convention, in January, 1775." Every school child is familiar with William Wirt's re-creation of Henry's brilliant appeal for "Liberty or Death," but Wilson's sober speech deserves attention as a careful exposition of the legal basis upon which the rebellion rested.[1]

When nearly every assembly opened its legislative debates to the public after the mid-eighteenth century, the Whig leaders were given an opportunity to appeal to the populace directly from the floors of assemblies, for "a speech well adapted to the gallery, was oftentimes of more service to the cause of liberty than if its purport had been confined to the members of the house." Furthermore, "frequent hints are thrown out, that if they are not able by their votes and resolves, there is, however, virtue and valour enough in the people to effect all that is desired. . . . "[2] Opening the galleries to Adams's "Mohawks and Hawcubites" in Massachusetts, or in any colony, "meant the virtual end of freedom of speech" for the Tory faction.[3]

In addition to ordinary legislative debates, the assemblies acted as courts. During the trial of the Philipse election case in 1737, "by the mere dint of eloquence," the New York lawyer William Smith (1697–1769) carried a resolution against the suffrage for Hebrews, although he lost the case for his client Van Horne.[4] In 1777 the legislature of Georgia received a South Carolina delegation, which proposed a union of the two states. In the ensuing debate between William Henry Drayton and Button Gwinnett (*ca.* 1735–1777), the former received little support for his plan.[5] The Con-

---

[1] William Wirt, *Sketches of the Life and Character of Patrick Henry* (15th ed., Hartford, 1854), pp. 138–142; James Wilson MSS, Vol. II, Historical Society of Pennsylvania.

Other legislative speech texts of this period include, prior to the formation of state governments [Crean Brush], *Speech of a Member of the General Assembly of New York, at Their Session, in 1775* (New York, 1775); and from the same debate on the appointment of congressional delegates, "Speech of Mr. Isaac Wilkins of Westchester County," February, 1775, 4 *American Archives* I, 1293. Under state governments, *Mr. [William] Tennent's Speech on the Dissenting Petition, Delivered in the House of Assembly, Charles-town, So. Car., Jan.* 11, 1777 (Charlestown, 1777); *The Speech of the Hon. Wm. Henry Drayton, Esquire, Chief Justice of South Carolina . . . Twentieth January, 1778 . . . upon the Articles of Confederation . . .* (Charlestown, 1778).

[2] Josiah Quincy, Jr., "Journal," *Massachusetts Historical Society Proceedings*, 49: 476; *cf.* Etting, *op. cit.* (2nd ed.), p. 88 and 88n; Eddis, *Letters*, p. 204, Apr. 26, 1775; *North Carolina Historical Review*, 2: 60; Hutchinson, *op. cit.*, III, 120; and Thomas Hutchinson, *Diary and Letters* (P. O. Hutchinson, ed., Boston, 1884–1886), I, 116.

[3] Miller, *op. cit.*, p. 110; Thomas Hutchinson, *History*, III, 218–220.

[4] William Smith *History of the Late Province of New York* (New York, 1829), II, 37–40. This is one of the fullest analyses of a single speech available in the Colonial period.

[5] George White, *Historical Collections of Georgia* (New York, 1854), pp. 203–205.

gresses of 1775 and 1786 sent commissions to plead personally with the assemblies of Pennsylvania, New Jersey, and Massachusetts.[1]

On various occasions, short speeches of thanks and response were delivered in the assemblies. William Henry Drayton and Rawlins Lowndes (1721–1800) of South Carolina briefly thanked delegates to Congress and retiring presidents of the Provincial Congress; Richard Henry Lee (1732–1794) replied briefly to a resolution of thanks, June 20, 1777, in the Provincial Congress of Virginia; in 1779, Ezra Stiles was introduced into the Rhode Island Assembly to speak in behalf of the Newport sufferers; and the incoming speakers of the Virginia Burgesses made traditional short "disabling speeches," which, in Chinese fashion, pointed out the speaker's inability but his willingness to undertake the task thrust upon him.[2]

The custom of Colonial governors to appear personally before the two houses of the general assemblies in joint session for speeches began at least as early as Governor Berkeley's (1606–1677) militant speech to the Virginia House of Burgesses, March 15, 1650/1.[3] Beginning with 1691 in New York, 1686 in Massachusetts Bay, 1689 in Pennsylvania, 1697 in Maryland, and 1701 in South Carolina, these utterances and the answers from the assemblies record in vivid detail the vicissitudes of the governors and assemblies in their relations with each other and the Crown. (1) The governors customarily spoke at the opening of a legislative session to acquaint the assembly with the policies and views of the executive with respect to pending legislation. (2) Some governors personally prorogued and dissolved their assemblies in short speeches, sometimes congratulatory but more often

---

[1] 4 *American Archives* III, 1874–1875, and *The Historical Magazine*, 11: 25; E. C. Burnett, *Letters of Members of the Continental Congress* (Washington, D. C., 1921–1936), VIII, Nos. 500n, 516, 543; hereinafter referred to as *Burnett*, cited according to volume and serial number of document.

[2] Drayton, *op. cit.*, I, 207, Rawlins Lowndes, thanks of House to Delegates to Continental Congress, from *Journals*, Aug. 2, 1774–Sept. 15, 1775, p. 12; *ibid.*, 2: 168–171, Drayton's thanks to the Delegates, from *Journals*, Feb. 8, 1776; R. H. Lee's short remarks, *Journal of House of Delegates, Provincial Congress of Virginia*, June 20, 1777, p. 84; Ezra Stiles, *Literary Diary* (F. B. Dexter, ed., New Haven, 1901), II, 320; *Journals, House of Burgesses, Virginia*, 1695–1702 (Richmond, 1913), 1696, p. 57; 1698, p. 120, William Randolph; 1699, p. 132, Robert Carter; 1700, p. 206, Peter Beverly; *Journals*, 1727–1740 (Richmond, 1910), 1734, p. 175, John Randolph, also separately printed (Williamsburg, 1734); 1736, p. 239, John Randolph; *Journal of Senate, Virginia*, 1778–1779, p. 4, Speaker Archibald Cary; *Journal of House of Delegates, Virginia*, 1781–1787, p. 4, Speaker Benjamin Harrison. See also Pargellis, *op. cit.*, VII, 73–74; Robert Proud, *History of Pennsylvania . . .* 1681–1742 (Philadelphia, 1797), II, 217–219.

[3] "Printed by Samuel Broun, English Bookseller, Hach, 1651," reprinted in H. R. McIlwaine, *Journals of the House of Burgesses of Virginia*, 1619–1658/9 (Richmond, 1915), pp. 75–79. See also the "Little Speech," 1645, by Governor Winthrop, of Massachusetts Bay, *History of New England* (Boston, 1853), II, 227; but the two governorships are hardly comparable.

expressive of disgust or severe disapproval. (3) Occasionally, personal appearances replaced written messages for communication between governor and assembly during the session.[1] The speeches varied in length from a paragraph to several pages and usually were read or spoken from a prepared manuscript.[2] This practice had distinct advantages, as the charges against Governor Nicholson (1655–1728) of Virginia readily demonstrated.[3]

Some governors sent written messages either because they were poor speakers or because they wished to avoid a personal appearance during a heated controversy. In a speech of June 10, 1743, Governor William Shirley (1694–1771) clearly stated the case for those who appeared in person: "Notwithstanding I have but very lately met you here, yet as I am now desirous that what I now have to communicate may have all the weight with you that I can give it, I choose to do it by speaking to you rather than by message."[4]

As the contentions became more bitter, conscientious governors were impelled to present a full statement of the case of the Crown, and, in the light of study a century and a half later, these belated efforts to enforce the imperial system deserve praise for clear and orderly presentation even when they lack tact. These speeches were usually prepared with great care.[5]

Not only did the royal appointees vary so widely in ability in delivery that generalizations are impossible but their applications of persuasion theory ranged from flattery and commendation to a highly efficient use of the known means of making legislators angry. Robert Hunter's (? –1734) brusqueness and his direct question form of outlining his policies, the sharp and often inaccurate language of Francis Bernard (1712–1779), the violent tempers of Benjamin Fletcher, Alexander Spotswood (1676–1740), and Arthur Dobbs (1689–1765) only increased the stubborn independence of the assemblies.

However, even in the trying years preceding the Revolution, such men as Henry Ellis (1721–1806), James Habersham (1712–1775), and James Wright (1716–1785) of Georgia, Robert Eden (1741–1784) of Maryland, Baron de Botetourt (1718–1770) and Francis Fauquier (1704?–1775) of Virginia, Cadwallader Colden (1688–1776) of New York, and, surprisingly, Thomas Hutchinson (1711–1780) of Massachusetts either made reasonable

---

[1] See the speech of Governor Francis Bernard proroguing the difficult Massachusetts assembly, July 15, 1769, *Journals . . . Massachusetts Bay*, 1769 (Boston, 1769), pp. 84–85.

[2] An exception may be found in Smith, *op. cit.*, II, 283.

[3] *Virginia Magazine of History*, 3: 375.

[4] *Journals . . . Massachusetts Bay*, 1739 (Boston, 1739), pp. 45–49.

[5] *Massachusetts Historical Society Collections*, 6th series, 6, Part I: 473; *New York Historical Society Collections*, 68: 26 and 121.

conciliatory appeals or attempted to avoid all controversy, in the hope of retaining the loyalty of the moderate liberals in their colonies.[1]

The eloquence or the success with which the governors achieved the control they sought could be easily exaggerated. The strength and persistence of the opposing parties made the task almost impossible as long as the Ministry continued to demand submission to the trade laws. Yet judged by the wisdom, directness, and simplicity with which numerous governors did apply conciliatory techniques, many of their speeches are superior to the florid, inflammatory popular speeches of the same era.

Although the French wars had produced an intercolonial congress at Albany and several meetings of groups of governors, it required the realization of common interests in the controversy against British policies, deliberately encouraged by means of newspaper articles, pamphlets, personal letters, and the efforts of committees of correspondence, coupled with the Boston Port Bill and the threat of British arms, to bring delegates together in a Continental Congress.

On September 5, 1774, the delegates met at the Merchants ' Coffee House in Philadelphia 'and proceeded to Carpenters' Hall. In a chamber only 20 by 30 feet, upwards of fifty delegates chose the venerable Peyton Randolph president and Charles Thomson secretary; Patrick Henry rose to speak of the common distress that brought them together; James Duane moved the appointment of a committee to draw up regulations of procedure; and the first debate had begun.[2]

The Second Congress met in the State House in Philadelphia, May 10, 1775. Here, in the former chamber of the Pennsylvania Assembly, a room about forty feet square, with a high ceiling and paneled walls, the Congress sat until December, 1776, from March to September, 1777, and from July, 1778, to June 21, 1783. Facing the entrance doors, the president of Congress was seated behind a table or desk; below and in front of him was a table for the secretary and his clerks; and on either side, quite filling the room, were tables, usually covered with green cloths, and chairs for the delegates.[3]

[1] *William and Mary Quarterly*, 31: 171; *Maryland Historical Magazine*, 2: 231–232; *cf* also speech of Jan. 18, 1775, Governor James Wright of Georgia.

[2] *Reminiscences of Carpenters' Hall* . . . (Philadelphia, 1858), Frontispiece. See the *Journals of the Continental Congress* (Washington, D. C., 1904–1937), Sept. 5, 1774 (hereinafter referred to as *Journals*); *American Quarterly Review*, 1: 30; and John Adams, *Works*, II, 365; III, 29*n*. See also T. H. Matteson's painting, "First Prayer in the Continental Congress" and *Recording the Celebration of the Two-hundredth Anniversary of the Institution of the Carpenters' Company* . . . (Philadelphia, 1925), pp. 18–23 and 63.

[3] The high ceiling and paneled walls at one time produced an echo that so annoyed the Pennsylvania Assembly that it ordered a committee "to take efficient measures so that the members may better hear one another." Etting, *op. cit.*, pp. 24 and 190. See Prince de Broglie's

In the intervals when Congress was forced away from Philadelphia, it met in the long room of Jacob Fite's tavern, Baltimore; the Lancaster and York, Pennsylvania courthouses; the second-story library and occasionally the larger prayer hall in Nassau Hall, Princeton, New Jersey; the southeast room of the State House, Annapolis, Maryland; the Long Room of the French Arms Tavern, Trenton, New Jersey; and the room later reconstructed into the Senate Chamber of the City Hall, New York City. None of the rooms was larger than about forty by sixty feet and probably none smaller than twenty by thirty feet. The furnishings of each of the rooms, except in the two courthouses, were similar to those in the Declaration Chamber of the Pennsylvania State House. Whenever public audiences were held, the members' tables were moved to the sides, and a portion of the room was reserved for guests.[1]

Until the Revolution was nearly over, the congresses spent long and tedious days in session, customarily from 9 or 10 o'clock in the morning until 4, 5, or 6 o'clock in the afternoon, except for an hour or two for a midday meal.[2]

Although it lacked the power to force its own members' attendance, Congress governed itself by custom, common agreement, and a few simple rules.[3] Without leave of Congress, no member might speak twice on the same subject; if any colony desired postponement, no question would be "determined the day on which it is agitated and debated," and the debates were to be private and secret.[4] Freedom of debate within Congress existed by common agreement, reinforced in 1780 by a rule adopting the fifth

---

description, 1782, quoted *ibid.*, p. 193; [Carroll Frey] the *Independence Square Neighborhood* (Philadelphia, 1926), which considers the painting of Pine and Savage, "Continental Congress Voting Independence," a more accurate representation of Congress in session that the more famous Trumbull.

[1] For partial descriptions of the rooms in which Congress sat, see Anna M. L. Sioussat, *Old Baltimore* (New York, 1931), p. 91; J. T. Scharf, *The Chronicles of Baltimore* (Baltimore, 1874), pp. 141, 153; G. R. Prowell, *Continental Congress at York* (York, 1914); V. L. Collins, *The Continental Congress at Princeton* (Princeton, 1908); Ridgely, *op. cit.*, p. 146; [Trenton Historical Society] *A History of Trenton, 1679–1929* (Princeton, 1929), Chap. 4; T. E. V. Smith, *The City of New York in the Year of Washington's Inauguration, 1789* (New York, 1789); and I. N. P. Stokes, *Iconography of Manhattan Island* (New York, v.d.). The original protest of Congress against interruptions by "the passage of carriages," *Journals*, July 20, 1785; *Burnett*, VIII, 939.

[2] *Burnett*, I, 150, 382, 580, 691; III, 494. In addition to formal appointments, there was the inevitable "out-of-doors" discussion.—*Burnett*, III, 64 and 535; IV, Preface, xxvi; IV, 512; VII, 247.

[3] *Journals*, Apr. 10, 11, 24, 25, 1778; *Burnett*, III, 195 and 494.

[4] *Journals*, Sept. 6, 1774; *Burnett*, I, 11. See also the *Journals*, Oct. 19, 24, 1774, and May 11, 1775; July 10, 17, 1776; May 26, 1778, Rules 3, 4, 5, and 6; May 4, 1781; May 17, 1784.

article of the Articles of Confederation: "Freedom of speech and debate in Congress shall not be impeached or questioned in any Court or place out of Congress, and the members of Congress shall be protected in their persons from arrests and imprisonments. . . . "[1]

John Adams attempted to open the debates to the public during discussion of the Articles of Confederation, but "neither party was willing." Except for public audiences for generals and foreign ministers, the sessions remained closed, and this fact, together with the reluctance to employ shorthand for detailed reports of the debates and the scanty private notes of the debates, makes evaluation of them difficult.[2]

The members of the congresses were generally acknowledged to be men of virtue, "good intentions," earnestness, and sometimes "superior abilities." All were experienced in public affairs locally, but "dangerous prejudices," personal, local, and state interests often superseded the national interest. After the Declaration of Independence and the Articles of Confederation had been completed and noted members went abroad or returned home to set up state governments, the quality of wisdom and political skill waned.[3]

Despite evidence of informality in committees and occasionally on the floor, the rules adopted by Congress imposed an atmosphere of formality that neither the restrictions of the small chambers, the absence of a gallery, nor the attendance of less than fifty members could dissipate. Various members presented speeches over whose preparation they had labored long and hard, but only John Witherspoon ordinarily wrote out and read speeches to Congress. Actually, speaking ranged from the most formally prepared to impromptu discussion. For public audiences with Indian chiefs, generals, or foreign ministers, speeches of the presidents were written by committees and, often with the proposed address of the visitor at hand, approved by the whole Congress.[4]

[1] *Journals*, Aug. 24, 1780; text of the Articles, as ratified, *Journals*, 1781, pp. 214ff. It will be noted that the rules used by Congress were in essential agreement with those of the British House of Commons and the Colonial assemblies. See precedents and later American rules in Thomas Jefferson, *Manual of Parliamentary Practice* (Philadelphia, 1850).

[2] John Adams, *Works*, III, 69; *Burnett*, II, 84n. Members jealously guarded their immunity from outside attack.—*Journals*, June 12, 13, 14, 1777. For an evaluation of information left by the members, see the prefaces to the volumes of *Burnett*.

[3] *Burnett*, II, 162; V, 383; VI, 23, 476n, 583; VII, 99.

[4] Witherspoon, *op. cit.*, and *Miscellaneous Works* (Philadelphia, 1803), for texts of his speeches. *Journals*, June 16, 1775, George Washington's speech accepting command of the armies. *Journals*, Sept. 28, 1774, Galloway's "Plan of Union" speech. *Journals*, Oct. 29, 1777, President Hancock's resignation and farewell speech. *Journals*, Dec. 9, 1778, Henry Laurens' speech upon resigning as President. Laurens also kept notes or texts of speeches he made Jan. 9, and Jan. 19, 1779. *Journals*, Aug. 3, 1786, John Jay on the Treaty with Spain; Aug. 16, 1786, Charles Pinckney in answer to Jay; *Burnett*, VIII, 480, William S. Johnson's speech

Members characterized debates as "learned" and "formidable," "conducted with . . . deliberation and solemnity" but more frequently wrote that "more than necessary debate ensued," that "it was battled for divers Hours with much Heat and much Oratory," that the discussion was "very warm, loud, and long," "fierce," "trifling," or "desultory."[1] Thomas Burke expressed a common complaint when he wrote of "the noise of loud incessant Declamation" in the York courtroom, which, together with the part he "was obliged to take in the Debate occasioned so violent a pain in my head that I was totally unable to attend any longer. . . . "[2]

Another common complaint was that the discussions were tedious, delaying, and wasteful of time. John Adams wrote: "The business of Congress is tedious beyond expression. . . . Every man in it is a great man, an orator, a critic, a statesman: and therefore every man upon every question must show his oratory, his criticism, his political abilities."[3] The rather pompous democrat James M. Varnum, who sinned often by talking heedlessly, concluded that "great Bodies move slow; and the Tediousness of their Deliberations forms a Sacrifice to be offered up at the Shrine of Freedom."[4] If the debates were unnecessarily tedious in accomplishing truly representative government, the causes were the frequent changes of members, the size of Congress, even with less than fifty members ordinarily present, ineffective leadership, the fondness of almost all the members for talking, and the limited powers of the Congress.

A third characteristic complaint against contentious bickering and the "spirit of party" in debates was raised more and more often as the discussion of Vermont, the Western lands, army pay and pensions, a permanent capital, and finances followed sharp but more dramatic clashes in the early years over voting powers of delegates, final attempts at reconciliation, the formation of state governments, the Declaration of Independence, and

---

on the Treaty with Spain. *Journals*, June 13, 1775; June 6, 11, 1776; Dec. 3, 1777; May 2, 1786, for various texts and plans for speeches and conferences with the Indians. *Journals*, Nov. 28, 1781, Washington's audience at Congress; Aug. 26, 1783, Washington's audience; Dec. 23, 1783, Washington resigns his commission as General. *Journals*, Aug. 5, 1778, reception of Minister Gerard; Sept. 17, 1779, Gerard's farewell; Nov. 17, 1779, reception of Minister Luzerne; May 13, 1782, minister's reception; Oct. 31, 1783, reception of Minister Van Berckel; July 2, 1785, reception of Chargé d'affaires Gardoqui.

[1] *American Historical Review*, 1: 292, 307, 309; John Adams, *Works*, III, 7; *Burnett*, III, 481; IV, 268, 337; V, 29.

[2] *Burnett*, III, 253. Next morning Burke was back in the fray, however. Also, *Burnett*, VI, 203; VII, 203.

[3] *Burnett*, I, 89; III, 605, Nov. 3, 1778.

[4] *Burnett*, VI, 29, Mar. 16, 1781; Oliver Ellsworth put it more simply: "We all know that such a body as Congress is can't move otherwise but slow." *Burnett*, IV, 512; III, 470, 534, 572; IV, 361, 258, 310; V, 376; VI, 14, 57; John Adams, *Works*, II, 395, 401; III, 43.

the Articles of Confederation. John Fell remarked that Congress had "long debates on the title to be given the President of Congress whether Excellency or Honor."[1] Everyone had a "psalm and Doctrine in finance."[2] The bitterest debates followed the Lee-Deane affair, and strong-tempered men such as Thomas Burke, Henry Laurens, and William Henry Drayton let their personal feelings run high until censured for indecorous behavior.[3]

However, before reaching an unfavorable conclusion regarding congressional debates, consider evidence of well-composed argument, appropriateness, coherence, deliberate preparation, and skillful refutation in scattered notes of debates taken by John Adams, James Duane, Charles Thomson, Richard Smith, Henry Laurens, and James Madison, as well as contemporary estimates of the debaters. Jefferson served with Washington and Franklin and "never heard either of them speak ten minutes at a time, nor to any but the main point, which was to decide the question."[4] Jefferson also admired in his former teacher George Wythe "a logical style of reasoning; for in pleading he never indulged himself with a useless or declamatory thought or word," and in debate, he was "methodical in the arrangement of his matter, learned and logical in the use of it, and of great urbanity . . . not quick of apprehension, but with a little time, profound in penetration, and sound in conclusion."[5] On the other hand, Caesar Rodney criticized Thomas Burke, who did not "attend sufficiently to system, order and arrangement, in a general view but confined himself too much to particular Objects." Likewise, Rodney found fault with Colonel Bland, who seemed "not very systematical not always of the best judgment and is rather rustic in debate," and Governor Hawley, of Georgia, a man of great reading, "which he generally displays without system or design straying far from the object in question so that he often leaves it in doubt which side of the question he is on."[6] John Adams (1735–1826) made a distinction between the deliberators in debate such as Johnson of Maryland, Galloway, Duane, Dickinson, and Paca, and those passionate, zealous speakers who lacked penetration and clarity. Only in Richard Henry Lee and Patrick Henry did

[1] *Burnett*, IV, 600, Oct. 14, 1779; I, 89, 188.

[2] *Burnett*, V, 73, Mar. 4, 1780; see also *Burnett*, I, 224.

[3] *Journals*, Apr. 3, 1779, censure of Burke; Dec. 9, 1778, Laurens's speech of resignation. See also heated discussions of Franklin, Washington, General Lee, General Gates, Laurens, and General Greene; *Burnett*, V, 128, Philip Schuyler to George Washington, Apr. 5, 1780; Thomas Jefferson, *Writings*, I, 58, described a member "afflicted with the morbid rage of debate, of an ardent mind, prompt imagination, and copious flow of words, who heard with impatience any logic which was not his own." But see *Burnett*, V, 460, " . . . spirit of party is much abated."

[4] Thomas Jefferson, *Writings*, I, 58.

[5] *Ibid.*, I, 112–114.

[6] *Burnett*, VI, 23.

Adams find a desirable combination of sound argument and moving eloquence.[1]

An analysis of the notes of two dozen debates in the first three years of Congress shows that Richard Henry Lee, Samuel Chase (1741–1811), Patrick Henry, John Adams, Christopher Gadsden, John and Edward Rutledge, John Jay, Thomas Lynch (1727–1776), James Duane, James Wilson, and Benjamin Franklin spoke most frequently. Eliphalet Dyer (1721–1807), Benjamin Harrison (1726?–1791), William Hooper, Thomas Stone, R. R. Livingston, and John Joachim Zubly (1724–1781) took considerable parts. For quality of speaking, however, a recapitulation of the criticisms leaves Patrick Henry and Richard Henry Lee the foremost speakers. Among the others, John Adams, George Wythe (1726–1806), James Wilson, and to a lesser degree the Rutledges (1739–1800 and 1749–1800), Samuel Chase, Thomas McKean, and probably Thomas Lynch, John Jay (1745–1829), Benjamin Harrison, J. J. Zubly, William Hooper (1742–1790), John Dickinson, and James Duane (1733–1797) did pleasing, dependable, and capable speaking in one debate after another. The Rutledges had to overcome first impressions of defects in delivery. Roger Sherman (1721–1793), Eliphalet Dyer, and Christopher Gadsden bored their audiences with heavy, tiresome, lengthy speeches, as did John Witherspoon's low-voiced reading from manuscript. Samuel Adams took less part in debate than had been expected, and except for the debate upon the Articles of Confederation, Jefferson (1743–1826) and Franklin (1706–1790) had a well-confirmed reputation for silence.

In the absence of Henry, Lee, the Rutledges, Gadsden, Dyer, Hooper, Franklin, and John Sullivan (1740–1795), after the first three years, Henry Laurens, William Henry Drayton (until his death in 1779), Thomas Burke (1747–1783), John Mathews (1744–1802), and James Varnum (1748–1789) became prominent, but their speaking, though at times earnest and often heated and noisy, did not compare with that of the early leaders. Witherspoon, Duane, Sherman, Samuel Adams, Jay, and James Madison (1750/1–1836) remained for several years, and, toward the end of the life of the Congress, debates were occasionally enlivened by the young Alexander Hamilton (1757–1804), Charles Pinckney (1757–1824), Rufus King (1755–1827), and the returning Richard Henry Lee.[2]

[1] See John Adams's various notes of the First Congress and brief estimates of the leading members in 1774.

[2] Some useful references to individual speakers include:

Richard Henry Lee: *Burnett*, I, 30, 315; II, 547; IV, 106; John Adams, *Works*, III, 32.

Patrick Henry: *Burnett*, I, 30; John Adams, *Works*, II, 396; III, 29–30n., and *American Quarterly Review*, I: 30.

The Rutledges: John Adams, *Works*, II, 361, 364, 396, 401, 422; *Burnett*, I, 4, 15.

For remainder of footnote see next page.

3. LEGAL SPEAKING. Until the beginning of the eighteenth century, courts were so irregular in procedure, judges so poorly trained, and lawyers so few that little significance can be attached to speeches upon legal occasions.[1] An adequate legal education was difficult to obtain, because law books were scarce and law colleges unknown in America. Those who could afford it attended the Inns of Courts in London, but the majority relied upon a general education and the reading of law in a private office.[2] In New York, just before the Revolution, a legal club, the Moot, held "weekly debates on legal and constitutional topics."[3] Wythe, while teaching at William and Mary, developed a similar club for his students.[4] Great impetus was given legal education when such training was required for judges in most of the colonies after 1750, as a part of the general plan of strengthening royal government in America.[5]

Too often it is hard to draw the distinction between eloquent pleading and other legal abilities. However, legal eloquence received its share of praise, so that a list can be made of men whose speaking filled courtrooms with large audiences or won them acclaim through either clever or thorough

---

Samuel Chase: John Adams, *Works*, II, 395, 422, 506.

Roger Sherman: John Adams, *Works*, II, 395, 423; *Burnett*, II, 533, 547; Roger Sherman Boardman, *Roger Sherman* (Philadelphia, 1938), pp. 115ff.

Eliphalet Dyer: John Adams, *Works*, II, 422–423; *Burnett*, I, 485.

John Witherspoon: *Burnett*, VI, 23.

James Duane: *Burnett*, IV, 240; VI, 23; John Adams, *Works*, II, 350, 357, 396.

Thomas Johnson (Maryland): John Adams, *Works*, II, 395, 506.

Benjamin Franklin: *Burnett*, I, 242; John Adams, *Works*, II, 511.

Thomas Jefferson: *Virginia Magazine*, 43: 113; John Adams, *Works*, II, 511.

William H. Drayton: *Burnett*, III, 317, 370; IV, 380.

Henry Laurens: *Burnett*, II, 584; III, 146; IV, 240.

James M. Varnum: *Burnett*, VI, 23, 61.

John Mathews: *Burnett*, VI, 23, 383.

[1] No printed speeches or trial reports from the courts appeared until the last years of the seventeenth century, with the efforts of the Crown to regularize government.

[2] P. M. Hamlin, *Legal Education in Colonial New York* (New York, 1939), fully discusses the education of New York lawyers. By 1767, in New York, nearly all lawyers were college graduates.—*Ibid.*, p. 118, note 6, and list of lawyers, Appendix II. See also *ibid.*, Appendix VII, for law books in the best private libraries in New York City, and Chap. V, Library Facilities.

[3] For a full discussion of the Moot, see R. M. Morris, ed., *Select Cases of the Mayor's Court of New York City*, 1674–1784 (Washington, D. C., 1936), pp. 5–6; Peter Van Schaack, Jr., *Life of Peter Van Schaack* (New York, 1842), pp. 14ff.; Hamlin, *op. cit.*, Appendix IX.

[4] Among Wythe's notable students were Jefferson, Marshall, and Clay.

[5] The best general discussion of legal education is given by Charles Warren, *History of the Harvard Law School and of Early Legal Conditions in America* (New York, 1900), Vol. I. See also Hamlin, *op. cit.*, Appendix VIII, pp. 197–198, "William Smith's Course of Study for Law Students," in which he recommended Dr. Watts' *Logic* and *The Art of Speaking*, together with readings and listening to the best preaching.

arguments. A few of these achievements are discussed later in the chapter, but the following is a general list of some two score prominent lawyer-speakers, arranged in roughly chronological groups:

Early eighteenth century: Daniel Dulany, Sr. (1685–1733), and Charles Carroll, Sr. (*ca.* 1657–1720), of Maryland; William Byrd of Westover (1674–1744), Sir John Randolph (*ca.* 1693–1736/7) and John Holloway (*ca.* 1666–1734) of Virginia; Joseph Read (1679/80–1749) of Massachusetts; Andrew Hamilton (?–1741) of Pennsylvania.

Mid-eighteenth century: Joseph Murray (*ca.* 1694–1756), William Smith, Sr. (1697–1769), James Alexander (1691–1756), and William Smith, Jr. (1728–1793), of New York; Jeremiah Gridley (1701/2–1767), Edmund Trowbridge (1709–1793), and James Otis, Sr. (1702–1778), of Massachusetts.

Of prerevolutionary and Revolutionary fame: James Otis, Jr. (1725–1783), and John Adams (1735–1826) of Massachusetts; William Livingston (1723–1790) of New York; Thomas McKean (1734–1817), Tench Francis (?–1758), Joseph Galloway (*ca.* 1731–1803), John Dickinson (1732–1808), and James Wilson (1742–1798) of Pennsylvania; Daniel Dulany, Jr. (1722–1797) of Maryland; Patrick Henry (1736–1799), George Wythe (1726–1806), Peyton (*ca.* 1721–1775), and John Randolph (*ca.* 1727–1784) of Virginia; James Iredell (1751–1799) and William R. Davie (1756–1820) of North Carolina; John Rutledge (1739–1800), Peter Manigault (1731–1773), and William H. Drayton (1742–1779) of South Carolina.

Of postrevolutionary fame: Oliver Ellsworth (1745–1807), of Connecticut; John Jay (1745–1829), Alexander Hamilton (1757–1804), Gouverneur Morris (1752–1816), Aaron Burr (1756–1836), and Edward Livingston (1764–1836), of New York; James Varnum (1748–1789) and Henry Marchant (1741–1796), of Rhode Island; and C. C. Pinckney (1746–1825), of South Carolina.[1]

Two speech occasions arising in court procedure produced the important legal speeches of which we have record: (1) charges delivered by judges to grand juries and (2) pleas of lawyers in ordinary trials.

Charges. The charges, an ancient English custom, (1) explained the functions of grand juries to men often ignorant of them; (2) stimulated grand juries to act against specified crimes regarding which the judge's wrath had been kindled, either for personal reasons or by the home government; and (3) offered opportunities for the judges to make political speeches that would (*a*) serve the Crown, (*b*) promote the personal desires of the judge, and (*c*) in prerevolutionary days, add fuel to the controversy over colonial liberties.

---

[1] Another recent treatment of American legal concepts and the leaders of the American bar is Richard B. Morris, *Studies in the History of American Law with Special Reference to the Seventeenth and Eighteenth Centuries* (New York, 1930).

An examination of the texts of the charges, some twenty of which were printed as pamphlets or broadsides for general circulation or published in the newspapers, reveals a well-standardized, abstract, formal style in all but a few. Brevity, plenty of moralizing, and many perfunctory words and phrases were common characteristics. The charges delivered in times of public stress, however, read well. Samuel Chew's speech *On the Lawfulness of Defense against an Armed Enemy, Delivered to the Grand Jury at Newcastle* [Pennsylvania], November 21, 1741, is a direct attack upon the Quaker doctrine of nonresistance in the French wars. It was reprinted during the Revolution.[1] In his charges, Governor Robert Dinwiddie (1693–1770) of Virginia adds to polished phrases that outline the duties of juries, flattery of their "Probity and Good Sense," which will merit not only the "Praise of Men but also the Blessing of God."[2] Four years later his speech is full of brusqueness and irritation with the excessive wickedness, immorality, and profaneness, "so epidemical that Nothing but a strict Discipline and wholesome Rigour can prove a cure for it."[3] Especially in political crimes, juries frequently disregarded the pleas of Thomas Hutchinson and others for respect for the law and sometimes, as in the case of James De Lancey, of New York, ordered the charges printed to expose the judges to public disdain.[4]

The most noted charges in Revolutionary times were those delivered by the liberal Justice William Henry Drayton, of South Carolina, in 1774, 1776, and 1777. These four charges reveal a deeply philosophical but dynamic statement of the political and legal theory upon which the rebellion and independence were based. The last three were heard by large audiences in Charleston and were delivered several times on the circuit. Today, the charge of October 15, 1776, entitled *The Rise of American Empire* is widely read, but the vivid claim of April 23, 1776 that the King had by his unconstitutional acts dissolved the ties between Britain and America deserves first rank for its timeliness, its influence in developing the spirit of independence in the colony, and the strong, but careful logical development of its argument. In it, the charge seems to have reached the peak of its peculiar usefulness in political controversy.

In addition to the charges to grand juries, judges also delivered speeches charging the petit juries and read opinions in nonjury cases. These latter were usually brief and well-reasoned statements, but on one occasion Robert Auchmuty (?–1788), in vice-admiralty court, gave an awkward but vigorously phrased condemnation of all illegal trade practices, "a

[1] *The Speech of Samuel Chew* . . . (Philadelphia, 1741, 1775).
[2] *Virginia Historical Collections*, n.s., 3: 34–35, Apr. 10, 1753, and 35–37, Oct. 16, 1753.
[3] *Ibid.*, 4: 608, Apr. 11, 1757.
[4] *New York Historical Society Collections*, 68: 319, and *Some Observations on the Charge of the Hon. James De Lancey* . . . (New York, 1734), regarding the charge of Jan. 15, 1734.

sermon that must have made many of the Rhode Island merchants slightly uncomfortable."[1]

Trials. The major portions of some fifty trials, in which the public interest was great, were published as pamphlets, beginning with the trial of Thomas Southerland, of West Jersey, for murder in 1691/2.[2] In certain trials this interest became so intense that the sessions were held in the evening in such relatively large auditoriums as Fanueil Hall in Boston.[3] Contemporary writers noted large audiences at the political trials in New York City in the 1730's and at Charleston in vice-admiralty cases. Numerous witness accounts tell of the effect that some lawyers had upon both the audiences and juries. The speeches of the two Otises on opposite sides in *Fletcher v. Vassall* are given special treatment in the appeal-narrative, and William Smith, Jr., Cadwallader Colden, and others heard and wrote their impressions of the famous plea of Andrew Hamilton in the Zenger case.[4]

Although Hutchinson is careful to point out that "Mr. Otis' zeal [in the writs of assistance trial] . . . was deemed as meritorious as if it had sprung from a sincere concern for the liberties of the people [and] [h]is resentment against the governor was not charged against him as the motive,"[5] the arguments of this young Boston lawyer, who spoke between four and five hours, show a scholarly treatment, and what witness accounts remain indicate that the speech deserves a place among the best specimens of trial pleading in this period. It seems to have crystallized opposition at the very beginning to the increasingly imperialistic policies of the Ministry just when Colonial interest was turning from military to domestic affairs. Howard believes this trial dates the beginning of the prerevolutionary era.[6]

The following is a list of a few trials prior to 1787 that excited popular interest, often far outside the colony where they occurred. Some of the noted lawyers involved are named.

[1] D. S. Towle, ed., *Records of the Vice-admiralty Court of Rhode Island*, 1716-52 (Washington, D. C., 1936), pp. 94ff.

[2] [Thomas Southerland] *Blood Will Out, or an Example of Justice in the Tryal, Condemnation, Confinement, and Execution of Thomas [So]utherland, Who Barbarously Murdered John Clark of Philadelphia, Trader* . . . (Philadelphia, 1692), Evans No. 588. Another early printed trial was narrated in *New England's Spirit of Persecution Transmitted to Pennsylvania* . . . *Tryal of Peter Boss, George Keith, and Thomas Budd and William Bradford* . . . 1692 ([New York], 1693). See Eames, *New York Imprints* No. 1 (facsimile in D. C. McMurtrie, *New York Printing*, 1693, Chicago, 1928).

[3] *Cf. The State of the Action Brought by William Fletcher and William Vassall for Defaming Him* . . . (Boston [1753]), p. 34.

[4] Smith, *op. cit.*, II, 20-22; *New York Historical Society Collections*, 68: 337-339.

[5] Thomas Hutchinson, *History*, III, 69.

[6] G. E. Howard, *Preliminaries of the Revolution* (New York, 1905), pp. 78ff. Other events with which to begin the prerevolutionary era might be the fall of Quebec, the accession of George III, the Treaty of 1763, or the resistance to the Stamp Act (1765).

1703—*The Case of William Atwood*, New York City.

1717—*The Trials of Eight Persons for Piracy*, Boston.

1718—*The Tryals of Major Stede Bonnet and Other Pirates*, Charleston.

1726—*The Tryals of Five Persons for Piracy, Felony and Robbery*, Boston.

1726—*The Tryals of Sixteen Persons for Piracy*, Boston.

1733-1734—*The Case and Tryal of Peter Zenger, Printer*, New York City (Andrew Hamilton, defense).

1741—[Negro] *Conspiracy . . . for the Burning of the City of New York*.

1752— . . . *The Action Brought by William Fletcher and William Vassall, for Defaming Him*, Boston (Trowbridge, Otis Sr. *v.* Gridley, Otis, Jr.).

1761—Writs of assistance, Boston (Gridley *v.* Thacher, Otis, Jr.).

1763—Parson's cause, Hanover Co., Virginia (Patrick Henry, defense).

1770—*The Trial of Wm. Wemms* [Boston Massacre], Boston (Robert T. Paine, Samuel Quincy *v.* John Adams, Josiah Quincy, Jr.).

1784— . . . *A Cause between Elizabeth Rutgers and Joshua Waddington*, New York City (Benson *v.* Hamilton).

1786—*The Case of Trevett v. Weeden*, Newport Co., Rhode Island (James Varnum, Henry Marchant, defense).

In addition to these civil trials, the several courts-martial of the American generals St. Clair, Lee, Howe, and Schuyler, 1778–1781 were published in full. They contain several long, and to us, uninteresting speeches in summary by the various defendants.[1]

4. ACADEMIC SPEAKING. Upon quarter days and at the annual public commencements, college students publicly performed declamations, orations, dialogues, and disputations that had been practiced in weekly performances throughout the year as the essential parts of the program of speech training. Occasionally, too, the public was invited to the colleges for lectures on subjects of general or scientific interest.

The commencements, at first held in the fall but later advanced to midsummer, attracted large crowds of alumni, friends, and townspeople. The uneducated must have understood very little of the Latin that was used almost entirely in the early Harvard exercises and that never completely disappeared from the program. Commencement began about 10 a. m., with an oration in Latin by the presiding officer, forensic and syllogistic disputations, and orations by the candidates for the bachelor's degree. After an official dinner for the notables, often beginning as late as 4 p. m., there were similar exercises for the candidates for the master's degree. In later years, the orations might be in Latin, English, Hebrew,

---

[1] *Proceedings of a General Court Martial . . . for the Trial of Major General St. Clair, August 25, 1778 . . .* (Philadelphia, 1778), pp. 6–34, speech of John Laurance, Judge Advocate; pp. 123–169, speech of St. Clair in his defense. *Proceedings of a General Court Martial . . . for the Trial of Major General Howe, December 7, 1781 . . .* (Philadelphia, 1781), pp. 285–310, Howe's speech in summary.

Chaldee, or French, but the syllogistic disputes were regularly in Latin. After the mid-eighteenth century, dramatic dialogues and sometimes anthems enlivened the exercises.

Ezra Stiles recorded the time schedules of several commencements. He noted, for example, a Latin salutatory oration of 36 minutes, a forensic dispute of 43 minutes, a Latin syllogistic dispute of 8 minutes, a dialogue of 22 minutes, and a Latin oration of 16 minutes. In the afternoon, after a funeral oration for a lately deceased professor, the exercises included a syllogistic dispute of 10 minutes, a forensic dispute of 44 minutes, and, following the granting of degrees, a valedictory oration of 16 minutes.[1] The orations written by college students dealt with political, literary, religious, and philosophical subjects that covered almost the whole field of knowledge and controversy. Prerevolutionary agitation reflected itself in many orations and disputes, of which the Varnum, Williams, and Rogers disputation of 1769, "Whether Americans, in their present Circumstances, cannot with good Policy, affect to become an Independent State," is one of the more famous.[2]

After the Revolution began, such prominent domestic problems as religious liberty, disestablishment of the clergy, public education, free press, female academies, standing armies, trials by jury, amnesty for the Tories, the power of Congress, and imprisonment for debt received the attention of the young graduates.[3]

Among the Latin orations extant, Professor Morison has found that many at Harvard, especially those delivered by the acting President Urian Oakes (*ca.* 1631–1681) in the 1670's, are full of timely, clever passages that must have delighted the more intellectual listeners at those early commencements.[4]

5. POPULAR SPEAKING. Prior to 1760 the New England town meeting was the only established institution of popular speaking in the colonies. Because the population was widely scattered there were few meetings not held under the auspices of the church, court, assembly, or school, and out-

---

[1] Ezra Stiles, *Literary Diary*, Sept. 11, 1782.

[2] *Rhode Island Historical Collections*, 7: 265ff.

[3] The fact that students were compelled to speak on either side of thesis questions occasioned the opposition of many conservative clergy in Massachusetts, because students in some instances had to deny immortality, the supremacy of God, and other fondly held doctrines. See A. Creswell, *Testimony against the Prophaneness of Some of the Publick Disputes on the Last Commencement-day* . . . (Boston, 1760) and the answering letters of President Holyoke.

[4] *Cf.* Leverett's Book of Latin Orations (MSS), Harvard Archives; S. E. Morison, *Harvard College in the Seventeenth Century* and "Harvard College Records," Vols. I–III, *Publications Colonial Society Massachusetts*, 15, 16, 31 (Boston, 1925–1935). Translations of Oakes's orations by Professors Morrison and Kittredge make good reading.

side New England, local governments did not develop along democratic lines. Public meetings were infrequently used in campaigns for public offices. Commemorative speaking was almost entirely the function of the churches. After-dinner speaking, as we know it, was discouraged by the custom of offering dozens of brief, formal toasts instead of one or two longer speeches.

Aside from town meetings, there is evidence of some popular speaking before 1760. In tumultuous days in 1671 in South Carolina, when the governor called a meeting of freemen, William Owen, rejected as councillor, "p'suaded the people, to elect a Parliamt among themselves (which they did) & returned to the s'd Gov'nor," but the Governor "having patiently heard what the s'd Owen had ill advised the people, directed his Speech to the s'd people," and "all or most of the freemen" were satisfied, and "left quietly."[1] Nathaniel Bacon (1647–1676) repeatedly harangued his troops at Green Spring, in 1676. Governor William Shirley (1694–1771) and others, on the balcony of the Province-House, tried in vain to disperse a Boston mob gathered in 1747 to protest the impressment of seamen. In the same year, Benjamin Franklin proposed a militia association to two Philadelphia meetings and obtained nearly a thousand signers to the instrument of association. As a leader in promoting civic improvements, Franklin frequently spoke to groups of his fellow citizens. Otherwise, talk, though plentiful, was not commonly formal enough to be called a speech outside the church, law courts, colleges, legislatures, and on these few popular occasions.[2]

The New England town meeting, which developed from the earlier plantations and corporations to meet the needs of local communities for a method of controlling their affairs, was the first American institution of popular debate and discussion.[3] With modifications from within and from provincial legislation, the town meeting came into general use in the colonies of Massachusetts Bay, New Hampshire, Connecticut, and Rhode Island. Theoretically, the town suffrage was limited in varying degrees, by property holdings, income, and church relationships, to freeholders and freemen, but in actuality it appears that many other men and even boys who were present at meetings participated without question in the deliberations and votes. The Body of Liberties of 1641 in Massachusetts provided:

[1] *South Carolina Historical Society Collections*, 3: 293–294.

[2] *A True Narrative of the Late Rebellion in Virginia*, by the Royal Commissioners (London, 1677); Thomas Hutchinson, *History*, II, 331; Benjamin Franklin, *Autobiography*, I, 277; Bernard Faÿ, *Franklin, the Apostle of Modern Times*, on the Junto club and other social and civic interests in Philadelphia during this period.

[3] Upon the origin of Massachusetts towns, see J. F. Sly, *Town Government in Massachusetts* (Cambridge, 1930), p. 89, and numerous articles in *Massachusetts Historical Society Proceedings*, as well as Charles F. Adams, *Three Episodes in Massachusetts History* (Boston, 1892), Vol. II, an analysis of the history of the town of Braintree.

Everyone whether Inhabitant or Forreiner, free or not free, shall have libertie to come to any publique Court, Councel, or Town Meeting, and either by speech or writeing to move any lawfull, seasonable, and materiall question, or to present any necessary motion, complaint, petition, Bill or information, whereof that meeting hath proper cognizance, so it be done in convenient time, due order, and respective manner.[1]

Under the Charter of 1691, duties, powers, times for regular meetings, the selection of moderators, and penalties for disturbing meetings were provided by law. As late as 1786 the penalty for speaking without leave or acting disorderly was a fine but, if persisted in, might be the stocks or cage for three hours "unless the town shall sooner adjourn or dissolve."[2] The office of moderator was created, "that all the assembly shall address and direct their speech unto him and shall be attentive unto the business of the assembly."[3] Even relatively, it is difficult to determine how orderly was the average town meeting. "The records of Boston offer the clearest examples of well-regulated procedure."[4] Except during occasional intense debates, however, discussion became prolonged, dull, and tedious; attention lagged; disorder increased. Often, when no important business was at hand, moderators who were chosen because they were "wheel-horses" of the town or church conducted their meetings with much informality and sometimes in downright confusion. Despite an early fine of 1 peck "Indian corne" for not "staying with the assembly," men came and went at will from the meetings.[5] Altogether, decorum was little better than the minimum needed to keep a meeting going at a particular time.

In most of the towns, meetings were small. Samuel Sewall records only 90 votes cast for deputies in the Boston meeting of 1685 and only 200 votes during the first decade of the eighteenth century. In this, the largest town of New England, the average vote at annual election meetings by decades was: 1710's, 340 votes; 1720's, 200 votes; 1730's, 410 votes; 1740's, 510 votes; 1750's, 470 votes; 1760's, 690 votes; 1770's, 460 votes; 1780's, 910 votes. Only in hotly contested elections were more than a thousand votes cast, and then the polls were open for a half day, so that the number

[1] Quoted from the Body of Liberties, 1641, Art. 12, in Charles F. Adams, *et al.*, "Genesis of the Massachusetts-Town, and of Town-meeting Government," *Massachusetts Historical Society Proceedings*, January, 1892, pp. 37ff.

[2] *Acts and Resolves*, Massachusetts, I, 64–65; Act of Mar. 23, 1786, *General Laws*, I, Chap. 75, pp. 250–255.

[3] "Dorchester Town Records," Jan. 27, 1645, *Report of Boston Record Commissioners* (Boston, 1883), IV, Document 9.

[4] Sly, *op. cit.*, p. 95.

[5] Charles F. Adams, "Genesis of the Mass. Town," *Massachusetts Historical Society Proceedings*, January, 1892, pp. 37ff., from the Dedham Records; "Dorchester Town Records," Oct. 18, 1642; Dec. 24, 1645; Jan. 27, 1645/6.

of men in actual attendance at discussions was probably considerably smaller.[1]

The meetinghouses of New England also served for town meetings, for sessions of the courts, and for any other public occasion. Boston built its first town house in 1658, using a room only 25 by 36 feet both for town meetings and for the lower house of the General Court, until somewhat greater attendance forced the town to meet on the exchange floor, about 36 by 60 feet. The New Town House (present Old State House), built after the fire of 1711, had rooms almost twice as large. This sufficed until the town entered Fanueil Hall in 1742, in whose auditorium about a thousand persons could be accommodated. Except for occasional adjournments to the Old South Meetinghouse in the heat of revolutionary agitation, Fanueil Hall remained the site of town meetings through the rebuilding in 1806 to the end of town government in Boston, 1822.[2]

Until the 1730's, the two regular meetings for the election of town officers and routine town business and for the election of deputies to the General Court, with an occasional special meeting to consider school problems, a new street, a housing law, a smallpox epidemic, or a tax proposal, took an average of no more than 4.4 days or part days a year in Boston. But after 1730 the time spent in meetings steadily increased: 1730's, 7.7 days or part days; 1740's, 9.9; 1750's, 5.8; 1760's, 9.3, increasing markedly after 1763; 1770's, 19.4; 1780's, 19. Town interest in the problems of defense, resistance to British trade policies, the Revolutionary War, and urban projects such as schools, sanitation, fire protection, streets, and taxes justified additional time in town meetings, but the real significance of the time spent is that the citizenry was wont to spend as much time in town meetings as was needed to talk a matter out before a final vote. Day after day the clerks would write, "after a very long debate" or "after full debate" or "after an animated and extended debate, it was resolved. . . . " or, frequently, "after long debate, the meeting was adjourned to. . . . "

The quality of these discussions varied greatly from day to day and town to town. Occasional superior speeches or debates were overbalanced by tedious and pointless remarks of considerable length. Honyman reported a Boston meeting on the smallpox epidemic, March 28, 1775:

At three o'clock went to a Town meeting called by the Selectmen to consider what is to be done in regard to the S[mall] Pox which is at present in town. The

---

[1] The detailed voting statistics appear in the Boston Town Records after 1715. Prior to these, Sewall's largest figure is 340 votes in 1698.

[2] J. H. Benton, *The Story of Old Boston Town House 1658–1711* (Boston, 1908); *The Old State House Memorial* (3d ed., Boston, 1885) and A. E. Brown, *Fanueil Hall and Fanueil Hall Market* (Boston, 1901).

meeting was in Fanueil Hall, & it was very full. . . . One Whitwell was chosen Moderator; and there were a good many spoke, but all of them very indifferently, & some even very ungrammatically, though they were mostly men of note.[1]

Few individual speeches have been identified or the texts preserved from the town meetings of New England. When John Wilson (1591–1667) "in his zeal gat up upon the bough of a tree" at the election meeting in 1637 " . . . and there made a speech, advising the people to look to their charter. . . . His speech was well received by the people, who presently called out Election, election, which turned the scale."[2] In a "short speech to the freemen" of Boston, in 1683, Increase Mather persuaded the town to refuse to submit to the surrender of the charter.[3] Boston newspapers printed a digest of at least one of James Otis' (1725–1783) several long speeches as moderator of town meetings during the critical period 1765–1769.[4]

Although full debate generally occurred with considerable spontaneous participation in important meetings, the political clubs, such as the Caucus in Boston and merchants' or mechanics' associations, usually selected the leading speakers, and the whole debate was subject to a degree of management through cooperation between such leaders as Sam Adams and the moderator, clerk, and selectmen.[5]

Under such conditions, the town meetings proved immensely valuable to radical and merchant leaders in promoting measures of resistance to British policies. Mobs, general assemblies, the press, and town meetings were almost constantly controlled by the Whigs. Resolutions and instructions adopted at town meetings were utilized in coordination with petitions, statements of remonstrance and rights, letters, and essays to be published in pamphlets, newspapers, broadsides, and official journals and passed by word of mouth all over the colonies. The meetings gave legal sanction to

[1] Padelford, *op. cit.*, p. 53. Among the best accounts of Boston town meetings are those in the diary of John Rowe, a Tory, in *Proceedings in Masonry* (Boston, 1895). His account of the meeting of June 27, 1774, reads: "Town Meeting. The Hall so full they adjourned to Old South Meeting house. The Debates were for & against the Committee of Correspondence, very warm on both sides it Lasted all day and adjourned till to morrow 10 of Clock. . . . The Speakers in Behalf of the Committee were Saml Adams, Josiah Quincy jr. Dr. Warren, Dr. Young, Willm Molineux, Banja Kent. The Speakers against the Behaviour of the Committee were Treasr. Gray, Thos Gray, Saml Eliot, Saml Barrat, John Amory, Edward Paine, Francis Greene, Ezek Goldthwait."

[2] Thomas Hutchinson, *History*, I, 54n.

[3] A text of Mather's speech appears in Cotton Mather, *Parentator*, p. 91.

[4] Moderators and chairmen of meetings were wont to outline the proposed business of meetings in speeches often lasting an hour or two.

[5] Miller, *op. cit.*, interestingly correlates these factors in Boston politics. See also A. M. Schlesinger, *Colonial Merchants and the Revolution* (New York, 1918).

committees of correspondence and safety and to provincial assemblies and, indirectly, to the Continental Congress.[1]

A by-product of merchant agitation and radical activity against British rule was the rising interest of the lower middle class in both imperial policies and domestic reforms. When merchant conservatism threatened the Whig majority in town meetings, the radical leaders ensured their control over popular meetings by extending their scope to include all classes in "body-meetings." Where the town meeting never existed, "city-county meetings," "county assemblies," "public meetings," and even provincial conventions served as instruments in which inflammatory speeches or prolonged debates with astute management brought about the passage of resolutions and the creation of extralegal committees.[2] The committees themselves sometimes held hearings at which members and accused Tories spoke.[3]

In the summer of 1775, the Charleston Committee of Safety, following a pattern also used in North Carolina, South Carolina, and Pennsylvania among the Germans, sent the Reverend William Tennent III (1740–1777) and William Henry Drayton (1742–1779) on a tour of the conservative back-country settlements of Scots Highlanders. Tennent preached, and both men harangued their audiences for as much as three hours at a time, with varying success in obtaining signatures to the Association of South Carolina.[4]

Later, numerous meetings were held all over the colonies to support separate state governments and the Declaration of Independence.[5]

---

[1] Although Davidson, *op. cit.*, points out that the Tories well used what facilities they had, the control of all important vehicles of propaganda by the Whigs was a strong weapon.

[2] "Massachusettensis," *Massachusetts Gazette & Postboy*, Jan. 2, 1775; John Adams, *Works*, II, 325*n*.

[3] Jonathan Boucher, *Reminiscences*, pp. 105–108, a vivid story of his appearance before an Annapolis committee in 1775: " . . . sundry of the members harangued long and loudly. . . . It was on this occasion that for the first time in my life I attempted to make a public speech [outside the pulpit]. . . . What it was that I did say I perhaps could not have told the moment after it was said. . . . I remember also that in whatever I said I addressed myself more to the multitude around me than I did to those who were sitting as my judges. In such an emergency this was fair policy, and it had its effect. Many bawled out aloud that what I had said was quite satisfactory, and I was accordingly acquitted [but] my thus coming off with flying colours served but to heighten the ill-will of my particular enemies." Hence Boucher soon fled America.

[4] R. W. Gibbes, *Documentary History of the American Revolution* (Charleston, 1855), I, 225–239; John Drayton, *Memoirs*, I, 326–394. Seven sermons and seventeen major speeches by Tennent and nine major speeches by Drayton are noted in twenty-three meetings. In ten meetings all or a majority signed; in nine meetings few or none signed. Drayton's militia faced down a force led by opposing Tory agents who had followed him on the tour and temporarily pacified the back country.

[5] *Journal of Elias Boudinot* (Philadelphia, 1894), pp. 4–8.

Some prepared speeches were delivered at public meetings. At New-castle, Del., in 1774, the chairman Thomas McKean "opened the occasion of the meeting with a speech of about two hours in length." Before a meeting of June 18, 1774, the moderate Quakers of Philadelphia obliged William Smith (1727–1803), Joseph Reed (1741–1785), and Charles Thomson (1729–1824) "to write down what they intended to say and submit their several speeches to the revision of the Presidents," John Dickinson, Thomas Willing, and Israel Pemberton.[1]

Just as in town meetings, the discussions in other popular meetings throughout the colonies were sometimes brief and cold, sometimes pro-longed and heated, but usually successful in adopting resolutions either in the original form or as compromised after long and tumultuous debate.[2]

Special-interest groups, whose meetings after 1764 were large, well-publicized, and characterized by debates and discussions similar to those in town meetings, played a part in preparing the way for general political action. "Merchants' meetings" were held in all the important cities to consider attitudes toward policies of resistance and to formulate plans of self-administration of nonimportation agreements. In Boston, Charleston, and Philadelphia, permanent mercantile associations grew up, holding regular meetings of as many as a thousand members. For two of these groups, John Dickinson and Daniel Roberdeau (1727–1795) delivered pre-pared speeches.[3]

---

[1] *Pennsylvania Journal* and *Pennsylvania Gazette*, July 6, 1774. See also *Pennsylvania Journal*, Aug. 3, 1774, "Heads of a speech," at Lewes, July 28, 1774; *Pennsylvania Gazette*, Aug. 3, 1774, text of the Reverend Samuel Magaw's speech at a meeting of Kent County, Dover, Del., July 20, 1774; *Pennsylvania Journal* and *Pennsylvania Gazette*, June 22, 1774, text of the Reverend William Smith's speech; Charles Thomson, letter to William H. Drayton, 1774, variously printed: *Pennsylvania Magazine of History and Biography*, 2: 411; *New York Historical Society Collections*, 11: 278.

Other texts delivered at popular meetings included Henry Laurens' speech on the Associa-tion of South Carolina, Provincial Congress, June 4, 1775, *South Carolina Historical and Genealogical Magazine*, 8: 142–150; an anonymous "Speech of a Farmer to His Neighbors," *ca.* May, 1776, Almon's *Remembrancer*, III, 1776, Part II, pp. 249–252; portions of texts of speeches of Isaac Low, New York City, May 19 and 23, 1774, *Pennsylvania Gazette*, May 25, 1774, and 4 *American Archives*, I, 294; Josiah Quincy's partial text of his speech at the Boston Tea Party mass meeting, Dec. 16, 1773, *Massachusetts Historical Society Proceedings*, 1873, p. 197; William Tennent III, *An Address Occasioned by the Late Invasion of the Liberties of the American Colonies by the British Parliament, Delivered in Charleston, South Carolina* (Phila-delphia, 1774).

[2] A. M. Schlesinger, *The Colonial Merchants and the American Revolution, 1763–1776*, p. 291, and *passim; New York Historical Society Collections*, 11: 219–220; J. Drayton, *Memoirs*, I, 100, Jan. 7, 1774; I, 173.

[3] John Dickinson, "An address Read At a Meeting of Merchants to Consider Non-impor-tation," *Writings* (P. L. Ford, ed., Philadelphia, 1895), I, 411–417. Speech of Daniel Roberdeau as president of a meeting to establish a fund for an "American Manufactory of Woollens,

Separate meetings of mechanics or joint meetings of "mechanics and merchants" or "planters and mechanics" were advertised, but after the lower middle class groups began to exert strong influence at body and other popular meetings, their separate meetings sufficed chiefly to prepare plans of action.[1]

The Stamp Act led to the organization of Sons of Liberty, through which radical leaders and the disenfranchised classes promoted anti-British feeling by dedicating liberty trees, holding popular demonstrations with toasts and speeches, and directing mobs to terrify British officials and destroy stamps.[2]

Because so few of their speeches or detailed witness accounts of popular meetings remain to guide the choice, any list of the leading speakers is inconclusive. Among the men best known, however, for their frequency and capability of their participation in popular discussions were: Samuel Adams, Joseph Hawley (1723–1788), Dr. Samuel Cooper (1725–1783), Joseph Warren (1741–1775), Thomas Young (1731/2–1777), Josiah Quincy, Jr. (1744–1775), William Molineux, James Otis, John Adams, John Hancock (1736/7–1793), of Massachusetts; John Witherspoon, Elias Boudinot (1740–1821), of New Jersey; Charles Thomson, John Dickinson, Thomas Mifflin (1744–1800), Thomas McKean, and Caesar Rodney (1728–1784), of Pennsylvania and Delaware; Mathew Tilghman (1718–1790), Thomas Johnson (1732–1819), William Paca (1740–1799), Samuel Chase, Charles Carroll, of Maryland; Patrick Henry, Richard Henry Lee, George Mason, of Virginia; Hugh Waddell (1734–1773), John Ashe (1748–1802), Cornelius Harnett (1723?–1781), William Hooper, of North Carolina; Christopher Gadsden, William Tennent III, Edward Rutledge, Rawlins Lowndes, William Henry Drayton, Henry Laurens, Thomas Lynch, and John Rutledge, of South Carolina; and Joseph Wood, of Georgia.

Commemorative speaking on popular, nonreligious occasions developed much more slowly than popular meetings themselves. Aside from religious services, the only regularly observed speech occasion with a commemorative purpose was the Boston Massacre oration, presented annually to the town meeting on March 5, from 1771 to 1783. Before the war, the town com-

---

Linens, and Cottons," in Carpenters' Hall, Philadelphia, Mar. 16, 1775, 4 *American Archives* II, 140–144.

[1] *Pennsylvania Gazette*, Aug. 31, 1774, text of a purported speech at a mechanics' meeting; cf. *Pennsylvania Journal*, Sept. 21, 1774.

[2] The clergy, at lengthy toast programs, were excused or excused themselves after the third toast. A few dedicatory speeches were published, including [Benjamin Church] *Liberty and Property Vindicated, and the St..mpm..n Burnt* (New London, Conn., 1765, etc.); [Pro Patria] *Discourse, Addressed to the Sons of Liberty, at a Solemn Assembly* (Providence, 1766); [Silas Downer] *Discourse Delivered in Providence . . . 25th Day of July 1768, at the Dedication of a Tree of Liberty, from the Summer House In the Tree* (Providence, 1768).

mittee used these orations to nurture the flame of resistance by calculated appeals to the stronger passions, while studiously avoiding open acts of rebellion; during the war, lagging interest was stirred anew; and as success came, the glories of the past and future of America were extolled. The fact that the orations reeked of classicism and florid, emotional appeals and were delivered from memory, with stiffly formal gestures and inflections, by speakers clad in academic robes did not deter crowds from filling the auditorium and even the windows and pulpit stairs of Old South Meeting-house. These orations were printed and widely read throughout the colonies.[1]

On March 25, 1783, the town of Boston adopted a resolution authorizing an annual oration on the Fourth of July instead of the fifth of March, "in which the Orator shall consider the feelings, manner, and principles which led to this great National Event as well as the important and happy effects whether general or domestick, which already have, and will forever continue to flow from this Auspicious Epoch." Thus began the oldest regularly celebrated popular commemoration in the United States.[2]

Other commemorative popular speeches were delivered at the installation of militia officers by such provincial leaders as Joseph Hawley, John Dickinson, and Joseph Warren;[3] celebrations of the surrender of Cornwallis and the treaty of peace;[4] the annual meetings of the American Philosophical Society in Philadelphia;[5] and the festival days of masonic lodges.[6]

[1] Each of the Boston Massacre orations was printed and widely circulated both in pamphlets and newspapers soon after delivery. All appear in *Orations Delivered at the Request of the Inhabitants of the Town of Boston* (Boston, 1785, 1807).

[2] *Boston Town Records*, Mar. 25, 1783. See J. S. Loring, *The Hundred Boston Orators* (Boston, 1852 *et seq.*). The first of these orations was delivered by Dr. John Warren, July 4, 1783, but the first popular Fourth of July oration appears to have been delivered by David Ramsay in Charleston, S.C., July 4, 1778. See the manuscript note by Ramsay on the Massachusetts Historical Society copy, *Oration on the Advantages of American Independence*, July 4, 1778 (printed 1800). A few extemporaneous speeches and numerous commemorative sermons were delivered July 4, 1777. The Society of the Cincinnati sponsored early Fourth of July speeches. See also Cedric Larson, "Patriotism in Carmine: 162 Years of July 4th Oratory," *Quarterly Journal of Speech*, 26 (1940): 12–25.

[3] Joseph Hawley, "To a Company of Minute Men at Northhampton," *Magazine of American History*, 22: 492–496, from a manuscript; *Burnett*, I, 501; John Adams, *Works*, III, 277.

[4] Ezra Stiles, *Diary*, Vol. II, Nov. 5, 1781, oration of Josiah Meigs in New Haven, separately published (New Haven, 1782); Nathan Fiske, *An Oration Delivered at Brookfield, November 14, 1781, in Celebration of the Capture of Lord Cornwallis* . . . (Boston, 1781), reprinted *Magazine of History*, Extra No. 101: 61–67, but sometimes called a "sermon." The distinction between a popular commemorative oration delivered by a minister in a church and a sermon is rarely clear. Levi Frisbie, *An Oration Delivered at Ipswich* . . . *on the Twenty-ninth of April*, 1783; *on Account of the Happy Restoration of Peace* . . . (Boston, 1783).

[5] Several orations of the American Philosophical Society were published. For the occasions see the *Early Proceedings*, 1744–1838 (Philadelphia, 1884).

[6] Masonic charges and orations were delivered by local masters or visiting orators. Previous

Somewhere between the classes of popular and legislative speaking are the hundreds of speeches delivered by British governors, commissioners, and agents and Indian chiefs at ceremonial conferences and treaties that characterized every effort of the whites to penetrate farther on the frontier or to secure peace for exposed settlements. The British and, later, the Americans carefully prepared the texts of speeches to be read at such conferences. Purportedly accurate translations of the Indian speeches are also included in the reports of the negotiations. Contemporary critics described Indian orators as "eloquent," "giving an artful turn to affairs, and . . . expressing their thoughts in a bold figurative manner . . . with gestures equally violent, but often extremely natural and expressive."[1] However, Alexander Kellett doubted that the Indians were eloquent, because "their ideas are few, and their language is unpleasingly guttural, and extraordinarily barren . . . of necessity throwing the Indians into . . . vehement gesticulation."[2]

BIBLIOGRAPHICAL NOTE

Those who wish to dig more deeply into the subject of Colonial public address will find in the footnotes to this essay the titles of many of the best or most readily available sources, both primary and secondary. For further research, the major bibliographies and studies in the Colonial period of American history, Charles Evans, *American Bibliography* (to 1800), Joseph Sabin, *Dictionary of Books Relating to America*, and numerous check lists and guides to manuscript collections, including those still in preparation by the Historical Records Survey, will need to be consulted.

Printed Colonial speech texts are limited to some 2,000 sermons; 50 narratives of trials; and 300 popular, legislative, academic speeches and charges to grand juries, of which about

---

to Joseph Warren's selection as Grand Master, sermons rather than orations were the custom. All such speeches followed conventional, exceedingly abstract patterns of composition. See M. M. Johnson, *Beginnings of Freemasonry in America* (Washington, D. C., 1924) for references in early newspapers to masonic sermons. Printed orations included James M. Varnum, Providence, Dec. 28, 1778 (Providence, 1779); Isaiah Thomas, June 24, 1779, Lancaster, Mass. (Worcester, 1781); Ezra Styles, Charlestown, Dec. 27, 1781 (Westminster, Vt., 1782); John Warren, Boston, June 24, 1782 (Boston, 1782); Oliver Lewis, Middletown, Sept. 30, 1783 (Hartford, 1783); St. John Honeywood, *Address*, Albany, N. Y., June 24, 1785 (Albany, 1785); Josiah Bartlett, Charlestown, Mass., Mar. 14, 1786 (Charlestown, 1786).

Among miscellaneous commemorative speeches whose texts remain are Count Rochambeau's "Farewell Address to the Citizens of Williamsburg, on display in the restored capitol at Williamsburg; John Cruger, speech on retiring from the mayoralty of the City of New York, Sept. 28, 1782, *Bristol Gazette*, Oct. 10, 1782, reprinted in broadside; copy at New York Historical Society.

[1] "Account of the North American Indians," *American Magazine*, 1757–1758, p. 13, copied from the *Universal Magazine*, May, 1757.

[2] Alexander Kellett, "A Letter from North American about the Indians," *The Mental Novelist and Amusing Companion* . . . (London, 1783), pp. 27–28. Kellett likewise criticizes the accuracy of interpreters of Indian speeches. See also Carl Van Doren, *Indian Treaties Printed by Benjamin Franklin, 1736–1762* (Philadelphia, 1938), Introduction, pp. x, xvii.

250 are listed in Evans and 25 more in Sabin. All but a few are available in American libraries; almost all the remainder in the Public Record Office or British Museum, with transcripts in the Library of Congress. Approximately 130 of the group of 300 speeches printed are separately issued pamphlets of governors' speeches to assemblies; a dozen are speeches of legislators in assemblies; 40 more are classifiable as academic speeches, including scientific lectures and college memorial orations; 20 are charges to grand juries; and the remainder are popular speeches, masonic orations, and reports of Indian conferences.

Many sermons, a large number of academic speeches, and a few each of the other types may be found in manuscript.

Most secondary sources of texts are extremely unsatisfactory reproductions of original manuscripts or printed pamphlets. This is especially true of the standard collections of American oratory. However, some usable texts for classroom study may be found in Peter Force, *American Archives;* Almon's *Remembrancer;* Hezekiah Niles, *Principles and Acts of the Revolution in America* (1822 ed. only); and E. B. Williston, *Eloquence of the United States* (5 vols., 1827). A partial bibliography of the principal prerevolutionary political speeches is included in the author's "Political Oratory in Pre-Revolutionary America," *Quarterly Journal of Speech,* 23 (1937): 243–250.

2

The Early National Period: 1788-1860

by BOWER ALY *and* GRAFTON P. TANQUARY

I. *Introduction*[1]

The history of public speaking in America is not simply the biography of great orators. It is also the experience of the plain citizens who, unhonored in song and story, have nevertheless had their talk embedded into the warp and woof of American culture. The pettifogger securing the release of a farmer imprisoned for debt; the circuit rider whose zeal for preaching the gospel led him into a frontier settlement where his scalp was lifted by hostile Indians; the people's candidate for sheriff of Atchison County, talking to the voters; the auctioneer persuading an assembled crowd to buy a Negro slave—all these and many more, as well as the orators of the Senate chamber, belong to the history of speechmaking in America. And the people who listened, as well as those who commonly did the talking, they too belong.

In understanding American speechmaking during the period of great expansion, 1788–1860, one may begin by looking at the three generations of Americans: the founders, 1788; the second generation, 1820; and the third generation, 1850. Concerning each generation, certain questions may underlie any inquiry, as, for example, the following: Under what conditions did the Americans talk? On what occasions did they make speeches? What did they talk about? What kind of people were they?

II. *The Founders: 1788*

In the first number of *The Federalist* Alexander Hamilton noted the common belief that the people of America have been called on "to decide the important question, whether societies of men are really capable or not

[1] The following is a list of graduate students and other persons to whom the authors are indebted for assistance with the manuscript of this study: Verna B. Andrews, Floy Roberson Bennett, Dudley J. Bidstrup, Mariana Reagan Bidstrup, L. Gray Burdin, Marie Hochmuth, Charles E. Jones, Audrey Miles, Henry L. Mueller, Helen Thompson Newman, Helen Scott, Lucille Scott, William E. Seelen, Dean B. Smith, J. G. Westover.

of establishing good government from reflection and choice, or whether they are forever destined to depend for their political constitutions on accident and force."[1]

Upon the answer to this question, Hamilton believed, rested "the fate of an empire in many respects the most interesting in the world."[2] Hamilton's empire was more prepossessing to the eye of the prophet than it ever could have appeared to an unimaginative observer. It was not so much an empire as a loose confederation of thirteen sovereign states, each jealous of its own prerogatives, each governed by local officers unwilling to part with any bit of authority, and each related to its neighbors by petty suspicions fully as much as by the strongly remembered adventures of the past. Rival claims to Western land had offered a ready opportunity for disagreement until the titles of the several states were defined by the Northwest Ordinance. Other reasons for disagreement were not wanting: petty trade rivalries between citizens of different states, like those between New York and Pennsylvania; misunderstandings over customs duties and local tariffs, like those between New Jersey and New York; conditions approaching civil war over land titles, like those in the upper counties of New York. Franklin, Hamilton, and Washington were among the relatively few men truly national in spirit. Even the nationalists, in order to breathe the air of their time, had perforce to be primarily Pennsylvanians, New Yorkers, or Virginians. For the ordinary citizen the general government was a vague abstraction. The South Carolinian thought of himself as a citizen of South Carolina. If his government, that is, the government of South Carolina, thought it well to enter discreetly into an alliance with other governments, well and good; but he remained a son of South Carolina, and as such he was hardly more concerned with Massachusetts than he was with France. The Confederation was not a government of the people. It was rather a league of young republican nations.

The thoughtful citizen who looked upon the conditions surrounding these young republics in 1788 found little reason for cheer. On every side they were surrounded by enemies. To the north of them lay Canada, securely in the control of Britain, the world's greatest power, with which the young republics had recently been at war and with which even now they maintained only an insecure peace. Indeed, Britain still held for ransom the frontier forts, including Detroit, Oswego, and Michilmackinac, from which marauding Indians could be sent forth, as they had been in the past, to burn and to kill. To the east the seaboard was exposed to the

[1] Alexander Hamilton, John Jay, and James Madison, *The Federalist* . . . (sesquicentennial ed., with an introduction by Edward Mead Earle, Washington, D. C., National Home Library Foundation, 1937), p. 3.
[2] *Ibid.*

power of the British Navy. To the south the Spanish possessions, including Florida and every foot of land opening on the Gulf of Mexico, as well as the port of New Orleans, offered a base of operations for Spain whenever latent hostilities should be fanned into flame. On the west the boundary was presumably the Mississippi River, with Spanish and British territory beyond it. The American states were thus truly encircled by potentially hostile powers.

The situation gave the citizens strangely little concern. Supremely confident of their ability to defend themselves against any foe, they maintained no standing army, but expended their energies in industry, in trade, and in talking of every sort. More immediately significant to the people than any great power was the ever-present threat of the Indian. The white settlers on the frontier, and even those well within its limits, lived with the rifle always at hand, with disciplined fear as a constant companion, and with the plans and provisions for Indian warfare ready for the day of deadly earnest. When Daniel Boone spoke to the newcomers in Kentucky about the best way to kill an Indian, he was discussing no academic subject.

CONDITIONS AFFECTING PUBLIC DISCUSSION

Life was neither so strenuous nor so dangerous in other areas as it was on the frontier. In the Dutch villages along the Hudson the patroons and their tenants lived quietly, tilling their fields. The plantation owners and their slaves along the Carolina seaboard, unworried by the threats of Indian warfare, produced cotton and tobacco and exchanged them for English manufactures. The citizens of New England had assimilated alien immigrants and successfully maintained a distinctly New England culture cut from the pattern of their motherland. Boston, an English visitor observed, bore "considerable resemblance to an old city in England."[1] The folkways, the language, and the government, moreover, were English transplantations born of an earlier and forgotten time when Indians had howled in New England as they now whooped in distant settlements.

It was easy for the comfortable citizens of seaboard Massachusetts or New York or Virginia to lose interest in the backwoods people. In 1788 many inhabitants of Charleston, Boston, and Philadelphia had never seen an Indian, and few had ever heard a war whoop. Most people stayed at home nearly all the time. A trip from New Haven to New York was a matter for serious planning. A journey from New York to Pittsburgh was undertaken only under dire necessity after the greatest deliberation. The frontier settlements were far away, and the men who peopled them were a rough lot. Why were they unable to stay at home and tend to their own

[1] C. W. Janson, *The Stranger in America:* 1793–1806 (New York, Press of the Pioneers, 1935), p. 29.

business? Why must they go off to the edge of nowhere stirring up the Indians?

The frontiersman, in turn, cherished few illusions about the land he had left. Unlike later colonists of other empires, he had little sentimental attachment for "back home." His home was in the wilderness, and his friends were other frontiersmen as forthright as himself. The new country over the mountains attracted him, not the old lands near the sea.

The cleavage between the seaboard and the frontier influenced every political discussion of the time; for the differences in culture, in point of view, and in economic interest between the back-country people and those of the seaboard were fundamental. Massachusetts townsmen long remembered the back-country revolt led by Daniel Shays in 1786. The New Yorkers over the border from Massachusetts likewise remembered Shays when in 1788 they had to consider what to do with the rebellious Green Mountain Boys. The conditions that were to produce the Whiskey Rebellion in Pennsylvania were already in being in 1788, as were those for the secession of the state of Franklin from North Carolina. George Washington was truly justified in his fear of a possible separation between the Atlantic states and the Western territory.[1]

In the Virginia legislature, in the New England town meeting, in the Congress, in every public assembly the conflicting interests of the frontiersmen and the settled citizens frequently had to be considered and somehow compromised. Indeed, the Constitutional Convention of 1787 had been developed in part from Washington's interest in a great canal from the Chesapeake to the West that would serve to bind the Western men to the seaboard with commercial ties and with the habits of trade.

SOCIAL DISTINCTIONS

The distinction between the people of the new settlements and the older land was partly economic—but only partly so. The true frontiersman was hearty and often uncouth, but he was rarely a ne'er-do-well. His task was an exacting one demanding specialized skills and an armamentarium of trades. As he moved deeper into the wilderness, he was likely to carry with him, in one form or another, the proceeds of his clearing, sold to an incoming settler. Nor were the people who followed him into the settlement naked of goods and supplies. Nevertheless, the substantial capital of the American people in 1788 was certainly not held by the frontier folk. Furthermore, albeit the commonwealths were all primarily rural and the great majority of the people lived on farms, the working capital was not held by the small farmers. It was largely held by merchants in such towns as

[1] Letter, Washington to Lafayette, July 25, 1785, in George Washington, *Writings* . . . (J. C. Fitzpatrick, ed., Government Printing Office, Washington, D. C., 1931-), XXVIII, 207.

Charleston, New York, and Philadelphia, by shipowners in such centers as Salem, Boston, and Portland, and by the slaveowners of the South.

The differences between owner and tenant, between shopkeeper and workman, between master and slave were present and they showed no signs of diminishing. The rich and well born in the towns and cities, as well as on the great plantations, constituted themselves a native aristocracy. But the lower orders of men, who for the most part could not vote, did not share John Jay's belief that the men who owned the country should govern it. They were for demanding and getting the right to vote without the restriction of property. An English visitor observed with regret how "the people in general know too much, and too little."[1] The spectator was perturbed that these "political tinkers think themselves capable of governing a universal monarchy; speak with contempt of their legislators as *the servants of the public;* and declaim with more than royal pride on *the majesty of the people.*"[2]

The class distinctions chiefly set up by economic status deflected the courses of many streams of public opinion in 1788, and the reconciling of fundamental antagonisms among economic groups was in 1788, as it continued to be for succeeding generations, a primary function of the discussion of public affairs.

THE COLOR OF THE TIMES

Obviously no sound generalizations are possible concerning the state of the American public mind in 1788, for it contained more of diversity than of unity. The rich and well born, who had been educated at Harvard, Yale, or King's College or even at universities abroad, were of one order; the mechanic and the farmer were of another. The mind of the seaman differed from that of the woodsman; the basic beliefs of the Virginia slave were naturally different from those of the independent farmer of New Hampshire. But if certain special group characteristics be set off, there will remain some fundamental assumptions held so freely in common by the citizens as to warrant their being called national.

THE MIND OF THE FRONTIERSMAN. Concerning the frontiersman, one must reckon first of all with his lack of "book larnin'." Among the back-country people the ability to read at all was an intellectual distinction. Even the skill necessary to write one's name was more than the frontier required. Accordingly the teller of yarns was in great demand. To be called a "liar" was, in one meaning of the term, a compliment; for a "liar" was a storyteller, one who could either invent or embroider a tale. Dramatic narrations, such as the story of Jack the Giant Killer, in which Jack, always

[1] *Daily Advertiser* (New York), Aug. 13, 1787 *et seq.*
[2] *Ibid.*

the hero, overcame great obstacles and conquered the giant, were a source of prime entertainment during leisure hours.[1] The well-remembered ballads brought from England and Scotland by word of mouth and thus transmitted through the old colonies to the new country were told again and again by frontier singers whose hearers hung on every word.[2] Such ballads as the mournful story of Lord Randal, the dolorous tale of the Three Ravens, and the tragic song of bonny Barbara Allen were recited, along with countless others, before the open fireplace in many a frontier cabin.

It was the English Bible, however, that chiefly influenced the ideas, if not always the conduct, of the frontiersman. The Bible was a common denominator of history, philosophy, and literature, an unfailing treasure house of song, story, and moral axiom. Sometimes men who knew the Holy Book exceedingly well never knew much of any other. The Book, read or preached, formed the law and the gospel of the new Americans of the frontier. Dependence on the Bible was not incompatible with the common acceptance of superstition. Life in the backwoods was primitive, hard, and dangerous. Superbly educated for his difficult task, the frontiersman was constrained nevertheless to find solutions for perplexing personal problems to which no rational answer was possible.[3]

Although the frontiersmen were superstitious, not all of them, certainly, were pious. Those evildoers who not only were rough according to the manner of the time and place but also were disobedient to the frontier code were dealt with heartily, whether by formal or informal justice. The punishment for minor crimes and misdemeanors was "hating the offender out." This mode of chastisement was a continuing public expression of indignation against those persons who violated the code by lying, dishonesty, and ill fame generally. Commonly the offender was either reformed or banished.[4] The frontier customs in these respects were drawn more from the Old Testament than from the New: Men are obviously of two kinds, good and evil. Evil men are sinners who must be reformed or condemned. For a friend a good man will give his life, if necessary; but a good man may take the life of an enemy in fair quarrel. And all Indians are enemies. The only good Indian is a dead Indian.

[1] For an account of the social life of the frontier, see Joseph Doddridge's "Notes on the Settlement and Indian Wars of the Western Parts of Virginia and Pennsylvania . . . ," in Samuel Kercheval, *A History of the Valley of Virginia* (Strasburg, Va., Shenandoah Publishing House, 1925).

[2] For a recent collection of traditional songs and ballads, including many that were doubtless known on the frontier of 1788, see "Ballads and Songs Collected by the Missouri Folk-lore Society," *The University of Missouri Studies: A Quarterly of Research*, 15, No. 1 (Jan. 1, 1940).

[3] Doddridge, *op. cit.*, pp. 280–283.

[4] *Ibid.*, pp. 284–285.

The same code that banded the community together to chastise a reprobate or to fight the Indians operated also to enforce communal enterprise. At a house raising or a harvest party everyone was expected to contribute his share of labor. Anyone who failed to do so was likely to receive the disapprobation of his neighbors and, when it came his turn for help, to have his call denied. Thus, while the hunter on the remote outskirts might have to depend on himself alone, the frontier families who lived in the border country often developed a strong bond of cooperation. At hog-killing time or at a log rolling, a man showed himself for what he was and was reckoned accordingly in the community books.[1]

In such a society the basis of persuasion was inevitably personal. The arguments of the frontier were little concerned with proofs of policy and expediency, except perhaps in finely chopped reasonings concerning the metaphysics of baptism. In politics actions were likely to be determined not so much by the arguments John Sevier or Simon Kenton used as by the answer to such questions as: How good a man is he? How many Indians has he killed? Can he hit the bull's-eye at 100 yards? Is he one of us?

THE MIDDLING CLASSES. In 1788 the middle classes of men in America were divided concerning the nature of the world in which they lived. The Revolution had brought the seaboard people especially in direct contact with the French, and the irreligious works of Voltaire had been widely distributed. Thomas Paine, who had gone abroad following the Revolution, published *The Age of Reason* in France and sent it over to America, to be sold if possible and if not, to be given away.[2] Many public men made no bones about proclaiming their infidelity. General Charles Lee carried his opposition to Christianity so far as to request that he not be buried "in any church or churchyard, or within a mile of any Presbyterian or Anabaptist meeting-house."[3] Chancellor Kent, the eminent jurist, observed that in his younger days "there were few professional men who were not infidels, or at least so far inclined to infidelity that they could not be called believers in the truth of the Bible."[4] The men who cast off the old doctrine of divine revelation frequently adopted a mild deism associated with the new doctrines of the rights of man. A substantial body of citizens, however, regarded the "new views" emanating from France with nothing short of horror. Such a substantial middle-class merchant, farmer, and officeholder as Melancton Smith, for example, continued unabated in his religious zeal. The religious views of a candidate for office were a matter of public concern, and, despite the evidences of growing disbelief, the clergymen, particularly

[1] *Ibid.*

[2] F. G. Beardsley, *The History of Christianity in America* (New York, American Tract Society, 1938), p. 94.

[3] *Ibid.*, p. 95.

[4] *Ibid.*

those of New England, continued in their sermons to exert something of the substantial influence on the electorate that had characterized their efforts before and during the Revolution.

Substantially divided as they were on the question of their cosmos, the middling classes of Americans approached agreement on other matters. The Tories having been driven off or quieted, the middle-class citizens generally agreed on the iniquity of the Tory opposition in the late war. Although men were in some doubt about the advantages of the carrying trade, they commonly accepted the mercantile theories of commerce among nations. Nearly all were agreed on the advantages of freedom from the British yoke, of some kind of union among the states, and of the dangers of a leviathan that was likely to raise one's taxes or send one's sons to fight a foreign war.

In these circumstances the speaker who looked for some basic assumptions on which to build his argument was not likely to find them in religion, except for a limited audience and except as the religion of the time expressed itself in platitudes. He was more likely to find common ground with all his middle-class hearers in a prophetic account of the future of these states; or in a glowing tribute to the heroes of the Revolution; or still better, in an energetic twisting of the lion's tail.

THE LOWER ORDERS. In the South the lower orders were constituted principally of Negro slaves who were not citizens and had presumably no minds of consequence. The "white trash" exerted little influence. The people of the lower orders in the other commonwealths worked mostly as servants in the towns or as hired hands or tenants on someone else's farm. The state of the poorer people in New England was wretched almost beyond belief, and the fishermen who sailed from her ports often endured unimaginable hardships for small return. These people were usually either too busy trying to escape from their low status to ponder much about the world in which they lived or too drunk to realize what was happening. The poorer people were often indifferent to religion, and, despite the efforts of missionary societies, they tended to remain so.[1] The drunkenness of the time led to the creation of a Temperance Society by a group of Connecticut farmers in 1789; and the theme of temperance furnished a common topic for sermons, as well as for other speeches, not only for the lower classes of men but for all orders.[2]

From the poorer classes came the men who could be found in the town jail, imprisoned for debt. There was, however, another kind of poor—those who might be called poor but honest. The young apprentice was often

[1] M. L. Hansen, *The Immigrant in American History* (Cambridge, Mass., Harvard University Press, 1940), p. 106.

[2] *Beardsley, op. cit.*, p. 124.

received in his employer's house; he might even marry his employer's daughter. The son of a neighboring farmer who went to another town as hired man was accepted by the family and the community. The experience of an Englishman who visited New England late in the eighteenth century accurately reflected the republican attitude that prevailed in 1788:

> The Arrogance of domestics in this land of republican liberty and equality, is particularly calculated to excite the astonishment of strangers. To call persons of this description *servants,* or to speak of their *master* or *mistress,* is a grievous affront. Having called one day at the house of a gentleman of my acquaintance, on knocking at the door, it was opened by a servant-maid, whom I had never before seen, as she had not been long in his family. The following is the dialogue, word for word, which took place on this occasion:—"Is your master at home?"—"I have no master." "Don't you live here?"—"I stay here."—"And who are you then?"— "Why, I am Mr. _____'s *help.* I'd have you to know, *man,* that I am no *sarvant;* none but *negers* are *sarvants.*"[1]

The significant factor in the minds of the lower orders of America in 1788 is told in the phrase of the help. Somewhat aloof, often feverishly concerned to get on in the world, the lower orders of men held persistently in common the dominating idea of the white man in the new world: *I have no master.*

THE RESPECTABLE CHARACTERS. The American aristocracy in 1788 was not established by law, it was not recognized by authority, it was not always admitted to exist. But exist it did, despite all talk of republican institutions, of human equality, and of the leveling of men before God. The phrases commonly used in 1788 to describe the aristocracy and upper middle class were "the rich and well-born" and "the respectable characters." The respectable characters consisted by and large of (1) all educated persons, including generally lawyers and physicians, (2) all great landholders, (3) the clergymen of the older churches, particularly the Episcopal, (4) most of the holders of public office, (5) all wealthy men whose money was not of recent acquisition. A "respectable character," more likely to be of English than of any other origin, was probably a man of Colonial background. To be sure, many respectable characters had fled the country when the British left in 1783. Those who remained had, more likely than not, restored themselves to the good graces of other aristocrats by 1788. But the rank and file of Americans continued to distrust former Tories and to resent their being preferred for high office.

The aristocracy in 1788 was to be found in the rapidly forming Federalist party, of which George Washington was chief. The leaders of this party generally assumed that the people were incapable of self-government.

[1] Janson, *op. cit.,* p. 88.

They favored a *republic* rather than a democracy. Alexander Hamilton probably expressed the opinion of this aristocracy when he wrote:

> For my part, I am not much attached to the *Majesty of the multitude*, and therefore wave all pretensions (founded on such conduct) to their countenance. I consider them in general as very ill qualified to *judge* for themselves what government will best suit their peculiar situations; nor is this to be wondered at:—The science of Government is not easily understood.[1]

The aristocrats who had been schooled at all were educated in the classics, including those of rhetoric and oratory. Those who, like Jay, Otis, Hamilton, and Morris, had been educated in the colleges had ordinarily undergone "restrictions to learn the art of public speaking"; and those who had not been formally educated often had endeavored to learn the art. Although they were influenced by classical learning, the educated citizens in 1788 were probably more directly indebted to John Locke for their ideas than to any other single source. The writings of Rousseau and Hobbes were influential, but the seventeenth century rationalism of Locke made a special appeal to the judgment of Madison, Hamilton, and other intellectual leaders of the period. Even Jefferson, notwithstanding his debt to the French, probably owed even more to Locke.

THE NATIONAL MIND

Without respect to social status or location, some assumptions were held so generally in 1788 as to warrant their being used to characterize the national mind. The first of these was the assumption of perfectibility out of which, apparently, grew the prevailing buoyancy of spirit amid hardship and the belief in progress. The doctrine of progress was not a facile optimism. It was rather a basic attitude toward the value of struggling for a better time. Among the westward-moving frontiersmen this characteristic wrought itself into an *au-delà*, a sense of the over-beyond, which doubtless made more tolerable the world in which they lived. Among the more stable peoples of the seaboard its expression frequently was found in the ambitions of young men to better themselves, and among nearly all kinds and conditions of men the basic assumption of progress in an expanding order was reflected in a feverish desire to get ahead, to acquire capital. Along with the assumption of perfectibility, to be sure, there existed laziness, drunkenness, and despair.

A second prevailing assumption was that kings and regal institutions are wicked in the nature of things. To call a man a *monarchist* was in almost any society to level a charge against him. The belief in democracy,

[1] *Daily Advertiser*, Oct. 17, 1787.

however, was not widely held: fraternity and equality were matters of argument.

There was no argument on the question of liberty. The new French view of the rights of man merely served to confirm the old tradition of the rights of Englishmen. The American of 1788 believed in liberty, that is, his own liberty, with a passionate attachment difficult to describe. For the word *liberty* to him was not a semantic confusion. It was a symbol of concrete realities. It meant a freedom from every manner of restraint; a freedom to believe what he wished about God and to worship him or not as he chose; a freedom to speak whatever he pleased, including profanity, without hindrance; a freedom to move about whenever he wished without interference by officers; a freedom from special assessments and, insofar as possible, from any taxes whatsoever. Not the least element of his concept of liberty was the freedom to hold property and to defend it against all comers.

A fourth and highly significant mental trait common to the people generally was an ethical equality relative not so much to questions of religion or personal morals—although such questions were often in the fore—as to the primary question of fair play or sportsmanship. Even in the wilderness there was a pervasive feeling that, while a man should have his rights, he should be willing to accept the consequences for any use that he made of them. By analogy one who entered into a controversy should be willing to accept the consequences without bad temper. This ethical quality naturally is of the utmost importance to persuasion. If by unanimous consent a group has shared an agreement to arbitrate issues by persuasion rather than by other forms of force, the power of persuasion either in the written or spoken word is infinitely increased. If, however, persuasion is practiced in a social order where the resort to arms in the settling of questions has not been interdicted by an almost universal ethic, the art of persuasion may become simply the handmaiden—perhaps the concubine—of the warrior.

EXPERIENCES IN SPEECHMAKING

In the year 1788 the Americans had the benefit of a long experience in the various uses of speechmaking.

In spite of a native distrust of lawyers, they were perhaps as litigious as any people who ever lived. They busied themselves in the courts not only about such major crimes as murder, rape, and larceny but also about such petty matters as property lines, damage done by stock, and minor breaches of contract. During the year 1788 the controversies continued: In Connecticut, Christopher Crandall was suing Samuel Hall to recover the state's bounty of £6, which Hall allegedly had agreed to pay him for performing a tour of duty in the Continental army.[1] In South Carolina, the learned chancellors reached a decision in a suit brought by the Presbyterian Church of Bethel in St. Bartholomew's Parish, against the executors of the church's trustee, who had directed the use of part of the funds of the Bethel Church to support a minister at Saltcatcher.[2] In Kentucky, the Supreme Court, on hearing a complicated case involving the ownership of 1,000 acres of land on the Rolling Fork of Salt River, decided simply that the "defendant hath a better right to the land in controversy than the plaintiff."[3] In Virginia, William Graves and John Hague brought an information against the ship *Cyrus*, James Dawson, master, alleging that Dawson had imported salt, loaf sugar, rum, and soap from Philadelphia to the port of Norfolk without reporting the entry truly to the collector of the revenue.[4] In every one of the thirteen states forensic oratory was constantly employed in the dispensation of justice.

The churches required the regular use of speechmaking: the reading of the service, the preaching of the sermon, the prayer, the exhortation of sinners, the testimony of the saved. In the church, as in other institutions, there were great differences both in men and in practice.

In the seaboard cities, ministers of many creeds preached each Sunday to congregations of sober citizens. In Boston, for example, the Reverend Samuel Stillman, D.D., preached moving sermons, as he had done since 1765, to an appreciative congregation. A thin, spare man, dressed with the utmost neatness, he wore a large, bushy wig; his motions were quick, and there was about him a nervous impatience that seemed to say to his hearers, "I long to be at my work."[5] Like other ministers, Dr. Stillman had duties that extended beyond the pulpit. He was once observed to enter the jail in Court Street, where a criminal was confined, awaiting execution. Darting, almost pushing through the crowd, he appeared to say by his very motions: Make way, gentlemen, make way; your business cannot be equal to mine. I have but one work to do; it must be done; I go to rescue a sinner from the darkness of his ignorance and the pangs of the second death. Make way, gentlemen, make way.[6]

The ministers in the backwoods were no less energetic than their brothers in the cities. Indeed, some of the pioneer preachers were believed to hold a certain contempt for the fair-weather Christianity of the seaboard, where neither ministers nor laymen had to endure any inconvenience for

[1] *Hall against Crandall*, Kirby 402, 1788.

[2] *Presbyterian Church of Bethel v. Executor of Donnom*, 1 Desaus. 154, March 1788.

[3] *John Reed, Assignee, etc. v. Samuel Lawrence*, Hughes (Ky.) 19, November 1788.

[4] *Dawson v. Graves & Hague*, 4 Call 127, May 1788.

[5] J. S. Loring, *The Hundred Boston Orators* . . . (Boston, John P. Jewett and Company, 1852), pp. 222–227.

[6] *Ibid.*, p. 227.

their God. Francis Asbury, earnestly engaged in advancing Christianity on the frontier, was one of many who had to undergo the greatest hardship. In December, 1788, Asbury reported a bad passage through the Allegheny Mountains in Virginia:

> Our course lay over mountains and through valleys, and the mud and the mire was such as might scarcely be expected in December. . . . I lay along the floor on a few deer skins with the flees. . . . O, how glad should I be of a plain, clean plank to lie on, as preferable to most of the beds; and where the beds are in a bad state, the floors are worse. The gnats are almost as troublesome here, as the moschetoes in the lowlands of the sea-board. This country will require much work to make it tolerable. The people are, many of them, of the boldest cast of adventurers, and with some the decencies of civilized society are scarcely regarded.[1]

In addition to the perennial requirements of the courtroom and the church, the public address had long been employed to commemorate the great occasion. The Boston Massacre, the Fourth of July, and anniversaries of victory were, by custom, duly celebrated with an appropriate speech. The death of any citizen of merit called not only for a funeral sermon but also for eulogies delivered in other parts of the country. The conduct of associations like the Massachusetts Society of the Cincinnati required such ceremonial oratory as that which William Hull delivered before the Society on July 4, 1788.[2] The offering of toasts and the response to them was an accepted custom that offered an opportunity for wit, humor, and courtesy.

Inasmuch as the governments were legislative, they depended for their force upon the communication of ideas in public address, in conference, and in discussion. In every state, the political leader was required periodically to submit his candidacy to the suffrage of a qualified, if somewhat restricted, electorate. Accustomed by the habits of a hundred years and more to solving problems by discussion, the Americans had established the parliamentary forms necessary to legislative government. Even more than the English shires, the new lands had become the home of free speech. Indeed, the humblest citizen in the New World had and was inclined to exercise that liberty of utterance which in England was permitted only to members of Parliament.

Throughout the year 1788, there was ample opportunity for citizens of both high and low degree to exercise their right to speak. The Constitutional Convention which met in 1787[3] had submitted a proposal for a new

[1] Francis Asbury, *Journal* (New York, 1821), II, 35–36. Quoted from C. B. Goodykoontz, *Home Missions on the American Frontier* . . . (Caldwell, Idaho, The Caxton Printers, Ltd., 1939), p. 101.

[2] Loring, *op. cit.*, pp. 218–222.

[3] The convention organized itself for business on May 25, 1787, and dissolved on Sept. 17, 1787.—Jonathan Elliot, ed., *The Debates in the Several State Conventions* . . . (Philadelphia, J. B. Lippincott Company, 1891), I, 120–122.

government, and although Delaware, Pennsylvania, and New Jersey had ratified in short order,[1] most of the states, as the new year began, had still to consider the proposed Constitution.[2]

During the course of the debates in the several state conventions, the citizens held their own discussions. According to report, the password of the day was *new constitution*, the countersign was *state conventions*, and the rage of the season was "Hallow, damme, Jack, what are you, boy, FEDERAL or ANTIFEDERAL?"[3] One observer noted that the "wretched dialogues on politics, so frequent in taverns and elsewhere, please the mirthy not less than the novels of Peregrine Pickle, while they enrage the splenetic, and grieve the serious patriot."[4]

The popular discourse abounded in personalities. In New York, on April 28, 1788, "A Flatbush Farmer" answered the "King's County Farmer" with a handbill stating that he "has trod again in the same dirty path in which he first set out, as if he expected to carry his point by mere abuse."[5] On April 30, an election handbill, urging the citizens of New York to vote in numbers, made invidious comments on the amount and source of Governor Clinton's private fortune.[6] One of the factors in the popular discussion was the hard-times argument. The times were bad for shop-keepers, butchers, and farmers, it was alleged; but they were never better for brokers, usurers, aldermen, constables, and coiners of circulating cop-pers. The remedy was to be found in a new constitution.[7]

The private opinions that the controversialists held of each other were not always flattering. Abraham Lansing, determined Antifederalist, de-clared that disappointed Federalists would do anything.[8] Robert Livingston complained to James Duane about those Antifederalists who went about poisoning the minds of the tenants, admitting that considerable mischief was done among the ignorant.[9] Hugh Williamson believed that the Anti-federalists had in many cases carried the elections for the state conventions

---

[1] Delaware and Pennsylvania on Dec. 12 and New Jersey on Dec. 18, 1787.—*Ibid.*, I, xi.

[2] The ratifications during 1788 occurred in the following order: Georgia, Jan. 2; Connect-icut, Jan. 9; Massachusetts, Feb. 6; Maryland, Apr. 2; South Carolina, May 23; New Hamp-shire, June 21; Virginia, June 26; New York, July 26. North Carolina ratified on Nov. 21, 1789, and Rhode Island on June 16, 1790.—*Ibid.*

[3] *New York Journal and Weekly Register*, Dec. 27, 1787.

[4] *Daily Advertiser*, Aug. 13, 1787 *et seq.*

[5] "A Flatbush Farmer, Flatbush, 28th April, 1788," handbill, Broadside Collection, New York Public Library.

[6] "To the Citizens of New-York, New-York, April 30, 1788. One of Yourselves," handbill, Broadside Collection, New York Public Library.

[7] *New York Packet*, Feb. 12, 1788.

[8] Letter, Abraham G. Lansing to Abraham Yates, June 1, 1788, New York Public Library.

[9] Letter, Robert Livingston to James Duane, Apr. 30, 1788, New York Historical Society.

by propagating impudent lies.[1] Ædanus Burke, explaining the ratification of South Carolina to Col. John Lamb, complained that every former Tory was "zealous for the new Constitution. From the British Consul (who is the most violent Man I know for it) down to the British Scavenger, all are boisterous to drive it down."[2]

The debaters in convention, though they employed somewhat different arguments, were no less determined than their constituents. The Antifederalists generally viewed with alarm the tyranny that could be practiced by a government given complete jurisdiction over a Federal town 10 miles square. They feared the powers of a vice-president; they thought it unwise to elect representatives for so long a period as two years; they disliked to contemplate the idea that a senator might succeed himself in office. The Antifederalists believed that a strong central government could grow out of the new system; and they wanted no part of any scheme that might raise their taxes or send their militia to fight a foreign war. Patrick Henry, in Virginia, and Melancton Smith, in New York, spoke well the fundamental objection of the Antifederalists to the new system: it surrendered the sword and the purse to a government too far removed from the people.[3]

On the Federal side, the debaters in convention spent their time in answering the objections offered to the new plan, in appealing to the emotional currents set up by the Revolution, and in viewing with dismay the situation of petty American states caught up in fratricidal wars, falling prey to European nations. Hamilton, in New York, and Madison, in Virginia, presented the case for the new constitution: it was strong enough to secure an ordered liberty, yet not strong enough to be a tyranny.[4]

The cause of James Madison and Alexander Hamilton rather than that of Patrick Henry and Melancton Smith triumphed in the conventions. On July 2, 1788, the president of the old Congress sitting in New York announced that the necessary nine ratifications had been secured and proposed that steps be taken to initiate the new government. Therewith not merely did he mark the close of an era in politics. He signaled also the approaching conclusion of one of the most noteworthy discussions of which mankind has any record: the debates in the Federal and in the state conventions concerning the American Constitution. The Americans of that moment were capable, if any people ever were, "of establishing good government from reflection and choice."

[1] Letter, Hugh Williamson to James Iredell, July 26, 1788, New York Public Library.
[2] Letter, Ædanus Burke to John Lamb, June 23, 1788, New York Historical Society.
[3] Elliot, *op. cit.*, III, 395*ff.*; II, 336*ff.*
[4] *Ibid.*, III, 394*ff.*; II, 366*ff.*

III. *The Second Generation:* 1820

The Fourth of July, 1788, was a day of rejoicing throughout the American nation. To be sure, there were some untoward incidents like the pitched battle between Federalists and Antifederalists in Albany, in which one man was killed and eighteen injured.[1] But such unhappy events, perhaps the result of too much alcohol and buoyancy of spirit, were the exception. Generally the day was celebrated with processions, with merriment, and with speeches. Many orators doubtless spoke in the patriotic vein that moved the young Harrison Gray Otis, the elected Orator for the Town Authority of Boston: "A review of the history of the North American settlements exhibits an early and almost a continual struggle between tyranny and avarice upon one side, and an ardent sense of native liberty upon the other."[2] The Crown of England, he went on to say, had consistently oppressed the Colonial citizens, even in the earliest days; and the high-spirited American colonials, actuated by the highest principles, had uniformly resented the despot's encroachments on their liberties.[3]

As young Otis and his brother orators throughout the country celebrated for their fellow citizens the glories of their common ancestors, a new generation of boys was being inducted into citizenship, a generation whose earliest memories would be of nationhood rather than of Colonial status. In Virginia young Henry Clay was growing up in Hanover, the first of all the counties of Virginia to raise troops against the British. In 1788 three six-year-old boys—Daniel Webster in New Hampshire, John Calhoun in South Carolina, and Thomas Hart Benton in North Carolina—were hearing such stories as Otis told the crowd at Boston.

By 1820 these three had come to vigorous manhood. Henry Clay, member from Kentucky, was Speaker of the United States House of Representatives. John C. Calhoun was Secretary of War in the Cabinet of President Monroe. Daniel Webster, practicing law in Boston, was preparing to go to Congress as Representative from Massachusetts. Thomas Hart Benton was waiting on the new frontier to represent the state of Missouri in the Senate. Looking backward, Webster, Calhoun, Clay, and Benton, with other men of their generation, could remember vividly the history of their country: the establishment of the new government, with Washington as chief; the creation of a fiscal policy; the Whiskey Rebellion; the admission of new states into the Union; wars with the Indians; the War of 1812 with Britain; the acquisition of Louisiana Territory in 1803 and of Spanish Florida in 1819. They could remember also the growth of the leveling spirit

[1] *Daily Advertiser*, July 10, 1788.
[2] Loring, *op. cit.*, p. 188.
[3] *Ibid.*

in the people, and always they could remember speeches: speeches by politicians, speeches by preachers, speeches by lawyers—speeches by any American who wanted to talk.

THE STATE OF AFFAIRS

The country which the young men of 1820 saw was radically different from that which they had seen as boys in 1788. British Canada still held the boundary to the north, but since the British Navy had learned to respect the American seamen during the War of 1812, there was perhaps less danger from the sea. Spain had agreed to give up Florida, and every foot of the exposure of the Gulf of Mexico, including the great port of New Orleans, was becoming American. Beyond the Mississippi a new Northwest, tremendous in size and portent, extended vaguely toward the Pacific. The Indians had been pushed back and back again. The frontier had moved westward from the Alleghenies to the Ozarks and beyond. In a single generation the Americans had become a strong nation of ten million people, possessing a great territory vast in extent and rich in promise. The call of the American land without men was being heard by the European men without land, and every Fourth of July orator spoke in the foreknowledge of the peopling of the continent.

THE NEW STATES

In addition to the thirteen states along the seaboard that had joined together to form the new United States of America, eight states had been created in the region of the old frontier: Alabama, Illinois, Indiana, Kentucky, Louisiana, Mississippi, Ohio, and Tennessee.[1] The new states had been admitted to the national Union with every right and prerogative held by the older commonwealths. In 1820 Missouri, the first of the commonwealths to be formed from territory completely beyond the Mississippi River, was ready for admission. The most important public question of the day was: Should Missouri be admitted? Henry Clay, sitting in the Speaker's chair of the House of Representatives, observed that Spanish affairs, manufactures, and every other matter of public concern gave way to the "Missouri question." It engrossed the whole thought of the members and constituted almost their only topic of conversation. A most unhappy question, in the opinion of Henry Clay, it awakened sectional feelings and exasperated them to the highest degree. Those abominable words *civil war* and *disunion* were uttered in the very halls of Congress almost without emotion!

---

[1] Vermont was formed (1791) from territory once controlled by New York. Maine was created (1820) from the upper counties of Massachusetts.

However regrettable the Missouri question may have been, it was not lacking in abiding interest, for the central issue was not simply that of admitting a new state. It was: What shall the nation do about slavery? That is why the debates seemed to the aging Jefferson at Monticello to be "like a firebell in the night." That is why a spectator could report crowds, listening with rapt interest to the ardent debates, in daily attendance at the sittings of the Senate.[1] The debates were concluded after the characteristic fashion of democracy by a compromise that left the status of slavery ambiguous. In part slavery was perpetuated; in part it was barred. Missouri was admitted to the Union.

Before, during, and after the speechmaking of the great orators in the Senate chamber, the people of the states went right on talking not only about slavery but also about every other subject imaginable. Governor William Findlay, in a speech to the legislature of Pennsylvania, urged adequate punishment for kidnaping and complained that *"our laws regard the stealing of a horse a more heinous offence than the stealing of a man."*[2] In Arkansas Territory, James Miller, the first governor, apologized to the legislature for his delay of almost a year in taking his office and outlined briefly the public business requiring the attention of the territorial assembly.[3] In St. Louis, Judge Tucker delivered a message to the grand jury of the St. Louis circuit, pointing out the special responsibilities of the jury to the new state and the Union.[4] In Massachusetts, Ralph Waldo Emerson, listening to William Ellery Channing, observed that the "charm of his preaching is not to be discovered by reading his sermons; whenever he spoke it seemed to [be] an occasion; the heart of his audience rose to meet him; here was something sufficient; the multitude found it good to be there, and went away fed, satisfied."[5] In Wisconsin, the Reverend Jedediah Morse, a Presbyterian divine, preached the first Protestant sermon ever heard in that territory.[6] In New England, Story, the eminent jurist, delivered a learned charge, in the course of which he declared that the "existence of Slavery under any shape is so repugnant to the natural rights of man and the dictates of justice, that it seems difficult to find for it any adequate justification."[7]

[1] *Missouri Herald* (Jackson), Feb. 19, 1820, reprinted from the *National Intelligencer*, Jan. 20, 1820.

[2] W. C. Armor, *Lives of the Governors of Pennsylvania* . . . (Philadelphia, James K. Simon, 1872), p. 331.

[3] *Missouri Herald*, Mar. 11, 1820, reprinted from the *Arkansas Gazette*.

[4] *St. Louis Enquirer*, Dec. 23, 1820.

[5] M. D. Conway, *Emerson at Home and Abroad* (Cambridge, Houghton Mifflin Company, 1889), p. 56.

[6] R. G. Thwaites, *Wisconsin: The Americanization of a French Settlement* (Boston and New York, Houghton Mifflin Company, 1908), p. 255.

[7] *St. Louis Enquirer*, Aug. 16, 1820, reprinted from *Portsmouth Oracle*, June 10, 1820.

OCCASIONS FOR SPEAKING

For the America of 1820 the multitude of speeches can be classified in part by the institutions in which they were delivered. Such speechmaking as has been reported centered chiefly in the courts, the legislature, and the church. Other speechmaking occasions, somewhat fewer in number so far as records go, derived from the schools, from business, trade, and labor, and from the multitude of causes that were coming into being, mostly out of the fertile minds of the sons of New England. In addition to other types, there was the speech delivered for its own sake. Americans liked to listen to speeches, and if no sufficient reason presented itself otherwise, a "speakin'" could be arranged for out of hand.

FORENSIC SPEAKING. During the first generation of nationhood America was a lawyer's paradise. The break with Great Britain, which left the precedents and practices of the courts to be re-established, the litigious character of the people, the expanding order—all combined to give the lawyers abounding prosperity. As the center of population shifted westward other conditions added to their business. The rough-and-ready character of Americans during the first two decades of the nineteenth century made for the courts long dockets of indictments for such crimes of violence as murder and mayhem. Breaches of contracts, the theft of hogs, the denial of a right of way over a disputed road, and kindred actions at law brought citizens into court and gave briefs to lawyers. Along the seaboard the maritime law and the beginnings of a law of corporations were the mainstays of some attorneys. In the Southern and border states "the peculiar institution" gave rise to cases of the utmost significance to forensic speaking as well as to the national politics.

Court Day. Not only on the frontier but also in the rural regions of the settled country generally, the sessions of court, usually lasting three or four days, were a time of "gathering in." Everyone with any business at the courthouse and everyone wanting to meet neighbors from another part of the county, together with an assortment of riffraff who wanted only to drink, fight, and gamble, came riding on horseback or in country wagons to the county seat at court time. If a murder trial was on the docket, the crowd was likely to take sides, mildly or violently, as the facts and prejudices warranted. There was none so poor as to have no opinion about the facts. There was no one who did not know what penalty should be assessed against the accused. And everyone spoke his mind. Such a trial, whether for murder, for highway robbery, or for the theft of a dog, might be and often was more of an issue between the defendant and the relatives of the accused than it was a case of the *State v. Doe.* At intervals between the hearing of testimony and the discussing of the case the assembled country-

73

men engaged in games: cock fighting, foot races, and "scuffling." This latter diversion, a kind of playful fight, might get out of hand and go so far as the hideous "gouging," in which each combatant tried to punch out the other's eye.

The judge and the members of the bar alike rode circuit, moving from county seat to county seat as the sessions of the court demanded. The judge was often the friend and companion of the several attorneys at the bar, and, on the frontier particularly, he was sometimes their inferior in his command of language and of law. In these circumstances the persuasive powers of a lawyer were distinctly useful in getting a verdict from a jury. In one class of cases at law this conclusion stands out in bold relief.

Land Cases. In a number of the states, particularly in those south of the Ohio, some of the most lucrative business for attorneys concerned the ownership of land. In the first place, the records of ownership in the new counties often left much to be desired. In the second place, the law was not always clear; and even when it seemed to be clear, it was not easy to enforce against a public opinion that held strongly for squatters' rights, especially when public opinion was enforced by men with long rifles, strong in their conviction that possession is nine points in the law. In the third place, land titles were often involved in a veritable maze of contradictions. For example, a settler moved onto his land without establishing a claim and, being without the necessary cash, neglected to have it surveyed. Even when the survey was made, the description was sometimes of doubtful value; for corners listed as 20 *rods beyond a painted rock by the Blue spring* or *to a great elm about half a quarter beyond the bee-gum tree* were not easily adjudicable in a country full of painted rocks and bee-gum trees.[1]

The upshot of the whole matter was that the ownership of land was involved in public opinion. The community gathered at the trial, as well as the jury impaneled to hear the case, was the object of the lawyer's argument. Even the judges, who were not universally educated in the law, were susceptible to the frontier rhetoric. The law thus became identified with the personality of the officer of the court. When the back-country man said to his neighbor, "I'll have the law on you," he intended literally to call the attorney or the constable as the law's embodiment.

The Peculiar Institution. Another class of cases, less important to lawyers than those involving land but even more important to public policy, were

---

[1] The following citations are to cases that exemplify some of the forensic problems of land ownership in 1820: *Allison vs. Allison,* 1 Yerger 16, November 1820; *Thomas Newman et al. v. William Kendall,* 2 A.K. Marsh. 642, April 1820; *John Cowan, Sr., et al. v. Jacob Hite et al.,* 2 A. K. Marsh. 645, April 1820; *Ray v. M'Ilroy et e. contra,* 1 A. K. Marsh. 455, June 1819; *Gallion v. M'Caslin,* 1 Blackf. 91, November 1820; *P. C. Barbour et al. v. Thomas Watts,* 2 A. K. Marsh. 683, May 1820.

74

the actions at law that involved that other kind of property: Negro slaves. Such actions naturally were taken principally in the courts of Southern and border states. In 1820 the Negroes, free or slave, had a legal status, and actions at law involving Negroes offered opportunity for argument and for court orders that established precedent, influenced public opinion, and set up the state policy. The issues were frequently complex and their determination difficult. Ordinarily the trials involved a jury, and the persuasive techniques of attorneys were thus influential in setting up decisions. And decisions made precedent, and precedent made law. In Kentucky, for example, the courts had to decide the following matter: Could the woman Lydia, born a slave in Kentucky in 1805 and taken as a child to the free territory of Indiana, be restored to bondage when her master removed her, against her will, from Indiana to Kentucky?[1] In North Carolina, a jury had to decide what should be done with one Tackett, a white man charged with the murder of Daniel, a slave, whose wife, a free colored woman, was alleged to have been the object of Tackett's attentions.[2] A South Carolina case involved the following issue: To what recompense, if any, was the owner of a slave entitled, it being established that the defendant, on suspecting the Negro woman slave of the plaintiff of stealing chickens, had beaten and kicked her so violently that a miscarriage resulted?[3] In Tennessee, the courts had to decide a question of utmost social, as well as political, importance: What should be done with a man who had harbored a runaway slave?[4]

The Grand Juries. In the American states the people, through their proper representatives, were called on not only to terminate but also to initiate actions of the courts. The grand jury was an active force in indicating and executing public opinion. As foreman of a grand jury in Philadelphia, Richard Henshaw made a speech to the judges of oyer and terminer disclosing that 470 convicts were confined in the Walnut Street apartment and 250 untried prisoners in the Prune Street apartment of the prison. He complained that

although much attention is paid to cleanliness . . . prisoners are indiscriminately assembled together without regard to age and crime. The young offender, whose sense of propriety solitude might restore, is utterly lost by unceasing lessons from the worst of men; and the old convict, by his associations day and night, is literally prevented from reflection. . . . The punishment of confinement for offences, to produce reformation in the delinquent, must be solitary, and his person so secure

---

[1] *Rankin v. Lydia (a pauper)*, 2 A. K. Marsh. 813, October 1820.
[2] *The State v. Tackett*, I Hawks 210, December 1820.
[3] *Mary Lloyd vs. Honore Monpoey*, 2 N. and McC. 446, May 1820.
[4] *State vs. Jones, and others*, 2 Yerger 22, May 1820.

that escape is hopeless. These ends cannot be obtained by the present state and construction of the prison.[1]

POLITICS AND LEGISLATURE. It was a time of making and revising constitutions. The new states had perforce to set up the basis of government. The older ones, subject to the growing democratic pressure, had to consider replacing old orders with new. The process of democratization in the seaboard states was not carried on without argument. John Phillips, who was elected in 1820 to the Massachusetts convention for revising the state constitution, doubtless represented the prevailing conservative opinion resisting change. In urging the indefinite postponement of an article concerning which there was a great diversity of opinion, Mr. Phillips hoped the convention would remember the adage, "When you know not what to do, take care not to do you know not what."[2] He also ventured to hope that the convention would not resemble the man who had the epitaph on his tombstone: "I was well; I would be better, and here I am."[3]

The conservatives were merely postponing the inevitable. The democratic spirit, continually renewed on the frontier, stirred the seaboard artisans and small farmers to action. In the meantime state business had to be carried on under the existing forms of government. The state legislatures had problems that could not wait: What should be done about the school funds? Should the pending bill for increasing the governor's salary be passed or rejected? Does the state have a right to set up loan offices, and, if so, what penalty should be provided for disparaging the credit of loan-office certificates? For the members of the legislative bodies there were, to be sure, occasional releases from tension like the dinner given by members of the Virginia legislature for Henry Clay and G. M. Bibb, at which "great hilarity and good feeling prevailed."[4]

The legislatures of the several states were by no means similar in their membership. A visitor to the legislature of Massachusetts or Virginia could expect to hear deliberative speaking of dignity. In the new states, however, albeit there were sometimes legislators of good judgment and independent spirit and occasionally also a man of considerable learning, the bearing of the members and the conduct of the assembly were likely to be forthright and informal. At the first meeting of the legislature of Missouri, for example, some of the rural people were represented by an assemblyman whose countrified manners of speaking were made the more noticeable by contrast with those of the cultured gentlemen of old Ste. Genevieve and

[1] *Niles' Weekly Register* (Baltimore), June 24, 1820.
[2] Loring, *op. cit.*, p. 250.
[3] *Ibid.*
[4] *St. Louis Enquirer*, Mar. 16, 1822, reprinted from the *Richmond Enquirer*.

St. Louis. Jacob Groom, honest backwoodsman, introduced himself to the new legislature in St. Charles with the following speech:

> You don't know me I 'spose; well, it's no matter. I tell you my name is Jacob Groom—live at the Big Spring Post-office, Montgomery county (I air the postmaster), and bein' a Jackson Dimocrat of the upright principle. You see I am a big man—can eat a heap—can eat green persimmons without puckerin'. Salt don't keep me, nor liquor injure me. I am a tearin' critter of the catamount school, and a most decided and total porker in pollyticks. In religion I am neutral, and am decidedly masculine on the upright principle. . . .
>
> I am no book larnt man, but there is few who can beat me swapping horses or guessing at the weight of a bar. I have come here because my people voted for me, knowing I was a honest man, and could make as good whisky and apple brandy at my still as any man. . . . [1]

ELECTIONEERING. Before one could be a legislator one had first to be elected. In a land where public dignity as well as public emolument was granted annually at the polls, it was desirable to be able to speak well enough to get votes. Electioneering was a useful art. Many an up-and-coming fellow studied it, no matter whether his ambitions extended toward the legislative or some other office. The readers of the *Jeffersonian Republican* were doubtless amused if not edified by an article entitled "How to Electioneer." In the Western states, so it was said,

> the more impudent a candidate appears before the public, the greater is his chance of success. Here the friends of the candidate are expected to hold forth on his character and qualifications, but there the candidate holds forth himself.—He assembles his constituents, and mounting a stump, harrangs on his merits, with unblushing effrontery.[2]

The *Indiana Weekly Messenger* described the art of electioneering as one John Shaddy put it into practice:

> Friends and fellow-citizens—I am a candidate for school commissioner. . . . was a soldier in the Revolutionary War—bore arms in defence of my country before my opponents for this office were thought of.
>
> Me thinks I can hear my fellow citizens with united voices say, 'Let's to the Polls, and vote for the old vetran John Shaddy. . . .
>
> My wife, who has been jogging on through the last fifty years with me, express— it would do you hearts good to see the old body when I come in from my daily labour, take her white napkin, and wipe the sweat from my face, accompanied generally with a stanzy or two of an old song altered by her:

[1] W. S. Bryan and Robert Rose, *A History of the Pioneer Families of Missouri* . . . (St. Louis, Bryan, Brand & Co., 1876), p. 503.

[2] *Jeffersonian Republican* (Jefferson City), Oct. 26, 1833.

Oh! Johnny Shaddy, dear John.
When first we were acquaint,
Your locks were like the stoe, John,
Your bonny brow was brent;
But now your brow is bald, John,
You locks are like the snow,
Yet blessings on your frosty prow,
Dear, dear Johnny, oh my Jo.[1]

When William Harrison, of Washington County, Illinois, wished to state "his claims for the *Sheriffism* of that county," he told of his experience with the Indians around Grave Creek and Ft. Lawrence and of having killed a buffalo bull for a hide to make a bed. He told of all the troubles he had seen and of the service he had rendered to his country as soldier, as sheriff, and as magistrate; and finally he asked to be elected to the sheriffism.[2]

The successful officeholder did not stop electioneering after he was elected. As a good politician he "ran all the time." Glad of an opportunity to talk to an audience, the officeholder or the candidate—East, West, North, South—was a ready speechmaker. The inhabitants of the South Congressional District in the County of Worcester, Massachusetts, met to hear the Honorable Benjamin Adams attempt to influence their opinions on the subject of tariffs.[3] Likewise the citizens of Floydsburg, Kentucky, and the surrounding country heard the candidates for public office give their opinions on the replevin and endorsement laws and on the power of the legislature to remove a judge from office.[4]

Resolutions. The politicians did not do all the speaking themselves. They were sometimes spoken to emphatically by groups that met with varying degrees of indignation to pass resolutions for forwarding to the legislator, the senator, or the congressman. The people of Charette township, for example, met at Marthasville, Missouri, "to take into consideration the currency of *Loan Office money*."[5] Judge Stuart "made a speech about two hours long against Loan Office certificates and the replevin law." The meeting resolved, however, that "attempts made to disparage the credit of Loan Office Certificates, are from mercenary and speculative motives."[6] A few weeks later the citizens of Femme Osage township met at Mrs. Zumalt's home and took directly contrary action. The good people

---

[1] *Jeffersonian Republican*, Oct. 26, 1833, reprinted from the *Indiana Weekly Messenger*.
[2] *St. Louis Enquirer*, Aug. 9, 1820.
[3] *Independent Patriot* (Jackson, Mo.), Jan. 13, 1821.
[4] *St. Louis Enquirer*, Aug. 19, 1822, reprinted from *Louisville Advertiser*.
[5] *Ibid.*, Mar. 16, 1822.
[6] *Ibid.*

of Femme Osage resolved "that the act establishing Loan Offices, is in the opinion of this meeting, unconstitutional and impolitic." Furthermore they resolved not to "support any person that is in favor of the Loan Office and Replevin laws, as a candidate for the next General Assembly."[1] The habit of calling meetings to pass resolutions was countrywide. A meeting was held in Boston *"to take into consideration the decision of the Congress of the United States, on the Missouri Question!"* A commentator observed that "'Boston folks are full of notions' and pretty queer ones too"; but it made no difference. The Boston people had met and decided the Missouri issue for themselves.[2] On April 10, 1820, a group of 100 citizens met in St. Louis to oppose the extension of the slave trade in Missouri.[3] Some weeks later in Kensington, Pennsylvania, a meeting of the citizens passed resolutions deprecating the violent and quixotic zeal for the abolition of domestic slavery.[4]

Resolutions meetings were not always peaceful. Sometimes they were troubled, like the meeting held in Philadelphia on November 21, 1820, by a vocal opposition. This meeting, called by a group who were against extension of slavery, was disrupted by Mr. Simpson, who charged that "some of the partizans of James Monroe were present, and they were not invited." He was answered by James C. Biddle, who declared the president to be a long-tried patriot, an able statesman, and a faithful public servant. But Biddle was answered in his turn by Col. Duane, who styled Monroe "a perjured traitor, the tool of George IV." When Mr. Biddle tried to answer again, he was stopped by cries from the audience. He tried three more times but was stopped each time because the meeting "was intended to be exclusively a meeting of the enemies of James Monroe." After much demonstration, the chairman, the secretary, and some other persons went to Overhot's Tavern to draw up an opposition electoral ticket.[5]

In the Western country questions concerning the public land and land titles were a frequent subject of resolutions. Missouri, for example, had no sooner got into the Union than Mr. Barton began introducing into the Congress of the United States resolutions from the people of Missouri "requesting the Senators and Representatives in Congress, from that state, to endeavour to obtain the passage of a law to extend to all the actual [settlers] on the upper Gasconade who may have erected saw-mills on the public lands, the right of pre-emption. . . . "[6] Not long after, Senator

---

[1] *Ibid.*, Apr. 20, 1822.
[2] *Ibid.*, May 6, 1820.
[3] *Ibid.*, Apr. 15, 1820.
[4] *Ibid.*, Nov. 25, 1820, reprinted from *The Philadelphia American Centinel.*
[5] *St. Louis Enquirer*, Nov. 25, 1820.
[6] *Ibid.*, Mar. 23, 1822.

Benton made a speech in the Senate supporting his bill to "*perfect French and Spanish land titles in Missouri, late Upper Louisiana.*"[1]

THE CONGRESS. The Senate and the House of Representatives in Washington attracted the ablest legislative speakers of the day. Among the foremost of the parliamentarians was Henry Clay, Speaker of the House. An observer described his speaking from the point of view of the foreigner:

As an orator, Mr. Clay stands high in the estimation of his countrymen, but he does not possess much gracefulness or elegance of manner; his eloquence is impetuous and vehement; it rolls like a torrent, but like a torrent which is sometimes irregular, and occasionally obstructed. Though there is a want of rapidity and fluency in his elocution, yet he has a great deal of fire and vigour in his expression. When he speaks he is full of animation and earnestness; his face brightens, his eye beams with additional lustre, and his whole figure indicates that he is entirely occupied with the subject on which his eloquence is employed.[2]

One of Clay's fellow countrymen, although employing somewhat different language, confirmed the foreigner's observation:

He [Henry Clay] is warm, vehement, and, when fairly engaged, is almost headlong in his eloquence. To use a *back-woods* simile, he seems as tho' he would "*fly off the helve,*" during the paroxisms of declamation. He sometimes descends to *mimic* the manner of his opponents. . . . The language of Mr. C. though seldom select, and scarcely ever classically published, is always forcible. He is unquestionably a powerful speaker; and will always have considerable influence in a popular assembly.[3]

Another speaker of great contemporary reputation was William Pinkney. One who heard Pinkney speak on the Missouri question wrote about his speech as follows:

I yesterday attended the Senate, and heard Mr. Pinkney speak on the Missouri question. Such a burst of oratory, I never before witnessed. The lofty, impressive and elegant arguments he adduced—his unbroken chain of reasoning, his flights of fancy, his metaphors and allusions, were all of that *ne plus ultra* standard, which we are taught to admire and reverence in the Orators of Ancient Rome at her proudest era.[4]

To all this Mr. Faux agreed:

At the first glance, you would imagine Mr. Pinkney was one of those butterflies of fashion, *a dandy,* known by their extravagant eccentricities of dress, and pecul-

[1] *St. Louis Enquirer,* Apr. 27, 1822.

[2] William Faux, "Memorable Days in America," in R. G. Thwaites, *Early Western Travels* . . . (Cleveland, Arthur H. Clark Company, 1905), XII, 28–29.

[3] *Missouri Herald,* Apr. 1, 1820, reprinted from *The Downington Republican.*

[4] Letter signed "R." *Missouri Intelligencer* (Franklin), Mar. 11, 1820, reprinted from the *Baltimore Patriot.*

iarities of manners. . . . But Mr. Pinkney is indeed a wonderful man, and one of those beings whom the lover of human nature feels a delight in contemplating. His mind is of the very first order; quick, expanded, fervid, and powerful. The hearer is at a loss which most to admire, the vigour of his judgment, the fertility of his invention, the strength of his memory, or the power of his imagination. . . . This singular union of the rare and precious gifts of nature, has received all the strength which education could afford, and all the polish and splendour which art could bestow.[1]

Another speaker who attracted the attention of the gallery was Mr. Holmes, of Massachusetts, who was

what would be called a *cute* speaker. . . . He affects a great deal of *point* in his sentences; and is often pretty successful. His manner evidently indicates, that he expects the full force of his arguments and sarcasms, to be duly appreciated by the audience. A certain tone of voice, almost bordering upon whine, has a prejudicial influence upon his oratory—though, by the way, it is not very uncommon among the public speakers of New England. Take him altogether, I think Mr. H. a pretty shrewd sort of a politician; and although I may think him neither correct nor profound in his views yet he is generally ready and apt in his replies, and tolerably ingenious in his arguments.[2]

According to one observer, Representative Lowndes of South Carolina

is undoubtedly the most influential member in the House of Representatives. His eloquence is neither showy nor graceful; but his mildness and candour, superadded to the useful information which he brings into the discussion of every important topic, win upon the confidence of the House, and give a weight to his opinions which can never be acquired by declamatory vehemence, nor pointed sarcasm. . . . A suggestion from him, will often-times avert a proposition of menacing aspect; and change the direction of a debate which promises nothing better than angry repartee, or noisy harrangue. . . . [3]

Concerning the redoubtable John Randolph, of Virginia, no two observers agreed. Cynical, bitter-tongued, eloquent, and fearless, the inimitable Randolph spoke without fear and without friends. The editor of the Lexington Reporter received and printed a letter saying that

Mr. RANDOLPH entirely failed in his attempt to be eloquent on the Missouri question, though he occupied part of two days. He was wild, diffuse, & sometimes perfectly incoherent.[4]

To another listener, however, Randolph was the orator *sui generis:*

[1] Thwaites, *Early Western Travels*, XII, 32–33.
[2] *Missouri Herald*, Apr. 1, 1820, reprinted from *The Downington Republican*.
[3] *Ibid.*
[4] *Missouri Intelligencer*, Mar. 25, 1820, reprinted from the *Lexington Reporter*.

While the eloquence of Mr. Clay gushes forth like the mountain torrent, impetuous and foaming—that of Mr. Randolph glides along like a pellucid streamlet, discovering, in its devious meanderings, every curious gem and pebble in its bed, and reflecting . . . rays of attic wit and humour. Mr. R. does not seem to find himself *at home*, as a politician, among the republicans of modern times. He . . . refers continually to the administration of Thomas Jefferson, as the golden age of our Republic. . . . He is in fact exceedingly prone to find fault with the present state of things, and to praise the times that are past.—One reason for this may be, that he was then a conspicuous leader of the majority; but now belonging in reality to no party, he criticises upon all sides. . . . [1]

From a foreigner Randolph's oratory received compliments that would have been of doubtful merit west of the Alleghenies:

I again went to Congress, where I heard Mr. Randolph's good speech on the Missouri question. This sensible orator continually refers to English authors and orators, insomuch that all seemed English. These American statesmen cannot open their mouths without acknowledging their British origin and obligations. [2]

The American people of 1820, despite many obvious diversities of belief and conduct, had this trait generally in common: They took their politics seriously. The great body of them believed implicitly and put into daily practice the lessons they had learned from their fathers of 1788, to wit, that the

disposal of your reputation, and of your lives and property, is more momentous than a contract for a farm, or the sale of a bale of goods. [3]

Fully as ardent believers in liberty as their fathers had been, the men of 1820 were extending in the political sphere the concept of equality.

RELIGIOUS SPEAKING. Despite their abiding interest in politics, the Americans of 1820 did not want it mixed with their religion. [4] In the aristocratic churches of the seaboard, the minister was expected to read the service prescribed. In the churches of New England, the sermon had sometimes become in its own way an art form. The older members of a Unitarian

---

[1] *Missouri Herald*, Apr. 1, 1820, reprinted from *The Downington Republican*.

[2] Thwaites, *Early Western Travels*, XII, 23.

[3] Governor George Clinton, writing as Cato, *New York Journal and Weekly Register*, Sept. 27, 1787 *et seq.*

[4] Even so, there was no serious objection to Everett's addressing the Congress. Witness Faux's observation, made on February 13, 1820: "From the Speaker's chair in Congress-hall, I heard the young, learned, and reverend professor Everett, of Cambridge University, (aged 29) preach most eloquently to the President and legislature of this great empire. His voice, bewitchingly melodious, yet manly, filled the house, and made every word tell, and every ear hear. *Time is short*, was the subject. . . . Independent of its moral instruction, this sermon was a fine specimen of oratory, and greatly interested the members of both houses, who very cordially shook the preacher by the hand."—Thwaites, *Early Western Travels*, XII, 54–55.

congregation, on hearing a new minister, experienced something of the critical pleasure that another generation might have found in the appreciation of poetry or the enjoyment of the theatre. The careful structure, the cadenced prose, the chosen figure of the New England minister's sermon contrasted sharply with the direct and vigorous preaching of his colleagues in other churches. The learned Unitarian divine was not likely, as a Methodist minister at a camp meeting in Delaware did, to provide for his congregation a homely translation of the familiar metaphor of the rich man getting into heaven: "It is as impossible for an unregenerated soul to enter into the kingdom of heaven, and be saved, as it would be for the best horseman among you, to ride down the clouds upon a thunderbolt, through the branches of a crab apple tree, without getting scratched."[1]

The New England minister's function was often that of justifying the ways of God to man while refraining from interfering with the orderly functioning of the universe in so doing. In the rural regions and on the frontier generally, the preacher—frequently an itinerant Methodist or Baptist—was expected to and usually did "preach Christ and him crucified." The theme was perennially the way of salvation, the spirit was evangelism, and the method was persuasion.

Throughout the country popular favor was thus generally withheld, albeit for different reasons, from the political parson. So pronounced was the public feeling that John M. Peck, one of the most influential Baptist ministers, felt obliged to publish the following letter:

BRETHREN,

A report has been started by an individual who *knew* its falsity, and that report has been seized upon and published by the editors of the *St. Louis Enquirer*, that the Rev. Mr. Welch and myself have been engaged in "*political preaching* and circulating anti-slave tickets." Whatever may be my private sentiments on the subject of slavery itself, or the policy or expediency of its limitation, I have had too much regard to the cause of religion, the interests of the country, and my own public and private reputation, to preach on slavery or any other subject of party politics. . . . [2]

Years later, the Reverend Mr. Milton of Newburyport, New York, was to look back upon the good old days: "When I came into the pulpit, and for years after, Religion used to be the principal topic preached upon; now, it is all rum and niggers![3]"

In 1820 the Mormons had not yet risen; and the Catholic Church, commonly viewed with suspicion by the other denominations, was not

---

[1] *Jeffersonian Republican*, Mar. 15, 1834.

[2] Letter from J. M. Peck to the members of the Baptist Society in Howard and Cooper Counties, *Missouri Intelligencer* (Franklin), June 17, 1820.

[3] *Jeffersonian Republican*, July 29, 1837.

highly influential. The great migration had not yet brought the Lutherans and other immigrant religious groups. The forms of religious worship or the lack of them were native; and on the frontier they emphasized the hope of heaven and the dangers of hell-fire. The primary emotional appeal was frequently that of fear. Dr. R. H. Manier once described the effective sermons of Peter Cartwright, one of the greatest preachers of the West:

He was absolutely fearless, and upon entering a community would in his first sermon scorch the people for their sins, particularizing the vices of that neighborhood. 'You are hair-hung and breeze-shaken over hell,' he would say, with indescribable force and emphasis, shaking his great fist at his congregation; 'and when you get there your ribs will only be a gridiron for the devil to roast your souls in.' He literally scared thousands of his hearers into salvation.[1]

In 1820 the frontier region still had vivid recollections of the famous hen-egg revival, which had stirred the wilderness between 1797 and 1805. During this extraordinary revival of religion, congregations numbering thousands of men and women had been stirred by religious fervor and mass hysteria to the point of hugging, kissing, barking like dogs, dancing ecstatically, laughing the Holy Laugh, and speaking with tongues. A common manifestation of the religious emotion was "the jerks," a violent spasm of the head, which was the special affliction of women. The religious revivals had been characterized in some places by a rebellion against the constituted churches, and the established order of religion, in turn, had frequently deplored and deprecated the uses to which the "heavenly confusion" was put.[2] By 1820, however, the unusual rush of religious fervor had run its course or had found manifestation in other ways.

For the several denominations it was a time of organizing. The churches in the East, particularly the Baptist, Methodist, and Presbyterian, were busy creating societies to save the unregenerate West. The American Education Society had been founded in 1815 and the American Bible Society in 1816. Some years later, in 1824, the Sunday School Union was formed. It was followed in 1825 by the American Tract Society, in 1826 by the American Society for Promoting Temperance, and in 1828 by the American Peace Society. But the most successful religious organization was doubtless the American Home Mission Society, founded in 1826. To the American Home Mission Society and its predecessors the West was indebted for the financial support that made possible the establishment of churches and

---

[1] W. B. Stevens, *Centennial History of Missouri* . . . (St. Louis, S. J. Clarke Publishing Company, 1921), I, 169.

[2] The religious revival in Kentucky is well described by Bernard Mayo in his book *Henry Clay: Spokesman of the New West.* (Boston, Houghton Mifflin Company, 1937), pp. 122–127.

the support of ministers. The missionaries in the West were busy trying at one and the same time to do the work of God and to live on their meager salaries. Many a tale of stern devotion to duty could be told of those New Englanders who, like the young graduates of Andover Seminary, left their own peaceful communities in order to gather the resources "of philanthropy, patriotism and Christian sympathy throughout our country, into one vast reservoir, from which a stream shall flow to Georgia, to Louisiana, to Missouri and to Maine, fertilizing every barren spot and causing our whole country to flourish like the garden of the Lord."[1]

Despite the devotion of the missionaries and despite the more spectacular revivals, the substantial advance of the churches was made in the unremitting effort Sunday by Sunday and weekday by weekday. The story of the conquering of the frontier by the churches is told in countless thousands of cards that appeared, like the following example, in the little country newspapers: "The Rev. Thomas P. Green will preach at the Court House in this place, at candle light to-morrow (Sunday) evening."[2]

The preachers, to be sure, established themselves and their faiths among the back-country men in other ways also. In performing a marriage ceremony or in preaching a funeral, the minister had an opportunity to make friends and eventual converts.

CELEBRATIONS. In 1820 the public address in some form was almost invariably a part of every celebration. Accordingly, when, on the Fourth of July, 1820, "a respectable party, consisting of gentlemen, natives of *seven different countries,* dined together, in the long room, over the Public Baths, in C Street" in Washington, D. C., John Wright made a lengthy speech that included a reading from the Declaration of Independence and a lament for freedom in a country where more than 900,000 individuals were held in bondage.[3] In every part of the country the reading of the Declaration of Independence and the listening to a patriotic speech were accepted ceremonials for Independence Day. Even in the small villages the people forgathered, as did the inhabitants of Marthasville on the Fourth of July, 1820, when they heard an oration, ate a sumptuous dinner, drank many toasts, and closed the evening with a ball.[4]

Washington's Birthday was another occasion for great public celebrations. The orator on such an anniversary was likely to point with pride to all things American and to view with alarm all things European, as did the young man whom Adlard Welby heard on February 22, 1820:

---

[1] John Maltby, "Connexion between Domestic Missions and the Political Prospects of our Country," quoted from Goodykoontz, *op. cit.,* p. 177.

[2] *Missouri Herald,* May 6, 1820.

[3] *St. Louis Enquirer,* Aug. 16, 1820.

[4] *Ibid.,* July 19, 1820.

At ten A.M. we repaired to Washington Hall, where an oration was to be delivered . . . by a young student in the law, one of which profession is annually chosen for the task; this being an opportunity of becoming known, and a trial of ability, may be of much advantage to a young man. . . .

Yankee doodle over, the Orator, a fine young man but of very inadequate strength of voice, advanced and commenced his address, in which I was surprised to hear but little of the great character we were met to recal to respectful memory. It was a rapid panoramic sketch of the political situation of the several principal powers of Europe, with all of whom he found fault; . . . he concluded with an unqualified approbation of the men and measures at home; not excepting the late decision of Congress on the Missouri question, which perpetuates slavery in the United States: in short, he boldly affirmed that *their* nation was alone the favoured one under heaven where true liberty was understood and enjoyed.[1]

The ceremonial occasion was not always sound and fury. Webster's "Plymouth Oration," delivered in 1820, translated the feelings of a patriotic audience into words of dignity and did so with notable effect. George Ticknor had never been so excited by public speaking in his life as he was by the "Plymouth Oration." "Three or four times," Ticknor said, "I thought my temples would burst with the gush of blood."[2] The themes of Daniel Webster were mighty ones; and his was a personal power commensurate with his task.

Toasts. In the early decades of the nineteenth century, the patriotic speech was frequently one part of a program that included an important counterpart: the drinking of toasts and the response to them. In 1820 the citizens of St. Louis demonstrated their Americanism beyond the cavil of the meanest critic:

The 44th anniversary of American Independence was celebrated in this town, by the volunteer company of 'Saint Louis Guards' who paraded at an early hour, after going through the various evolutions of the day and firing 24 rounds, they marched to the court house (where a dinner was prepared for the occasion,) accompanied by a number of the most respectable citizens of the place. Lieut. A. J. Bruce was called to the chair, as President, and col. E. Rector, Vice President. The Declaration of Independence being read, the following toasts were drank.

The Day we Celebrate—May it ever be remembered and venerated, as giving birth to a republic of freemen.
   [Washington's march, 3 cheers.
George Washington—The father of his country, the brightest ornament of the human family. Who executed and maintained the noblest system of freedom and republicanism.
   [Hail to the chief.
The United States—The stars of freedom—may their lustre be as permanent as it is brilliant.
   [Yankee doodle, 6 cheers.

[1] Thwaites, *Early Western Travels*, XII, 316–318.
[2] H. C. Lodge, *Daniel Webster* (Boston, Houghton Mifflin Company, 1891), p. 118.

The Early National Period: 1788–1860

The Martyrs of the Revolution—May the alter on which they offered their lives a sacrifise, be duly appreciated by Americans.

[Hail Columbia.

The Union of the States—Accursed be the politician, who harbors from mercenary or ambitious views the idea of a dissolution.

[American Eagle, 3 cheers.

Our Navy—The admiration of the world. The intrepidity of our seamen, has taught foreign nations to respect and fear us.

[Decatur's victory, 3 cheers.

The Army—Our protectors from foreign encroachments in peace, in war the brave and intrepid defenders of our rights.

[Star spangled banner, 3 cheers.

The Yellow Stone Expedition—The chosen vanquished of the revolution.

[Successful campaign, 3 cheers.

Agriculture—The noblest employment of freemen.

[Speed the plough, 3 cheers.

Commerce—The flags of our merchants wave on every sea, their name is known to every nation.

[America, commerce & freedom.

Internal Improvements—National Roads and Canals, the surest means of connecting the interests of the different sections of our country.

[Logan water, 3 cheers.

Public Education—The grand object of a republican government—The diffusion of knowledge is the surest safe guard to our political blessings.

[Life let us cherish 3 cheers.

The Treaty of 1803, which gave us the Pacific for our western boundary, and secured to us the blessings of liberty, without bloodshed.

(Jefferson and Liberty. 6 cheers.

Missouri—She rose into public notice, by the assertion of her political rights—may her future deeds prove her a star of the first magnitude.

(Missouri Bugle Quick Step. 9 cheers.

Missouri and Mississippi Rivers—Gushing from the mountains of the north, they roll in blended majesty until mingled with the mighty waves of the atlantic, teeming with the productions of every clime—step stones to the future wealth of the west.

Missouri state convention—On their wisdom, justice and republican principles repose the hopes of their country.

(N. constitution, 6 cheers 2 guns.

The President of the United States—The honest friend of his country, unbiassed by local politics

(Presidents march, 3 cheers.

The Ex-Presidents—May they be as happy in private life, as they were useful in public.

(Marseilles Hymn. 3 cheers.

John Scott, our delegate—unawed by the array of a most formidable opposition—he never relaxed his labours. in supporting the rights of Missouri—he deserves well of his countrymen.

(Scott's o'er the border, cheers.

Emigration—may its rapid march soon cross the Rocky Mountains, and civilization and improvement extend to the pacific.

(Bugle Quick Step 1 cheer.

The Late War—It transformed the citizen into the soldier—its glorious result manifested our superiority over veteran troops of Europe.

(Perry's Victory. 3 cheers.

The Patriots of South America—Engaged in freedoms cause may they soon plant the standard of liberty and be hailed the republicans of the South.

(The Tree of Liberty 6 cheers.

Gov. Clark—The star which first gleamed in the western horizon through the trackless deserts of the Rocky Mountains; now illumines the political world with all the splendor of a meridian sun.

The fair of Missouri—appreciated as bestowing the greatest blessings on society.

(Rural felicity.

The day proved very inauspicious, but it passed very pleasantly, perfect harmony and order prevailed throughout.[1]

BUSINESS GATHERINGS. During the early part of the nineteenth century the American people were almost perpetually in motion, not simply toward new land but also toward new improvements and inventions. The changes were occasioned by and were the occasion of speechmaking. Did a growing town need a fire department? Then a meeting of the citizens was held, and rousing speeches were made. The newspaper accounts of such meetings become almost a formula: A committee of three was appointed to solicit signatures, and a further meeting was called for the following week.[2] Speechmaking was accompanied by action. One will read in the columns of contemporary newspapers accounts of meetings to establish fire companies and of resolutions adopted concerning the officers at fire drills.[3] Was it desirable to raise funds for a town library? Then a meeting was held, ways and means were discussed, and actions were taken. At a meeting in St. Louis held on January 4, 1820, resolutions were passed to force members to pay the installments, and those who would pay their second and subsequent installments in books were told to report to the office to have the examiners see the offering: "The Directors beg leave to inform the public that it is their object to collect the sum of 2000 dollars as speedily as possible, for the purpose of sending to the East for books, which may arrive here in the ensuing spring, when the river becomes navigable. . . . "[4]

Great public interest was universally manifested in public improvements and manufactures. The meeting held at Pittsburgh in June, 1820, was only one of many:

At a meeting held in the court house at Pittsburg, Penn. without distinction of parties, and composed of from two to three hundred citizens, resolutions were passed which evinced the sentiments of the meeting to be highly friendly to the promotion of *manufactures* and *internal improvement*. The thanks of the meeting were given to *Henry Baldwin*, esq. for his able endeavors on the floor of congress,

[1] *Missouri Gazette and Public Advertiser* (St. Louis), July 12, 1820.
[2] *St. Louis Enquirer*, Aug. 2, 1820.
[3] *Ibid.*, July 26, 1820.
[4] *Ibid.*, Jan. 12, 1820.

to advance those great interests, and he was nominated for a re-election. *Walter Lowrie*, esq. also obtained the acknowledgments of the meeting for his aid of the manufacturing interest.[1]

PREVALENCE OF SPEECHMAKING

Any classification of speeches by occasions is likely to leave the false impression that the Americans spoke only on occasion. The fact is, however, that speechmaking went on in the daily exercise of life in situations and under conditions that defy classification. And if no situation requiring speechmaking was at hand, then one was invented. The literary society, the "bee," the debating society, and the lyceum were largely given over to speechmaking in one form or another.

Among the presumably unlikely occasions for speechmaking, the hanging is one of the most interesting. In the early decades of the nineteenth century, executions were plentiful and public. People gathered from the countryside for miles around to see justice at work; and often the hanging of a convicted person was merely a central act in a day of drama. The condemned man, among others, was commonly permitted, if not actually expected, to make a speech confessing or denying his crime. Such a play, with an unusually happy ending, was enacted in Indiana when a crowd assembled to witness the hanging of one Samuel Fields, an old white-haired veteran of the Revolutionary War. At the appointed time and place the "Rev. Augustus Jocelyn rose, and delivered an eloquent and appropriate sermon. . . . Some well adapted remarks, were made by the Rev. Mr._____, and divine service was then concluded. . . . "[2] Just as the sheriff was about to perform his official duty, his Excellency, the Honorable James B. Ray, acting governor of the state of Indiana, stepped forward and made a speech, addressed presumably to the prisoner:

"Take this, sir, (handing him a PARDON,) and remember . . . I am responsible to my country for your future good behavior. . . . remember, that I am your security for your conduct. . . .

"I do not do so, under the belief, that you have committed no crime. . . . I have no power to commute, to change your punishment—no, none, but to forgive you. . . . "

Never had *electricity* more influence upon the human frame, than this act had on the prisoner and the spectators [three or four thousand people]. The throb of universal approbation was instantaneously felt, and some even shouted with joy. The poor old man raised his head, from the most stupid lethargy, and at once became animated: gratitude was immediately seated on his heart. But few seemed dissatisfied with this magnanimous act of the Governor.[3]

[1] *Niles' Weekly Register* (Baltimore), June 17, 1820.
[2] *Independent Patriot*, July 16, 1825, reprinted from *Brookville Enquirer*.
[3] *Ibid.*

In all their public meetings and in every public expression of opinion, the Americans of 1820 found a growing preoccupation with the problems of slavery. Presumably the great Compromise of 1820, by which Missouri was admitted to the Union, settled all such questions permanently. Yet when Alexander McNair, the first governor, addressed the first general assembly of Missouri on September 19, 1820,[1] there were doubtless many citizens who were still perplexed with forebodings for the future.

IV. *The Third Generation:* 1850

It was the custom of good Methodist people in Virginia and throughout the South to usher in the New Year with a watch-night party. In the church or in a friendly home the neighbors gathered to await the coming of the New Year, and after testimony and prayer and perhaps an appropriate sermon, they knelt for a few moments before and after midnight, rising to sing the "New Year's Hymn":

> Come let us anew
> Our journey pursue,
> Roll round with the year
> And never stand still till the Master appear.
>
> His adorable will
> Let us gladly fulfil,
> And our talents improve
> By the patience of hope, and the labour of love.[2]

As the pious parishioners sang out the "New Year's Hymn" at midnight, December 31, 1849, to mark the turn from the earlier to the latter half of the nineteenth century, they celebrated in a land markedly different from that which they had seen a generation earlier. The vigorous young men of 1820 had become the elder statesmen of 1850: Webster, Clay, Benton, and Calhoun were all in the Senate and were universally respected, if not universally liked. Webster had come to stand in the public mind for New England and for that nationalism in which many New England men believed. Clay represented the Old West, beyond the Alleghenies, and Benton stood for the New West, beyond the Mississippi. Calhoun spoke for the South, that is, for the part of the South that knew its own mind.

When the venerable Senators from the North, South, West, and Far West recalled the thirty years of their prime, they could remember event after event full of meaning for their country: the revolutions in Mexico

---

[1] *Missouri Gazette and Public Advertiser*, Sept. 20, 1820.

[2] M. D. Conway, *Autobiography* . . . (Boston, Houghton Mifflin Company, 1905), I, 24–25.

and South America; the development of liberalism in Europe; and the rise of Jacksonian democracy in the United States. Since the prolonged debate concerning the admission of Missouri into the Union in 1820, the Congress had many times deliberated, not always without murmurings and protests, about the admission of still other states. Michigan, Wisconsin, Arkansas, and Texas had come into the Union, along with Florida and Iowa.

THE NATIONAL EXPANSION

The population of less than ten million in 1820 had grown to more than twenty-three million in 1850.[1] Two notable factors were observed: (1) the great migration from Europe and (2) the growth of the cities. Of the twenty-three million Americans in 1850, almost one million had been born in Ireland, and more than one-half million had been born in the various German states. Three-quarters of a million had come from other countries, including England, Scotland, and Wales. The major tendency of newcomers was toward the free states.[2] Although many of the immigrants settled in the rural counties, Chicago, Milwaukee, and St. Louis numbered more foreigners than native Americans; and Cincinnati, New York, and New Orleans, for example, counted almost as many foreigners as native sons.[3]

Certainly one of the most striking differences between the United States of 1850 and that of 1820 was the rapid increase in the number and population of the cities. New York, which had numbered 123,706 people in 1820, had become in 1850 a metropolitan center of more than one-half million inhabitants. Philadelphia and Boston, with other Atlantic cities, showed marked increases in population. Chicago, which hardly existed in 1820, had become by 1850 a boom town of nearly 30,000 people. Detroit, with a population of 21,019, and Milwaukee with 20,061, had come into being. St. Louis had increased in population from fewer than 5,000 in 1820 to more than 75,000 in 1850.[4]

The Pacific Northwest, virtually an unknown country in 1820, was firmly fixed within the national boundaries. In the Southwest the victory over Mexico had added an immense expanse to the public domain and had provided, in California, the gold mines that led ambitious men and boys the country over into the gold rush of 1849.

Fully as remarkable as the growth in the nation's territories and population had been its internal development. Whereas in 1820 there had not been a single mile of railroad anywhere in the country, by 1850 the East

[1] J. D. B. De Bow, *Statistical View of the United States* . . . (Washington, D. C., A. O. P. Nicholson, Public Printer, 1854), p. 39.

[2] In 1850, almost five times as many foreign-born persons lived in free as in slave states. —*Ibid.*, p. 115.

[3] *Ibid.*, p. 399.

[4] *Ibid.*, p. 192.

and West had been firmly linked with a large and expanding network of steel railroads. Furthermore, the steamboats on the rivers and the steamships on the seas had made the American nation and the world immeasurably smaller. The Erie Canal, the most spectacular of a great number of public improvements, had been completed and celebrated with appropriate speechmaking in 1825. The invention and rapid development of telegraphy had changed every aspect of communication.

POLITICAL DEVELOPMENT

All the while the Americans had been pushing back their physical frontiers and developing their economic resources, they had likewise been pushing back the frontiers of democracy and expanding the ideas of equality. The accession of Andrew Jackson to the Presidency in 1828 had marked the triumph of equalitarianism; and the central tendency since his day had been toward equal political rights for every freeman. The common American had reason to declare himself as good as any man anywhere. He had not advanced himself without a struggle, and his weapon had often been the spoken word. By the use of this instrument the commoner, with the aid of such friends as Horace Mann, had gone far toward establishing the right of every citizen to a free public education.

The labor unions, despite strong opposition, had grown immensely in power and influence, and they lent their support to the public-school movement. The unions, most influential in the cities of the North and West, had also been largely responsible for the abolition of imprisonment for debt, for the establishment of the 10-hour day, for the enactment of laws concerning mechanics' liens, and for the prevention of convict labor. In their agitation the union men had used many means: the strike, the formation of working men's caucuses and parties, and the sponsoring of newspapers. Certainly not the least effective agent of the working man was the private consideration of his problems in his own union hall and the public expression of his point of view in legislature and town meeting.

The rise of the common man involved some casualties. The United States Bank, which had fought against the policies of Andrew Jackson, was perhaps the most notable. The aristocracy had suffered a loss of influence in forming public opinion.[1] Many of the better men had turned from politics to economics, from government to business.

REGIONALISM

Despite the phenomenal physical and political changes in the nation, however, the sectional divisions had not been ameliorated. The complaints

---

[1] D. R. Fox, *The Decline of Aristocracy in the Politics of New York* (New York, Columbia University Press, 1918).

that Southern men had uttered in 1820 were in 1850 still unremedied. The significant feature of the time was the continuing expansion of sectionalism. Indeed, the other characteristics of the period seemed to contribute to the rise of a sectional as opposed to a national spirit. The tendency of the European immigrants to prefer the free to the slave states and the consequent growth in wealth as well as in population of the free territories in the North and West; the establishment of new lines of transportation prevailingly from east to west rather than from north to south; the divisions between the developing urban economy of the North and West and the continuing rural economy of the South—all these tended to make possible, if not actually to perpetuate, the spirit of controversy between the regions.

THE NORTH, THE SOUTH, AND THE WEST

By 1850 the trans-Allegheny West of Henry Clay had been largely swallowed up by the North and the South. Ohio and Indiana had become Northern rather than Western; Mississippi and Alabama had become Southern rather than Western. The Ohio River tended to form a natural line of cleavage between the regions. The West in 1850 was the New West of Benton, rather than the Old West of Clay. The West was now the vast territory beyond the Mississippi, greater in extent than the North and South combined, richer in opportunity than either, and even more filled with the hope of the future. The West was the country desired by the dreamers of the North and South, and, in fact, the whole American struggle from 1820 to 1850 can be viewed from one vantage point as a thirty years' war between North and South for the new lands beyond the great river.

THE WEST. In 1850 the West still had a quarrel with the North; for the central politico-economical issue in the West continued to be the public land and its exploitation. Thomas Hart Benton, suspicious of Eastern capital, had fought during his 30 years in the Senate for a policy of Western expansion. The means was obvious: Let the men who will use and maintain the land have it free of charge. Nevertheless, when in 1820 applications had been made for the establishment of the preemptive system, the applications had been made without effect and without the prospect of eventual success.[1] But, as Benton declared, perseverance was successful. The new states continued to press the question and finally prevailed.[2] Under the Western plan for a land system, the settler got a choice home in a new country, and the nation got a body of cultivators whose labor gave value to the surrounding lands as their courage gave protection to the new country.

[1] T. H. Benton, *Thirty Years' View* . . . (New York, D. Appleton and Company, 1854) I, 12.
[2] *Ibid.*

The Western land policy was enacted in spite of active opposition from other sections. Many Southerners had no interest in expanding a territory likely to compete with the slave economy. Likewise, there were interests in the North and even in the Old West that were unfavorable toward an expansion of the new territory. It was believed that the growth of the new country must be made at the expense of the land values in the old. The task of the Western men was finally accomplished by persuasion—not by any single speech or by any single act but by the constant effort of such persevering men as Benton, who left no opportunity unused to develop their policy. They were aided by events: the expanding economy of the country; the transportation interests; the development of communication; and most of all by the immigration that made possible the peopling of the West without undue disruption of values in the older states.

The common interest in the land, as well as a common frontier spirit, served as well as any other single factor to form the West of 1850 into a nation neither North nor South, possessing attributes common to neither. The allaying of the hostility of Western men toward the North, which grew out of the following of the more liberal policies concerning public lands and public improvements, had the widest possible implications for the Union. The Western men had generally held the North, rather than the South, responsible for frustrating their desires for expansion. The removal of the land question as a matter of hostility between North and West left the real differences between the free West and the slave South exposed and made the Western men more amenable to Northern persuasion.

The preoccupation with the land occasioned many a debate, discussion, and public address in gatherings more humble than those of Senators in Washington, but in the aggregate not less influential.

The Growth of Western Culture. The citizens bound for California or other Western points were likely to require advice, if not persuasion. All those citizens in Cooper County, for example, who planned to leave for California held a meeting at the courthouse in Boonville, Missouri, on March 2, 1850, to select a suitable route and time and place of rendezvous. Officers were elected, and a gentleman who had been to California the previous year was called upon "to address the meeting as to the most practicable route, place of meeting, and suitable time of starting."[1]

When the United States took over the trans-Mississippi River country, it was not virgin territory. The French and Spanish settlements were established and, although not rapidly expanding, were well developed in their culture. The old Spanish cities of California, the pueblos of Arizona, and the French towns along the Mississippi in Missouri and Louisiana were

---

[1] *Boonville Observer*, Mar. 21, 1850.

wholly different from the wild country that the pioneers had faced in other areas. Nevertheless, the coming of the Americans had brought a new kind of civilization and an expanding order that required the development of a new society.

The application of the American culture to the Western lands was made in diverse ways, of which one of the most clearly discernible is that of the minister of the gospel and the missionary. It was such a purpose that the Reverend M. Hickey served in 1850, when he preached a sermon to a crowd of professed sinners in Portland, Michigan,[1] to get 500 feet of lumber for a mission house.[2] Elder S. S. Church similarly propagated an American culture when in January, 1850, he preached his sermon entitled "Influence of the Spirit."[3] In Wisconsin, the citizens united in forming the Wisconsin Historical Society, and on January 15, 1850, "they listened to a discourse from Gen. Wm. R. Smith, elaborated in its researches and felicitous in its style."[4] The first conception of the society was that it should be an institution for the delivering of addresses upon historical subjects. The idea of gathering historical material was subsidiary.[5]

The public school, an American contribution to the Western country, was heavily involved in speechmaking. It was the custom to examine students publicly, even in the common schools. On stated occasions the teachers, pupils, and patrons met in circumstances like the following:

EXAMINATION.—An examination of the pupils of the common school, under charge of Mr. J. Scott, will take place on Thursday and Friday, 14th and 15th insts. The friends of education and the public generally, are respectfully invited to be present.[6]

The movement for public education had come so far by 1850 that the states were beginning to provide a free university education for every citizen prepared to take advantage of the opportunity. In new states like Michigan and Wisconsin the Westerners had outstripped their teachers. The public university provided and required much speechmaking: inauguration ceremonies, exercises at graduation, and public lectures were the order of the day.[]

[1] Although Michigan is east of the Mississippi, it possessed in 1850 the characteristics of the Western lands and was distinctly a part of the new West.

[2] *Report of the Pioneer Society of the State of Michigan. . . .* (Lansing, Michigan, W. S. George & Co., 1883), IV, 25.

[3] *Glasgow Weekly Times*, Jan. 24, 1850.

[4] L. C. Draper, ed., *Collections of the State Historical Society of Wisconsin* (Madison, 1903), I, xxxix.

[5] Louise Phelps Kellogg, "The Services and Collections of Lyman Copeland Draper," *Wisconsin Magazine of History*, 5 (1921–1922): 246.

[6] *Glasgow Weekly Times*, Mar. 7, 1850.

The new country, like the nation generally, abounded in moral lectures and serious discussions. Father Matthew, the great apostle of temperance, lectured and administered the temperance pledge.[1] Mr. Wood delivered a lecture on the physical, moral, and intellectual natures of man, phrenologically considered.[2] General Lewis Cass, Michigan statesman and patriot, addressed the Kalamazoo Agricultural Society.[3] The Glasgow Lyceum met in the basement of the Methodist Church to consider whether "the signs of the times indicate a dissolution of the present Political Parties?"[4]

Religious Meetings. Camp meetings and revivals were common throughout the West. The General and Quarterly Conferences of the Methodist Church were regularly announced in the papers. Religious meetings were sometimes involved in debate. The Baptist American and Foreign Bible Society, for example, passed resolutions against any revision of the commonly received English version of the Scriptures.[5] On November 4, 1850, Elder S. S. Church affirmed, and the Reverend C. D. Simpson denied the question, "Is Division in the Church of Christ Sinful?"[6] A large audience was present, and the reporter thought it worthy of remark that the debate was conducted with order and good feeling. Such order and good feeling were not always found in theological controversy. Elders M. P. Wills and W. W. Keep conducted an extended argument during 1850–1851 over remarks alleged to have been made by Elder Keep in a public discourse as follows:

"That a Preacher of the Gospel near Millersburg in Callaway County had induced an individual to believe that if he would submit to be baptised he should receive the gift of the Holy Ghost; that said individual was baptised, and after waiting in the water fifteen minutes remarked to the preacher that he had deceived him—that he felt no change, except he went into the water dry and came out wet" or words to that amount.[7]

Business Meetings. In the expanding West the necessities of business and professional life were frequently the occasions for speaking: The directors of the Home Mutual Fire and Marine Insurance Company met for the regular conduct of its business.[8] The president of the Pacific Railroad made an address to his board of directors, stating the facts of the commercial

[1] *Glasgow Weekly Times*, Oct. 3, 1850.
[2] *Boonville Observer*, Aug. 8, 1850.
[3] *The Semi-centennial of the Admission of the State of Michigan into the Union* (Detroit, Detroit Free Press Printing Company, 1886), p. 397.
[4] *Glasgow Weekly Times*, Nov. 21, 1850.
[5] *Ibid.*, June 13, 1850.
[6] *Ibid.*, Nov. 7, 1850.
[7] *Missouri Statesman* (Columbia), Apr. 4, 1851.
[8] *Glasgow Weekly Times*, May 16, 1850.

situation in such a vivid way that he roused the people to action.[1] At a meeting held in Hannibal, Missouri, in October, 1850, the disposition of the people of Missouri to stand idle and wait for their neighbors to do all their work and supply all their wants was very happily hit off by Col. Richmond, of Hannibal, in a speech made concerning the Hannibal and St. Joseph Railroad: "Just look over the water at our enterprising neighbors. I declare I was almost led into the belief, the other day, that every thing we possessed came from Quincy! and I recollect remarking, down on the Levee, that, after awhile, Quincy and Alton would undertake to furnish us with hot cakes, ready buttered for breakfast every morning."[2]

Public Improvements. Everyone in the Western country was interested in public improvements. The phrase covered a diversity of subjects, including, for example, the "constructing a plank road between Huntsville and Glasgow, and Fayette and Glasgow," as well as "a railroad and highway from St. Louis to San Francisco." The latter project was a favorite one with Senator Benton, who introduced a bill concerning it in the Congress. The railroad was to be 1,600 miles long, and the whole grant of land was to come to 1,500,000 acres.[3]

Ceremonial Meetings. Every new development was an occasion for speechmaking, and no project was considered auspiciously opened without a public speech. In the Western country every anniversary was the occasion for a celebration. Accordingly, on July 4, 1850, John L. Blair, Esq., delivered in Madison, Wisconsin, "a beautiful and spirited composition, creditable alike to the head and heart of the author, and was listened to with intense interest by an immense audience."[4] On the same day, at Me-shim-ne-kab-ning Mission at Danby, Ionia County, Michigan, a celebration was held by the whites and the Indians. Short addresses "were delivered, both by the whites and Indians, which were interpreted, to the mutual edification of all."[5]

No one should suppose, however, that an occasion was required for public speaking in the West in 1850. It was still the common practice to have public speaking for its own sake. The citizens of Boonville, for example, learned that on "Saturday the 13th there will be public speaking at Big Lick, and on Saturday the 20th inst. at New Salem Camp Ground."[6]

Forensic and Legislative Speaking. The courts continued to require the services of the ablest speakers. The Westerner charged with murder was

---

[1] Walter Williams and F. C. Shoemaker, *Missouri: Mother of the West* (New York, American Historical Society, Inc., 1930), I, 555.

[2] *Boonville Observer*, Oct. 10, 1850.

[3] *Ibid.*, Dec. 19, 26, 1850.

[4] *Wisconsin Argus* (Madison), July 9, 1850.

[5] *Report of the Pioneer Society of the State of Michigan*, IV, 32.

[6] *Boonville Observer*, July 11, 1850.

likely to make every effort to get the most able attorney and the best jury pleader. A man who had acquired a reputation as a trial lawyer was likely to be an attractive candidate for public office, so that the forensic and political speaker was frequently found in the same person. There was, in addition to the ordinary legislatures, a constant business of making and revising constitutions. At Santa Fe, for example, a convention met for the purpose of drawing up a constitution for the territory of New Mexico.[1]

Union Meetings. Throughout the West the citizens engaged more and more in a consideration of the state of the Union. The Westerners were disturbed. Many a meeting was held:

> There will be a procession formed, and the citizens of the county, and of the neighboring counties, and all friends of the Union, are invited to attend. The Reverend Clergy of the city and county, and the Schools with their Teachers and Pupils, are respectfully invited to join in the procession. The Ladies *especially*, are requested to contribute their presence and approbation.[2]

As the quarrel between the North and South became more and more aggravated, as the Massachusetts men moved into Kansas and the Southerners moved into Missouri, the controversies were led by the Kansas-Missouri War, which preceded the breaking out of the War between the States. In 1850, however, many of the Western people continued to view both slavery and fratricidal war with abhorrence and thus found themselves somewhat estranged from both the North and the South and gained the complete sympathy of neither the one nor the other.

THE NORTH. In 1850, the section called the North or the East could be more easily described in negative than in positive terms: It consisted of those elements of the nation that had neither a Western nor a Southern spirit. Diverse in its ways, various in its peoples, divided in its mind, the North was becoming a nation, partly at least, in opposition to the growth of the separatist movement in the South. The North included, but did not embrace, New England; for Boston was the hub of New England's separate universe.

In the North were the major cities of the country; but the North had more improved agricultural land in use than the South. In the North resided the major part of the foreign born, the recent immigrants; but the North had a greater number of native-born white citizens than the South. In the North were the leading manufacturers of the country; but even so the products of the Northern farms were probably more valuable in dollars and cents than those of the agricultural South.[3]

[1] *Boonville Observer*, July 4, 1850.
[2] *Ibid.*, Apr. 4, 1850.
[3] De Bow, *op. cit.*, pp. 170, 115, 171.

The Early National Period: 1788–1860

The Mind of the North. The diversity of the North extended throughout the fields of public opinion. Since slavery was nonexistent in the states north of the Ohio, there was no strong local interest in its behalf in the North. Yet the South had many sympathizers, and many Northerners deplored the agitation of the slavery issue. The North was presumably nationalist in outlook; yet the secessionists in the North were fully as vocal as those in the South, albeit for different reasons. William Lloyd Garrison, as between Abolition and the Union, chose Abolition. If necessary, he said, Massachusetts men should "let the Union slide."[1] Yet of all the Northern states only those in New England gave to Negroes the full political rights of freemen. In the other states Negroes were hedged about with restrictions; and even in Massachusetts a Negro was perhaps not wise to presume too much on his legal rights.

The North appeared to have no unity, no common cause to which an orator could appeal. The public mind was divided, atomized, unsynthesized. A foundation had still to be set on which a structure of opinion could be built; but once such a foundation was discovered, the North, with its powerful resources in men, money, and spirit, it was safe to predict, would become a well-nigh irresistible force. The foundation for the opinion of the North was being slowly discovered in New England and in Illinois. It was being constructed of two different materials: (1) the whole reforming zeal of New England, all directed into the single channel of abolition, and (2) the almost mystic devotion to the Union that stirred the spirit of the men on the prairies. From this amalgam of freedom and union was to be created the basis of Northern nationalism.

The Middle East. Anyone who seeks examples of public speaking in the Middle East is embarrassed with plenty. The land was one of intellectual curiosity, and the ante bellum years were an inquiring era. In New York and in Pennsylvania, as well as in the West or the North, lecturers were in great demand. There were lectures on the employment of discharged convicts, on the opera, on women, on phrenology, on psychology, and on arctic exploration.

The public was agitated by such questions as the murder trial of Professor Webster, the death of President Taylor, the invention of the steam shovel, and by the visit of Jenny Lind. In the city of New York, the newspapers run by Bennett and Greeley kept everyone informed as well as exercised. Grave consideration was given to such questions as the propriety of vegetarianism and the expedience of abolishing flogging in the navy. Union laborers held regular meetings to discuss their common prob-

---

[1] W. L. Garrison, "The Union and Slavery," address delivered at the celebration of independence Day, 1850, *The World's Best Orations* (David J. Brewer, ed., St. Louis, Ferd P. Kaiser, 1899), VI, 2241.

lems. The fraternal orders, like the Mohegan Tent of the I O R M, met regularly and occasionally passed resolutions. Indignation meetings were not uncommon. All the while the regular business of the city was carried on by the Aldermanic Council. A listing of the questions discussed and debated would constitute a panoramic social and intellectual history of the time, astonishing in its complexity and diversity.[1]

New England. The New England of 1850 was a land of fulfilled promises. The intellectual curiosity of the fathers had begot wisdom and learning in the sons, and with wisdom had come understanding, tinctured with indignation. New England in 1850 was the home land of Thoreau, of Alcott, and of Emerson. It was the country of Lowell and Whittier and Holmes. It was, moreover, still the nation of the Adams family, of the Quincys, and of the Channings. Everett and Phillips were the orators of New England; Choate and the godlike Daniel were her advocates. Theodore Parker was her prophet. Motley had spent his days writing the history of the Dutch Republic, Parkman had told the story of the Oregon trail, and Prescott that of the conquest of Mexico. Hawthorne and Longfellow, Story and Norton, Bryant and Higginson, each in his own way expressed the vital force that characterized the New England renaissance. At Harvard College, Asa Gray, Benjamin Peirce, and Louis Agassiz lectured and created knowledge as they spoke. Truly, there were giants in the New England earth in those days.

The New England Reformer. New England from 1815 to 1860 was filled with reformers, of whom some stayed at home and others went out to save various corners of the nation and the world at large. The world was to be reclaimed by mesmerism, by phrenology, by psychometrists, by vegetarianism, by hydropathy, by women's rights, by Bloomerism, by communal ownership of land,[2] and by a host of other remedies. Transcendentalism, as it had found expression in Brook Farm, was only one of the many cures offered to a troubled world. Emerson well described the reforming urge:

What a fertility of projects for the salvation of the world! One apostle thought all men should go to farming, and another that no man should buy or sell, that the use of money was the cardinal evil; another that the mischief was in our diet, that we eat and drink damnation. These made unleavened bread and were foes to the death to fermentation. It was in vain urged by the housewife that God made yeast, as well as dough, and loves fermentation just as dearly as he loves vegetation; that fermentation develops the saccharine element in the grain, and makes it more palatable and more digestible. No; they wish the pure wheat, and will die but it

[1] For accounts of speeches, see especially the *New York Herald* and the *New York Daily Tribune.*
[2] T. L. Nichols, *Forty Years of American Life:* 1821–1861 (New York, Stackpole Sons, 1937), pp. 40–46.

shall not ferment. Stop, dear Nature, these incessant advances of thine; let us scotch these ever-rolling wheels! Others attacked the system of agriculture, the use of animal manures in farming, and the tyranny of man over brute nature; these abuses polluted his food. The ox must be taken from the plow and the horse from the cart, the hundred acres of the farm must be spaded, and the man must walk, wherever boats and locomotives will not carry him. Even the insect world was to be defended,—that had been too long neglected, and a society for the protection of ground worms, slugs and mosquitoes was to be incorporated without delay. With these appeared the adepts of homeopathy, of hydropathy, of mesmerism, of phrenology, and their wonderful theories of the Christian miracles! Others assailed particular vocations, as that of the lawyer, that of the merchant, of the manufacturer, of the clergyman, of the scholar. Others attacked the institution of marriage as the fountain of social evils. Others devoted themselves to the worrying of churches and meetings for public worship; and the fertile forms of antinomianism among the elder puritans seemed to have their match in the plenty of the new harvest of reform.

With this din of opinion and debate there was a keener scrutiny of institutions and domestic life than any we had known; there was sincere protesting against existing evils, and there were changes of employment dictated by conscience.[1]

Critical of reforms and reformers, Ralph Waldo Emerson was nevertheless spiritually akin to the reformers of his time. From his lectures had flowed a steady stream of ideas and inspirations. George William Curtis heard the man speak and reflected on his experience:

Many years ago the Easy Chair used to hear Ralph Waldo Emerson lecture. Perhaps it was in the small Sunday-school room under a country meeting-house, on sparkling winter nights, when all the neighborhood came stamping and chattering to the door in hood and muffler, or ringing in from a few miles away, buried under buffalo skins. The little, low room was dimly lighted with oil-lamps, and the boys clumped about the stoves in their cowhide boots, and laughed and buzzed and ate apples and peanuts and giggled, and grew suddenly solemn when the grave men and women looked at them. At the desk stood the lecturer and read his manuscript, and all but the boys sat silent and inthralled by the musical spell.[2]

Not everyone understood the philosopher. Parents were heard to say, "I don't go to hear Mr. Emerson; I don't understand him. But my daughters do."[3] It was not necessary to understand Emerson. One could go and hear him for other reasons, as did Madame Hoar's servant, who, on being questioned about quitting her work early, replied:

[1] Ralph Waldo Emerson, "New England Reformers," a lecture read before the Society in Amory Hall, Mar. 3, 1844. *The Complete Works of Ralph Waldo Emerson* . . . (Boston, Houghton Mifflin Company, 1876), III, 252–253.

[2] G. W. Curtis, "Emerson Lecturing," *From the Easy Chair* (New York, Harper & Brothers, 1891), I, 21.

[3] *Ibid.*, p. 22.

"Yes, I've got to go now. I'm going to Mr. Emerson's lecture."

"Do you understand Mr. Emerson?"

"Not a word, but I like to go and see him stand up there and look as if he thought every one was as good as he was."[1]

When Emerson rose in public meeting to attack Daniel Webster, the idol of his youth, he symbolized the forces that were to make *union* and *freedom* the indispensable attributes each of the other and to provide the North with an agent of unity. Amid the groans and hisses of the young Southern sympathizers in Boston, Emerson stated the case against Webster's apostasy: "Nobody doubts that Daniel Webster could make a good speech. Nobody doubts that there were good and plausible things to be said on the part of the South. But this is not a question of ingenuity, not a question of syllogisms, but of sides. *How came he there?*"[2]

But the time was not yet. Governor Johnson, of Pennsylvania, speaking on slavery, declared that the South should not be disturbed in its institution and that slavery must not be extended.[3] And the North generally did not share Emerson's feeling about the great address of Daniel Webster. An observer in Washington described the speech: "Spark after spark, flash after flash, it warmed and trilled the breast of every listener, till, when he closed, the pent-up enthusiasm of the audience manifested itself in a round of applause that the place and presence could not suppress."[4]

The Washington *Republic* reported that 125,000 copies of Senator Webster's speech had been published and circulated, and that 50,000 more were ordered.[5] When Webster spoke in Bowdoin Square, following his "Seventh of March Speech," an observer declared "he never received greater applause, nor ever spoke with greater power and boldness."[6]

In 1850 Mr. Emerson's crusade against slavery was still lost in a welter of other business, petty and great, but great or petty, concerned with speechmaking. In Pittsburgh, for example, Joseph Barker, convicted and pardoned of street preaching, was elected mayor on an anti-Catholic ticket.[7] In Philadelphia, a national railroad convention elected officers and passed a resolution favoring Congressional support for a railroad from the Mississippi to the Pacific.[8] In New York, on April 13, 1850, "the avenues and large

[1] Edward Waldo Emerson, *Emerson in Concord* . . . (Boston, Houghton Mifflin and Company, 1890), p. 148.

[2] *Ibid.*, p. 79.

[3] *Glasgow Weekly Times*, Jan. 24, 1850.

[4] *Boonville Observer*, Mar. 21, 1850, reprinted from the Washington *Republic*.

[5] *Glasgow Weekly Times*, Apr. 25, 1850.

[6] *Ibid.*, May 16, 1850.

[7] *Missouri Statesman*, Jan. 18, 1850.

[8] *Glasgow Weekly Times*, Apr. 11, 1850.

saloons of Niblo's spacious theatre were filled to overflowing" with an assemblage of the personal and political friends of Henry Clay, come to celebrate his seventy-third birthday.[1] In Cincinnati, the General Assembly of the Old School Presbyterian Church met, deliberated, and adjourned.[2] In Washington, D. C., the statesmen considered many a question, including the distribution of "the public lands among the States in which they are located for the use of actual settlers. . . . "[3]

In Worcester, Massachusetts, a Women's Rights Convention, with delegates from almost all the states east of Illinois and north of Virginia, elected officers and heard speeches.[4] In Peoria, Illinois, a crowd of people assembled to witness the hanging of two murderers, not knowing that a stay of execution had been granted. Disappointed in their expectation and egged on by exciting speeches, they got possession of the scaffold, erected it in front of the jail, and prepared to hang the culprits.[5] In Pennsylvania, a convention of editors petitioned Congress, "asking for the circulation of newspapers postage *free*. . . . "[6] In Boston, young Andrew D. White heard Theodore Parker, the great minister of the gospel, pray and preach with inspiration before more than four thousand people who gathered in the music hall.[7]

The uses of rhetoric were thus so amply demonstrated in such a variety of causes that a single theme was likely to be lost in a multitude of voices. But even so, the cause of Emerson, Whittier, and the New Englanders was penetrating more and more into the Northern, if not into the national consciousness. Before the year was out the Common Council of Chicago had met and passed resolutions condemning the fugitive-slave law. Even though Judge Douglas shortly afterward addressed a mass meeting and, in a speech of $3\frac{1}{2}$ hours, condemned fanaticism, the record was made.[8] Abolition and union, rather than slavery and union, it was beginning to be believed, would capture the mind of the North. Once the two—abolition and union—were associated, they would gain strength from each other and enhance in prestige and volume that devotion to the Union made manifest in New York by a very large and respectable meeting;[9] in Cincinnati, where an enthusiastic Union meeting was held;[10] in Philadelphia, where

[1] *Ibid.,* Apr. 18, 1850.

[2] *Ibid.,* June 6, 1850.

[3] *Boonville Observer,* Aug. 22, 1850.

[4] *Glasgow Weekly Times,* Oct. 31, 1850.

[5] *Missouri Statesman,* Jan. 3, 1851.

[6] *Glasgow Weekly Times,* Feb. 14, 1850.

[7] A. D. White, *Autobiography* (New York, Century Company, 1907), II, 535.

[8] *Glasgow Weekly Times,* Nov. 7, 1850.

[9] *Boonville Observer,* Nov. 14, 1850, reprinted from the *Courier & Enquirer.*

[10] *Ibid.,* Dec. 5, 1850.

extensive preparations were made for a Union meeting;[1] and in Manchester, New Hampshire, where Whigs and Democrats joined in calling a Union meeting.[2] Indeed, Union meetings were "all the go in the Eastern and Northern cities."[3]

THE SOUTH. There were speeches, mass meetings, and conventions in the South also, but the talk was quite different from that of the Federal Union men of the North. Instead of "Union Forever," one was likely to hear "Disunion" applauded. The Honorable Barnwell Rhett made a speech to the people of Charleston in which he "frankly and boldly unfurled the flag of *Disunion*" and declared, "there is no remedy but the severance of our connection with the north."[4] A disunion meeting, held in Macon, Georgia,[5] was addressed by Messrs. Rhett, Yancey, Colquitt, and Stiles. The editor of the *Citizen*, published at Macon, disapproved of the disunion meeting and was ordered by that body to leave the city within 10 days, and his paper was ordered to be discontinued.[6]

People in the West were shocked in September to receive a telegraphic dispatch revealing the fury of the people at Charleston at the passage of the territorial bill. According to the dispatch, a public demonstration had been held, and the United States flag had been trampled on.[7] Meetings were called in a number of districts of South Carolina "to take action upon the present state of affairs."[8] Although the story of South Carolinians' treading on the flag was later believed to be a humbug,[9] it was clear that South Carolina was in earnest. In October, a Union Southern-rights meeting held in Savannah, Georgia, passed resolutions stating that the people of Georgia would resist any aggressive legislation against Southern rights.[10] In November, the constituents of the Honorable William F. Colcock, member of Congress from South Carolina, desiring to express their entire approbation of his course in Congress, gave him a dinner.[11] The toasts, as represented in the Charleston *Courier*, breathed "secession and disunion in every line."[12] One speaker even stated at what distance he could kill a

---

[1] *Boonville Observer*, Nov. 22, 1850.
[2] *Glasgow Weekly Times*, Dec. 5, 1850.
[3] *Ibid.*, Nov. 28, 1850.
[4] *Boonville Observer*, July 25, 1850.
[5] *Ibid.*, Sept. 12, 1850.
[6] *Ibid.*, Sept. 19, 1850.
[7] *Ibid.*, Sept. 19, 1850, reprinted from the Washington *Evening Bulletin*.
[8] *Boonville Observer*, Sept. 19, 1850.
[9] *Glasgow Weekly Times*, Sept. 26, 1850.
[10] *Ibid.*, Nov. 14, 1850.
[11] *Boonville Observer*, Nov. 28, 1850.
[12] *Ibid.*

Yankee, and another declared that when it came to fighting, he wished to be put down for two chances.[1]

So much were the Southerners in earnest that a convention of the South, in which nine Southern states were represented, was held to determine a Southern policy. South Carolina and Mississippi were for drastic action, but they were restrained, and the delegates contented themselves with passing resolutions.[2] While the Southerners sat in convention at Nashville, the Congress in Washington was debating the omnibus bill, which embodied the great Compromise of 1850.

The Compromise. On January 29, 1850, Henry Clay, the great compromiser, who had secured a measure of peace with the Missouri Compromise in 1820, introduced a group of resolutions. Clay's resolutions were designed, so he thought, to alleviate the dangers of disunion and, by mutual concession, to set the nation again on a solid basis. In brief, his compromise provided:

1. That California be admitted as a free state.

2. That Utah and New Mexico be created as territories without restriction as to slavery.

3. That on the relinquishment by Texas of her claim to Eastern New Mexico, the debt of Texas contracted prior to annexation should be assumed by the Federal government.

4. That the slave trade should be prohibited in the District of Columbia, but only on the consent of Maryland.

5. That a more effectual means be found to return fugitive slaves to their masters.

6. That Congress should go on record declaring that it had no right to forbid interstate slave trade.

Clay spoke for two full days in favor of his compromise measures, appealing with great effect for concessions from North and South, in order that the Union of the fathers might be preserved. On March 4, 1850, John C. Calhoun got up from his sickbed and went up to the capital to hear a friend read for him a speech that he was too weak to deliver.[3]

The Mind of the South. Calhoun's speech exhibits as perfectly as any speech can the point of view with which the influential Southerners regarded the Union and their position in it. Significantly, whereas Clay's speech had been a plea for compromise, Calhoun's speech was a warning of danger. It was a last, a final appeal to the North to beware and to the South to stand firm.

[1] *Ibid.*

[2] *Boonville Observer*, Nov. 21, 1850; *Glasgow Weekly Times*, May 16, 1850 *et seq.*

[3] W. M. Meigs, *The Life of John Caldwell Calhoun* (New York, G. E. Stechert & Company, 1917), II, 449–450.

As Calhoun represented his own views—and those of the Southern leaders—the Union had begun as a league of balanced powers. The North and the South in the beginning had maintained an equilibrium. Now, however, that equilibrium was destroyed. The coming census would show, he declared, a great preponderance of population for the North—a preponderance due not to natural causes but to three deliberate policies of the federal government: the exclusion of slavery from the Northwest Territory under the Ordinance of 1787; the levying of duties to protect manufactures; the increasing centralization of the powers of government in Washington. Striking out against the antislavery agitation, Calhoun declared that the destruction of slavery would disrupt the South. It was the agitator, not the slaveowner, who endangered the Union. Already, he noted, the Methodist and Baptist churches are divided, and the same divisive tendency is to be seen in the political parties. If the agitation continues, he said, disunion is inevitable.

Calhoun then addressed himself to the question, "How can the Union be saved?" and to his question he gave the Southern answer:

. . . there is but one way by which it can be—and that is—by adopting such measures as will satisfy the States belonging to the Southern section, that they can remain in the Union consistently with their honor and their safety. There is, again, only one way by which this can be effected, and that is—by removing the causes by which this belief has been produced. Do *this*, and discontent will cease—harmony and kind feelings between the sections be restored—and every apprehension of danger to the Union removed. The question, then, is—How can this be done? But, before I undertake to answer this question, I propose to show by what the Union cannot be saved.

It cannot, then, be saved by eulogies on the Union, however splendid or numerous. The cry of "Union, Union—the glorious Union!" can no more prevent disunion than the cry of "Health, health—glorious health!" on the part of the physician, can save a patient lying dangerouly ill. So long as the Union, instead of being regarded as a protector, is regarded in the opposite character, by not much less than a majority of the States, it will be in vain to attempt to conciliate them by pronouncing eulogies on it.[1]

Calhoun came to the end of his argument with his solution of the question—a Constitutional Amendment that would "restore to the South . . . the power she possessed of protecting herself." And he gave a final warning of the consequences of inaction:[2] "If you, who represent the stronger portion, cannot agree to settle them on the broad principle of justice and duty, say so; and let the States we both represent agree to separate and

[1] J. C. Calhoun, "Speech on the Slavery Question," *Works* . . . (R. K. Crallé, ed., New York, D. Appleton and Company, 1888), IV, 559.
[2] *Ibid.*, p. 572.

part in peace. If you are unwilling we should part in peace, tell us so, and we shall know what to do, when you reduce the question to submission or resistance."[1]

Calhoun's warning was his last, for within a month he was dead. Not long after his death meetings were held in the parishes of South Carolina to take measures for the erection of a monument in his honor, by popular contribution.[2]

Union Sentiment in the South. Although Calhoun's speech accurately represented the prevailing opinion of the South, it was not the only opinion. Moderate men in the South, like moderate men in the North, were for compromise; and they expressed themselves in public meetings and in public speeches. In 1850, a meeting of Union men was held in Jackson, Mississippi, and another was scheduled in Natchez. Governor Crittenden, in his message to the Kentucky legislature, declared that the nation to which Kentuckians belong is the Union, not Kentucky. Even in Nashville, seat of the Southern convention, a "large meeting, without distinction of party," declared by an overwhelming majority the inexpediency of appointing delegates. On November 27, 1850,

there was a most enthusiastic Union Meeting at New Orleans, attended by one of the largest crowds ever assembled in that city. J. Labatut presided, assisted by seventy Vice Presidents. The immense concourse was addressed by Senators Downs, of La., and Foote, of Miss., both of whom delivered eloquent speeches, which were most rapturously applauded.[3]

Nevertheless, many people in the South felt that, come a final decision all Southerners would stick together. Indeed, the governor of Maryland had already formulated the ultimate answer of the moderates in the South in the declaration of the "determination of the State to stand in the crisis, which he anticipates, by the South, should a choice of alternatives be precipitated on her."[4]

The Speeches of the Day. Despite the Southern excitement over slavery and the Union, the practiced routine of daily living was carried out; and in the custom of the South the public speech was a habit of life. The sermon on Sunday, the trial in the courthouse, the deliberations of the legislatures went on in their accustomed manner, but little disturbed by the anti-Union feeling. One member of the Methodist Episcopal Conference in Virginia found time during the year (1850–1851) to travel upward of 3,800 miles in the discharge of his duties, to preach 321 sermons, to pay 380 visits, to

[1] *Ibid.*, p. 573.
[2] *Glasgow Weekly Times*, May 9, 1850.
[3] *Ibid.*, Dec. 19, 1850.
[4] *Ibid.*, Jan. 24, 1850.

witness 279 conversions in his various congregations, and to admit 260 members into the church.[1] On the Fourth of July, 1850, the governor of Virginia being unavoidably detained, the Honorable Charles James Faulkner, member of Congress from Virginia, delivered an address at the examination of the cadets of the Virginia Military Institute, and an observer reported that the address "increased greatly and justly his already high reputation as an orator and scholar."[2]

At Lynchburg, the people celebrated the construction of their first railroad—the Virginia and Tennessee—with a speech by the Honorable James K. Irvine; and although the weather was cold, it did not cool their ardor.[3] Upon the death of President Zachary Taylor, the citizens of Lynchburg paid him a fitting tribute:

> . . . when the day arrived business was suspended from ten to one o'clock, the bells of the town tolled, a salute was fired, and the houses were draped in mourning. A hearse, drawn by six black horses, led the procession, then came the veterans of the Mexican War, temperance organizations, hose company, military companies, citizens, etc. They marched to the Third Street Methodist church, where the Rev. George W. Longhorne conducted the religious services and N. H. Campbell delivered the address.[4]

At Richmond, a convention met for reforming the constitution of Virginia.[5] In Texas, public opinion was aroused not only about the Union but also by the incorporation of lands claimed by Texas in the new territory of New Mexico. The legislature, in special session, heard the governor declare that all Texas rights should be defended.[6] At San Augustine, General Houston and General Henderson made speeches concerning the actions of the late Congress in respect to the Texas boundary.[7]

Throughout the South speechmaking for every occasion, or for no particular occasion, was the custom of the country; and the custom continued undisturbed by the gloomy forebodings spoken by the great Calhoun or by the loud calls for action emanating from Barnwell Rhett.

V. *Conclusion*

Mr. Clay's compromise was enacted and became the law of the land. But the compromise was a palliative, not a remedy; and the very necessity

[1] *Missouri Statesman*, Apr. 11, 1851.
[2] *Democratic Review Magazine*, 41 (March, 1858): 225.
[3] W. A. Christian, *Lynchburg and Its People* (Lynchburg, Va., J. P. Bell Company, 1900), pp. 146–147.
[4] *Ibid.*, p. 149.
[5] *Boonville Observer*, Oct. 31, 1850.
[6] *Ibid.*, Sept. 12, 1850.
[7] *Glasgow Weekly Times*, Dec. 5, 1850.

for such a compromise ratified the actual if not the legal fact of two emerging nations. The evolving nations of North and South were coming into being just as those elder statesmen who had been lads when the Constitution was formed were passing away. Calhoun, of the South, died in 1850; Webster, of the North, and Clay, of the Old West, lingered on until 1852; and Benton, exponent of the New West, who met his political death in 1850, came to final dissolution in 1858. The death of the sages who had literally grown from childhood through manhood on into old age with the nation was in itself an omen of impending evil. The conflict did indeed appear to be irrepressible. The need for discussion, the opportunity for persuasion had passed, and men turned to the final arbitrament of the sword.

The close of the war ushered in a new era in which life became more and more complex and Americans, becoming perhaps more sophisticated, found public speaking relatively less important than it once had been. But of the founders of the American Republic and their sons and grandsons, this much is clear: They believed in a government, even in a life, based on discussion and on the forms of public address. Not only on state occasions but also in their daily lives they exemplified the republican virtues, both social and political, of living in groups bound together by talk. Since the ancient Athenians, no people had spoken so fully, so freely, or, on the whole, so well. Perhaps it was because the Americans, like the ancient Athenians, really believed with Pericles "that any proposal is foredoomed to failure if undertaken undiscussed."

BIBLIOGRAPHIC NOTE

The influence of speechmaking in American life during the period 1788–1860 was so pervasive that few historical sources will fail to yield relevant data. Diaries, letters, newspapers, magazines, legislative journals, church records, legal briefs, minutes of assemblies, and countless other materials must be consulted by the historiographer of American public address.

With so great a mass of information available it is impossible here even to cite specific works. The interested student should consult the bibliographies in American history and the studies in historical method. Many of the works in American history will provide a guide to materials that, when studied by one who has the point of view of rhetoric, will amplify the history of speechmaking. Nevins,[1] for example, has appended to his *American States during and after the Revolution* a useful bibliography that is available as freely to the student of the history of speechmaking as to anyone else.

Every library of standing will have available certain special devices suited only to that particular library. These will naturally be consulted by careful students. In addition to these devices there are guides to American history that should be readily available to any investigator. The following list includes those thought to be most generally useful:

[1] Allan Nevins, *The American States during and after the Revolution* 1775–1789 (New York, The Macmillan Company, 1927).

Beers, Henry P.: *Bibliographies in American History: Guides to Materials for Research,* New York, The H. W. Wilson Company, 1938. (This work should be consulted by anyone doing research in the history of American public address.)

Bolton, Herbert E.: *Guide to Materials for the History of the United States in the Principal Archives of Mexico,* Washington, D. C., Carnegie Institution, 1913.

Channing, Edward, A. B. Hart, and F. J. Turner: *Guide to the Study and Reading of American History,* rev. ed., Boston, Ginn and Company, 1912. (See especially pp. 28–189.)

Evans, Charles: *American Bibliography,* 12 vols., Chicago, 1903.

Greene, Evarts B., and Richard Morris: *Guide to the Principal Sources for Early American History* (1600–1800) *in the City of New York,* New York, Columbia University Press, 1929. (Lists, among other collections, those of the New York Public Library, the New York Historical Society, and the Library of Columbia University.)

Griffin, A. P. C.: *Bibliography of American Historical Societies, the United States and the Dominion of Canada,* 2d ed., revised and enlarged. Washington, D. C., 1907. (The second volume of the *Annual Report of the American Historical Association* for 1905. The first edition, published in 1895, formed pp. 677–1236 of the *Annual Report of the American Historical Association* for 1895.)

Griffin, Grace G., and Dorothy M. Louraine: *Writings on American History,* 1936: *A Bibliography of Books and Articles on United States History Published during the Year 1936,* Washington, D. C., Government Printing Office, 1941. (Issued as the second volume of the *Annual Report of the American Historical Association.* See also earlier volumes in the series, compiled by Grace G. Griffin *et al.,* 1908–1935.)

Hart, A. B., ed.: *The American Nation: A History,* 28 vols., New York, Harper & Brothers, 1904–1918. (Vol. XXVIII is an analytic index.)

Larned, J. N., ed.: *The Literature of American History: A Bibliographical Guide,* Boston, published for the American Library Association by Houghton Mifflin Company, 1902. (See also the Supplement for 1900–1901, edited by P. P. Wells, published for the American Library Association by Houghton Mifflin Company, Boston, 1902.)

Matteson, D. M.: The Decennial Indexes of the *American Historical Review,* 1895–1925, 3 vols., New York, The Macmillan Company, 1906–1926.

Parker, David W.: *Guide to the Materials for United States History in Canadian Archives,* Washington, D. C., Carnegie Institution, 1913.

Sabin, Joseph, *et al.: Bibliotheca Americana* . . . , 29 vols., New York, 1868–1936. (See the introduction to Vol. XXIX for a statement concerning the scope of the work.)

Schlesinger, Arthur M., and Dixon Ryan Fox, eds.: *A History of American Life,* New York, The Macmillan Company, 1927 *et seq.* (Ten of the projected twelve volumes had appeared in January, 1943; Vols. IV and V have not yet been published.)

Trent, W. P., *et al.,* eds.: *The Cambridge History of American Literature,* 3 vols., New York, The Macmillan Company, 1936.

Winsor, Justin, ed.: *Narrative and Critical History of America,* 8 vols., Boston, Houghton Mifflin Company, 1884–1889.

The Later National Period:
1860-1930

by KENNETH G. HANCE, HOMER O. HENDRICKSON, and EDWIN W. SCHOENBERGER

Introduction

The Civil War and its aftermath ushered in a new epoch of American life. In it the nation progressed toward political union, made a transition to the Machine Age, witnessed the closing of the frontier, and became a world power. In short, modern America was emerging.

The modern steel age, born in 1856 with the invention of the Bessemer process, gained a foothold in 1867. Other industries soon expanded to the scope of Big Business. Transportation, banking, and other agencies of commerce expanded rapidly. There was a strong westward march, first of the farmer, then later of the manufacturer. There was increased demand for labor by the expanding corporations, resulting in problems of wages and hours that had repercussions in labor organizations and labor unrest. In all, this epoch saw an industrial boom, the rapid development of the city, the "taming of the West," the revolt of the farmer, many attempts at social reform, and increasing attention paid to relations with other nations.[1]

In public address this was the period typified by such historically prominent persons as Henry Ward Beecher, Ralph Waldo Emerson, Wendell Phillips, Robert G. Ingersoll, Phillips Brooks, Henry W. Grady, James G. Blaine, Roscoe Conkling, L. Q. C. Lamar, Carl Schurz, William Jennings Bryan, Theodore Roosevelt, Albert J. Beveridge, Woodrow Wilson, Charles W. Eliot, Henry George, Samuel Gompers, Eugene V. Debs, Jane Addams, and Clarence Darrow. It was, like the period that preceded it, one in which there was abundant deliberative, forensic, and ceremonial speaking. In fact, it was a period in which there was perhaps more speechmaking than at any previous time in the history of the United

[1] See, for instance, Allan Nevins, *The Emergence of Modern America* (New York, The Macmillan Company, 1927).

States. Yet strangely, this period has been characterized by an observer as being of little significance with respect to public address.

> Down to the last half-century, oratory was one of the most potent forces in moulding public opinion and in arousing popular enthusiasm in America. Since then our susceptibility to the power of human speech has gradually declined and with this loss has come a deterioration in the quality of our oratory.[1]

To understand the place of public address in this period and to appraise Morison's observation, we should inquire: What significant relation, if any, is apparent between public address and the events of the period? Furthermore, to understand the distinctive forms or uses of public address in this period, we should ask: Were there any trends in the use of public address that appeared in the years 1860–1930 or that received especial emphasis in this era? The answer to the first question suggests a survey of the more prominent speakers in terms of the events of the period. The latter is concerned with those forms and circumstances which were distinctive.

I. *Public Address and the Events of the Period*

A. THE RECONSTRUCTION PERIOD (1865–1885)

The Reconstruction period is remembered not only for the division between the North and South as to the means of solving the problem created by the war but also for the intense division between factions in the North. Some of these groups proposed bloody reprisals upon the South; others advocated a policy of amnesty and cooperative rebuilding. Interwoven with these problems were conflicts over party politics, political reforms, means of regulating industrial expansion, social reforms, and means of controlling corporate wealth.

Public address was concerned with these events. Such speakers as Sumner and Thaddeus Stevens, for example, spoke frequently on the need for Northern domination of the South and on the need for the immediate granting of citizenship to the Negro.[2] Andrew Johnson made a now famous "Swing around the Circle" speech in conjunction with this issue. The Bloody Shirt Republicans, headed by such speakers as Blaine, George F. Hoar, Roscoe Conkling, Ingersoll, and Henry Cabot Lodge, became spokesmen for one group of considerable influence. The Liberal Republicans, also, were represented by distinguished speakers. Beecher, Schurz,

---

[1] Samuel Eliot Morison, *The Life and Letters of Harrison Gray Otis, Federalist,* (Boston, Houghton Mifflin Company, 1913), I, 248.

[2] For a statement of the influence of Sumner and Stevens, see James Truslow Adams, *The Epic of America* (Boston, Little, Brown, & Company, 1931), pp. 284–285.

and Phillips spoke upon such issues as amnesty, governmental reform, social reform, and means of solving the Negro problem.

In the field of social reform, speechmaking was closely identified with the humane movement, temperance, and woman suffrage. Henry Bergh was one leader who relied on speechmaking to effect his ends. Beginning in 1866 with the chartering of the American Society for the Prevention of Cruelty to Animals, he was instrumental in securing legislation in many cities and states to protect dumb animals. Bergh made a speechmaking tour as far west as Chicago and St. Louis in the years 1871–1873, and shortly thereafter societies of the A. S. P. C. A. were incorporated in city after city.[1]

Public address and the temperance movement were also closely identified. Such lecturers as John B. Gough, Frances E. Willard, Col. J. J. Hickman, and Anna Howard Shaw campaigned in opposition to the liquor business. Of Gough's prominence in speechmaking we observe:

In his later life, Mr. Gough ceased to be a temperance lecturer, but his enthusiasm infused all his lectures with his principles and interest of temperance. Whether he lectured on "Life in London" or on "People I have met" or on "Power," he always had something to say on his favorite theme, and his audience never failed to receive some warning against the dangers of drink, or some inspiration toward the practice of temperance. He was unquestionably the most popular orator in America,—a popularity which was steadily on the increase.[2]

From Gough's own records we learn that in the years 1862–1870 he delivered 2,080 lectures and that in his career, which ended with his death in 1886, he made 9,600 addresses before approximately nine million hearers.

Colonel Hickman, to cite another temperance speaker, toured his native state of Missouri, the state of Texas, and others in the Middle West and West. On one trip to Texas he delivered seven lectures at seven different places on successive evenings, organized seven temperance lodges, and enlisted 600 members. A dispatch from Fort Worth, Tex., comments: "He has been heard on both sides of the continent with great acceptance, and our citizens may congratulate themselves upon this opportunity to hear him."[3]

[1] Nevins, *op. cit.*, p. 334.

[2] John B. Gough, *Platform Echoes* (Hartford, Conn., A. D. Worthington and Company, 1887), pp. 64–65. (Introduction by the Reverend Lyman Abbott.)

[3] *Weekly Missouri Statesman*, Feb. 1, 1884, p. 1. From the same periodical we learn of Col. Hickman's conducting a series of meetings in St. Louis, Mo., under the auspices of the Grand Lodge of Good Templars and of his giving lectures in Centralia, St. Joseph, Cumberland, La Plata, Hannibal, Fulton, and other communities in Missouri; also, of arrangements made by the Women's Christian Temperance Union of Columbia, Mo., to conduct temperance meetings at various points in the state.

Anna Howard Shaw spoke in Michigan, Ohio, Illinois, Pennsylvania, and adjoining states on behalf of temperance. She describes one experience in these words:

> We were working for a prohibition amendment in the State of Pennsylvania, and the night before election I reached Coatesville. I had just completed six weeks of strenuous campaigning, and that day I had already conducted and spoken at two big outdoor meetings. . . . Three times in my life, and only three times, I have made speeches that have satisfied me. . . . The speech at Coatesville was one of those three. At the end of it the good-natured crowd cheered for ten minutes. The next day Coatesville voted for prohibition, and, rightly or wrongly, I have always believed that I helped to win that victory.[1]

That the temperance movement utilized many speakers and attracted large crowds can be surmised from a report of a temperance picnic in Missouri: "The temperance pic-nic at Brookline last Saturday was a highly successful affair, the attendance being estimated at from 1,000 to 1,200 persons. . . . Speeches were made by Capt. D. C. Dade, Rev. C. H. Briggs, and J. H. Dobbs, and Prof. W. P. Hampton. . . . "[2]

Closely identified with the temperance movement was that of woman suffrage, with such speakers as Susan B. Anthony and Anna Howard Shaw. In the years from 1882 to 1893 they campaigned in Kansas, Ohio, New York, West Virginia, South Dakota, Idaho, Utah, California, and Washington.[3]

Similarly, the leading representatives of the South in the Reconstruction era were speakers. Henry W. Grady, both a journalist and a speaker, delivered eight speeches in both the North and the South from 1886 to 1889 on phases of problems of reconstruction.[4]

Booker T. Washington, probably the leading representative of the Negro race in this period, used public address on many occasions to urge support for Negro education and for his solution of the race problem. In his autobiography he comments as follows: "Meetings were held in New York, Brooklyn, Boston, Philadelphia, and other large cities . . . At these meetings an especial effort was made to secure help for the building of Alabama Hall [at Tuskegee Institute], as well as to introduce the school to the attention of the general public."[5]

[1] Anna Howard Shaw, *The Story of a Pioneer* (New York, Harper & Brothers, 1929). (Quoted by permission.)

[2] *Springfield Express*, July 15, 1881, p. 3.

[3] Shaw, *op. cit.*, pp. 182, 242–243.

[4] Grady spoke in 1886 on "The New South," in 1887 on "The South and Her Problems" ınd "The 'Solid South,' " and in 1889 on "The Race Problem in the South" and "Plymouth 'ock and Democracy," for example.

[5] Booker T. Washington, *Up from Slavery* (New York, Doubleday, Doran & Company, Inc., 1920), p. 180. (Copyright, 1900, 1901. Reprinted by permission of Doubleday, Doran & Company, Inc.)

B. THE POPULIST PERIOD (1885–1895)

An almost inevitable outgrowth of the confusion of the Reconstruction period was the Populist era. In particular, this period was a reflection of the contest between agriculture and expanding industrialism and of many political and social excesses of the years from 1870 to 1885. More than merely an agrarian revolt or a local movement, it was essentially a cry for reform in many social and political areas. It was a challenge to the industrial East and to both major political parties. Populism is said to have changed the course of the Democratic party as early as 1896 and that of the Republican party by 1904.

Public address was closely related to the events of this period. In fact, the Populist revolt was as much a speaking crusade as a political movement. Not only renowned public figures like Bryan but the heretofore largely inarticulate farmer became spokesmen for the movement. In the rural areas, farmers' societies, the Grange, the Farmers' Alliance, and similar organizations held frequent meetings that hotly debated the needs of agriculture; and the leaders of the political parties likewise debated the issues presented by the "revolt of the farmer."[1]

Bryan, largely through his speechmaking, gained the leadership of the Populist forces in Nebraska and eventually of the Democratic party in the convention of 1896. In the years 1887–1889 he spoke on every possible occasion; and in 1889 he and the Republican candidate for Congress entered into a joint debate, speaking in nearly every city and town in the district. His speeches in various sessions of the Democratic party, including his famous Cross of Gold speech, suggest further his reliance upon this means of attempting to reach both his party and the nation.

C. THE ERA OF IMPERIALISM (1895–1910)

As the United States grew in size and strength and as her industrial plant began to outgrow the home market, agitation for expansion took definite form in the years soon after 1890. On one side were those who saw the "star of empire" and who advanced the thesis that the United States should assume the "white man's burden" in the Philippines and should look to Central and South America as areas of expansion.[2]

Speechmaking was widely used by the leaders of this period. The activities of Senator Beveridge and his colleagues constitute a good case

[1] For a detailed account of this important use of public address, see *infra*, the second half of this study. Also, see Arthur M. Schlesinger, *The Rise of the City* (New York, The Macmillan Company, 1933), p. 18.

[2] It should be noted that the decade 1890–1900 was the first after the end of the frontier in the United States and hence saw the beginning of the tendency to look overseas for the development of new enterprises.

in point. In fact, the record of Beveridge's public life is essentially a roll call of his prominent speeches. A firm believer in imperialism (he termed it *expansion*), he spoke at the Middlesex Club in Boston, April 27, 1898, with such apparent effect that "the audience in Boston applauded his [Dewey's] victory before it was won; applauded the policy we were to pursue before it had officially been defined, and applauded through the prophecy of Beveridge. Imperialism, defiant, unified, had found a voice."[1]

Shortly thereafter he made the keynote of his campaign of 1898 the theme of his Indianapolis speech, entitled "The March of the Flag." (The Republican state committee ordered 300,000 copies of this speech for distribution as a campaign document.) Later (February, 1899) he spoke in Philadelphia on "The Republic that Never Retreats"; then there followed a speech on "The Star of Empire, or America a World Republic," together with a series of debates in the Senate on this issue. This series was marked by such representative addresses as Beveridge's in 1899 on "The Republic that Never Retreats," Roosevelt's "Strenuous Life" (1899), two by Beveridge in 1900, Bryan's opposition speech on "America's Mission" (1899), another opposition speech by Schurz in 1899, one by Hoar in 1900, and Bryan's speech in 1900 accepting the nomination for the Presidency of the United States.

D. THE PERIOD OF REFORM (1900–1914)

This period, representing a culmination of a movement begun about 1880, was marked by agitation for far-reaching social, economic, and political reforms. During this era legislation was passed creating, for instance, a Department of Commerce and Labor, pure-food laws, and numerous controls upon individual and corporate practices. It was, in addition, a period of conflict between parties and between groups within parties. Beveridge and Robert M. La Follette, for example, were opposed to the more conservative wing of the Republican party; and the policies of Theodore Roosevelt were essentially those of the Populist-Democratic party of 1896 and 1900.

These issues were reflected in a large body of the public address of the period. Such speakers as Roosevelt, Beveridge, La Follette, to mention only a few of the "progressives," and Joseph Choate, Chauncey M. Depew, and Henry Cabot Lodge, representing the opposing point of view, debated the issues at length. For example, Roosevelt, who in 1902 inaugurated a campaign of exposure against a number of practices that he considered antisocial, began a speaking crusade in 1902 with a tour through New England, continued in 1906 with his "Muck Rake Speech," continued

[1] Claude G. Bowers, *Beveridge and the Progressive Era* (Boston, Houghton Mifflin Company, 1932), p. 70.

with a series on "The New Nationalism" in 1910, presented a "Charter for Democracy" in 1912, and the "Armageddon Speech" in 1912. In these and other speeches he frequently attacked the trusts and public utilities or argued for the income tax, the conservation of national resources, and other reforms.

Similarly, Beveridge agitated in Congressional debate and on the platform for reforms in the meat-packing industry, for child-labor legislation, for reforms in the national forest service, for a lower tariff, for control of corporate practices, and for other reforms advocated by the Progressive party. Jonathan P. Dolliver and Albert B. Cummins, of Iowa; Joseph L. Bristow, of Kansas; Moses E. Clapp, of Minnesota; William E. Borah, of Idaho; and La Follette were other spokesmen for public-utility legislation, the income tax, the direct primary system, and a tariff for revenue only.

E. THE FIRST WORLD WAR PERIOD (1914–1918)

This period in American history is marked by the curtailment of the reform program of the Wilson administration, as well as by the war itself. In it were pressures for and against American participation in the conflict, attempts to create national unity once the United States had entered the war, and appeals for the support of war enterprises.

In the speechmaking of Wilson, Samuel Gompers, and Herbert Hoover, as well as in that sponsored by such organizations as the Committee on Public Information and the Liberty Loan committees, the events of the period are closely identified with public address.[1]

For instance, the important steps in the development of the war situation were occasions for speeches by Wilson: (1) the outbreak of the war in 1914 was followed by his speech "A World League for Peace"; (2) the inauguration of Germany's submarine warfare, by his message to Congress in February, 1917; (3) the growing emergency, by his "Request for Power"; (4) the pressure of hostile actions, by his "War Message" on April 6, 1917; (5) the need for development of morale, by his "Flag Day Address" on June 14, 1917; (6) the need to consolidate labor, by "What Democracy Means," delivered to the American Federation of Labor on November 12, 1917; (7) the "Second War Message," on December 4, 1917; (8) the outline of his Fourteen Points in a plea for world peace on January 8, 1918; and (9) the series of addresses on the League of Nations in 1919.

Similarly, public address was identified with other events by other speakers. Gompers, president of the American Federation of Labor,

[1] The Committee on Public Information, for example, directed 75,000 speakers, who delivered more than 750,000 speeches.

appeared before a national convention of that organization on February 22, 1918, and appealed to labor to unite in the war effort under the slogan, "Unity, solidarity, energy, and the will to fight and win." Hoover, director of the Food Administration, spoke on "Food and the War"; Franklin K. Lane, Secretary of the Treasury, opened a Liberty Loan campaign with "The Message of the West"; and General Enoch Crowder, director of the draft, opened this phase of the war campaign by speaking to the eligible men of the nation on "Begin Now." In addition, William Howard Taft, Borah, Lodge, and Hiram Johnson, to mention only a few other speakers, used public address in several instances to develop their points of view for or against the League of Nations.[1]

F. THE POSTWAR PERIOD (1918–1930)

This period may be roughly described as the era of reconstruction and of postwar prosperity. There were various proposals for reconstruction, such as the League of Nations. Further, there was the continuation of the high plane of industrial activity maintained during the First World War (an exception was the depression of 1921); there was the period of "normalcy" as described by President Warren G. Harding; and finally, there was the era of Coolidge and Hoover prosperity. The issues faced by the American people during these twelve years were primarily the treaty of peace and the League of Nations, war debts, "good-neighbor" policies, and relations with Russia. By and large, domestic issues were not accorded the same prominence by the American people, for there was "normalcy" at home. Even the vigorous attempts of such reformers as La Follette made little progress in dislodging the major parties from a conservative position.

Perhaps the most notable instance of the use of speechmaking in the period of reconstruction was that made by Wilson. After virtually failing to gain support in Congress for his League of Nations proposal, he planned a tour of the nation, a tour that would include speeches in the Middle West, the Northwest, and the West, in particular. Engagements in twenty-five cities were planned, but the trip was suddenly halted at Pueblo, Colo., by Wilson's serious illness; he was forced to return to Washington to see his plan defeated in the Senate. It would be interesting to speculate concerning the possible turn of events had Wilson been able to take his proposal to the people in all parts of the nation.

---

[1] See, for example, Taft's speeches entitled "Why a League of Nations is Necessary," "Answer to Senator Knox's Indictment," and "America Can't Quit"; see Borah's speeches entitled "Americanism" and "The League of Nations"; see Lodge's "The Senate and the League of Nations" and his debate with A. Lawrence Lowell, Mar. 19, 1919; see Johnson's "League of Nations."

The colorful Presidential campaign of 1928 brought public address to the fore more vividly than in several previous campaigns. The picturesque Alfred E. Smith, a dynamic, dramatic speaker, presented a marked contrast to the more stolid Hoover; and the former campaigned in a vigorous, appealing manner reminiscent of a former day.

Two other uses of public address during this period are worthy of our consideration here. The first is the use of speech by the public-relations counsel; the other is the use of speech by "pressure groups." The former is described by a counselor himself:

> The lecture platform still retains its place for the public relations counsel. . . . The public relations counsel can, for instance, suggest to his client to secure a prominent person, who because of interest in a cause will be glad to undertake a lecture tour. . . .
>
> Then there is the lecture tour managed by the client himself and arranged through the booking of engagements with such local groups as might be interested in assuming sponsorship for what he said. . . .
>
> The lecture field offers another means of communication inasmuch as it gives the public relations counsel a range of group leaders to whom he can furnish the facts and ideas he is trying to propagate.[1]

The campaign of the Mid-West Utilities Corporation is another interesting case. Using the radio and armed with the best techniques of persuasion, the Old Counselor served as a spokesman for that organization. He imitated the best manner of a trusted adviser, answering questions on family finances and giving homely advice on problems of investment.

In addition, various "pressure groups" used public address in a variety of ways and reached millions of listeners. For example, the Anti-Saloon League, the Lord's Day Alliance, the National Security League, and the Citizens' Union developed campaigns that largely concentrated upon the public platform. Using the forum, the lecture program, and meetings of such organizations as the church, the women's clubs, and the men's "service" clubs, they sought to arouse public opinion on behalf of their programs.

Thus the era of prosperity and of high-pressure methods adapted public address extensively to the service of business and special-interest groups. The public-relations counsel is but one example of the former, and the Anti-Saloon League campaign well illustrates the latter.

CONCLUSION

The history of the years from 1860 to 1930 could conceivably be written in terms of the themes and the arguments of the speechmakers. Public

---

[1] Edward L. Bernays, *Crystallizing Public Opinion* (New York, Liveright Publishing Corporation, 1923), pp. 201–203.

address was inextricably woven into the achievements of the majority of responsible leaders of this period. In social and political reform, imperialism, war, and reconstruction, it was the instrument of leaders and lesser figures who spoke to hundreds of millions of people in their efforts to shape and direct public thought. It was far indeed from being dead or dying, as many septuagenarian autobiographers complained, but was in fact more widely used than ever before in American history. Nor was there any indication of its decrease in influence on American thought.

II. *Certain Distinctive Aspects of Public Address*

During the years 1860–1930, public address retained, as we have observed, the traditional forms and uses that were present in former periods. Deliberative oratory (on the political platform and in Congress, for example), forensic oratory (in the law court), and ceremonial oratory (on the special occasion) were, of course, in constant use. They will no doubt always be integral parts of a free society. Of especial interest, however, are certain distinctive aspects—sometimes in type, sometimes in use, and sometimes in the person of the speaker. To some of these we shall now direct our attention.

Specifically, we are concerned here with four aspects: (1) the development of the Lecture Platform; (2) the rise of the farmer as an articulate member of society; (3) the increasing displacement of Congressional debate by committee deliberations and party caucuses; and (4) the increasing prominence of speaking on behalf of labor and by representatives of labor. These developments were peculiar to, if not observed solely in, the period under consideration. They represent probably the distinctive aspects of public address as a form of force in these years.

A. THE LECTURE PLATFORM

The lecture platform, especially in relation to the commercial lecture bureaus, reached its climax in the years from 1870 to 1900, with subsequent popularity in the Chautauqua, which continued until about 1920. We shall consider it from the point of view of three periods: (1) its beginnings to the Civil War; (2) its development from that time to 1900; (3) its evolution in recent years.

THE BEGINNINGS TO THE CIVIL WAR. The beginnings of American lecturing as a distinct phase of public address cannot be definitely established. It is certain, however, that long before the colonies won their independence, the lecture platform was in existence. In its early history it probably consisted primarily of traveling evangelists who went from one community to another, not only as preachers but as bearers of news. Their job was essentially that of the lecturer of later years—to tell of the latest events, to interpret news, and to lead discussions on topics of current interest.

Not until 1826 did the lecture platform assume a well-defined status. When Dr. Josiah Holbrook, an early agitator for free public education, began the lyceum movement, he organized a tremendous influence not only upon the lecture platform but also upon American life. He organized the first lyceum in Millbury, Mass., in 1826; and by 1828 there were approximately one hundred branches of the American lyceum. By the end of 1834 there were 3,000 town lyceums, which were affiliated with county lyceums, which were, in turn, affiliated with state lyceums and a national lyceum. By 1839, however, this institution had markedly declined; and except for a few local units, the majority of the organizations had become inactive.

THE PERIOD FROM 1867 TO 1900. In 1867 an organization of 110 lyceums, calling itself the Associated Literary Societies, was formed. The formation of this institution marks the beginning of the lecture "business" and is in many respects the first commercial lecture bureau, a distinct innovation in the field of American public address. Its purpose was to make some of the better Eastern lecturers available to the West, and in the first year of its existence it booked thirty-five lecturers. In 1870 this group amalgamated with the American Literary Bureau of New York.

Meanwhile, James Clark Redpath, one of the most important men in the lecture business, founded, in collaboration with George L. Fall, the Boston Lyceum Bureau. Redpath was an immediate success, for he met a long-felt need—a central bureau that could supply lecturers to local lyceums. Just as Holbrook gave the lyceum its initial impetus, so did Redpath give it its beginning as a big business, making well-known lecturers available to almost any community. A successor of Redpath says of this development:

The bureau . . . has done more than any other agency to revive the lecture system, which was rapidly dying out all over the country. Since the establishment of this bureau, the number of lectures given in the United States has increased tenfold, chiefly under the impulse which it gave to the system. It has more than quadrupled the number of lectures that were given in New England when it was organized.[1]

On the basis of a 10 per cent commission, Redpath managed most of the American lecturers from 1867 to 1875. Among the more prominent persons under his direction were Wendell Phillips, William Lloyd Garrison, Charles Sumner, John B. Gough, Ralph Waldo Emerson, John Greenleaf

---

[1] James B. Pond, *Eccentricities of Genius* (New York, G. W. Dillingham Company, 1900), p. 536.

Whittier, Elizabeth Cady Stanton, Susan B. Anthony, Anna Dickinson, Henry Ward Beecher, and Charles Dickens, the English novelist. Putting lecturers on a commercial basis, Redpath helped some of his clients to clear handsome sums for their efforts. Gough, for example, cleared $40,000 for the season of 1871–1872; Phillips averaged from $250 to $500 per lecture (often returning the fee to the sponsors); Beecher received as much as $1,000 for a single lecture; and Dickens' tour of 1867–1868 took in $228,000.

The full development had not, however, been reached even at this point. The combination of favorable circumstances in the nation and of a lecture-bureau manager of unusual ability made the years 1875–1900 even greater for commercial bureaus than were those of a previous period. The favorable circumstances were essentially the following: the rise of the Machine Age with its era of comparatively greater prosperity, the spread of the temperance and the woman-suffrage movements, the growth of the city, an increasing interest in literary and scientific matters, and the improvement of transportation. And to this set of circumstances should be added the second factor: the presence of James Burton Pond, a lecture-bureau manager of great ability.

What transpired is little short of phenomenal. From 1875 to 1900 the number of larger bureaus increased from 1 to 100. Fees increased to the point where lecturers received as much as $1,000 for a single performance. Lecturing became a big business.

In this wise the informal, serious-minded and spontaneous gathering of the villagers at the school house or tavern has become the prosperous commercial lecture bureau of today. First the local light, then the exchange of local savants between lyceums of neighboring communities, then the payment of small fees and the emergence of the professional lecturer, then the combination of many lyceums or literary societies to engage lecturers jointly and on tour, then the formation of bureaus engaging and booking lecturers as a business.[1]

We shall now consider three questions: What were the important developments in the lecture platform in this period? How did this institution operate? Who were some of the prominent figures?

By 1875 the old lyceum had virtually disappeared, only thirty of the old organizations remaining. Taking its place was this new commercial lecture bureau with its new practice of booking and of providing means of stimulating public interest. In 1887 these bureaus began the practice of sending advance agents on the road to help build up interest in the coming lecturers. By the end of the century a half dozen of the largest bureaus

---

[1] John S. Noffsinger, *Correspondence Schools, Lyceums, Chautauquas* (New York, The Macmillan Company, 1926), p. 106. (Quoted by permission.)

were booking more than three thousand lecture dates apiece; and the hundred other bureaus and scores of independent groups were also doing a large business.

The Chautauqua circuit was another important phase of this development, being both a complement and a competitor of the lecture business. Even though it may have been a factor in the later decline of the commercial lecture platform, it was a complementary force in the years 1875 to 1900 in that it helped to popularize the lecture business and expand the demand for its talent. Another factor that was also both a complement and a competitor was the system of free public lectures established in 1888 in New York City. Sponsored by the New York school board, this system grew until by 1898 there were forty-five centers, where in one year more than two thousand lectures were given to approximately 1,200,000 persons. Other cities, especially in the East, followed the example of New York.[1]

Nor was the business limited to speakers. The bureaus introduced popular singers, players, and even opera companies into the talent available. Among the actors who were booked by lecture bureaus were Joseph Jefferson, William Winter, Sir Henry Irving, Charlotte Cushman, and Ellen Terry. Dr. A. Conan Doyle, Sir Edwin Arnold, Hall Caine, and George W. Cable were among the author-readers also booked by the Pond Bureau.[2]

The operation of the lecture-bureau system is interesting. It was customary for the bureaus to send out agents armed with sample photographs and circulars. These agents would round up a committee of enterprising citizens who wanted to do something for their community and persuade them to guarantee a fund to secure a course of lectures and entertainments.

They listen to the bureau agent's recommendations of "the greatest orator of the time, Mr. Breeze," and "the great traveller and adventurer, Mr. Push," "the latest and most original dialect poet, Mr. Verse," "Miss Wonder, whose dramatic recitations have captivated metropolitan audiences in all the large cities," and "Miss Good, who is a direct descendant of a great-grand-niece of Oliver Wendell Holmes's cousin." The course is made up, and contracts are signed before the agent leaves town. Then for six months the course is being talked up. The bureau agent remains for a few days to assist the local canvassers in getting started, telling them who the celebrities are that are to make the town so famous by their visit, etc.

Over fifty such courses are already announced for the State of Michigan the coming autumn, August, 1900, over two hundred in the State of Illinois, nearly as

[1] Anna L. Curtis, A Brief History of the Lyceum, *Who's Who in the Lyceum* (A. Augustus Wright, ed., Philadelphia, Pearson Brothers, 1906), p. 31.

[2] Pond, *op. cit.*, classifies the talent made available by the bureaus as orators; pulpit orators; women lecturers and singers; humorists; explorers, travelers, and war correspondents; actors and dramatic critics; literary lecturers; miscellaneous; author readers and lecturers.

many in Iowa, and so proportionately all over the country. More than $6,000 a week is now being disbursed by bureaus to agents 'selling courses.'[1]

The system sponsored two types of talent, the lesser light or "simon-pure lecturer," and the "star" of the platform. As a general rule, the lesser light received from $75 to $300 per lecture. He was usually a fairly well-known person who devoted the greatest part of his career to lecturing and was usually managed by a bureau that would pay a stipulated amount for each lecture plus traveling expenses. The following description is typical.

The simon-pure lecturer . . . is a man or woman to whom lecturing is the chief, or at least, one of the chief ways of earning a living. He is nearly always a native American. He is lecturing steadily from five to eleven months of the year. He is constantly moving, living in hotels and sleeping-cars (when he is lucky enough to be "making a jump" where the latter luxuries may be found). . . .
This sort of lecturer receives from his bureau his railroad expenses and half his fees, if he is in lyceum work, or his railroad expenses and a flat salary if he is in Chautauqua. In short, the genuine, dyed-in-the-wool lecturer is the lecturer of the organized lyceum and its offspring, the Chautauqua, which, with some modifications, is merely a lyceum in a tent.[2]

This was the type of lecturer that probably exerted the strongest influence upon the smaller communities, in particular. In the days when there were no radios and motion pictures, when newspapers and magazines were less widely circulated than in 1930, the lecturer who reached the small cities and towns was not only a purveyor of information but a molder of opinion. It is estimated that lyceum lecturers alone reached an audience of five million persons each year during the years 1875–1900, and the Chautauqua and the free lecture bureaus reached an equally large number.

The money-makers of the system, however, were usually not the "simon-pure lecturers" but the "stars" of the platform. Invariably they were the famous men and women of the pulpit, leaders in political and social movements, explorers, scientists, and authors who devoted only a small portion of their time to the lecture business. They were usually booked for the large cities, and ordinarily each of them would undertake one tour per season.

The principal figures of the lecture platform were virtually a "Who's Who" of the period. They included the "great triumvirate of lecture

---

[1] Pond, *op. cit.*, pp. 300–301.
[2] Gregory Mason, "Quenching America's Mental Thirst," *Scribner's Magazine*, 75 (1924): 553.

kings," Gough, Beecher, and Phillips, as well as others whom we shall consider at this point.[1]

John B. Gough, who began his lecture career about 1842 and continued to the time of his death in 1886, delivered more than 9,600 addresses before an estimated nine million hearers. His popularity was tremendous; and as a result he frequently received from $500 to $1,000 per lecture in the years from 1874 to 1886. In many instances, sponsors of lecture courses would rely upon Gough's popularity to make up what had been lost on other speakers on a season's program.

Henry Ward Beecher was also one of the great figures of the lecture platform. In the years 1875 to 1887, during which he was connected with the Pond Bureau, he delivered 1,261 lectures in every state and territory in the Union except Arizona and New Mexico, covering approximately 300,000 miles "by every conceivable mode of travel, in special Pullman cars, the regular passenger trains, mixed trains, freight trains, on steamboats and rowboats, by stage and on the backs of mules."

Likewise, Wendell Phillips participated for forty years in lyceum work under the sponsorship of the commercial bureaus. In two respects he was distinctive among the lecturers of his era: in the breadth of his repertoire and in his attitude toward the financial end of the lecture business. His prepared lectures embraced such subjects as travel, science, current politics, reform, labor, abolition of slavery, education, biography, religion, and foreign affairs. Among his more popular titles were "The Lost Arts," "Temperance," "Woman," "Agitation," "Law and the Lawyers," "Courts and Jails," "The Irish Question," "Sumner," and "Christianity a Battle, Not a Dream." His attitude toward finances was different from that of many bureaus and of other lecturers. He did not earn so much money from his lecturing as he might have made, for he never permitted lecture sponsors or committees to lose money if he knew it. "In case of bad weather, or a disappointment of any kind . . . he would invariably insist that he receive only an equitable portion of the profits."[2]

Among the pulpit orators who spoke on the lecture platform were, in addition to Beecher, such men as Lyman Abbott, Newell Dwight Hillis, T. DeWitt Talmage, and two English preachers, Joseph Parker and

---

[1] Pond lists the following orators, pulpit orators, and women lecturers, *op. cit.*, Contents: Gough, Phillips, William Lloyd Garrison, Charles Sumner, Chauncey M. Depew, Gen. Horace Porter, Col. Robert G. Ingersoll, Frederick Douglass, Booker T. Washington; Beecher, the Reverend Dr. Lyman Abbott, the Reverend Newell Dwight Hillis, the Reverend Dr. Joseph Parker, the Reverend T. DeWitt Talmage, the Reverend Charles H. Spurgeon, the Right Reverend Bishop Henry C. Potter, the Very Reverend S. Reynolds Hole, the Right Reverend Dr. Boyd Carpenter, the Very Reverend Charles William Stubbs; Susan B. Anthony, Julia Ward Howe, Anna E. Dickinson, Mary A. Livermore, Lucy Stone.

[2] Pond, *op. cit.*, p. 11.

S. Reynolds Hole, who was on a lecture tour in the United States during the season 1894–1895.

T. DeWitt Talmage, in addition to conducting several lecture tours in England and preaching during a long career, was a popular figure on the American platform. Said James B. Pond of him in 1900:

> Dr. Talmage has the greatest congregation of readers of his sermons of any man living, and this is his means of advertising. To gather up a large audience for him in the western country all that is needed is a railroad junction where cars can be run from all directions, the erection of a temporary amphitheatre, and the announcement that Dr. Talmage is to preach, and all the facilities for bringing out crowds will be tested to their fullest capacity. Under these conditions the doctor is the greatest one-man attraction in America. . . . [1]

Nor was the lecture platform limited to men. In the years 1875–1900 women came into prominence both as lecturers in the traditional sense and as protagonists for temperance and woman suffrage. They used the commercial lecture platform to present their points of view.

Mrs. Ann Elizabeth Young, the first lecturer booked by Pond, began her career in 1873 in New England and other Eastern states, lecturing "nightly to as large audiences as were being drawn by the most popular lecturers of the period. . . . At the end of the season she had earned over $20,000."

Miss Susan B. Anthony and Dr. Anna Howard Shaw constituted one of the most noted teams in the history of the American platform. In addition to doing extensive speaking under other auspices and on other subjects, they joined in 1882 and proceeded to concentrate on the cause of woman suffrage. Dr. Shaw says of their activities: "In 1890, '92, and '93 we again worked in Kansas and in South Dakota with such indefatigable and brilliant speakers as Mrs. Catt, Mrs. Laura Johns of Kansas, Mrs. Julia Nelson, Henry D. Blackwell, Dr. Helen V. Putnam of Dakota, Mrs. Emma Smith DeVoe, Rev. Olympia Brown of Wisconsin, and Dr. Mary Seymour Howell of New York."[2]

An instance of Miss Anthony's speaking on the suffrage issue and of her popularity is cited in a dispatch from Leavenworth, Kans. "Susan B. Anthony occupied the pulpit of the Rev. E. R. Sanborn, pastor of the Free Congregational Church in this city, last night. Every available seat was occupied. The aisles were filled, and hundreds were turned away, unable to gain admittance. She spoke upon the moral results of the franchise to woman."[3]

---

[1] Pond, *op. cit.*, p. 110.
[2] Shaw, *op. cit.*, pp. 242, 243. (Quoted by permission.)
[3] *The Boonville, Missouri, Advertiser*, Dec. 31, 1875, p. 4.

Among the other prominent women lecturers were Julia Ward Howe, who for thirty years lectured in all parts of the United States, Anna E. Dickinson, and Mary A. Livermore. Miss Dickinson was said to be so popular that "only Gough and Beecher rivalled her as a lyceum favorite"; and Mrs. Livermore rivaled Phillips in the scope of her repertoire, which included woman suffrage, biography, history, politics, religion, and reform. The first woman to be listed by the Redpath Bureau, she lectured on an average of one hundred times a year in the lyceum in addition to over a thousand times on temperance and a similar number of times on woman suffrage.

THE EVOLUTION IN RECENT YEARS. By about 1900, the commercial lecture platform entered into another phase. While some lecture bureaus continued to exist, the trend was toward the Chautauqua, the free public-lecture system, the forum, and the University Extension movement, as well as toward competing institutions such as the press and the theatre. In the years from 1920 to 1930 the development of the radio, the motion picture, and improved transportation from smaller communities to the city served further to curtail comparatively the scope of the organized lecture program.

A great part of the lecturing talent went over to the Chautauqua. For example, Bryan, President McKinley, Theodore Roosevelt, La Follette, James Bryce, and William Allen White appeared with Chautauqua rather than with the regular lyceum bureaus.[1]

The University Extension movement was also a factor. When Provost Pepper, of the University of Pennsylvania, brought from England in 1890 the idea of an extension service, he inaugurated a movement in adult education that quickly spread to many leading institutions, including nearly every state university in the United States. This movement, which now has units in more than fifty centers, paralleled the work of the commercial lecture bureaus and soon was one of the means of displacing them.

Other factors that served to minimize the importance and the popularity of the lecture platform were the increasing availability of newspapers and magazines and the development of the opera house with the traveling operatic and theatrical companies on tour. Whereas in 1875, magazines were of limited circulation, in 1900 they had increased several-fold. In 1875 the machinery for printing 1,000 newspapers per hour was exceptional; by 1900, however, 100,000 papers could be printed in the same time. In 1885 there were approximately eighty traveling operatic and theatrical combinations on the road, whereas in 1900 there were nearly fifteen hundred going from town to town on "one-night stands." In cities like New Haven, Hartford, Springfield, and Worcester, for instance, theatres booked their time

[1] Upton Close, "The Lecture Business," *Saturday Review of Literature,* 21 (1940); 15.

solid with these traveling groups from August to May, leaving little opportunity for the lecture course to arrange a program or to attract a following.

Subsequent to 1900, the emphasis changed in many instances to the forum, the radio, and the motion picture, all of which furnished either greater variety or more accessible entertainment. The forum movement, with a somewhat different emphasis and type of program, came into a position of prominence after 1900. A few representative institutions were Ford Hall Forum, Boston (1908); Old South Forum, Boston (1915); Chicago Forum (1925); Town Hall, New York (1921, established originally as The League for Political Education in 1894); Sinai Temple Forum, Chicago (1914); Commonwealth Club of California (1912).[1]

In addition, the radio was instituting such features as America's Town Meeting of the Air (in conjunction with Town Hall) and similar forum programs made available to all persons having access to receiving sets. The entertainment field, both in the radio and in the motion picture, was also an increasingly important competitor of the lecture platform. The motion-picture industry, for example, in 1924 embraced 17,836 theatres and is said to have attracted 20 per cent of the population of the United States each day and 68.2 per cent more or less regularly.[2]

The situation in the third decade of the twentieth century was, therefore, essentially this: Many lecture bureaus were doing an extensive business, many lecturers were on the road, and perhaps even more persons were attending lectures than ever before, but comparatively the lecture platform did not occupy the distinctive position that it did in 1885.[3] Even though it had assumed the proportions of a "big business" and attracted many of the leading platform personages,[4] it had largely disappeared from the smaller communities, and in the larger cities it was rivaled by such other agencies of education and entertainment as the motion picture. The typical city, for instance, might have a number of motion-picture theaters drawing

---

[1] See Mary L. Ely, *Why Forums?* (New York, American Association for Adult Education, 1937). See also Reuben L. Lurie, *The Challenge of the Forum—The Story of Ford Hall and the Open Forum Movement* (Boston, Richard A. Badger, 1930).

[2] *World Almanac*, 1925, p. 539.

[3] Among the more prominent bureaus were Alber and Wickes, Inc.; Columbia Lecture Bureau; William B. Feakins, Inc.; Forum Lecture Bureau; Clark H. Getts, Inc.; Lee Keedick; W. Colston Leigh, Inc.; Harold R. Peat, Inc.; Program Associates, Inc.; Redpath Bureau; Shearwood-Smith, Inc. See Close, *op. cit.*, p. 3.

[4] Among the lecturers listed in a typical issue of *Program* (published by the Pond Program Company, Inc., 2 West 45th St., New York City) were Louis Adamic, Stuart Chase, Upton Close, Will Durant, Irving Fisher, Hugh Gibson, Frank Kingdon, André Maurois, Anne O'Hare McCormick, Harry A. Overstreet, Ruth Bryan Owen, William Lyon Phelps, Carl Sandburg, Lew Sarett, Ralph W. Sockman, Vilhjalmur Stefansson, Norman Thomas, and Albert Edward Wiggam.

large crowds each day, whereas it would have one or two lecture courses offering perhaps fortnightly programs during the fall and winter season. Be that as it may, the lecture platform was an important medium of public address in America from 1865 to 1930; and it contributed much to the life of the nation. "From it [lecturing] came the main stimulus to American adult education, reading courses, book clubs, correspondence schools, the immense business-book publishing business. It has been the firing line of our anti-slavery, temperance, woman's rights, and anti-narcotics crusades."[1]

B. THE FARMER BECOMES ARTICULATE

The Plight of the Farmer. During and after the Civil War the Middle West rose to a position of agricultural dominance. The population of the four new grain states and territories (Minnesota, Dakota, Nebraska, and Kansas) increased from 300,000 in 1860 to nearly two and a half millions in 1880. This development created at once serious social and political problems. The pioneer life was one of hardship; the economic status of the farmer was precarious, especially when overproduction drove down the prices of grain; and the economic philosophies of the major political parties were hardly suited to meet the needs of the frontier people or to attract their support. Added to these circumstances were disasters and near disasters that occurred all too frequently—prairie fires, blizzards, plagues of locusts and Hessian flies, and recurrent droughts. Ultimately the crisis came.

The farmer lived from half-year to half-year in fear that he could not meet the payment on his mortgage, and that foreclosure would ruin him. In contrast with his own lot he pictured the enviable position of the Eastern business classes in the flush years before 1873, with their carriages and comfortable homes, their assured income from an ever more prosperous trade. There has never been an Anglo-Saxon population which would endure such conditions without revolt, and the bitterness of the Middle Western farmer rapidly ripened into open rebellion.[2]

The objects of the attack were, in general, the "capitalists," but more specifically the middlemen (grain dealers and stock buyers), the bankers, the manufacturers of farm machinery and other goods, and the railways. The government was also held responsible for the currency system, the tariff, and the tax system.

Reprisals began in 1867 when in Illinois the farmers opposed an attempt to crush the independent elevator companies, and were continued in 1871 with the passage in Illinois, by the farmer-controlled legislature, of a railway law that prohibited rate discrimination. The "revolt of the farmer"

---

[1] Close, *op. cit.*, p. 15.

[2] Nevins, *op. cit.*, p. 162. (Quoted by permission.)

soon gathered momentum. The Grange, a powerful organization of farmers, was expanding to the point where by 1874 it had a million and a half members and 15,000 local units, with only four states in the Union not represented. Even in the South it had 6,400 local units by 1875.

At length the movement led to a political flare-up, with the emergence of third parties. In some instances it was the Farmers' Alliance; in Minnesota, the Anti-Monopoly party; in Wisconsin, the Reform party; in Kansas, a combination of Reformers and Democrats; in many states, the Populists; at last, in 1896, the Democrats with many features of Populism. In 1874 there were independent agrarian parties in nine prairie states as well as in Oregon and California. In Illinois in the fall of 1874 the farmers' party elected four members to Congress; in Wisconsin, three; and in Iowa, one.[1] And the movement continued for twenty years.

In the South, also, the revolt was in evidence. In the years 1878–1888 farmers' clubs and societies were organized largely for the purpose of discussing the problems of agriculture and of training people for leadership in the new crusade. There were upheavals in Virginia and South Carolina as well as in Texas, where in 1890 the agrarian revolt elected "Jim" Hogg as governor. "Thus, as the decade ended, the Southern agrarian leaders were ripe for cooperation with their Western brethren in demands upon the federal government for remedial action."[2]

PUBLIC ADDRESS IN THE REVOLT. The Populist revolt "was a religious revival, a crusade, a pentecost of politics in which a tongue of flame sat upon every man and each spake as the spirit gave him utterance. . . . The farmers, the country merchants, the cattle-herders, they of the long chin-whiskers, and they of the broad-brimmed hats and heavy boots, had also heard the word and could preach the gospel of Populism."[3] Not only were there the leaders who organized political parties and engineered movements but there were the rank and file of rural people who used every opportunity to speak out upon the issues that affected their very existence.

Furthermore, in the Kansas campaign in 1890, for instance, scores of persons who had been trained as lecturers for the Farmers' Alliance toured the state, spreading the doctrine of Populism. There were huge meetings of farmers at which there was speech after speech "that came straight from the hay-fields and the corn-rows, speeches that were an echo of the daily experience of the farmer and the farmer's wife."[4] The Alliance encouraged

[1] Nevins, *op. cit.*, p. 175.

[2] Arthur M. Schlesinger, *The Rise of the City* (New York, The Macmillan Company, 1933), p. 20. (Quoted by permission.)

[3] John D. Hicks, *The Populist Revolt* (Minneapolis, University of Minnesota Press, 1931), p. 159. (Quoted by permission.)

[4] Vernon L. Parrington, *Main Currents in American Thought* (New York, Harcourt, Brace, and Company, 1930), III, 266.

people to talk of their common problems. Nearly every local organization had a "lecturer," who not only spoke to the group but also prepared other members to make speeches. Study groups were formed; speakers were provided for every conceivable occasion; in short, the revolt was a speaking crusade.

The crusade spread as far eastward as Indiana. A letter written June 5, 1889, by James M. Washburn to S. A. Lancaster describes a farmers' meeting at Princeton:

> I had a very interesting visit to Princeton, Indiana. . . . There were 6000 to 7000 persons at the meeting. Mr. Moore, President of our Organization, and myself addressed the meeting or a part of it. Of course not half of them could hear us. . . . The farmers over there are much more lively to their interests than in Williamson County.

The announcement of a farmers' meeting in Hopewell, Mo., contains similar details. The Farmers' and Laborers' Union was the sponsor; and speeches "will be made by county lecturer R. P. Matthews, Judge Wm. McKerall, Judge H. G. Millings and T. S. Wilson who will present and fully explain the aims and objects of our organization."[1]

Audiences were invariably large, and the speakers were almost exclusively farmers or persons close to the farmers in point of view and interests. The mass meetings in Nebraska in 1893 that were described by a correspondent writing to the *People's Party Paper* were typical of farmers' gatherings throughout the Middle West.

> The Populists are holding mass meetings all over the State in support of their judicial candidate. At these meetings there are songs sung by the glee clubs, composed generally of pretty country maidens. . . . When the orator takes the platform he awakens the echoes with his thunderous denunciations of the existing order of things. His audiences are always silent and attentive to a degree rarely if ever found in the political gatherings of either of the old parties. After the speaking comes more music. . . . [2]

A Few of the Prominent Speakers. Of the scores, even hundreds, of colorful speakers in this movement, we shall discuss here only a few who were representative of the Populist revolt of the 1890's. Ignatius Donnelly, of Minnesota; Jerry Simpson, of Kansas; Ben Tillman, of South Carolina; Davis Waite, of Colorado; and James B. Weaver, of Iowa, all picturesque and vigorous figures of the West and South, were typical of the men. Mrs. Annie L. Diggs and Mrs. Mary Elizabeth Lease, of Kansas, and Mrs. Eva McDonald-Valesh, of Minnesota, were among the more prominent women.

[1] *Springfield Express*, May 23, 1890, p. 3.
[2] Hicks, *op. cit.*, p. 286. (Quoted by permission.)

The colorful, dynamic leader of the revolt in Minnesota was Ignatius Donnelly, a hot-headed, keen-witted agitator who came within about five thousand votes of winning the governorship of the state in 1874. Called by many of his neighbors the "Minnesota Sage," Donnelly was both a popular lecturer on such topics as "Wit and Humor" and a persuasive speaker on any subject that had to do with politics or economics. Three times he ran for Congress on the Republican ticket, and three times he was elected. But in the late 1880's, he went over to the People's party and immediately led the uprising of the farmers in Minnesota.

In the campaign of 1890, he spoke in nearly every town in the state, in many of them on several occasions, vigorously denouncing the capitalists and the "oppressors in Wall Street." In one speech he harangued his audience by saying, "We meet in the midst of turbulent times. This government was founded by plain men, not millionaires. But . . . we now have two parties arrayed against each other, Aristocracy against Commonality. Thirty thousand families own one-half the wealth of the country, and they have no part in producing it. They have stolen it from the labor and toil that has produced the nation."[1]

Nor was Donnelly merely a state figure. He was a leading agitator in the Populist party and one of the principal speakers at the Omaha convention of 1892. As the author of the preamble to the platform adopted there, he aroused the 10,000 delegates to a fever pitch. Cheers and shouts greeted his words, and in an almost fanatical frenzy the people crowded about him to grasp his hands. A campaigner of boundless energy, a speaker with a striking personality and the gift of picturesque language, Donnelly was a powerful figure in the revolt of the farmer.

"Sockless" Jerry Simpson, of Kansas, the People's party candidate for Congress in 1890, was equally humorous, quaint, and appealing. Distinctly rural in appearance, he at one time dubbed his well-dressed opponent (Col. James R. Hallowell) "Prince Hal, the wearer of silk stockings." Immediately Simpson's habit of being without socks became publicized; and from that time on, he was called "Sockless Jerry."

One-eyed "Pitchfork" Ben Tillman, of South Carolina, was attracted to the Populist movement as a result of his personal contacts with the physical and economic hardships endured by the farmers in those bitter days. He was a farmer, and he made the most of it in his speaking. In appearance, in manner, in language he adapted his presentation to the "none-too-squeamish rural classes." He and his opponent, Earle, debated the issues of the day before excited crowds in various parts of South Carolina, Earle presenting the point of view of the well-to-do classes and Tillman denouncing the "capitalist oppressors." Constantly Tillman would appeal to the farmers to

[1] Hicks, *op. cit.*, p. 331. (Quoted from *Representative*, July 18, 1894.)

put their faith in the Populist party. Constantly the audiences would interrupt and try to shout down Earle, at the same time wildly demonstrating their faith in Tillman.

The debates between Earle and Tillman attracted crowds of turbulent citizens from far and near, some of whom were so eager for the fray that they arrived on the scene the day before the speaking was to take place. . . . Usually the majority was with Tillman, and the county-to-county canvass that he made demonstrated clearly the strength of the movement for which he stood.[1]

"Bloody Bridles" Waite, governor of Colorado in 1893, was probably the most profane and bitter speaker in the crusade. It was while he was campaigning in the summer of 1893 on the issue of the repeal of the Sherman Silver Purchase Act that he prophesied dramatically the impending revolution and asserted, "It is better, infinitely better, that blood should flow to the horses' bridles rather than our national liberties should be destroyed." From that moment on, Waite was known as "Bloody Bridles," a hysterical, capitalist-baiting radical who delighted in arraying the farmers and laborers against the "money interests."

So vigorous was his crusade and so bitter his invectives that frequently he brought upon himself and his doctrines adverse criticism from persons who were sympathetic with his objectives but not with his methods. Typical of this reaction is an editorial in a national journal, which said in part, "They [Waite and the people in Colorado] are determined to sail straight into the desired harbor against a head wind, when the only possible way to get in is by a course of well calculated tacking."[2]

General James B. Weaver, of Iowa, became famous in 1880 when, as the Greenback nominee for the Presidency of the United States, he toured the country from "Arkansas to Maine, and from Lake Michigan to Mobile." Not only in that year but in 1881 and on to 1890 this "commanding, gesticulating" crusader argued for unlimited free coinage of silver, the abolition of all banks of issue, the issuance of all money by the government, and higher taxes upon the "wealthy capitalist."

Using a plentiful array of jokes, he would invariably try to win his listeners by humor and bitter tirades of abuse upon the Democratic and Republican parties for "their sins of omission and commission." Typical of his approach was that in Fort Scott, Kans., in 1881, as reported by a press correspondent who apparently was none too sympathetic with the Greenback cause.

Gen. Weaver's speech on Friday was remarkable in one respect at least that he said nothing new. In some respects at least Gen. Weaver is a remarkable man, and

---

[1] Hicks, *op. cit.*, p. 172. (Quoted by permission.)
[2] *Review of Reviews*, 8 (1893): 247–248.

it was to be expected that his utterances would have been in keeping with his character as a man and ex-candidate for the Presidency. Unfortunately for his party they were not. He opened his speech with a complaint at an Associated Press reporter at Lincoln, Nebraska, whose estimate of the General's audience at that place was too small. Next he denounced the subsidized Republican press of the country. Told how the prosecutors of the Greenback party were going over the country tearing down their bills. He evidently believes that the blood of the Martyrs is the seed of the church. After this kind of peroration he opened upon the Republican party and the National Banking system, and for an hour and a half did a deadly work of destruction to both. . . . [1]

An account of a speech in Springfield, Mo., in 1890, shows Weaver's analysis of the ills of the farmer and the laborer and his remedies for the oppressive conditions that he said were victimizing the middle classes of the Middle Border.

Gen. James B. Weaver of Iowa spoke to a large and enthusiastic audience at Music Hall in this city at 1 o'clock yesterday afternoon. He spoke under the auspices of the Farmers' and Laborers' Union of this county and for nearly three hours ably handled the important political questions of the day, frequently eliciting hearty applause from the hearers. . . . From the records of the National Treasury he showed that the people today (62½ millions of them) have only half as much money in circulation as the 25 millions of people in the North had at the close of the war, and declared that the only remedy to relieve the people of hard times and enable them to get out of debt was more money in taxes, both direct and tariff. . . . [2]

Mrs. Annie L. Diggs, of Kansas, and Mrs. Eva McDonald-Valesh, of Minnesota, were earnest, vigorous spokesmen of the embattled farmers and laborers. One of the best known of the Farmers' Alliance women, Mrs. Diggs overcame her slight stature and her mere hundred pounds by her unusual gift for words and her tremendous vitality. Mrs. Valesh, known as "the jauntiest, sauciest, prettiest little woman in the whole coterie of women in the Alliance," attempted in the campaign of 1890 to rally both the farmers and the Knights of Labor to the Populist cause.

Perhaps the outstanding woman in the Populist revolt was Mary Elizabeth Lease, of Kansas. She it was who "struck from the common bitterness a phrase that embodied the militant spirit of Populism. Week after week she travelled the prairie country urging the farmers to 'raise less corn and more hell'."[3] "A tall, slender, good-looking woman of thirty-seven years," she was the most spectacular of the colorful advocates of revolt. Combining personal knowledge of the bitter hardships of the frontier with a study of the law, she worked effectively and tirelessly for the Union Labor

[1] *Springfield Express*, Aug. 26, 1881, p. 2.
[2] *Ibid.*, Apr. 25, 1890, p. 3.
[3] Parrington, *op. cit.*, p. 266

candidates in the campaign in 1888, for the Farmers' Alliance, and for the Populists in 1890. It was in this last campaign that she made 160 speeches. Later she went to the Rocky Mountain states, where she "progressed from one triumph to another." In Nevada at one time in the campaign in 1892, she made eight speeches in one day; and in Nebraska, in 1893, she made an extensive tour on behalf of the Populist candidates.

Mrs. Lease's theme was "Wall Street owns the country." At the root of all the farmers' troubles, she declared, were the giants of banking and of transportation and the old-line political parties. Her solution was, "We want money, land, and transportation." Wipe out private finance and the foreclosure system, and prosperity will come to the farmer, she declared. Her message and her style are portrayed in a portion of a speech in the Kansas campaign of 1890.

Wall Street owns the country. It is no longer a government of the people, by the people and for the people, but a government of Wall Street, by Wall Street and for Wall Street. The great common people of this country are slaves, and monopoly is the master. The West and South are bound and prostrate before the manufacturing East. . . . The common people are robbed to enrich their masters. . . . We want the abolition of the National Banks, and we want the power to make loans direct from the government. We want the accursed foreclosure system wiped out. Land equal to a tract thirty miles wide and ninety miles long has been foreclosed and brought in by loan companies of Kansas in a year. We will stand by our homes and stay by our firesides by force if necessary, and we will not pay our debts to the loan-shark companies until the Government pays its debts to us. The people are at bay, let the bloodhounds of money who have dogged us thus far beware.[1]

Nor were these the only speakers of the Populist revolt. "Cyclone" Davis, of Texas; Tom Watson, of Georgia; the Reverend J. B. Kyle, of South Dakota; W. A. Peffer, of Kansas; and "Calamity" Weller, of Iowa, were other men who made the Middle Border of the West and South fairly ring with denunciations of the capitalists. And as for the women,

The great political victory of the people of Kansas would not have been won without the help of the women of the Alliance. Women who never dreamed of becoming public speakers, grew eloquent in their zeal and fervor. Farmers' wives and daughters rose earlier and worked later to gain time to cook the picnic dinners, to paint the mottoes on the banners, to practice with the glee clubs, to march in procession. Josh Billings' saying that 'wimmin is everywhere' was literally true in that wonderful picnicking, speech-making Alliance summer of 1890.[2]

The 1870's, 1880's, and 1890's, then, saw the farmer revolt against his real or fancied oppressors. Through the Grange, the Alliance, the Reform

[1] Hicks, *op. cit.*, p. 160. (Quoted by permission.)
[2] Annie L. Diggs, *Arena*, 6 (1892): 163–165.

party, and the Populist party he organized for action. He elected his supporters to the state legislature and to Congress; in many instances he demanded—and received—remedial legislation; ultimately he forced the major political parties to recognize his claims. But more than that, he and his fellows spoke and listened to others—not to staid, dignified orations but to "speeches that came straight from the hay-fields and the corn rows, speeches that were an echo of the daily experience of the farmer and the farmer's wife."[1] He gave speeches that were vigorous, colorful, almost fanatical, delivered by shouting, haranguing zealots of a cause that to them was as vital as property or even life itself. The farmer became articulate—in large numbers and with a fervor that was eventually heard in the councils of the major parties.

C. PUBLIC ADDRESS IN CONGRESS

The years 1860–1930 also witnessed the development of another trend in public address—the changing character of speechmaking in Congress. Public debate continued, of course, on the floors of the House and the Senate; but its significance in contrast to that of the great debates of the triumvirate of Clay, Calhoun, and Webster, for example, appeared to be considerably diminished.

Exceptions, to be sure, can be observed. There were the speeches of Beveridge on "Imperialism"; there were notable speeches by Borah on phases of foreign policy; and there was a speech in 1893 by Senator William V. Allen, of Nebraska, which lasted for 16 hours. Senator Thomas H. Carter, of Montana, spoke for nearly 20 hours on March 3 and 4, 1901; and Senator Carmack, of Tennessee, spoke for 2 days (March 3 and 4, 1907) against the ship-subsidy bill. Others in the Senate filibustered for long periods at a time. These speeches were long rather than good.

The trend, however, was in the other direction. Specifically, fewer reputations as statesmen and orators were being won by Congressional debates; fewer "great debates" were in evidence; and in general, the fate of bills in Congress was being determined less and less by what transpired on the floor of either house than by other phases of the legislative process.

This trend was noted in a study made by Champ Clark at the time that he was leader of the Democratic party in the House of Representatives. In essence he observed that oratory was falling into disuse, particularly on the floor of Congress, and that the short speech of information or of reply in debate was replacing it. He recognized that longer speeches were still being delivered in the Senate, but he emphasized that long speeches were not the rule even there, for "the really great debaters in that body never waste time."[2]

[1] Parrington, *op. cit.*, p. 266.
[2] Champ Clark, "Is Congressional Oratory a Lost Art?" *Century*, 81 (1910): 307–310.

The *Nation* magazine observed the trend in an editorial in which it listed three reasons for the lessening of debate in Congress. Even though he disagreed with the point of view that this trend was desirable, the writer considered three forces at work: (1) Weariness with long "set" speeches; (2) impatience with deliberation when the decision has already been made in the mind of virtually every member; (3) dependence upon those persons who draft bills.[1]

Several other explanations might be made. It would be possible, for instance, to say that the speakers of this era were inferior to those of the previous years. That, however, is at best only an inconclusive explanation, for there were many strong statesmen in Congress, men who on various occasions did speak effectively.[2] It would also be possible to say that the issues and the occasions were not so auspicious for great speaking as formerly. This explanation, however, is offset by the presence of such great issues as those enumerated in Part I—Reconstruction, Populism, Imperialisms, and others. And certainly the League of Nations issue in 1920 was as momentous as the Foote Resolution in 1830.

The explanation appears to lie rather in a number of factors inherent in the Congressional organization and procedure or in closely related factors. Some of these became increasingly important as Congress grew in size and as the amount of business increased; others appeared with changes in rules or even in the place of meetings. Because these are significant to a student of public address, we shall consider several: (1) a number of features that distinguished the Congress of pre-Civil War days from that of 1885 and later; (2) the relation of these variables to deliberations in Congress.

CHANGES IN CONGRESS. The Congress of the late nineteenth and the early twentieth century was vastly different from that of the earlier days. Size, quantity of business, number of standing committees, place of meeting, limits upon debate (by rule), and use of the privilege of extension of remarks are only a few of the factors that should be considered.

Place of Meeting. Prior to 1859, the Senate met in a much smaller hall than that now in use. The original meeting place was used later by the Supreme Court. Prior to 1857, the House of Representatives met in what is now the Hall of Statuary, a much smaller hall than the one provided in a new wing of the Capitol, now used.

Limits upon Debate. Of significance to us here was the placing, in 1841, of a limit of one hour upon speeches in the House. Other factors of limitation were included primarily in the status of the committees.

Extension of Remarks. Increasingly the practice of printing in the *Congressional Record* the texts of speeches not actually delivered on the

[1] *Nation,* 90 (1910): 154.
[2] Beveridge, Borah, Bryan, Hoar, La Follette, and Schurz, to mention only a few.

floor of Congress has been used. Called *extension of remarks*, this practice permits a member to express himself upon controversial issues without necessarily participating in oral debate.

EFFECTS UPON SPEECHMAKING. Three types of factors are immediately apparent in analyzing the reasons for the trend in Congressional speechmaking: (1) Those which are somewhat superficial or are not inherently related to the organization of Congress; (2) those which are essentially the outgrowth of the size of organization of the legislative body; (3) those which arise from forces outside of Congress. Each of these had the effect of limiting or minimizing the speaking on the floor of Congress; and in combination they served merely to intensify the trend.

The first category includes the place of meeting, the limits placed upon debate by rule, and the use of extension of remarks. The second embraces the size of the Congressional bodies, the quantity of business, the number and importance of committees, and the increasing importance of the party caucus (with the practice of *quid pro quo*). The third includes the increasing popularity and use of polls of public opinion and the increasing use of what is termed "a specific program of legislation."[1]

The Place of Meeting. Both the American and the English political scientists have observed the effect of this factor upon Congressional debate. Both emphasize the situation conducive to good public speaking in the former meeting places and the equally poor circumstances in the halls in use since 1857 and 1859. Wilson comments particularly upon the House, observing that certain rules designed to stifle debate "were at a greater disadvantage in a room where oratory was possible than they are in a vast chamber where the orator's voice is drowned amidst the noises of disorderly inattention." Again, he says:

A speaker must needs have a voice like O'Connell's, the practical visitor is apt to think, as he sits in the gallery, to fill even the silent spaces of that room; how much more to overcome the disorderly noises that buzz and rattle through it when the representatives are assembled—a voice clear, sonorous, dominant, like the voice of a clarion.[2]

Bryce similarly comments upon the physical conditions:

Less favourable conditions for oratory cannot be imagined, and one is not surprised to be told that debate was more animated and practical in the much smaller room which the House formerly occupied.

[1] In this analysis we shall be guided in a large measure by two eminent political scientists Woodrow Wilson and James Bryce, both of whom carefully studied Congress and its operations and reached essentially the same conclusions with respect to matter under consideration, here.

[2] Woodrow Wilson, *Congressional Government* (Boston, Houghton, Mifflin and Company, 1885), pp. 90 and 97.

Not only is the present room so big that only a powerful and well-trained voice can fill it, but the desks and chairs make a speaker feel as if he were addressing furniture rather than men. . . . "Speaking in the House," says an American writer, "is like trying to address the people in the Broadway omnibuses from the curbstone in front of the Astor House. . . . The natural refuge is in written speeches or in habitual silence, which one dreads more and more to break."[1]

The Limits Placed upon Debate by Rule. When the House, in 1841, placed a time limit upon debate, it at once set up restrictions that need to be considered by a student of speechmaking. Clark comments upon this in contrasting the freedom in the House prior to Henry Clay's term as Speaker to the practice in later years. He observes that John Randolph, a speaker who frequently wandered far from the resolution at hand, could indulge in his favorite practice in the former era but would in all probability be restrained under the hour limit unless he could secure unanimous consent to speak more fully.[2]

The Use of Extension of Remarks. Another in the set of forces affecting Congressional speaking is the increasing use of extension of remarks. Wilson says of this practice:

Nowadays would-be debaters are easily thrust out of Congress and forced to resort to the printing-office; are compelled to content themselves with speaking from the pages of the "Record" instead of from their places in the House. Some people who live very far from Washington may imagine that the speeches which are spread at large in the columns of the "Congressional Record," or which their representative sends them in pamphlet form, were actually delivered in Congress; but everyone else knows that they were not; that Congress is constantly granting leave to its members to insert in the official reports of the proceedings speeches which it never heard and does not care to hear. . . . [3]

The Size of the Congressional Bodies. The increase in the size of the house. of Congress has, of necessity, placed serious limitations upon public addresss This is especially true of the House, but it is also noted to some extent in the Senate. "The early Congresses had time to talk; Congresses of to-day have not." There is a "scantiness of time which hurries the House; and the weight of business which oppresses it."[4] As a result, business must be transacted elsewhere; and as we shall observe, that place is in the committee.

The Quantity of Business. The sheer weight of the volume of business before Congress in any session has, quite clearly, an influence upon the

[1] James Bryce, *The American Commonwealth* (abridged ed., New York, The Macmillan Company, 1922), p. 109. (Quoted by permission.)

[2] Clark, *op. cit.*, pp. 307–310.

[3] Wilson, *op. cit.*, pp. 90–91. Bryce has a similar comment, *op. cit.*, p. 110.

[4] Wilson, *op. cit.*, p. 90.

SIZE OF CONGRESS

Date	Total number of members	Senate	House
1821	233	48	185
1836	280	48	232
1883	406	76	330
1895	447	90	357
1903	447	90	357
1925	531	96	435

QUANTITY OF BUSINESS

Date	Total number of bills introduced	Senate	House
1861	1,026	413	613
1889	19,646	5,318	14,328
1903	27,369	7,295	20,074

NUMBER OF STANDING COMMITTEES

Date	Total	Senate	House
1821	38	16	22
1836	49	20	29
1883	79	32	47
1895	106	49	57
1903	115	57	58
1925	98 (plus 16 committees of special investigation)	35	63

amount of deliberation and debate possible. The inevitable result of this volume has been to direct the business to the standing committees, which have become nearly all-powerful.

The Number and Importance of Committees. This factor is probably the most significant of all in determining the reasons for comparatively less speechmaking on the floor of Congress. Both the increasing strength of the committees and the factor cited just above—the quantity of business—have tended to focus attention upon the standing committee in particular. That this is true of both the Senate and the House is observed by Wilson.

It would seem as if the seer had a much more favorable opportunity in the committee-room than the orator can have, and with us it is the committee-room which governs the legislative chamber. The speech-making in the latter neither makes nor often seriously affects the plans framed in the former; because the plans are made before the speeches are uttered. This is self-evident of the debates in the House; but even the speeches made in the Senate, free, full, and earnest as they seem, are made, so to speak, after the fact—not to determine the actions but to air the opinions of the body.[1]

Bryce observes the same shift of emphasis, especially in the House, when he says, "The very habit of debate, the expectation of debate, the idea that debate is needed, have vanished, except as regards questions of revenue and expenditure, because the centre of gravity has shifted from the House to the committees."[2]

But there is something more fundamental than the mere transfer of certain functions. Two significant effects upon public address are observed: (1) the fact that the real debate is in the committee; (2) the fact that when bills are reported out of committee, the debate upon them is largely an "airing of opinions," because in general the committees are all-powerful.

Speaking of the House, in particular, Wilson says:

One very noteworthy result of this system is to shift the theatre of debate upon legislation from the floor of Congress to the privacy of the committee-rooms. Provincial gentlemen who read the Associated Press dispatches in their morning papers as they sit over their coffee at breakfast are doubtless often very sorely puzzled by certain of the items which sometimes appear in the brief telegraphic notes from Washington. What can they make of this for instance: "The House Committee on Commerce today heard arguments from the congressional delegation from 'such and such States' in advocacy of appropriations for river and harbor improvements which the members desire incorporated in the River and Harbor Appropriations Bill"? They probably do not understand that it would have been useless for members not of the Committee on Commerce to wait for any opportunity to make their suggestions on the floor of Congress, where the measure to which they wish to make additions would be under the authoritative control of the Committee, and where, consequently, they could gain a hearing only by the courteous sufferance of the committeeman in charge of the report. Whatever is to be done must be done by or through the Committee.[3]

Wilson has already suggested the second effect upon speechmaking in the legislative chamber—the tendency to turn speeches into utterances "after the fact," not to determine the course of action but "to air the opinions of the body." Bryce observes that in many instances "the question

[1] Wilson, *op. cit.*, p. 216.

[2] Bryce, *op. cit.*, pp. 119–120. (Quoted by permission.)

[3] Wilson, *op. cit.*, pp. 81–82. Speaking of the Senate, he says, "Its functions, also, like those of the House, are segregated in the prerogatives of numerous Standing Committees. In this regard Congress is all of a piece."—P. 212.

at issue is sure to have been already settled, either in a committee or in a 'caucus' of the party which commands the majority, so that these long and sonorous harrangues are mere rhetorical thunder addressed to the nation outside."[1] The cause of this circumstance may be discovered in the written and unwritten laws that give the committees power to "dictate the course to be taken, prescribing the decisions of the House not only, but measuring out, according to their own wills, its opportunities for debate and deliberation as well."[2]

Wilson observes that "we are ruled by a score and a half of 'little legislatures,'" and the trend has been toward "a government by the chairman of the Standing Committees of Congress."[3]

In consequence, there have been a restricting of the opportunities for debate in the legislative chambers and a shifting of the bulk of the important speechmaking to the committee rooms.

The Increasing Importance of the Party Caucus. Designed as an antidote to the power of the Congressional committees, as well as a means of maintaining party solidarity, the caucus has had significant effects upon speechmaking in Congress. Wilson believed the caucus to be nearly as important as the standing committees. In fact, he regarded it as a means of "resisting the centrifugal force of the committee system" in that it "is designed to supply the cohesive principle which the multiplicity and mutual independence of the Committees so powerfully tend to destroy."[4]

Two questions concerning the caucus suggest themselves at this point: (1) What effect does it have upon legislation? (2) What effect does it have upon speechmaking? In general, whenever there appear differences of opinion among members of a party or uncertainties in the minds of members of the same party, the party hastens to remove the disrupting or revealing debate from the floor of Congress "where the speakers might too hastily commit themselves to insubordination, to quiet conferences behind closed doors, where frightened scruples may be reassured and every disagreement healed with a salve of compromise or subdued with the whip of political expediency."[5] In other words, the deciding votes, at least of a party, concerning a piece of legislation are likely to be cast in the caucus.[6]

---

[1] Bryce, *op. cit.*, p. 89. (Quoted by permission.)

[2] Wilson, *op. cit.*, pp. 78–79.

[3] *Ibid.*, pp. 113 and 102.

[4] Wilson, *op. cit.*, p. 326.

[5] *Ibid.*, p. 327. See also Bryce, *op. cit.*, pp. 152–153. "It [the party caucus] is used whenever a line of policy has to be settled, or the whole party to be rallied for a particular party division." (Quoted by permission.)

[6] The practice of *quid pro quo*, of promising patronage or support for other bills in return for votes upon the measure under consideration, is frequently mentioned in describing the party caucus or its equivalent.

The caucus also has an effect upon speechmaking. (1) It tends to make the debate on the floor of the assembly "merely the movements of a dress parade, for which the exercises of the caucus are designed to prepare." (2) It tends to make the debate in the caucus of supreme importance. In fact, it is safe to say that the debates in the caucus, like those in the committees, constitute the essence of the deliberations pertaining to the bulk of legislation. Wilson observes that the speeches in the caucus

> would constitute interesting and instructive reading for the public, were they published; but they never get out except in rumors often rehearsed and as often amended. They are, one may take it for granted, much more candid and go much nearer the political heart of the questions discussed than anything that is ever said openly in Congress to the reporters' gallery.[1]

The caucus, it is true, is nearly as old as Congress itself (it was used in the Eighth Congress); but it has become in recent years a more significant institution than it was earlier.[2] The factors of size, number and strength of the committees, and volume of business have served to render the caucus a means of determining the outcome of legislation. Just as the "centrifugal force" of the committees increases, so does the resistance of the caucus operate. Concurrently, speechmaking in that body increases in quantity and importance as the opportunity for the practice of it on the floor of Congress declines in inverse ratio.

The Use of Polls of Public Opinion.[3] Within recent years polls of public opinion have become increasingly numerous. The *Literary Digest* poll (1920), the Psychological Barometer developed by Dr. Henry C. Link (1932), the *Fortune* survey (1935), and the Gallup poll (1935), to name only a few, were originated for the purpose of "feeling the pulse" of the American public and of forecasting as accurately as possible the outcome of elections. This method, which differs from long-used samplings of public opinion largely in its scope and in the application of scientific principles, has in two respects affected speechmaking in Congress. (1) It has entered into the content of debate itself. "The *Congressional Record* is liberally sprinkled with the name of Gallup, and the *Fortune* survey has figured importantly in Congressional debates.'[4] (2) It has acted in much the same way as have the committee and the caucus. It has tended to minimize the significance of

---

[1] Wilson, *op. cit.*, p. 329.

[2] Wilson points out that in the early days persons censured the caucus for stressing party pledges and that "the censure may have seemed righteous at the time when such caucus pledges were in disfavor as new-fangled shackles, but it would hardly be accepted as just by the intensely practical politicians of to-day."—P. 328.

[3] In order to make this survey as complete as possible, this factor is included here, even though in its fullest development it did not operate until 1932 or later.

[4] Robert R. Updegraff, "Democracy's New Mirror," *Forum*, 103 (1940): 11–14.

debate as a means of influencing opinion and to encourage the members of Congress to study the polls and to vote as the public—particularly their constituency—would do.

The Use of a Specific Program of Legislation. In recent years, especially under the influence of strong and energetic leaders in the White House, there has arisen a tendency to lay out a specific legislative program sponsored and designed in detail by the Administration. This program, which takes precedence over all other legislation as far as possible, involves a comparatively few simple steps: (1) The necessary measures are drawn up. (2) The appropriate committee chairmen introduce them. (3) There is a clear track through to ultimate passage. Party machinery, including the caucus and other pressures, provides for the smooth functioning of these proceedings insofar as the majority party can maintain control.

The effects upon speechmaking are, again, essentially those of the committee and the caucus. What deliberation there is takes place in the committee and the party sessions, leaving little that needs to be used, or is even permitted, on the floor of Congress.[1]

For better or worse, therefore, the trend in Congressional speechmaking during the years 1860–1930 was from debate on the floor of the Senate and the House of Representatives to deliberations in the committee or in the party caucus. The trend has followed the growth of the nation and of the Congress, and the correlation between committee-caucus speaking and that in the legislative chambers has been constant.

D. PUBLIC ADDRESS AND THE LABOR MOVEMENT

The nationalization of American economic life and the Machine Age following the Civil War inevitably led to labor problems, and the men and women who attempted to lead labor in the solution of these problems were dependent on speech, whether they sought to agitate and educate workers, arouse and inform the public, or negotiate with employers. The story of labor speaking in the United States is the story of relative degrees of adaptation by labor leaders to these audiences in different periods.

Scattered local meetings and labor lectures before 1860 helped to produce labor unity later by frequently giving the worker his first opportunity to meet more men of his own class. Some early speaking had a less desirable influence; much of it came from assorted reformers, idealists, and intellectuals who did not labor but merely sought audiences for the spread of their teachings. Cooperation, Fourierism, agrarianism, and Utopian socialism shaped the thinking of labor officials for many years, and intel-

[1] See Bertram Benedict, "The Odyssey of a Bill through Congress," *New York Times Magazine*, Feb. 2, 1941, p. 8.

lectuals continued to insist on speaking for the workingman. One labor editor protested:

> We are and ever have been in favor of developing the latent strength of our own ranks in preference to chasing after a professional bore every time a public exposition of our aims is demanded. It is true that many of our representatives lack the polish of the college graduate, the turned periods of the scholar, or the fluency of the hot-house politician yet in the army of labor may be found men who can command the attention of the audience, who speak from the heart to the heart . . . the great drawback is the deplorable lack of self-assurance.[1]

More than assurance, however, was required. Labor leaders needed an understanding of the reason for speaking. They needed knowledge of the new industrial forces and a practical labor program. Labor waited for more than two decades after the war for these. In the meantime speakers from the army of labor used rhetoric to hide their confusion in the face of reality.

William Sylvis, treasurer of the International Union of Iron Moulders, may be considered typical of labor speakers during the sixties. To the Moulders, in 1864, he remarked that "burning words and thrilling eloquence cannot alone accomplish our purpose. . . . Works are what we want; great noble and brave deeds." His own burning words were quenched by the vagueness of his remedy of cooperative shops for labor's ills. This simple solution inspired him to conclude:

> Shall he not dwell in palaces who raises palaces? Shall she not go in rich attire whose fingers wind the silk of the toiling worm. Shall the ruby, the diamond and the red, red gold not glitter on the miner's manly breast. . . . Yes, by the living God shall they. . . . Then the carrolling birds, the whispering winds, the gorgeous clouds, the perfumed flowers, the sunny earth, the mighty ocean, man's glorious beauty, speak seraphed-toned his ineffable destiny, the faint foreshadowings of his final home.[2]

Though Ira Stewart, the great propagandist for the 8-hour movement of the sixties and seventies, did not indulge in grandiloquence, his proposal for labor seemed as elusive as that of Sylvis. One laborer who had heard him recalled that "he never spoke one word in all the lecture that we could take practical hold on. I was choked with bitter disappointment when he stopped." During this period labor papers were reporting some "very interesting speeches upon the dignity of labor and the union of capital and labor!"

[1] From an unidentified newspaper clipping in a labor scrapbook at the John Crerar Library, Chicago, Ill. Internal evidence indicates this article probably appeared in the early seventies.

[2] James C. Sylvis, *The Life, Speeches, Labors, and Essays of William H. Sylvis* (Philadelphia, Claxton, Remsen, and Haffelfinger, 1872), p. 172.

Labor distress became more acute in the depression of 1873–1879. Cities where factory workers and miners were massed became sounding boards for unrest and revolutionary talk. The old national trade-unions either collapsed or had a nominal existence, and workers became impatient with speeches about "golden sweatdrops upon the laborer's honest brow." One agitator of this period described his task at Leadville, Colo., in 1880 as "simple, and a man with ordinary intelligence and a 'gift of gab' had no difficulty in holding a street audience, especially if he was a radical in his denunciation of the operators and sympathetic in depicting the wrongs of labor."[1] Workers in the Middle West were stirred by the flaming speeches of Albert R. Parsons—speeches that later helped to convict him of a responsibility in the Haymarket bombing in 1886. Parsons was associated with many labor groups, and at one time several trade-unions united in sending him on a tour to present the 8-hour question. Parsons and the other Chicago anarchists "availed themselves of every opportunity and before every society to disseminate their doctrines, whether before the Liberal League or the Methodist ministry." If his words captivated underpaid workers, they likewise aroused fear and antagonism among conservative classes, for Parsons did not hesitate to give cutting and defiant speeches before Chicago's "elite."[2] The courts silenced anarchists after the Haymarket incident; but what is more important, the whole environment of the United States was hostile to anarchism and revolution.

Many workers, dissatisfied with the old unions, turned to the Knights of Labor, which had a meteoric rise and decline during the eighties. Terence V. Powderly, who became Grand Master Workman of the Knights in 1879, was one of labor's outstanding speakers for more than a decade.[3] At one time requests for him to lecture were coming in at the rate of ten a day, and in 1887 he received over four hundred invitations to speak on Labor Day. The order, moreover, could boast of a number of lesser lights who were popular speakers and were constantly touring the nation.

As early as 1885 Powderly complained that his excessive speaking was too much for his health, but apparently this was not his only reason for protesting. "I will talk at no picnics," he proclaimed. "When I talk on the

[1] Joseph Buchanan, *The Story of a Labor Agitator* (New York, Outlook Company, 1903), pp. 15–16.

[2] George Schilling, A Short History of the Labor Movement in Chicago, in Lucy Parsons, *Life of Albert R. Parsons* (2d ed., Chicago, 1903), p. xxx.

[3] The Knights, starting as a secret organization in 1869, had a total membership of little more than nine thousand by 1879. The organization dropped its secrecy in 1882 and within 4 years claimed a membership of over 700,000. The order declined to 100,000 members by 1890. See Norman J. Ware, *The Labor Movement in the United States: 1860–1895* (New York, 1929). Ware describes Powderly as a rabble rouser and street-corner orator but credits him with being a successful agitator.

labor question I want the individual attention of my hearers and I want that attention for at least two hours and in those two hours I can only epitomize. . . . At a picnic where . . . the girls as well as the boys swill beer I cannot talk at all. . . . Those who are not members attend the picnic to see the men . . . advertised but no one goes to a lecture."[1] If Powderly found some audiences disappointing, they, in turn, possibly discovered his shortcomings. True, Powderly seemed to realize that labor audiences had changed since the day of Sylvis. At Faneuil Hall, in 1890, he began by assuring the workers, "I am not here to give you taffy. I am not here to say you are grand and noble men." But immediately he added, "You must do better things than ever in the past, and among these things is to study the transportation question, and ask why you pay $5 to $7 for coal when I can have it put in my cellar for $2.65." Powderly could not escape the confusion of the sixties! His attacks on liquor were probably recalled more vividly than anything he said about wages. Powderly had no permanent goals. He could talk only about ending the wage system, yet he was no radical; therefore, he blew both hot and cold. In most of his speeches he deplored violence and discouraged strikes; on other occasions he sounded as dangerous as Parsons. Once he warned: "It has been demonstrated that two-thirds of the regiments of each state are members of the Knights of Labor and when their time expires they will not re-enlist. Let the men who are in the banks and the railroads—let the men who oppress labor fill up their ranks. Then when the two sides are arrayed against each other, we will see who will win."[2] It is not surprising that the Knights, puzzled but restless with growing power, engaged in many unsuccessful, poorly organized strikes that left the workers disillusioned and led to the fall of the order.

While Powderly was a national figure, John Swinton published in his labor paper an editorial entitled "Wanted: An Orator." "We need a great orator. . . . " he wrote in 1885. "Oh, for another Wendell Phillips."[3] For more than two months Swinton was receiving replies that give an insight into the problems of the labor speaker. Many readers nominated "orators"

[1] *Journal of United Labor,* Mar. 16, 1885, p. 931.

[2] *John Swinton's Paper,* July 25, 1886. Swinton copied the report of this speech from another paper. A week later Powderly indignantly described the original account as an "augur-hole speech." He had not given permission for the reporting of this address; and "some parts," he said, "I repudiate entirely." He neglected, however, to say what parts.

[3] *Ibid.,* July 19, 1885. Swinton was managing editor of the *New York Times* during the Civil War and became the chief writer for the *New York Sun* in 1871. He started his paper in 1883 to champion the cause of labor but stopped publishing it 4 years later. He engaged in much speaking in behalf of labor, particularly during the strikes of 1877. It was once said that Swinton "being a man of wide reading and great powers of expression, with matchless powers of gesticulation and facial expression . . . could make himself profoundly felt and understood even by those who knew no English." See Robert Waters, *Career and Conversation of John Swinton: Journalist, Orator and Economist* (Chicago, 1902).

from their section. The *Chicago Sentinel,* however, was skeptical of the reception this orator would receive: " . . . the dollar-a-day breadwinners would not even allow him to sleep on their door-steps . . . every would-be-orator in the house would malign or belittle him." Another editor observed that Phillips had turned his sympathy toward labor after the slavery issue but that he was seldom heard because he lacked an audience. "Give an audience and we will bring you plenty of orators." The *Winsted* (Conn.) *Press* exclaimed: "Fudge! You have orators enough. The truth plainly spoken is its own orator. You want a constituency of workingmen who care more for justice and liberty than they do for a cockfight. The seed which mere oratory sows falls for the most part in stony places." Another contributor wisely observed that "any cause that has no better support than the mere force of oratory has little to recommend it to the intellects of those educated classes who rule everywhere. . . . What is most wanted is a brain that is able to present the true philosophy of the labor problem."

All these views contain some truth. Leaders who had never discovered a labor philosophy compatible with American institutions talked glibly of ending the wage system. They led laborers through a maze of cooperatives, trade-unions, labor unions, and political parties. On the other hand, the rank and file may have been partly responsible for these vague, idealistic goals. Many workers seemed to be as eager as their leaders for experimentation. Their enthusiasms and loyalties were continually shifting, and at times they showed little interest in any labor issue. These faults were all the more glaring when leaders attempted to organize and speak for one big union of class-conscious workingmen. There was no such obvious group in those formative years, and when leaders attempted to find the common denominator for some vast working-class movement their speeches became as ethereal as the group itself.

A new order came with the American Federation of Labor in 1886. Samuel Gompers, its president from the beginning until his death in 1924, with the exception of a single year, was convinced that trade-unions offered the only stable foundation for a permanent labor organization. In his speeches we may find such statements as the following: "Trade unionism is neither fantastic nor visionary"; "the trade unionist is not likely to stake his future hopes on the fond chance of the many millions turning philosophers in a twinkling of an eye"; and "if the lesser and immediate demands of labor could not be obtained from society as it is, it would be mere dreaming to preach and pursue that will-o-the-wisp, a new society constructed from rainbow materials." No previous labor leader had seen so clearly the problem of labor in the American setting. Gompers eschewed labor parties, cooperative shops, temperance, and other paraphernalia that had been attached to the labor movement before. He explained his program simply

148

as one "to make today a better day than yesterday, tomorrow a better day than today . . . not by tactics or politics that are destructive but by a constructive, rational, and natural goal." In 1920 when the regulation of labor was frequently discussed, Gompers reminded the Boston Chamber of Commerce that if trade unions "go by the board . . . then instead of having a movement of men and women loyal and cooperative . . . you will have to deal with an irresponsible body. . . . It is a question of choice."[1] Gompers was not interested in meaningless rhetoric in the promotion of his philosophy. Workers had to be educated to trade-unionism, and a public opinion sympathetic with labor had to be created. Gompers recognized the role that was played in such a program by effective speaking. In addition to labor groups his audiences included ministerial associations, colleges, fraternal organizations, Chambers of Commerce, American Legion groups, and countless public mass meetings. He was undoubtedly pleased when John Kirby, president of the National Association of Manufacturers, objected to Federation speakers appearing before women's clubs.

Gompers was only one of a galaxy of Federation speakers. John Mitchell, president of the United Mine Workers from 1901 to 1911, was among the most prominent of these spokesmen. After he retired from the presidency of the miners he lectured for two years to the public at large. A biographer has described his speaking and its effect as follows:

He had learned . . . that a responsible leader, with wage negotiations always in the offing, cannot say reckless, even if glorious things, because his own people would then judge him by his own avowed aspirations or condemn him for a radicalism greater than their own, and because the employers were always eager to seize on the pretext of radicalism. . . . He did not stir the occasional listener who might have responded to the evangelism of a Debs or an Emma Goldman. To the large masses of the common people who flocked to the Chautauqua or the average student who heard him in the universities, he brought a revision of the then common belief that the labor movement was a purse-stealing, black-jacking, bomb-throwing raid on American institutions. . . . [2]

In 1888 Gompers conceived of the idea of commissioning organizers to assist him, and by 1919 the Federation had over two thousand of these, of whom almost all were volunteers. Childs has contended:

The work of these organizers if told in full would undoubtedly portray one of the vivid and dramatic phases of modern industrial life. . . . The volunteers work at their trade during the daytime and then devote their leisure hours to discussion, persuasion, speaking, holding mass-meetings, and in general doing whatever may seem expedient.[3]

[1] *American Federationist*, 27 (1920): 30.
[2] Elsie Glück, *John Mitchell* (New York, The John Day Company, 1929), pp. 240–241.
[3] Harwood Childs, *Labor and Capital* (Columbus, Ohio University Press, 1930), p. 19.

By the turn of the century radicalism was breaking out again in the labor movement. The A.F. of L. was criticized and charged with dividing the workers by rigid lines. The leaders of this revolt believed that the rapid elimination of skill by the machine was resulting in a degradation of the workers that called for an array of all labor in one great industrial union. Deplorable conditions of unorganized workers in the textile mills of New Jersey and migratory workers in the West provided fertile soil for this new unionism. What was needed was successful agitators, and many of these appeared. The outstanding figure in this new movement was William D. Haywood. In 1915 he was elected secretary-treasurer of the Industrial Workers of the World, but he was of national importance almost ten years before that. Haywood boasted; "I liked speaking; I liked the way I could handle a crowd, the way they responded."[1] No other statement could reveal better the characteristics of his speaking. He endeavored always to describe the workers' distress vividly. In 1903, when he sought to call attention to the high infant mortality in the smelter district of Colorado, he compared the rustling silk of the wives of the smelter owners with the clatter of babies' skulls.[2] During the textile strikes at Paterson, N. J., he staged his speeches in the setting of huge pageants. Ramsay MacDonald described him as

useless on committees; he is a torch amongst a crowd of uncritical, credulous work-men. I saw him at Copenhagen amidst the leaders of the working class movements drawn from the whole world, and there he was dumb and unnoticed. I saw him addressing a crowd in England, and there his crude appeals moved his listeners to wild applause. He made them see things, and their hearts bounded to be up and doing.[3]

While Gompers, Mitchell, and others of the Federation were busy molding public opinion, Haywood was refusing offers of $7,000 for a week's appearance in vaudeville. He explained that if he limited his addresses to working-class organizations, every step he made would be upward in the estimation of the workers. "In vaudeville I should be talking to mixed audiences, not carrying the message to the working class." Haywood's leadership passed when he fled to Russia in 1920 rather than serve a prison sentence for obstructing the war. The I.W.W., however, had discovered before this that there were inherent obstacles to a permanent organization of those workers for whom they had been fighting.

[1] *Bill Haywood's Book: An Autobiography* (New York, International Publishers Co., Inc., 1929), p. 228.

[2] *Ibid.*, p. 101.

[3] Quoted by Louis Adamic, *Dynamite* (New York, 1931), pp. 135–136.

The history of the American labor movement is a strange amalgam of social and economic forces and personalities. The speaking by some leaders seems to indicate that they blundered in adapting to their environment, and their influence was at the best only transitory. The public addresses of others appear to reflect clearly the attitudes and thinking of the workers and society of their time. The former group, however, undoubtedly modified their environment to some extent; and the task of the latter group was more than that of mere conformity with existing ideas and institutions. Effective speakers were to be found in both groups. Some of these were merely agitators, but the speaking by these men, nevertheless, played a part in the shaping of the American labor movement. A few were not only successful agitators but also rational leaders and ambassadors to the public.

CONCLUSION

The years 1860–1930 witnessed no diminution in the wide-spread use of public address by persons in all walks of life. The forms and uses that had been observed in previous eras of American life persisted throughout the nineteenth century and into the twentieth; and the deliberative, forensic, and ceremonial types of speaking were closely identified in theme and occasion with the events of history.

Of perhaps even greater significance were the distinctive trends in public address in which new uses were found for it and in which many persons and groups heretofore largely inarticulate became exponents of the spoken word. A student of American history from 1860 to 1930 will undoubtedly discover, therefore, not that "the power of human speech has gradually declined" but that, while its form may in some instances have changed, it was used even more widely and by more persons than in former years.

SELECTED BIBLIOGRAPHY

Arnet, Alex M.: *The Populist Movement in Georgia*, New York, Columbia University Press, 1922. (Doctoral dissertation, Columbia University.)

Bill Haywood's Book: An Autobiography, New York, International Publishers Co., Inc., 1929.

Bryce, James: *The American Commonwealth*, New York, The Macmillan Company, 1922.

Buchanan, Joseph: *The Story of a Labor Agitator*, New York, Outlook Company, 1903.

Clark, John B.: *Populism in Alabama*, Auburn, Ala., Auburn Printing Company, 1927. (Doctoral dissertation, New York University.)

Commons, John R. and associates: *History of Labour in the United States*, 2 vols., New York, The Macmillan Company, 1918.

Ely, Mary L.: *Why Forums?* New York, American Association for Adult Education, 1937.

Faulkner, Harold U.: *The Quest for Social Justice*, New York, The Macmillan Company, 1931.

Garland, Hamlin: *Main-Travelled Roads*, New York, Harper & Brothers, 1918.

———: *A Son of the Middle Border*, New York, The Macmillan Company, 1925.

Glück, Elsie: *John Mitchell*, New York, The John Day Company, 1929.
Gompers, Samuel: *Seventy Years of Life and Labor*, 2 vols., New York, E. P. Dutton & Company, Inc., 1925.
Harper, Ida M.: *The Life and Work of Susan B. Anthony*, Indianapolis, The Hollenbeck Press, 1898-1908.
Hicks, John D., *The Populist Revolt*, Minneapolis, University of Minnesota Press, 1931.
Lurie, Reuben L.: *The Challenge of the Forum—The Story of Ford Hall and the Open Forum Movement*, Boston, Richard G. Badger, 1930.
McConachie, Lauros G.: *Congressional Committees*, New York, The Thomas Y. Crowell Company, 1898.
Morgan, W. Scott: *History of the Wheel and the Alliance, and the Impending Revolution*, St. Louis, C. B. Woodward Company, 1891.
Nevins, Allan: *The Emergence of Modern America*, New York, The Macmillan Company, 1927.
Noffsinger, John S.: *Correspondence Schools, Lyceums, Chautauquas*, New York, The Macmillan Company, 1926.
Parrington, Vernon L.: *Main Currents in American Thought*, Vol. III, "The Beginnings of Critical Realism in America," New York, Harcourt, Brace, and Company, 1930.
Parsons, Lucy E.: *Life of Albert R. Parsons*, 2d ed., Lucy Parsons, Chicago, 1903.
Paxson, Frederic L.: *History of the American Frontier*, 1763-1893, Boston, Houghton Mifflin Company, 1924.
——: *The New Nation*, Boston, Houghton Mifflin Company, 1915.
Perlman, Selig, and Philip Taft: *History of Labor in the United States*, 1896-1932, Vol. IV, "Labor Movements," New York, The Macmillan Company, 1935.
Pond, James B.: *The Eccentricities of Genius*, New York, G. W. Dillingham Company, 1900.
Powderly, Terence V.: *Thirty Years of Labor*, Columbus, Excelsior Printing House, 1889.
Riddick, Floyd M.: *Congressional Procedure*, Boston, Chapman & Grimes, Inc., 1941.
Schlesinger, Arthur M.: *The Rise of the City*, New York, The Macmillan Company, 1933.
Shaw, Anna Howard: *The Story of a Pioneer*, New York, Harper & Brothers, 1929.
Sheldon, William DuB.: *Populism in the Old Dominion*, Princeton, N. J., Princeton University Press, 1935.
Stanton, Elizabeth Cady, Susan B. Anthony, and Matilda J. Gage: *History of Woman Suffrage*, New York, Fowler and Wells, 1881-1922.
Sylvis, James C.: *The Life, Speeches, Labors, and Essays of William H. Sylvis*, Philadelphia, Claxton, Remsen, and Haffelfinger, 1872.
Vincent, John H.: *The Chautauqua Movement*, Boston, Chautauqua Press, 1886.
Ware, Norman J.: *The Labor Movement in the United States, 1860-1895*, New York, D. Appleton-Century Company, Inc., 1929.
Wilson, Woodrow: *Congressional Government*, Boston, Houghton Mifflin Company, 1885.

4

Women's Introduction to the American Platform

by Doris G. Yoakam

The Age of Experimentation

In the exuberant young America of the early nineteenth century almost anything could happen—even public speaking by women and the resultant crumbling of St. Paul's authoritative dictum, which, through the many centuries, had kept women silent in public meetings. Brimming over with ideas that seemed as limitless as the vast unexplored frontier, stimulated by a surge of achievement in scientific inventiveness that introduced such conveniences as the sewing machine, the locomotive, the rotary printing press, the telegraph, and the automatic reaper, confident of unbounded opportunity for all in economic security and advancement, and inspired by belief in the rights and capabilities of the common man and in the perfectability of all mankind, everywhere the people of this new republic were eagerly seeking new worlds to conquer. It was a period—this Middle Period of American history—of unprecedented experimentation and exploration in social, economic, and political life, of an intellectual curiosity that led to widespread and thorough investigation (possible only in a republic) of all spiritual and moral institutions, and of an insatiable thirst for knowledge that ignored the rotting barriers of tradition. Upon the banners leading the inevitable march of progress were emblazoned the inscriptions "Freedom," "Equality," and "Opportunity."

Woman's Sphere. And yet, when the woman of this period peered through the ruffled curtains of her well-protected home, she saw a world in which she had little place. In spite of the thrilling opportunities for action in the outside world, woman's "sphere" was in the home, where, as a humble and retired individual in the shade of domestic duties, it was believed she could yield to society the greatest returns.[1] Her educational program prepared her for this career, including, as it did, little other than instruction in music, sewing, and domestic science and insisting that privileges of higher educa-

[1] *Cf. Godey's Lady's Book,* 40 (March, 1850): 209–210.

153

tion were unnecessary and extravagant. Her training from childhood taught her that marriage was not only the crowning, but the only suitable aim and end of a woman's life. Custom required that she marry at an early age, for to be an old maid meant probable dependency on male relatives and a life spent in trying to be as little in the way as one could manage.[1]

The professions were closed to her, and if she had to earn money she must resort to needlework, teaching, or taking in boarders. Dressmakers earned from 33 to 50 cents a day, and a teacher in summer school "boarded around" and was given a dollar a week for her teaching efforts. Salaries for women were about half, or sometimes two-thirds, of what were paid to men holding corresponding positions.[2] What she did earn, if she happened to be married, belonged to her husband by right of legal control.

She saw that, in accordance with the jurisdiction of the English common law (still predominant as late as 1850), women had no political existence and that as citizens of the democracy they were likewise nonexistent. Upon marriage they could no longer hold property; they could maintain no legal relationships nor bring any action at law independent of their husbands. They could rarely obtain divorces. Their husbands were responsible for their conduct and might, in controlling their actions, punish them in the same degree as their children. Even their personal liberty was dubious, as may be illustrated by the fact that the right of a man to imprison his wife in his own house was not often questioned until after 1890.

Women Listen—and Speak. So general was the acknowledgment that those of the "weaker sex" were the inferiors of men that the majority of the women themselves believed this to be true. They strove to achieve the ideal qualities that the age thought ought to be possessed by women—meekness, gentleness, forbearance, kindness, charity, and long-suffering patience.[3] A small minority of women, however, who possessed courage, ambition, and curiosity to investigate existing conditions (as have individual and representative women throughout history), continued to chafe under the legal, economic, and social restrictions imposed by a society formed and controlled by men. Surely, these women reasoned, there must be something they could do for humanity besides superintend the already well-organized machinery of their homes—could they but learn what and how.

In the escort of benevolent husbands, many women indulged their intellectual cravings with lectures. Oratory, at this time, was enjoying

---

[1] *Cf.* Charles Butler, *The American Lady* (Philadelphia, Hogan and Thompson, 1836), pp. 222–223.

[2] Virginia Penny, *The Employments of Women: A Cyclopaedia of Woman's Work* (Boston, Walker, Wise and Co., 1863), p. 50.

[3] *Ladies' Morning Star* (New York), May 4, 1836.

its heydey of glory, its supreme authority as instructor and propagandist among a curious people who had limited facilities for acquiring news and knowledge, and its unrivaled popularity as entertainer] of a religious people who worked hard and, believing such frivolities as the theatre to be immoral and degrading, had few avenues of amusement. Oratory filled the ears of the city as resonantly as the church bells on Sunday. Philip Hone, a theatre lover, resentfully recorded in his diary in 1841 that lectures seemed to furnish the necessary evening amusement for the people other than "poking the fire and playing with the children" and that, as a result, the theatres were "flat on their backs."[1] During the 1852 lecturing season alone, New Yorkers might listen to at least thirteen different courses of lectures, ranging from those of Professor Adolphus L. Koeppen, "of Kentucky Cave memory," and of Mrs. E. Oakes Smith on women, down to the "Polyglot Lectures" in Italian, Spanish, French, and German.[2]

[Oratory boomed out from village green, from country lane and meadow. Few were the rural communities that had no meetinghouse or failed to produce an audience for any kind of lecture, even in the "most unpropitious weather." In wagon or sleigh, on horseback or afoot, the farmers and their wives came, not to spend one bored hour but to give an eager evening, not to appraise the attire of their neighbors but to fill a poignant gregarious need, not to carry away the pleasing sound of rhetorical phrases but to sift out fertile grains of thought as they reluctantly turned again homeward.]

Casting a reflective glance backward as he wrote in 1852, William Goodell felt that the rail car and the electric telegraph of the two preceding decades were scarcely greater innovations or greater curiosities than were the voluntary lecturers and the free public conventions.\Was it strange, he asked, at a period when laymen were finding that they had tongues and when laborers of almost all classes were giving free utterance to their thoughts, that the morality of unpaid and forced labor began to be questioned—the chivalry of whipping women and the civilization of selling babes at auction by the pound began to be scrutinized? No, for hand in hand came the new spirit of moral inquiry and the appropriate methods of their manifestation and culture among the masses of the people.[3] Reforms of every kind conceivable at the time, sponsored in the earlier years by individuals, evolved into well-organized movements for peace, communistic experimentation, care of the poor and of the insane, temperance,

[1] Philip Hone, *The Diary of Philip Hone* 1821–1851 (Allan Nevins, ed., New York, Dodd Mead & Company, Inc., 1927), II, 515–516, 572–573.

[2] *The Home Journal* (New York), Nov. 20, 1852.

[3] William Goodell, *Slavery and Anti-Slavery* (New York, William Harned, 1852), pp. 389–390.

universal equality and suffrage, and free inquiry. And to clarify thought, win converts, and resolve action upon these moral enterprises came the increasing barrage of free-discussion meetings, annual convention weeks, anniversaries and celebrations.

With their men or, more boldly, in unescorted groups, women also went to hear these lectures on free inquiry and attended the early conventions called for the purpose of combining individual humanitarian interest into the powerful machinery of organized endeavor. Here, at these reform meetings, ambitious and courageous women found not only purposes with which they were in complete accord, purposes that expressed their inherent desire to contribute to the improvement of mankind, but a very atmosphere that was somehow different from the stuffy darkness of traditional circles. They found that even the procedure of the meetings was novel and exciting.[1] There was singing, but the songs were new and alive and original under such titles as "Freedom's Summons," "The Fraternity of Man," "Temperance War Song," and "I am an Abolitionist—I Glory in the Name." There were prayers, spoken with confidence in God's help in righteous crusades. There were speeches, teeming with spontaneity and freshness, directness and earnestness, enthusiasm and aggressiveness, and engaging everybody's attention and feelings, either for or against what was said. Consecrated to freedom of speech and action, equality of the individual, tolerance and democracy of thought was this reform platform. Somehow, women sensed that they were actually welcome at these meetings—that they belonged.

Here the women learned that there was a world to be done for mankind and that there were many directions in which they might spread their work. As advocates of the antislavery movement, destined from the first to overshadow all other reforms of the Middle Period, they could contribute money and prayers to the cause. They could get signatures to petitions and "engage men to write poetry and short pieces in prose, to be printed on fire boards, on cards, on silk, and on ivory for parlor ornaments" to keep the subject constantly before the attention of all observers.[2] They could daily diffuse information by conversing on the subject at home and in social circles. With the enthusiastic support of those who were "in the front of the battle," the ladies could hold benefit bazaars and fairs and could form themselves into auxiliary female antislavery societies. And last, but not least, they could induce reticent husbands to open prejudiced ears by themselves attending the antislavery meetings.[3]

[1] *Cf. New York Christian Inquirer*, cited in *The Liberator* (Boston), May 25, 1849.

[2] *New Hampshire Anti-Slavery Convention Proceedings*, 1834 (Concord, N. H., Eastman, Webster and Co., Printers, 1834), pp. 8–9.

[3] *Ohio Anti-Slavery Society Report of the First Anniversary*, 1836 (Cincinnati, Ohio Anti-Slavery Society, 1836), p. 26.

Women's Introduction to the American Platform

This was all very fine. All very proper and within the dictates of "the sphere." It was a chance for women to do something—to be of service in the cause for humanity. The decade of the 1830's may well be called the preparatory period of women's activity in public life. They learned, through observation and with the assistance of the men reformers, how to organize and conduct their own meetings. They learned by trial and error how to plan activities, how to cooperate. Individuals among them, practicing before audiences of the "female associations," learned the rudiments of public speaking and of the art of persuasion. And while many were content, not so the individual women who felt that there must be more that they could do besides pray and give money, that somehow there must be a way they could get to the front lines of this conflict whose chief weapon of warfare was the stirring up of popular sentiment. The methods of reform open to women were too slow for the time, for the need. All the pent-up energies, all the rebellion against degradation and submission, all the desires to effect radical changes could no longer be held in submission. They, too, must use the public platform to disseminate their ideas, to create and stimulate a public sentiment so strong that eradication of oppression and inequality could be the only ultimate result. There would be opposition to such a daring step, perhaps even within the ranks of the reform societies themselves, certainly in the opinion of the public at large. But few accomplishments worth while are ever won easily. With the backing given from the start by the Garrisonian lefts, by the ultra press, and by the foremost liberals of the church, including Channing, Parker, May, and Higginson, they could at least emulate the brave and glorious career of Frances Wright, their predecessor and the first orator among women to appear before the American public.

Frances Wright. It was during the summer of 1828, almost a decade before an American woman gained any prominence upon the platform, that Frances Wright, attractive, red-haired, and fiery-natured Scotch woman, began to create a sensation throughout the North as a public speaker of extraordinary ability. Well known as an author and philanthropist, she had come to America to realize dreams of social reform that she believed could be effected in this enfranchised republic. She had founded the well-planned but short-lived community for the gradual emancipation of slaves at Nashoba, Tenn., identified herself with the idealistic experiment of Robert Owen, and started to promulgate her radical views to the public as editor of the New Harmony *Gazette* before she discovered her ability at oral persuasion.[1] On the Fourth of July, 1828, she had the honor of giving a patriotic address in New Harmony and the good fortune of finding her latent oratorical talents. Eagerly, though not without misgivings, she

[1] *Cf. The Pandect* (Cincinnati), Aug. 19, Sept. 2, 1828.

directed her enthusiasm toward the public platform as a means of propagating her one reform. Frances Wright's belief was that could she but educate the people to question and investigate existing institutions, she would start the wheel of social reform revolving, and soon its momentum would surmount all obstacles of tradition and lethargy.[1]

Frances began her campaign by hiring a hall in Cincinnati and giving a series of lectures on free inquiry that she hoped would offset the unhappiness caused there by the current revival meetings of the old school. The people, drawn by curiosity concerning the subject and the fact that a woman dared to speak, crowded the courthouse but failed to accept her doctrines. Instead, opposition to her materialistic principles became invective even before she left Cincinnati.[2] Because she advocated investigation of the existing autocratic institution of the church, she was soon branded as an atheist, and the "priestess of infidelity." Because she preached birth control as a means of alleviating suffering and poverty—in an age that did not even countenance divorce—she was accused of being a disciple of free love.

If her lectures aroused opposition, Frances Wright knew that they also would incite thought and interest. Was not her mission to stimulate people to think and question that they might be led to action? Was not her Cause, that of human improvement and happiness, more important than personal reputation or fortune?[3]

Undaunted, she enlarged her lecturing field and went east in the autumn of 1828 to set up her headquarters in New York City. There she edited the *Free Enquirer*, bought a hall of her own in answer to the closing of all city halls against her, and carried on her campaign throughout the East until 1830. She returned to the American platform again in 1836 after a 6-year absence in Europe (the departure of which was instigated by the unfavorable influence she felt she was bringing to the Workingmen's party in her sponsorship of its activities), only to meet increased abuse. The coals of prejudice and conservatism had been stirred into flame during her absence by the growing antislavery agitation. The fact that she was a foreigner was played upon by such newspapers as the *Philadelphia Evening Courier*, in an appeal to the old American antagonism against Great Britain. Because she returned with a third name, that of D'Arusmont, she was accused of inconsistency by those who denounced her as an enemy of marriage. A seemingly increased consciousness of the one sphere of women added to the opposition.

[1] *The Free Enquirer* (New York), Mar. 4, 1829.
[2] *Cf.*, for example, *Pennsylvania Gazette*, cited in *The Pandect* (Cincinnati), Aug. 19, 1828.
[3] Frances Wright, *Course of Popular Lectures* (London, James Watson, 1829 and 1834), p. 18.

Women's Introduction to the American Platform

As enthusiastic as ever, Frances determined to speak on her old-new theme and to add such discourses as "Chartered Monopolies" and "Southern Slavery" to the old ones upon "Existing Evils and Their Remedy," "Religion," "Morals," and "Of the More Important Divisions and Essential Parts of Knowledge." For two years she persevered in her attempt to carry the truth to the people. When, after her first lecture in Philadelphia, Frances was prohibited by the mayor from speaking in that city, she called an outdoor meeting at Fair Mount, on the outskirts of the city.[1] This meeting broken up by rioters, she turned to the courthouse at York, Pa., and here she was able to complete her lectures, but not without difficulty. The mobocrats and the press dogged her footsteps to the end of her career and were instrumental in creating pandemonium at two of her last attempted meetings in New York in October, 1838.[2] Then, questioning the wisdom of continuing in the face of such odds and believing that a large part of her purpose in stirring up free inquiry had been accomplished, Frances Wright D'Arusmont retired from public activity and spent the remaining sixteen years of her life in Cincinnati.

And yet, in spite of all the calumny bestowed upon the head of Frances Wright, in no available record was anything but recognition and praise accorded to her ability as a public speaker. The reports of her first lecture in Cincinnati were to the effect that all expectations fell far short of the "splendor, the brilliance, the overwhelming eloquence" of the speaker and added that "if chaste diction, and logical deduction from assumed data, delivered with an air of determined purpose, breathing an indomitable fortitude, that seemed to court persecution and martyrdom, heightened by persuasive smiles and earnest gestures be eloquence, she possesses it.[3] Comments on one of her first lectures in New York City, given early in January, 1829, at Masonic Hall to an audience of nearly two thousand, admitted that while her message was fanatical and should be condemned, and she should be prevented from repeating such an "exhibition" in public, she had skilfully and eloquently expressed her ideas in a voice of remarkable sweetness, distinctness and power.[4] Recognition of the fiery persuasion of her speech in the same city on October 16, 1836, upon "twaddle" as "miserable and ignorant" as the editorials of William Cullen Bryant in the *Evening Post* or the bulletins of the Anti-Slavery Society attested to the belief that her power had not abated during her years abroad.[5] To the very

[1] *Philadelphia Saturday Courier*, July 23, 1836.

[2] *New York Gazette*, cited in *The Liberator* (Boston), Nov. 2, 1838.

[3] Frances Trollope, *Domestic Manners of the Americans* (Whittaker, Treacher and Co., 1832), I, 94–98; *Saturday Evening Chronicle* (Cincinnati), Aug. 30, 1828.

[4] *New York American*, Jan. 5, 1829.

[5] *New York Herald*, Oct. 18, 1836.

end of her career, Frances Wright's eloquence was acclaimed by friend and foe alike. Even those who were most infuriated at her insistence in expressing ideas that were in actuality only too advanced for their comprehension and those who were most insulted by her willful desecration of the sphere of women could not but yield to her a place in the ranks of the orators. And this success of Frances Wright, coupled with admiration for her courage and fortitude, contributed a mighty advance step toward the breaking down of women's barriers.

Angelina Grimké. Somewhat different was the introduction to the public platform experienced by Angelina Grimké, who was to become the most prominent woman orator of the 1830's. With her older sister Sarah, Angelina made frequent visits to Philadelphia from the luxurious seclusion of her Charleston, S. C., home and came to view the institution of slavery, and even the traditional practice of it in her home, with abhorrence. Both she and Sarah wrote pamphlets and appeals upon the subject and upon attending an antislavery convention in New York City in November, 1836, were welcomed as able supporters of Abolitionism and invited by leaders of the movement to speak to groups of women in the North. As Southerners, telling of actual experiences witnessed at home, they could do a great work in winning sympathizers and converts to the Cause. Parlor meetings were quite in order; so Angelina accepted Elizur Wright's plea and made a great hit with her women audiences. Sarah, sincere and earnest, though not a very fluent speaker, served as auxiliary, and soon the numbers attending the Grimké meetings forced them into churches and halls. Husbands, drawn out of curiosity at their wives' enthusiastic reports, began to dot the audiences, and by June, 1837, the Grimké sisters were speaking to mixed audiences. In this manner came the transition from conversing with parlor circles to speaking to crowded audiences like the ones of three and four thousand that filled Boston's Odeon in the spring of 1838.[1]

Recognition of Angelina's eloquence grew as her fame spread. Audiences such as those in Charlestown, Mass., in August, 1837, sat spellbound for the two hours or more of her discourses and found that the graceful chestnut-ringleted, blue-eyed daughter of the South "in propriety of manner and gesture, beauty of elocution, and excellence of arrangement and conclusiveness of reasoning, satisfied even the most fastidious."[2] They realized that it required more of a speaker than mere learning in schools to enable him to rouse tears in the eyes of audiences with "the unaffected pathos, the sound and comprehensive intelligence, the magnanimous and meek spirit,

[1] *Cf. The Liberator* (Boston), Apr. 20, 1838.
[2] *Ibid.*, Sept. 1, 1837.

the sweet eloquence" that characterized the oratory of Angelina Grimké.[1] Dr. Spofford, editor of the *Haverhill Gazette* and a senator in the Massachusetts legislature, who likened Angelina's eloquence to that of Birney, could not decide which he thought was the better speaker.[2] And Wendell Phillips believed that Angelina was gifted with an eloquence of emotional power rarely equaled, and felt that her experiences had so ripened her wonderous faculty of "laying bare her own heart to reach the hearts of others" that she could not but captivate her audiences.[3]

Even the callous reporter for the *Boston Morning Post*, who had known the "misfortune" of hearing hundreds of lectures in the Massachusetts Hall of Representatives, admitted that seldom had he heard better speaking than that of Angelina Grimké when she appeared there before capacity houses in February, 1838, in support of a petition against slavery.[4] "We heard her speak of LIBERTY," said the *Boston Reformer*, "and as she pronounced the word, chains rattled in our ears—the wife calling for her husband—the husband for the wife—and the parent for the offspring."[5] With a thrilling beauty of intonation, her deep, rich, melodious voice penetrated to every part of that many-cornered and difficult hall.

Angelina's audiences responded not only to the word artistry of her pictures of Southern slavery but felt a tug at their hearts when she explained that she and Sarah were a part of the system—a penitent part, educated in early life to all connected with slavery, but come now to plead for the slave. They felt that she was so familiar with slavery in "all its heart-rending details of suffering and of wretchedness" that there was little danger of her falling into the common practice of exaggeration.

They were startled by her denunciation of the North as a supporter of slavery. Was not slavery practiced at the very "seat of government," she asked. Did not Northern soldiers participate in quelling servile insurrections? Did the North not permit the return of fugitive slaves to their masters without jury trial? Did the North not buy slave products? Did the North not educate ministers in its theological seminaries without instilling in them the spirit of liberty? The North could not ask the South to free the chains of the slave, while the black man at the North was bowed down by the iron bonds of prejudice. Wake up, said Angelina Grimké, showing neither quarter to the system of slavery nor mercy to its supporters—wake up, people of the North, to your responsibilities.[6]

---

[1] *Mercantile Journal*, cited in *The Liberator*, Apr. 20, 1838.

[2] *The Liberator*, Mar. 2, 1838.

[3] Theodore D. Weld, *Angelina Grimké Weld* (Boston, George H. Ellis, 1880), p. 28.

[4] *Boston Morning Post*, cited in *The Philanthropist* (New Richmond, Ohio), Apr. 3, 1838.

[5] *Boston Reformer*, cited in *The Liberator*, Mar. 9, 1838.

[6] *Cf. Boston Courier*, June 26, 1837.

Surprisingly, the meetings of the Grimkés were rarely disturbed by the missile throwing, fire threats, light extinguishing, and noisy outbursts so common at those of Frances Wright. As late as April 6, 1838, a commentator in the *Liberator* remarked that never was the reception of a speaker more respectful or orderly than that of Angelina Grimké in Boston on the preceding Thursday. Wherever the Grimkés were able to find a place to speak, be it hall, church, or barn, crowds composed mainly of abolitionists listened attentively to their speaking.

Opposition expressed itself vigorously, however, in the newspapers, and even reports lauding Angelina's eloquence mirrored objections to women in public, as did the *Boston Reformer* in commenting that if men would perform their duties these women would not need to leave their proper duties to plead for the slave, and the *Boston Morning Post* in stating that Angelina could reel off an antislavery speech of two and a half hours in length in excellent offhand style as easily as if she were engaged at the spinning wheel, where she should have been occupied.[1]

Opposition to the Grimkés caused the church to flare up in its most overt action against the appearance of women on the American public platform. The orthodox brethren charged the antislavery movement with a tendency, if not an actual design, to put women out of their sphere and to disturb the sacred foundations of social life. They were more afraid of these two women, said Oliver Johnson, prominent abolitionist, than they would have been of a dozen lecturers of the other sex.[2] And was it any wonder? Here were two representatives of the very sex of parishioners upon the control of whom the prestige and authority of the minister in the community was largely dependent, succeeding in their quiet disregard of sacrosanct biblical injunctions and daring to steal the thunder of moral persuasion learned in the church and to apply it to principles uttered independently of clerical instruction.

The ministers first addressed themselves to the work of communicating their disapproval to the minds of their congregations. They preached sermons on the one sphere of woman, on her duties to God and man, and her subsequent downfall should she step outside the bounds of her province.[3] And in July, 1837, the orthodox clergy dealt its heaviest blow. When the General Association of Congregational Ministers met at West Brookfield, they put their heads together and decided to make the usual annual pastoral

---

[1] *Boston Reformer*, cited in *The Liberator*, Mar. 9, 1838; *Boston Morning Post*, cited in *The Philanthropist*, Apr. 3, 1838.

[2] Oliver Johnson, *William Lloyd Garrison and His Times* (Boston, B. B. Russell and Co., 1880), p. 261.

[3] *Cf.*, for example, the Reverend Hubbard Winslow, *The Appropriate Sphere of Woman* (Boston, Weeks, Jordon and Co., 1837); *Boston Courier*, June 26, 1837.

letter the vehicle of an assault upon the obnoxious women who were causing such havoc in their well-ordered lives.[1]

The result was the famous Brookfield Bull, the longest and weightiest division of which was devoted to the serious situation of women.[2] "The power of woman is her dependence, flowing from the consciousness of that weakness which God has given her in those departments of life that form the character of individuals, and of the nation," said the ministers. Women may wield much influence in the home and rightly offer prayers in the cause of advancing religion; they may participate in the Sabbath school and ask their ministers for instruction. But when women assume the place of men as public reformers and when they so far forget themselves as to itinerate in the character of public lecturers and teachers, their characters become unnatural, and they sever themselves from the protection and care that are their right. "If the vine, whose strength and beauty is to lean upon the trellis-work, and half conceal its clusters, thinks to assume the independence and the overshadowing nature of the elm, it will not only cease to bear fruit, but fall in shame and dishonor into the dust." The ministry deplored the direction that these women had taken toward degeneracy and ruin and hoped that in making public its sentiments it would help to secure such reformation as it believed was scriptural and would be permanent.

The "Papal Bull" succeeded, at least in part, in accomplishing what it had set out to do. Many men and women who had acted with the abolitionists were persuaded to return to the fold, the force of their religious prejudices and fears superseding their more liberal inclinations. Scores of churches or vestries that might have been opened to the Grimké sisters were rigidly closed. Preachers refused to give notices of antislavery meetings from their pulpits.

On the other hand, the Brookfield Bull had the salutary effect of furthering the activities of the Grimkés and of strengthening the claim of women to public life. The inconsistency of the pastoral letter in advocating candid discussion of slavery "and all other proper methods of diffusing light and promoting correct moral sentiment" and in seeking to prohibit women from speaking threw the spotlight of individual rights upon the discrepancy.[3] "We allow our women liberty of the press—why should we deny them liberty of speech?" reasoned the author of an article on "Female Liberty of Speech" appearing in the *Liberator* on October 20. Another writer complimented the Grimkés not only for disseminating sound first-hand

---

[1] Wendell P. Garrison and Francis J. Garrison, *William Lloyd Garrison* (New York, The Century Company, 1885), II, 133.

[2] *Cf. The Liberator*, Aug. 11, 1837.

[3] *Emancipator*, cited in *The Liberator*, Aug. 18, 1837.

doctrines but also for bringing to clearer light the proslavery spirit and clerical persecution. "Though ministers may abuse and denounce them, it is gratifying to believe the people will sustain them. The days of Popery are numbered."[1]

["The whole land seems aroused to discussion on the province of woman, and I am glad of it," said Angelina, who herself felt that her womanhood seemed to be as objectionable to the public as her abolitionism; "we are willing to bear the brunt of the storm, if we can only be the means of making a breach in the wall of public opinion, which lies right in the way of woman's true dignity, honor and usefulness."[2]

[And Angelina Grimké followed the advice of the *New England Spectator* that "women must fulfill their duties according to the talents God has given them, and are responsible to Him alone,"[3] speaking in more than sixty towns in answer to an overwhelming pressure of invitations from people who "were glad to hear women," until ill-health forced her from the antislavery arena. Then, after her marriage to the prominent reformer Theodore Weld in 1838, she returned to a private life filled with reform activities.

Abby Kelley. The second week in May in the year 1838 was an exciting one in Philadelphia. The event was the dedication of the famous Pennsylvania Hall, built by the reformers of the city in answer to violent opposition to the antislavery movement. The hall was to be consecrated to freedom of speech, liberty, and the "rights of man," and the occasion brought together leading abolitionists from far and near. During the three days between May 14, the day of the dedication of the hall, and May 17, the day of its burning by the mob, a small band of courageous reformers held the meetings of the Anti-Slavery Convention. [Antislavery was a most unpopular subject in 1838, and it is probable that only the warm-hearted enthusiasm and determination of the leaders enabled them to hold their meetings in spite of the increasing mob outside, and to attempt to carry out their program in spite of howling threats and showers of rocks, brickbats, and rotten eggs hurled through the windows.]

At the evening meeting on May 16, the bride Angelina Grimké Weld gave her last public address before as difficult an audience situation as any reformer could be called upon to face. And at the same noisy meeting an attractive Irish girl, graceful in manner and earnest in purpose, made her

---

[1] *The Liberator*, Aug. 25, 1837.

[2] Catherine H. Birney, *Sarah and Angelina Grimké* (Boston, Lee and Shepard, 1885), pp. 194–195; *cf.* also Gilbert H. Barnes and D. L. Dumond, eds., *Letters of Theodore Dwight Weld, Angelina Grimké Weld and Sarah Grimké 1822–1844* (New York, D. Appleton-Century Company, Inc., 1934) I, 427.

[3] *New England Spectator*, cited in *The Liberator*, Oct. 6, 1837.

public speaking debut. The initiation of this newcomer into the ranks of antislavery leadership, amidst the excitement of a violent outbreak of public sentiment, was a prophetic sign of the stormy career that was to follow. Abby Kelley was a born fighter. Her life as an antislavery orator contributed the technique of verbal warfare, and as a lecturer she created more turbulence, perhaps, than any other advocate of the cause of Negro freedom in her times. From the day Abby Kelley gave up her teaching position in Worcester, Mass., to join the antislavery crusade in the spring of 1838, throughout her long speaking career, her life seemed to be "a continual holocaust on the altar of human freedom."

As an agent or traveling public speaker for the Anti-Slavery Society, Abby Kelley quickly gained notoriety. In 1839 her appearance in Washington, Conn., caused a temporary disruption in the community church. The conservatives and progressives became irreconcilable in the dispute over whether she should be allowed to lecture there. In the same year, at the Peace Convention in Boston, Abby so far forgot that she belonged to the subordinate sex that she publicly called to order one of the ministers present. In 1840 her nomination to an executive committee at the national Anti-Slavery Convention was the final straw that split the organization.[1]

To the ranks of the Garrisonian abolitionists Abby Kelley was welcomed as an able and inspired crusader. In October, 1840, Garrison remarked upon Abby's growing "eloquence and impressiveness," and Rogers proudly commented that "Abby is taking the field like a lion."[2]

From 1840 to 1845 Abby Kelley spent a large portion of her energy in spreading antislavery propaganda throughout Massachusetts. She attended local and national conventions. She lectured throughout Rhode Island and western New York and appeared in a number of towns in New Hampshire and Pennsylvania.

In June 1845, Abby ventured to the frontier state of Ohio. Her reception there was just as unfavorable as it had been in the East. On September 7, for instance, she was dragged out of the Quaker Church in Mount Pleasant, having felt prompted to deliver a message to her fellow church members on slavery. The argument that followed Abby's expression of a desire to speak resulted in the withdrawal of a large number of the members of the congregation to the home of Aquilla Hurford; and from her friend's porch, Abby Kelley spoke to her audience for an hour and a half "in an earnest and forcible manner."[3]

As early as 1842, Abby Kelley's name began to be associated with that of Stephen S. Foster. Foster was a leftist among radicals. No measure that

---

[1] *Cf. Herald of Freedom* (Concord, N. H.), May 23, 1840; Weld, *op. cit.*, p. 29.

[2] Garrisons, *op. cit.*, II, 418–420.

[3] *The Liberator*, Sept. 19, 1845.

would forward the antislavery cause was too hazardous for him to undertake, and probably no reformer was thrown out of more meetings. He was jailed more than once for disturbing the peace by the excitement he caused in meetings. But nothing could stop this utterly fearless young man, so consecrated was his life to the cause for which he was crusading.

It was a common occurrence for the agents of the Anti-Slavery Society to appear upon the same platform when lecturing in the same vicinity, and in this manner the friendship of Stephen Foster and Abby Kelley flourished and finally culminated in their marriage at New Brighton, Pa., on December 21, 1845.

With a radical antislavery reformer for a husband and traveling companion, Abby Kelley's speaking career was for a time, if anything, more turbulent than before. Instead of mellowing the fierceness of Stephen Foster, Abby seemed to become more violent and outspoken herself. Armed with unvanquished faith in their Cause and strengthened by a oneness with Stephen in purpose, Abby would sally forth with him from the refuge of their quiet, harmonious farm home near Worcester, Mass., to battle against the slavery ogre.

Abby and Stephen Foster were ridiculed by the newspapers. They were abused and called vile names, and their lectures were often broken up by mobs and rioters. At other times their meetings were disturbed by strange actions from their audiences, including hissing, shouting, and stamping. Abby learned how to dodge every kind of missile, from rotten eggs on down to tobacco quids, but only once was she ever stopped in the midst of a lecture. The Fosters were traveling in Massachusetts during the latter part of 1848 and found a troublesome audience at Warren on the evening of December 16. While Abby was speaking a group of rowdies busied themselves by sprinkling pepper on the floor, overturning benches, and throwing corn and beans about the audience. Then an overgrown lad of around twenty-five fired a bullet at Mrs. Foster. The bullet whizzed clear, and Abby appealed to the audience for protection; but in vain; and so for once disconcerted, she asked Stephen to continue with the meeting.[1]

By 1850, however, Abby Kelley was able to remark that the taste of the public had improved and that more audiences were throwing fresh eggs instead of rotten ones. By this time, too, more communities were becoming conditioned to the haranguing methods of the reformers. Greater numbers of individuals were questioning the inability of the supporters of slavery to answer the challenge of antislavery and were insisting upon a showing of respect for the opinions of such people as Abby Kelley, who followed their course out of a sense of duty and belief in its integrity.

[1] *Ibid.*, Dec. 29, 1848.

Women's Introduction to the American Platform

Contemporary records tend to establish the belief that Abby Kelley Foster was the most persecuted of all the women taking part in the anti-slavery struggle. The reason is obvious. Abby Kelley asked for trouble. Like Frances Wright, Abby saw in the American people a great power to be awakened from lethargy by sharp verbal thrusts and to be galvanized for battle against the fetters of oppression by pointed truths based upon the persuasion of sound evidence and logical reasoning. To arouse the people, by whatever action it required, was her objective, and in spite of trouble little foreseen at the beginning of her career, Abby could not allow public disapproval to divert her from her purpose.

Abby Kelley believed in telling her audiences, to their faces and in no uncertain terms, exactly what was wrong with them. Because they tolerated slavery, she accused her auditors of being "thieves," "robbers," "liars," "adulterers," "murderers," "pirates" and "cradle-plunderers."

In denunciation Abby Kelley was supreme. Her tongue was sharp and merciless. She denounced the existing institution of the church because it passively accepted the institution of slavery. She stigmatized ministers as "hireling priests" and "ambassadors of the devil" because they welcomed slaveholders into their congregations. Churches whose doors were closed to the propagation of antislavery she characterized as "whited sepulchres." All organized institutions that passively endured slavery came in for a share of her anathemas. Political parties, she said, were dirty and corrupt. And at the Liberty Party Convention held in Cazenovia, N. Y., in 1842, Abby told the delegates in plain language that their party was the dirtiest of all political parties.[1] Nor did she forget to pay her respects to the political leaders of the day who tolerated slavery. In her lecture at Blackstone, Mass., on July 23, 1848, she spoke of "praying Polk, bloodhound Taylor and spaniel Cass." She opposed Henry Clay even more than she did Calhoun, threatening one evening in her most excited manner to "flay Mr. Clay alive with her keen dissecting knife and to hold up his 'sheep clad wolf skin' for the terror of other prowling wolves."[2]

Abby Kelley denounced the Constitution of the United States because it, too, permitted slavery. "No Union with Slaveholders" was her theme, and she urged the immediate dissolution of the Union. At a meeting in Cadiz, Ohio, in October, 1845, she not only went so far as to present a petition for the dissolution of the Union but, to the horror of the conservatives of the town, charged a fee of 2 cents for the privilege of affixing a signature to the petition. By 1846 Abby was predicting civil war and, in such lectures as the one given in Salem, Ohio, in April, describing in glow-

[1] *Cazenovia Abolitionist*, cited in *The Liberator*, Aug. 5, 1842.
[2] *Boston Daily Atlas*, cited in *The Liberator*, Aug. 18, 1848; *The Liberator*, Nov. 18, 1842.

167

ing terms the horrors of such a war.[1] Is it any wonder that Abby Kelley was persecuted?

And yet, all the while, Abby Kelley was loved by the members of her own reform groups. From the liberal antislavery point of view, she was preaching sound arguments. "How the slave would rejoice," wrote an auditor of one of her lectures in Fitchburg, Mass., "could he have heard her. She pleads in his behalf, and O, how sincerely! God grant that it may be effectually." And added, "Her last lecture at Leominster exceeded, for moral sublimity, clearness and force of truth, anything I have ever heard."[2]

Abby Kelley was welcomed as an able speaker at women's rights and temperance meetings. She was admired by both friends and foes for her courageous, fighting spirit. And those who knew her best had only the highest of praise for her.

In private life Abby Kelley felt kindly toward her fellow men. She was sweet and unassuming and had a grand sense of humor.[3] In 1842, although already beset with opposition, she reported to the *Liberator* that the events of her trip into Rhode Island were not clearly impressed in her mind, from the fact that she could not persuade herself that people were really so wicked as to be guilty of such atrocities. She added, "'Tis all a farce, me thinks."[4]

As a public speaker Abby Kelley is to be remembered as a particularly eloquent debater. She was praised by friends and enemies for her great ability at argument. Her talent and power as an orator were agreed to be of an uncommon order. Her speeches were always given extemporaneously. Contemporary reports rarely fail to characterize her voice as being excellent in quality, "full" and "mellow," and she was said to have unusually clear enunciation. Infrequently, she was criticized as being overemphatic in her speaking and too effusive in quality, but as the *Albany Tocsin* added, "her elocution is quite graceful, and . . . she is nevertheless a very interesting and efficient lecturer."[5]

Perhaps the greatest compliment received by Abby Kelley during her public-speaking career was uttered by Henry Wright, who, in writing to Garrison concerning the American Anti-Slavery Convention of 1848, said, "The *woman* is forgotten when she . . . speaks; the grandeur and glory of the theme is all that is thought of."[6]

---

[1] *Salem Bugle*, cited in *The Liberator*, Apr. 24, 1846.

[2] *The Liberator*, Oct. 22, 1841.

[3] *Cf.* Sallie Holley, *A Life for Liberty* (John W. Chadwick, ed., New York, G. P. Putnam's Sons, 1899), p. 130.

[4] *The Liberator*, Jan. 21, 1842.

[5] *Albany Tocsin*, cited in *The Liberator*, July 15, 1842.

[6] *The Liberator*, May 19, 1848.

Women's Introduction to the American Platform

Lucretia Mott. It is probably fortunate for the progress of women in public life that there were women like Lucretia Mott to salve the wounds of public prejudice upon which such women as Abby Kelley poured the vinegar of denunciation. Lucretia Mott was the diplomat among pioneer women orators. In her gentle Quaker manner, with a voice of remarkable clarity and sweetness, this sprightly, delicate little lady in the dove-colored dress and prim little Quaker cap preached the humanity of brotherly love. She rarely denounced anything, but with a calm, though invigorating, eloquence which came from a full conviction that her hearers could not help but respond to that which irresistibly controlled her, made positive suggestions for courses of action as radical as any proposed by the left-wing reformers of the day.[1]

Lucretia Mott never dreamed of trying to be eloquent. Her single thought was to express her own convictions simply and plainly, holding the truth "equal to its own support." Her appeals were, for the most part, to the reason, and her logical acumen so keen that once admitting her premises, there was no escape from her conclusions.[2] An uncommon ability at "rounding off the periods" of sentences, of neat and correct style of expression and of choice of language elicited much comment, and her careful articulation and pronunciation seemed to compensate for any lack of strength in vocal quality. Said Thomas Guill aptly, in criticizing her speech before the New England Anti-Slavery Convention of 1847, "Her matter was well arranged; her language simple, but critically correct; and she stitched on proposition to proposition as adroitly, yet calmly, as if she were at home knitting a pair of socks for her sleeping grand-child, while she gently jogged its cradle with her well-employed toe."[3] Another testimonial to Lucretia's manner of speaking was offered by Samuel Longfellow, who said:

Her simple, straightforward words went right to the mark of the truth, right to the heart of the evil. There was a divine force in that "still small voice" of reason, of conscience, of unselfish purpose. No whirlwind of passion, or lightning of eloquence; it was rather the dawn of clear day upon dark places and hidden. She had the enviable but rare power of "speaking the truth in love, without in the least abating the truth."[4]

The fact that Lucretia Mott had been testifying and preaching with great favor in Quaker congregations from the early date of 1818 abetted

---

[1] *Cf.*, for example, *Anti-slavery Bugle*, cited in *The Liberator*, Oct. 1, 1847; *Baltimore Clipper*, cited in *The Liberator*, June 29, 1849; *The Liberator*, Dec. 3, 1852; Dec. 9, 1853.

[2] *Nantucket Inquirer*, cited in *The Liberator*, July 22, 1842.

[3] *Boston Post*, cited in *The Liberator*, June 4, 1847.

[4] Anna D. Hallowell, *James and Lucretia Mott, Life and Letters* (Boston, Houghton, Mifflin Company, 1884), p. 469.

her self-assurance before lay audiences and reform groups. From early childhood Lucretia had been accustomed to the equality of sex practiced in her home and by her sect and to the freedom and spontaneity of speaking customary in Quaker meetings. Her father had educated her, had believed that she should be a useful citizen and applauded her self-assumed duties as a teacher. Her husband, also a Quaker, regarded her as his equal and was glad for her success as a reformer, which overshadowed his own. Perhaps it was the Quaker influence that caused her always to speak extemporaneously, believing as she did that "fixed speeches are not to be compared to spontaneous discussions," and to have faith in the light within "to speak as the spirit giveth utterance."[1]

Lucretia Mott was a splendid example of the universal reformer. In common with her compeers, she held herself consecrated to the spirit of reform, of which the various agitations were but subdivisions. She dedicated herself to all causes, and in the company of her reformer husband—tall, benevolent, distinguished James Mott—traveled about as a free agent, employed by no reform society, but helping everywhere she could. She spoke for antislavery and in antislavery circles, beginning with the meeting which organized the American Anti-Slavery Society in 1833. She advocated women's rights, was one of the formers of Women's "Declaration of Independence" and one of the organizers of the Woman's Rights Society in 1848, and made what is probably her best known speech upon this subject when she refuted Richard Dana's lecture on woman's sphere on December 17, 1849, in Philadelphia, in her lucid and convincing "Discourse on Woman." She was an active participant at the numerous nonresistant meetings and conventions. Religious creeds and disciplines she considered of little importance in comparison with the freedom of the soul. She attended and spoke at Anti-Sabbath conventions. And she held meetings in practically every town she visited for the colored citizens, to urge them to educate themselves and to elevate their own condition. Lucretia preached sermons, using as one of her favorite texts, "If the truth make you free, Ye shall be free indeed." She spoke often upon one of her most cherished lecture subjects, "Reforms of the Age," in which she skillfully wove together discussion of theology, slavery, peace, capital punishment, and temperance.[2] On one tour in 1847, Lucretia and James traveled more than 2,400 miles in 70 days and attended seventy-one meetings devoted to various reforms of the day and the worship peculiar to their sect.[3]

Of course, Lucretia Mott met with much of the same kind of criticism that her other "forward sisters" encountered. Diplomatic as she might be,

---

[1] *Ibid.*, p. 387.
[2] *Cf. The Liberator*, Sept. 17, 1847; Aug. 25, 1848.
[3] *Baltimore Cor. of Era*, cited in *The Liberator*, Dec. 3, 1847.

she was, after all, a proponent of radical reform—and she was a member of the "weaker" sex. She was snubbed by the conservative Quakers who could find no principles in her doctrines for which they could expel her from her church, and she was hurt by the closing of doors that had once opened wide for her at the Yearly Meetings. She was hailed by the press as a "decidedly old girl" and a frump with a skull cap and a puny, shrill voice.

But in spite of all difficulties, there were—in a career that lasted until two years before her death in 1880—the calmness, the hopefulness for and faith in humanity of the speaker, mirrored in speeches of well-arranged content and concrete language, and the shining goodness of the woman, whose business of living was "to do good and communicate," to win for Lucretia Mott her deservedly high place as an American woman orator.

Ernestine L. Rose. The long career—one that spanned almost half a century—of that "matchless orator" and unusual woman Ernestine L. Rose also began in the 1830's. Ernestine Rose was born a Polish Jewess, and the forces that impelled her to preach reform came from experiences with inequality in the Old World. The first 16 years of her life were spent in the atmosphere of a wealthy ecclesiastical home, where she watched her beloved father, the Rabbi Potoski, follow such severe religious practices that Ernestine came to doubt the value of a religion that demanded so much sacrifice, and became professedly an infidel. At seventeen, she left her home to travel in Europe, where she undertook reform issues. Then she spend considerable time in England, where she identified herself with liberal movements.[1]

In the spring of 1836, Ernestine came to America with her recently acquired husband, William E. Rose, and settled in New York City. She lost no time in identifying herself with the reform activities going on about her. With unusual handicaps—a foreign accent, a Jewish ancestry, and an outspoken creed of infidelity—Ernestine set out to find her place in the ranks of American reform. Soon she was lecturing on the evils of the existing social system, the formation of human character, and the rights of women. The subjects of her talks during her first year in America included the "Science of Government," "Political Economy," and the "Equal Rights of Women"; and although the announcements of her lectures brought ridicule, because it was considered audacious for a woman to attempt to treat such subjects, much curiosity was aroused, and many went to listen. Among the male auditors, as a result, there was much admiration for the speakers's clear, strong intellect and excellent logic.[2]

[1] *The Excelsior*, cited in *The Liberator*, May 16, 1856.

[2] Paulina W. Davis, *A History of the National Woman's Rights Movement* (New York, Journeymen Printers' Co-operative Association, 1871), p. 11.

Ernestine Rose became an ardent participant in the many free-inquiry meetings, so popular during her time. She was among the speakers of the Sunday meetings held in Boston and occupied the platform at the morning and evening meetings on March 24, 1844, with the subject "Social Reform." Her avowal of infidelity caused her to become the target for the grossest interruptions at the free-discussion convention in Hartford, Conn., in June, 1853. But on a Sunday evening in April, 1861, she spoke to a crowded hall of respectful and patient listeners in Milford, Mass., upon an "Inquiry into the Existence of a God," and effectively repudiated "pseudo Christianity."

Although she lectured on religion, government, and other subjects and spoke frequently upon human rights, as upon one occasion an address in Washington, D.C., revolved upon "The Nebraska Question, as Deduced from Human Rights," Ernestine Rose seldom spoke directly upon the subject of antislavery. The rights of women was her especial Cause, and from the time she presented the first petition for women's property rights to the New York legislature in 1836 forward, she devoted her talents to the amelioration of their wrongs. As early as 1856, she had lectured in twenty-three states of the Union, had appeared before legislative bodies a number of times to plead for women, and had won international renown.

In spite of much prejudice against her opinions, seldom was there any outward demonstration of antagonism at her meetings. Fears concerning the nature of her propaganda were often voiced upon announcement of her arrival in a community, but the appearance of the lecturer usually dispelled these apprehensions. Her manner before audiences was graceful, dignified, and self-assured. She immediately enlisted the attention of her audiences, and her poise demanded respect. Her earnestness and enthusiasm were of a nature "which strangely impresses a popular audience," and as Paulina Wright Davis, a contemporary speaker of repute, said, "Whoever hears her, feels that she believes what she says, that it is a truth to her of the utmost moment."[1] Ernestine herself admired courage of conviction and openly complimented her foes for speaking out what they believed to be the truth in opposing her doctrines.

There were, of course, jibes at her decided foreign accent, at the way she pronounced even the title of her Cause—"woman's errights"—and sometimes Ernestine herself begged her audiences to have a little charity on its account. For, after all, was she not an example "that not only American women, but the down-trodden women of Poland, and even the down-trodden people, the Jews, were sensible of the wrongs inflicted upon women?"[2] More frequently, however, newspaper reports complimented

[1] *The Una* (Providence, R. I.), 2 (April, 1854): 251.
[2] *The Liberator*, Oct. 8, 1852.

172

her upon a grammatical choice and distinct enunciation of words that rendered her speaking entirely intelligible. For one born and educated in Poland, she spoke the English language with surprising precision and accuracy. Dr. Harriot Hunt believed that Ernestine's accent added interest to the truths she uttered.[1]

Much of Ernestine Rose's speaking was of a bombastic nature, illustrated with much gesticulation. Her dark eyes would often flash with indignation and her jeweled fingers emphasize important arguments. She moved about the platform a good deal, ignoring speaker's stand or table, and earned a reputation of being theatrical in manner and ornate in dress. But to offset these criticisms, her "rhetorical ability, logical power of mind and mental independence" in speeches two hours long, given with no reference to notes or manuscript, won admiration for her speaking ability. Among the reformers themselves, who avoided all personal ostentation, Ernestine was regarded with great acclaim. Sallie Holley found her to be splendidly clear and logical and added, "I cannot give any idea of the power and beauty of her speech. I can only stammer about it a little." And Joseph Barker claimed that "her eloquence is irresistible. It shakes, it awes, it thrills, it melts—it fills you with horror, it drowns you in tears. . . . To hear her reason, you might fancy she was all intelligence; to hear her plead, you would think her an incarnation of benevolence."[2]

And thus Ernestine L. Rose, foreigner, Jewess, radical, infidel—Ernestine L. Rose, orator, crusader in the American vanguard of human rights, accomplished for elevation of her sex, for amelioration of social conditions, for aggrandizement of intellectual freedom a work that can be ascribed to few women of her time.

The Auspicious Forties

The 1840's witnessed increased activity of women upon the public platform. While feminine speaking was still more or less confined to reform agitation, eloquent individuals came to address large public assemblies often, and frequently to occupy half of evening programs with such famous men orators as Wendell Phillips and Ralph Waldo Emerson and to share equal contemporary acclaim. Inspired by the example of their leaders and encouraged by the American Anti-Slavery Society after its reorganization in 1840, a number of women were finding their tongues at reform meetings, overcoming the fear of St. Paul's misinterpreted dictum and gaining in determination to express their opinions and wishes in conventions. (In

[1] Cf. Washington Sentinel, Mar. 29, 1854; Harriot K. Hunt, Glances and Glimpses (Boston, John P. Jewett and Co., 1856), p. 251.
[2] Holley, op. cit., pp. 127-128; The Liberator, Nov. 24, 1854.

addition to crusading for the all-important antislavery movement, women saw their names begin to appear as speakers at the Anti-Sabbath, Philanthropic, Anti-Capital Punishment, Temperance, and Peace meetings. And perhaps the most outstanding development in this decade was the hiring of women as reform agents. This meant that individual women were considered by their reform groups to be eloquent and to be well able to undertake the assiduous duties of traveling public speakers.

Lucy Stone. In 1847, a new star appeared among women orators when Lucy Stone joined the reform crusade upon her graduation from Oberlin College. Lucy had been a reformer at heart since childhood, when she had noticed the firm, though benevolent, hand with which her father dominated her own home, and since the time she had experienced inequality at school with her brothers. Lucy's blood had boiled when her father had calmly made plans for his sons' higher education and then had turned upon her in consternation when she told him that she intended to gain more instruction than that usually accorded to the "weaker" sex. Her dream of an education consumed years for realization, years spent in working and saving money, years spent in breaking down her father's prejudice so that by the time she was a junior he was willing to help defray her college expenses.

Lucy was twenty-eight years old when she finished at Oberlin and was well accustomed to fighting her way even at this one liberal college that allowed Negroes and women to enter upon equal terms. She had bravely announced her intention of entering the profession of public speaking and had struggled against the shocked determination of the Ladies' Board to keep women students within "proper restrictions." She had managed one very successful debate in which coeds participated instead of serving merely as audience and also had joined a secret debating society.

Lucy planned to teach and to lecture upon reform at every opportunity, but, assisted by Abby Kelley Foster, to whom she announced her intentions, she was able to become an agent of the Massachusetts Anti-Slavery Society immediately upon graduation. In speaking for women's rights Lucy Stone was put on her own initiative, for there was no suffrage association strong enough to back her during these early years, and to make expenses she finally accepted the method of charging a small fee for her lectures, often asking no more than 12½ cents admission.

As with the other reform speakers, Lucy Stone's work took her over a good deal of territory in the North and West; and she extended her efforts into Canada, where she attracted audiences that equaled Jenny Lind's and were the largest ever collected in Toronto.[1] She appeared before

---

[1] *The Una,* 3 (April, 1855): 59.

the Massachusetts Constitutional Convention in 1853 to speak for woman's rights and was the center of attraction not only because of her presence but because of the success of her speaking, in spite of the fact that she shared the platform with Wendell Phillips. She lectured upon both woman's rights and antislavery to audiences as far south as Louisville, Ky., and St. Louis, Mo., and excited heartfelt admiration and utmost respect from crowds who came in curiosity and intended to deride. These audiences, in the highly excitable borderline region between North and South, found that the messages of the feminine lecturer abounded "in matters worthy of reflection."[1]

It was not long before Lucy Stone discovered that life as an itinerant was neither easy nor monotonous. There were times like the night in Montgomery, in 1850, when she and Parker Pillsbury hiked through a Massachusetts snowstorm, baggage in hand, after a late antislavery meeting, in search of a night's lodging at a neighborhood farmhouse. There were nights such as the one at Ledyard, Conn., when the meetinghouse was neither lighted nor warmed and where candles had to be procured to "make the darkness visible" and a fire kindled while the audience gathered.

Upon occasions such as the one in East Bridgewater, Mass., in 1848, coppers, dried apples, smoked herring, beans, and tobacco quids "were a part of the logic with which, in great profusion," the gallery answered her arguments and those of Parker Pillsbury. At the close of this meeting a fellow in a green jacket hurled a prayer book at Miss Stone with great violence, and the blow would have prostrated her on the floor had not the force of the object been abated by one end striking her shoulder.[2] At Mystic Bridge, Conn., in 1852, Lucy found not only the gallery ovation but pranksters who bolted the lecture hall doors from the outside before the close of a meeting and one who became so frolicsome at the Saturday evening meeting that he aimed a squirt gun from a window near the platform and drenched her with water while she was speaking. "This was a thing quite unnecessary," said Lewis Ford, with whom she was conducting the meeting, "inasmuch as she received the ordinance of baptism at an early period in life."[3]

However irritating these experiences may secretly have been to Lucy Stone, she found that her popularity with audiences completely overshadowed vestiges of disfavor. Antislavery audiences, having once heard her lecture, clamored to hear her again and filled columns of the Liberator

---

[1] *Cf. Louisville Democrat*, cited in *The Liberator*, Nov. 18, 1853; *St. Louis Intelligencer*, cited in *National Anti-Slavery Standard* (New York), Dec. 31, 1853.

[2] *The Liberator*, July 14, 1848.

[3] *Ibid.*, Mar. 26, 1852.

with letters of praise and encouragement, and exhortations to all who had an opportunity, not to fail to hear her. In the West and Southwest, Lucy's speaking soon dissipated any prejudice that may have been created against her by abusive articles that appeared "too frequently" in Eastern papers. Her propaganda for women's rights stirred audiences there as they seldom had been moved upon any subject, and to her lectures in the large cities people flocked by the thousands to listen in respectful and enthusiastic admiration.[1]

Even when Lucy Stone adopted the shocking Bloomer costume, the fad of the dress reformers in the early 1850's, her audiences held to her, and newspapers commented upon her courage in following her convictions on dress reform. She looked charming in spite of the fact that the general adoption of the fad was to be deprecated.[2] And when, in upholding her advocacy of women's rights, she went so far as to retain her own name after her marriage to Henry Blackwell in 1855, and to publish a declaration of rights in which both she and Henry protested the existing status of married women, she failed to topple from her enviable place as one of the most popular woman orators of the pre-Civil War period.

For Lucy Stone made either conscious or unconscious use of the many persuasive techniques and employed the many emotional and intellectual appeals. She used the tricks of her trade. One critic believed that "her solid Seward-like logic, her keen sarcasm, her earnest appeals, and volumes of facts, are wholly irresistible to every person who cares for reason or justice."[3] Another found that the plainness of her "priestly" gown, the severity of her hairdress were forgotten when Lucy began to speak, and that soon her audiences were intent upon the theme she appeared before them to unfold.[4] A third was inspired to extravagant praise by the sight of the "noble little woman, small in stature but large of soul, and grand in the magnitude of a lofty purpose; her bearing modest and dignified, her face radiant with feeling, and speaking all over, as it were, in eloquent accord with her earnest voice."[5]

Lucy Stone had no superior in the art of storytelling. She illustrated her lectures with appealing and colorful stories of slave circumstances, of women's wrongs, and of personal experiences with cowardice and prejudice and told them in a spicy fashion with splendid use of dialogue. She revealed excellent study and preparation in her allusions and quotations. And

---

[1] *Practical Christian* (Milford, Mass.), Jan. 14, 1854.

[2] *Cf. East Boston Ledger*, cited in *The Liberator*, June 10, 1853; *Prentice's Daily Journal*, cited in *The Liberator*, Nov. 18, 1853.

[3] *Norristown Olive Branch*, cited in *The Liberator*, Dec. 8, 1854.

[4] *St. Louis Intelligencer*, cited in the *National Anti-Slavery Standard*, Dec. 31, 1853.

[5] *Pennsylvania Freeman*, cited in *The Liberator*, July 1, 1853.

especially was Lucy Stone an artist of words—a painter of word pictures, carrying always a palette of vivid metaphors and similes.[1]

In 1853, the Reverend Jehiel Claflin appropriately commented:

> The secret of Miss Stone's eloquence is, she speaks from the *heart*. Hers are "thoughts that breathe and words that burn." Her soul is in the subject. Her heart and mind seem all radiant and luminous with love and truth, so elevating and soul-stirring, that she holds her hearers in perfect captivity, and in the language of another, it is beautifully true, that her "words sway the multitude as pendent vines swing in the summer breeze." Under her stirring appeals, the consciences of the people have been painfully aroused.[2]

Antoinette Brown. Lucy Stone was but the first among pioneer women orators to graduate from Oberlin College. Antoinette Brown, her devoted friend, finished the literary course of the college in 1847 and continued with professional work until 1850. For Antoinette wanted to enter the ministry and at Oberlin she could pursue theological study. Of course, she was granted no license upon her graduation—because even at Oberlin there was discrimination against her sex—but Antoinette persevered toward her goal, accepted the invitations of various ministers to fill their pulpits, and in 1852 was able to accept the appointment as pastor of the Congregational Church at South Butler, N. Y., as the one she preferred among several offerings.

During these two years Antoinette spent much effort in lecturing and study and soon identified herself with the popular reforms of the day. Frequently she would visit a community to lecture on a reform topic, usually woman's rights, at a Saturday evening meeting, and to preach in the community Sunday forenoon, afternoon, and evening. At other times she would preach on Sunday morning and afternoon and speak in the evening on a reform subject. She attended and addressed conventions and preached at such gatherings upon invitation. At the Plymouth County Anti-Slavery meeting in West Bridgewater, Mass., in 1851, for example, she was asked by the Reverend J. G. Forman, Congregational minister, to occupy his pulpit on Sunday afternoon. Antoinette spoke on "The Signs of the Times," and then the next session of the antislavery meeting was resumed in the basement of the church.[3]

Four thousand people assembled in Metropolitan Hall, New York City, on Sunday morning, September 4, 1853, to hear the Reverend Antoinette

---

[1] *Cf.* for example, speech before the American Anti-Slavery Convention, New York City, May 11, 1853, in *The Liberator*, May 27, 1853; speech before New England Anti-Slavery Convention, Boston, May 25, 1853, in *The Liberator*, June 17, 1853; "Taxation without Representation," address at Orange, N. J., Feb. 8, 1858, in *The Liberator*, Feb. 19, 1858.

[2] *The Liberator*, Sept. 2, 1853.

[3] *Ibid.*, Feb. 28, 1851.

Brown preach. To the citizens of the city, this was somewhat in keeping with the events of the season. It was Convention Week in New York City, and from near and far delegates had come to participate in reform meetings and to cause a disturbance in the peaceful existence of the community. As a representative delegate, Miss Brown, the twenty-eight year old minister, the capable lecturer, abolitionist, temperance worker, and women's righter, had been called upon to be the speaker at this Sunday-morning gathering, and Miss Brown acquitted herself well in a sermon based on Jeremiah XLIV:4, "O! do not this abominable thing, which I hate." The entire service was conducted in a spirit of solemnity and without turmoil of any kind.

Not so the meetings that Antoinette attended the following week. She endured, with the other reformers, the unfriendly notoriety of the Vegetarian Dinner and the scurrilous actions of spectators at the antislavery meetings, the Women's Temperance meeting and the Women's Rights convention. And when she attempted to exercise her right, as a duly appointed delegate from her local organization, to speak at the World's Temperance Convention, she excited a din of argument in the meetings that was the talk of Convention Week. The ridiculous part of this, as Antoinette herself confessed, was that she had intended merely to rise and thank the convention for its liberal attitude toward women in preparatory meetings. It was reaction toward the insolence of the convention members that caused her determination to show to the public the true nature of the temperance convention by attending and attempting to speak at later meetings.[1]

The result was an avalanche of newspaper articles and a great amount of public discussion, both vilifying and defending Antoinette's actions and the whole question of women's sphere and women's rights. Without a doubt, this attempt of Antoinette Brown to defend feminine liberty of speech won a great deal of sympathy for the women's cause in general.

Although Antoinette Brown's pastoral duties terminated in 1854, because of ill-health, and she returned to reside with her father at Henrietta, N. Y., for a while she continued to speak and to preach. In making a public explanation of her reasons for resigning her pastorate, Antoinette further exploded the traditional joke of feminine frailty by explaining clearly that a professional woman needed physical strength far beyond that of a professional man, because, in order to succeed, she had not only to fulfill the duties of his office but must continue a woman's duties of household activities, sewing, and feminine social obligations.[2]

[1] *The Una*, 1 (October, 1853): 148–149.
[2] *Ibid.*, 3 (March, 1855): 35–36.

Women's Introduction to the American Platform

Her marriage to Samuel C. Blackwell, brother of Lucy Stone's husband, in 1856, in no way impeded Antoinette's career, and from her new home in Newark, N. J. she continued to go forth to preach the gospel and to propagate reform. She preached upon such subjects as "Forgiveness of Sin," "Atonement," "Rewards and Penalties," "Redemption," and from such texts as "He that ruleth his spirit is greater than he that taketh a city," and "Prove all things, hold fast that which is good." Her reform lectures included discussions on "Slavery—Its Influence on Woman, and Her Duties in Relation to It" and "The Actual Existing Relationship of Women to Politics and Legislation and the Changes Needed." She lectured occasionally upon literary subjects and directed a portion of her energy to the writing of several books upon theological and other subjects.

In company with Susan B. Anthony, Antoinette campaigned in New York State for the temperance cause. With Miss Anthony and Ernestine L. Rose she went before the assembly committee of the New York state legislature to plead for just and equal rights for women. And to the cause of women's rights, the reform in which her chief interest lay from the beginning of her work, she continued to give her aid and was still speaking in its defense at the turn of the century.[1]

Antoinette Brown Blackwell was acclaimed as a model lecturer, whose speaking gave much strength to the cause of reform by supporting it with arguments based upon religious and moral teachings. Her oratorical power seemed to have emanated especially from her originality of expression and from the deep devotional sincerity with which she followed her self-appointed Christian duties. Her style was characterized as being classically elegant, her ideas clothed in "sentences superbly framed," and her lectures "sprinkled all over with rich metaphors and graphic figures." Her simplicity of manner and modest deportment, her gentleness of speech, "to which may be added her sound words of truth and soberness, plainly spoken," made her an able advocate for "down-trodden humanity." With very few gestures, no notes or manuscript, and with ease and beauty of diction, Antoinette impelled her audiences to the highest opinion of her superiority as a finished scholar and a high-minded woman—a compliment indeed for a nineteenth century woman.

As a minister, Antoinette Brown Blackwell filled her position with utmost grace and dignity. In answer to ribald jests about the "she-minister" and the "reverend miss in petticoats who administered sacraments in a night cap," her supporters united in upholding that her appearance upon the platform accorded with the sternest requirements of propriety and that

[1] *Cf.* Elizabeth C. Stanton, *et al.,* eds., *The History of Woman Suffrage* (Indianapolis, The Hollenbeck Press, 1902), IV, 292–293.

her services were conducted with the utmost dignity and in a very interesting manner.

The chief objection was that it just "didn't seem right to see a woman in the pulpit," but few refused to admit that she did not "acquit herself more than manfully." Said Harriet Beecher Stowe, in the minister's defense, "Can any one tell us why it should be right and proper for Jenny Lind to *sing* to two thousand people 'I know that my Redeemer liveth' and improper for Antoinette Brown to *say* it?"[1] And another admirer added, "In real eloquence, effective appeals and cogent reasoning, she is infinitely superior to three-fourths of those who now minister our pulpits."[2]

In thinking over the problem of women and the ministry, Antoinette concluded in 1854 that, in spite of candid and earnest opposition to be expected as long as honest and conscientious men believed that the Bible excluded women from the office of the ministry, and in spite of contumely and misrepresentation of every variety to call forth the fullest exercise of Christian patience and philanthropic magnanimity, any woman of talent could find ample work in the ministry, and because of the novelty of her position become more prominent before the public than if she were a gentleman. Confidently said this pioneer woman, who pointed the steps of women further in the direction of freedom of professional activity, "It is cheering to be able to say that there are many indications of a growing sentiment in favor of as various methods of explaining the teachings of St. Paul upon the position of woman, as there are of interpreting the nature of Jewish slavery. . . . The strong desire to hear a woman preach more than over-balances the disabilities under which she labors."[3]

Sallie Holley. The third of Oberlin's trio of pioneer women orators was Sallie Holley, daughter of Myron Holley, the famous reformer and founder of the Anti-Masonic party. Her father's favorite, Sallie experienced from childhood a companionship that ranged from listening ardently to his preaching in the Rochester Sunday morning courthouse meetings to helping him plant flowers in the family garden. She acquired many features of her father's mind—his liking for good books, for liberal religion—his passionate humanity and his courage in speaking out his convictions.[4]

The death of Myron Holley in 1841 brought upon Sallie the serious problem of what she was to do with herself—how she was to make the most of her talents. She could not imagine herself married and leading the usual life of a housewife, and even the most promising of her suitors she had to reject because "he had black eyes and voted for Henry Clay." And so

---

[1] *Frederick Douglass' Paper* (Rochester, N. Y.), Feb. 9, 1855.

[2] *Madison County Journal* (New York), cited in *The Liberator*, Feb. 25, 1853.

[3] *The Liberator*, Dec. 15, 1854.

[4] Holley, *op. cit.*, p. 35.

Sallie finally decided in favor of a career. Attracted by the coeducational advantages obtainable at Oberlin College and encouraged by the recommendations of the Rochester Unitarian minister, the Reverend Holland, and his gift of $40, Sallie made her way westward to Ohio. Her college career, begun in the winter of 1847, was a colorful one. When her money ran out, Sallie contributed to her own support by doing everything from washing dishes and baking bread at her boardinghouse to giving private lessons in arithmetic to young colored men who were trying to keep up with their classes.

Besides her scholastic studies, Sallie received training in the ways of reform agitation while she was at Oberlin. In company with Caroline Putnam and other progressive friends, she attended the antislavery and women's rights meetings held in the vicinity. To go to a woman's rights convention in Akron, for instance, they hired a horse and buggy for three days at the extravagant charge of 50 cents a day.

It was at an antislavery meeting in Litchfield, Ohio, that Sallie first heard Abby Kelley Foster speak. Sallie was so impressed that at the close of the meeting she offered herself for the Cause in answer to Mrs. Foster's plea for abolition advocates. Mrs. Foster welcomed the offer with warmth and gratitude, and begged Miss Holley to join her instantly on a campaign through Ohio. When Sallie replied that she could not join the Cause until she finished college the next year, Mrs. Foster suspected that the offer had been prompted by a mere overflow of youthful enthusiasm. But from that day forward, Sallie's plans were made toward the fulfillment of her promise. To her friend Miss Putnam she wrote, "Putty, I've decided to be an anti-slavery lecturer."[1]

In the summer of 1851 Sallie Holley began her career by joining in the Ohio campaign, and participated in holding conventions with Parker Pillsbury, Charles Burleigh, Sojourner Truth, and others. By September, she wrote to friends at home, "You are aware that I have already entered upon my work of anti-slavery lecturer. My love and interest in the great cause increases and swells and brightens every hour. It does seem to me that I have at last found out my 'sphere.'"[2]

It was not long before the abolitionists began to recognize the speaking ability of the new crusader, and word of the persuasiveness of the daughter of Myron Holley began to presage interest in and attendance at Sallie's lectures. In announcing a series of conventions to be held in western New York, the *National Anti-Slavery Standard* stated, for example, that

the privilege of hearing Miss Holley will for the first time be granted at these conventions; and we are quite sure that it will be esteemed as such when it is once

[1] *Ibid.*, pp. 59–60.
[2] *Ibid.*, p. 80.

enjoyed. The testimony which reaches us in regard to her is of the highest character. She is praised for great power of expression, for keen logical faculty, and for unusual graces of declamation; a combination, which renders her an eloquent, as well as persuasive and convincing speaker.[1]

On August 26, 1852, Sallie wrote to a friend from Abington, Mass., saying, "An anti-slavery lecturer's life has something apostolic in it, if it only be in going from town to town to preach the everlasting gospel. Today I was entertaining myself making out a memorandum of all the places and times I had lectured. I made out one hundred and fifty-six times."[2] Such a record, in addition to attending conventions and in light of the hardships of travel, was no mean record for an abolitionist's first year. And the eight years that remained before antislavery agitation was converted into active work for the Union forces in the Civil War witnessed an increasing amount of activity by Sallie Holley, accompanied by widespread renown.

Sallie's travels took her over much of the same ground as did those of the other antislavery agents. She lectured principally in Massachusetts and Delaware during 1852. In 1853 she traveled in Rhode Island, New Hampshire, and Michigan. Much of the time in the 1854 lecture season she spent in New York State, and the entire year of 1855 she devoted to work in Massachusetts. In 1856 and 1857 she again lectured in Rhode Island, western New York, and Michigan. In the summer of 1858 she held a series of meetings in Vermont, and as she wrote to Abby Kelley, "I never enjoyed a lecturing summer so much, though I have spoken more than forty times to the people. . . . Full of rural occupations as the month of August is, enough of the inhabitants have attended our meetings to make it well worth while to have continued them." In 1859 Sallie spent considerable time in Rhode Island, and traveled into Maine, where she was received so favorably that she joyfully exclaimed, "Anti-slavery is walking in silver slippers" in Maine.[3]

It seems that everywhere Sallie Holley went she was received with warm friendliness and that praise of her popularity and ability preceded her to the next town. If we look for evidence of opposition directed at Sallie Holley, we search in vain. And here is the reason. Sallie Holley's antislavery lecturing was different from that of the majority of agents. She lectured to the characteristically religious-minded folk of the middle nineteenth century in a manner that could not fail to appeal to them. She preached religious antislavery sermons.

[1] *National Anti-Slavery Standard*, cited in *The Liberator*, Mar. 26, 1852.
[2] Holley, *op. cit.*, 87.
[3] *The Liberator*, Sept. 10, 1858; Oct. 7, 1859.

Sallie opened her meetings with prayer, either given by herself or by a member of the audience in answer to her plea for a volunteer. She then usually read a portion from the Bible and, using the Scripture as a text, proceeded to give her lecture. For example, Thomas Garret's report of Sallie's lecture in Wilmington, Del., on October 29, 1852, tells us that

at the opening of the meeting, Sallie read a few verses, both from the Old and New Testament, showing that Jesus and His apostles, with the ancient patriarchs, were opposed to slavery and oppression of every kind; and she commented these passages in a very appropriate and effective manner. She then closed the book, and invited anyone who felt qualified, and wished to do so, to offer vocal prayer. After a short pause, she arose, and addressed the assembly for nearly an hour, with one of the most thrilling anti-slavery discourses I have ever listened to. She drew such a picture of the cruelty and inhumanity of slavery . . . as I have seldom listened to; particularly the outrages committed on her own sex, by irresponsible slaveholders and their overseers. Notwithstanding several hundred had to stand during her address, the audience remained quiet and attentive to the close.[1]

We are told that so captivating was Sallie's manner and so lovely her melodious voice that she led her audiences on to listen quietly to as radical antislavery principles as those preached by any of the Garrisonian abolitionists. The secret of Sallie's success was, without a doubt, in her method of approach and in her direct appeals to the sympathy of her listeners. So earnest was her fervency of appeal, so adequate her fund of argument and illustrative facts, so keen her logical reasoning, so delightful her grace of declamation that she was able everywhere to command attention, admiration, and belief. At a meeting held in Portsmouth, N. H. on April 17, 1853, for instance, Sallie addressed her audience for over an hour and received "close attention to the end." A newspaper report of the occasion added, "We never knew such sweeping statements as she made—such scathing rebukes—such bitter denunciation as hers, received so quietly."[2]

Sallie's method of speaking found great favor among her audiences. "What we want," wrote an auditor at her lecture in Hingham, Mass. on April 8, 1853, "is earnest, faithful, heart-searching, revival preaching—and that was the character of our friend Miss Holley's discourse." Mr. Noyes, in writing to Garrison concerning the same lecture, exclaimed, "Oh that we had a thousand such women as she to go through the length and breadth of this guilty nation, proclaiming the gospel of freedom and Christianity."[3]

One of the most interesting reports of Sallie's lectures tells of an outdoor meeting held in a grove near Buxton, Me., on August 16, 1859. The meeting was said to be

---

[1] *Ibid.*, Nov. 12, 1852.
[2] *Portsmouth Daily Chronicle*, cited in *The Liberator*, May 6, 1853.
[3] *The Liberator*, Apr. 15, 1853; Apr. 22, 1853.

far the most numerous and successful anti-slavery meeting ever held in Buxton. For an hour and a half Miss Holley held her audience in rapt attention by the sincere and heart-felt truths she uttered. The people seemed taken by surprise. Instead of a declaiming female fanatic, they met one who had a message from God to them. . . . Even the youth were affected deeply by her truthful words. . . . Except a few old political fogies, who believed that slave-holding and pro-slavery voters can be good Christian church members, none found fault. . . . There was a great amount of prejudice against female speaking that found a grave that day, which will not be soon resuscitated.[1]

And so labored Sallie Holley—preacher of reform—begging to be allowed to carry the one Cause to which she had consecrated her life, not to the cities of the United States but to the out-of-the-way communities—to the people who had few opportunities to hear antislavery "truth." As a report in the *Liberator* of April 25, 1856, stated, "We should call her a preacher of anti-slavery righteousness, rather than a lecturer. All that we hear speak of it say they never heard such preaching. She is an anti-slavery revivalist, full of a wonderful mastery over the heart."

The Final Emergence, 1850–1865

Sallie Holley and her seven compeers mentioned above are but representatives of a large group of pioneer women orators. To record adequately the history of women's oratory even of this early period would require several volumes.

The 1850's alone saw a great expansion of public-speaking activity among women. As reform movements gained in strength, so the participation of women as speaking advocates increased. Temperance organizations, among which was the famous Daughters of Temperance Society, grew in strength. The Women's Temperance Society of New York was able, in 1852, to hire a half dozen agents, at salaries of $25 per month and expenses, to lecture throughout the state, to secure membership to the society, signatures to "the pledge," and petitions to the legislature.[2] The Women's Rights movement, organized in 1848, offered countless opportunities during the next decade for the development of public-speaking ability among women.

As agitators, women continued largely to be universal reformers, embracing all reforms in their interest and specializing in one or two. As speakers, they won notoriety or acclaim by various modes of action or methods of persuasion. Emma Coe, one of the first women lawyers, enhanced the effectiveness of her arguments by applying legal knowledge

[1] *Ibid.*, Sept. 2, 1859.
[2] D. C. Bloomer, *Life and Writings of Amelia Bloomer* (Boston, Arena Publishing Co., 1895), pp. 85–86.

184

in lectures such as those on "The Pecuniary Position of Women" and "American Slavery and the Fugitive Slave Law" and seeking to win her audiences by solid reasoning and an obvious lack of anathemas. Amelia Bloomer, attired in the costume that had been named after her, attracted huge crowds to her temperance lectures in 1853 and still spoke to large audiences a few years later, when she no longer wore the Bloomer dress and no longer relied upon carefully written manuscripts. Mrs. Charles Spear illustrated her lectures for prison reform with realistic prison scenes. Jane Elizabeth Hitchcock and Jane Grey Swisshelm rivaled Abby Kelley in ability at denunciation. Mrs. Lydia A. Jenkins elicited favorable comment for her attainment of a place in the Unitarian ministry and for her work for temperance. Jane Elizabeth Jones, Mrs. C. I. H. Nichols, and Rebecca M. Sandford combined their lecturing activities with newspaper editorship. Among the Negro women orators, so ably bringing honor to their sponsors, the abolitionists, were Sojourner Truth, that unrivaled artist of native wit, Frances Ellen Watkins, writer and poet, and Sarah P. Remond, scholar in the history of human rights.

The expansion of women's public-speaking activity in the 1850's was not only in numbers but in variety of subjects propounded. Women, following the belief that if knowledge of the human body and its functioning were propagated, the prevailing delicacy among women (a potential reason for their subordinate state as literally the "weaker" sex) might be overcome, continued to lecture upon health and medicine to audiences composed of women. Mary Gove, Paulina Wright Davis, Mary Ann Johnson, Dr. Harriot Hunt, and other "physiology lecturers," who had pursued medical study in spite of all obstacles, were in great demand as health lecturers. Such women as Elizabeth Oakes Smith, Caroline H. Dall, Sarah Jane Lippincott, and Frances D. Gage gave, in addition to their lectures upon reform, public speeches on cultural subjects, upon literature, and upon travel. Other women, including Anna Cora Mowatt, Fanny Kemble Butler, and Mary Webb, the "Black Siddons," gained renown as elocutionists.

Women's names began to appear in the lists of professional lecturers advertised in the newspapers at the beginning of lecture seasons. The *New York Daily Tribune's* lyceum list for 1859 contained the names of 203 lecturers "ready for engagement as public lecturers the present season," and twelve of the names on this list were those of women.[1] That the names of twelve professional woman lecturers appeared in one advertisement assumes significance if compared with the fact that only two decades earlier women were not allowed to speak before the general public.

---

[1] *New York Daily Tribune*, Sept. 9, 1859.

With the beginning of the Civil War, endeavor in the North was immediately directed toward furthering the effectiveness of the Union forces. To this the women reformers at once turned their attention. They contributed their skill to help marshal clothing and supplies for the army. Through the medium of such organizations as the Sanitary Commission, the Christian Commission, and the Woman's Central Relief Association of New York, they aided in providing for the physical and spiritual needs of the soldiers. In the hospitals they worked valiantly and raised their voices to comfort and entertain the wounded men. They participated in the formation and activities of the Woman's Loyal League, the purpose of which was to awaken public sentiment by writing and speaking and to secure signatures to petition Congress demanding a Federal amendment forever abolishing slavery in the United States.[1]

Between 1861 and 1865, Anna E. Dickinson, the lyceum star of the late nineteenth century, gained unparagoned fame throughout the North as an orator upon war questions and political issues. She was often termed the Joan of Arc of the Union and of Republicanism, was said to be a walking encyclopedia of the events of the Rebellion, and was praised as one of the most outstanding orators of either sex of the time. Early in 1862 Anna Dickinson was pleading for a proclamation of Negro freedom and for united effort to bring the war to an immediate end. She proved to be an invaluable aid in the Republican campaign of the same year. In 1864 she aided the cause of the Negro by benefit lectures such as the one for the National Freedman's Relief Society, given in the Hall of the House of Representatives in Washington, D.C., to a throng that numbered among its members President and Mrs. Lincoln. And the year 1865 saw her pleading for a moral battle that would vanquish the "idea" of slavery left unconquered at the end of the war. Said a report of her lecture in Portland, Me., in February, 1865, "It was certainly the strongest illustration of woman's power on the platform—and the *power* carried with it the *right* to be there—that we ever witnessed."[2]

The Significance

The end of the Civil War brought with it the end of the first chapter of women's oratory. And although the exciting days of anti-slavery agitation were forever at an end, the new period immediately following was to bring forth a continuation of the public-speaking activities of women along every conceivable line, especially those of the ever-new old reforms. The one

[1] Elizabeth C. Stanton, *et al.*, eds., *The History of Woman Suffrage* (Rochester, N. Y., Charles Mann, 1887), II, 50.

[2] *Portland Transcript*, cited in *The Liberator*, Mar. 3, 1865.

all-important connecting link between the work accomplished by the pioneer women orators and the activity undertaken by the group of women public speakers of the new era was the struggle for the emancipation and enfranchisement of women. And serving as transition orators, their actions based upon the experiences of their work and associations in the 1850's, such women as Susan B. Anthony, Elizabeth Cady Stanton, Caroline Severance, and Matilda J. Gage became the leaders of the second period and with the many new recruits, including Julia Ward Howe, Frances Willard, Isabella Beecher Hooker, Carrie Chapman Catt, Dr. Lee Anna Star, Dr. Anna H. Shaw, and others, furthered the art of eloquence among women and completed the emancipation of women upon the American public platform as a heritage for the Ruth Bryan Owen Rohdes, Aimee Semple McPhersons, and Dorothy Thompsons of the 1930's and 1940's.

Viewed from the historical approach, with the perspective that even the brief span of intervening years provides, the first period of women's oratory in America assumes a significance that has been flagrantly neglected. To date, historians and sociologists have failed to emphasize the importance of the public platform in the history of women's rights and emancipation. They have overlooked voluminous evidence that women's speaking in public is a factor as worthy of consideration in the study of the progress of American women as the inventions of the Middle Period that began to provide women with leisure time and the humanitarian movement that pointed the way to greater individual equality.

It was the reform platform, occupying only a small area of activity in North and West but offering equality of individual participation and freedom of speech—the reform platform engendered by the need of the Age of Experimentation—together with the profession of public speaking, occupying its place of paramount importance in the lives of nineteenth century America, that proved to be one of women's most helpful stepping-stones from the obscurity of the domestic circle to the joys and woes of public life. In claiming the public platform for their use, the pioneer women orators set the precedent for and helped to establish the propriety of women as participants in and not merely spectators of public life. For in 1828 speaking in public by women was an unheard of practice in America, and in 1860 it was a common occurrence, if not happily accepted, at least countenanced by public opinion. In the years between these dates the change came, gradual enough if considered in the light of contemporary events, but startingly swift if viewed as a part of the long history of women. By their insistence on facing and conquering hazardous obstacles of public disapproval and opposition toward both their actions and their incendiary subject matter, which would try even the most courageous, pioneer women

187

orators proved the sincere determination of women to fight for their alleged rights. By speaking and lecturing they exemplified women's true intellectual and physical capabilities, helped to incite thought that led to the improvement of the legal, economic, and educational status of women, and not only hastened but helped to render inevitable the ultimate emancipation and enfranchisement of American women.⌉

⌈And to reform speaking pioneer women orators gave an eloquence based not upon a knowledge of rhetorical rules and oratorical fashions but upon the inspiration of an impelling need to be heard, upon the fervor of religious and moral conviction and upon the spontaneity of enthusiasm in purpose, that enabled them to appeal from their hearts directly to the great heart of the people. For women, in order to become orators, must bury themselves in themes greater than ordinary subjects—in crusades that demand individual selflessness—and these women of the Middle Period were fighting not only for unpopular reform issues but for the right to prove themselves as public speakers.⌉

Likewise have chronologists omitted giving credit to women public speakers for worthy contributions to the reform movements of the humanitarian era. To balance the additional notoriety they brought to reform propagation, women orators stirred up increased thought and questioning upon the subjects of freedom and equality and converted many who saw in their difficulties the inconsistencies between principles and practices of democracy. To countervail the disorderliness they often caused in meetings, they brought to a short stop any tendencies among reform leaders to exhibit variance between policies and practices in upholding equality of speech and participation. To compensate for the dissension they created in reform organizations, causing, as they did in large part, the split of the American Anti-Slavery Society in 1840, they helped to keep the vision of the reform goals unimpeded by vested power and political and individual interests. To make amends for the numbers their speaking deleted from support of reform movements, they persuaded the opening of the pocketbooks in many homes by creating confidence among timid members of their sex; they gave liberally of their own substance and, in such cases as that of Abby Kelley, of their entire patrimony; and they won financial support by their pleas from the platform. To equiponderate the radical tendencies they provoked in left-wing doctrines, they gave inspiration and consecration of purpose and spurred on the crusading spirit, for their own status constantly reminded them of the goals for which they themselves must never-ceasingly agitate.

⌈Only recently have those concerned with the history of oral persuasion in this country begun to ponder over the possibility that women may have made some contribution to this field of speech. Contemporary reports and the few accurately reported speeches available at the present time substantiate the skill of the pioneer women speakers. In a word, these women were versatile extemporaneous persuaders with inspiring messages and fine voices. To oratory—an art characterized by ornamental style and exaggerated eloquence—they brought simplicity of expression, sincerity of purpose, and enhancement of goal over speaker. They helped mightily in toppling oratory off its rhetorical stilts and in guiding it toward a more natural, straightforward, and conversational means of communication. They helped to make it possible for oratory to enjoy the conversational camaraderie and warm psychological persuasion it possesses today.

CRITICAL ESSAY ON SELECTED AUTHORITIES

Contemporary Periodicals

A study of more than ninety contemporary periodicals, including practically every variety from penny dailies to religious monthlies, reveals that the reform newspapers are the chroniclers of the history of women's oratory. In their pages also are to be found many of the records of meetings and conventions that are less easily accessible in pamphlet form. If the bibliography of the first chapter of women's speaking were limited to one source, it would be the famous abolition weekly, *The Liberator*, edited by William Lloyd Garrison at Boston from 1831 to 1865, in which women orators received what appears to be their greatest amount of recognition. The many "exchange articles," printed verbatim from other newspapers of every political and reform policy, the "Refuge of Oppression," a first-page section devoted especially to the printings of the opposition press,[1] and the advocacy of women's speaking that resulted in a careful chronology of their activities, praise for worthy representatives, and frank but kindly criticism for speakers of lesser ability render *The Liberator* a less prejudiced source and a more valuable aid than cursory examination would predict.

Among the other reform newspapers that yield helpful information upon women's speaking are *The Practical Christian* (Hopedale, Mass.), the *Herald of Freedom* (Concord, N. H.), the *Anti-Slavery Bugle* (Salem, Ohio), the *National Anti-Slavery Standard* (New York), *Frederick Douglass' Paper* (Rochester, N. Y.), the *Pennsylvania Freeman* (Philadelphia), and *The Free Enquirer* (New York). *The Emancipator* (New York),[2] *The Friend of Man* (Utica, N. Y.), and the *Philanthropist* (New Richmond and, later, Cincinnati, Ohio) are helpful in depicting antislavery and reform activities but contain little specific information upon women.

---

[1] Garrison, writing in *The Liberator*, Jan. 8, 1847, explained that all articles found in the "Refuge of Oppression" were to be branded with condemnation and added: "We are satisfied that, while no part of *The Liberator* is more carefully perused than this novel one, it has done more to shame our assailants, to demonstrate the righteousness of our course, and to secure for us co-operation of thoughtful and reflective minds, than the most able articles that have been written in our defence. The future historian of the abolition of American slavery, on being furnished with the files of *The Liberator* will find nearly all the materials he can require to complete his history on both sides of the question."

[2] The name of this paper was changed to *Emancipator and Free American* in 1842.

The more conservative newspapers often followed the policy that to ignore women's speaking was one highly effective weapon of opposition. Whether or not this is the reason, the following papers aid only by presenting an occasional report, rebuke, or exchange article: *Daily Evening Transcript* (Boston), *New York Daily Times*, *New York Daily Tribune*, and *New York Weekly Herald*. The *Home Journal* (New York) is especially good for reports of lectures and entertainment taking place in New York City.

The *Lily* (Seneca Falls, N. Y.) and *The Una* (Providence, R. I.), contain a number of articles on women speakers and from all observations, seem to be the only periodicals devoted especially to women that upheld their activities upon the platform. *Godey's Lady's Book* (Philadelphia) is an invaluable source for a picture of the social life of the times, for the life and interests of women in general, and for a sane, middle-of-the-road policy about women's rights.

Letters, Memoirs, and Speeches

A dearth of material of this nature greets the bibliographer, for many of the women orators so opposed publicity that they burned personal materials, had little use or time for the popular custom of keeping journals, and very infrequently recorded the content of their speeches. *Course of Popular Lectures* (London, James Watson, 1829 and 1834), by Frances Wright; *Discourse on Woman . . .* (Philadelphia, W. P. Kildare, 1869), *A Sermon to the Medical Students* (Philadelphia, Merrihew and Thompson, 1849), by Lucretia Mott; *An Address on Woman's Rights . . .* (Boston, J. P. Mendum, 1851), by Ernestine L. Rose; *Address to the Legislature of New York* (Albany, N. Y., Weed, Parsons and Co., 1854), *Address Delivered at Seneca Falls and Rochester, New York, July 19th and August 2, 1848* (New York, Robert J. Johnston, 1870), by Elizabeth Cady Stanton; *The College, the Market and the Court* (Boston, Lee and Shepard, 1867) and *Woman's Right to Labor* (Boston, Walker, Wise and Co., 1860), by Caroline H. Dall number among the few speeches printed outside newspaper columns. Letters, reminiscences, and several speech texts are to be found in the following: Lucy N. Colman, *Reminiscences* (Buffalo, H. L. Green, 1891); Gilbert H. Garnes and D. L. Dumond, eds., *Letters of Theodore Dwight Weld, Angelina Grimké Weld, and Sarah Grimké 1822-1844* (2 vols., New York, D. Appleton-Century, Company, Inc., 1934); Anna D. Hallowell, ed., *James and Lucretia Mott, Life and Letters* (Boston, Houghton, Mifflin Company, 1884); John W. Chadwick, ed., *A Life for Liberty, Anti-Slavery, and Other Letters of Sallie Holley* (New York, G. P. Putnam's Sons, 1899); Harriot K. Hunt, *Glances and Glimpses* (Boston, John P. Jewett and Co., 1856); Frances Ann Kemble, *Records of Later Life* (New York, Henry Holt and Company, Inc., 1884); Mary A. Livermore, *The Story of My Life* (Hartford, Conn., A. D. Worthington and Co., 1899); Elizabeth C. Stanton, *Eighty Years and More* (New York, European Publishing Co., 1898); and Sojourner Truth, *Narrative of Sojourner Truth* (Boston, J. B. Yerrinton and Son, 1850).

Biographies

A few individual biographies, largely eulogistic, but of value in their factual and background material are Catherine H. Birney, *Sarah and Angelina Grimké* (Boston, Lee and Shepard, 1885); Alice S. Blackwell, *Lucy Stone* (Boston, Little, Brown & Company, 1930); D. C. Bloomer, *Life and Writings of Amelia Bloomer* (Boston, Arena Publishing Co., 1895); Amos Gilbert, *Memoir of Frances Wright* (Cincinnati, Longley Brothers, 1855); Florence H. Hall, *Julia Ward Howe and the Woman Suffrage Movement* (Boston, Dana Estes and Co., 1913); I. H. Harper, *The Life and Work of Susan B. Anthony* (3 vols. Indianapolis, The Hollenbeck Press, 1898-1908); William R. Waterman; *Frances Wright* (Columbia University Studies in History, Economics and Public Law, Vol. 25, 1925); and Mary Alice Wyman, *Two*

Women's Introduction to the American Platform

American Pioneers: Seba Smith and Elizabeth Oakes Smith (New York, Columbia University Press, 1927).

Supplementary Materials

In books upon many themes, written by contemporary nineteenth century authors and by modern writers who concern themselves with people and events of the Middle Period, a paragraph here—a page there—unexpectedly pops up to tell about women's activities in public and upon the platform. The many English travel books, such as the following, furnish frequent and helpful comments: Fredrika Bremer, *The Homes of the New World* (Mary Howitt, translator, 2 vols., New York, Harper & Brothers, 1853); J. S. Buckingham, Esq., *America, Historical, Statistic, and Descriptive* (3 vols., London, Fisher, Son and Co., 1841); George Combe, *Notes on the United States of North America during a Phrenological Visit in* 1838-9-40 (2 vols. Philadelphia, Carey and Hart, 1841); Marianne Finch, *An Englishwoman's Experience in America* (London, Richard Bentley, 1853); Harriet Martineau, *Society in America* (2 vols., New York, Saunders and Otley, 1837); Mrs. Trollope, *Domestic Manners of the Americans* (2d ed., 2 vols., London, printed for Whittaker, Treacher and Co., 1832).

The many autobiographies, letters, lectures, and reminiscences of prominent men of the nineteenth century and the numerous books written about them, yield information upon the women. Among the most accommodating are Oliver Johnson, *William Lloyd Garrison and His Times,* (Boston, B. B. Russell and Co., 1880); Wendell P. Garrison and Francis J. Garrison, *William Lloyd Garrison* (4 vols., New York, The Century Company, 1885 and 1889); Frederick Douglass, *Life and Times of Frederick Douglass* (Hartford, Conn., Park Publishing Co., 1884); Robert Dale Owen, *Threading My Way* (New York, G. W. Carleton and Co., 1874); Henry B. Stanton, *Random Recollections* (New York, MacGowan and Slipper, 1886); Philip Hone, *The Diary of Philip Hone,* 1828-1851 (Allan Nevins, ed., 2 vols., New York, Dodd, Mead & Company, Inc., 1927); Wendell Phillips, *Speeches, Lectures and Letters* (2d series, Boston, Lee and Shepard, 1894); Samuel J. May, *Some Recollections of Our Anti-Slavery Conflict* (Boston, Fields, Osgood and Co., 1869); and Parker Pillsbury, *Acts of the Anti-Slavery Apostles* (Boston, Cupples, Upham and Co., 1884).

In the books advocating "women's sphere" and denouncing "women's rights" is interesting and colorful material, and to this lore belong the contributions of Timothy S. Arthur, *Advice to Young Ladies on Their Duties and Conduct in Life* (Boston, G. W. Cottrell and Co., 1851); Charles Butler, *The American Lady* (Philadelphia, Hogan and Thompson, 1836); Morgan Dix, *Lectures on the Calling of a Christian Woman and Her Training to Fulfill It* (New York, D. Appleton-Century Company, Inc., 1883); and the Reverend Hubbard Winslow and Mrs. John Sanford, *The Lady's Manual of Moral and Intellectual Culture* (New York, Leavitt and Allen, 1854).

Antislavery books are of value: Maria W. Chapman, *Right and Wrong in Massachusetts* (Boston, Henry L. Devereux, 1840); James F. Clarke, *Anti-Slavery Days* (New York, John W. Lovell Co., 1883); William Goodell, *Slavery and Anti-Slavery* (New York, William Harned, 1852); and Eliza Wigham, *The Anti-Slavery Cause in America and Its Martyrs* (London, A. W. Bennett, 1863).

The most useful work upon woman's rights, the first two volumes of which contain a wealth of factual material upon the activities of the pioneers, is *The History of Woman Suffrage,* (Elizabeth Cady Stanton, *et al.*, eds., 2 vols., Rochester, N. Y., Charles Mann, 1887, Indianapolis, The Hollenbeck Press, 1902, New York, J. J. Little Ives and Co., 1922). Mary Woolstonecraft, *A Vindication of the Rights of Woman* (Philadelphia, William Gibbons, 1792) should preface any study of the history of women. Virginia Penny, *The Employments of Women: A Cyclopaedia of Woman's Work* (Boston, Walker, Wise and Co., 1863) tells of the economic side of women's early progress. Thomas W. Higginson's *Common Sense about*

Women (London, Swan Sonnenschein and Co., 1891) gives a common-sense liberal reaction toward women's rights. Other helpful books upon women's activities include L. P. Brockett *Woman's Work in the Civil War* (Philadelphia, Zeigler, McCurdy and Co., 1867); Carrie C. Catt and Nettie R. Shuler, *Woman Suffrage and Politics* (New York, Charles Scribner's Sons, 1926); Paulina W. Davis, comp., *A History of the National Woman's Rights Movement* (New York, Journeymen Printers' Co-operative Association, 1871); Lydia H. Farmer, *What America Owes to Women,* (New York, Charles Wells Moulton, 1893); Phebe A. Hanaford, *Daughters of America* (Augusta, Me., True and Co., 1883); and May W. Sewall, ed., *The World's Congress of Representative Women* (Chicago, Rand McNally & Company, 1894).

The Teaching of Rhetoric in the United States during the Classical Period of Education

by OTA THOMAS

General Overview

Education, it has often been contended, reflects the temper of the age in which it exists. Certainly this seems true of the development of the teaching of speech in America. The New World, founded partly because of religious dissension in the old, felt that one of the immediate needs was for spiritual leaders. Accordingly, schools were established to train ministers of the gospel, and the curriculums of those schools followed the principles currently accepted for theological training. The classical languages, logic, and rhetoric constituted part of that preparation. At the outset, college students were required to speak in Latin, not only in their formal speech appearances but in their conversation as well.[1] Scholastic debates were couched in the Roman tongue and carried on in the stilted manner of formal logic. But Colonial Americans faced a hard life, with little time for such luxuries as conversational command of an outmoded language. Before long the vernacular triumphed as the method of informal communication in the college. Subsequently, as governmental and political institutions developed and it became apparent that leaders were needed for affairs other than the saving of men's souls, the colleges turned their attention more directly to the training of lawyers, doctors, and teachers. From the beginning, it must be remembered, colleges were functioning as professional schools no less than as liberalizing institutions. Before the opening of the nineteenth century, courses in surveying, navigation, anatomy, and geography were recognized and accepted in the New England colleges. For

[1] The first laws of Harvard as set forth by President Dunster in *New England's First Fruits*, in 1642, demanded that "the Scholars shall never use their Mother toungue except that in publike Exercises of oratory or such like, they bee called to make them in English." The Yale laws of 1726 contained a similar provision.

men with secular interests, speech training based only on the Latin of Cicero and the syllogisms of Aristotle served little practical need. Thus, on demand of student and layman alike, the study of English grammar, literature, and speech was introduced into the higher institutions.

During the Revolution, the British occupied many college towns. William and Mary, Princeton, Yale, Harvard, Pennsylvania, and King's colleges were among those to feel the impact of invasion. In the midst of death, destruction, and hunger, students turned from abstractions to the immediate problems at hand. Ready and forceful discussion of contemporary issues demanded a free, flexible form of argument delivered in the vernacular. The difficulty of expression in the Latin language and the rigidity of the syllogistic forms were inhibiting to thought. Thus the trend toward anglicizing and informalizing speech training in the colleges was hastened by the political turmoil of the eighteenth century. The demand was for the solution of legal and governmental problems, and in adjusting its techniques to this demand speech training seemed to justify itself.

The greatest practical changes in speech education during the first two centuries of American collegiate history were, then, the transfer from the Latin to the English medium of communication and the inauguration of training in forensic debate during the latter half of the eighteenth century.

With the changes in the practical aspects of speech training came changes in the theories that governed the practices. When debate was confined to formal logic and speech performances were delivered in the classical languages, the preeminent rhetorical concepts posed for student mastery dealt primarily with stylistic perfection. Disputations were the legitimate offspring of logic, and proficiency in defending a conviction in these student arguments was relatively little related to mastery of rhetorical principles. In other oral exercises collegiate speakers strove for elegance of language. Then, as the training modified its goal and concerned itself with the development of effective speakers, using the vernacular, the theoretical precepts in turn were modified to conform to the necessity for persuasion in lay speaking. As college students attempted to perfect the art of convincing others, the four divisions of rhetoric as conceived by Aristotle once more gained ascendancy. The tool of this broader rhetoric was oratory; its primary medium of communication was speech.

With the increasing demand for effectual lay speaking, writers for the first time devoted whole books to discussions of delivery—an aspect of rhetoric that Aristotle, Cicero, and their followers had largely ignored. During the late eighteenth and nineteenth centuries the enthusiasm for working principles of oral presentation flourished both in England and America. The writers on elocution refined and detailed their treatments.

194

The Teaching of Rhetoric in the United States

With the growing emphasis placed on delivery, rhetoric became more and more associated with the written word, and spoken language became considered chiefly a matter of elocution. During the nineteenth century, speech training was largely conceived as learning and practicing mechanical rules for oral communication.

By the middle of the nineteenth century student speech performances were conducted mainly in the English language. The classical rhetorical principles expounded in the American colleges found practical application in frequent disputes, as well as in the older, accepted types of collegiate speaking exercises. Furthermore, specialized and intensive training in elocution supplemented the persuasive techniques acquired in the rhetoric classes.

Speech in the Curriculums

From the time the first classes met on the Harvard campus, training in the theory and practice of speechmaking held an acknowledged place in higher education. The early laws of William and Mary did not specify any definite courses in rhetoric, yet the statutes of 1792 provided that candidates for the bachelor's degree must "be well acquainted with Logic, Belles Letters [*sic*], Rhetoric," as well as other prescribed subject fields.[1] According to the Harvard laws of 1643 and 1655 and those of Yale in 1726, the study of rhetoric was required of all students throughout their undergraduate preparation. Later statutes[2] of these colleges demanded only one year's classwork in that branch of learning—that year to be completed before reaching junior standing.

Following the curtailment of time devoted to rhetoric, certain other important curricular adjustments relating to speech education occurred. The first of these changes was the introduction of the study of English grammar, composition, and literature into the curriculums. Yale first hesitantly granted classroom recognition to English speech and language on October 26, 1776, when the Corporation, at the request of the seniors, voted that Timothy Dwight be allowed "to instruct them in rhetoric, history, and the belles lettres, provided it may be done with the approbation

[1] Auguston Davis, "Statutes of the University of William and Mary, Richmond," reprinted in *William and Mary Quarterly*, 25 (1792): 58.

[2] The Laws of Harvard College, 1767, MS in Harvard Archives; *Laws of Harvard College*, (Boston, Samuel Hall, 1790); *Laws of Harvard College*, (Boston, Samuel Hall, 1798); Laws of Yale College Made and Established by the President and Tutors, 1745, MS in Yale Library; *Laws of Yale-College in New Haven, in Connecticut, Enacted by the President and Fellows* (New Haven, Thomas and Samuel Green, 1774); *Laws of Yale-College in New Haven, in Connecticut, Enacted by the President and Fellows, the Sixth Day of October, A.D.* 1795 (New Haven, Thomas and Samuel Green). When the official curriculum was first formally set forth at Dartmouth in 1796 rhetoric was required only during the freshman year.

of the parents or guardians of said class."[1] Harvard had legislated regarding the teaching of English in 1766, when the tutorial plan of the college was changed from a class to a subject-matter basis. The ruling provided that all students report to their tutors on Saturday morning to be instructed in "Theology, Elocution, Composition in English, Rhetoric, and other Belles Lettres, according to the direction of the Corporation from time to time."[2] Seemingly, English had been taught in the Grammar School at William and Mary since its founding, and specific reference is found in 1772 to "a course of lectures on . . . poetry, including the general principles of composition."[3]

The introduction of such courses was important. The English language had been accepted as a recognized medium for speech performances. Naturally, facility in handling the mother tongue was imperative to students in oral performances, particularly because most of these exercises were written in full and read aloud.

The second important development was the inauguration in the early 1800's of courses devoted to the delivery of speeches. E. D. North, who wrote his book in 1846 outlining the procedure by which elocution was taught at Yale, had been instructing in that subject for more than a quarter of a century at New Haven, and plainly he considered the course as a complement to the study of rhetoric.[4]

Another compensation attending the reduced emphasis on rhetoric in the curriculum was the increased opportunity for actual student participation in speaking exercises, particularly in declamations. In the last half of the eighteenth century authorities at both Yale and Harvard encouraged more students to declaim each week.[5]

Still another significant development in the teaching of speech was its recognition as a separate and distinct subject field, organized in course form. In 1806 John Quincy Adams was appointed to the Boylston Chair of Rhetoric and Oratory at Harvard. It was the first such appointment in the United States. Previously the subject had been taught by some tutor

[1] Yale Corporation Records, cited in Wm. L. Kingsley, *Yale College*, (New York, Henry Holt and Company, Inc., 1879), I, 99.

[2] Harvard College Records, II, 271.

[3] *The Virginia Gazette*, Jan. 2, 1772.

[4] E. D. North, *Practical Speaking as Taught at Yale* (New Haven, T. H. Pease, 1846). For a full treatment of the diversification of courses in speech after 1835, see the study by Thomas E. Coulton noted in the bibliography at the end of this chapter.

[5] The Yale laws of 1745 required six students to declaim each week; by 1755 twelve declamations were demanded weekly. Harvard provided in its early laws for such weekly performances also, but did not specify a definite number of participants. On Nov. 10, 1766, additional speaking opportunities were provided by a vote of the Corporation asserting that "Sophimores and Freshmen shall on Fryday mornings thro' ye year declaim in the chamber of their Tutors respectively."

who also instructed in numerous other fields and was frequently not specifically prepared for teaching speech. But after Adams began his duties, other colleges established similar professorships. From this meager beginning have sprung the speech departments of the present day.

Speech Practices in the Colleges

In addition to the classes devoted to the acquisition of theory, students were required to demonstrate the practical application of rhetorical concepts in frequent speaking exercises. The 1727 statutes of William and Mary, which did not call for the study of rhetoric, required of all students both declamations and disputations. The declamation, which originally had meant a short composition in one of the ancient languages, written and delivered *memoriter*, had been one of the most popular of these weekly exercises. Not until 1751 do any indications appear that the English tongue was permissible. At that time Benjamin Franklin wrote to one of the Yale trustees: "I am glad you have introduced English declamation into your college. It will be of great service to the youth, especially if care be taken to form their pronunciation on the best models. . . . It is a matter that hath been too much neglected."[1] The legalizing of English for speech exercises was accompanied by the introduction of English grammar and composition into the curriculums, for the common medium of expression was increasingly regarded as worthy of study. The clamor for a "practical" education was already producing tangible results. After the lapse from Latin, the term *declamation* was enlarged to include the delivery of an excerpt from another author. Thus John Quincy Adams delivered at Cambridge in 1786 a cutting from *As You Like It* to fulfill his curricular declamation requirement;[2] members of the Harvard Speaking Club recited bits of composition from such varied sources as English histories, Demosthenes' orations, all types of poetry, and contemporary sermons. Students were probably encouraged in this activity by the elocutionists, who included in their books practice selections for the mastery of specific dicta.

In the earliest days of the colleges, *commonplacing*, or the delivery of original sermons, had been required, as well as the repeating of the context of sermons attended. As the institutions became more secular and the purpose of education became broader than that of preparing ministers, this requirement was abandoned.

Another type of oral activity, destined for enormous popularity, was the disputation. Until the mid-point of the eighteenth century the disputes,

[1] *The Writings of Benjamin Franklin* (Albert Henry Smyth, ed., New York, The Macmillan Company, 1907), III, 61.

[2] John Quincy Adams, college diary, cited in Henry Adams, "Old Cambridge and New," *North American Review*, 114 (1872): 132.

though presented orally, had been exercises in formal logic, conducted by means of syllogisms in the Latin tongue. After 1750 the more utilitarian forensic debate was gradually substituted as a classroom procedure; by 1800 it had superseded the traditional form of argument.[1] Not only was this exercise demanded of the juniors and seniors in their course of study but the students began to debate extracurricularly.[2] In fact, it is in its extracurricular use that we find the first distinction made between a forensic and an extemporaneous dispute.[3] The students, of their own volition, attempted to free themselves from their manuscripts.

But perhaps the most significant adaptation of the forensic dispute was found in the law school of the College of William and Mary, where the students conducted regular legislative exercises. Jefferson wrote to James Madison on July 26, 1780 regarding this activity: "Wythe's school is numerous, they hold weekly Courts & Assemblies in the Capitol. The Professors join in it, and the young men dispute with elegance, method & learning. This single school by throwing from time to time new hands well principled, & well informed, into the legislature will be of infinite value."[4]

In addition to speech performances that were demanded as a part of the weekly recitation routine, the more excellent students were allowed to appear at commencement and at special class-day exhibitions held three or four times throughout the year. One of the most popular entertainments on such occasions was the English dialogue.[5] The terminology

---

[1] On July 21, 1789, President Stiles, of Yale, recorded in his diary: "The seniors have had but one syllogistic disputation this year, and perhaps half a dozen last year. There was one only last Commencement—none this. Thus farewell syllogistic disputation in Yale College much to my mortification."—*The Literary Dairy of Ezra Stiles* (Franklin B. Dexter, ed., New York, Charles Scribner's Sons, 1901), III, 360. The commencement programs at both Dartmouth and Harvard show that the Latin disputes disappeared at those colleges, also, before 1800.

[2] See the section in this chapter on Literary Societies.

[3] On Nov. 26, 1776, the Linonia Society at Yale voted to introduce extemporaneous disputes into their meetings. The constitutions of the chapters of Phi Beta Kappa distinguished between "opposite composition" and extemporaneous disputation. The constitution of the United Fraternity at Dartmouth provided at each meeting "one written and two extemporaneous disputes" should be given. The Code of Laws of the Brothers in Unity at New Haven, in 1783, contained the provision that on the third gathering of the month "one-half of the disputants shall perform in writing; the other extempore." John Quincy Adams, in 1786, recounted that in the classroom forensic dispute the arguments were written out and totaled two or three pages in length. *Writings of John Quincy Adams* (W. C. Ford, ed., New York, The Macmillan Company, 1913), I, 21.

[4] *Writings of Thomas Jefferson* (P. L. Ford, ed., New York, G. P. Putnam's, 1894), II, 322.

[5] Like the declamation and disputation, the dialogue was originally confined to the classical languages, though it had never been received enthusiastically by the students. Always the parts assigned to be delivered in the mother tongue had been those most coveted by the contending scholars.

was so indefinite, however, as to extend over a number of meanings. At times it designated a conversational technique after the Socratic method. The interrogations might be so directed as to secure information, or the purpose of the inquisitor might be to wring such concessions and admissions from his speaking colleagues that the latter would be forced into an indefensible position. Or it might be a discussion written and prearranged by two or more persons. As applied to this latter activity, *dialogue* was freely interchangeable with the *colloquy* or *conference*. Occasionally, students memorized and delivered an excerpt from some classical model, such as Erasmus' *Colloquies* or Cicero's *De oratore*. This exercise, too, was known simply as a dialogue. And a fourth usage for the word was its application to plays written and produced by the students.[1]

Two other activities presented on special occasions were so closely related to the original declamation that their respective boundaries can hardly be disentangled. These were the oration and the dissertation. Apparently the term *dissertation* referred to a rather lengthy persuasive speech. Orations, on the other hand, although primarily persuasive, might include inspirational and eulogistic performances. The cliosophic, valedictory, salutatory, and funeral orations, for example, were all concerned less with producing action than with the inculcation of an attitude or an appreciation.

The Literary Societies

After 1750 one of the most important forces promoting better speech in the college emanated not from the faculty and governing bodies but from the students themselves. This force was the literary society, which assumed, during the latter half of the eighteenth century, a distinguished and powerful place in educational institutions. Kingsley, the Yale historian, says that the New Haven Linonia Society was one "which for more than a hundred years was to exert a marked influence on the institution; and which, in the opinion of some of the most distinguished of the living alumni, has been scarcely second in its advantages to the regular instruction of the officers of the college."[2]

---

[1] The term *dialogue* was deliberately used by the Linonia Society at Yale to camouflage the production of plays. On Dec. 21, 1782, the secretary recorded that since the college authorities had forbidden the enacting of plays at the society's anniversary, each of the four classes should present a dialogue for the event. The account of the celebration that took place on Apr. 8, 1783, states that they performed a humorous dialogue, the characters of which were "Esquire Grimsey, an avaricious miser who has two sons educated; Johnny Grimsey, the eldest son, a profligate rake who was married to Susy Princost; Solomon Grimsey, the youngest son, a sober-minded studious youth, unmarried," etc.

[2] Kingsley, *op. cit.*, p. 78.

At Yale, where these groups first appeared in a significant role, two of the societies, the Linonia and the Brothers in Unity, were of primary importance. At Harvard, the Hasty Pudding and the Speaking clubs, at Dartmouth, the United Fraternity and the Social Friends, at William and Mary the F.H.C. Society, and at Princeton the American Whig Society were the representative organizations.

The Linonia, organized in 1753, was the oldest of all such fraternities, and its program was in essence the outline followed by later groups, including the Phi Beta Kappa chapters in their early years. These organizations served three important purposes. (1) They provided an opportunity for students to participate frequently in speech activities. (2) They encouraged a systematic attempt to criticize the performances constructively. (3) Each of the societies established and maintained a library for the use of its members.[1]

An indication of the abundant opportunities for student performance is provided by the records of the Linonia Society. On November 9, 1781, the program of the meeting consisted of five compositions, eleven speeches, and several dialogues, with two or three members speaking in each. The next week eight speeches and two dialogues were given. The constitution of 1785 specifically enjoined that each "member shall at every meeting have an opportunity of offering whatever exercises he pleases, which if approved by the Society, shall be exhibited at the next meeting." Written compositions were examined by a committee of student critics, any member violating proper grammatical usage during the meeting to be corrected by his confreres.

By 1800 the literary societies had assumed such importance on the Yale campus that students entering college were automatically allocated by the authorities to one of the two major organizations. For thirty years this practice was continued.

As the nineteenth century progressed, records show that the literary societies became less dominant and that members became increasingly uninterested and irresponsible. But it should be remembered that during the period in which colleges had provided little other opportunity for studying the English language and speech, these groups had done vital and dynamic work to promote the improvement of speechmaking.

Rhetorical Theory

A. AS REVEALED BY STUDENT READING

The Ramean Rhetoric. Until approximately 1720 the Ramean concept of rhetoric occupied a lofty position in the Harvard curriculum. Ramus

---

[1] By 1869 the combined libraries of the Linonia and Brothers in Unity Societies at Yale numbered 30,000 volumes. Edward B. Coe, "The Literary Societies," in Kingsley, *op. cit.*, p. 321.

believed that *inventio* and *dispositio,* as processes of the mind, belonged to the field of logic, whereas rhetoric proper was concerned chiefly with the ornamentation of ideas. To him rhetoric had two parts—expression and action. Expression included the study of tropes and figures; action dealt with voice and gesture.[1] Evidence indicates that the classical rhetoricians were largely ignored while the abbreviated rhetorics of Talaeus and Dugard, disciples of Ramus, were widely known and venerated.[2] Both these authors considered *elocutio* and *pronuntiatio* in general, but their chief emphasis was upon elegancies of style, especially the use of tropes and figures.

In addition to Dugard, Harvard freshmen in 1726 studied the grammar-school text of Thomas Farnaby. Farnaby, a student of the seventeenth century English rhetorician Vossius, naturally reflected in his *Index rhetoricus et oratorius cum formulis oratoriis et indice poetico* the classical view of his teacher. Dull, abbreviated, and yet crowded with information, the work fell far short of providing a self-explanatory, interesting text. It did, however, contain adequate discourses on all four divisions of the classical rhetorical doctrine during an era in which two of those divisions were woefully neglected.

Outside the Ramean tradition, the *Formulae oratoriae* of John Clarke was also read in the New England colleges. In treatment less complete than Farnaby's text, it contained more detailed helps and illustrations for composition of specific types.

After 1720 the *Port Royal Art of Speaking* attracted considerable interest in America. Though this book is by no means a restatement of classical doctrines, nevertheless the fivefold division of rhetoric is proposed and discussed in the second section, The Art of Persuasion. The treatment of delivery is slighted, the discussion of memory is negligible, and matters of style, particularly the use of trope and other figures, are grossly emphasized. But invention and arrangement, long neglected in popular colleges texts, are given full recognition as parts of the art of persuasion.

The Rhetoric of Oratory. With the *Port Royal Art of Speaking* serving as a transition from the abbreviated to the classical concept of rhetoric in collegiate circles, the mid-eighteenth century marked a turning point in the history of speech education. Parallel with the change from Latin to English speechmaking, with the shift from syllogistic to forensic debate, and with the increasing student enthusiasm for improved speech, came a general familiarity of students with the classical rhetorical doctrines. In the latter half of the eighteenth century, although Quintilian and Aristotle still remained comparative strangers, Cicero's *De oratore* obtained wide

[1] Frank Pierrepont Graves, *Peter Ramus and the Educational Reformation of the Sixteenth Century* (New York, The Macmillan Company, 1912), p. 138.
[2] The investigations of Warren Guthrie and P. G. Perrin confirm this conclusion. For full treatment concerning the early curriculums, see these studies.

circulation. Until the publication of Blair in 1783, the most influential contemporary reformulation of the classicist viewpoint was Ward's *System of Oratory*. This text, a massive synthesis of the Greek and Roman rhetorical concepts, considered oratory as the medium of the art and its aim as the influencing of the minds of men. Despite its tedious length, the students liked it and read it of their own volition. In 1767 a member of a student-organized group for the promotion of oratory at Yale tells us that we "purchased Ward's System of Oratory for our director." After the speeches given at each meeting, the same student continues, "We read a lecture in Ward, and, as we go on, are careful to digest and incorporate it."[1]

This awakened interest in Aristotelian principles of speaking does not mean, however, that the abbreviated rhetoric with its concentration on tropes and other figures had been discarded. Holmes' *Art of Rhetoric Made Easy* and the section on rhetoric in R. Dodsley's *The Preceptor*[2] were devoted largely to style. Both were read, and Holmes was particularly popular. Library records, available at Dartmouth during the period from 1774 to 1777, show that the *Art of Rhetoric Made Easy* was the only text in rhetoric among the books most frequently withdrawn;[3] and before the adoption of Blair's *Lectures*, Holmes had been one of the texts in use at Yale.[4] Though Holmes did not confine his treatment to *elocutio*, the sections devoted to other aspects of rhetoric were superficial and perfunctory.

In addition to these rhetorical concepts, students were exposed to still a third point of view. The late eighteenth century saw the origin and amplification of a new theory of rhetoric—in the elocutionary school. Arising out of the oft-repeated criticisms of the standard of English oratory, the proponents of this new movement argued for the improvement in speech through better delivery. As to how this effective communication should be achieved they differed, and accordingly ranged themselves into two opposing camps.

The first of these groups was the naturalistic school. It posed the tenet that the most effective delivery was that which followed the natural, conversational method. Its most famous exponent was the English author

[1] Letter of David Avery, cited in E. H. Gillette, "Yale College One Hundred Years Ago," *Hours at Home*, 10 (February, 1870): 334–335.

[2] The rhetorical section in this book was not of Dodsley's own composition but was abstracted from the Reverend Anthony Blackwall's *Introduction to the Classics*, published in 1750.—R. Dodsley, *The Preceptor* (London, R. Dodsley, 1754), I, 405.

[3] Herbert D. Foster, Webster and Choate in College, *Collected Papers* (privately printed, 1929), p. 236.

[4] J. C. Schwab, "Partial List of the Text-books Used in Yale College in the Eighteenth Century," broadside in Yale Library. Simeon Baldwin had an abstract of this book in his Commonplace Book or System of Learning, compiled during his sophomore year at New Haven, in Yale Library.

Thomas Sheridan, whose works were widely known in the American colleges.[1] William Enfield's *The Speaker*, which followed the same tradition, was circulated less extensively. In the nineteenth century the naturalistic school, widely known in the eighteenth century, was almost entirely ignored.

The second, or mechanistic, concept of elocution, destined to receive overwhelming popularity in the 1800's, had not been greatly emphasized in the Colonial educational institutions in the previous century. Adherents of this school held that the way to achieve an effective, and eventually natural, delivery was to classify didactically the various elements of oral communication and to seek proficiency in their use by means of mechanical practice. Thus, with varying emphasis, each of the authors set forth specific instructions concerning the use of pitch, intensity, rate, and quality of the voice, as well as movements of hands, head, eyes, and other parts of the body. John Walker, the English writer, penned a series of books after 1781 and was the first thoroughgoing "mechanist" to become really famous, though his influence had no important effect upon the American schools until the last years of the century. The most widely known mechanistic protagonist in the colonies was James Burgh, in his *Art of Speaking*. First published in 1761, it was in the Harvard library by 1767 and a few years later was purchased by student literary societies at both Yale and Harvard. Burgh's doctrines were not so mechanical as those which were to follow, yet even before the dawn of the nineteenth century the rhetorical *theses* bear testimony to the fact that American collegians were learning specific injunctions relative to the manipulation of voice and body in speaking.[2]

During the latter half of the eighteenth century, it is apparent that the classical rhetorical concepts which the students read were supplemented by acquaintance with the stylistic and elocutionary rhetorics. In addition to the works already cited, Rollin's *Belles Lettres*, Priestley's *On Oratory*, Blair's *Lectures*, Campbell's *Philosophy of Rhetoric*, Mason's *Essay on Elocution*, Lawson's *Lectures Concerning Oratory*, and the several compositions of both Walker and Sheridan were readily available for student use. Throughout this period oral communication was the medium through which the art of rhetoric found its expression. Rhetoric and oratory were consistently coupled both in the curriculums and in the thinking of the period.

[1] Sheridan's *Lectures on Elocution* appeared in the Harvard Library catalogue of 1765 and according to the library charging record was withdrawn more frequently in 1767 than any other rhetorical text—three times! Members of the United Fraternity at Dartmouth purchased a copy for their use, and in his diary, a Hanover collegian, Ephraim Smedley, recorded for posterity his diligent reading of the *Lectures*.

[2] See below, pp. 208–209.

Ascendancy of the Elocutionary School. In the late years of the eighteenth century certain influences converging gradually wrought a change that was to culminate in the nineteenth century with the virtual isolation of *pronuntiatio* as a part of rhetoric. Probably one of these potent influences was the publication in 1783 of Hugh Blair's immediately popular *Lectures on Rhetoric and the Belles Lettres*. Yale adopted the book as a text in 1785; Harvard chose it three years later. The library of William and Mary today contains a copy of this book that bears the signature of John Gilchrist, who was a student there in 1791; so at that time it was at least known at that institution if not actually used, and before 1817 it had been adopted as a textbook. Until the middle of the nineteenth century it was one of the most widely used textbooks of rhetoric. The only authors who rivaled Blair were Campbell and Whately.

Blair's work in the transition of rhetorical thought had a double significance. First, it associated rhetoric with belles-lettres; furthermore, like the volumes of Aristotle and Cicero, it largely ignored the matter of delivery. This text, it must be remembered, was achieving signal successes in America at a time when the democratic spirit was high and the country was in the midst of the tremendous ordeal of formulating and maintaining a stable government. The demand was for effective speakers who could gain the confidence and could sway the beliefs of voters. When, concurrent with this demand, the popular school rhetoric ignored *pronuntiatio* and the writers of the elocutionary school became more prolific and precise, the stage was set for the coupling of rhetoric with composition and written communication and for the establishment of elocution as a distinct discipline. The college at Hanover, for example, furnishes a pertinent illustration. The Dartmouth curriculum in 1822[1] required a course in English during the sophomore year and specified the text for that subject as Blair's *Lectures*.

Nor did the rise to popularity of Campbell's *Philosophy of Rhetoric*[2] and Whately's *Elements of Rhetoric* greatly alter the scene. Both these men made contributions to the art of persuasion that have been frequently and amply reviewed in later criticisms; their contributions, however, did not include treatments of *pronuntiatio* significant enough to retard the distinctly growing discipline of elocution. Campbell, like Blair, held to the natural mode of delivery but placed little emphasis upon oral presentation as such. Whately was more definitive, assigning oral presentation to a position of greater importance, but his work did not appear until 1828,

[1] Dartmouth College Catalogue of 1822, cited in Leon Burr Richardson, *History of Dartmouth College* (Hanover N. H., Dartmouth College Publications, 1932), pp. 376–377.

[2] Campbell's treatise was published in 1776 but did not achieve a circulation comparable to Blair's until after 1830.

by which time the mechanistic elocutionary school had consolidated its prestige. Furthermore, the catalogues of Colby, Middlebury, South Carolina, and Yale colleges specified that Whately was studied "except Part IV"—the section dealing with *pronuntiatio*, which argued for the naturalistic concept.

Before analysis of the amazing growth of the elocutionary movement, it should be noted that American college professors were publishing rhetorics of their own. None of these editions, it is true, was widely circulated, but as documents they are important because most of them are compilations of lectures; they indicate what was taught to groups of American college students in the period between the Revolutionary and Civil wars. Seemingly, the first major New World contribution was that of President Witherspoon at Princeton,[1] whose lectures on rhetoric, delivered at the New Jersey college from 1758 to 1794, were posthumously collected and printed. He maintained that the orator was made, not born, and that the best method of training was wise study coupled with intimate knowledge of great models. His discussion of rhetoric was in the classical tradition.[2] From 1819 to 1851 Edward Channing delivered the prescribed Boylston lectures. They were published in 1856, but, though they too conformed to the letter of the classical doctrine, they emphasized the development of literary taste and the perfection of style. Channing was interested more in the literary than in the oratorical aspects of the subject.[3]

Two other early nineteenth century American professors were responsible for rhetorical publications of more limited scope. Samuel P. Newman, instructor at Bowdoin from 1822 to 1839, is the only one of the whole group of American authors whose work[4] was originally intended as a text; soon after publication it was adopted by several American colleges. Newman stressed primarily matters of style, virtually ignoring both oral communication and the persuasive goal of rhetoric. The second document is the little known rhetoric of Ebenezer Porter, *Lectures on Eloquence and Style*. It is not surprising that Porter, holder of the Bartlett Professorship of Sacred Rhetoric at Andover Academy from 1813 to 1831, famous for his

---

[1] The Reverend High Jones, of William and Mary, had as early as 1724 published his *Accidence to the English Tongue*. While the book was not a comprehensive rhetoric text, Dean Grace Warren Landrum hails the work as "the first grammar in English hitherto discovered to have been written in His Majesty's colonies."—*William and Mary Quarterly*, 19: 272.

[2] John Quincy Adams, *Lectures on Rhetoric and Oratory* (2 vols., Cambridge, Hilliard and Metcalfe, 1810) "His *Lectures* though confused in some matters of detail, were an admirably organized summary of classical rhetoric—probably the best such summary ever made by an American."—Horace Rahskopf, John Quincy Adams' Theory and Practice of Public Speaking (Ph.D. dissertation, State University of Iowa, 1935), p. 40.

[3] Edward Channing, *Lectures on Rhetoric and Oratory* (Boston, 1856).

[4] Samuel P. Newman, *A Practical System of Rhetoric* (Portland, Me., 1827).

treatises on elocution, should indicate in these lectures that he considered delivery one of the most important aspects of rhetoric and that he cherished style.[1]

As rhetoric became allied with written composition, training in speech per se was by no means neglected, but the details of the instruction were dramatically modified. Following the publication of his *Elements of Elocution* in 1781, John Walker produced a series of books that set and amplified the pattern for the new and prospering mechanical elocution: detailed analyses of all the movements of head, hand, arm, and body; minute descriptions of shades of facial expression; intricate calculations of the uses of the human voice; and all these embroidered and beset with innumerable rules allegedly derived from nature.

Following in his wake came a host of elocutionary writers, American as well as English.[2] The influence of the new tradition felt in the colleges in the late 1700's was reflected in the rhetorical *theses* posed for commencement exercises. But it was not until the nineteenth century that strenuous training in vocal and physical communication became an end in itself. So great was the fervor for specific instructions in speaking that the more vague and philosophical naturalistic teachings were largely forgotten or despised.

The development of the elocutionary theory can be traced in general contour by a few keystone treatises. After Walker had definitely set the pattern, Gilbert Austin published in 1806 his *Chironomia*.[3] The book is significant because it carried to quintessential refinement the mechanistic treatment of gesture and bodily action. In addition to the inclusion of more than a hundred plates to illustrate the gestures, a system was charted for marking and designating movements, in much the fashion of Steele, who in his *Prosodia rationalis*[4] had earlier worked out such techniques for the voice. For several decades Austin was to be considered the source book on physical action in speaking. Author after author patterned his content from the plan so amply provided.

[1] Lambertson, in his study of homiletics before 1860, concludes that the advances made in the theory of preaching centered around delivery. He maintains that Porter, together with Russell, Rawson, Taylor, Meade, "and a few others in the final period present the first well-rounded discussion of sermon delivery."—F. W. Lambertson, A Survey and Analysis of American Homiletics Prior to 1860 (Ph.D. dissertation, State University of Iowa, 1930), p. 266.

[2] All the important and many of the less important elocutionary treatises are reviewed in the works of Robb, Guthrie, and Blanks.

[3] Gilbert Austin, *Chironomia; or a Treatise on Rhetorical Delivery: Comprehending Many Precepts, Both Ancient and Modern, for the Proper Regulation of the Voice, the Countenance, and Gesture* (London, T. Cadell and W. Davies, 1806).

[4] Sir Joshua Steele, *Prosodia Rationalis: An Essay Towards Establishing the Melody and Measure of Speech to be Expressed and Perpetuated by Peculiar Symbols* (London, J. Almon, 1775).

The Teaching of Rhetoric in the United States

Although William Russell, in 1823,[1] and Ebenezer Porter, in 1827,[2] and in the years following, had produced texts on elocution, their contributions were significant mainly as representing the theories of important American teachers whose influence was felt on more than one campus. Essentially they were both Walker adherents who merely reiterated, with minor variations, the standard mechanistic philosophy.

In 1827 appeared the American document destined to be a unique contribution. Probably the *Philosophy of the Human Voice*, by Dr. James Rush, of Philadelphia, was the greatest single influence upon the development of elocution in America. Dr. Rush divided the treatment of voice into sections on quality, force, time, abruptness, and pitch.[3] He further analyzed each of these attributes and made suggestions for their specific application in the reading of sentences and phrases of various kinds. In other words, he attempted to reduce the use of voice to a definitely describable pattern in much the fashion used by Austin in treating bodily action. The book was immediately popular, and, despite attacks by various adverse critics, it remained the supreme authority on voice through most of the nineteenth century.

With the publication of Rush's volume, the essentials in the story of elocutionary theory were completed. Walker had built the framework for the system; Austin had reduced bodily action to a formula; and Rush had made voice usage an exact science. Henceforth students were to be taught specific, hard-and-fast dictums for the oral presentation of material. The mechanical school flourished and grew despite the occasional protests of those who objected to its supposed artificiality. The movement gathered such swift momentum that it reached the period of the Civil War without having its supremacy seriously threatened.

B. AS REVEALED BY THE THESES

The rhetorical tenets published yearly at commencement time tell generally the same story. Until 1720 almost all the propositions considered as defensible dealt with matters of style. Tropes, metaphors, synonyms, epithets, hyperboles, and other figures frequently constituted the subject matter of the assertions to be maintained by graduating students.

[1] William Russell, *The American Elocutionist* (Boston, Jenks and Palmer, 1840).

[2] Ebenezer Porter, *Analysis of the Principles of Rhetorical Delivery as Applied in Reading and Speaking* (New York, Leavitt, 1827). This was Porter's most popular and important work. It was one of the most widely used college elocutionary texts before 1850.

[3] James Rush, *The Philosophy of the Human Voice* (4th ed., Philadelphia, Lippincott, Grambo and Co., 1855), p. 49.

After 1720 a gradual change in the *theses* of the New England Colleges indicated the return of *dispositio* and *inventio* to the realm of rhetoric. This return to the long-neglected phases of rhetoric was probably due in some part to the increasing disrespect toward logic. Cotton Mather, as early as 1726, had advised students of theology not to spend too much time on logic, contending that its processes ended merely in confirmation of the obvious. The Boston minister argued, "The most valuable thing in Logic, and the very Termination of it, is the Doctrine of Syllogisms. And yet it is notorious, that . . . all Syllogizing is only to confirm you in a Truth which you are already the owner of. . . . "[1] Seventy years later, another Boston clergyman, John Clarke, wrote: "Logic, I am sorry to observe, has with many persons, a doubtful reputation. The time was when it triumphed over other arts; and the time has come, when the usurpation is too much resented. . . . Syllogisms seem now to be passing into oblivion."[2]

Concomitant with the broadening vista of rhetoric came a modification in the tenets affecting *elocutio*. From 1720 to the end of the century a constantly recurring warning appears against sheer copiousness and ornateness as a standard for style. "Tropes, unless for expressing ideas more aptly, ought not to be used more than common words."[3] "Tropes and figures, although influential and persuasive when correctly used, nevertheless make the oration obscure and become tedious to the listeners when piled up with affectation."[4] "A profusion and redundance of metaphors tend to debase language and speech."[5]

Figures and tropes were still sought, but the *theses* reflected the growing turn toward moderation in the use of such rhetorical devices. Brevity and simplicity were beginning to be heralded as attractive qualities.

A third change in rhetorical discipline reflected in the *theses* occurred during the latter half of the eighteenth century. Propositions dealing directly with the delivery of speeches increased rapidly. This was, of course, a direct effect of the new English elocutionary school, the importance of which, even before 1800, had been felt so vividly as to presage its nineteenth century popularity.

Pronuntiatio tenets set forth were frequently specific injunctions relative to the use of voice and body. "The head should always be inclined towards the moving hand except in renouncing."[6] "Wrath is detected by a

[1] Cotton Mather, *Manuductio ad Ministerium* (Boston, Thomas Hancock, 1726), pp. 35 and 36.
[2] John Clarke, *Letters to a Student in the University of Cambridge, Massachusetts* (Boston, Samuel Hall, 1796), pp. 80 and 84.
[3] Harvard *Theses*, 1770.
[4] Harvard *Theses*, 1758.
[5] Yale *Theses*, 1790.
[6] Yale *Theses*, 1751.

harsh, violent and broken voice."[1] Others were more general and philo-sophical. "The facial expression is more powerful in expressing the emotions of the mind than is the whole body."[2] "Polished delivery demands move-ments of the body, control of voice and language, and a facial expression appropriate to one's speech."[3]

A fourth development revealed by the same source testified to the growing association of rhetoric with written communication. Criticisms of belles-lettres are occasionally included as defensible propositions, and after 1781 the definition of rhetoric at Yale is consistently set forth as the teaching of "finer literature and the art of speaking."

Publication of *theses* ended in the early years of the nineteenth century, but until that time, these exercises corroborated the story of the texts— the early ascendancy of the Ramean rhetoric of style, the transition to the classical doctrines, the growing importance of delivery, and the linking of rhetoric with belles-lettres.

Conclusion

Speech education was from the beginning a recognized part of col-legiate training in America, though the details of that education were altered by the demands of the contemporary civilization. During most of the Colonial period college graduates were almost exclusively members of the clergy, whose speaking was confined to a limited subject field with a limited purpose. While this condition obtained, students' attention was directed toward the beauty and "elegancy" of language in oral per-formance. The language utilized was one of the classical tongues. With the conflicts and problems of the middle eighteenth century came a democ-ratizing of society, evident in education as well as in other aspects of living. Its implication for speech was that leaders must learn to talk to all types of people in a manner that would achieve tangible results. Rhetorical theory expounded was once again concerned with practical persuasion. The English language was seen to be the medium through which this persuasion could be accomplished. As the desire for effective speaking increased, more. and more energy was centered on an aspect of rhetoric hitherto relatively neglected—*pronuntiatio*. Excellent content was futile if one could not present it tellingly. The objective, scientific attitude was growing, in speech delivery as elsewhere. The result was the mechanical, elocutionary school, which flourished and in the nineteenth century produced a distinct speech discipline.

[1] Harvard *Theses*, 1783.
[2] Yale *Theses*, 1769.
[3] Harvard *Theses*, 1776.

BIBLIOGRAPHICAL NOTES

Sources consulted in the preparation of this material included official documents of the colleges: the list of *Theses* and *Quaestiones* published each commencement at Yale and Harvard; the Harvard commencement programs printed after 1794; the statutes and laws governing Yale, Harvard, William and Mary, and Dartmouth; the Corporation, Faculty, and Over-seer's records at Harvard College; the catalogue of books in the Yale library in 1755 and 1791 and in the Harvard Library in 1790.

Many accounts of contemporaries furnished valuable information. By far the most important of these was *The Literary Diary of Ezra Stiles*. John Quincy Adams's *Writings* and student diary, the manuscript diary of Ephraim Smedley, Samuel Swift's *Reminiscences of College Life*, and Jonathan Trumbull's *Memoirs* were also useful. Manuscript commonplace notebooks of material abstracted during college attendance by Simeon Baldwin, Perez Fobes, Joseph Goffe, Benjamin Wadsworth, Nathan Fiske, and others, gave further insight into college reading and texts.

The files of the written performances delivered at Dartmouth commencements, the 110 student manuscripts of Joseph Goffe, the Baldwin manuscripts, Napthali Daggett's book of student forensic speeches, Daniel Haskel's composition book, and the Orations and Dissertations of the Linonia Society in the Yale Library, together with miscellaneous speeches in the college archives, provided extensive samples of the speaking performances in New England colleges.

Invaluable information concerning extracurricular speaking activities was revealed in the manuscript records of the Phi Beta Kappa societies, of the Linonia and Brothers in Unity societies at Yale, of the Speaking and Hasty Pudding clubs at Harvard, of the Social Friends and United Fraternity at Dartmouth. In addition, short records were available of minor students groups at Yale and Harvard.

Graduate research in fields related to American speech education has been of indispensable assistance. The following studies were consulted: Anthony F. Blanks, An Introductory Study in the Teaching of Public Speaking in the United States; Thomas E. Coulton, Trends in Speech Education in American Colleges, 1835 to 1935; Charles A. Fritz, The Content of the Teaching of Speech in the American College before 1850; with Special Reference to Its Influence on Current Theories; W. A. Guthrie, The Development of Rhetorical Theory in America, 1635 to 1850; F. W. Lambertson, A Survey and Analysis of American Homiletics Prior to 1860; Alice Moe, The Changing Aspects of Speech Education in the United States from 1636 to 1936; P. G. Perrin, The Teaching of Rhetoric in the American Colleges before 1750; Mary Margaret Robb, *Oral Interpretation of Literature in American Colleges and Universities;* W. P. Sandford, *English Theories of Public Address,* 1530–1828; and Ota Thomas, The Theory and Practice of Disputation at Yale, Harvard, and Dartmouth from 1750 to 1800.

II

Leaders in American
Public Address

·· 6 ··

Jonathan Edwards

by ORVILLE A. HITCHCOCK

Born in East Windsor, Conn., on October 5, 1703, Jonathan Edwards entered Yale College at the age of thirteen, and was graduated four years later, in 1720. He studied theology in New Haven, 1720–1722. He accepted his first pastorate (New York), 1722; returned to Yale, 1724, as tutor, but left in 1726 to become assistant to his grandfather, Solomon Stoddard, then pastor at Northampton, Mass. In 1729 he succeeded his grandfather and remained in Northampton until 1750. This was his most productive speaking period; the Northampton revivals occurred in 1733–1734, and the Great Awakening reached its height in 1740–1741. In 1750 he became engaged in a dispute with his congregation over the question of admission requirements to the church and was asked to resign. He accepted a charge in the frontier town of Stockbridge, Mass. Here, because of the large Indian population, much of his work was of a missionary nature. He remained in Stockbridge until 1758. Some of his best known books were written during this period. In 1758 he became president of Princeton College, but died on March 22, 1758, shortly after taking office.

In 1748 Joseph Emerson, a young Colonial minister, stopped off at Northampton, Mass., to spend the night with the Reverend Jonathan Edwards and his family. Emerson, along with several other ministers, was on his way home from the commencement exercises at New Haven, Conn. That evening, and the next, he wrote in his diary this interesting short account of the Edwards household: "wen 21 Spent the Day very pleasant the most agreable Family I was ever acquainted with much of the Presence of God here. . . . thurs 22 We sat out for home Mr. Edwards was so kind as to accompany us over Connecticutt River and bring us on our way we took our leave of him, he is certainly a great man."[1]

In calling Edwards "a great man" Emerson was simply echoing the popularly held view. In 1748 Jonathan Edwards had reached the peak of his ministry, and many of his contemporaries looked upon him as the outstanding theological leader of the time.[2]

---

[1] Joseph Emerson's Diary, *Proceedings of the Massachusetts Historical Society*, 1910–1911, 44, series 3: 267. (Published by the society, 1911.)

[2] Joseph Tracy, *The Great Awakening* (Boston, 1842), p. 99; William D. Sprague, *Annals of the American Pulpit* (New York, 1857–1869), I, 334.

Today, while literally dozens of scholars attest to Edwards's preeminence in the fields of philosophy, theology, and literature,[1] most people, strangely enough, do not really know and understand him. As Carl Van Doren has put it: "Edwards survives, so far as he may be said to survive at all, outside technical histories of Calvinism and metaphysics, chiefly as a dim figure preaching sermons full of awful imprecations. . . . "[2]

No one has undertaken to study Edwards as a speaker. Not one of the seven major biographies contains an adequate treatment of his public speaking.[3] Yet Edwards was a speaker first and a writer afterward. Most of his time was employed in the preparation and delivery of sermons. These religious addresses were the most important things in his life, and toward them he directed most of his energy. Over his Sunday and midweek discourses he labored long and carefully. More than twelve hundred of them have been preserved in the closely written scrawl of his own hand.[4] They show us that we must look at Edwards first as a speaker; that we must remember that he evolved his doctrines to meet real speaking situations; that his ideas, before they found their way into his books, were preached to actual congregations. A critical study of Edwards the speaker should serve to make him a more human figure by throwing light on one aspect of the important, and hitherto neglected, social side of his life.

[1] " . . . Jonathan Edwards, the greatest theologian that American Congregationalism has produced. . . . "—Williston Walker, *A History of the Congregational Churches in the United States* (New York, 1894), p. 253.
" . . . Certainly the most able metaphysician and the most influential religious thinker of America, he must rank in theology, dialectics, mysticism and philosophy with Calvin and Fenelon, St. Augustine and Aquinas, Spinoza and Novalis; with Berkeley and Hume . . . ; and with Hamilton and Franklin as the three great American thinkers of the . . . century of more than provincial importance."—Jonathan Edwards, *Encyclopaedia Britannica* (11th ed.), IX, 5.
A. E. Winship, *Jukes-Edwards: A Study in Education and Heredity* (Harrisburg, Pa., 1900), p. 17, includes a series of tributes to Edwards: "'The Freedom of the Will,' by Mr. Edwards, is the greatest achievement of the human intellect."—Daniel Webster. "A prince among preachers. In our day there is no man who comes within a thousand miles of him."— Lyman Beecher. "The greatest of theologians. . . . "—Dr. Chalmers.
A. S. Hoyt, *The Pulpit and American Life* (New York, 1921), p. 19, quotes George Bancroft: "He that would know the workings of the New England mind in the middle of the eighteenth century and the throbbings of its heart, must give his days and nights to the study of Jonathan Edwards"; Dr. Fairbairn, of Oxford, "We are fain to confess that in this lone New Englander . . . [we] have one who holds his place amid the most honorable of the doctors of the Church, of the philosophers of his century, and of the Saints of God."
[2] Carl Van Doren, ed., *Benjamin Franklin and Jonathan Edwards: Selections from Their Writings* (New York, 1920), p. ix.
[3] See lives by Hopkins, Dwight, Allen, Miller, Parkes, McGiffert, Christie.
[4] In the library at Yale University.

The Speaking Situation

To understand Edwards's oratory it is necessary first to get a picture of the speaking situation in which he found himself. If a stranger had ridden into the little frontier town of Northampton at a quarter of nine some summer Sunday morning about 1740, he would have discovered most of the citizens making their way piously toward the central spot of the village, the Congregational Church.[1] He would have found himself in the midst of a rather large company, because in Colonial days five-sixths of the population attended church regularly. On one Sabbath 1,460 persons were counted in the Northampton congregation.[2]

The Northampton people were of hardy Colonial stock, honest and thrifty farmers of simple manners and pious natures. Most of them went to church on foot, but there were always many on horseback, husbands and wives often on the same horse. Occasionally some of the young people would walk together. This practice later gave rise to the afterchurch "frolicks" and "visitings" against which Edwards railed so bitterly. It was partly responsible for his controversy with the Northampton congregation, which led to his dismissal in 1750.

The Northampton farmers enjoyed their religion. Church services were to them the most serious business of life, and they followed the sermons closely. While many of them were not well educated, nearly all could read and, in general, they knew the Bible thoroughly. Most of them were amateur theologians. The frequent scriptural references, the involved religious doctrines, the basic appeals to reason did not escape them. They remembered the arguments, turned them over in their minds, discussed them with their friends. The children were encouraged to memorize portions of the Sunday sermons and to repeat them at home during the week. Edwards's preaching was deliberately designed to meet just such a situation.[3]

In 1740 the Northampton church was comparatively new. It had been erected in 1737 to meet the needs of the growing congregation. Constructed

[1] A. B. Hart, Extracts from Capt. Francis Goelets' Journal, *American History Told by Contemporaries* (New York, 1899), II, 63. The captain, in describing Boston of 1750, says, "In Boston they are very Strict Observers of the Sabath day and in Service times no Persons are allow'd the Streets but Doctors if you are found upon the streets and the Constables meet you they Compell you to go either to Curch or Meeton as you chuse. . . . "

[2] The Reverend Solomon Clark, *Antiquities Historical and Graduates of Northampton* (Northampton, 1882), p. 36.

[3] E. H. Byington, *The Puritan as a Colonist and Reformer* (New York, 1899), pp. 192 and 193; ——, *The Puritan in England and New England* (Boston, 1896), pp. 221–277; W. F. Bliss, *Side Glimpses from the Colonial Meeting House* (Boston, 1896), pp. 20–43; G. F. Dow, *Everyday Life in the Massachusetts Bay Colony* (Boston, The Society for the Preservation of New England Antiquities, 1935), p. 102.

after the usual Colonial pattern, it was a square boxlike structure with three entrances. The high pulpit, canopied by a large sounding board, was placed against the north wall, facing the principal door. The front entrance formed the lower part of a tower which rose high above the building. It housed the church bell and a clock, newly installed. Inside, the church was two stories high, galleries having been constructed around three sides of the interior. Rough seats and pews crowded around the pulpit from every angle.[1]

Men and women did not sit together in the meetinghouse in Colonial Northampton. Men were seated in the south end and women in the north end of the building. As late as 1737 the town forbade men and their wives to be placed side by side unless "they incline to sit together." Pews for Negroes were built near the gallery doors, those for men being labeled *BM*, those for women, *BW*. Children of various ages were herded together on benches in different parts of the meetinghouse under the watchful eyes of appointed guardians. Pews were assigned by a committee of the elders. A copy of one of these seating plans, still extant, shows the exact audience situation that Edwards faced.[2]

On Sunday there were two services, the first in the morning at nine o'clock, the second in the afternoon at two or earlier. In the larger towns like Northampton the congregation usually went home for the midday meal after the first service, but in the smaller communities many of the parishoners stayed at the church until both services were concluded. The minister opened the meeting with a prayer, usually about fifteen minutes in length. This was followed by a Bible reading, sometimes by the minister, sometimes by the teacher (if the church was large enough to have one), but more often by some young student preparing for the ministry. Then came the first hymn, "lined out" by the ruling elder. In Edwards's time there was practically no instrumental music in the churches and little singing by note. After the psalm there followed the sermon, which in Jonathan Edwards's case was nearly always about an hour in length. The services were concluded with another prayer (short), sometimes a second hymn, and the invocation.[3]

[1] There is a drawing of this church in *Early Northampton* (Springfield, Betty Allen Chapter of the D. A. R., 1914), p. 41.

[2] *Early Northampton*, pp. 30 and 31; Bliss, *op. cit.*, pp. 87–90; the Reverend Solomon Clark, *Historical Catalogue of the Northampton First Church, 1661–1891* (Northampton, 1891), pp. 40–67, contains a record of the names of those admitted to the church during Edwards' pastorate.

[3] In addition to the two Sunday sermons there were "lectures," usually on Thursday evening of each week. In 1720 most Congregational churches adopted the practice of holding Friday-afternoon lectures, preparatory to the Lord's Supper.—Joel Hawes, *A Tribute to the Memory of the Pilgrims* . . . (Hartford, 1836), pp. 34 and 35; Walker, *op. cit.*, pp. 238–

In the crowded wooden church, with the audience pressing closely about him, Jonathan Edwards would lean on the desk of his high pulpit, take his carefully prepared manuscript in his hand, lean toward the audience and toward the sermon (so that he could see it clearly), and in clear, precise tones begin to explain the Biblical passage which he was using as a text. As he got into the body of the sermon, with its regular unfolding of closely integrated material, he would speak with a seriousness and a solemnity that kept the audience constantly intent on his thesis. With the "application" would come a change in his tone. He would speak with a tenseness and an earnestness that he had not before attained. He would lean closer toward the audience, speaking to each one directly, painting word pictures with a terrible finality. After the last practical point had been driven home, he would deliver a short prayer and step down from the pulpit while the ruling elder led the audience in the final song.

Such were the circumstances under which Jonathan Edwards made his reputation as a speaker.

Training

Edwards's preparation for the ministry was in the usual Colonial style. His first training was received at home, at the hands of his father and his four older sisters. (He had ten sisters. "My sixty feet of daughters," his father called them.) After this preparatory education he entered Yale College. Here he was subjected to the usual heavy classical and theological instruction. Edwards, however, refused to be limited to the regular academic routine and on his own initiative read widely in many varied fields. He was always intellectually curious and did much to educate himself, even after he was graduated from college.

The biographers of Jonathan Edwards, in considering his intellectual development, have not emphasized sufficiently the important role played by his father, himself a minister. This influence was doubly important because it was exercised during the formative years of the boy's life. Edwards attended no public school, and until he entered Yale at thirteen he had no other instruction than that given him at home. Timothy Edwards seems to have taken care of the educational needs of practically all the promising young men of East Windsor.[1] His daughters assisted him in this work. There is evidence that Timothy was regarded as a man of more than usual learning. Church historians agree that he was well acquainted with Hebrew

241; Albert H. Dunning, *Congregationalists in America* (New York, 1894), pp. 150 and 151; *Meadow City's Quarter Millenial Book, Prepared and Published by Direction of the City of Northampton* (1904), *passim*.

[1] John A. Stoughton, *Windsor Farmes* . . . (Hartford, 1883), pp. 77 and 580; *Notebook of Timothy Edwards*, Library of New York Historical Society, *passim*.

literature and was particularly distinguished by his accurate knowledge of the Greek and Roman classics. It was this type of learning that was emphasized in the Edwards household, and we can be sure that Jonathan received a sound classical background.[1]

Jonathan received something more from his father than a thorough grounding in the classics. Timothy was fond of his only son, and the two remained close friends throughout life. They often exchanged pulpits,[2] and Jonathan had frequent opportunity to hear his father preach. From him he gathered much inspiration. There was a close similarity between their views. Both were strict Calvinists. Both believed in a personal religion, a religion of revivals and conversions, and both had a tendency to stress the mystical, idealistic elements. A comparison of Timothy's only published sermon with those of his son reveals, moreover, that they both employed the same general methods.[3]

From his grandfather Solomon Stoddard, one of the leading theological figures of the period, Jonathan Edwards received very little in the way of direct training and influence. Indeed, he disagreed violently with his grandfather's theological views and spent all his life in combating them. While he respected his elder's piety and learning, Jonathan could not conform to the easy-way Arminianism that he taught from the pulpit.[4] Stoddard's influence on Jonathan Edwards was essentially negative.[5]

Edwards's basic training at Yale did not go much beyond the classical and theological. Dr. Ames's theological treatises were the standard textbooks.[6] Latin, Greek, and Hebrew were heavily emphasized. In 1701 the trustees had instructed the rector to "Ground Them well in Theoretical Devinity . . . take Effectual Care that the said students be weekly . . . Caused memoriter to recite the Assemblies Catechism in Latin and Ames' Theological Theses of which as Also Ames' Cases He shall make or Cause to Be made from time to time such Explanations as may be. . . . [necessary]." The trustees went on to declare that "the said Rector shall also Cause

[1] Henry R. Stiles, *The History and Genealogies of Ancient Windsor* . . . (Hartford, 1891), pp. 578–582.

[2] *Edwards Correspondence*, Andover Theological Seminary Collection.

[3] His only published sermon was preached at the general election in 1732. See Stoughton, *op. cit.*, pp. 43, 53; Sprague, *op. cit.*, I, 230–232.

[4] For a discussion of Arminianism see below, pp. 221, 222.

[5] Jonathan Edwards, *Works* (Leeds, 1810), VII, 3. The influence of Edwards' mother must also be mentioned. Sprague, *op. cit.*, p. 578, talked with some people who knew her. Briefly, they said that she had received a superior education in Boston; that she was affable and gentle and was regarded as surpassing her husband in native vigor of understanding; that she was possessed of remarkable judgment, extensive information, and a thorough knowledge of the Scriptures and theology in general; that she was of singular conscientiousness, piety, and excellence of character.

[6] Perry Miller, *Orthodoxy in Mass.* (Cambridge, 1933), p. 159.

Scriptures . . . morning and evening, to be read by the Students at the time of prayer in the School . . . and upon the Sabbath Shall either Expound practical Theology or Cause the Students non-graduated to Repeat Sermons. . . . "[1]

This repetition of sermons on the Sabbath, together with the Colonial practice of weekly declamations and occasional public disputations, seems to have constituted the students' practical training in public speaking.[2]

The library at Yale in 1719 was one of the largest, most liberal, and best selected in Connecticut, plentifully endowed with theological books of both the orthodox and nonorthodox varieties.[3] Edwards read extensively in both types. Most of his reading, however, as shown by entries in his early journals, was in the Bible.[4] His sermons, with their copious quotations and variety of texts, show the result of this study.

Edwards did not limit himself to theological reading. His notebook, in which he entered the books that he had read and intended to read, shows that his literary tastes were exceedingly varied. His active mind sent him searching into every field of knowledge. History is well represented. So are geography, mathematics (including astronomy), and general literature. A few representative authors and titles are Pope, Milton, Vergil, and Addison; Richardson's *Clarissa* and *Pamela*, Fielding's *Amelia*, Young's *Trigonometry*, Rollin's *Roman History*, Locke's *On the Human Understanding*, Plato's *Works*, Watts's *Art of Reading and Writing English* (the nearest approach to a speech text, apparently, aside from Plato's dialogues), a *Universal History of the Arts and Sciences*, a book on shorthand, and, of all things, *An Essay on Mid-wifery!* And this is only a small part of the list![5]

Jonathan Edwards thus was well read; he was acquainted with the classical writings, including Hebrew; he knew the Bible thoroughly; he delved critically into most of the important theological treatises; his interests extended beyond the theological field. In speech he had little

[1] F. B. Dexter, *Documentary History of Yale University* (New Haven, 1916), pp. 32 and 33.

[2] The disputations were similar to those at Harvard. See Cotton Mather, "The History of Harvard College," *Old South Leaflet* (Boston), 8, No. 184: 143 and 144.

[3] Dexter, *op. cit.*, pp. 240, 241; letter from Jeremy Dummer to the Reverend Timothy Woodbridge. Concerning Harvard, see *Massachusetts Gazette*, Thurs., Feb. 2, 1764.

[4] Edwards, *Representative Selections* (New York, 1935), pp. 40 and 47.

[5] From a photostatic copy of the notebook in the Yale Library. The scope of his special interests may be shown in this quotation from the notebook: "Books to be enquired for—the best geography; the best history of the world; the best exposition of the Apocalypse; the best general Ecclesiastical history from Xt. to the present time; the best upon the types of the Scripture; which are the most usefull & necessary of the Fathers; the best Chronology; the best historical Dictionary, of the nature of Boyle's dictionary; the best that speaks of the Ecclesiastical learning of the Jews; the best History of Lives of Philosophers."

academic training. We know only that he read Plato's works and Watts's little book on English, actually a manual of pronunciation. That he had some practical speech training in disputation, Bible reading, and repetition of sermons is certain. Most of his practical training, however, must have been received after he entered the ministry, at the expense of his early congregations.

The Sermons

Ideas. Jonathan Edwards was a strict Calvinist, an archconservative in an age that was becoming increasingly liberal in theological ideas. He was a true Congregationalist, who adhered to the doctrines of the vigorous theology of more than a century before. His philosophy had its beginnings in the works of Calvin.[1] He taught the religion of the first generation of Puritans, when the spirit of Congregationalism was strong and dynamic. In the days of a lowering of standards and a lessening of restrictions, Jonathan Edwards stood out as a successful defender of strict Calvinistic orthodoxy.[2] Because of his influence, and that of others like him, the older Calvinism had one great final flare-up before it died out almost completely.

It must be noted, however, that there runs through Edwards's sermons a more pronounced strain of mysticism and pathos than is to be found in the works of most of his orthodox predecessors. Edwards set forth the Congregational theology in all its grimness, but he went beyond the other ministers in the emphasis of complete inner conversion and in the addition of human appeal to the traditional severely logical theology. As John Fiske says, "The distinction between the converted and the unconverted became in his hands more vitally important than the older distinction between the elect and the non-elect."[3] It was this holding forth of the possibility of conversion that set the stage for the great revivals which developed from Edwards's preaching.

What were the doctrines which Edwards preached? Analysis of his sermons reveals that eight fundamental theological tenets form the basis of his theology. He taught (1) that the entire truth of religion is contained in

---

[1] *Massachusetts Colonial Records*, iii, 419; Cotton Mather, *Magnalia*, v, 63; *Collections Connecticut Historical Society*, ii, 51–125; Samuel Mather, *An Apology* . . . . (pamphlet), 32.

[2] Williston Walker, *Ten New England Leaders* (New York, 1901), pp. 232 and 233; ———, *Great Men of the Christian Church* (Chicago, 1908), pp. 347 and 348; Samuel Miller, *Jonathan Edwards* (New York, 1902), p. 245; A. E. Dunning, *Congregationalists in America* (New York, 1894), p. 237.

[3] John Fiske, *New France and New England* (Boston, 1902), p. 224.

the Holy Scriptures;[1] (2) that man is a lowly, mean creature, tainted with the guilt of Adam's sin;[2] (3) that man is completely and universally dependent upon God;[3] (4) that the invisible church is composed of a small number of elect, who will continue to be saints throughout eternity;[4] (5) that these elect become aware that they are saints through divine revelation in conversion;[5] (6) that for the elect the practice of true religion is "sweet" and "pleasant";[6] (7) that the remainder of mankind are doomed to eternal suffering, which they can escape in part through prayer and repentance, partaking in a sort of "common grace";[7] and, finally, that God is sovereign and supreme.

These eight principles, aside from the emphasis on common grace, were fundamental to the strictest Calvinism. They were the principles that had motivated the establishment of the Congregational Church.[8] Theoretically, the church still clung to these tenets, but actually, by Edwards's time, Arminianism had made great inroads. Arminianism had a more optimistic tone than Calvinism. It made the admission requirements to the church less strict (conversion was not required); it offered more hope to the

[1] "The light of nature teaches no truth as it is in Jesus. It is only the word of God, contained in the Old and New Testament, which teaches us Christian divinity."—Edwards, *Practical Sermons Never Before Published* (Edinburgh, 1788), p. 5.

[2] "From which I infer that the natural state of the mind of man . . . is corrupt and depraved with a moral depravity, that amounts to and implies their utter undoing."—Edwards, *Representative Selections*, p. 321. There are many references to "vile, unworthy, hell-deserving creatures," "stupid, blind, hardened wretch," etc.

[3] "The nature and contrivance of our redemption is such, that the redeemed are in everything directly, immediately and entirely dependent on God: they are dependent on Him for all, and dependent on Him every way."—Edwards, *Works*, VI, 471. Throughout the chapter, for *Works*, see the Leeds ed.

[4] "When heaven was made, it was intended and prepared for all those particular persons that God had from eternity designed to save."—Edwards, *Selected Sermons* . . . (New York, 1904), p. 69. "The good works of the Saints will also be brought forth . . . as for their evil works, they will not be brought forth against them . . . for the guilt of them will not lie upon them, they being clothed with the righteousness of Jesus Christ."— ———, *Practical Sermons* . . . , p. 171.

[5] "That there is such a thing as a Spiritual and Divine light, immediately imparted to the soul by God, of a different nature from any that is obtained by natural means."—Edwards, *Twenty Sermons on Various Subjects* . . . , p. 248.

[6] This is a phase of his so-called "mysticism." "An inward, sweet sense of these things, at times, came into my heart; and my soul was led away in pleasant views and contemplations of them."—Edwards, *Representative Selections*, p. 59.

[7] "The Scripture teaches, that the wicked will suffer different degrees of torment, according to the different aggravation of their sins." Edwards, *Works*, VII, 512. See also pp. 543–554.

[8] Thomas Branagan, *A Concise View of the Principal Religious Denominations of the United States* (Philadelphia, 1911), pp. 9 and 10; Dunning, *op. cit.*, pp. 141 and 142; Robert Baird, *Religion in the United States of America* (Glasgow, 1844), p. 98.

sinner (anyone could be saved); it gave man more faith in himself (man had a certain freedom of will); it permitted a more passive moral attitude; and it affirmed that saints could fall from grace.[1] Calvinism was doomed to give way to it. That it held on as long as it did was due partly to the speaking and writing of Jonathan Edwards.

Organization. Jonathan Edwards's sermons are highly organized, exaggerating the early American practice. Each is divided broadly into four large sections; the thesis is carefully stated; the discussion is developed in three or four main points; these main points are arranged according to a definite system (the order is usually logical or topical); and each tends to establish the principal thesis; the transitions from one idea to another are smoothly and easily made; frequent summaries occur. This meticulous arrangement extends even to minor details. So carefully articulated are the parts that to change the position of one idea would seriously disturb the effectiveness of the whole. Clear organization is one of the outstanding characteristics of Edwards's speaking.

The theses are always clearly stated. Edwards sums up his principal objective in one sentence and tells the audience directly that this will be the keynote of his talk. Then he proceeds to analyze it into its important parts and to assert, again directly, that these will be the main heads of his exposition. The thesis thus is stated twice, once as a whole and once in the form of an outline of its component parts. In the body of the sermon the thesis is referred to frequently. Edwards never loses sight of his primary objective; he never forgets that he has an idea to drive home. Nor does he let the audience forget it. This constant hammering of one idea throughout an hour's exposition serves to set it up as something vital. Through sheer repetition he makes the listeners remember the doctrine that he is expounding.[2]

The discussion proper is always organized into points, and these points are stated definitely at the beginning of the sermon. Three is the average number, although sometimes there are as many as seven or as few as two. These principal points stand out clearly in the body of the text. Usually they are numbered and are referred to as first, second, and third. They are presented according to a definite order and often cannot well be interchanged. Point two follows logically from point one and cannot precede it. All these main points pertain to, and help establish, the thesis. There are no digressions. Edwards maps a course of thought, states it definitely, and then adheres to the plan throughout the speech. There are no wasted arguments,

[1] George L. Walker, *Some Aspects of the Religious Life in New England* (Boston, 1897), pp. 72–74; Dunning, *op. cit.,* p. 243.

[2] Edwards, *Works,* VIII, 3–21; VII, 355–382, are typical sermons. The organization described above can be readily traced.

no deviations from the main thread of logic; all is a unified whole, with every part contributing to the complete picture.[1]

Edwards makes use of a variety of methods of presentation. Sometimes he begins the development of a main proposition somewhat formally: "I would show how hypocrites often continue for a season in the duty of prayer." In other sermons he states the argument baldly, with little preamble, "Many persons remain exceedingly undetermined with respect to religion." In still other instances he uses a combination of methods. Witness the handling of the seven major points in the May, 1735, discourse.[2] In this sermon summaries and transitions are employed with maximum effectiveness.

All introductions are of the expository type. They explain the Biblical text, analyze it into parts, and prepare the way for the statement of the doctrine. In most cases the conclusion consists of an appeal for action based upon an evaluation of the thesis. It is a practical appeal, an attempt to reach a specific audience. Although not a summary, it contains summary elements. In effect, it consists of a final emphasis of the thesis through a practical application of that thesis to the lives of the individual members of the audience.[3]

Types of Proof. Concerning the types of proof, let Edwards speak for himself: "It is impossible that their teaching and preaching should be a means of grace, or of any good in the hearts of their hearers any otherwise than by knowledge imparted to the understanding."[4] He consistently followed this dictum. His discourses are collections of compact reasoning. There are, of course, a number of sermons in which pathetic proof predominates, but on the whole Edwards relies mainly upon appeals to the understanding. Nearly every point is supported by multitudes of reasons and examples; nearly every argument has behind it a pattern of proof that is almost bewildering in its completeness. He unfolds a chain of logic that in most instances compels belief. Generally, his emotional arguments serve as adornments.

Edwards's argumentative method is essentially inductive.[5] Of the types of logical proof, he makes greatest use of authority, generalization, explica-

---

[1] *Ibid.*, VII, 427–437 and 438–446. Two typically organized sermons.

[2] *Ibid.*, VII, 465–475, 413–426, 439–446.

[3] Contemporary writers emphasized clear organization. Two of the many references: Joseph Glanville, *An Essay Concerning Preaching* (London, 1678), p. 38, maintained that a preacher should be methodical if he were to reach the understanding of his audience. Thomas Foxcroft, *A Practical Discourse Relating to the Gospel Ministry* (Boston, 1718), p. 27, says, "Order is the strength and glory of all things," and advocates effective organization of sermons.

[4] Edwards, *Practical Sermons*, p. 6.

[5] This is true in spite of the fact that practically all his arguments can be traced back

tion, analogy, and causal relation. Deductive methods are employed, also. Many instances of syllogistic reasoning can be found. Categorical, hypothetical, and disjunctive enthymemes appear in every sermon. The general approach, however, is inductive rather than deductive. Edwards works mainly through the use of example, quotation, comparison, explanation, cause to effect, and effect to cause.

Argument from authority greatly predominates. As one would expect, the principal source, almost the only source, is the Bible. It is the one great authority. Rarely is any other cited. A detailed examination of 15 typical sermons reveals a total of 374 Biblical quotations, about 25 per sermon. The highest number in any is 59; the lowest is 11. In all, 52 books of the Bible are mentioned. In one sermon he refers to 27 different books. Biblical authority is employed in 8 cases out of 10 in which logical arguments are presented.[1]

Proof by authority is used in several ways. In most cases both the Biblical reference and the complete quotation are given. An example is found in one of his early sermons (1736) on "The Most High a Prayer-hearing God": "Others worship devils, instead of the true God: I Cor. X, 20. 'But I say, that the things which the gentiles sacrifice, they sacrifice to devils.' "[2] Examples could be multiplied endlessly. For instance, in the sermon "God Glorified in Man's Dependence": "Thus in redemption we have not only all things of God, but by and through him, I Cor. viii, 6. 'But to us there is but one God, the Father, of whom are all things, and we in him. . . . ' "[3] Direct Biblical quotations of this type appear on nearly every page of every published sermon.[4]

Usually Edwards is not satisfied to draw his conclusions from just one citation of Biblical authority. Often two or three references will be made. In "God Glorified" one of the closing arguments is developed in this fashion:

This is the sum of the saints' inheritance; and therefore that little of the Holy Ghost which believers have in this world, is said to be the earnest of their inheritance, 2 Cor. i. 22. "Who hath also sealed us, and given us the Spirit in our hearts." And chapt. v. 5. "Now he that hath wrought us for the self same thing, is God,

---

to the fundamental principles of Congregationalism. In most of his sermons Edwards manages to give the impression that a multitude of ideas, examples, and Biblical references have led him to his conclusions, not that his preconceived conclusions have been supported by laborious development of logic and evidence.

[1] See especially Edwards, *Practical Sermons*, pp. 67-85.

[2] Edwards, *Practical Sermons* . . . , p. 74.

[3] Edwards, *Representative Selections*, p. 98.

[4] Even though Edwards undoubtedly added some citations as he prepared the sermons for publication, the extent of Biblical reference in the unpublished sermons indicates that this was typical of his method.

who also hath given unto us the earnest of the Spirit." And Eph. i. 13, 14. "Ye were sealed with that Holy Spirit of promise, which is the earnest of our inheritance . . . . "[1]

Sometimes the authority reference is given, but the quotation itself is omitted. An example will make clear the method: "They are made partakers of the divine nature, or moral image of God, 2 Pet. i. 4. They are holy by being made partakers of God's holiness, Heb. xii. 10."[2] Usually, however, the quotation is given in full. Of the twenty-five Biblical citations in the average sermon, not more than three or four give the reference without the quotation.

Argument from generalization is widely employed, but since the examples on which the generalization is based are usually drawn from the Bible, this method of proof also is of an authoritative nature. The evidence is established by authority, and the conclusion is reached, from the evidence, by the inductive method of generalization. In a 1731 sermon, for example, Edwards says:

> The redeemed have all their good of God. It is of God that Christ becomes ours, that we are brought to him, and are united to him. It is of God that we receive faith to close with him, that we may have an interest in him. Eph. ii. 8. "For by Grace ye are saved, through faith; and that not of yourselves, it is the gift of God." It is of God that we actually receive all the benefits that Christ has purchased. It is God that pardons and justifies. . . . The ministers of the Gospel are sent of God . . . 2 Cor. iv, 7.[3]

Argument by explanation also becomes an important instrument of proof. Explication is used throughout but occurs most frequently in the introductions. Here Edwards's primary purpose is to explain the Biblical text and from it to deduce a thesis or doctrine. In the body of the sermons argument by explanation is used primarily for the development of ideas that are either unimportant or obvious. Occasionally it is used to establish a small part of a larger, more complex argument. It is a schoolteacher type of approach, used by those who speak from a vantage point of superior knowledge. Since the Colonial minister was also an ecclesiastical pedagogue, explanation naturally suited the speaker-audience relationship. A typical passage of this type: "There are two kinds of knowledge of the things of divinity, viz. speculative and practical, or in other terms, natural and spiritual. The former remains only in the head. No other faculty but the understanding is concerned in it. It consists in. . . . "[4]

---

[1] *Ibid.*, p. 100.

[2] *Ibid.*, p. 99.

[3] Edwards, *Works*, VI, 472.

[4] Edwards, *Practical Sermons*, p. 5.

Two other inductive devices appear frequently: analogy and causal relation. The latter argument follows this form: "Your evil ways of living [cause] will soon lead you to the hellfire of damnation [effect]"; or "Your present miserable existence [effect] is due to your life of sin [cause]." These patterns of reasoning, from cause to effect and from effect to cause, are carried out again and again. The analogies cover an even wider territory. They are on all subjects and are nearly always apt and pertinent. Sentences like this abound: "The Gospel is as a glass, by which this light is conveyed to us" . . . . "You are in a poor famishing state, and have nothing wherewith to feed your perishing soul" . . . . "A wicked man is a servant of sin . . . . "[1] Often they are expressed in poetic language. Observe how Edwards contrasts the spiritual and material legacies: "This legacy of Christ to his true disciples is very different from all that the men of this world ever leave to their children when they die. The men of this world . . . . have great estates to bequeath to their children, an abundance of the good things of this world, large tracts of ground, perhaps in a fruitful soil, covered with flocks and herds. . . . But none of these things are to be compared to that blessed peace of Christ which he has bequeathed to his true followers."[2]

Consider another example, from the more famous "Sinners in the Hands of an Angry God":

Unconverted men walk over the pit of hell on a rotten covering, and there are innumerable places in this covering so weak that they will not bear their weight, and these places are not seen. The arrows of death fly unseen at noon-day; the sharpest sight cannot discern them.[3]

It will not be possible to examine in detail the more complicated deductive lines of reasoning. These, however, proceed, in most cases, from the eight major premises discussed in the section on Ideas. The categorical form is favored, but hypothetical and disjunctive developments are also employed.

Finally, two other attributes of Edwards's sermons deserve mention: the compact, condensed reasoning and the complete exhaustion of the subjects under discussion. He speaks much in small compass and drains the lines of inference. His work is epigrammatic; it is inexorable in its logical penetration. He exhausts his propositions by accumulation of subdivisions until the entire field of classification is set forth. In a sermon of June, 1735,

---

[1] Edwards, *Representative Selections*, pp. 110, 128, 134.
[2] Edwards, *Works*, VII, 536.
[3] Edwards, *Representative Selections*, p. 159.

for example, in enlarging the thesis that sinners have mean thoughts of God, he makes use of twenty-six separate subarguments.[1]

Although Edwards emphasized appeals to the understanding, he recognized the importance of the emotional approach. In one of his later works (*A Treatise Concerning Religious Affections*), he says, "True religion in great part consists in the affections."[2] In his funeral sermon for David Brainerd, he gives further indication of a realization of the value of pathetic proof: "He had extraordinary knowledge of men, as well as things; and an uncommon insight into human nature . . . a peculiar talent at accommodating himself to the capacities, tempers, and circumstances, of those whom he would instruct or counsel."[3]

While Edwards uses a great many pathetic arguments, these appeals are, in general, subordinated to the logical elements. Even in those sections in which pathetic proof predominates there is a strong substructure of logic. Seldom do these appeals to duty, fear, jealousy appear alone. They seem to be added "for good measure." Overlooking no avenue of conviction, first he appeals to the understanding and then interweaves into this fabric of logic appeals to motives and desires. Emotional arguments, as we should expect, appear principally in the "applications." Only when Edwards wishes to apply the thesis does he resort to motivation. Logical proof is used to secure belief and pathetic proof to ensure action. This combination of logic and persuasion partly explains his skill in handling argument, evidence, and audience factors.

The principal appeals are to fear, shame, desire for happiness, security, and pride. Gratitude, common sense, emulation, greed, and courage receive less emphasis. In appealing to fear, Edwards frequently refers to hell. It is a very real hell that he pictures, a hell of endless burning of the flesh. He is not content with merely describing the nature of hell and eternal punishment. He drives home the horrors of the torment to each of his listeners. He paints a fearful picture and then sets the audience squarely in the middle of it. It is a positive, powerful suggestion. Everyone has read this famous illustration: "O sinner! Consider the fearful danger you are in: It is a great furnace of wrath, a wide and bottomless pit, full of the fire of wrath, that you are held over in the hand of that God, whose wrath is provoked . . . against you. . . . You hang by a slender thread, with the flames of divine

---

[1] Edwards, *Practical Sermons*, pp. 39–53; Contemporary writers emphasized logical argument. Typical examples: John Wilkins, *Ecclesiastes* . . . (London), pp. 102ff., advised emphasis on logical proof, with plenty of scriptural quotations; Nathaniel Appleton, *Superior Skill and Wisdom Necessary for Winning Souls* (Boston, 1737), p. 12, said that "a sermon without a good blaze of thought, a bright flame of reason, and the sinews of good argumentation is but a lifeless image. . . . "

[2] Edwards, *Works*, IV, 13.

[3] Edwards, *Representative Selections*, p. 175.

wrath flashing about it, and ready every moment to singe it, and burn it assunder. . . . "[1]

He developed variations of this theme. In the passage following, the first phrase shows that he used the device consciously: "But to help your conception, imagine yourself to be cast into a fiery oven, all of a glowing heat, or into the midst of a glowing brick-kiln, or of a great furnace, where your pain would be as much greater than that occasioned by accidentally touching a coal of fire, as the heat is greater. Imagine also that your body were to lie there for a quarter of an hour, full of fire. . . ."[2] As a last example, consider this unpleasant picture: "What will it signify for a worm, which is about to be pressed under the weight of some great rock . . . to collect its strength, to set itself to bear up the weight of the rock. . . . Much more in vain will it be for a poor damned soul, to endeavor to support itself under the weight of the wrath of Almighty God."[3]

Next to fear the most common emotional reference is to shame and its positive counterpart, pride. Edwards seeks to make the sinner ashamed because he has violated the commandment of God, in spite of all that God has done for him. Sometimes shame and fear are used together; more often the appeals are handled separately. A brief excerpt: "And consider, what a shameful thing it is for such rational beings as you are, and placed under such advantage for usefulness, yet to be wholly useless, and to live in the world to no purpose."[4]

The essence of the appeal to pride is that man should be proud of his heritage, proud of the place that God has accorded him and of the graces that have been bestowed upon him. This motive logically and theologically accompanies the reference to shame and desire for happiness. It is best illustrated in a single sentence from a 1736 sermon: "The greater part of mankind are destitute of this privilege; they are ignorant of this God; the Gods whom they worship are not prayer-hearing Gods."[5]

But if the parishoner is subjected to these strong fear appeals, he is also stimulated by sentiments of love and happiness. Happiness is set up as the state or condition that will replace fear, as a positive reward for the absence of sin. Love, a sentiment very real to Edwards, refers primarily to love of God and is used both as a means to, and an end of, this happiness. If we love God, we shall achieve happiness, and one of the elements of happiness will be the pleasure of loving God. Edwards does not use the appeal to love as part of a social code. Little reference is made to love of one's fellow man.

---

[1] Edwards, *Works*, VI, 494.
[2] Edwards, *Representative Selections*, p. 146.
[3] *Ibid.*, p. 144.
[4] Edwards, *Practical Sermons*, p. 217.
[5] *Ibid*, p. 80.

God is the supreme and only object of love. In the following passage, from "The Christian Pilgrim," the main appeal is the emotional one, "Love God." But notice also the varied use of comparison:

> Then we shall perfectly give up ourselves to God: our hearts will be pure and holy offerings, presented in a flame of divine love. . . . Fathers and mothers, husbands, wives, or children, or the company of earthly friends, are but shadows; but the enjoyment of God is the substance. These are but scattered beams; but God is the sun. These are but streams; but God is the fountain. These are but drops; but God is the ocean.[1]

Coupled with the appeal to fear is the reference to security. Obey Christian precepts and your life will be one of peace and security. The reference is often pointed: " . . . be defended from all storms, and dwell above the floods, Psalms xxxii. 6, 7; and you shall be at peace with everything, and God will make all his creatures throughout all parts of his dominion, to befriend you, Job v. 19, 24. You need not be afraid of anything that your enemies can do unto you, Psalms iii, 5, 6."[2]

Edwards also frequently refers his arguments to statements that are obviously reasonable. Among these appeals to common sense are such propositions as: "How unreasonable is it to think that God stands bound to his enemies"; and, "to continue thus undetermined and unresolved in the things of religion, is very unreasonable. . . . ," and, "Nothing is more agreeable to the common sense of mankind, than that sins committed against anyone, must be heinous proportionably to the dignity of the being offended and abused. . . . "[3] The other minor appeals—courage, emulation, greed, and hate—follow the same pattern.

Jonathan Edwards, then, uses pathetic proof often, but depends primarily upon logical argument. The emotional elements usually are found in the exhortatory passages and lead to action, while the logical arguments are doctrinal and establish belief. Few emotional appeals are used without a logical background. Often the two are inextricably woven together. Few clergymen succeeded as did Edwards in elaborating such irresistible doctrinal argument and enforcing it with such dramatic motivating material. In his sermons are elements that stimulated the listeners to run the entire gamut of Puritan religious experience, from fear, shame, longing for salvation, to gratitude and beatific contemplation.[4]

[1] Edwards, *Representative Selections*, p. 131.

[2] *Ibid.*, p. 143.

[3] Edwards, *Practical Sermons*, p. 52; ———, *Works*, VII, 417; ———, *Representative Selections*, p. 114.

[4] Colonial speakers, in general, used many emotional appeals. As Thomas Foxcroft, *Some Seasonable Thoughts on Evangelical Preaching* (Boston, 1740), p. 28, puts it, "Press every duty with the most impelling motives, and with all the artifices of persuasion. . . . "

The term *ethical proof* is used broadly to cover all attempts of the speaker to establish himself as a man of good character and intellectual honesty, to set himself up as an authority on the subject of discussion, to secure the good will of the audience. Naturally, therefore, all speakers use ethical proof. The life and record of the speaker, insofar as they are known to the audience, constitute a measure of ethical persuasion. What he says in his speech and what he omits also add to the ethical appeal. Edwards, in this respect, presented a strong ethical argument. His life was exemplary; he followed a strict moral code; his friends and neighbors thought well of him. His speeches, moreover, helped to establish him as one unrelenting in his attacks on evil, as one always constant in the glorification of the good. This type of ethical proof Edwards employed well.

But there is a more obvious type of ethical proof, consisting of direct statements by the speaker in support of his own authority, character, and good will. Practically no ethical proof of this sort appears in Edwards's sermons. Personal references are seldom used. The notable exceptions are the "Farewell Sermon" and one or two funeral discourses. Most of the others are coldly impersonal.[1] Edwards speaks as a teacher to a group of children, withholding details of his own life but carefully examining theirs.

It may be, however, that Edwards omitted direct ethical proof on principle. One of his primary beliefs was that man should not strive to glorify himself. Proof is found in his journal: "[I am] . . . too dogmatical . . . too much of egotism. . . . " "To mark all that I say in conversation, merely to beget in others a good opinion of myself, and examine it. . . . "[2]

Style. Edwards wrote his sermons in a precise, plain, exact style. Nothing of fine writing or of excessive display creeps into his text. Nor are there classical allusions or other learned references. The language is the language of the audience; it is constantly toned down to the listeners' level. The analogies and comparisons are of an everyday type, apt and exact, yet often of the commonest form. The quotations are Biblical and are cited with a matter-of-factness that appealed to the most unlearned listener. Even Edwards's own language has a Biblical flavor. His style can best be described as common and precise, patterned after that of the Scriptures.

It is not enough to say that Edwards's style is precise: it is sometimes mechanically awkward. Occasionally his language flows smoothly and freely, in an almost poetic manner, but usually he is so much concerned with

---

[1] Edwards, *Works*, VII, 355–382; *Manuscripts* (Yale Univ.), XXXVI, Letter to Joseph Bellamy, Dec. 6, 1749.

[2] Edwards, *Works*, I, 21; *Representative Selections*, p. 52. Many of Jonathan's contemporaries made great use of personal references. Compared with the style of these men, his sermons are cold and aloof. See John Brown, *Puritan Preaching in England* (New York, 1900), p. 63.

the mechanics of the logical development of his case that the niceties of diction are neglected. The words are hewn out of solid rock; idea follows idea with exacting precision. The result is clear, but stiff and heavy. Its disjointed, rasping qualities, not its beauty, compel attention. Edwards, in most of his sermons, did not appeal to man's finer literary sense.

Yet the style seems suited to the speaking situation. The sentences, when read aloud, fit nicely together; the pauses are natural; the repetitions add effect. In short, the sermons exhibit an excellent oral quality but an indifferent literary style. They were written to be heard, not to be read. Although they look awkward in print, they "listen" well. Observe this typical passage:

> I invite you now to a better portion. There are better things provided for the sinful miserable children of men. There is a surer comfort and more durable peace . . . a peace and rest that you may enjoy with reason and with your eyes open; having all your sins forgiven, your greatest and most aggravated transgressions blotted out as a cloud, and buried as in the depths of the sea, that they may never be found more. . . . [1]

The language is the simplest possible. Most of the words are short, a majority being of only one syllable. A detailed study of 200 words, selected at random, reveals that more than 82 per cent are made up of five letters or less; 25 per cent are three-letter words; 23 per cent are two-letter words. The average for the entire passage is about four letters. A brief excerpt will establish this as an element of Edwards's short, curt style: "Offer a saint what you will, if you deny him God, he will esteem himself miserable. His soul thirsts for God, to come and appear before God. God is the center of his desires; and as long as you keep his soul from its proper center, it will not be at rest. The true saint sets his heart on God as the chief good."[2]

Biblical words appear frequently. Even the figures of speech are similar to those found in the Gospels. Everyday expressions abound. Edwards's sermon vocabulary was not unusually large, and therefore he repeats the same words over and over. Synonyms are seldom employed. In speaking of the wrath of God, for example, he will describe it as "dreadful," and "dreadful" it will remain throughout three or four pages. This constant repetition of one term has a rather profound and disturbing effect.

While the sentences appear long in print, they are actually made up of many short, separable clauses. Read aloud, the sermons seem short and curt in style. They move briskly, with rapidity and vehemence. Parallel structure is frequently used, one idea strung after another, the fragments being held together with a sentence thread. Rhetorical questions and

---

[1] Edwards, *Representative Selections*, p. 142.
[2] Edwards, *Practical Sermons*, p. 29.

exclamatory statements often appear. The style is fast-moving, nervous, logical. It is antagonistic, penetrating. For example:

Now God stands ready to pity you; this is a day of mercy; you may cry now with some encouragement of obtaining mercy. But when once the day of mercy is past, your most lamentable and dolorous cries and shrieks will be in vain; you will be wholly lost and thrown away of God, as to any regard to your welfare. God will have no other use to put you to, but to suffer misery; you shall be continued in being to no other end. . . . [1]

Edwards's images are of the homely and obvious variety. Some have a Biblical basis, but most are founded in Colonial life and events. The comparisons are always made in terms that even the meanest member of the audience can understand. The images thus are vivid, readily understood, and easily retained. Expressions like "drop in the bucket," "against the grain," "rack their brains" occur frequently. They are characteristic. Even the more fully developed illustrations have this same quality.

Edwards's style may be said to be four-sided. Most of the writing is hard and logical. This driving appeal to reason is broken occasionally, however, by three types of passages: passionate appeals to basic motives; serene, mystical exhortations; and involved, technical explanations of doctrine. These passages occur in about that order of frequency. In general, his use of language is plain, exact, repetitious. No embellishments, no ornaments appear. He drives home his ideas with a minimum of effort. He follows the usual eighteenth century practice but tends to emphasize the logical at the expense of the emotional. The cumulative, disjointed sentences; the frequent repetition of ideas; the direct, forceful manner; the parallel structure—all point toward an oral style.

Methods of Preparation and Delivery. One of the earliest of the resolutions that Edwards formed was, "Resolved, Never to lose one moment of my time, but to improve it in the most profitable way I possible can." And immediately following this, "Resolved, to live with all my might while I do live."[2] In the preparation and delivery of his sermons he followed this intensive pattern.

An examination of his manuscripts is revealing. The twelve hundred or more sermons in the Yale collection are carefully written out in a small, scrawly hand on tiny, uniform squares of paper. In accordance with Puritan thrift and the scarcity of writing materials, there are practically no margins. Since Edwards began to date these manuscript sermons in 1735, we have

[1] Edwards, *Representative Selections*, p. 167.
[2] Edwards, *Representative Selections*, p. 38.

thus a complete record of his methods of preparation. Most of those before 1746 are completely and meticulously written. Some contain many corrections and erasures; most show only slight revision.[1]

After 1746 Edwards began to depend more on outlines. At first they were complete and full, almost sermons in themselves. Later came notes of a more and more sketchy nature. The outlines for some of his last sermons at Stockbridge are very incomplete. They cover little more than the main heads of the speeches.[2]

Dr. Samuel Hopkins, a pupil and disciple of Edwards, who had access to much material now lost, tells us that Edwards commonly spent 13 hours a day in study. His only exercise was vigorous wood chopping for a half hour each morning and a horseback ride after lunch each afternoon. Usually he carried pen and ink with him on his rides and jotted down any ideas that occurred to him concerning the sermon that he was preparing. These notes he would stuff in his pockets or fasten to various parts of his clothing, so that he would not forget them.[3]

His careful preparation is reflected in the sermons themselves. We have before referred to the complete, detailed organization, the well-worked-out logical arguments, the copious support from Scripture, and the multiplicity of interconnected ideas. Sermons such as these could not have been composed hastily.

In the pulpit Edwards adhered rather closely to his notes. Hopkins tells us that he was accustomed to read the greater part of his sermons. At times, however, he interjected extemporaneous material, "often with greater pathos, and attended with a more sensibly good effect on his hearers as any part he had written." His voice was not strong, yet it had a pleasant, penetrating quality. It was a product of his general frailty of physique. His vitality, voice, and bodily action suffered. He made little motion of his head and hands. He appears, however, to have spoken with such gravity, solemnity, and distinction that he gave the impression of dynamic delivery. He was over six feet, with sharp, clear-cut features and piercing eyes (as his portraits show) and undoubtedly carried himself with an easy, solemn grace. The dynamic qualities of his delivery seem to have come from his seriousness, knowledge, and earnestness of purpose rather than from any cleverness in vocal manipulation and action. His lack of activity was in

---

[1] In Edwards's time the practice varied. Some ministers read their sermons; others delivered from memory; still others spoke from notes. Memorization seems to have been most favored. Edwards himself preferred memoriter and extempore preaching, and later in life he followed both techniques. See Glanville, *op. cit.*, p. 84; Wilkins, *op. cit.*, p. 107; Increase Mather, *The Work of the Ministry Described* (Boston, 1718), pp. 97–138.

[2] Edwards, *Manuscripts* (Yale Univ.), XXXVI.

[3] Edwards, *Works*, I, 43.

conformity with the seriousness of the speaking situation as he conceived it.[1]

Effect. Edwards's preaching had a powerful and immediate effect. Observe some of the testimony from his own writings:

> The young people declared themselves convinced by what they had heard from the pulpit, and were willing of themselves to comply with the counsel that had been given; and it was immediately, and, I suppose, almost universally complied with; and there was a thorough reformation . . . which has continued ever since. . . .
>
> . . . a great and earnest concern about the great things of religion . . . became universal in all parts of the town, and among persons of all degrees, and all ages. . . .
>
> Our public assemblies were then beautiful . . . everyone earnestly intent on the public worship, every hearer eager to drink in the words of the minister as they came from his mouth; the assembly in general were, from time to time, in tears while the word was preached; some weeping with sorrow and distress, others with joy and love, others with pity. . . . [2]

That this was the usual effect of the sermons is indicated by Trumbull's account, collected from an actual member of the audience, of the sermon preached at Endfield on July 8, 1741. He says, "There was such a breathing of distress and weeping, that the preacher was obliged to speak to the people and desire silence, that he might be heard. This was the beginning of the same great and prevailing concern in that place, with which the colony in general was visited."[3]

The emotional reactions of the listeners naturally led to some unfortunate results. Some of them were so carried away by their feelings that they attempted to commit suicide, and a few succeeded. The religion taught by Edwards was not an easy one. To those who could not fully appreciate his point of view, it was a religion of despair. They saw little joy on earth and little chance for joy in heaven. Edwards himself confirms this suicidal mania: " . . . Satan seemed to be more let loose, and raged in a dreadful manner. The first instance wherein it appeared, was a person putting an end to his own life by cutting his throat . . . and many who seemed to be under no melancholy, some pious persons . . . had it urged upon them as

---

[1] *Ibid.*, I, 50. Edwards was opposed to the bombastic type of delivery. In his funeral sermon for David Brainerd, he commended Brainerd for avoiding both "an affected noisiness and violent boisterousness in the pulpit" and "a flat, cold delivery, when the subject required affection and earnestness."—Edwards, *Representative Selections*, pp. 176, 178. We can be sure that Edwards himself sought the golden mean. He apparently preached with terse earnestness that captured and held the audience.

[2] *Ibid.*, III, 12, 14, 16.

[3] J. Tracy, *The Great Awakening*, p. 216.

234

if somebody had spoke to them, 'Cut your own throat, now is a good opportunity.' "[1]

The larger effect of Edwards's preaching is well known. The revival that started in Northampton[2] soon spread up and down the colonies and became known as the Great Awakening, the greatest revival in American history. Jonathan Edwards was its prime mover.

There is direct evidence, too, of the more lasting effects of Edwards's oratory. In 1835, 85 years after he had been dismissed from Northampton, two English ministers visited the town for the express purpose of discovering whether his influence had lapsed. They found that his labors were still "visibly and happily over the people." The people, they discovered, were very pious and carried themselves with much gravity and steadiness of character and inclined "after their great leader, to metaphysical distinctions; require to be addressed through the understanding; and look vigilantly to their motives for action." These were the very things that Edwards emphasized![3]

Conclusion

Such was the oratory of Jonathan Edwards. A preacher for 36 years, he prepared and delivered hundreds of sermons. These sermons were well organized, packed with logical argument and scriptural evidence, and motivated by vivid persuasive appeals. Written in a plain and direct style and delivered with sincerity and earnestness, they had a profound effect on the people who heard them. Today organized religion has moved away from many of the principles for which Edwards stood; yet his influence still is felt. The man who, with George Whitefield, was responsible for the Great Awakening, one of the most important religious revivals of all time, cannot be said to have spoken in vain.

SELECTED BIBLIOGRAPHY

Edwards's Writings

Edwards, Jonathan: *Works*, 8 vols., 1st Am. ed., S. Austin, ed., Worcester, Isaiah Thomas, 1808–1809.
———: *Works*, 8 vols., E. Williams and E. Parsons, eds., Leeds, E. Baines, 1811.
———: *Works*, 10 vols., S. Dwight, ed., New York, H. Carvill, 1830.
———: *Letters*, Andover Theological Seminary Library.
———: *Letters*, Boston Public Library.

[1] Edwards, *Works*, III, 67, 68.

[2] I have carefully gone over the records of the Northampton First Church, which are admittedly not complete, and have counted the names of more than four hundred people admitted to Communion during Edwards's pastorate.

[3] A. Reed and J. Matheson, *A Narrative of the Visit to American Churches* . . . (London, 1838), I, 270–273. Timothy Dwight, *Travels in New England and New York* (New Haven, 1821), I, 329.

———: *Manuscript Sermons and Letters*, Yale Library.

———: *Notebook*, photostatic copy, Yale Library.

———: *Practical Sermons Never Before Published*, Edinburgh, H. Gray, 1788.

———: *Representative Selections*, C. Faust and T. Johnson, eds., New York, American Book Company, 1935.

———: *Selected Sermons*, H. Gardiner, ed., New York, The Macmillan Company, 1904.

———: *Selections from the Unpublished Writings . . .* , A. Grosart, ed., privately printed, 1865.

———: *Twenty Sermons on Various Subjects*, Edinburgh, George Kline, 1803.

General

Allen, Alexander: *Jonathan Edwards*, Boston, Houghton Mifflin Company, 1891.

Appleton, Nathaniel: *Superior Skill and Wisdom Necessary for Winning Souls*, Boston, Kneeland and Green, 1737.

Baird, the Reverend Robert: *Religion in the United States of America*, Glasgow, Blackie & Son, Ltd., 1844.

Bliss, W. F.: *Side Glimpses from the Colonial Meeting House*, Boston, Houghton Mifflin Company, 1896.

Branagan, Thomas: *A Concise View of the Principal Religious Denominations of the United States*, Philadelphia, John Cline, 1911.

Brown, John: *Puritan Preaching in England*, New York, Charles Scribner's Sons, 1900.

Byington, E. H.: *The Puritan as a Colonist and Reformer*, Boston, Little, Brown & Company, 1899.

———: *The Puritan in England and New England*, Boston, Roberts Bros., 1896.

Christie, Francis: Jonathan Edwards, *Dictionary of American Biography*, New York, Charles Scribner's Sons, 1931, Vol. VI.

Clark, the Reverend Solomon: *Antiquities Historical and Graduates of Northampton*, Northampton, Gazette Printing Co., 1882.

———: *Historical Catalogue of the Northampton First Church*, 1661–1891, Northampton, Gazette Publishing Co., 1891.

Dexter, F. B.: *Documentary History of Yale University*, New Haven, Yale University Press 1916.

Dow, G. F.: *Everyday Life in the Massachusetts Bay Colony*, Boston, Society for the Preservation of New England Antiquities, 1935.

Dunning, A. H.: *Congregationalists In America*, New York, Hill, 1894.

Dwight, S. E.: (For *Life*, see Vol. I of the Carvill ed. of Edwards's *Works*.)

Early Northampton, Springfield, Bassette, Betty Allen Chapter of D.A.R., 1914.

Encyclopaedia Britannica, Hugh Chrisholm, ed., Cambridge, University Press, 1910–1911, 11th ed., Vol. IX.

Foxcroft, Thomas: *A Practical Discourse . . .* , Boston, Brettolph, 1718.

———: *Some Seasonable Thoughts . . .* , Boston, Rogers and Fowle, 1740.

Glanville, Joseph: *An Essay Concerning Preaching . . .* , London, Grome, 1678.

Hart, A. B.: *American History Told by Contemporaries*, New York, The Macmillan Company, 1899, Vol. II.

Hawes, Joel: *A Tribute to the Memory of the Pilgrims*, Hartford, Burgess, 1836.

Hopkins, Samuel: (For *Life*, see Vol. I of the Leeds ed. of Edwards's *Works*.)

Hoyt, A. S.: *The Pulpit and American Life*, New York, The Macmillan Company, 1921.

Mather, Cotton, "*The History of Harvard College*," *Old South Leaflet* (Boston), 8, No. 184.

Mather, Increase, *The Work of the Ministry Described*, Boston, Green, 1718.

McGiffert, A. C.: *Jonathan Edwards*, New York, Harper & Brothers, 1932.

Meadow City's Quarter Millenial Book, prepared and published by direction of the City of Northampton, 1904.

Miller, Perry: *Orthodoxy in Massachusetts,* Cambridge, Harvard University Press, 1933.

Miller, Samuel: *Jonathan Edwards,* New York, Harper & Brothers, 1902.

More, Paul Elmer: Edwards, *Cambridge History of American Literature,* I, 57–71, New York, 1917.

Notebook of Timothy Edwards, Library of New York Historical Society

Parkes, H. B.: *Jonathan Edwards, the Fiery Puritan,* New York, Minton Balch, 1930.

Reed, A., and J. Matheson: *A Narrative of the Visit to American Churches* . . . , 2 vols., London, Jackson and Walford, 1838.

Sewall, Samuel: *Letter Book,* Collection of Massachusetts Historical Society, Boston, 1886, 6th Series, Vol. II.

Sprague, W. D.: *Annals of the American Pulpit,* New York, Carter, 1857–1869, Vol. I.

Stiles, H. R.: *The History and Genealogies of Ancient Windsor,* Hartford, Lockwood and Brainard, 1891.

Stoughton, J. A.: *Windsor Farmes,* Hartford, Clark and Smith, 1883.

Tracy, Joseph: *The Great Awakening,* Boston, Tappan and Donnet, 1842.

Upham, William P.: *On the Shorthand Notes of Jonathan Edwards,* Massachusetts Historical Society Proceedings, second series, XV, 514–521, Boston, 1902.

Van Doren, Carl, ed.: *Benjamin Franklin and Jonathan Edwards, Selections from Their Writings,* New York, Charles Scribners' Sons, 1920.

Walker, G. L.: *Some Aspects of Religious Life in New England,* New York, Silver Burdett Company, 1897.

Walker, Williston: *A History of the Congregational Churches in the United States,* New York, Christian Literature Co., 1899.

———: *Great Men of the Christian Church,* Chicago, University of Chicago Press, 1908.

———: *Ten New England Leaders,* New York, Silver Burdett Company, 1901.

Whitefield, George: *A Continuation of the Rev. Mr. Whitefield's Journal from His Arrival at Savannah to His Return to London,* London, 1739.

———: *A Continuation of the Rev. Mr. Whitefield's Journal from His Leaving New England, October, 1740, to His Arrival at Falmouth in England, March 11, 1741,* Boston, 1741.

Wilkins, John: *Ecclesiates* . . . , London, Collebrand.

Winship, A. E.: *Jukes-Edwards: A Study in Education and Heredity,* Harrisburg, Myers, 1900.

Zenos, A. C.: *A Compendium of Church History,* Philadelphia, Presbyterian Board of Publications, 1907.

7

Theodore Parker

by ROY C. MCCALL

Theodore Parker was born in Lexington, Mass., August 24, 1810, the youngest of eleven children. Educated: four months of two summers and three months of ten winters in the district school; three months in Lexington Academy. He taught four years in district schools; Harvard University, 1830–1834, but not officially enrolled because of inability to pay tuition; taught in private school for three years; Harvard Theological Seminary, 1834–1837; chief education attained through his own reading; mastered twenty languages. He was ordained a Unitarian minister, 1837; West Roxbury parish, 1837–1845. He preached the famous sermon on "The Transient and Permanent in Christianity" May 19, 1841, which denied the special authority of the Bible and the supernatural origin of Christ and which resulted in most pulpits being closed against him. His own church supported him, however. He became minister of the Twenty-eighth Congregational Society, January, 1845, and began to preach to large audiences in Melodeon Theatre; moved with his church members to Music Hall, 1852; preached the famous philippic on Webster, November, 1852. Throughout life he agitated against fundamentalism in theology, espoused the doctrine of intuition, flayed social abuses and class distinction, and in later years fought vigorously against slavery. He wrote voluminously for the *Dial* and the *Massachusetts Quarterly Review*; died in Florence, Italy, May 10, 1860.

Introduction

During the twenty-two years of his ministry Theodore Parker wrote 925 sermons and preached approximately fifteen hundred times,[1] and he commanded consistently during the last 15 years of his ministry weekly audiences of 3,000.[2] In addition to his regular Sunday preachings, Parker "appointed" himself "a home missionary for lectures and lectured eighty or a hundred times each year in every Northern state east of the Mississippi. . . . "[3]

Standing as he did at the critical juncture of American philosophical thought and social, religious, political, economic, and educational reform; representing also the change in the function of the pulpit, Parker deserves

[1] Record of Preachings, MSS, Boston Public Library.

[2] *Boston Saturday Evening Express*, Nov. 13, 1858.

[3] *Centenary Edition of the Works of Theodore Parker* (15 vols., Boston, American Unitarian Association, 1907–1910), XIII, 349. Cited hereafter as *Cent. Ed.*

consideration as the embodiment of a national revolution that found its expression in homiletics and rhetoric as well as in other fields. He was no mere freak of nature but a scholar who consciously applied rhetorical technique to the business of speechmaking.[1] Therefore, although the chief purpose of this study is to reflect his speaking powers, effort will be made to allow the reader to see also Parker's conscious application of principles. The author has preferred to include reference to what might be called "Parker's rhetorical consciousness," even though he wrote no systematic treatise on either rhetoric or homiletics, for investigation has led to the belief that from his own words, gathered piecemeal from his Journal and from his letters and criticisms, may be garnered sufficient information to give some expression to the theory by which he worked. If a study of the apparent methods and eventual nature of an artistic production are of value to the student of rhetoric, even more should insight into the conscious working principles of the artist be helpful.

Invention

The Man. The only rhetorically significant inheritance of Parker was a philosophical cast of mind from his father and an active religious instinct from his mother.[2] As we shall see, these traits were operative in determining his reading, his religious outlook, the direction of his attempts at reform, and, both directly and indirectly, his rhetorical practice.

Parker himself tells us that as he grew up among the New England hills, where nature so strongly impressed him,[3] he applied his mind early to books far beyond his age, reading "Homer and Plutarch before I was eight. Rollins' *Ancient History* about the same time, and lots of Histories, with all the poetry I could find, Pope, Milton, Cowley, Dryden, before ten."[4] The family took great care that his potential powers of observation, memory, and judgment should not fail of their development and at the same time taught him "to respect the instinctive promptings of conscience as the 'voice of God in the soul of man.'"[5]

Although Parker's early schooling offers nothing particularly suggestive of his later developments,[6] his total boyhood experience combined with his

[1] *Cent. Ed.*, XIII, 304.

[2] *Ibid.*, XIII, 10–11; also, Parker Genealogy, prepared by Theodore Parker, Boston Public Library.

[3] Journal: Parker's diary-notebook, MSS, Boston Libraries and Societies, cited hereafter only as Journal.

[4] Paper prepared at request of Ripley for biographical notice of Parker, September, 1854.

[5] *Cent. Ed.*, XIII, 291.

[6] Parker "learned to read at home, went to school at five or six, (in May 1816) a woman's

inherited qualities to prepare him for his later career as ecclesiastical and social reformer.

Until Parker entered Harvard Theological School in 1834, his education was largely a matter of his own reading.[1] Even during his sojourn there books apparently held a larger place in his studies than did the lectures of his professors. Likewise were books his staple throughout life. It is appropriate, therefore, that we should give careful consideration to Parker's reading as influencing his thinking and as a process of preparation for his speaking.

One who has thumbed the 20,000 volumes of the Parker library, now in a special section of the Boston Public Library, will answer the question of what Parker read with the one word—everything. Upon the dusty shelves are books in thirty languages; books of history, literature, theology, philosophy, logic, mathematics, zoology, chemistry, physics, law, biography; books rare and ancient, books that were modern in his day; books of all the great masters. Practically all of them show evidence of use, though few are annotated.

Now as to the portion of this vast array that early affected Parker's thinking: The story is most briefly told by pointing out that with a background of English literature and Greek and Roman classics he began his theological study at Harvard by entering upon a critical study of the Bible, using as authority the leading German and French transcendentalists, the English rationalists, and the English transcendentalists. In addition, he read the early church fathers, the mystics, the humanists, and the scholastic group.[2] In such reading is easily discerned the likely bias toward transcendentalism, the tempering of rationalism, the eclecticism of contact with many schools.

Parker's more specifically rhetorical reading was in the *English State Trials*, the classical orations and books of rhetoric, Campbell's *Philosophy of Rhetoric*, Whately's *Elements of Rhetoric*, and Adams's *Lectures on Rhetoric and Oratory*. "Here [in the *English State Trials*] and in the Greek and

---

school, kept 12 to 16 weeks in summer. To a man's school 1816–17, kept *twelve weeks* . . . Academy ten or eleven weeks, but profited little by it." Here was taught only "the pronunciation of Latin."—Paper for Ripley, *op. cit.* See also John Weiss, *Life and Correspondence of Theodore Parker* (New York, D. Appleton and Company, 1864), I, 45, for full but not wholly accurate account.

[1] On Parker's twenty-second birthday (Aug. 24, 1832) he wrote to William P. Huntington, who had been his teacher at Lexington Academy: "My own education, since attending at your school, has been pursued in *Private* and *alone*. I have read all the Greek and Roman authors used at Cambridge and many more. In Geometry and Algebra, I have used the Cambridge course. This has been effected without the *assistance of any teacher.*"

[2] Letters from Parker to Silsbee; also, *Cent. Ed.*, VI, 191; XIII, 315.

Latin orations I got the best part of my rhetorical culture."[1] Thus his rhetorical training manifests a definitely classical base, though he appears to have admired greatly some American speakers and recommends them as valuable study.[2]

Concerning the leading ideas that motivated Parker's behavior, our first observation is that his whole philosophy was based upon his renunciation of the prevailing sensational ideology and his complete dependence upon conscience, or intuition, as "the last standard of appeal" beyond rational processes. He summarizes the matter well thus: "I often find I can *feel* farther than I can *see*, and accordingly I rest the great doctrines of Christianity not on Reasoning—but Reason on Intuition."[3]

Out of this rational-intuitive subsoil grew the following beliefs: (1) God is everywhere and always present; (2) God is infinitely powerful and perfect; (3) God reveals himself to man through nature, through reason, but most often, and most clearly, through the conscience; (4) man's purpose upon earth is to improve himself physically, intellectually, morally, spiritually, that is, in "God-consciousness"; (5) since God operates always by natural law, revealing himself to all through natural channels, it is the preacher's function as a teacher of religion to break down false conceptions of theology and to build from the "emotional germ" of "feeling" and the "intellectual blade of thought" a rational religion of intellect, conscience, "good deeds" and "moral fruits," which shall not end in the church, but *shall extend to every act of life and to every branch of social relationship.* " . . . he is to promote the application of this consciousness of religion to all the departments of human life,—individual, domestic, social, national, and universal. . . . It is idle to say the minister must not meddle with practical things. . . . he must have an eye to the business of the nation. . . . "[4]

Here, then, is the framework for Parker's activity as preacher and lecturer, and likewise his homiletic theory of the function of the preacher. We must add description of the two directions of reform upon which his philosophy launched him. That for which he still enjoys a share of fame was his relentless and uncompromising attack upon slavery. Like the majority.

---

[1] *Cent. Ed.*, XIII, 304; VII, 246. See also letter from Parker to Joseph Allen, Feb. 14, 1854; letter from Parker to the Reverend H. A. Keach, Sept. 3, 1851, hereafter cited as letter to Keach.

[2] Although Parker corresponded and associated with the leading thinkers and writers of New England, it is probably fair to assume that his own thinking was not measurably influenced by them; he was too independent and too critical. See *Cent. Ed.*, VIII, 140–142, 159–163; letter to Silsbee, Aug. 10, 1838; letter to George H. Ellis, May 27, 1838.

[3] Letter to Caroline H. Dall, Sept. 21, 1846. See also *Cent. Ed.*, IV, 301; VI, 152–153, 188, 352–353; XI, 292; XIII, 301.

[4] *Cent. Ed.*, XIII, 90–97; III, 118, 282–283, 287, 330, 337; IV, 285, 301, 305, 320, 326; VI, 162, 326–327; IX, 53–54.

of New England abolitionists, he denounced slavery largely upon moral grounds, but, unlike many of them, he also attempted to dislodge it with arguments social and economic.[1] Basically, though, the moral sin was the evil in slavery. He wrote to his congregation from his death bed: "I have spoken against slavery more than any other concrete wrong, because it is the greatest of all, 'the sum of all villainies.'" . . . [2] Though his efforts at Abolition have given him to posterity, his attacks upon the current theology hoisted him from the obscurity of the little West Roxbury parish and gave him popular power. His sermon on "The Transient and Permanent in Christianity," preached at the ordination of Charles C. Shackford, in South Boston, 1841, created a stir equal to that created by Emerson's famous message less than three years earlier and resulted in such controversy as to bar Parker from the great majority of Unitarian pulpits; but it placed him upon the pages of newspapers and theological publications and eventually upon the stage of the Melodeon Theatre, where he preached to unprecedented congregations. In the letter last quoted he explains the motive in his persistence: "I have preached against the errors of the ecclesiastical theology more than upon any other form of wrong, for they are the most fatal mischiefs in the land."

Parker's own theory was that to be a "*permanently impressive*" speaker, one must be a man of "superior ideas."[3] A Boston news writer, comparing Parker with Chapin, Cheever, Vinton, and Beecher, thought "their stature by no means so formidable." In fact, he considered Parker "among the less than half dozen living great minds of the age."[4] Convers Francis thought his "learning is far outdone by the riches of profoundly significant thought."[5]

Parker's memory apparently outdistanced even his profundity of thought. The man who could as a boy "repeat a poem of 500 to 1000 lines after a single reading," continued throughout life to excite admiration and wonder for his feats of memory.[6] Although power of recall is frequently most valuable as an attribute of delivery, it seems in Parker's case to be far more significant as an inventive process, for it was in marshaling his materials into systematic form that Parker found most employment for the faculty of memory. James Freeman Clarke says of him: "His memory of details was astonishing; but his power of systematizing those details—making them

---

[1] *Ibid.*, XI.

[2] *Ibid.*, XIII, 377.

[3] Letter to Keach.

[4] *Boston Saturday Evening Express*, Nov. 13, 1858.

[5] Letter from Convers Francis, Jan. 18, 1841.

[6] Ripley paper. See also O. B. Frothingham, *Theodore Parker* (Boston, James R. Osgood and Co., 1874), pp. 572–573, for a number of such incidents; also, *Newark Daily Advertiser*, Sept. 29, 1860.

drill in companies, and march in squadrons, and take on the order of battle
—was equally striking."[1]

Parker's phenomenal powers of memory gave him complete and ready
control of his remarkable breadth of reading.

His ability to concentrate is best illustrated by the incident of his
student days when he became so absorbed in conversation with two of his
classmates as he walked along, "working his sturdy limbs, his head inclined
downward," that he bumped his forehead with such force against a high
stump as to knock him completely unconscious.[2] Imaginatively, he had
perhaps not the power of Emerson, but probably no less than most of his
prominent contemporaries. He is held to be equal in this respect to his
intellectual company by virtue of his creative ability in effecting new and
living combinations of old bodies of knowledge. Of his depth of conviction
there can be little doubt; every act attests it, and contemporaries almost
without exception proclaim it.[3] In fact, the strength of his convictions was
in all probability the basis of his apparent radicalism.

One cannot read a volume of Parker's Journals without being fully
convinced of his high moral character. It is true that he often referred to
himself as the "best hated" man in America, but the criticisms of his views
almost without exception spare the moral man. Whatever his reputation, in
all fairness we must say that he fulfilled admirably the traditional "good-
man" qualification.

Parker believed that the necessary complement of "superior ideas," his
first criterion of greatness in speakers, was "superiority of sentiment."[4]
Whether he possessed that quality is difficult to determine. That he was
emotionally sensitive is not to be questioned. He professed never to feel
anger but was easily wounded and as quickly driven to tears as a child.[5]
"His intellect was so diluted with passion that one lost sight of the intellect
in the volume of the passion."[6] He is often pictured in the Music Hall as one
who "thundered and lightened and tore down."[7] Whether the controversialist in him was at odds with the sentimentalist, though, seems not to be the
important question; rather, the enigma is whether his emotional flurries
were compatible with that depth of sentiment which he considered essential
to great speaking. The only substantiable conclusion is to ascribe to him

---

[1] James Freeman Clarke, *A Look at the Life of Theodore Parker*, delivered June 3, 1880
(Boston, George H. Ellis Co., 1910).

[2] *The Dial*, 1 (1840): 446.

[3] Letter to Silsbee, Mar. 24, 1843; *Boston Daily Times*, Aug. 14, 1841.

[4] Letter to Keach.

[5] Journal; *Boston Daily Atlas and Bee*, June 18, 1860; letter to Caroline Dall, Jan. 25, 1845.

[6] *Boston Post*, Dec. 20, 1860.

[7] *Christian Inquirer*, June 16, 1860.

emotional quantity beyond the ordinary and to leave to conjecture the quality thereof.

The total man is perhaps fairly to be declared intellectually great, morally stable, emotionally intense.

The Process of Preparation. It is nothing to say of a man that his preparation for a given speech was the work of a lifetime; and in Parker's case a consideration of any phase of his preparation must return to his reading. Breadth of informational reading we must grant him. "We know the writings of no man which display such wealth of allusion, except those of Macaulay. . . . This man commands at every touch the literature of the world. . . . "[1] "It is thought, by those competent to judge, that over and above his theological learning, Mr. Parker—although now but thirty-six years of age—has a more extensive general knowledge than any other man living, except it may be Lord Brougham."[2] The philosophical groundwork, built from childhood,[3] suggests rational processes and reference to universal laws or fundamental principles; his study of law,[4] history, literature, and the sciences equipped him to bridge the gap between pulpit and politics, at the same time that it afforded him wealth of allusion and a systematic view of every problem.

From this general reading came upon him multitudes of sermon subjects, which marched rapidly into position, assuming their places always as a part of a larger plan. To illustrate his method of planning, we reproduce here his lecture plans for 1845–1846:

SCHEME OF LECTURES FOR 1845–1846

1. History of the growth of the Roman Hierarchy till 1517
2. History of the growth of the Roman Dogmatics till 1517
3. State of Europe—1511 Polit. not phil. moral. rel.
4. Formation of a power hostile to the hierarchy and dogmatics of the R. C.
5. The Reformation—Antagonistic to the Rom. C.
6. The Church's defense—Loyola.
7. Luther ⎫
8. Calvin ⎬ The 3 fold division of the Ref. movement.*
9. Zwingli ⎭
10. Political consequences of the Ref.

[1] *Richmond* (Va.) *Examiner*, Nov. 6, 1842.
[2] *Streeter's Weekly Boston Star*, April 11, 1846.
[3] *Cent. Ed.*, XIII, 300–301; letter to Silsbee, Aug. 10, 1838.
[4] "His acquaintance with civil law equals that of our most eminent lawyers. . . . "—*Streeter's Weekly Boston Star*, Apr. 11, 1846.
   According to W. H. Fish, a lawyer friend of his considered Parker's exposition of jury trial in his *Defence* "the best to be found."—Letter from W. H. Fish.

11. Its moral and intellectual consequences—effects, etc.
12. The Catholic Refor—Council of Trent.
   * Develope this further as I have time & give the life of Erasmus, Melanchthon, etc.[1]

Concerning his preliminary reading for these lectures, he said: "Last night I began a course of study of Eccl. Hist. preparatory to the special study of the Reformation. I shall study: I. (1) Tillemut—as far as he goes. (2) Review the ground in Tully & follow down to 1517, with occasional readings in Dupin, Neander, de Porter, etc. II. Then I shall take the Dogmas, & III. The Heretics."[2]

In preparation for a specific sermon or lecture he apparently drew heavily upon preliminary reading and in addition probed assiduously every source of information or inspiration. Emerson said of him, "It looked as if he was some president of council to whom a score of telegraphs were ever bringing in reports. . . . "[3] Wendell Phillips doubted "if any workman in our empire equalled him in thoroughness of preparation."[4] He was continually writing to Sumner, Wilson, Seward, Chase, Mann, and others for firsthand information.[5] Parker's sources of information included all that he might learn from books, documents, and men.

The reflective process undoubtedly contributed much original thought to information from other sources at the same time that it gradually wrought the materials into the general form of the discourse. In his words:

I did not abandon my scholarly work while traveling and lecturing. The motion of the railroad cars gave a pleasing and not harmful stimulus to thought, and so helped me to work out my difficult problems of many kinds. . . . [6]

It is a good plan before writing anything, to think over the subject and see what you know about it, then to make a plan of your work, putting down the points you intend to make in their order, and under them the propositions, the proofs, illustrations, facts, etc. Time spent in the plan is time saved in filling it up. . . . [7]

I have no receipt for writing, except to think the *subject* all over long before writing—then to think over the *Form* of the thing, arrange the parts, and see if they are well proportioned, and make up a whole. Then I write. . . . [8]

He further confirmed in his paper to Ripley that "nothing was commenced until a scheme or outline" had been worked out. When "reading and meditating and taking copious notes" had furnished him with a "view

[1] Journal, undated.
[2] Journal, Dec. 3, 1844.
[3] *Boston Daily Atlas and Bee*, June 18, 1860.
[4] *Ibid.*
[5] See, for example, letter from Sumner, Feb. 6, 1854; letter from Wilson, July 23, 1855.
[6] *Cent. Ed.*, XIII, 352.
[7] Letter to Keach.
[8] Letter to Miss Grover, Oct. 8, 1857.

of the whole subject," so that he "saw not only the end from the beginning, but the details and subdivisions of each head," he began to write. Peter Dean concluded: "He generally wrote his sermons at the beginning of the week, and left a page or two for after-thoughts to be written on Saturday night."[1]

Further conception of Parker's methods may be gained from examination of his Journal. It will be noted that, true to his theory, he first sketched the headlands, sometimes filling in the spaces at a later date, or at others simply reproducing the outline in more complete form just beneath his original framework.[2] The actual writing he apparently did rapidly and without the delay of interruption when opportunity allowed (*cf.* page 255). In the case of his long discourse on Webster, he said: "At eleven o'clock Wednesday not a line of it was written; at two p. m. Saturday not a line unwritten."[3] One may thus readily infer the relatively extemporaneous character of his writing; but comparison of first drafts with later printings, or of final printings with shorthand newspaper reports, reveals clearly that Parker's revisions were few and doubtfully valuable.

Although he testifies to having "added extemporaneously" at the time of delivery and refers repeatedly to having preached less than was written,[4] the author finds no conclusive proof that the process of preparation for any important engagement ever ended with anything short of a finished manuscript. Those manuscripts yet available are written out fully, in large script, and compare almost identically with the final printings.

Logical Proof. Inspection of the main propositions of Parker's speeches will readily justify the expectation of logical procedure. His "Sermon of War," outlined on pages 253–254, falls easily into three simple syllogisms.[5] The same may be said of his sermons "Of Immortal Life," "The Laboring

---

[1] Peter Dean, *The Life and Teachings of Theodore Parker* (London, Williams & Norgate, Ltd., 1877), p. 144.

[2] Note the influence of Henry Ware, Jr., Parker's instructor in homiletics at Harvard. Ware wrote to his brother in January, 1831: " . . . the Senior Class . . . bring me plans and skeletons once a fortnight on given subjects, which I criticize; and I sometimes require them to write out at length one of the heads, for example, the Exordium or the Conclusion." In 1833 Ware wrote to Dr. Carpenter: "In the second year, the *Art of Composition*, including, first the finding of thoughts, or the art of discussion; secondly, arrangement, and thirdly, style. This is followed by a course on the *Composition of Sermons*, accompanied by criticisms and remarks, and by exercises of the students in drawing up plans and arranging skeletons."— John Ware, *Memoir of the Life of Henry Ware, Jr.* (Boston, James Munroe and Co., 1854), pp. 105–106.

[3] Journal, Oct. 31, 1852.

[4] Journal; letter to Lydia Cabot, Aug. 22, 1836; letter to Caroline Healey, Nov. 29, 1842; letter to W. H. Fish, Dec. 25, 1853.

[5] The first syllogism, for example, would read: Whatever is a waste of property should be abolished; war is a waste of property; war should be abolished.

Classes," "The Chief Sins of the People," "Transcendentalism,"[1] in fact, practically all those which are argumentative in nature. The five main propositions in which we have attempted to encompass Parker's philosophy appear in somewhat modified form throughout the majority of his speeches.[2] His logical proof, then, is set in the simple framework of his philosophy, and all inductions and deductions are made thereto or therefrom.

Since the argumentative materials of any discourse may be superficially cast in syllogistic form, the evaluation of Parker's logical proof is not to be completed in terms of mere prevalence; but we must inquire into the soundness of his reasoning from premises to conclusion and into the validity of his major premises.

To validate a man's reasoning by offering a dozen samples from any hundred of his speeches would be to indulge in the fallacy of insufficient number; but to produce as many instances of fallacious reasoning would be unquestionably to invalidate his powers. It is the inability to produce the latter that leads the author to conclude that if one accepts Parker's premises the critic can hardly deny the conclusions. In any case, the prevailing force of Parker's implications is sufficient to constitute logical proof for demonstrative speaking occasions.

The validity of Parker's major assumptions, or premises, was, of course, the crux of the controversies that enveloped him. Science has to some extent justified some of Parker's supporting arguments,[3] but his major theses remain as enigmatical today as then.[4]

[1] *Cent. Ed.*, III, X, IX, VI, respectively.

[2] The institutional nature of religion is his thesis for "A Discourse of the Religious Element and Its Manifestations"; its universality and its compatibility with man's philosophical nature become proofs of its validity. In his "Sermon of Providence," the infinite perfection of God becomes proof of His universal providence, the thesis. So may one go through all Parker's sermons, finding that his deductions are consistently based upon the five major premises of his philosophy.

[3] Parker's proposition of improving the relation between man and God was based upon the argument that man's existence upon earth is an evolutionary process of approaching ever nearer to perfection and so to infinite Perfection, God. A portion of his evidence lay in his belief in evolution in the animal and vegetable world.—Theodore Parker, *West Roxbury Sermons* (Samuel Barrows, ed., Boston, Robert Bros., 1892). His support of Spencer and his anticipation of Darwin give some hint of the broad and inclusive trend of his theological system.

[4] Although Parker did not use the inductive method of arrangement to effect his persuasions, it is evident to all students of rhetoric that the inductive process as a method of proof can scarcely be avoided. In Parker's case the large process was basically inductive, for always he aimed at a generalization. His deductions were the complements of his inductions. He was fully aware of these relationships and of the dangers inherent in each. In his own words, there are "two methods of inquiry, deductive and inductive"; and "two forms of error,—the assumption of a false fact as the starting-point of deduction, the induction of a false fact by the inductive process."—*Cent. Ed.*, VI, 6.

We have already noted that Parker's sources of evidence were in no sense restricted. The questions now to be answered concern his use of this evidence as an inductive procedure.

In his use of example the necessary considerations are (1) frequency and (2) nature. Parker's rhetorical view was: "Things well known require no illustration except for beauty and the delight it gives; things new or abstruse and hard to grasp require illustrative figures, etc."[1] His practice was to employ the first portion of his discourse for building a framework of philosophic cast and then to support his thesis with a series of topical divisions, each developed by examples and deductive arguments. The examples were most often of prominent people well known to his audience,[2] or of familiar scenes of New England's natural phenomena. When a friend wrote and asked him why he had used the example of the Cohasset Rocks in his lecture on John Quincy Adams, Parker replied:

> You object to the "Cohasset Rocks"—the words are not in the Manuscript, but I selected the figure at the moment and for this reason: I once went a fishing with Mr. Adams (and others) on the Cohasset Rocks, they are large and extend a long ways on the coast and are much assailed with storms. Everybody at Boston knows the Rocks, and Mr. Adams often went down there and so they were in my mind connected with him. I prefer the "Cohasset Rocks" in such a connection to "Gibraltar," because they are an object well known and the other not well known by the sight. If I were to speak of Birds in a Sermon I should not mention the *Nightingale* and the *Sky Lark*, but the Brown Thrasher and the Black-bird—for the same reason. . . . [3]

Since his use of specific instance was rarely for the purpose of debate, but more largely to make clear his expositions and inspirational appeals, which were argumentative only as part of the larger purpose, the usual tests for such argument are scarcely applicable.[4]

Since Parker relied so heavily upon intuition and rational processes for his ultimate authority, his preachings were predominantly didactic.

[1] Letter to Keach.

[2] It was said of him, "He keeps all his scalps in the desk at the Music Hall. While you are listening to him he suddenly draws one forth, shakes it at the audience, and puts it up again. It was the scalp of a clergyman. You recollect the sin for which he was slain, and grimly recognize and approve. Pretty soon forth comes another, and another; scalps of marshals, eminent lawyers, democratic officer-holders, and Southside clergymen."—Weiss, *op. cit.*, II, 198.

[3] Letter to W. H. White, Mar. 11, 1848.

[4] In a letter to Silsbee, Feb. 23, 1841, Parker throws some light on his understanding of the nature of *proof*, when he speaks of his method of testing the writings of the Apostles: "The proof is *external* and *internal*. . . . So much for the *external*, now for the internal. Look at the testimony *itself* without regard for the authors. The (1) *contradictions*, (2) inconsistencies, and (3) *statements of themselves incredible*. . . . Thus I prove the minor of the next syllogism. . . . "

Hence his source of quoted authority rarely went beyond his own person. In one volume of eleven representative sermons, for example, authority is used not once. Even the Bible, which is the ultimate source of authority for most ministers, he used for texts and inspiration but not for authoritative reference. Great religious leaders of the past he used more often as objects of criticism than as support for his statements.

As for his use of causal relation, it must be borne in mind that his whole philosophy was based upon a God in His universe, working by natural law from within rather than by miraculous power from without. Thus his sermons are almost invariably in the larger sense causal chains; and the sermon plans that fill the pages of his Journal are replete with such phrases as "show causes," "show effects of."

Since the basis of analogy is resemblance, or comparison, it follows that through interpretation the scope of analogy may be broad or narrow. In the narrow sense of literal analogy obviously used to support an argument, Parker's employment of the process is rare; in the sense of figurative analogy, sometimes used to include metaphor, his indulgence frequently approaches excess.[1]

Other than the orthodox inductive and deductive processes of marshaling argument and evidence to accomplish logical proof are certain aspects of the total implicative process often more efficacious as persuasive forces than are the traditional modes. Such are definition, comparison, exposition, narration, description. They are not "in the . . . generally accepted sense argumentative" but are "in a very true sense," since their "aim is to convince and persuade. . . . "[2] Although descriptive analysis of such processes is more properly a function of pathetic, ethical, and stylistic considerations, and will be treated in those divisions, mention of them as factors in the logical process is appropriate here. Our only specific consideration will be a general measurement through testimony of their worth in Parker's employ and of his own attitude toward such elements. He said of Webster: "He always addressed the understanding, not the reason, . . . not the imagination . . . he laid siege to the understanding. Here lay his strength—he could make a statement better than any man in America."[3] Eight years later another said of Parker: "His great power lay in his

---

[1] The extent to which Parker's analogies scurry to and fro between simplicity and obvious design, metaphor, and decoration may be typically illustrated from his sermon "Of the Culture of the Religious Powers": "That smoky chimney of an ill-temper is a torment to Mr. Fiery. . . . dead bodies are stirred in the bosom of the sea. . . . there are such men stationed along the line of human march; cities set on a hill, which no cloud of obloquy can hide . . . they are beacons on the shore of the world, . . . lighthouses . . . street-lamps. . . . " *Cent. Ed.*, III.

[2] Gladys Murphy Graham, *Quarterly Journal of Speech*, 11 (1925): 330.

[3] *Cent. Ed.*, VII, 359–360.

ability to make a statement, not in his sound wisdom, not in his useful learning. . . . It was the clearness in them, and the will behind them, that made them the very element of eloquential power."[1] Parker's lucid style was ostensibly one of his strongest contributions to logical proof.

Fully conscious of deductive and inductive methods, Parker uses them well, if one grants the generic propositions of his philosophy.

Pathetic and Ethical Proofs. In accomplishing proof through the pathetic mode, Parker appealed often to New England's historical pride, particularly in his speeches upon the issue of slavery.[2] The natural concomitant of such appeals was his frequent attack upon proponents of slavery and upon the South as the embodiment of the evil.[3] The element of fear, so prevalent in early Puritan preaching, Parker did not use; neither did he appeal to the economic well-being of the individual. Justice and love of fellow men he kept in the foreground as general positive aims; but as pathetic modes he employed the embodiment of their opposites.

Although the present reading of Parker's speeches gives little indication of his use of humor, the testimony is that his audiences were visibly amused by his flashes of wit. Assuredly one cannot read his Journal and letters without fully appreciating that his sense of humor was a lively one; but to all appearances the pulpit circumstance subordinated it quite fully to the serious vein. Adornment at its best was a pathetic aid; at its worst it appears to the contemporary reader only as "purple patches." The chief error of which he was guilty was irrational statement in matters upon which he felt strongly.[4] Parker was conscious of the audience factor in determining the desirable proportion of emotional elements;[5] but the instructional nature of his talk and the power of his thought combined to relegate the

[1] *Boston Post,* Dec. 20, 1860.

[2] A typical example is offered by his speech on "The Slave Power": "Will Massachusetts conquer her prejudices in favor of the 'unalienable rights of man'? . . . she will have to forget two hundred years of history. She must efface Lexington and Bunker Hill from her memory, and tear the old rock of Plymouth out from her bosom."—*Cent. Ed.,* XI, 268.

[3] See *Cent. Ed.,* XI, 373; IX, 11; VII, 337, 346. In his speech on "The Free Soil Movement," XI, 206, he says: "Who is most blustering and disposed to quarrel? The South. Who made the Mexican War? The South. . . . The South . . . why the South, the South."

[4] For criticisms of Parker's tendency in this direction see letter to Parker from W. H. Fish, Apr. 19, 1858; letter to Parker from Luther Griffing, July 4, 1854; letter from Parker to Caroline H. Dall, Jan. 25, 1854; *Boston Trumpet and Freeman,* Apr. 9, 1864.

[5] See *Journal,* Nov. 10 and 11, 1844; letter to Silsbee, Aug. 10, 1838.

Parker's own classification of persons is interesting: "Men in respect to their *mobility*—or passion faculty of being moved, may be divided into three classes, viz. 1. the *ductile* who can be led by the hand, 2. the *tractile,* who can be *drawn by the nose,* and 3. the *projectile,* who can be *kicked by the part which is wanting in cherubs but fully developed in school boys.*"—Letter to Convers Francis, May 26, 1844.

strictly pathetic burden, with the exception of his constant attack upon every representation of evil, preponderantly to *Style*.

Of the three Aristotelian obligations of ethical proof Parker had most occasion to establish his good sense and good will. It has been pointed out that his moral character was above reproach but that for his radicalism he enjoyed national fame. The latter reputation cast doubt upon his judgment. This circumstance was so constant, however, that Parker's direct ethical proofs were reserved largely for his special attacks. In general, it may safely be said that Parker's speeches upon slavery, politics, and such related topics employ both ethical and pathetic proof to a greater extent than do his properly sermonic efforts, though the generalization must reserve many exceptions. His consciousness of the nature of ethical appeal is evident in his reference to Webster: "In his oratory there was but one trick,—that of self depreciation."[1]

Parker had ample cause to use ethical appeal; he was sensitive to its value; he used it freely on special occasions to establish his fair judgment and good intention but in general avoided it.

Arrangement

Parker's idea of the nature and importance of arrangement in public discourse becomes more clear than any other of his rhetorical concepts. He says: "[Emerson] lacks the power of orderly arrangement to a remarkable degree. Not only is there no obvious logical order, but there is no subtle psychological method by which the several parts of an essay are joined together; his deep sayings are jewels strung wholly at random. This often confuses the reader; this want appears the greatest defect of his mind."[2] Channing's "arrangement is frequently unphilosophical." Beecher did not "put the ultimate facts in a row and find out their causes or their law of action. . . . "[3] In some instances even J. Q. Adams's "productions are disorderly, ill-compacted, without 'joints or contexture.' . . . "[4]

Such criticisms serve largely to indicate Parker's sensitiveness to order in discourse and assure us that he did not pass over the suggestions of Campbell, Whately, Cicero, Quintilian, and Aristotle or miss the examples offered by Cicero, Demosthenes, the Attic Ten—all sources that he recommended to others.[5] That his chief source of instruction in arrangement lay

---

[1] He extends this ethical theory in describing the proofs within Webster's person: "His noble form, so dignified and masculine; his massive head; the mighty brow, Olympian in its majesty; the great, deep, dark eye, . . . these all became the instruments of such eloquence as few men ever hear."—*Cent. Ed.*, VII, 358–361.

[2] *Ibid.*, VIII, 95–96.

[3] *Ibid.*, pp. 160, 435.

[4] *Cent. Ed.*, VII, 246.

[5] Letter to Keach; letter to Joseph Allen, Feb. 14, 1848.

in the *English State Trials*, however, is certain. He says: "Here and in the Greek and Latin orations I got the best part of my rhetorical culture."[1]

Examination of the classical sources that Parker recommends will reveal that their suggestions for arrangement differ essentially only in the extent to which they would subdivide the discourse. The *State Trials* exhibit remarkable uniformity of arrangement and agree closely with the recommendations of both earlier and later rhetoricians mentioned. In addition to the influences already suggested, it must further be noted that Henry Ware, Jr., Parker's teacher of rhetoric at Harvard, refers freely to the classical sources,[2] so that Parker undoubtedly met the same determining forces in his instruction as in his study. Ware's advice was that a student should "investigate carefully the method of every author he reads, marking the divisions of his arrangement, and the connection and train of his reasoning."[3] The task now is to examine Parker's practice to discover whether it conforms to his theory.

A not uncommon procedure was to state early in his discourse, sometimes in the opening sentence, what one might call his "Subject."[4] The occasional bluntness and brevity of this announcement were in no sense "introductory." The definitions, history, explanation, or philosophy with which he usually elaborated upon his opening statement fulfilled adequately the functions of the exordium, except that rarely did he include either ethical or pathetic elements. The whole purpose of the introduction appears to have been to clear the ground for what followed, not primarily to put speaker and audience on common ground.

More often he omitted the opening announcement and proceeded as we have just indicated, until such time as he could state a definite thesis. This proposition he invariably stated openly, frankly, clearly,[5] thus conforming to the first Aristotelian requirement and to the homiletic advice of the period.[6] The partition he sometimes omitted but frequently stated

[1] *Cent. Ed.*, XIII, 304. In addition to this testimony, he recommends their study for assistance in clearness of arrangement and distinctness in the use of terms on at least two different occasions and included them in his record of studies for 1836.—Letter to Keach; letter to Allen, Feb. 14, 1837; Journal, 1837; *cf.* also p. 240 supra.

[2] Henry Ware, Jr., *Hints on Extemporaneous Speaking* (Boston, Cummings, Hilliard and Co., 1824) pp. 27, 32, 39.

[3] *Ibid.*, p. 43.

[4] For typical examples see *Cent. Ed.*, IX, 288; IV, 342, 365, 391.

[5] For example, "Let us, therefore, devote a few moments to this subject, and consider what is *transient* in Christianity, and what is *permanent* therein."—*Cent. Ed.*, IV, 2. See also *ibid.*, I, 1; VI, 39; IX, 1, 326; XI, 1, 249.

[6] Aristotle, *Rhetorica* (translated by W. Rhys Roberts, Oxford, Clarendon Press, 1924), p. 1414; Alexander Jameison, *A Grammar of Rhetoric and Polite Literature* (New Haven, A. H. Waltby and Co., 1821), p. 267; Alexander Vinet, *Homiletics: Or the Theory of Preaching* (translated and edited by Thomas H. Skinner, 2d ed., Chicago, S. C. Griggs and Co., 1854),

fully.[1] If the partition was not formally made immediately following the thesis, the main divisions of the discussion were carefully pointed out in their place.

The topic sentences of the paragraphs of the discussion enable one readily to write almost without exception a symmetrical outline to the second and third subheadings, as is illustrated in the pages at the end of this section, verbatim from his printed sermons. In progressing from one point to another within the speech, Parker employed transitions that at once summarized, moved, and pointed forward. For example: "To sum all this up in one formula: . . . "[2] Minor summaries are employed continually throughout his discourses, and a major summary is almost invariably the first indication of his conclusion.[3] Immediately following his final summary, Parker frequently falls into a true peroration.[4]

As models of clear and logical outline, Parker's sermons are scarcely excelled. Whatever may be said of the other qualities of his composition, his organization is adequate. Some might criticize it for its sameness of "stating the proposition and then proving it" and for its invariable adherence to the fourfold method of introduction, thesis, discussion, and conclusion; but as a means of fundamental exposition that aims at persuasion as the remote end, this traditional outline probably will not soon be improved.

OUTLINE FROM PARKER'S SERMON

A SERMON OF WAR[5]

SUBJECT, OR INTRODUCTION: I ask your attention to a Sermon of War (opening sentence).

THESIS: Let me speak, and in detail, of the Evils of War.

DISCUSSION: I. . . . I begin by considering war as a waste of property.

    A. It paralyzes industry.

    B. Then, too, the positive destruction of property in time of war is monstrous.

    C. . . . See the loss which comes from the misdirection of productive industry.

        1. Your fleets, forts . . . are unprofitable.

        2. Your soldier is the most unprofitable animal you can keep.

---

pp. 262–263; Austin Phelps, *The Theory of Preaching* (New York, Charles Scribner's Sons, 1883), p. 39; William G. T. Shedd, *Homiletics and Pastoral Theology* (New York, Charles Scribner's Sons, 1867), p. 144.

[1] *Cent. Ed.*, VI, 289; IX, 139, 180, 327; XI, 2, 250.

[2] *Ibid.*, IX, 62; see also *ibid.*, VI, 329; IX, 67, 77, 100, 104, 349.

[3] *Ibid.*, VI, 326; IX, 90; XI, 284.

[4] "O Boston! thou wert once the prayer and pride of all New England men, and holy hands were laid in baptism on thy baby brow! . . . O Massachusetts, noble State!"—*Ibid.*, IX, 47–48.

[5] *Ibid.*, IX, 288–325.

II. But the waste of property is the smallest part of the evil. The waste of life is yet more terrible.
    A. . . . to spill . . . men's blood is an awful sin.
    B. But it is only the smallest part that perish in battle.
    C. Others not slain are maimed for life.
III. Yet more: aggressive war is a sin. . . .
    A. It lives only by evil passions.
    B. In war the state teaches men to lie, to steal, to kill.
IV. (Long analogy of possible war between two sections of Boston; many vivid pictures.)
V. We are waging a most iniquitous war. . . .
    A. In the general issue . . . we are in the right.
    B. . . . in this special issue . . . we are wholly in the wrong.
        1. . . . the whole movement . . . has been a movement . . . to extend slavery.
        2. . . . no reference has been made in this affair to Christian ideas. . . .
VI. What shall we do?
    A. We can hold public meetings in favor of peace.
    B. We can . . . spread the sentiment of peace.
CONCLUSION: "Though hand join in hand, the wicked shall not prosper."

OUTLINE FROM PARKER'S SERMON

THE TRUE IDEA OF CHRISTIANITY[1]

INTRODUCTION: For nearly a year we have assembled within these walls from week to week. . . .

THESIS: . . . what do we design to do? We are here to establish a church. . . .

DEFINITIONS: And a Christian church, as I understand it, is a body of men and women united together in a common desire of religious excellence. . . .

PARTITION: The action of a Christian church seems to me to be twofold:
    I. . . . first on its members. . . .
    II. On others out of the pale.

DISCUSSION: I. The first design of a church then is to help ourselves become Christians.
    A. If Jesus be the Model-man, then should a Christian church teach its members to hold the same relation to God that Christ held.
    B. We can attain this relation to God and man only on condition that we are free.
    C. . . . every truth is of God, and will lead to good. . . .
    D. Here too should the spirit of devotion be encouraged.
    E. Here too should be had the best instruction. . . .
    F. . . . another way in which a church should act on its own household is by direct material help in time of need.

[1] *Ibid.*, XIII, 19–49.

II. But the church must have an action on others out of its pale.
 A. A church should be a means of reforming the world. . . .
 B. . . . it should be a society for the promotion of good works.
CONCLUSION: . . . let us be true to our sentiments and ideas. . . . you can make this church a foundation of life. . . .

Style

Sources of Parker's Style. The chief determinants of Parker's style were (1) example, (2) practice, (3) the audience. Behind these external circumstances was, of course, the individual personality of Parker; but this conditioning influence must be revealed as a permeating factor, not as a separate consideration.

Although Parker believed that "no man can be a *model* for another," he did favor "study of the Roman and the Attic Orators" and comparison of "them with the American as an exercise, not forgetting the English and the French."[1] He was exposed to the embellishment of the Gorgias school, the strength of Demosthenes, the copiousness of Cicero, the simple precision of Quintilian,[2] the extravagance of the early church fathers,[3] the beauty of Milton and Plato, the fullness of Burke, the dry precision of Bacon, the plainness of the Puritans, and the original freshness of his own new soil.[4] Considering that he studied always critically, accepting the preference of taste and not the dictum of tradition, the natural inference is that his style should be eclectic, yet bear the peculiar mark of Parker.

As a second means of improving style, Parker believed practice efficacious.[5] As to his method of practice in early years, we know only that he studied composition of sermons with Ware and that he gave attention to style. The author finds no evidence of labored revision in these early years, and assuredly Parker's later sermons were written hastily and once only. He said, "I write swiftly though I think slowly, and so many of the literary defects of *all* my writing are no doubt the result of haste."[6] His only "Receipt for writing" was to "think the *subject* over long before . . .

[1] Letter to Joseph Allen, Feb. 14, 1848.
[2] Journal; letter to Joseph Allen, Feb. 14, 1848; letter to Silsbee, Aug. 21, 1836.
[3] "I think there is no writer of that period whom I do not know something of."—Letter to Joseph Allen, Feb. 14, 1848.
[4] The prose works of Milton in the Parker Collection at Boston are heavily marked and otherwise give evidence of much use but do not compare with the worn and marked pages of Plato's *Republic*. Of the *Phaedrus* Parker said, "I was appalled by the . . . beauty of the style. . . . I read and reread and read again."—Letter to Silsbee, Dec. 19, 1837.
Francis Bacon's works show considerable marking but no annotation. In speaking and writing, Parker makes reference to the English philosopher no fewer than sixteen times. The Puritans of England he refers to continually.
[5] Letter to George H. Ellis, Nov. 9, 1836.
[6] Letter to E. Peabody, January, 1841.

then . . . the *form* . . . arrange the parts to see if they are well proportioned. . . . Then I write!"[1]

His practice, then, was much, but not meticulous. In the fullest sense, his writing was extemporaneous, thus contributing to its oral character.

That Parker consciously endeavored to suit his style to the listening audience is his own testimony: "I feel bound to communicate my views just so fast and so far as men can understand them,—no farther. If they do not understand them when I propound them, the fault, I think, is mine, and not theirs."[2] "The good folks at Spring Street" were "not men of dictionaries. . . . Hence come words, and things, and illustrations and allusions, which are not in good taste when viewed from any point except the pulpit at Spring Street."[3] In fact, throughout all Parker's statements that touch upon rhetoric is continual reference, direct and indirect, to the audience as the primary factor in conditioning style. The one statement that best epitomizes his theory is: "In the expression of the thought, the shortest way is generally best, and it is better to state one thing once and no more."[4]

Qualities of Parker's Style. Rhetorically, the most significant contribution of Parker's sensitiveness to audience is the oral quality of his style. Add to the staccato effect of his short, terse sentences the directness achieved by the frequent use of "I," "we," "you," and one has named only the more evident factors that so amply justify Parrington's statement that "he was always the speaker rather than the writer and his printed pages bear the unmistakable marks of impetuous oral discourse."[5] In Parker's more purely literary contributions, where the obvious keys to audience-speaker relationship are subordinated and a superficial detachment thus accomplished, the reader still feels the personal drive of Parker and the presence of a living audience as the object of persuasion.

In giving to his style the concreteness so essential to popular discourse, Parker again considered his audience. For the "good folks at Spring Street" he would "never use a word of Latin Origin" when he could "find one of native birth."[6] To his Music Hall congregation he said:

In my preaching I have used plain, simple words, sometimes making what I could not find ready. . . . I have always preferred to use, when fit, the every-day words in which men think and talk, scold, make love, and pray, so that generous-

---

[1] Letter to Miss Grover, Oct. 6, 1857.
[2] Letter to Silsbee, 1838.
[3] Letter to E. Peabody, January, 1841.
[4] Letter to Keach.
[5] V. L. Parrington, *The Romantic Revolution in America*, 1800–1860, (New York, Harcourt, Brace and Company, 1927), p. 425.
[6] Letter to E. Peabody, January, 1841.

hearted philosophy, clad in common dress, might more easily become familiar to plain-clad men. It is with customary tools that we work the best, especially when use has made the handles smooth. . . . I have . . . on my side the example of all the great masters of speech . . . Homer, Dante, Shakespeare . . . Luther, Latimer, Barrow, and South. . . . [1]

The plainness and simplicity of these words did not mean the dry plainness of abstraction; rather, they were words that should quicken the dormant life experiences of his middle-class New England hearers into new imaginative patterns. He well states the difference himself: "It is better to use the definite than indefinite terms; to say a *man*, and not an individual or human being. I love specific terms, such as Ellen, or a *man* or *woman*. . . . "[2] He used the Cohasset Rocks in preference to Gibraltar "because they are an object well known." If he "were to speak of birds in a sermon," he would "not mention the Nightingale and the Skylark, but the Brown Thrasher and the Black-bird for the same reason."[3] Classical and Biblical names, objects, persons, and incidents were by no means barred from Parker's speaking vocabulary, but each had its companion in a Boston shop or market, the Massachusetts shore line, or the New England countryside.

Although figurative language has power in effecting the concreteness to which attention has just been given, it deserves separate consideration for its value in accomplishing clearness, illustration, and pleasure of the imagination. Parker's specific statement is that "things well known need no illustration except for beauty and the delight it gives. . . . "[4] But a more complete exposition of his theory may be inferred from his long, heavy pencil mark beside the following passage in the copy of Whately's *Elements of Logic*, bequeathed by him to the Boston Public Library:

It is not improbable that many indifferent sermons have been produced by the ambiguity of the word "plain"; a young divine perceives the truth of the maxim, that "for the lower orders one's language cannot be too plain" . . . and when he proceeds to practice, the word "plain" indistinctly flits before him, as it were, and often checks him in the use of *ornaments* of style, such as metaphor, epithet, antithesis, etc., which are opposed to "plainness" in a totally different sense of the word, being by no means necessarily adverse to perspicuity, but rather, in many cases, conducive to it. . . .

[1] *Cent. Ed.*, XIII, 398–400. Not only the audience and the great masters but also Parker's inward nature determined his preference for these simple but image-compelling words. He said: " . . . for this I must plead the necessity of my own nature, delighting in common things, trees, grass, oxen.—*Ibid.*, XIII, 399.
[2] Letter to Keach.
[3] Letter to the Reverend William H. White, Mar. 11, 1848.
[4] Letter to Keach.

In addition to the pencil mark, significant in itself, Parker has written, "I will grant this in part."

Giving his theory full rein in practice, Parker indulged freely in all types of figures, particularly the metaphor. That occasional excess resulted cannot be doubted. He said of himself: "In all my sermons is an excess of metaphors, similes, and all sorts of figures of speech. But this is my nature— I could not help it if I would." He took "illustration from the common objects" even though they were "not in good taste when viewed from any point except the pulpit . . . "[1] and criticized great preachers of the past for drawing "their figures from the schoolmen" rather than from life.[2] Some of his metaphors are at the same stroke both beautiful and powerful;[3] perhaps the great majority possess power of imagery but are doubtfully elegant;[4] rarely one is obscure or unfitting. Abundance of figurative passages does not, however, characterize the whole of Parker's speeches. They are most frequent in the conclusions, least prevalent in those introductions which are of philosophical nature, but are never absent and rarely scarce. Thus his work has been variously characterized. To one his style is "conventional, tame, dull";[5] to another it is "Beautiful, superbly beautiful,"[6] and yet again "like the music of Mozart."[7] His "eloquence became

---

[1] Letter to E. Peabody, January, 1841; see also letter to S. P. Andrews, Mar. 16, 1837.

[2] "The writings of Taylor, or Barrow and South, of Bossuet, Massillon, and Bourdaloue . . . always presuppose a narrow audience of men of nice culture. So they drew their figures from the schoolmen, from the Greek anthology, from heathen classics and the Christian Fathers. Their illustrations were embellishments to the scholar, but only palpable darkness to the people."—*Cent. Ed.*, VIII, 17–18.

[3] "Memory rakes in the ashes of the dead. . . . "—*Cent. Ed.*, III, 343.

"I saw why Webster caught at the Fugitive Slave Bill; it . . . was the red-hot iron hook to a man falling like Lucifer, never to hope again."—*Ibid.*, XII, 373.

"Mr. Webster stamped his foot, and broke through into the great hollow of practical atheism. . . . The firm-set base of northern cities quaked and yawned with gaping rents. Penn's 'sandy foundation' shook again, and black men fled from the city of brotherly love, as doves, with plaintive cry, flee from a farmer's barn when summer lightning stabs the roof. There was a twist in Faneuil Hall, and the doors could not open wide enough for Liberty to regain her ancient cradle. . . . "—*Ibid.*, VII, 338.

[4] "How noisy is this great channel of business, wherein humanity rolls to and fro, now running into shops, now sucked down into cellars. . . . "—*Ibid.*, VIII, 420.

"Slavery, the most hideous snake which southern regions breed, with fifteen unequal feet, came crawling north; then avarice, the foulest worm which northern cities gender in their heat, went crawling south. . . . "—*Ibid.*, VII, 336–337.

"How ill those gaudy ruffles become the withered dewlap that hangs beneath her chin! . . . "—*Ibid.*, X, 195.

[5] *Boston Daily Atlas and Bee*, Nov. 7, 1851.

[6] Letter from Wm. H. Seward, Apr. 21, 1854.

[7] Letter from Chas. Sumner, 1850.

a . . . brilliant scene painting—large, fresh, profuse, rapid, showy. . . . "[1]
but was invariably judged the fulfillment of his own demand for clarity.[2]

Parker's use of comparison and contrast bridges the uncertain gap
between analogy and metaphor and may for all practical purposes be
illustrated in both frequency and quality by reference to those divisions
(*cf.* pages 249, 258). Accumulation of incident Parker did not obviously
or consistently employ. Climax he achieved largely by sudden bursts of
description, exclamation, figurative language, and emotional appeal.
Repetition he avoided, in keeping with his theory of saying a thing well
once and no more. Humor is not discovered, though it is sometimes referred
to as characteristic of his speech.[3]

Rich in Anglo-Saxon words, abounding in illustrations of native cast,
concrete with the description of things rather than abstract principles, his
style was yet a kaleidoscope of the ages of culture, now simple and plain,
suddenly rich and full, putting "feelings into words before they have been
cooled by the intellect," so that it had "at times a torrent-like rush to it
as if it came right from the heart."[4] Reminiscent of many schools, Parker's
style yet represented his own enthusiasm and eccentricity; it reflected at
once the anomaly of his personality, the rationality of his mind, the richness of his reading; its faults were the faults of many of his activities—the
lack of finish consequent to attempting too much. Effective but inelegant,
rhetorical but not literary—this was Parker.

Presentation; Reception and Results

Paucity of evidence is in itself sometimes occasion for positive inference.
In the case of Parker, about whom so much has been written, the fact that
only rarely is mention made of his platform manner suggests that his
"power over an audience" was "not . . . in his manner, *but in what he
says.*"[5] Fortunately the evidence available is sufficiently definite to permit
a clear, though brief, description of his speaking presence.

"Short and sturdy in figure," with "a trim and well packed body and
limbs,"[6] Parker was "five feet, eight inches high" and weighed "about

---

[1] Thomas W. Higginson, *Contemporaries* (Boston, Houghton Mifflin Company, 1899),
p. 52.

[2] Letter to Keach; letter to Convers Francis, Jan. 8, 1839; Weiss, *op. cit.*, I, 178; O. B.
Frothingham, *Theodore Parker* (Boston, James R. Osgood and Co., 1874), p. 554.

[3] James F. Clarke, *A Look at the Life of Theodore Parker* delivered June 3, 1880 (Boston,
George H. Ellis Co., 1910); *Boston Evening Transcript*, Jan. 26, 1861.

[4] *National Intelligencer*, Aug. 14, 1841.

[5] *Boston Saturday Evening Express*, Nov. 13, 1858.

[6] *Boston Daily Atlas and Bee*, Nov. 7, 1851; *Christian Register*, May 26, 1910.

150 pounds."[1] Early in life the larger portion of his head was bald,[2] appearing as "a flesh colored mask,"[3] while at the back of his head hung long, slightly curling hair, light brown in 1846, but soon turning gray. His head was large, his forehead high and broad and "massive"; in all, "a head that phrenologists would not be apt to find fault with." His "regular" features,[4] so "quiet" that they gave him an "almost bashful look,"[5] yielded to a "somewhat more than current beard," silvery gray as early as 1848.[6] His eyes were blue, "not large, but . . . keen and piercing," except as they were obscured by his "gold mounted spectacles." Altogether his "simple and uncharacteristic" dress[7] and his "plain, modest," unassuming manner gave him somewhat more of the appearance of "schoolmaster or farmer,"[8] or "ploughman, than priest."[9]

Although Parker studied elocution under the direction of Henry Ware, Jr., at Harvard,[10] he believed that there were "no tricks in real eloquence; they belong . . . only to the low practice of the stage. . . . An impressive mode of delivery . . . will depend on qualities that lie a good deal deeper than the surface." As for gestures, "to some men they are natural and useful; to others not at all. Nature is the guide."[11] Apparently nature guided him to use little action. As he rose slowly and leaned "upon the desk,"[12] his manner was "modest, yet showing a familiarity with the business."[13] He had "no graces in action . . . his gestures" were "few, and some of them awkward."[14] In short, it seems that Parker relied almost wholly upon subject matter and voice to carry his persuasions.

[1] Letter to Frances P. Cobbe, Apr. 22, 1848.
[2] Letter to Desor, Aug. 24, 1854.
[3] *Medford Lyceum*, Mar. 6, 1857.
[4] *Streeter's Weekly Boston Star*, Apr. 11, 1846.
[5] *Manchester Mirror*, Mar. 8, 1852.
[6] *Boston Saturday Evening Express*, Nov. 13, 1848.
[7] "He always wore at church the plain, dark dress which he thought befitting the service." —Weiss, *op. cit.*, I, 409.
[8] *Manchester Mirror*, Mar. 6, 1857, and Nov. 8, 1852.
[9] James Russell Lowell, *A Fable for Critics* (Boston, Houghton Mifflin Company, 1891), p. 55.
[10] John Ware, *Memoir of the Life of Henry Ware, Jr.* (Boston, James Munroe and Co., 1854), p. 105; letter to E. Greene, July 11, 1834.
[11] Letter to Keach.
[12] *Manchester Mirror*, Mar. 8, 1852.
[13] *Boston Daily Atlas and Bee*, Nov. 7, 1851.
[14] *Manchester Mirror*, Nov. 8, 1852; *Banner of Light*, June 28, 1863.
Lowell said, "If not dreadfully awkward, not graceful at least, his gestures all downright and same, if you will, as of brown-fisted Hobnail in hoeing a drill."—Lowell, *op. cit.*, p. 55. E. S. Gannett described him as "quietly standing" and using "little or no gesture."— *Christian Register*, May 26, 1910.

Parker recommended that one *"speak distinctly* and in the natural tones of conversation as far as possible. In most (country) churches we need not speak above the natural tones of voice in order to be heard."[1] It is readily evident that his "natural tones of voice" referred largely, if not wholly, to intensity. That he meant to imply also the avoidance of affectation in either pitch or quality may be inferred from general knowledge of the man. As to his practice, one observer said, "He speaks distinctly" but has not "much compass of voice."[2] Another testified that he read "monotonously and dryly. . . . His voice level and monotonous"; but in the same description, "pleasant."[3] He had "little voice," and in that was "nothing in the charm of intonation."[4] He did not use, then, and probably did not possess great range of pitch, quality, or intensity in ordinary discourse.

Most descriptions of Parker begin by saying, "He was not an orator as the world goes,"[5] or, "He certainly has no graces of oratory. Whatever he is and has fame for, it is certainly *not* for any oratorical possession, in the sense in which that term is usually understood."[6] Or, "He is not an orator."[7] Most writers, however, eventually say, "And yet there is a certain winningness of manner which attracts and gratifies the hearer"; or, "Yet there was something in the power of his thought which controlled all who listened to him";[8] or, there is "entire absence of display in his . . . sociable style of delivery."[9] Or, "One soon finds his attention arrested by a certain something in the matter and style of the speaker which steals upon the sympathies unawares, . . . "[10] It would appear, then, that somewhere within this freedom from ostentation or artificiality was a quality or power of personality that reached out to take its hold upon the audience. Power of thought, yes; and power of oratorical composition; but yet something more that is purely an aspect of delivery. The answer lies probably in the observation of one correspondent, that "It is his deep earnestness that chains you."[11] Parker's own testimony supports the conclusion: "If you have felt with vigor and thought with vigor, you will . . . speak with

---

[1] Letter to Keach.
[2] *Manchester Mirror*, Mar. 8, 1852.
[3] *Boston Saturday Evening Express*, Nov. 13, 1858.
[4] *Banner of Light*, June 28, 1863.
[5] *Ibid.*
[6] *Boston Saturday Evening Express*, Nov. 13, 1858.
[7] *Manchester Mirror*, Mar. 8, 1852.
[8] *Ibid.*, June 28, 1863.
[9] *Medford Lyceum*, Mar. 6, 1857.
[10] *Boston Daily Atlas and Bee*, Nov. 7, 1851.
[11] *Manchester Mirror*, Mar. 8, 1852.

vigor."[1] Indeed, one who has studied the real Parker knows that he went into the pulpit feeling deeply what he had to say. That "nature" was a sufficient guide for him is not a matter of astonishment.

Although Professor Ware was one of the earliest exponents of the extemporaneous mode of delivery, believing that it "favors the concentration of the powers" and that the "presence of the audience gives vitality to composition,"[2] Parker was unquestionably a manuscript preacher.[3] This fact does not mean, however, that his preaching was devoid of extempore quality. In his early preaching, he "delivered the written word, but added much that was better and more reaching extemporaneously."[4] In later years the practice was to write more than he had time to preach and to omit portions at the time of delivery.[5] He invariably read from manuscript, but his dependence thereon was not so complete as to rob his speech of extempore freshness and audience adaptation.

In general, Parker's theory that delivery should arise from the nature of the man and should take the conversational mode as its point of departure receives application in his unaffected and unostentatious manner of presentation.

Attesting Parker's immediate power over an audience, ample evidence is available;[6] that he created a substantial theological stir in his time likewise is obvious;[7] that he exerted no inconsiderable pressure against the social ills of his day is probable; that he was a significant factor in the movement against slavery is supported by the protests of the proslavery group;[8] but an accurate measure of his immediate or ultimate effect upon the behavior of men is scarcely feasible. The 60,000 to 100,000 persons who heard him each year[9] signed no contract of allegiance to him, his

[1] Letter to Keach.

[2] Ware, *op. cit.*, pp. 27, 31.

[3] Letter to Caroline Dall, undated; letter to Keach; *Christian Register*, May 26, 1910; Journal, Oct. 31, 1852.

[4] Letters to Miss Lydia Cabot, Aug. 10, 1836, and Aug. 22, 1836.

[5] Journal, Oct. 31, 1852; letter to Caroline Healey, Nov. 29, 1842.

This practice of omission is readily evident upon comparing newspaper reports with his later printings, in which the whole was included. The omissions were most frequently paragraphs but occasionally sentences.

[6] *Commonwealth*, Jan. 6, 1853; *Boston Index*, Aug. 28, 1886; *Boston Daily Atlas and Bee*, Nov. 7, 1860; *Boston Saturday Evening Express*, Nov. 13, 1858; *Fortnightly Review*, 8: 147; Emily Dickinson, *Letters of Emily Dickinson* (M. L. Todd, ed., Boston, Roberts Bros., 1894), p. 194; letter from Charles Sumner, undated.

[7] Journal, Jan. 23, 1843; letter to Miss Healey, Dec. 3, 1841; *Christian Review*, 7: 161, 321; *Brownson Quarterly Review*, 2: 222; *The New Englander*, 2: 321, 528; 16: 575; *British Quarterly Review*, 11: 1.

[8] *Fortnightly Review*, 8: 147; Chadwick, *op. cit.*, p. 387; *Richmond* (Va.) *Examiner*, Nov. 6, 1852; *The Liberator*, Nov. 2, 1852; *National Intelligencer*, Nov. 16, 1852.

[9] *Cent. Ed.*, XIII, 349

theology, or his philosophy; they gave no official vote of approval or rejection to his proposals; but'the undeniable fact is that audiences of 3,000 did come each week to hear him. Thus the rhetorical effect of Theodore Parker must be measured in terms of attention, not demonstration, not conversion, not in votes; in terms of social and political agitation, not constructive organization of institutions or principles. He was a great popularizer of thought and knowledge,[1] a demolisher of conservatism in religious thought, a relentless agitator against all he considered evil, a stimulator of audiences; but "with the personal presence of Mr. Parker the chief element of his power over men has passed away. . . . "[2] His was the transiency of rhetorical effect, not the permanence of measurable contribution.

BIBLIOGRAPHICAL NOTE

Although quantities of material upon Theodore Parker are available in a variety of libraries, some explanation should be made of the present distribution of secondary and original sources.

In the Parker Collection at the Boston Public Library are approximately twenty thousand volumes of books and pamphlets once owned by Parker. Among them are all his own works ever published either in pamphlet or book form. Most of these printed works are also available at the Library of the Massachusetts Historical Society, at the Harvard University Library, and in lesser quantities elsewhere. A relatively complete bibliographical outline of Parker's published works and of publications concerning him is in Vol. XV of the *Centenary Edition*.

The present condition of original sources is gratifying in the sense that much is yet available but disappointing because so much has been unnecessarily lost. In the Boston Public Library are a few original letters, some copies of others that Mrs. Parker had transcribed for the biographers of Parker, several volumes of scrapbooks, a few original sermon manuscripts, including the first draft of his "Experience as a Minister," and the one small volume in which he kept a record of his preachings. Here also are available many of the newspapers in which Parker's speeches were often fully reported, accompanied occasionally by enlightening comment.

In the Library of the Massachusetts Historical Society are eighteen volumes of his manuscript Journals and letters. In the Library of the Unitarian Association are two more volumes of his Journal, some manuscript sermons, and a few letters. One volume of Parker-Sumner correspondence is at the Harvard University Library. A collection of Parker-Herndon correspondence is in the University of Iowa Library. A small collection of miscellaneous papers for 1856 is in the Yale University Library. A half dozen letters to Senator Wilson are in the Library of Congress. Forty letters are at the Clarke-Hancock House in Lexington.

His records of marriages and deaths during his ministry at Boston, together with some few letters, are at the Unitarian Church in West Roxbury. Parker's Journal for the last year of his life is in the possession of the Reverend John Haynes Holmes, of New York City.

On April 23, 1918, a quantity of Parker manuscript materials was sold at auction and, unfortunately, scattered beyond recovery.

[1] *Atlantic Monthly*, 6: 453–457; *Richmond* (Va.) *Examiner*, Nov. 6, 1852.
[2] *Bibliotheca sacra*, 22: 620.

SELECTED BIBLIOGRAPHY

Manuscript Documents

Journal: Parker's diary-notebook.
Letters to and from Parker (see Bibliographical Note).
Paper prepared at request of Ripley for biographical notice of Parker, September, 1854.
Parker Genealogy, prepared by Theodore Parker.
Record of preachings.
Sermons.

Works of Theodore Parker

Centenary Edition of the Works of Theodore Parker, 15 vols, Boston, American Unitarian Association, 1907–1910.
The Collected Works of Theodore Parker, Frances P. Cobbe, ed., 14 vols., London, Trubner and Co., 1863.
Speeches, Addresses, and Occasional Sermons, 3 vols., Boston, Horace B. Fuller, 1867.
West Roxbury Sermons, Samuel Barrows, ed., Boston, Robert Bros., 1892.

Secondary Sources

Chadwick, John W.: *Theodore Parker*, Boston, Houghton Mifflin Company, 1900.
Dean, Peter: *The Life and Teachings of Theodore Parker*, London, Williams & Norgate, Ltd.. 1877.
Frothingham, O. B.: *Theodore Parker*, Boston, James R. Osgood and Co., 1874.
Reville, Albert: *The Life and Writings of Theodore Parker*, London, Simpkin, Marshall, and Co., 1865.
Weiss, John: *Life and Correspondence of Theodore Parker*, 2 vols., New York, D. Appleton and Company, 1864.

Books

Addison, D. D.: *The Clergy in American Life and Letters*, London, Macmillan and Company, Ltd., 1900.
English State Trials: A Complete Collection of State Trials and Proceedings upon High Treason from the Reign of King Richard II to the Reign of King George II, 8 vols., 3d ed., London, 1742.
Higginson, Thomas W.: *Contemporaries*, Boston, Houghton Mifflin Company, 1899.
———: *Letters and Journals 1846–1906*, Mary T. Higginson, ed., Boston, Cambridge University Press, 1921.
Howe, Julia Ward: *Reminiscences*, Boston, Houghton Mifflin Company, 1900.
Lambertson, F. W.: A Survey and Analysis of American Homiletic Theory Prior to 1860, Ph. D. Thesis, University of Iowa, not published, 1930.
Ware, Henry, Jr.: *Hints on Extemporaneous Speaking*, Boston, Cummings, Hilliard and Co., 1824.
Ware, John: *Memoir of the Life of Henry Ware, Jr.*, Boston, James Munroe and Co., 1854.

8

Henry Ward Beecher

by LIONEL CROCKER

Henry Ward Beecher was born in Litchfield, Conn., June 24, 1813, the son of Lyman Beecher. He was educated at Amherst College, class of 1834; at Lane Theological Seminary, class of 1837; held pastorates at Lawrenceburg, Ind., 1837–1839; Indianapolis, 1839–1847; Plymouth Church, Brooklyn, 1847–1887. He visited England and Europe in 1850 and 1863 and England in 1886 on lecture tour; in 1863 he gave a series of addresses in England at Manchester, Glasgow, Edinburgh, Liverpool, and London. He supported Fremont for the Presidency in 1856, gave the oration at the raising of the flag at Fort Sumter in 1865, supported Cleveland for the Presidency in 1884; was editor of the *Independent*, 1861–1863; part owner and editor of the *Christian Union*, 1869–1880. In addition to his sermons, special lectures, extensive lyceum lectures, and newspaper writing, he also published twenty-four books between 1845 and 1887; died, Mar. 8, 1887.

I. *Family*

Henry Ward Beecher was the next child in succession to Harriet Beecher, the author of *Uncle Tom's Cabin*. These two children were the most famous of the large Lyman Beecher family, which included Catharine, a pioneer in education for women; William Henry Beecher, who might be said to have failed in the ministry; Edward Beecher, who became president of Illinois College and Knox College; Mary Foote Beecher, who was the only Beecher to live a private life; Charles Beecher, the heretic; Isabella Beecher, the suffragist; Thomas K. Beecher, the builder of the First People's Church and a friend of Mark Twain; and James Beecher, the sailor and soldier. All these Beechers are engagingly treated by Lyman Beecher Stowe, in *Saints, Sinners and Beechers*.[1] Lyman Beecher Stowe gives the right emphasis in portraying Henry Ward and Harriet by devoting six of his twenty-six chapters to Henry and five to Harriet, thus acknowledging that the pastor of the Plymouth Church and the author of *Uncle Tom's Cabin* were the most important of this unusual family. Albert J. Beveridge has said, "The Beecher family is one of the most eminent in American history, nearly all of the thirteen children of Lyman Beecher having attained distinction in literature and theology."[2]

[1] *Saints, Sinners and Beechers* (Indianapolis, The Bobbs-Merrill Company, 1934).
[2] *Abraham Lincoln*, 1809–1858 (Boston, Houghton Mifflin Company, 1928), p. 233.

II. *Chronology*

In 1826 Litchfield was given up by the Beechers for Boston, where Lyman was called to be pastor of the Hanover Street Church. In 1832 Boston was deserted for Cincinnati, an important city of the frontier, situated on the Ohio river, which communicated with points east and south. Lane Theological Seminary had called Lyman to help train preachers to save the West for Protestantism. During most of the years the Beecher family was in Boston, Henry Ward was at Amherst, passing through the academy and the newly formed college. On receiving his diploma in 1834, he joined the family in Cincinnati to study with his father. After his ordination in 1837, Henry Ward went down the river to Lawrenceburg, Ind., to take charge of a weak Presbyterian church, where, as he himself said, he did "everything but hear himself preach." After two hard years, he was called to the Second Presbyterian Church at the state capital, Indianapolis, a city of four thousand. Here he remained for eight fruitful years, developing as a preacher, as a citizen, and as a reformer. He became, for example, a trustee of Wabash College; he gave the commencement address at Asbury College, later known as DePauw University; he preached the funeral sermon at the death of General William Henry Harrison. Slavery, intemperance, and other social problems were attacked with a power that centered attention upon him. His talent demanded greater opportunities than the capital of a pioneer state could offer. The attention of the newly formed congregation in Brooklyn known as the Plymouth Church was drawn to him. He accepted their call at the age of thirty-four, in 1847.

To recuperate from the strenuous task of building a new church in 1850, Plymouth Church sent him to England and the Continent. Throughout his life, his congregation was exceedingly generous to him. In 1855 he published his *Plymouth Collection*, one of the first church hymnals to have a wide influence upon American church life. In 1856 he campaigned for John C. Fremont for the Presidency because of his stand on slavery; this endorsement launched Beecher on a national career in political circles. In 1860 his personal acquaintance with Lincoln began, although Beecher must have met Lincoln in Springfield in 1855 when on a lecture tour, and Herndon had some of Beecher's books, to which Lincoln had access. From 1861 to 1863 Beecher was editor of the *Independent*, a religious journal of national circulation, to which he contributed his "Star Papers." Many of his attacks on social questions and his sharpest criticisms of Lincoln found expression in this journal. While ostensibly on a trip to England for his health in 1863, a trip financed by his congregation, he was "prevailed" upon to deliver five addresses on the Civil War. These addresses, to which fuller reference is made later in this chapter, indissolubly connected his name with that national calamity.

In 1870 Beecher became editor of the *Christian Union*, with Lyman Abbott as an assistant editor from 1875 to 1881. The growth of the *Christian Union* at the expense of the *Independent*, of which Theodore Tilton was the editor, Beecher's friends believed, had much to do in 1874 with Mr. Tilton's suit against Beecher for alienating the affections of his wife. The trial dragged on for six months and ended in a disagreement of the jury, nine of whom affirmed their belief in Beecher's innocence.[1] His congregation paid the expenses of this trial, which were more than $100,000.

He published the first volume of his *Life of Jesus the Christ* in 1871. The first of the Yale Lectures on Preaching (by many thought to be the most valuable of the three series) was given in 1872. Henry W. Sage founded this lectureship for the express purpose of providing his pastor, Henry Ward Beecher, with an opportunity of discussing his theory of extemporaneous preaching. So important has this lectureship become in the life of the Protestant church that Edgar DeWitt Jones has declared, "To be chosen for this lectureship is the highest honor of the kind that can come to any minister."[2] In 1884 Beecher stepped out of his party and supported Grover Cleveland for the Presidency in order to bring about reform in government. In 1886 James B. Pond, his lecture manager, persuaded him to lecture in England during the summer.[3] The strain of eighty-four appearances, his friends felt, brought on his death on March 8, 1887. These, briefly, are the important dates in Beecher's career between the years 1813 and 1887.

III. *Preacher*

Influence. As this chronological outline is reviewed two major lines of endeavor are apparent: he was a preacher and he was a reformer. These two life interests will be taken up separately.

As a preacher he influenced the content of the sermon in America, and he influenced the manner of its presentation. Whereas the sermon had been concerned with the inculcation of a correct set of beliefs, he put the emphasis on the implications of religion in everyday living, and whereas the sermons had been argumentative he helped to make them illustrative.

[1] For accounts of the trial friendly to Beecher, consult Thomas W. Knox, *Life and Works of Henry Ward Beecher* (Hartford, Conn., Hartford Publishing Co.), Chaps. XIX and XX; and Lyman Abbott, *Henry Ward Beecher* (Boston, Houghton Mifflin Company), Chap. XII. For unfriendly accounts see Mark Van Doren, *An Autobiography of America* (New York, Albert & Charles Boni, Inc., 1929), pp. 648–662; and Paxton Hibben, *Henry Ward Beecher; An American Portrait* (New York, Doubleday, Doran Company, Inc., 1927).

[2] *American Preachers of To-day* (Indianapolis, The Bobbs-Merrill Company, 1933), p. 280.

[3] See James B. Pond, *A Summer in England with Henry Ward Beecher* (Fords, Howard & Hulbert), 1887.

Beecher's emphasis upon religion rather than upon theology was an outgrowth of his father's struggles at Lane Theological Seminary. Doctrines had split the Presbyterian Church on the frontier into the Old School and the New School. Lyman Beecher had brought the liberal spirit of New England into the West. He lined up Lane Seminary with the New School Presbyterianism. The struggle of the 1830's was a prototype of the fight between fundamentalism and modernism of the 1920's. When Henry Ward was called to the Lawrenceburg church, which was Old School, trouble began. Either Henry Ward had to join the Old School or the pulpit would be declared vacant. Realizing that in Henry Ward it had one preacher in a thousand, the Lawrenceburg church left the Old School Presbytery. Henry Ward's distaste for theological bickering dates from these early struggles. "My whole life," he says, "has more or less taken its color from the controversy which led to the division of the Old School and the New School Presbyterians."[1]

In those early years of heresy hunting, centered so largely around his father, Henry Ward saw that sectarianism was destroying the gospel of Jesus Christ. Early he vowed, "I will never be a sectary." An echo of this youthful determination is seen in his address at the centenary anniversary celebration of Channing's birth. "It seems to me that the consent of men, whether they are in the Mother Church or in any of the scattered sectarian churches,—orthodox, half orthodox, or heterodox,—is all gained tonight, and gained on one point: that a man who loves God fervently and his fellow men heartily, and devotes his life to that love is a member of every communion and of every church, and is orthodox in spite of orthodoxy and everything else"[2]—an all-inclusive statement that puts the emphasis not on belief but on action motivated by love. Further light is thrown on Beecher's thinking on religious matters in the following condemnation of Jonathan Edwards' theology:

Great as Edwards was, and far in advance of his age in many respects, he yet was unconsciously under the grossly materializing theological habits of the medieval schools. The monarchial figures of government in the Bible, and the figures of material punishment are full terrible enough. But to employ the imagination, as Edwards did, in inventing new horrors for hell, above all, in attempting to picture the Divine Heart as so in love with justice that it rejoices in the merited sufferings of the wicked, was a sad perversion of the functions of the imagination. In some respects Edward's terrific sermon, "Sinners in the Hands of an Angry God," may

[1] William C. Beecher, Samuel Scoville, Mrs. Henry Ward Beecher, *A Biography of Henry Ward Beecher* (New York, Charles L. Webster and Co., 1888), Chaps. VIII and IX, give in detail the controversy mentioned here.

[2] Newell Dwight Hillis, *Lectures and Orations of Henry Ward Beecher* (New York, Fleming H. Revell Company, 1913), p. 157.

be ranked with Dante's *Inferno* or Michael Angelo's painting of the "General Judgment." But who can look upon the detestable representations of the painter, or the hideous scenes of the Florentine poet, without a shudder of wonder that they should have ever come from such tender and noble hearts?[1]

Much testimony as to the effectiveness of Beecher's preaching, freed as it was from theological speculation, exists. Among the thousands that were attracted to his ministry, based on the love of God, was Michael Pupin, who was for years a professor at Columbia University. His reaction to Beecher's preaching reveals what one young man thought of Beecher's gospel: "I firmly believed that Beecher was preaching a new gospel, the American gospel of humanity, the same gospel which his great sister had preached. Every member of his congregation looked to me like a faithful disciple of this doctrine."[2] The historian Allan Nevins, in surveying the nineteenth century, believes that it was Beecher's adherence to a "theology adapted to the needs of the day" that helped make him one of the national leaders.[3] George A. Gordon, in his *Yale Lectures on Preaching*, credited Beecher with leadership in the break with Calvinism in America:

Henry Ward Beecher did more than any other preacher to break up and abolish the Calvinistic Moloch. He plead for the infinite Father of Mankind when all the seminaries of the land, with their prestige, their learning, their opportunity and power, were putting first God, the Sovereign, God, the Moral Governor of the world. It was an immense battle, like that of David and a host of Goliaths. Men in middle life well recall the opinion industriously disseminated, that Beecher was no theologian. It was said that the great preacher was neither a scholar nor a consistent thinker. The indictment of a whole generation of scholars and teachers seemed strong enough to send the great commoner into speedy and everlasting oblivion. Contrary to all expectation the professionals failed. Greater influence upon the religious belief of the people of the United States has been exerted by none than by William Ellery Channing and Henry Ward Beecher.[4]

When Harry Emerson Fosdick wanted a quotation to bring quickly into focus the belief of the nineteenth century in the Calvinistic Moloch, which he was condemning, he borrowed one of Henry Ward Beecher's attacks on this monster created by theologians. This is the quotation that Fosdick used:

To tell me that back of Christ there is a God, who for unnumbered centuries has gone on creating men and sweeping them like dead flies—nay, like living ones—into

---

[1] *Yale Lectures on Preaching* (1st series, New York, J. B. Ford, 1872), p. 261.

[2] *From Immigrant to Inventor* (New York, Charles Scribner's Sons, 1926), p. 107.

[3] *The Emergence of Modern America*, 1865–1878 (New York, The Macmillan Company, 1928), p. 344.

[4] *Ultimate Conceptions of Faith* (Boston, Houghton Mifflin Company, 1903), p. 341.

hell, is to ask me to worship a being so much worse than the conception of any mediaeval devil as can be imagined; but I will not worship the devil, though he should come dressed in royal robes and sit on the throne of Jehovah.[1]

In the epilogue to his *Saints, Sinners and Beechers*, Lyman Beecher Stowe calls attention to this service to theology rendered by all the Beechers:

The children of Lyman Beecher helped to build the intellectual bridge between the theologians of the past, who placed the emphasis upon holding the correct doctrines and leaving everything else to God's divine intervention, and the spiritual leaders of the present, who care nothing for doctrines and do not believe in supernatural intervention.[2]

In line with Beecher's break with traditional theology is his hospitality to the teachings of evolution. In his struggle to meet the needs of his generation, he attempted to reconcile the teachings of Christianity and evolution, and so important were his sermons that they were telegraphed verbatim every week to newspapers in Chicago. How far Beecher was ahead of the thought of other preachers in this regard can be judged by the inability of James B. Pond, Beecher's lecture manager, to secure a clergyman to preside at the lecture on "Evolution and Religion" at St. James' Hall in London in 1886. "I invited many clergymen and ministers to preside," he reports, "but they regretted that 'unavoidable circumstances prevented.'"[3] The historian Arthur Meier Schlesinger[4] makes special mention of Beecher's efforts to reconcile Christianity and evolution as early as 1880. Charles W. Gilkey, in his essay on "Protestant Preaching," remarks upon the importance of Beecher's receptivity to new truth. "It is highly significant that already in his later life Henry Ward Beecher had begun to face with open mind and forward-looking faith the bearing of the new scientific and biblical scholarship on the preaching of religion." A friendship grew up between Herbert Spencer and Henry Ward Beecher through their mutual interest in evolution, and at the farewell dinner to Herbert Spencer in New York in 1882 Henry Ward Beecher was the principal speaker. In the course of his address, Beecher declared, "To my father and mother I owe my physical being; to you, sir, I owe my intellectual being. At a critical moment you provided the safe paths through the bogs and morasses; you were my teacher."[5] No adequate treatment of the theological trends

[1] "Preventive Religion," *The Power to See It Through* (New York, Harper & Brothers, 1935), p. 64.

[2] *Op. cit.*, p. 392.

[3] James B. Pond, *A Summer in England with Henry Ward Beecher* (New York, Fords, Howard & Hulbert, 1887), p. 93.

[4] *The Rise of the City*, 1878–1898 (The Macmillan Company, 1933), p. 323.

[5] Hillis, *op. cit.*, p. 313.

of the nineteenth century will omit the significant part played by Henry Ward Beecher in breaking away from Calvinism and in preaching the gospel of humanity.

Beecher's concept of the preacher's mission was a logical outgrowth of his preaching of the love of God and the love of man. In Beecher's thought the preacher was not to prepare men for the enjoyment of a future life or to warn them of the dangers of hell but to ennoble man on earth. In speaking of the work of preaching, Beecher declares, "The thing the preacher aims at all the while is *reconstructed manhood*, a nobler idea in his congregation of how people ought to live and what they ought to be."[1] Two of the lecturers on the "Lyman Beecher Lectureship on Preaching" commend Beecher's definition of the preacher's relation to man. A. J. F. Behrends, in 1890, occupying the pulpit of the Central Congregational Church in Brooklyn, said of Beecher's definition: "In my judgment, no better and more helpful definition of the preacher's vocation has been given, in recent years, than the one to which the first incumbent of this lectureship gave expression, supporting it by an appeal to the words of Paul in his Epistle to the Ephesians. 'Reconstructed manhood,' was the vivid phrase into which he packed his theory of the sermon."[2] Similarly, a Scotsman, John Kelman, then minister of St. George's United Free Church, Edinburgh, declared, "In the great words of Henry Ward Beecher the ultimate aim of preaching is no less than 'reconstructed manhood.'"[3]

Besides influencing the content of the sermon, Beecher influenced its composition. The use of illustrations is the most distinctive single feature of Beecher's presentation, and since Beecher played an important part in ushering in the illustrative type of preaching, this significant aspect of his composition is worthy of consideration. Of his attempts to master the illustration as an instrument of persuasion that would bring his truths quickly to his audience, he says:

I can say for your encouragement, that while illustrations are as natural to me as breathing, I use fifty now to one in the early years of my ministry. For the first six or eight years, perhaps, they were comparatively few and far apart. But I developed myself in that respect; and that, too, by study and practice, by hard thought, and by a great many trials, both with the pen, and extemporaneously by myself, when I was walking here and there. Whatever I have gained in that direction is largely the result of education.[4]

[1] *Yale Lectures* (1st series), p. 6.
[2] A. J. F. Behrends, *The Philosophy of Preaching* (New York, Charles Scribner's Sons, 1890), p. 27.
[3] *The War and Preaching* (New Haven, Yale University Press, 1919), p. 17.
[4] *Yale Lectures* (1st series). p. 175.

Charles W. Gilkey,[1] in his essay "Protestant Preaching," already referred to, states that "the larger use and more careful study of the art of illustration is a marked characteristic of the best modern preaching." Testimony is available that supports the belief that Beecher was largely responsible for the introduction of this type of preaching into the American pulpit. Professor Louis Brastow,[2] one-time professor of homiletics at Yale Divinity School, declares, "The illustrative type of preaching has displaced the argumentative, and in it he [Beecher] was a pioneer." Similarly, W. M. Taylor, a Scottish preacher, one-time minister of the Broadway Tabernacle, New York City, credited Beecher with pioneering in the use of illustrations. "In former days, preachers were exceedingly sparing in their use of comparisons, but under the influence of the example of Guthrie and Beecher, and others, a great reaction has set in."[3] In his *Yale Lectures on Preaching* Beecher devoted one entire lecture to the uses of the illustration. His theory of the illustration is expressed in the following:

Experience has taught that not only are persons pleased by being instructed through illustration, but they are more readily instructed thus, because, substantially, the mode in which we learn a new thing is by its being likened to something which we already know. They are a kind of covert analogy, or likening one thing to another, so that obscure things become plain, being represented pictorially or otherwise by things that are not obscure and that we are familiar with.[4]

Beecher can be said to have influenced the thinking of the American pulpit in that he put the emphasis on noble living rather than on correct doctrines and that he influenced the presentation of the sermon in making it illustrative rather than argumentative.

Growth. Valuable as are these influences upon the thought of the sermon and its manner of presentation in the United States, they do not constitute Beecher's chief claim to a permanent place in the history of the Protestant church. Primarily, Beecher will be remembered as one of the greatest preachers produced in America, if not in the world. S. Parkes Cadman declared, "I place him at the summit of the sacred oratory of the last two hundred years."[5] A quick survey of the important landmarks in his growth as a preacher will help us to understand his eminence.

As a student at Amherst College Henry Ward's interests were varied rather than intensive. The limited curriculum of the young college failed to satisfy his intellectual curiosity; he was more consumed with finding

---

[1] *The Church through Half a Century* (New York, Charles Scribner's Sons, 1936), p. 222.
[2] *Representative Modern Preachers* (New York, The Macmillan Company, 1904), p. 187.
[3] W. M. Taylor, *The Ministry of the Word* (New York, Randolph & Co., 1876), p. 187.
[4] *Yale Lectures* (1st series), p. 155.
[5] *Ambassadors of God* (New York, The Macmillan Company, 1920), p. 80.

out the secrets of nature and mankind than in learning the formulas of mathematics and the conjugations of verbs. His book on conic sections was put up for auction at the end of the college year and brought a good price because its leaves were uncut. He jokingly said that the only time he stood next to the head of his class was when the class was arranged in a circle.

Botany, psychology (then called *phrenology*), political science, and public speaking attracted him. Unlike most geniuses, Beecher was always ready to admit the part that training played in his growth as an orator. His instructor, John Lovell, is frequently referred to by Beecher as the one who taught him the rudiments of public speaking.[1] In his eulogy on Wendell Phillips, Beecher declared that in debating the slavery question in college his life purpose was set. He was asked by his classmates to present a Bible to Henry Clay because he was the best speaker in his class. One $10 fee received for lecturing on phrenology was spent for a set of Burke, which became the nucleus of his large personal library, which numbered 15,000 volumes at his death. Indeed, Beecher had intellectual drives, but they were not the kind that led to a Phi Beta Kappa key.

In 1834 Henry Ward entered Lane Seminary and found himself again under the energizing influence of his father. Lyman Beecher's quarrel with the orthodoxy of the time was to leave its mark on his son's theology, as has been pointed out. His roommate was the productive young Biblical scholar Calvin Ellis Stowe, a member of the Lane faculty, who married Harriet Beecher in 1836.

Again the extracurricular activities claimed his attention, and they were of more consequence in determining his future than his study of church history and systematic theology. We find him making careful preparation for his Sunday-school class of young ladies in his father's church on Fourth Street. We find him shouldering a musket in 1836 in the Birney riots. Never would Beecher have been the antislavery crusader of the 1850's in Brooklyn if he had not seen the evils of slavery firsthand on the banks of the Ohio River. We find him editing the *Cincinnati Journal* for four or five months, and the wonder is that he did not turn to journalism as a career, for he was uncommonly successful as an editor. Later, in Indianapolis, his editorial interest found expression in his department, "The Western Farmer and Gardener," of the *Indiana Journal*. Throughout his career his pen supplemented his voice in proclaiming his views.

After two years at Lawrenceburg, Beecher was called to the state capital, Indianapolis. Here he learned directness in speaking, discovered the power of illustrations, and realized the value of timeliness. For example, when Beecher wanted to preach against slavery, a question that most preachers meticulously avoided, he waited until all the judges of the various courts

[1] *Yale Lectures* (1st series), p. 143.

were assembled in the capital. When Judge McLean was asked his opinion of Beecher's antislavery sermon, he replied, "Well, I think if every minister in the United States would be as faithful it would be a great advance in settling this question."[1] Nowhere was the factor of timeliness applied by Beecher with better effect than in England, in 1863, where he refused to speak until after the victories of Vicksburg and Gettysburg in July.

Feeling the restriction upon his influence of the four walls of his Indianapolis church, Beecher wrote out his *Lectures to Young Men* (1845) and had them published. The vitality of the thought and style of this book caused it to have a rapid sale in both the United States and England. The book is still in circulation. The attention of the newly formed Plymouth Church was directed to this son of Lyman Beecher; also, the Park Street Church in Boston issued an invitation. Although it had been Beecher's intention to stay in the West, he finally yielded to the persuasion of the Plymouth congregation and began to preach to great crowds from October 10, 1847, on. The cornerstone of the new church built under his aggressive leadership was laid on May 29, 1849, and the first services were held in the new church on the first Sunday of 1850. Plymouth Church stands today as one of the landmarks of America.

Beecher was fortunate in the beginning of his long career at Plymouth Church in being able to design a church especially for the purpose of public speaking. When the architect consulted with him he gave these instructions: "I want the audience to surround me, so that they will come up on every side, and behind me, so that I shall be in the centre of the crowd, and have the people surge all about me." The church was built upon the principle of personal and social magnetism that Beecher believed was the most important element of all the external conditions conducive to effective preaching. Charles Dickens, after giving one of his readings in Plymouth Church, sent Beecher word that the auditorium was perfect for speaking. The seating capacity was 2,100, which was thought an extravagant allowance; however, in 1857, folding seats were fitted to the ends of the pews, which accommodated 300 persons more. Counting the number who found standing room and those who sat on the pulpit stairs, the capacity could be stretched to 3,200.[2]

No preacher has ever equaled Henry Ward Beecher's record of 40 years in Plymouth Church. Imagine drawing an audience of 3,000 people Sunday morning and evening for 40 years! Charles Haddon Spurgeon, with 32 years at his tabernacle, Phillips Brooks, with 22 years at Trinity Church, T. DeWitt Talmage, with 25 years at his Brooklyn Tabernacle—all impres-

[1] Beecher, Scoville, and Beecher, *op. cit.*, p. 196.

[2] For a description of Plymouth Church, see the article in *The Atlantic Monthly* for January, 1867.

sive records but falling short of Beecher's achievement. In 1856, when Plymouth Church had been in operation only six years, Henry Fowler wrote an essay on Beecher in which he marvels at Beecher's drawing power. What superlatives Fowler would have had to employ had he written his essay in 1887, after 40 years:

Here gather, twice on every Sabbath of the year, except during the summer solstice, about twenty-five hundred people, and the audience sometimes numbers three thousand. It is not unusual for the capacious body of the church, the broad galleries, the second elevated gallery, the several aisles, and all vacancies about pulpit and doors to be occupied by eager listeners, and sometimes hundreds turn away, unable to find footing within the audience-room. Its persistence imparts to it the dignity of a moral phenomenon. It is unprecedented in the history of audiences, whether religious, literary, political, or artistical. What in truth is it? It is not that an orator attracts a crowd. That is often done. But it is, that twice on each Sabbath of six years, from two to three thousand people centre to an unchanged attraction. No dramatic genius, no melodious voice, no popular eloquence has ever done so much as that. Neither Macready, Garrick, nor Jenny Lind, nor Rachel, nor Gough, nor Clay, nor Choate has done it. The theatre must change its "Star" monthly, the singer must migrate often, the orator must make "angel visits" to concentrate three thousand people.[1]

Analysis. Why did the people throng to hear Beecher? One answer lies in Beecher's sympathy with men. Richard Storrs[2] gave this as one of the secrets of Beecher's power over men. Theodore Cuyler[3] found Beecher "a most fascinating companion, with the rollicking freedom of a schoolboy." Edward Bok[4] tells how he was drawn to Beecher. Speaking of himself in the third person, he says, "Edward Bok was in the formative period between boyhood and young manhood when impressions meant lessons, and associations meant ideals. Mr. Beecher never disappointed. The closer one got to him the greater he became—in striking contrast to most public men, as Edward had already learned." Beecher's acquaintance knew no bounds; he was a friend of P. T. Barnum, Andrew Carnegie, Jenny Lind, Dr. John Raymond, Dion Boucicault, Henry Irving, Ellen Terry, Robert G. Ingersoll. Beecher drew all classes of men to him because of the breadth of his sympathy. Julia Ward Howe tells of the sympathetic letter written by Beecher to Edwin Booth on the death of his wife. "Henry Ward Beecher,

[1] Henry Fowler, *The American Pulpit* (New York, J. M. Fairchild and Company, 1856), p. 141.

[2] "Silver Wedding Address," in Lyman Abbott and S. B. Halliday's *Life of Beecher*, p. 457. In this address, Richard Storrs developed these eight points: (1) thoroughly vitalized mind; (2) immense common sense; (3) sympathy with men; (4) mental sensibility; (5) animal vigor; (6) voice; (7) sympathy with nature; (8) enthusiasm for Christ.

[3] *Recollections of a Long Life* (New York, Baker & Taylor Co., 1902), p. 214.

[4] *Americanization of Edward Bok* (New York, Charles Scribner's Sons, 1924), p. 85.

meeting Mary Booth one day at dinner at my house, was so much impressed with her peculiar charm that, on the occasion of her death, he wrote a very sympathetic letter to Mr. Booth, and became thenceforth one of his most esteemed friends."[1] Walt Whitman met Beecher once at the Camden Ferry; they had a long visit. Afterward, Walt Whitman wrote, "He was more than commonly cordial, and I hope I was, too, for I felt more than commonly drawn to Beecher."[2] Collis P. Huntington was proud of Beecher's friendship, giving him four $1,000 bills when he had performed his second marriage. After Beecher's death, Huntington befriended his widow, providing her with railroad passes that she might visit her son who lived on Puget Sound.[3] Beecher was all things to all men.

Beecher's friendliness is a key to the subject matter of his sermons. People crowded to hear him because he knew the motives of his fellow men. He expressed their innermost yearnings; he told them things they had often felt but never expressed. He praised the type of conduct they admired and condemned the type of behavior they shunned. Beecher foraged upon people for his material as some preachers forage upon books.

If I know my own business—and the presumption is I do—it is to hunt men and to study them. Do you suppose I study old, musty books when I want to preach? *I study you!* When I want to deliver a discourse on theology, *I study you!* When I want to know more about the doctrine of depravity, *I study you!* When I want to know what is right and what is wrong, I see how *you* do; and I have abundant illustrations on every side.[4]

So important did Beecher believe the study of mankind was to the preacher that he spent one of his lectures at Yale on "Study of Human Nature."[5]

Testimony that Beecher studied human nature to good purpose is abundant. Michael Pupin admitted Beecher's conquest over him. "I felt thrills creeping over my whole body as I listened, and the effect was not only mental and spiritual but also physical, undoubtedly because of the quickening of the blood's circulation produced by the mental exhilaration."[6] Walt Whitman heard Beecher in Brooklyn in 1849, when the new church was being built. His appraisal is enthusiastic. "He hit me so hard, fascinated me to such a degree that I was afterwards willing to go far out of

---

[1] *Reminiscences*, 1819–1899 (Boston, Houghton Mifflin Company, 1900), p. 242.

[2] Horace Traubel, *With Walt Whitman in Camden*, March 28–July 24, 1888 (Boston, Small, Maynard Co.), p. 137.

[3] Oscar Lewis, "Men against Mountains," *The Atlantic Monthly*, June, 1938.

[4] N. A. Shenstone, *Anecdotes of Henry Ward Beecher* (Chicago, R. R. Donnelley & Sons Company, 1887), p. 434.

[5] *Yale Lectures* (1st series), Lecture IV.

[6] *Op. cit.*, p. 106.

my way to hear him talk."[1] John Burroughs used to run from the ferry to get to Plymouth Church in order to get a seat, for he could not bear to miss a word.[2] W. H. Herndon heard Beecher in Springfield, Ill., in 1855, and exclaimed to Theodore Parker, "He is a new rose, fresh from the garden of the almighty forces. This age is fortunate in having so beautiful a present. He is a man—'a fresh minister.'"[3] Such spontaneous tributes to Beecher's power over individuals it would be possible to multiply many times.

The British newspapers of 1863, although critical of his ideas, praised his speaking skill. The *Daily Post*, Liverpool, October 17, declared, "Without regard to the merits or demerits of his views, the greatest credit is due to Mr. Beecher for the tact, wholly devoid of reservation or flattery, with which he managed to have his say." The *Glasgow Examiner*, October 17, similarly expressed itself:

The Reverend Henry Ward Beecher has again visited Glasgow, and on Tuesday evening he addressed a crowded meeting in the City Hall, on American affairs. The subject was one in which there is a great diversity of opinion, but it was impossible not to admire the wonderful abilities and brilliant eloquence of one of the most gifted of America's sons, as he painted the blessings of liberty and the horrors of slavery.

The great throngs that crowded these mass meetings served to corroborate the judgment of the newspapers of his speaking ability.[4]

Since we have no moving-picture film of Beecher in action before an audience, the next best thing is to present the description of an eye witness.

When Mr. Beecher was speaking on Communism, in Chicago, a rather dramatic and very characteristic thing happened. His lecture was half finished. He was standing before an audience of ten thousand people in the old Tabernacle Building, a temporary structure on Franklin Street, put up to accommodate the vast audiences which thronged in those days to hear Moody and Sankey, then in the heydey of their early work and enthusiasm. The great room was packed. Beecher rolled out sentence after sentence in his most telling manner. Word after word fell forcibly

[1] Horace Traubel, *With Walt Whitman in Camden*, July 16, 1888–October, 1888 (New York, D. Appleton & Co., Inc.), p. 471.

[2] Clara Barrus, *John Burroughs, Life and Letters* (Boston, Houghton Mifflin Company, 1925), I, 48.

[3] Paul M. Angle, *Herndon's Life of Lincoln* (New York, Albert & Charles Boni, Inc., 1930), p. xxii.

[4] Although the income of a speaker is not an accurate gauge of his ability, it may be an indication of how greatly he was in demand by his fellow men. The fact that Plymouth Church paid Beecher $20,000 a year reveals in a way the value it placed upon his services. Joseph Howard estimates that Beecher's salary at Plymouth Church for the 40 years was $550,000, and his lectures totaled $465,000.—*Life of Henry Ward Beecher* (Philadelphia, Hubbard Brothers, 1887), p. 626.

upon the vast crowd, which grew more and more silent as he went on. A reporter at the table down in front of the platform dropped a lead pencil, and one could almost feel the noise that it made, so breathlessly were all in the audience listening to the orator's voice. He was telling the story of the rise of the power of the people. Presently he ended a ringing period with these words, pronounced in a voice so deep and fervid and full of conviction that they seemed to have been uttered then for the first time: "The voice of the people is the voice of God."

In the absolute and intense silence of the instant that followed fell the voice of a half-drunken man in the gallery: "The voice of the people is the voice of a fool."

Everybody fairly shivered. But Beecher was equal to the moment. He drew himself up, looked toward the place from whence the disturbing voice came, and "I said the voice of the people, not the voice of one man," he replied, with perfect simplicity.

It would be impossible to describe the responsive expression of the audience. It was not a laugh, it was not a cheer. It was a movement, a sound like one great sigh of relief and delight. The lecture went on; the air was full of electric sympathy, tingling toward an explosion of some sort. Beecher knew it and seemed waiting for a chance to put his finger on the key of the pent-up personal enthusiasm which moved his audience. The drunken fellow suddenly gave him a chance. He staggered to his feet, feeling that the odds were against him, and mumbled out some unintelligible words. Beecher paused a second time in his lecture. Then he said with that smile of his, at once winning and condemning, which so many people know; "Will some kind person take our friend out and give him some cold water—plenty of it—within and without?" Two policemen had hold of the disturber by this time, and the audience had liberty to cheer—and such a cheer as it was! The tabernacle shook with it, and it is probable that at least nine-tenths of the people who clapped with their hands supposed that they were cheering Mr. Beecher's wit, instead of that tremendous personal power which no one need try to analyze.[1]

This lecture on communism was one of the yearly lectures Beecher carefully wrote out and gave up and down the country. The most famous of such lectures were his "Wastes and Burdens of Society" and "The Reign of the Common People," which were in much demand. At the beginning of the lecture season Beecher depended on his manuscript.[2] Amos C. Barstow[3] remembers having seen Beecher turn over three or four leaves of his manuscript without reading. At the close of the lecture, Beecher was asked what was on those leaves, and he replied, "I don't know. This is a new lecture, and I have hardly got the hang of it. The next time I give it, perhaps I will read those leaves." Beecher was familiar with the usual types of composition and delivery, as is evidenced by both his practice and his discussion in his

[1] Shenstone, *op. cit.*, pp. 192ff.

[2] A number of these lecture manuscripts can be seen at Plymouth Church. On the margins of the lectures, Beecher wrote the names of the cities where the lecture had been given.

[3] Lyman Abbott and S. B. Halliday, Reminiscences of Amos C. Barstow, *Henry Ward Beecher* (Hartford, Conn., American Publishing Co., 1888), p. 310.

Yale Lectures on Preaching. Mr. Barstow, in the same article, records that on one occasion Beecher laboriously wrote out a twenty-page manuscript in longhand, and on still another occasion at Brown University he dictated to a stenographer as he paced up and down the room.

It will be noted that these types of speech preparation were devoted to speeches for special occasions; for his preaching in his pulpit Beecher depended upon extemporizing in the presence of his audience. His method is so peculiarly his own and so indicative of his genius that it must be described in some detail.

Beecher went into his study an hour before church time to work out the outline of his sermon. His belated preparation, or so it would seem to most speakers, was due not to carelessness but to his way of working. A quotation from his account of his method will throw light upon a practice that would spell ruin for most speakers.

I know what I am going to aim at, but, of course, I don't get down to anything specific. I brood it, and ponder it, and dream over it, and pick up information about one point and another but if I ever think I see the plan opening up to me I don't dare to look at it or put it down on paper. If once I write a thing out, it is almost impossible for me to kindle to it again. I never dare nowadays, to write out a sermon during the week; that is sure to kill it. I have to think around and about it and get it generally ready, and fuse it when the time comes.[1]

In that hour of outlining Beecher marked out the boundaries of his thought and left the filling out of the outline to the moment of speaking in the presence of his audience, when he collaborated with the thought of the people before him. So sensitive was Beecher to the thought of the audience that the completed sermon bore the imprint of the spiritual needs of the people before him.

No description of Beecher on the platform would be complete that did not mention his ability to pantomime. Beecher was not content to tell; he wanted to show. Shenstone gives an amusing example of Beecher's cleverness at mimicry. Henry Ward was speaking of his father Lyman playing his violin.

One day he was amusing himself on his favorite instrument, and struck up a genuine jig, which, unsanctified, had been running in his head ever since he was a boy.

Just at that moment the mother came in, and, catching the inspiration of the tune, placed her hands on her hips and actually danced a minuet.

Mr. Beecher described the scene. He stepped back on the platform, placed his hands on his hips, and showed the audience how his mother did it. He described the

---

[1] Abbott and Halliday, *op. cit.*, p. 211.

consternation of the children. He clasped his hands, rolled up the whites of his eyes like a regular maw-worm, opened his mouth, drew down his lips, and stood the personification of rustic horror.

The whole scene was irresistibly comic.[1]

Beecher's splendid voice was no small factor in his success. Partly a gift of nature and partly the result of hard work, his voice was capable of evoking the desired response in the audience. Beecher tells us that he and his brother Charles used to make the woods ring on Walnut Hills in Cincinnati as they practiced their vowel sounds. Delighted were Ellen Terry and Henry Irving[2] when they heard Beecher read Shakespeare. "He was gifted with a richly melodious voice," Theodore Cuyler reports, "which was especially effective on the low and tender keys."[3]

People liked Beecher on the platform because he had a physique that filled the eye. He was essentially an outdoor man, spending much time when weather permitted on his farm at Peekskill on the Hudson. An excellent swimmer, a capital horseman, and all-round athlete, he appreciated the value of perfect health. In the *Yale Lectures on Preaching*, he devoted one lecture to the preacher's health, incidentally, the only one in the whole series on the subject, in which he says, "A man in health is a fountain, and he flows over at the eye, at the lip, and all the time, by every species of action and demonstration."[4] As Beecher entered the pulpit he radiated robust health and impressed his congregation with his sense of well-being. When Beecher was in Glasgow in 1863 one reporter noted this good impression created by Beecher's presence so necessary to the successful speaker. "His quiet, self-possessed manner indicates great mental power, with a consciousness of possessing it. A stranger who had never seen or heard him would pronounce, when he rose to speak, that he had something worth saying, and worth listening to."[5]

His vigorous health and self-possession evinced themselves in his good nature. His even temper was noted by the English press in 1863, and unquestionably the success he achieved was as much due to this trait as to any other skill he possessed. The *Liverpool Chronicle*, on October 17, 1863, remarked, "We must give Mr. Beecher the credit of being one of the best tempered lecturers to whom we have listened." In 1872, in reflecting on how best to control a congregation, and with perhaps his English experience in mind, Beecher advised the young preachers at Yale Divinity School: "The great art of managing a congregation lies in this,—be good-natured

[1] *Op. cit.*, p. 174.
[2] Ellen Terry, *The Story of My Life* (London, Hutchinson & Co., 1913), p. 291.
[3] *Op. cit.*, p. 214.
[4] *Yale Lectures* (1st series), p. 184.
[5] *Glasgow Examiner*, Oct. 10, 1863.

yourself, and keep them good-natured, and then they will not need any managing."[1]

A survey of a few of the prominent characteristics of Beecher's composition may help to understand further why he was so successful in managing a congregation. He undoubtedly would have said with Spurgeon that he owed more to variety than he did to profundity.[2] "Sympathy with your people," Beecher declared, "insight of their condition, a study of the moral remedies, this will give endless diversity and fertility to your subjects for sermons. He that preaches out of a system of theology soon runs his round and returns on his track. He that preaches out of a sympathy with living men will sooner exhaust the ocean or the clouds of water, than his pulpit of material."[3] S. Parkes Cadman believed that variety was the secret of Beecher's superiority. "He always had a surprise in store. If he was philosophical in the morning, he was inspirational at night. He would sometimes astonish his congregation by his austerity or again by his exquisite tenderness."[4] Beecher aimed to ennoble mankind, and he used every device within his power to accomplish this purpose. Although diversity extended to every phase of his preaching—to the choice of his theme and materials, to the use of illustrations, to the choice of words, to the construction of his sermons, he always aimed at securing a single unified effect in his sermons. As long as his purpose was served Beecher cared little for the ordinary conceptions of logical development and symmetry taught in rhetorics. So necessary, for example, was variety in planning his sermons that Beecher developed the principle that "the greatest number of men, particularly uncultivated people, receive their truth by facts placed in juxtaposition rather than in philosophical sequence. Thus a line of facts or a series of parables will be better adapted to most audiences than a regular unfolding of a train of thought from the germinal point to the fruitful end."[5] Such a conception of planning permitted extempore speaking in the presence of his audience and the introduction of variety in all its phases into speech composition. He could seize upon the inspiration of the moment and weave it into the context of his sermon. When questioned if this practice would not make his sermons unsymmetrical, he answered, "Were you called to preach for the sake of the salvation of sermons?"[6]

[1] *Yale Lectures* (1st series), p. 256.
[2] C. H. Spurgeon, *Lectures to My Students* (3d series, London, Marshall, Morgan & Scott, Ltd.), p. 129.
[3] *Yale Lectures* (1st series), p. 40.
[4] G. Bromley Oxnam, ed., *Effective Preaching* (New York, Abingdon-Cokesbury, 1929), p. 245.
[5] *Yale Lectures* (1st series), p. 219.
[6] *Ibid.*, p. 165.

Variety was also served by the use of illustrations. Every walk of life could be drawn upon as a source of illustrations. "They must be on a level with your audience, so that they will surge back and draw your hearers to you."[1] Long years of trial and error, as has been suggested, gave Beecher command over this instrument of persuasion, so capable of variety. His introduction of Pinky, a slave girl, into his pulpit is his most famous use of illustration. Her freedom was bought several times over by a generous collection. Spurgeon, a master of the illustration, comments on the effectiveness of his illustration in his lectures to his students: "Still a live illustration is better for appealing to the feelings of an audience than any amount of description could possibly be. When Mr. Beecher brought a beautiful slave girl, with her manacles on, into his pulpit, he did more for the anti-slavery cause than he might have done by the most eloquent harangue."[2] Emerson, too, was captivated by Beecher's skillful use of the illustration. He records in his journal, after hearing Beecher speak at a special gathering: "Beecher, at breakfast, illustrated the difference between the impulsive mob in New York Cooper Institute and the organized mob in Liverpool meeting. 'In one you go by a corner where the wind sucks in, and blows your hat off, but, when you get by it, you go along comfortably to the next corner. In the other, you are on the prairie, with no escape from the irresistible northwester.'"[3]

Another instrument of persuasion that Beecher used with excellent effect was humor. Chiefly through the use of humorous illustrations Beecher swept his audiences with laughter. Sometimes, however, it was the clever turn of a phrase. Throughout the unedited "English Addresses" of 1863 the word *laughter* is frequently interpolated. The students at Yale Divinity School rocked with laughter at his reply to the question: "What is the occasion of the tendency toward short pastorates in churches nowadays?" Beecher flashed back, "Largely, I think, the divine mercy toward the parish."[4] Humor was not an end in itself, but if he could drive home his point by a good laugh he was not averse to it. Church etiquette frowned upon laughing, but Beecher was not bothered by this breach.

Indeed, it was not only *what* Beecher said but *how* he said it that kept his church filled. The ability to phrase is an important one in the success of any orator. Beecher attempted to say things in such a way that audiences would remember them and discuss them after the lecture or sermon was over. Many books were compiled from Beecher's remarks, all of which

[1] *Ibid.*, p. 172.

[2] Spurgeon, *op. cit.*, p. 48.

[3] Bliss Perry, ed., *The Heart of Emerson's Journals* (Boston, Houghton Mifflin Company, 1909), p. 302.

[4] *Yale Lectures* (1st series), p. 50.

found a good market. Such compilations as *Royal Truths*, *The Crown of Life*, and *Life Thoughts*, which sold 40,000 copies in England, are characterized by epigrams and maxims that say a good deal about life in a few words. It is not uncommon to run across quotations from him in current periodicals like the *Reader's Digest*, *Coronet* and the *Ladies' Home Journal*. The last-named magazine, for example, in October, 1939, carried the following dissertation by Beecher on apple pie: "Its capacity is endless. It will accept almost any flavor of every spice. Yet nothing is so fatal to the rare and higher graces of apple pie as inconsiderate, vulgar spicing. The final pie, though born of apple, sugar, butter, nutmeg, cinnamon, lemon, is like none of these, but the compound ideal of them all, refined, purified, and by fire fixed in blissful perfection." In such selections we see Beecher's familiarity with everyday things, his discerning comparisons, his imaginative power, his wit, his knowledge of mankind, his tenderness, and his gift of expression.

IV. *The Reformer*

At several points in this discussion it has been shown that Beecher differed from the nineteenth century conception of the duties of the preacher. In another particular Beecher departed from the current conception of what the preacher should speak about from the pulpit and from the platform. Beecher held that whatever concerned the good of man was his subject matter; thus he was interested in the social implications of the Gospel, and in this he was ahead of such men as Walter Rauschenbusch, Washington Gladden, and Harry F. Ward. Four of the leading questions of the day with which he identified himself were temperance, woman suffrage, good government, and the freedom of the slaves.

Temperance. Lyman Beecher lectured and wrote against the evils of intemperance; in London, in 1846, he addressed a huge mass meeting in Covent Garden. The father's profound convictions on this question became the son's, and from the time when Henry Ward was eighteen years old, when he delivered his first temperance lecture at Upton, Mass., he never lost interest in this reform. In the West in the 1840's, Henry Ward saw much hard drinking and learned firsthand about the relations of human nature and liquor. When we find him preaching on this question in 1874, we discover his mature reflections on a problem that has baffled solution. Since we have recently passed through a period of national prohibition, the following observation seems wise indeed.

In regard to what is called the "Maine Law," which absolutely forbids this traffic, that law is right. It is comformable to all the analogies of civil society. There is but one single fault to be found with it—you can not make it work. If you could, I think there would be an end to the argument. You may enforce it in neighborhoods, in particular communities, but, looking upon this nation, I anticipate that a hundred years will not see such an educated public sentiment, nor such conditions of general living and health, as will make it possible to maintain such a law.[1]

Temperance, not prohibition, was a lifelong interest with Beecher. It is interesting that the last public speech that Beecher gave was delivered at a demonstration in Chickering Hall, New York, on February 26, 1887, in favor of the Crosby High License bill.[2]

Woman Suffrage. One needs but glance through the index of *The Life and Work of Susan B. Anthony* to realize how thoroughly Henry Ward Beecher championed the cause of votes for women. At one time, he was president of the American Suffrage Association, then representing twenty-one states.[3] In 1860, he delivered a woman's rights speech at Cooper Institute, New York, which was used for a long time as one of the suffrage leaflets circulated by the association. Ida H. Harper tells the following incident, which illustrates Beecher's desire to see women get the ballot.

In her great need for funds, Miss Anthony decided to appeal to Henry Ward Beecher and she relates how, as she was wearily climbing Columbia Heights to his home, she felt a hand on her shoulder and heard a hearty voice say, "Well, old girl, what do you want now?" It was Mr. Beecher, himself, who the moment she explained her mission, said, "I'll take a collection in Plymouth Church next Sunday." The result was $200.00.[4]

Good Government. Beecher was interested in votes for women because their influence on the ballot would make for better government. Since the happiness of mankind depended upon good government, Beecher did all he could to secure it. When most churches were sidestepping slavery for fear they would split over the issue, Beecher attacked the moral and political aspects of the evil with all the eloquence at his command. In 1856, he took an active part in the formation of the Republican party and campaigned for John C. Fremont with the slogan, "The non-extension of slavery." The issues of the campaign were clearly drawn in his article "On Which Side Is Peace?" In conclusion, he wrote, "The only way to peace is that way which shall chain slavery to the place that it now has, and say to the Dragon, 'In thine own den thou mayst dwell, and lie down in thine own slime. But thou shalt not go forth to ravage free territory, nor leave thy trail upon unspotted soil.'"[5]

[1] *Plymouth Pulpit,* March–September, 1874 (New York, Fords, Howard & Hulbert, 1890), p. 225.

[2] Knox, *op. cit.,* p. 499.

[3] Ida H. Harper, *Life of Susan B. Anthony* (Indianapolis, Bowen and Merrill Co., 1898), p. 238.

[4] *Ibid.,* p. 234.

[5] John R. Howard, *Patriotic Addresses* (Boston, The Pilgrim Press, 1887), p. 202.

Beecher's interest in antislavery quite naturally led the Young Men's Lyceum Association of Plymouth Church to invite Lincoln, of Illinois, to lecture before them in the autumn of 1859. Because, undoubtedly, of the fact that Lincoln decided to speak on a political theme the appearance was finally booked for Cooper Institute on February 27, 1860.[1] Thus Beecher played an important part in introducing Lincoln to the East; this appearance greatly enhanced Lincoln's prestige. On the Sunday following the Cooper Institute Address, Lincoln went to Henry Ward Beecher's church, where a plaque now marks the pew he sat in, and dined with him at the home of a friend.[2] This acquaintance developed into a friendship that was to have its ups and downs during the next four momentous years. Beecher ardently advocated Lincoln's nomination in 1860 and in 1864.

When Mr. Lincoln became our candidate I gave all I had of time, strength, influence, and persuasion, and when his election was ascertained and efforts were made to intimidate the North to prevent his being inaugurated, I went up and down this country stiffening the backs of willow-backed patriots. I faced mobs. I preached day and night in my own church, to hold the North up to its rights and interests.[3]

For example, because of their tolerance of slavery, Beecher fought such interdenominational benevolent organizations as the American Sunday School Union, the American Tract Society, and the American Board of Commissioners for Foreign Missions. In the columns of the *New York Independent* Beecher attacked the cautious editing of tracts by the American Tract Society.[4]

Beecher was one of those who early in the Civil War urged an emancipation proclamation. Through the columns of the *New York Independent* Beecher attacked the policy of Lincoln: "The president seems to be a man without any sense of the value of time." . . . [5] "To put down rebellion first, and attend to slavery afterwards, is letting two serpents uncoil that may as well be stricken through with one blow." . . . [6] "Richmond deter-

[1] Emanuel Hertz, *The Hidden Lincoln* (New York, The Viking Press, 1938), p. 75.

[2] Nelson Sizer, one of the gallery ushers, gives this report of Lincoln's listening to Beecher: "As Mr. Beecher developed his line of argument, Mr. Lincoln's body swayed forward, his lips parted, and he seemed at length unconscious of his surrounding—frequently giving vent to his satisfaction, at a well-put point or illustration, with a kind of involuntary Indian exclamation, 'Ugh', not audible beyond his immediate presence, but very expressive! Mr. Lincoln henceforward had a profound admiration for the talents of the famous pastor of Plymouth Church."—F. B. Carpenter, *Six Months in the White House with Abraham Lincoln* (New York, Hurd and Houghton, 1867), p. 135.

[3] Beecher, Scoville, and Beecher, *op. cit.*, p. 581.

[4] E. D. Fite, *The Presidential Campaign of 1860* (New York, The Macmillan Company, 1911), p. 88.

[5] July 17, 1862.

[6] Aug. 28, 1862.

mines Washington reasons. Richmond is inflexible, Washington vacillates."[1]

What effect these attacks had on the policy of Lincoln it is impossible to say. We have, however, a report of Lincoln's reading these hostile criticisms and his reaction to them.

During the brief period that the Reverend Henry Ward Beecher was editor of "The Independent," in the second year of the war, he felt called upon to pass some severe strictures upon the course of the administration. For several weeks the successive leaders of the editorial page were like bugle-blasts, waking the echoes throughout the country. Somebody cut these editorials out of the different numbers of the paper, and mailed them all to the President under one envelope. One rainy Sunday afternoon he took them from his drawer, and read them through to the last word. One or two of the articles were in Mr. Beecher's strongest style, and criticized the President in no measured terms. As Mr. Lincoln finished reading them his face flushed with indignation. Dashing the package to the floor, he exclaimed, "Is thy servant a *dog* that he should do this thing?" The excitement, however, soon passed off, leaving no trace behind of ill-will toward Mr. Beecher, and the impression upon his mind by the criticism was lasting and excellent in its effects.[2]

Not content with his editorial attacks on Lincoln's delay in issuing the Emancipation Proclamation, Beecher, in company with Theodore Cuyler, a fellow Brooklyn clergyman, was about to start for Washington to urge upon the President in person the need for immediate action. Before the two could arrange to go, however, the proclamation was issued.[3]

Lincoln's death called forth a eulogy by Beecher that has found a permanent place in Lincoln literature. The final paragraph will give a glimpse of Beecher's impassioned, rhythmic prose style. No wonder Walt Whitman was captivated by Beecher!

Four years ago, O Illinois, we took from your midst an untried man, and from among the people. We return him to you a mighty conqueror. Not thine any more, but the Nation's; not ours, but the world's. Give him place, ye prairies! In the midst of this great continent his dust shall rest, a sacred treasure to myriads who shall pilgrim to that shrine to kindle anew their zeal and patriotism. Ye winds that move over the mighty places of the West, chant requiem! Ye people, behold a martyr whose blood, as so many articulate words, pleads for fidelity, for law, for liberty![4]

But leaders of public opinion in the North disagreed as to how law and liberty were to be maintained in reunion. Beecher's ideas are set forth in two of his public addresses—his "Fort Sumter Address" and his sermon on "Conditions of a Restored Union." He desired immediate restoration

[1] Sept. 11, 1862.
[2] Carpenter, *op. cit.*, p. 231.
[3] Cuyler, *op. cit.*, p. 150.
[4] Hillis, *op. cit.*, p. 263.

of the Southern states to the Union, thus aligning himself with President Johnson and the Democratic party; at the same time he agreed with the Republican party in desiring adequate protection for the rights and adequate promotion of the education of the colored people. No one can say whether the immediate readmission of the Southern states would have secured fair treatment for the Negro. History records that the Fourteenth and Fifteenth Amendments were ratified by the Southern states as the price of admission.

From his pulpit and from the platform and privately Beecher raised his voice in a plea for generous treatment for the South. He gave $1,000 to the college of which Robert E. Lee was president.[1] He praised Lee in words like these:

Robert Lee is the last man in the South ever again to rebel or incite rebellion. And I tell you we are not making friends, nor helping the cause of a common country, by raising the names of eminent Southern men, one after another, into the place of bitter criticism. It is not generous. We are the stronger party; we have been successful; and if there is to be magnanimity anywhere, we are the men to show it.[2]

Such words were rare in October, 1865.

During the administrations of Grant, for whom Beecher had campaigned, one leading question was that of sound money. Beecher shows his versatility and competence in discussing such an economic question. He must have been a student of currency for many years, for when he was in England in 1863 he was closely questioned on the financial side of the Civil War. In his account of these addresses in *Patriotic Addresses*, he says, "I had to discuss the question of taxation, the issues of such an enormous quantity of greenbacks, and the ability and the willingness of our people to pay; and I had to go into finance a good deal, and what little knowledge I had came wonderfully handy."[3] Beecher's interest in currency is a splendid example of how he interested himself in the live issues of the day and why he had such an extra-church following. Professor Arthur Meier Schlesinger must have considered Beecher more than an amateur in financial matters, for in attempting to show the thought of the times he repeats Beecher's prophecy that the chief danger of the future was one of money. "In 1871, Henry Ward Beecher, speaking in a prophetic sense declared, 'We are today in more danger from overgrown pecuniary interests—from organized money—than we were from slavery, and the battle of the future is to be one of gold and silver.'"[4]

[1] Douglas Southall Freeman, *R. E. Lee* (New York, Charles Scribner's Sons, 1935), IV, p. 205. See also Paul Buck, *The Road to Reunion* (Little, Brown & Company, 1937), p. 6.

[2] Howard, *op. cit.*, p. 731.

[3] *Op. cit.*, p. 649.

[4] *New Viewpoints in American History* (New York, The Macmillan Company), p. 250.

When it was proposed to pay the United States bonds in silver, Beecher replied from his pulpit in his Thanksgiving Day sermon on November 29, 1877:

Gold is king in commerce. All other money must represent gold. No vote of legislature can change the nature of commerce, the nature of property, the nature of its representative in money, or the relative superiority or inferiority of different currencies. . . . Gold came to its supremacy as a representative of property by the long established consent of mankind. The attempt to cheat capitalists by paying bonds in silver coin of less value than gold is hardly worse than the other attempt to derange and poison business by a renewal of the plague of greenbacks. No paper currency has any intrinsic value; no government can give it lawful power. Gold is the only basis.

In 1884, the strong reform element that had been growing within the Republican party made itself felt powerfully enough to influence the election of Grover Cleveland. When the Republican party had lost the election, one of the most brilliant and effective Republican workers in Plymouth Church said: "It cut me to the soul that Beecher was so wrong; but when it comes to denying his influence, that is simply absurd. We never worked so hard in our lives as we did to counteract him in this thing; but the effect of his personality and his power was evident on every side." In reviewing the campaign, Professor T. J. Wertenbaker says of this group of reformers:

The reformers were christened "Mugwumps," and in their ranks were included such lifelong Republicans as Carl Schurz, Henry Ward Beecher, William Everett, and George Ticknor Curtis. "They are not numerous but noisy," declared Blaine, "pharisaical but not practical, ambitious but not wise, pretentious but not powerful." None the less they played an important part in the approaching defeat of the Republican party.[1]

Plymouth Church, which through the years had been closely identified with the Republican party, criticized Beecher's campaigning for Cleveland, and many prophesied that Beecher was signing his death warrant in popular esteem by supporting Cleveland. Beecher's independence, a factor in his success as an orator, is revealed in this reply to his critics:

The alarm of friends, the party excitement of others, has no effect on me whatever. Any new and real information I shall be grateful for, but to tell me nothing, and only to express amazement, wonder, concern, et cetera, and let me know how damaging to my reputation and interests it will be if I follow my judgment, and not theirs, who love me as I am sure these brethren do, indicates how far gone in political excitement they are, and how little they understand the man whom they

[1] *The American People: A History* (New York, Charles Scribner's Sons, 1926), p. 399.

love. I shall do my duty as God reveals it to me, without a moment's consideration of its effect on me. I am ready to resign my pastorate at any hour's notice when I no longer have freedom to follow my convictions, or when doing so divides and scatters the congregation.[1]

But Beecher was not content to elect Cleveland to the Presidency; he wanted some assurance that the civil-service reform for which they had elected Cleveland was introduced. George William Curtis and Henry Ward Beecher personally interviewed President Cleveland on the retention of Mr. Pearson as postmaster of New York City. The Democrats wanted a partisan appointment. President Cleveland requested Beecher and Curtis to name some Democrat who would be acceptable to them. But they declined, saying that they sought the retention of Mr. Pearson on the grounds of civil-service reform, not partisan or personal; that he had proved himself an efficient and faithful official. President Cleveland listened to their wishes and reappointed Mr. Pearson.[2]

Antislavery. The fourth major reform to which Beecher dedicated his talents, and the reform with which his name will be forever associated, both in and out of the pulpit, was the emancipation of the Negro race. Cincinnati, Lawrenceburg, Indianapolis were milestones in his preparation for his fight on slavery from his Brooklyn pulpit. Beecher became a national figure in the antislavery crusade while attending an antislavery meeting at the Broadway Tabernacle in New York in protest to the attack of Preston S. Brooks upon Charles Sumner on May 22, 1856. Beecher had gone to hear such prominent orators as William M. Evarts, John Van Buren, and Daniel Lord, Jr. Beecher was sighted in the audience and called upon to speak. The event is important enough in Beecher's career to quote the description of the meeting given by his own family.

The speeches were able but tame and conservative. They did not meet the demand of the popular heart over that tremendous outrage. Just as the meeting was being adjourned Mr. Beecher was discovered in the back part of the room, having come in to listen to men whose reputation was so great but whom he had never heard. At once the cry from the unsatisfied audience was "Beecher, Beecher!" Scene after scene was depicted by his marvellous dramatic power, culminating in that outrage in the Senate Chamber on account of which they had gathered; and the audience, alternately moved by his pathos, fired by his passion, or swept by his humor, became one with the speaker. . . . The next day the press carried this impression to its multitude of readers, and, dismissing the other speeches of the evening with a formal notice, gave his nearly as possible verbatim.[3]

[1] Beecher, Scoville, and Beecher, *op. cit.*, p. 580.
[2] Knox, *op. cit.*, p. 230. Knox (p. 374) suggests that Beecher was at one time spoken of as a possible minister to the Court of St. James.
[3] Beecher, Scoville, and Beecher, *op. cit.*, p. 287.

By means of editorials in the *Independent*, as we have seen, as well as by his sermons and addresses, Beecher assumed a position of leadership in the North on slavery, which found its culmination in his British speeches of 1863. Because the British newspapers, for the most part, were closed to the Northern cause, the only way the sentiment of the unenfranchised millions, who were sympathetic with the Northern cause, could be shown was through public demonstrations. The caliber of the missionaries who were sent by the government can be judged by three who went in 1861: Thurlow Weed, Archbishop John Joseph Hughes, and Bishop Charles Pettit McIlvaine. The plan to send Wendell Phillips never materialized. Beecher's attacks on the administration were reason enough that he was not designated by the government as one of its propagandists. Beecher claims he went to England for a rest and had no intention of speaking but was persuaded to by the Emancipation Society of England.

To give an idea of the backdrop against which Beecher spoke in the autumn of 1863, it is necessary for us to remember that the newspapers and the upper classes, which they represented, were not fully aware of the implications of the Emancipation Proclamation which went into effect on January 1, 1863, and of the military victories of Vicksburg and Gettysburg. The *Weekly Express*, Manchester, October 11, 1862, scoffed at the proclamation which President Lincoln first announced on September 22, 1862. "After repeated declarations of his purpose to maintain slavery that he might reconstruct the Union, the Northern president has issued a proclamation for giving every slave his freedom—on paper." The newspapers reasoned that Lincoln had no jurisdiction over the South. Likewise, the significance of Gettysburg and Vicksburg was not fully appreciated. The *Manchester Courier*, September 5, 1863, wrote of Gettysburg: "It is evident that the repulse of Gettysburg did far more damage to the Federals than to their adversaries. . . . Now this orderly and deliberate retreat after three days at Gettysburg has turned out to be a wonderful success for the Southern army."

Other evidence suggests that public opinion in England during 1863 was divided. If Lincoln had thought the battle for neutrality had been won on January 1, 1863, he never would have sent in April, 1863, a set of resolutions against slavery to John Bright, asking him to have them adopted by popular assemblies in England.[1] If the Emancipation Society of England had not been afraid of the effect of the proposed campaign by the pro-Southern faction to influence public opinion, it never would have begged Beecher in July to undertake his series of addresses.[2] If Laird had felt that

---

[1] G. M. Trevelyan, *Life of John Bright* (Houghton Mifflin Company, 1914), p. 302.
[2] Howard, *op. cit.*, p. 485.

England was seriously determined to be neutral, he never would have continued to build his steam rams for the South up to the first week in September, when he received orders to cease.

That there was much sentiment in England against the North as late as October, 1863, is evidenced by the editorials appearing in the newspapers attacking Beecher. These editorials took the opportunity of denouncing the action of Lord John Russell for his detention of the rams. An example of this criticism is found in the *Albion*, Liverpool, October 12, 1863. The reference to Beecher as a Yankee braggart should be noted. Beecher spoke on October 9 in Manchester, and this editorial is one of many appearing in the Liverpool newspapers after that address.

If Earl Russell is satisfied, we feel pretty sure that England is not; we doubt extremely whether had Parliament been sitting, the menaces of America would have been thus attended to. Whatever is in accordance with law, domestic or international, by that we are ready to be bound, even in spite of our sympathies; but we are sure that Englishmen do not intend to be bullied into altering their laws; Yankee braggarts, and the half-hearted Englishmen who support them will find out their mistake whenever the sense of this country has an opportunity of expressing itself. Already have the latter well-nigh ruined the prospects of the Liberal party, by showing that democratic principles are dearer to their hearts than the dignity and greatness of England, we have no doubt, they will continue to sacrifice to the object of their affections, but of this, at least we are certain, that the great body of English liberals, if they must make a choice, will prefer to see the honour of their country safe in the hands of Lord Derby and a strong Tory administration, to having it dragged through insult and humiliation in the nerveless grasp of Russell.

But as the autumn wore on the cumulative effect of forces working for neutrality began to make itself felt, and such newspapers as the *Albion* became less hostile. We find, for example, on November 6, 1863, Charles Francis Adams writing to Mr. Seward, "I am rather hopeful of a better final result than I was in the Spring. There has been a marked alteration in the tone of the leading newspapers which will not fail to produce its effect on the classes they reach."[1] This change in sentiment, Brooks Adams has shown, influenced the leaders of Parliament to such an extent that they did not dare censure Lord Russell's action in retaining the rams.[2]

One of the many forces working to bring about this change in sentiment was the influence of Beecher's addresses, for they showed the extent of the feeling of the masses for the North. It was natural that partisans of the South should deny the importance of Beecher's mass demonstrations, but an editorial appearing in the *London Daily News*, October 21, 1863, refutes

[1] Letters of Charles Francis Adams to W. H. Seward, Archives, Washington, D.C.
[2] "The Seizure of the Laird Rams," *Massachusetts Historical Proceedings*, 45: 243.

the assertion of Southern sympathizers that Beecher's demonstrations were valueless in showing the sympathies of the common people.

If as the partisans of the South assert, this is not so, let them support their assertion in the only way that will be satisfactory to practical men—by counter demonstrations of a similar kind. If they can produce on their side any such genuine expression of popular feeling as that afforded by the meeting last night, they will do far more towards contraverting Lord Russell's declaration, at which they profess to be so aggrieved, than can be effected by any number of private assemblies of the elect of Liverpool and Manchester at club and parlour meetings from which reporters are carefully excluded.

But the challenge of this newspaper was never accepted by the pro-Southern group because, for one reason, it had no Henry Ward Beecher.

President Lincoln was so impressed with the results of these English addresses that he invited Beecher to give the address at Fort Sumter on the occasion of raising the flag on April 14, 1865. Oliver Wendell Holmes, in his article in the *Atlantic Monthly*, January, 1864, referred to Beecher as "Our Minister Plenipotentiary" and placed this estimate upon his efforts: "A more remarkable embassy than any envoy who has represented us in Europe since Franklin pleaded the cause of the young Republic at the Court of Versailles."

V. *Conclusion*

Beecher might have been a successful lecturer, a statesman, an author, or a journalist, but following in the footsteps of his father, he preached to the American people for 50 of the most important years of their history. His 40 years at Plymouth Church are his monument. His influence upon the content and composition of sermons in the United States, if not in the world, must be reckoned with by any historian of the Protestant church. The influence of his pulpit upon so many important men and movements of the nineteenth century has carved for Beecher a place in history. In the ceiling of the foyer of the Library of Congress his name has been set in the mosaic along with the names of his compeers: Channing, Mather, Brooks, and Edwards, a recognition of the worthy company to which he rightfully belongs. Historians who attempt to reconstruct the thought of his time find him a fertile source of reference. No American preacher has been so completely recorded. At the time of Beecher's death, Phillips Brooks said, "I know that you are thinking as I speak of the great soul that has passed away, of the great preacher, for he was the greatest preacher in America, and the greatest preacher means the greatest power in the land."[1]

[1] A. V. G. Allen, *Life of Phillips Brooks* (New York, E. P. Dutton & Company, Inc., 1901), III, 229.

SELECTED BIBLIOGRAPHY

Biographies

Abbott, Lyman: *Life of Henry Ward Beecher*, Boston, Houghton Mifflin Company, 1903.

——, and S. B. Halliday: *Life of Henry Ward Beecher*, Hartford, Conn., American Publishing Co., 1888.

Beecher, W. C., S. Scoville, and Mrs. Henry Ward Beecher: *Life and Letters of Henry Ward Beecher*, New York, Charles L. Webster and Co., 1888.

Hibben, Paxton: *Henry Ward Beecher: An American Portrait*, New York, George H. Doran Company, 1927.

Knox, T. W.: *Life of Beecher*, Hartford, Conn., Hartford Publishing Co., 1889.

Shenstone, N. A.: *Anecdotes of Henry Ward Beecher*, Chicago, R. R. Donnelley & Sons Company, 1887.

Stowe, Lyman Beecher: *Saints, Sinners and Beechers*, Indianapolis, The Bobbs-Merrill Company, 1934.

Works of Henry Ward Beecher

Lectures and Orations, Newell Dwight Hillis, Fleming H. Revell Company, 1913.

Lectures to Young Men on Various Important Subjects, New York, Doubleday, Doran & Company, Inc., 1879.

Patriotic Addresses, John R. Howard, ed., Boston, The Pilgrim Press, 1887.

Plymouth Pulpit, 10 vols., New York, Fords, Howard & Hulbert, 1890.

Plymouth Pulpit, Lyman Abbott, ed., New York, Harper & Brothers, 1868.

Summer in England with Henry Ward Beecher, J. B. Pond, ed., New York, Fords, Howard and Hulbert, 1887.

Yale Lectures on Preaching, New York, J. B. Ford, 1872–1873–1874.

9

Phillips Brooks

by MARIE HOCHMUTH *and* NORMAN W. MATTIS

Born in Boston, December 13, 1835, Phillips Brooks attended Miss Capen's Private School, public grammar school, Boston Latin School, Harvard (A.B. 1855), and the Virginia Theological Seminary. He was ordained deacon and priest, 1859, and served as rector, Church of the Advent, Philadelphia, 1859–1861; of Holy Trinity, Philadelphia, 1861–1869; and of Trinity, Boston, 1869–1891. Fire destroyed Old Trinity, 1872; new structure in Copley Square occupied, February, 1877. Brooks was a member of the board of overseers at Harvard for 18 years and of the Board of Preachers to the University from 1886 to 1891. He traveled much in Europe; preached before Queen Victoria, July 11, 1879; visited India, 1882; spent summer of 1889 in Japan. *Lectures on Preaching* appeared, 1877; first volume of sermons, 1878; the Bohlen lectures (*The Influence of Jesus*), 1779; second volume of sermons, 1881; third, 1883; many others thereafter. On October 14, 1891, Brooks was consecrated Bishop of Massachusetts. He died on January 23, 1893.

On July 21, 1865, Harvard held a memorial service for her sons who had died in the war. It was a great meeting, in which the most distinguished civil, military, and literary leaders of New England united to give thanks for victory and to pay homage to those who had made victory possible. Emerson, Mrs. Howe, and Dr. Holmes wrote poems for the occasion; and Lowell read the great ode that has made the service a part of American literary history.

Phillips Brooks, class of 1855, led in prayer. For six years he had been preaching in Philadelphia. He had made a deep impression on the citizens of that city, had attracted wide attention by a fine sermon on Lincoln, and had received many calls to important pulpits. But few in Boston knew of his work, and Col. T. W. Higginson wondered when he saw the program why a young man of whom he had never heard should have been chosen. The sequel may be told in the words of that most unemotional of men Charles W. Eliot. Nearly thirty years after the event he wrote of Brooks:

That day he stood up in the plain wooden church opposite the College gate, before the dignitaries of the State and the University, the soldiers returned from the war, the representatives of families of the dead heroes, and the throng of guests, graduates and students, and poured out to God an impetuous torrent of thanksgiving, praise, exultation, and aspiration. Private grief and public joy, tender memories and exalted hopes were blended in that glowing prayer. It was the most impressive utterance of a proud and happy day. Even Lowell's Commemoration Ode did not at the moment so touch the hearts of his hearers. That one spontaneous and intimate expression of Brooks' noble spirit convinced all Harvard men that a young prophet had risen up in Israel.[1]

Not a word of that prayer has been preserved. Brooks's only recorded reference to it, apart from a factual entry in his diary, was the remark that what touched him most was Senator Sumner's thanking him for it with tears in his eyes. It is perhaps symbolic that the utterance that first brought Brooks to the attention of those eminent in the social and intellectual life of the country should have been a prayer of which no trace remains. For Brooks's influence was forever a personal influence, traceable not in the record of events or even in the pages of his printed works but in the lives of men and women whom he inspired and strengthened.

The prayer had consequences, however, of practical import. From that time, Boston became interested in reclaiming her son. Four years later he reluctantly bade farewell to the Philadelphia scenes where he had labored happily since his ordination and returned to his native city as rector of its largest and wealthiest Episcopal church. There he remained, as pastor of Trinity and Bishop of Massachusetts until his untimely death at the age of fifty-seven, and there he won a unique place in the affections of the people. "What a pity that everybody cannot hear Phillips Brooks," said Julia Ward Howe.[2] A good part of the world did hear him, and it was an Englishman who called him "the noblest, truest, and most stainless man I ever knew."[3]

I. *Religious Unrest*

During the second half of the nineteenth century the impact of science on ways of thinking and of living produced changes that were deeply disturbing to all who cherished the spiritual and moral basis of Western culture. In the year Phillips Brooks was ordained and assumed charge of his first parish Charles Darwin published the *Origin of Species*. The theory of biological evolution associated with Darwin's name became the focal point of a momentous conflict between old and new conceptions of the universe and of man. The method and spirit of science, speedily spreading to all departments of study, and the enormous increase in verifiable knowledge of

[1] "What Phillips Brooks Did for the College," *The Harvard Monthly*, 15 (February, 1893): 5.

[2] Laura E. Richards and Maud Howe Elliott, *Julia Ward Howe*, 1819–1910 (2 vols., Boston, 1916), II, 126.

[3] Frederic William Farrar, "Phillips Brooks, Bishop of Massachusetts," *Review of the Churches*, 3, No. 17 (Feb. 15, 1893): 273.

physical phenomena, created a climate of opinion in which materialism, agnosticism, and skepticism flourished. For a time it seemed that an age of science could not be an age of faith, nor could the findings of science be reconciled with a belief in God, the dignity of man, and the moral order of the universe. The most fundamental issues were involved; as Brooks said of his own period, "It is not the difficulty of this or that doctrine that makes men skeptics to-day. It is rather the play of all life upon the fundamental grounds and general structure of faith."[1]

Every aspect of man's variegated activity revealed the pervasiveness of forces at best indifferent to religion and at worst actively hostile. The industrialization of Europe and America, proceeding at accelerated tempo, made it easy to regard men as soulless cogs in a machine, placed human relations on a profit-and-loss basis, and made common sense and expediency rather than idealism and spiritual faith the guiding principles of life. To Karl Marx all history could be interpreted as a sordid struggle for the goods of the earth, with no place left for "a spirit not ourselves that makes for righteousness." Poets and novelists surveyed humanity through the spectacles of biological or economic determinism. Some remained hopeful of man's destiny because he was proving his mastery of physical phenomena; some, incorporating in their work the scientific ideal of dispassionate description, produced the "realistic" novel. Some became darkly pessimistic at the thought of impotent man in a world in which no benevolent intelligence could be discerned; still others glorified a despairing hedonism. In every phase of life the most powerful forces operating on the mind of man tended to place religion on the defensive. In the words of Brooks:

The aspect of the world, which is fate, has been too strong for the fundamental religion of the world, which is providence. And the temptation of the world, which is self-indulgence, has seemed to make impossible the precept of religion, which is self-surrender; and the tendency of experience, which is hopelessness, has made the tendency of the gospel, which is hope, to seem unreal and unbelievable.[2]

The leaders of the great Christian denominations had special problems of their own, problems that grew largely out of the increasing gap between their static creeds and the knowledge of natural law. Tending to identify religion with the particular theology to which they subscribed, many of them were placed in the position, hopelessly indefensible to those impregnated with the scientific spirit, of being uncritical defenders of a traditional orthodoxy rather than seekers of truth. Their polemics were adapted to the resolution of doubts that could be debated without involvement of the totality of theological thought; now the very foundations of the edifice were

[1] "The Pulpit and Popular Skepticism," *Essays and Addresses* (New York, 1894), p. 63.
[2] *Ibid.*, p. 63.

being shaken. The growth of skepticism could no longer be stemmed by the buttressing of special doctrines. Apart from the agnosticism of science, discoveries of modern scholarship were claiming a disconcerted attention. The "higher criticism" of the Bible, archaeological research, and the comparative study of religions rendered untenable the belief in literal inspiration and shattered the complacent assumption that the Christian verities had been deposited in Palestine by special revelation nineteen hundred years ago. And to the disturbing effects of these studies must be added the profound consequences of world movements of the highest order in politics, philosophy, and art. The rise of political democracy after the French Revolution weakened faith in a despotic God ruling for his own arbitrary ends; the cult of the common man and the revelation of what he could do when left to govern himself ran counter to the theories of depravity and original sin; the poets' intimate communion with nature could not be reconciled to a belief that the world is essentially evil. A multiplicity of new interests competed for the time and energy formerly spent on theology, and as men became indifferent to the rationale of the creeds they became hostile to such specific articles of faith as the eternal damnation of the "unsaved."

The growth of agnosticism among the intellectual leaders of America is part of the historical record. Equally plain is the restiveness of clergymen and others who, while retaining their faith in the spiritual nature of man and their loyalty to Jesus as the supreme revealer of our divinity, could no longer accept the traditional formularies of their churches. The attitude of the masses is more difficult to assess. Schlesinger points out that even the spectacular controversy over evolution touched them but lightly, and a general tendency to segregate religion into a special compartment to be consulted on Sunday only made for a continued easy acquiescence in time-worn dogma.[1] Church membership bore up well. Nevertheless, many factors indicate a decline in the prestige and influence of organized religion. The minister was no longer vested with the sanctity that his position had once automatically conferred on him;[2] the distribution of space in the newspapers changed radically to the disadvantage of religion;[3] rapid shifts of population left vast numbers of the urban masses beyond the reach of the churches; and organized labor, irritated by clerical indifference to problems of social justice, was usually hostile.[4] Any assertion that the American people were

[1] A. M. Schlesinger, *The Rise of the City, 1878–1898* (New York, 1933), p. 321.
[2] Charles W. Eliot, "On the Education of Ministers," *The Princeton Review*, May, 1883, pp. 340–348, and Frank Luther Mott, *A History of American Magazines, 1865–1885* (Cambridge, 1938), p. 87.
[3] Schlesinger, *op. cit.*, pp. 198–201.
[4] *Ibid.*, pp. 330–333, and H. F. Perry, "The Workingman's Alienation from the Church," *American Journal of Sociology*, 4: 622.

growing indifferent to religion can be contradicted by selection of the right evidence. It can be shown, however, by reference to what was actually happening to religion that the message of Christianity had to be vitalized. The times were ripe for stripping it of "the mouldy husks of a dead theology" and bringing it into harmony with a view of the universe differing radically from that implied in the Bible and the classic creeds.

Matching the need for the rationalization of religion to fit modern conditions was the need for spiritualization. As faith in the dogmas dwindled, their capacity to move men decreased, and their presentation tended to become stereotyped and formal. In the early days of Phillips Brooks's ministry sermons still dealt mainly, in conventional phraseology, with such topics as original sin, sanctification, and second probation or with the perennial battle between orthodoxy and Unitarianism. Evangelical Episcopalians, with their "tempered Calvinism," droned on about "vicarious sacrifice, eternal life, sin, repentance, heaven, and sainthood"[1] or reiterated their ancient warnings against "Geneva on the one hand and Rome on the other." The hackneyed terminology of ancient controversy and the flat aridity of literal exposition competed in dullness, and neither possessed inspirational power.

In this confused, critical, and groping world Phillips Brooks had a double task. First, he had to combat the results of that "play of all life upon the fundamental grounds and general structure of faith" and strengthen man's confidence in the spiritual nature of his own constitution. And then, because he loved his own church and believed that its creed, liturgy, and institutional organization were useful instruments, when properly understood, for the cultivation of the spiritual life, he had to harmonize old doctrine with modern knowledge and his own convictions. In his method of accomplishing these tasks may be found the sources of his success both as minister to mankind and as a clergyman of the Protestant Episcopal church.

II. *The Religion of Phillips Brooks*

"Mankind are the Children of God," sang Phillips Brooks in a carol of moving simplicity,[2] and the whole of his message is implicit in that affirmation of the nature of humanity. To him, men were truly the sons of God, and their normal, natural, proper life was the religious life. Man may be

[1] William Lawrence, *Life of Phillips Brooks* (New York, 1930), pp. 50–52. For other descriptions and impressions of mid-nineteenth century preaching, see Thomas N. Clark, *Reminiscences* (New York, 1895), pp. 54–55, and Washington Gladden, *Recollections* (Boston, 1909), p. 62. Charles C. Tiffany calls attention indirectly to the deficiencies of this preaching by stressing the improvement, under the stimulus of new ideas, in the literary quality of works produced by Episcopalian clergymen after the Civil War.—*A History of the Protestant Episcopal Church in the United States of America* (New York, 1895), pp. 506–507.

[2] *The Voice of the Christ-child* (New York, 1891).

rebellious and ignorant, he may deny his divinity in thought or action, but he cannot escape it. When he sins, he sins against himself.[1]

To Brooks, therefore, religion was not a series of propositions about God, or a list of moral injunctions, but the totality of life lived in harmony with the universal order.[2] Such totality cannot be understood by one side only of our nature; neither the intellect, the will, nor the emotions can in isolation provide an avenue for the entry of ultimate wisdom. Religion may at any given moment present itself as a duty to be done, truth to be apprehended, or emotion to be felt, but it must start from a source that includes all these, and that also "has in itself a quality greater than the sum of all these elements which it includes, a quality answering to the unity or totality of the humanity to which religion proceeds and from which it offers itself."[3] Brooks found the fulfillment of these conditions in the concept of personality; in it, and in it only, all human faculties unite to form the complete man, who in his completeness is something more than the sum of his parts. The union of God and man cannot be made clear by definition and abstract statement, any more than can love, hope, fear, or life itself. Mysteries, without losing their mystery, become apprehensible when embodied in a person.[4]

In the personality of Jesus, Brooks found the supreme evidence of man's kinship to God. Jesus had the largest and deepest realization of that relationship ever attained, and displayed its full meaning in character and conduct.[5] Jesus did not create that relationship, nor had mankind ever been totally ignorant of it; the world had always had within itself its holiest potentialities and had always moved, though gropingly and with imperfect understanding, in its true directions. But Jesus knew perfectly what others glimpsed fitfully and provided both the supreme proof of the godhood of man and the supreme example of how much the full realization of that truth can mean.[6] In love and gratitude toward Him are to be found the most humanly valid and compelling incentives to the good life.

[1] Phillips Brooks, *The Influence of Jesus* (New York, 1879), pp. 13–14.

[2] "The Best Methods of Promoting Spiritual Life," *Essays and Addresses*, p. 21. See also "The Preeminence of Christianity," *New Starts in Life* (New York, 1897), p. 323.

[3] "The Teachableness of Religion," *Essays and Addresses*, pp. 206–207.

[4] " . . . Not all men are capable of arguing or of receiving argument; but all men are capable of living and appreciating life," he observed.—"Gamaliel," *Sermons Preached in English Churches* (New York, 1883) p. 261. He delighted to point out that the New Testament is a biography, saying: "Make it a mere book of dogmas, and its vitality is gone. Make it a biography, and it is a true book of life. Make it the history of Jesus of Nazareth, and the world holds it in its heart forever."—"Biography," *Essays and Addresses*, p. 428.

[5] *The Influence of Jesus*, p. 14.

[6] "The Light of the World," *The Light of the World and Other Sermons* (New York, 1890), pp. 3–5.

This statement of the mission of Jesus does not answer the moot question of his nature, so

To this combination of profound faith in the immanence of God with devotion to Jesus for his revelation of that immanence can be traced many of the characteristics of Brooks's ministry. It led him, first, to his conception of the function of the preacher. Since religion cannot be communicated to the intellect alone, the spiritual interpretation of the universal economy is to be proved not by argument or the scrutiny of "evidences" but by display of the consequences of its acceptance in the character of the individual. And as the most convincing evidence of character is found in conduct, it is "in the exhibition of their moral consequences and connections far more than in the discovery of their abstract truth or falsehood, or their proof or disproof from the Bible, that doctrines today must be established or refuted in the eyes of men."[1]

Second, it made him essentially indifferent to systematic theology. Exasperated literalists sometimes accused him of an absolute incapacity to understand theological distinctions. In reality he had a comprehensive knowledge of the imposing intellectual structures erected by Christian thinkers.[2] But the "simplicity which is in Christ" had little to do with the

---

significant in the Unitarian controversy. Was he a supremely gifted man who, "growing beyond his brothers, overlooked the battlements of heaven, and saw the place in the divine heart where man belonged, and then came back and bade his brethren follow him"?—"A Trinity-Sunday Sermon," *Sermons* (New York, 1878), p. 237. Or was he different in kind from the rest of men? It is hard to believe, from the totality of Brooks's work, that he considered the question crucial: the revelation was true no matter what its mechanism. Nevertheless, he accepted for himself the uniqueness of the Incarnation. Unitarians would have liked to claim him for their own, but one who regretfully admitted that they could not justly do so has spoken accurately of the orthodoxy of Brooks's position. "I have never seen any words of his which retracted or hesitated as to that interpretation of the nature, endowment, and office of Jesus which is distinctive of the orthodox position. He was not merely a supernaturalist of the Channing type. He was a full . . . believer in the *supreme* divinity of Jesus . . . Christ to him was God in the flesh; not merely as God spiritually is in us all, but peculiarly, particularly, as a unique incarnation of the divine being in the one man, Jesus. Christ, the God-man, was the essential link between men and God."—Joseph May, *Phillips Brooks* (Boston, 1893), pp. 65–66.

[1] "The Pulpit and Popular Skepticism," *Essays and Addresses*, p. 73. It must not be supposed that Brooks distrusted the reason or minimized its role in human affairs. On the contrary, he remarked: "The disbelief of reason is peremptory and absolute. The soul cannot hold what the reason declares to be untrue."—"Healthy Conditions of a Change of Faith," *ibid.*, p. 223. But the intellect is simply one of the avenues through which truth enters a man.

[2] The general conclusion is that Brooks made no important original contributions to theology. Leighton Parks, in *The Theology of Phillips Brooks* (Boston, 1894), and A. V. G. Allen, in *Life of Phillips Brooks* (2 vols., New York, 1900), made the most comprehensive investigations of his theology, and they attribute to him a certain originality of emphasis, Allen stressing particularly his constant desire to make thought and feeling operate on the *will* of man. But unquestionably Brooks's preeminence rests not on doctrinal originality but on his popularization of attitudes and interpretations common to many. Maurice, Robertson, and Bushnell probably exercised the most important immediate influence on his thought.

complexities of the theologians, and man is more in need of the simplicity than of the complexity. For orthodoxy in itself he had no respect: the test of a doctrine is its influence on life, not its antiquity or its internal consistency or its sanction by authority.[1] To that crystallization of thought in sharply defined propositions which constitutes dogma he attached importance, but it was an importance of a special sort. He refused to make acquiescence in any doctrine the test of a good man or of a Christian or even of a Protestant Episcopalian; on the other hand, he believed that the creeds of his church embodied spiritual truths formulated from the experience of mankind. They needed restatement and reinterpretation in every age, and every individual must be free to attach his own meaning to the words, but the fruitful attitude toward them is one of affectionate though critical inquiry rather than rejection. Hence one of his greatest tasks was to make traditional doctrines the symbols of the primary truths or to rediscover and restate the essential spiritual truth in dogmas whose presentation had grown hard and mechanical.[2] Always he strove to find the connection between dogma and life.[3]

Third, his rooted sense of the divinity of man determined the nature of his appeals and is the ultimate justification for the psychological motivation of his sermons. An invincible optimism governed his approach to men, as the Duchess of Bedford, with a different opinion of frail humanity, rather mistrustfully observed.[4] He summoned the world to the good life not by threatening punishment, or even by promising reward, but by revealing what each man knows instinctively, though darkly and uncertainly, con-

[1] He granted that an orthodoxy to which one clings may have utility at a low level of spiritual life. It keeps one in a certain routine of faith and action during periods of doubt and skepticism. "It does . . . seem to make capable of transportation and transmission truths which in their deeper spirituality it is not easy to think of except as the sacred and secret possession of the human soul." But it does so "only by the deadening of truth, as a butcher freezes meat in order to carry it across the sea."—"Orthodoxy," *Essays and Addresses*, pp. 193–194.

[2] See John W. Chadwick, *Phillips Brooks: A Sermon* (Boston, 1901), pp. 95–97.

[3] "Preach doctrine, preach all the doctrine that you know, and learn forever more and more; but preach it always, not that men may believe it, but that men may be saved by believing it."—*Lectures on Preaching* (New York, 1877), p. 129. Brooks's orthodoxy was sharply challenged at the time of his election to the bishopric. He was accused of denying the doctrine of the apostolical succession, of minimizing the importance of miracles, of Arianism, Pelagianism, of everything, as he said good-naturedly, except murder and theft. To requests that he clarify his views, he replied that they could be found in his published works. It is hardly surprising that the opposition did not find this answer satisfactory. They wanted categorical replies to questions that to Brooks's mind could not be answered categorically. For details of the controversy and of the extraordinary popular interest in it, see Allen, *Life*, II, 824–861. It should be added that the objections came from a small but vocal minority and for the most part from those who lived far from the scene of his immediate ministrations.

[4] Richards and Elliott, *op. cit.*, II, 171.

cerning his own nature. This serene faith in the responsiveness of man—described by Bishop Potter as "that enkindling and transforming temper which forever sees in humanity, not that which is bad and hateful, but that which is lovable and redeemable"[1]—linked closely with a change in Christian faith that was characteristic of his age. It has been well described by him: "It is a desire to escape from the severer, stricter, more formal, more exacting statements of truth and duty, and to lay hold of the gentler, more gracious, more spiritual, more indulgent representations of God and of what He asks of man. . . . The stern judge of the older dispensation is lost behind the gracious and merciful presence of the Christ. Pity is more than judgment, sympathy more than authority, persuasion more than rebuke, in the God of whom men are thinking, of whom men are preaching now."[2]

Brooks's faith has proved happily consonant with some of the highest manifestations of religious development, and admirably adapted to many of the difficulties of his age. Its all-pervasive principle of the immanence of God has been the determining element in the most progressive interpretations of Christianity. The classic theologies, both Protestant and Roman Catholic, have in general followed the Latin fathers. They, appalled by the social disorders and decaying culture of a declining empire, constructed a system in which God figured as governor and judge, controlling corrupt man "travelling in lonely probation to some distant throne" through fear of punishment and hope of reward. Throughout the history of Christianity, however, there have been men who have rejected the idea of an autocratic God administering laws valid only by reason of His arbitrary appointment. They have thought of Him as "a being whose presence pervades the world and with whose essential nature man has a constitutional kinship or relation."[3] Some of the Greek fathers of the early Church seem to have interpreted thus the words of Christ concerning his Father; Spinoza posited one world of reality, both nature and God; and mystics of all ages have borne witness to a continuing human protest against a theological mechanism that sets God apart from humanity.

In the nineteenth century the idea of immanence had a great renascence.[4] The rise of democratic ideals in politics, the deeper study of the Bible, the Romantic devotion to nature, and all the developments that

---

[1] Henry C. Potter, *The Mission and Commission of the Episcopate* (New York, 1892), p. 26.

[2] "The Mitigation of Theology," *New Starts in Life*, p. 339.

[3] A. V. G. Allen, "The Theological Renaissance of the Nineteenth Century," *The Princeton Review*, November, 1882, p. 264. Of this article Brooks wrote to his brother from a steamship in the Suez Canal: "I wonder who will be up to the mark of honestly admiring A. V. G. Allen's remarkable paper in the 'Princeton Review' and seeing how the change which he has described so ably is every whit as important and significant as the reformation of three hundred years ago."—*Letters of Travel* (New York, 1894), p. 228.

[4] The idea has never been absent from any Christian theology, but the systems of thought

produced doubt of specific doctrines of orthodoxy played a part; and as these movements stimulated thought of God as a pervasive and beneficent force, that thought in turn exercised a reciprocal influence, deepening and intensifying the movements that gave rise to it. Kant, with his reliance on self-consciousness as the most reliable source of truth, gave it impetus and authority; Goethe and Wordsworth expressed in poetry what Coleridge discovered by the speculative process; Emerson and the New England transcendentalists made it a vital force in American culture; and Maurice, Robertson, Thomas Arnold, Stanley, and many others in the Church of England labored to interpret Christ's message and the creed of their church in its light.[1]

When every aspect of life received its illumination from the concept of immanence,[2] as in the religion of Phillips Brooks, much that perplexed the people of his time and drove them to distressing doubt sank into insignificance. First, it provided a principle of universal unity. For a system that opposed saints to sinners, the saved to the damned, the world to God, natural law to special revelation, it substituted an organic unity of life and faith, nature and the "supernatural," God and man.[3] There could be no quarrel between science and religion in Phillips Brooks's cosmos; nor did he resolve the conflict, as many were doing, by dividing phenomena into two parts and assigning one to the scientists and the other to the theologians. Indeed, he took no active part at all in the attempts to reconcile particular doctrines or detached Biblical accounts with natural law;[4] the solution of the quarrel was implicit in the foundations of his thought.

---

that emerge if stress is placed upon God the Ruler and Judge, external to the universe, differ greatly from those which emerge if his interpenetration of all is emphasized.

[1] These men, however different, shared an intense apprehension of the unity of God and man. It is to this common denominator that William Mitchell refers in noting that Brooks's sympathies were with Clement of Alexandria and Origen, rather than with Jerome, Tertullian, Cyprian, or St. Augustine; with Cranmer, Coleridge, Robertson, Kingsley, Stanley, Emerson, Channing, and Schleiermacher rather than with Aquinas, Calvin, Jonathan Edwards, or even Cardinal Newman—*Phillips Brooks: A Study* (Kendallville, Ind., n.d.), p. 39.

[2] The idea of immanence came to be accepted widely during the latter part of the nineteenth century as "an improvement in the mode of theological statement" (necessitated by the findings of science), even by conservative theologians who refused to make it, as did Maurice and Brooks, the starting point for a recasting of the entire circle of doctrines. See Henry C. Hitchcock, "The Broad Church Theology," *Bibliotheca Sacra*, 48 (October, 1891): 643.

[3] Lawrence, *op. cit.*, pp. 37–39.

[4] Schlesinger, *op. cit.*, p. 468, cites Brooks as a clergyman who, while in no way hostile to the advances of science, stood aloof from discussions of its effect on theology and religion. Brooks was not scientific in his habits of thought and on some questions took positions that must have been irritating to those intent on discarding as fiction all that could not be explained by the science of the eighties. Thus the miracles gave him no trouble: he said simply that one might expect great accomplishments from a supremely great personality!

Second, it rejected completely the idea that there was any such thing as "an authoritative oracle of religious truth," a demand for which "haunts not merely the hills of Rome, but even the broad open Protestant pastures of our own communion. . . . "[1] All man's knowledge is limited by his own imperfections. God may have revealed himself perfectly, but man is only half-developed and has only half possession of his knowing powers.[2] Therefore insight into the spiritual nature of things is progressive, just as the understanding of physical phenomena is progressive. As man catches a glimpse of some higher truth, he abandons his former beliefs, not with contempt but with gratitude for their service as steppingstones to nobler conceptions.[3] In this rejection of the principle of authority and acceptance of the principle that all knowledge is provisional and subject to new discoveries, Brooks brought theology, the rationale of our thought about God, into harmony with science and modern scholarship and relieved it of the heavy incubus of approaching all problems to find support for preconceived dogmas rather than to discover the truth.[4]

Third, a religion based on immanence as interpreted by Brooks was tolerant. All men are the sons of God, good men everywhere are the servants of God, and men of every age and of every stage of culture have lived spiritual lives and belong to the fellowship of those who are faithful to their heritage of divinity. Brooks united in this tolerant acceptance of intellectual differences with those loosely referred to in his own church as Broad Churchmen. Though most of them were leaders in the reinterpretation and softening of Christian doctrine, they differed widely in their conclusions and can hardly be said to constitute a school. Their common denominator was a desire to enlarge the boundaries of the Church of England and of the Protestant Episcopal church of the United States so that men of the most diverse views could remain within those institutions. United in tolerance and in their desire to welcome to their membership all those who had "a cordial personal loyalty to Jesus,"[5] men like Dean Stanley in England and

[1] "The Sufficient Grace of God," *Sermons Preached in English Churches*, p. 128.

[2] "Healthy Conditions of a Change of Faith," *Essays and Addresses*, p. 226.

[3] " . . . there is no falsehood which man has once earnestly believed which has not in it truth enough to furnish a point of departure, and . . . there is no direction in which a man can earnestly look for truth in which he may not see some partial truth which is large enough at least to furnish him with temporary lodgment. . . . The healthy law of all change of opinion is not the abandonment of overthrown positions, but the pursuit of something still more attractive and important that is discerned beyond."—"Healthy Conditions of a Change of Faith," *Essays and Addresses*, pp. 219–220.

[4] For typical statements of this pervasive principle, see *The More Abundant Life* (New York, 1897), pp. 58–59; "Your Joy No Man Taketh From You," *Sermons Preached in English Churches*, pp. 303–307; "Healthy Conditions of a Change of Faith" and "The Purposes of Scholarship," *Essays and Addresses*, pp. 226–227 and 248.

[5] "The Mitigation of Theology," *New Starts in Life*, p. 347.

Brooks in America were often found defending those whose opinions they were far from sharing but whose right to hold those opinions within the portals of the church they stoutly maintained. That the two churches have remained truly catholic institutions is due in large part to the liberalizing influence of these men.

Fourth, the shift in emphasis from the depravity of man to his essential goodness as the Son of God led to a reshaping of the whole message of Christianity as interpreted by the major theologies, and in the process many of the doctrines whose harshness or irrationality had alienated increasing numbers were abandoned or received new meanings. The change in motivation to the good life from fear to love was in itself sufficient to alter drastically the character of much preaching. One can hardly say that an age in which agnostic, atheistic, and hedonistic currents flowed strongly was one peculiarly receptive to a religion of joy and optimism based on a hopeful reading of man's nature; one can say that the modification or denial of such doctrines as the eternal damnation of the wicked or, still worse, of the unbelieving helped greatly to stem the retreat from Christianity. Brooks did not have to denounce such doctrines: he simply ignored them. They became irrelevant or petty when viewed in the light of the nobler vision.

Fifth, the religion of Brooks transcended by its very scope many of the problems that were driving men to unbelief. It was no merely mystical intuition, proclaimed oracularly by those who had received the light; it saw in both the large movements of history and in the life of the individual proof that a spiritual Presence pervades all. Still, it was poetic and suggestive rather than intellectual and definitive and might at first thought seem helpless to stem the strongest tendencies of the modern world. It gained greatly, however, by abandoning doctrinaire formulations of what must at best be speculative and resting its case on the lessons of experience. To a man perplexed by the logical difficulties in the idea of an uncreated Creator or impressed with the discovery of man's kinship to the brutes or dismayed by the play of selfish instinct, Brooks and those who shared his beliefs said simply: Of course no one knows the final explanation of these mysteries.. But look within yourself for the evidence of your true nature, and corroborate what you find there by study of Christ and of the best men who ever lived. In the play of conscience, in the restlessness of man under sin, in the unceasing striving of humanity toward an ideal goal, sometimes dimly conceived but always existent, in the admiration bestowed by the worst of men on the best, you may find assurance of your own nature and of the reality of God.

To summarize: Phillips Brooks was one of many who, in their separate ways, labored to vitalize the message of Christianity for the modern world and to bring its theology into harmony with contemporary views of the universe. Stripping Christianity of obsolete accretions, they presented Christ as the supreme revelation of the divinity of man. In so doing they set themselves in opposition to some of the most powerful modern intellectual forces; but they allied themselves with other equally powerful forces, both intellectual and spiritual. They lifted religion far above the arena of ordinary theological combat, rejecting as historical relics the doctrines that offended the intelligence or shocked the conscience of modern man. That their attitude and spirit have not penetrated Christianity completely is patent. Great numbers of preachers and their congregations still carry on a rear-guard action with science, still measure a man's Christianity by his formal subscription to medieval dogmas, still preach a religion of fear, still draw fantastic conclusions from a literal reading of the Scriptures. But as Harry Emerson Fosdick says, the future is not theirs. "The movement goes on which, valuing as much as ever our fathers did the spiritual experiences that lie at the heart of Christianity, is rethinking and restating them in terms congenial with the modern mind."[1]

III. *Boston and Brooks*

Although Brooks preached successfully before all types of people in many parts of the world, he was in a special and very important sense a Boston preacher. In Boston he spent the years of his maturity; from Boston his fame radiated to the far corners; there he became a public fixture, the source of civic pride. There he found his spiritual home and the social and intellectual climate that fostered his genius.

The Boston to which Brooks returned in 1869 as rector of its wealthiest and most fashionable Episcopal church was still the cultural capital of the United States. The literary heroes of the Republic lived on to the middle of his tenure at Trinity; that genial autocrat of Boston amenities, Dr. Holmes, died the year after Brooks. The *Atlantic Monthly* continued as arbiter of the world of letters, managing to combine under William Dean Howells a surprising receptivity to new fashions with the maintenance of traditional flavor. The Saturday Club flourished, with scores of other societies dedicated to study and the exchange of ideas. To them Brooks added the Clericus Club, where intelligent clergymen met for companionship and discussion. In the mechanism of culture, as Van Wyck Brooks observes, as well as in its visible output, Boston's supremacy remained, subject only to an occasional half-envious challenge from other sectors of the sprawling nation.[2] Bostonians were still self-consciously absorbed in the

[1] "Recent Gains in Religion," *Recent Gains in American Civilization* (Kirby Page, ed., New York, 1928), pp. 240–242.

[2] *New England: Indian Summer, 1865–1915* (New York, 1940), p. 12.

finer things: the magnificent Gallery of Paintings and the Boston Symphony Orchestra are permanent memorials of the energy and public spirit of the seventies and eighties.

There were signs, indeed, that this admirable Boston was growing soft and emasculate and that its cultivated concern for art and letters was truly the Indian summer of a more vigorous cultural efflorescence. The genteel tradition preserved the form but lacked the sinew of the great New England enlightenment; it shrank from contact with the harsh realities that industrialism, mass immigration, and the dwindling supply of free land were creating. Bernard De Voto's biting characterization is seen in retrospect to possess some justification: " . . . literature was what the Brahmins wrote and life was dinner with watered Madeira on Mt. Vernon Street and the nightly gatherings of Bostonians before lecture platforms from which incurable schoolmasters read papers on the soul."[1] The two great passions, moral enlightenment and social reform, which had lent muscular force to even the wildest aberrations of an earlier day, had largely spent their force, and conservative characteristics of a long-established, opulent society, more interested in preserving what it had than in adventuring more, had begun to appear. Fathers like Thomas Apley established trust funds for their children and lamented the weakening in aggressive competency and even moral integrity that they observed in the new generation. A few fine old fighters like Wendell Phillips and Julia Ward Howe still battled for every good cause, but no such cause as Abolition appeared to rouse the crusading spirit.

Into the upper circles of this Boston, refined, even urbane, proud of the past, Brooks entered as into his natural home. His ancestry was unimpeachable. He numbered John Cotton among his forbears. His mother's family (the Phillips) had contributed many a clergyman and judge to New England, and his father's family had prospered for generations as farmers and merchants. In Brooks the mother's piety, a bit effusive in expression, was tempered by the reserve and practical sense of the father. His education, up to the theological seminary, was the best America offered: Boston Latin and Harvard. If the divinity school at Alexandria contributed little in the way of intellectual stimulus or discipline, it at any rate offered no impediments to study, and the other institutions had already implanted in Brooks a wide-ranging intellectual curiosity. He was an omnivorous reader; a mere list of what he read and annotated even before he was thirty would fill many pages. To this easy familiarity with the past—biography was his favorite subject, linking with his interest in personality—were added the happy results of constant travel. He knew the whole Continent of Europe; spent months in India; visited Japan, where his huge bulk amazed

[1] *Mark Twain's America* (Boston, 1932), pp. 183–184.

307

the diminutive Japanese. Brooks was a gentleman, not merely in the fundamentals but in the externals; in dress, manners, and poise he was a citizen of the civilized world. If he never became a true cosmopolite, that merely stamped him as the truer Bostonian. On his most enjoyable trips abroad he thought with longing of the excellencies of his native city.

If we disregard the essentially secular character of the whole age, we may say that the people of Boston were better prepared for the Episcopalianism of Phillips Brooks after the Civil War than at any time in their past history. Orthodox Congregationalism, though certainly not dead, had been sorely wounded by the Unitarian schism; it had been steadily losing the allegiance of the thoughtful; it was torn by internecine strife over such topics as the "second probation."[1] Unitarianism, the "Boston Religion," had lost much of the driving force it had possessed when it was a revolutionary movement. Distinguished men like James Freeman Clarke and Edward Everett Hale continued to occupy its pulpits, but its evangelical fervor had departed, and it became more and more indistinguishable from a lofty but somewhat arid system of ethical culture. For the basic lesson of trust in man as the sharer of divinity, Bostonians had been prepared by Emerson, the transcendentalists, even, in a special sense, by the Unitarians. For that message as presented by Brooks, with Episcopal accessories, formal retention of the old creeds, and the undogmatic elevation of Jesus to supremacy, they were now ready. He comforted those for whom the old doctrines held dear associations: if they heard no familiar accents, they at least heard no polemics against the ancient faith. The Unitarians could enjoy the color and warmth and tolerance without feeling that they were false to their intellectual convictions. They might even persuade themselves that Phillips Brooks was at heart a Unitarian!

For members of a comfortable society, vaguely idealistic and practically philanthropic, but quite content with the established order, Brooks was peculiarly well adapted. Throughout the second half of the nineteenth century the church in many of its branches had become increasingly aware of the misery created by industrialization and urbanization. Freed in its more progressive branches by the "new theology" from its preoccupation with the salvation of the individual from hell-fire, it turned its attention to the amelioration of conditions in the present life. The spiritualization and rationalization of religion were accompanied by the socialization of the church as an institution. In England Charles Kingsley, F. D. Maurice, and the others associated with the Christian Socialist movement plunged as early as 1848 into the organization of producers' cooperatives, challenged the competitive principle of capitalist economy, and preached a religion of

[1] H. K. Rowe, *History of Religion in the United States* (New York, The Macmillan Company, 1924).

social service.[1] In America, Washington Gladden, dedicated to a religion that proposed "to realize the Kingdom of God in this world," gave both precept and example to clergymen who wished to apply Christian principles to the solution of social and economic conflicts.[2] The world criticized Lyman Beecher about 1825 for preaching morality when he delivered six sermons on temperance; it criticized his son Henry Ward Beecher 25 years later for preaching politics when he presented a gospel of liberty. By the end of the century the clerical leadership of reforms was a commonplace feature of the national life. Even more symptomatic than the intervention of ministers in particular disputes was the development of the "institutional" church and of a bewildering variety of agencies for care of the underprivileged, guidance of youth, vocational training, and a score of other purposes. In Lyman Abbott's youth the Salvation Army was the greatest of evangelistic organizations; in his old age it specialized in practical philanthropy. "The church of today is not merely a teaching and worshipping organization, it is also a working organization. . . . "[3]

Brooks had little to do directly with this tendency. Under his administration Trinity developed some of the features of the institutional church, but its rector almost never preached on specific current issues. Early in his career he actively espoused certain measures growing out of the Civil War.[4] He took advanced ground on the enfranchisement of the Negro,[5] and labored for equality of treatment for the blacks in his own city of Philadelphia.[6] But from the end of the war to his death he rarely made the pulpit a sounding board for his own opinions of the immediate events of the passing scene. Occasionally a critic demanded the reason for this abstention. One rather overexcited clergyman traced it to the easy circumstances of Brooks's life, which had insulated him from the suffering of the masses, and concluded: "The men of our age are not wholly mean and envious . . . but, oh! they do yearn for a more equal arrangement of things, for less poverty, less misery, less suffering. They look at the Titanic stature, the cloud-reaching

---

[1] C. F. G. Masterman, *Frederick Denison Maurice* (London and Oxford, 1907), pp. 55–114.

[2] *Recollections*, especially pp. 58–63 and 250–255. See also Washington Gladden, *The Christian Pastor and the Working Church* (New York, 1898).

[3] Lyman Abbott, *Reminiscences* (Boston and New York, 1915), pp. 466ff.

[4] He was enthusiastically in favor of the war, being convinced that it was a just war designed to eradicate terrible evils from the national life, and was most indignant with the church for what he regarded as its temporizing. See Allen, *Life*, I, 94–95, 149–151, 368–370, 511–512, 517. Twenty years after the war ended Brooks described it in his address at the 250th anniversary of the Boston Latin School. "It was a war of principles. It was a war whose soldiers were citizens. It was a war which hated war-making, and whose methods were kept transparent always with their sacred purposes shining clearly through."—*Essays and Addresses*, p. 421.

[5] "Thanksgiving Sermon," 1864.

[6] Allen, *Life*, I, 424–431, 463–467; 519–520.

intellect, the heaven-encircling spirituality, and the universe-embracing liberality of such men as Phillips Brooks, and ask, What will you do for our cause?"[1]

The true explanation is no doubt in part temperamental: he had no hostility toward the reforming pastor but conceived that his own talents lay in a different direction. More important was his profound conviction that all improvement in society must be the product of a change in the character of the people who compose society. "Out of the heart are the issues of life," ran the old Jewish proverb. All efforts to end war, to abolish poverty, to establish equitable relations between employer and employee, to discourage intemperance will end in futility unless the will to righteousness is strong in the individual.[2] He had complete faith in the progressive amelioration of our earthly lot: the divine right of rulers and of priests, slavery, torture to extract confessions, praise of ignorance as a safeguard of social order had already been swept away, and so too would war, poverty, disease, mere money competition as a motive power of life. "I recognize in many a frantic cry the great growing conviction of mankind that nothing which ought not to be need be."[3] But never will these changes be accomplished by institutional tinkering, and the preacher must aim, in all that he says about public affairs, "not simply at securing order and peace, but at making good men, who shall constitute a 'holy nation.'"[4] The mission of Phillips Brooks was to make men aware of their divine heritage as revealed by Jesus. When that awareness exists, all other good things follow.

That this attitude was at least a negative factor in establishing his popularity with the rich, well-established circles of Boston can hardly be doubted. He would not have attained his extraordinary popularity with the most important people of an increasingly conservative city had not the fundamental premises of his religion kept him from making concrete applications that would have disturbed the comfortable members of his admiring audiences.

Nevertheless, Phillips Brooks was no preacher for the upper orders only. There are more ways than one of working for the improvement of our

[1] Thomas A. Hyde, "The Reverend Phillips Brooks," *The Arena*, 1, No. 6 (May, 1890) 729.

[2] For an explicit statement of the belief that "the real struggle for life is not with institutions or creeds, but with moral and spiritual dispositions, of which institutions and creeds are only the expressions," see "The Battle of Life," *Sermons* (6th series, New York, 1893), pp. 76–82.

[3] "The Egyptians Dead upon the Seashore," *Sermons* (6th series), p. 60.

[4] *Lectures on Preaching*, p. 141. One recurrent thought that malevolence (or communism!) might argue was designed to keep the poor docile is that every condition of life offers special opportunities for the cultivation of character.—"How to Abound" and "How to Be Abased," *The Light of the World*, pp. 140–158 and 159–176.

lot, and his appealed to the poor as well as the rich. The man who pleased Trinity, Windsor Chapel, Westminster Abbey, Harvard, and Wall Street also pleased Faneuil Hall and Moody's tabernacle and won the love of vast numbers from all walks of life. Most of the reasons for this extraordinary popularity emerge elsewhere; but it would be wrong to dismiss his relations with Boston without saying a word about his role as a citizen and as a pastor for whom preaching was only one of a multitude of duties.

It would be hard to exaggerate the extent of the demands made on his time or his willingness to meet them. No civic occasion, from a banquet for Prince Oscar of Prussia to a meeting in behalf of the Fine Arts Museum, could be complete without him. At one time during his short episcopate, every evening was filled with engagements for five months ahead.[1] Yet despite the enormous drain on his energies resulting from these public and ecclesiastical obligations, he never held himself aloof from the ordinary man, woman, or child who sought his advice or comfort. Supremely concerned by the premises of his faith with the personality of the individual, temperamentally sensitive to those about him, and endowed with the ability to make everyone feel at ease, he received all in need of sympathy, encouragement, or strength. Innumerable stories still circulate in Boston concerning his adaptability, his sense of humor, and his relations with children. He had the strength of the strong: he did not bare his innermost life to others, but he invited without conscious effort the confidence of others.

IV. *The Preacher*

Phillips Brooks was fortunate to live at a time when his thought of life was part of one of the great movements of the human intellect. He was equally fortunate to find himself placed in a community notably congenial to him, amidst people equipped by birth and training to appreciate him. His special eminence cannot, however, be attributed to these favorable circumstances. Many shared his views; forgotten clergymen proclaimed them from the pulpit. What qualities of personality, what characteristics of presentation made him tower above his contemporaries?

Consider for a moment a typical portrait of Brooks in the pulpit. It is 1878. The new Trinity, designed by the great Richardson and adorned with the splendid murals of John La Farge, is now the spiritual home of a people who lost historic old Trinity in the great fire of 1872. Seven hundred regular communicants compose the congregation. Although this is nearly twice as many as there were when Brooks first arrived in 1869, it is only half the number to be recorded at the time of his death in 1893. Even now, most of the space not occupied by regular communicants is occupied by

[1] Lawrence, *op. cit.*, p. 143.

visitors from other churches, other cities, and even other countries, eager to hear Brooks.

Six feet four inches in height, weighing over two hundred pounds, clad in the robes of the church, he hurries into the pulpit. His hair is brown and beginning to gray; his head superbly shaped; his eyes dark and deep-set. "He was the most beautiful man I ever saw," said Justice Harlan of the United States Supreme Court.[1] In his expression are the firmness, fulness, and compassion and truth that caused a Roman Catholic Sister of Charity to hang his portrait beside the Hofman "Christ," because it seemed so fitting there.[2] As the last notes of the preceding hymn are sounded, Brooks nervously places his neatly written manuscript[3] before him and begins with the announcement of his text, which, on March 31, 1878, was from Romans XV: 13: "Now the God of hope fill you with all Joy and Peace in Believing, that ye may abound in Hope through the Power of the Holy Ghost."[4] His voice is low at this point, scarcely reaching to all corners of the church. He elaborates his text for a moment, then proceeds to define peace by application to the different classes of men—the active man, the lazy man, the sluggish man, and finally the virtuous man, to whom it means harmony. His plan is topical rather than causal; glowing imagery in the form of examples drawn from common experience, travel, and reading takes the place of logical premises and logical conclusions. Questions are used to stimulate the thought, and answers shortly appear. Here and there is an exclamation; here and there a supplication. As he moves into the sermon, his voice increases in volume and tempo; his words roll out at the rate of 215 a minute, and now and then he stumbles or has to extricate himself from grammatical difficulty. There is little gesture other than a majestic dilation of the whole body as his feeling rises in intensity. All the fullness of heart and mind, the sympathy, the virtue, the will, the refinement, the gentleness, the delight in people that are in Brooks go into the sermon and find their climax in the last words: "Oh, then, that over us, perplexed and troubled and afraid, as over the disciple in the chamber long ago, the hand of Jesus might be stretched, and we, to-day, might hear Him saying, 'Peace I leave with you, My Peace I give unto you. Believe in Me.' Oh that our souls may say, 'Dear Lord, we do believe in Thee, and so we claim Thy Peace.'"

[1] Allen, *Life*, II, 778.

[2] Allen, *Life*, II, 779.

[3] Throughout his life Brooks preached both extemporaneously and from manuscript. While at the Church of the Advent in Philadelphia he wrote the sermon for the Sunday-morning service and spoke extemporaneously on Sunday afternoon and Wednesday evening. Toward the latter part of his life he relied more and more on the extempore method.

[4] "Peace in Believing," *Sermons* (6th series, New York, 1893), pp. 187–207.

This is the type of performance that one might have witnessed at Trinity almost any Sunday during Brooks's pastorate. It shows him as the consummate illustration of his own theory that religious truth should be transmitted by the evidence of its effect on character. He was a complete man, in whom thought, affection, and will really were harmonized by the power of his idea. Dedicated to the love of God and the service of man, he displayed in the smallest action as well as the greatest the beauty of the religious life, the life for which man is destined. The happiness and serene confidence that he gained from his faith communicated itself to others by means hardly susceptible of analysis. Simplicity and sincerity were the keynotes of his approach to humanity. There was no self-consciousness, for there were no inner conflicts; there were no clerical or ecclesiastical affectations.[1] Yet there was an air of unworldliness about him, a sense of high devotion, which rose at times when he stood in the pulpit to the exaltation of a mystical rapport with spiritual powers.[2] People felt with awe that he came closer to God, and through his closeness brought them closer, than any man they had ever known.

The conviction of the indissoluble connection between character and persuasiveness influenced every opinion on rhetorical or homiletical theory that Brooks ever expressed. A sermon, he observed, is an instrument of power designed for the "persuading and moving of men's souls."[3] It will do so only when the essential truth that has entered the preacher energizes every faculty and emerges with the unique stamp of his own personality. It is natural, therefore, for Brooks to turn to the cultivation of the whole man when he dwells on the training of the preacher. Effectiveness and grace in expression, he said, "must come through the cultivation of the man; not by mere critical discipline of language, which at the best can only produce correctness, but by lifting the whole man to a more generous and exalted life, which is the only thing that can make a style truly noble."[4] Of delivery he remarked that whatever the elocutionist might contribute, "the real power of your oratory must be your own intelligent delight in what you are doing. Let your pulpit be to you what his studio is to the artist, or his court room to the lawyer, . . . only far more sacredly let your pulpit be this to you, and you have the power which is to all rules

---

[1] Stopford A. Brooke says that this freedom from self-consciousness was rarer in Brooks's introspective, self-analyzing age than either greatness or goodness. He compares it to "the conscious stateliness" of Tennyson, the vanity of Ruskin, the morbid temper of Clough, the passionate pride of Carlyle.—*Phillips Brooks: A Sermon* (Boston, n.d.), pp. 4–5. Lord Bryce also commented on this quality.—Allen, *Life*, II, 809.

[2] See R. H. Newton, *The Critic*, March, 1901, p. 247.

[3] *Lectures on Preaching*, p. 110.

[4] *Ibid.*, p. 148.

what the soul is to the body. You have enthusiasm which is the breath of life."[1] Behind expression lies thought, "and behind thought deed and action. Nobody can truly stand as an utterer before the world unless he is profoundly living and honestly thinking."[2]

In thus urging the total cultivation of the man as the best means of developing skill in persuasive speaking, he never ignored the elementary truth that every occupation calls for the exercise of special skills. He marveled at his associates in the divinity school who, although they were studying for the Christian ministry, neglected their Hebrew and their Greek in order to "preach by the spirit" in neighboring chapels. His apparent distrust of the elocutionist must be equated with the fact that he took voice lessons for years under a Boston teacher.[3] In short, he did not disdain special techniques but believed that they must always be subordinate to total cultivation, comprehensive knowledge, and deep conviction.

[1] *Lectures on Preaching*, pp. 178–179.

[2] Address before the Curry School of Expression, quoted by Kenneth G. Hance, The Rhetorical Theory of Phillips Brooks (Ph. D. Thesis, University of Michigan, 1937), pp. 325–326.

[3] Allen, strangely, seems to have been unaware of these lessons, and lends his powerful support to the idea that Brooks accepted without qualification the doctrine that "if a man had something to say, he would find out for himself how to say it."—*Life*, I, 72. Influenced by Allen and by remarks of Brooks like the oft-quoted "Of oratory, and all the marvellous mysterious ways of those who teach it, I dare say nothing. I believe in the true elocution teacher, as I believe in the existence of Halley's comet, which comes into sight of this earth once in about seventy-six years" (*Lectures on Preaching*, pp. 178–179), recent critics either have misrepresented Brooks's attitude toward technical training or have felt it necessary to defend him against the charge of indifference or ignorance.—Lionel Crocker, *Henry Ward Beecher's Speaking Art* (New York, 1932), p. 48; Hance, *op. cit.*, pp. 325–326.

In reality, Brooks added to his understanding of the fundamental importance of thought and feeling a keen appreciation, forced upon him by personal necessities, of the value of voice training. Early in his Boston ministry he became conscious of discomfort when speaking, and a strain was sufficiently evident to excite the concern of parishioners, who feared that his career might be brought to an untimely end by vocal failure. Faced with this danger, he took the advice of a distinguished Boston physician, Henry I. Bowditch, and began to take lessons in October, 1875, from Miss Sarah H. Hooker. By mutual consent they decided to keep the lessons secret, meeting early in the morning at her studio. For nearly two years he worked faithfully with this woman, and throughout his career kept in communication with her. She often wrote to him after hearing him in church, long after the formal lessons had ended, making suggestions; and he welcomed them with graceful acknowledgments of the debt he owed her.

Miss Hooker, who died in 1924 at the age of ninety, had studied under Bassini, in New York, and abroad under Manuel Garcia, who had taught Jenny Lind. For the principles of her system, see Ralph M. Harper, *The Voice Governor* (Boston, 1940). For a full account of the circumstances surrounding the lessons, see the same author's series of articles "Phillips Brooks' Vocal Lessons," *The Churchman*, Mar. 14, 21, and 28, 1925.

The admirable *Lectures on Preaching* bear witness to the conscious attention that Brooks gave to homiletics.[1] That he worked out his sermons with scrupulous care is proved by his outlines, the completed sermons, and the testimony of those who knew him. Bishop Lawrence and Professor Allen have described his typical procedure. On Monday he would decide upon the topic of his sermon for the following Sunday and begin to jot down ideas, illustrations, phrases. On Wednesday morning he organized his material, casting it in the form of a carefully constructed outline and often indicating in the margins the number of pages to be devoted to each topic. On Thursday and Friday and on Saturday, if necessary, he wrote the manuscript, following his outline scrupulously, and

The last line done, he heaved a grateful sigh, gathered his sheets already cut for him in a special way, took from his drawer a spool of thread, and with quiet satisfaction deliberately bound them together in such a way that the pages would turn over without noise or distraction. The manuscript went into the drawer and rested there; mere paper and ink, but instinct with fire, pathos, reason, humor, and passion. The sermon, however, was in Brooks himself, like a banked furnace waiting to break forth with heat.[2]

Brooks never failed to plan his speeches carefully. "Leave to the ordinary Sunday-school address its unquestioned privilege of inconsequence and incoherence," he advised the Yale divinity students. "But give your sermon an orderly consistent progress, and do not hesitate to let your hearers see it distinctly, for it will help them first to understand and then to remember what you say."[3] The sermons are, therefore, easy to outline. The text is usually explained briefly and simply, not by way of exegesis but by a vivid and often moving picture of the circumstances under which it was uttered

---

[1] The following list of references gives but a slight indication of the continuing interest of homileticians in Brooks's theory and practice: T. Harwood Pattison, *The Making of a Sermon* (Philadelphia, 1902), pp. 62, 161, 355; Ozora S. Davis, *Principles of Preaching* (Chicago, 1924), pp. 191, 195, 214, 224, 227, 247, 248, 250; Andrew W. Blackwood, *The Fine Art of Preaching* (New York, 1937), pp. 27, 45, 75; Lewis O. Brastow, *The Work of the Preacher* (New York, 1914), pp. 23, 29, 45, 46, 288; J. Spencer Kennard, *Psychic Power in Preaching* (Philadelphia, 1901), pp. 30 and 58.

[2] Lawrence, *op. cit.*, pp. 101–106.

[3] *Lectures on Preaching*, p. 178. As a supplement to what has already been said about his method of working, Bishop Lawrence may be quoted again. "He built up his sermon with the industry and skill of an artist. The topic was whittled down to its narrowest limits, every word considered for the sermon must have direction and movement. . . . His introduction leading up to the topic was so framed as to catch attention and lead directly up to the topic. Thus stated, the frame-work and divisions were plainly marked out, one, two, three: and the subdivisions, a, b, c: suggestions, thought and phrases written under each: and finally a sketch of the conclusion."—*Op. cit.*, pp. 102–103. See also the same author's article in the *Harvard Monthly*, 15, No. 5: 194–195.

or with which it deals. Almost always it leads gracefully and without forcing into a statement of the theme,[1] expressed not in the form of an explicit proposition but as an invitation to consider together the true significance or the human applications of the topic of the sermon. Not infrequently a metaphor in the text becomes a unifying device for the whole, each part of the figure being related to some phase of man's life or some aspect of his character. There is often a formal partition, but even when that is lacking, care with transitions and summaries keeps clearly before us the immediate topic under consideration. Throughout there is reference to hypothetical persons typical of representative groups in the community: the business-man, the student, the working man. The conclusion, often introduced by a homely, "Well, what shall we say of it all?" usually summarizes the essential thought and often includes a final appeal or expression of hope that all will be strengthened to live as the Master lived.

Despite the emphasis on clear organization, the prevailing impression of a person reading Brooks's sermons is not that of rigidity but of fluidity. He progresses not by building up a case in which one part depends on the preceding but by expanding and amplifying. It is a swelling movement of depth and breadth, wherein the end is reached, not when he has stated his most significant point but when he has filled in the last detail of the broad outlines sketched at the beginning. Although the mind is rarely brought up short by a digression or a *non sequitur*, he achieves an emotional rather than a logical unity. Outlining is easy; briefing is difficult. His distrust of argument and refusal to rely upon it bear part of the responsibility. Perhaps equally important is his refusal to classify sermons by types. He says:

We hear of expository preaching and topical sermons, of practical sermons, of hortatory discourses, each separate species seeming to stand by itself. It seems as if the preacher were expected to determine each week what kind of sermon the next Sunday was to enjoy and set himself deliberately to produce it. It may be well, but I say frankly that to my mind the sermon seems a unit and that no sermon seems complete that does not include all these elements, and that the attempt to make a sermon of one sort alone mangles the idea and produces a one-sided thing.[2]

In his essays, where he relied chiefly on argument and addressed himself solely, or at least more largely, to the intellect of his hearers, Brooks proved amply that he could construct a closely knit, closely reasoned composition.

An outline of one of Brooks's sermons ("The Willing Surrender" in *Sermons Preached in English Churches*, pages 221–243) follows. The

---

[1] Brooks in his youth had indulged in the not infrequent clerical frivolity of selecting a text that bore a fantastic relation to the theme of the sermon. His published sermons give no evidence of this early *jeu d'esprit*.

[2] *Lectures on Preaching*, pp. 129–130.

material is presented.as it occurs in the sermon, with no attempt to reduce it to "logical" relationship.

INTRODUCTION

Text: "Thinkest thou that I cannot now pray to my Father, and he shall presently give me more than twelve legions of angels? But how then shall the scriptures be fulfilled, and thus it must be?"

I. The glory of Christ is in His willing surrender of that which belonged to Him, and which He might always have had and enjoyed, a surrender made evident in the text. (Pp. 221–223.)

    A. Momentarily when seized in the Garden of Gethsemane He seems to have thought of summoning aid from His Father, but

    B. Immediately He thought of His mission, and voluntarily went on to the trial and the scourging and the cross. (Pp. 222–223.)

II. I want you to think this evening of the nobleness of this surrender of Jesus, and of the paradoxical truth that no man has the right to take his full rights; all is not his to take which is his legitimately to own. (P. 224.)

Transition and proposition: Let us try to study this nobleness of voluntary surrender a little while to-night.

DISCUSSION

I. We must distinguish the noble and ennobling renunciation of things which we have the right and power to possess from two different kinds of renunciation which are unworthy of our human nature. (Pp. 224–227.)

    A. The first comes from idleness or lack of spirit.

        1. The world is full of people who might be rich or learned or famous, but who refuse to take the trouble to become so.

        2. In the world of faith there are always men who abandon thinking, that they may escape the disturbance of their opinions. (P. 225.)

    B. The second of the two base forms of voluntary surrender is the ascetic form. (Pp. 226–227.)

        1. It includes those renunciations of legitimate employments and pleasures made for the sake of their effect on ourselves . . . that we may be chastened by disappointment, or that restraint may whet the appetite for some desirable thing.

        2. It seems to imply a distrust of the relinquished object which defeats its own purpose and makes the surrender worthless. (P. 227.)

II. Casting aside these unworthy forms of renunciation, which had nothing to do with the action of Christ, who gave up what was truly His because He could not have it and yet do His work, we may illustrate our instinctive reverence for the highest type of surrender from common life.

    A. When a man who might be rich deliberately gives up the chance of wealth that he may be a scholar, all honor him. (Pp. 228–229.)

    B. The world loves the hard-working parents who deny themselves the pleasures of self-cultivation so that their children may have education. (Pp. 229–231.)

C. Properly understood, the voluntary abstinence from liquor by those who might without harm to themselves indulge in it, for fear that others following their example may be injured, deserves all honor. (Pp. 231–234.)

D. The beauty of such an act resides, however, in its voluntariness; it becomes worthless if imposed by law or by a despotic public opinion. (Pp. 233–234.)

Summary: Voluntariness is at the root of it all; the moral beauty of character resides in the power which was in us to be something else. (Pp. 234–236.)

III. This principle is operative in the laws which apply to thought as well as to action. (P. 237.) A man voluntarily surrenders mental comfort in order to face the hardest questions. (Pp. 236–237.)

IV. We may take comfort in the thought that wherever there is duty there is also possible joy. (Pp. 237–240.) Happiness sought for itself is elusive, but comes when we turn from it and seek something higher.

A. That is the message of Enoch Arden.

B. It is also the message of Jesus, who shows even that the very thing which is surrendered is not, in its spiritual essence, lost.

Conclusion

"This, then, is the sum of the whole matter. There will come to every manly man times . . . when he will see that there is something which is legitimately his, something which he has a right to . . . and yet something by whose voluntary and uncompelled surrender he can help his fellow-man and aid the work of Christ, and make the world better. . . . If he fails . . . nobody will blame him. . . . But if he is of better stuff, and makes the renunciation of comfort for a higher work, then he goes up and stands—humbly, but really—with Jesus Christ. . . . It is not a question of happiness with him at all; but gradually . . . he finds that the soul of the happiness which he has left behind is in him still. . . . " (Pp. 240–241.)

When Brooks started to write, his pen moved along with rarely a break, so completely had he worked out the details in his outline. All that he was found expression in a flexible medium, at once lucid and diffuse, chaste yet suffused with emotional warmth. He bent language to his will with never a trace of the effort showing, providing us with excellent examples of the style he himself admired, which "is like a suit of the finest chain armor, so strong that the thought can go into battle with it, but so flexible that it can hold the pencil in its steel fingers for the most delicate painting."[1]

He wrote as both speaker and poet. He had ever before him the persuasive end, to lead men to live better lives; but instinctively he extruded from his sermon every harsh and jarring note. He knew that only by the recognition of the supernal beauty of the highest truths could the doubts of a confused age be dissipated, the wayward desires disciplined, the antagonistic

Lectures on Preaching, pp. 163–164.

impulses harmonized. When he wrote a sermon he wanted to leave men with an exalted impression of their destiny or a clearer conception of how every walk of life, every action, every thought receives its meaning when seen in the Light of God. Smoothly, limpidly, with never a chance for the intrusion of doubt, he leads the reader along. Overclose scrutiny of details by the critically detached might be dangerous to the conception of the whole, as he said of the study of the Bible and Shakespeare; but few could remain critically detached in the face of this onward sweep, with its opulent imagery and its vistas of great hope.

The poetical temperament,[1] reenforced by his distrust of argument as a means of establishing or communicating the highest truths, led Brooks to a constant use of analogy. The very titles of sermons suggest the reliance on figures of speech: "The Candle of the Lord," "The Egyptians Dead upon the Seashore," "In the Light of God," "The Sea of Glass Mingled with Fire," "The Wings of the Seraphim." He possessed in marked degree the capacity to perceive the similarities in things dissimilar; images of light, the scudding clouds, the sparkling sea, the lofty mountain, the fruitful earth occur to him as natural figures for spiritual and moral truths. "There is a knowledge which is not light but darkness, just as there is a lustre on the surface of the ocean which keeps you from seeing down into the ocean's depths."[2] Sometimes the figures pile up.

There is a new tranquillity which is not stagnation, but assurance, when a life thus enters into Christ. It is like the hushing of a million babbling, chattering mountain streams as they approach the sea and fill themselves with its deep purposes. It is like the steadying of a lost bird's quivering wings when it at last sees the nest and quiets itself with the certainty of reaching it, and settles smoothly down on level pinions to sweep unswervingly towards it. It is like these to see the calm of a restless soul that discovers Christ and rests its tired wings upon the atmosphere of His truth, and so abides in Him as it goes on towards Him.[3]

The life of the Christian minister is the richest, most varied conceivable. "It is no dead break on the wheels of time. It is no burnt-out cinder among the glowing coals of life. It is a very wheel itself. It is the livest coal in all the furnace, making the other coals seem cold beside it."[4]

Such images, whether flashed in a phrase or worked out at length, are often so precisely the garb required for the idea that a more abstract re-statement is impossible. They clarify and, in combination with a vocabulary

[1] He wrote a great deal of poetry but wisely left most of it in his notebooks. Among the published verse is the universally popular "O Little Town of Bethlehem."—Phillips Brooks, *Christmas Songs and Easter Carols* (New York, 1904).

[2] *Sermons Preached in English Churches*, p. 95.

[3] *Sermons* (6th series), p. 300.

[4] *Sermons* (6th series), p. 339.

rich in words with happy associations—*joy, faith, hope, mercy, charity, love, spirit, courage, clear, shining, sweet, tender*—shed a lambent glow over his sermons. And yet this analogical habit is chiefly responsible for a sort of pervasive cloudiness that enshrouds much that Brooks has to say. The calm seas and the gushing fountains, the whispering trees and the silent mountains help immeasurably in creating the general impression; but if one attempts to state what he meant, one is driven to repeating the image. This is no defect in composition but rather a reflex of his deepest conceptions of the nature of religious truth. As a distinguished clergyman who knew him well said, "He loved clearness, and longed for it, when sometimes it seemed beyond his power; but he loved also the thinkers who recognize the mystery in which, as in blinding splendors, the highest ideas come to men."[1]

Despite the poetic coloration that Brooks gave to his compositions, he wrote with a vivid sense of an audience immediately before him. Repetitions and elaborations more common in speech than in writing designed solely for the eye recur;[2] questions abound; there is frequent use of direct address. A single illustration must suffice.

"Why do things seem so hard to me?" you say; "why does every conceivable objection and difficulty start up in a moment, just as soon as I attempt to lay hold upon the Christian's faith? Why is it so easy for these others to believe, so hard for me?" One cannot answer certainly until he knows you better. There is a willful and an unwilling unbelief. If it is willful unbelief, the fault is yours. Man must not certainly complain that the sun does not shine on him, because he shuts his eyes. But if it is unwilling unbelief; if you really want the truth; if you are not afraid to submit to it as soon as you shall see it, and it is something in your constitution, or in your circumstances, or in the side of Christian truth that has been held out to you that makes it more difficult for you to grasp it than your neighbor; then you are not to be pitied. You have a higher chance than he. To climb the mountain on its hardest side, where its rough granite ribs press out most ruggedly to make your climbing difficult, where you must skirt round chasms and clamber down and up ravines, all this has its compensations. You know the mountain better when you reach its top. It is a realler, a nobler, and so a dearer thing.

If there be such here, let me speak to them. The world has slowly learnt that Christianity is true. If you learn slowly, it is only the old way over again. The man who learns slowly learns completely, if he learns at last at all. If you can only keep on bravely, perseveringly, seeking the truth, saying I must have it or I die; saying that till you do die; dying at last, if needs be, in the search; then I declare not only that somewhere, here or in some better world, the truth shall come to you;

[1] George A. Gordon, *Phillips Brooks as the Messenger of God* (Boston, 1893), p. 15.

[2] Howe suggests that since the repetitions and elaborations were meant more for the ear than for the eye, the best effect is to be obtained by a very rapid reading, such as Brooks himself gave.—M. A. De Wolfe Howe, *Phillips Brooks* (Boston, 1899), p. 62.

but that when it comes the peace and serenity of it shall be made vital with the energy of your long search. Yours shall be that faith with which a pure, truth-loving soul may stand unashamed before the throne of God, and hear his work called "Well-done," and blessed and consecrated to perpetual value. You will believe better even in heaven for these earthly difficulties bravely met. . . . [1]

There are no bravura passages, no striving for dramatic effect, virtually no humor,[2] little use of such devices as antithesis to give pungency. Occasionally an apposite bit from his favorites Browning or Tennyson slips in, but Brooks disapproved of quotations on the ground that they usually indicated undigested knowledge. And yet, with never a display of erudition and few evidences of the stylist, the flavor of high literature pervades all. Hutchins Hapgood detected this while a student and remembered it fifty years later. He wrote:

In spite of what I may call my religious interest, it never occurred to me to go to church, except when Phillips Brooks was preaching. I never willingly missed one of his sermons. The natural flow of his eloquence, religious and untheological, the beauty of his physical person, the unconscious, almost untutored, beauty of his language, and yet his intimate relation to the esthetic traditional literature, fitted in perfectly with what Harvard meant to me.[3]

Sweetness and light without sentimentality bathe all that Brooks said in the pulpit. The sinew and muscle of the controversialist, the hammer blows of the reformer, the sarcasm, mimicry, and barbed irony of the hustings are not for him. For a mankind to whom "pity is more than judgment, sympathy more than authority, persuasion more than rebuke," he couched his message in a tone of high seriousness, confident of the response that never failed.[4]

[1] "The Sea of Glass Mingled with Fire," *Twenty Sermons* (4th series, New York, 1890), pp. 121–123.

[2] We do not find evidence to support Hance's statement (Thesis, pp. 247–248) that Brooks employs humor constantly in his sermons. One might read far to find a single instance. His letters and the *Lectures on Preaching* abound in drolleries, whimsicality, and homely illustrations that evoke a smile, and innumerable stories circulate of his flippancy and love of a joke outside the pulpit. But his sermons might well be cited as evidence of Beveridge's theory that the finest eloquence, dealing with the most vital issues, does not permit that dilution of intensity inevitable with the use of humor.

[3] *A Victorian in the Modern World* (New York, 1939), p. 81.

[4] These observations are primarily applicable to the sermons and to the lectures titled *The Influence of Jesus*. In his secular essays and addresses and in dealing with religious topics on secular occasions, there are marked changes. The structure of thought is much more rigid; there is more reliance on logical argument; the use of analogy is largely restricted to clarification, with little attention to its imaginative function; humor not infrequently creeps in. It is an excellent style for expository purposes or for argument conducted largely by means of exposition.

When Brooks began to speak, people unaccustomed to his delivery often felt bewildered. He raced on at the rate of more than two hundred words a minute,[1] and many experienced an initial difficulty in following him. Gradually, however, the perfect conjunction of expression and impassioned thought created its effect, and they listened raptly. William Cleaver Wilkinson had a reaction so typical that it may be allowed to stand here as representative of the popular verdict.

The preacher, from the very first word, begins his sermon, usually read from a manuscript, at a prodigious rate of speed in utterance. The words hurry out as if the weight of the Atlantic were on the reservoir behind them to give the escaping current irresistible head. There is no letup, there could be no acceleration, to the rush of the torrent. You feel at first as if you never should be able to follow at such a breakneck pace. But soon you find yourself caught up and borne forward, as it were, without your following, on the mighty breast of the onrushing flood. What is more, presently you enjoy riding so fast. There is a kind of impartation and transformation of personal living force, by virtue of which you not only understand everything uttered, but with ease understand it, more swiftly than your wont. The novel experience is delightful.[2]

This rapidity was interpreted by some as a defense against a tendency to stammer.[3] Occasionally Brooks seemed to become tangled in his own words, and the resulting blurring and confusion contributed to the notion that he stammered slightly under certain conditions. The truth seems to be that both the occasional stumbling and the rapidity were due to the eagerness of the preacher to drive his message home: he had so much to say and what he had to say mattered so greatly that the words tumbled out. He spoke extemporaneously as rapidly as he read, and an early attempt to control the tempo ended in failures. Weir Mitchell concluded that the speed of his extemporaneous utterance bore some relation to the rate of thinking, and that it in turn determined the rate of reading.[4] His voice teacher compared the phenomenon to that of a bottle filled with water, which when decanted gurgles and escapes with difficulty. She concentrated in her training on developing better control of the breath.[5]

Brooks's voice gave him considerable trouble, as has already been mentioned. Of its quality one must say what can be said of other aspects

---

[1] Thomas Allen Reed, an English stenographer, clocked him at 213 words per minute in a sermon preached at Westminster Abbey.—*Phillips Brooks: The Man, the Preacher, and the Author* (Boston, 1893), pp. 165–167.

[2] Edgar DeWitt Jones, *Lords of Speech* (Chicago and New York, 1937), p. 185.

[3] Some thought they had detected this tendency as early as his college days—Allen, I, 122; *Boston News*, Jan. 24, 1893, p. 4, col. 6.

[4] Allen, I, 633.

[5] Harper, "Phillips Brooks' Vocal Lessons," *The Churchman*, Mar. 14, 1925.

of his delivery: that it was subject to adverse criticism on technical grounds and yet seemed to be admirably expressive of the personality of the speaker. "The voice itself," says Mark Antony De Wolfe Howe, "may perhaps best be described as carrying with it rather too much breath to satisfy the most fastidious, yet so full of sympathy, tenderness, pleading, and conviction as to make one quite impatient of the elocutionary standards which would condemn it."[1] Occasionally people complained that they could not hear him, especially at the beginning of a sermon; and he seems to have misjudged the acoustics of Westminster Abbey completely when he first preached there. But such complaints and difficulties were exceptional and were heard less often as he grew older. No doubt both experience and the lessons of Miss Hooker had their effect.

As one first begins to read Brooks' sermons, one will probably be reminded of his opinion that "ordinarily, reading sermons is like listening to an echo." Presently, as one enters into the spirit of the man and his message one becomes aware that through the printed page a rich and rare personality is revealing itself. One keeps recurring to the idea of that "unconscious, almost untutored eloquence" which Hutchins Hapgood noted. The impression that here was a great man, totally lacking in self-consciousness and totally devoid of artifice, one receives vaguely and in varying degree from the cold print. Fortunately hundreds of those who heard him unite to confirm the opinion that every aspect of Brooks's presentation collaborated to make every word he uttered a revelation of the man and of the faith that made him the man he was. He was the living proof that the highest preaching is "truth through personality."

Conclusion

To adopt the words that Phillips Brooks often used when coming to a conclusion, what can we say about it all? He lived at a time when the currents were strong against the things for which he stood; but he profited from the reaction against the tides of skepticism and found hosts of people ready for the message he had for them. He did his primary work in a city peculiarly adapted to receive him gladly; but he won devoted followers throughout the world. His special clientele consisted of the prosperous and the cultivated; but he substituted successfully for Moody, and at Faneuil Hall captured

---

[1] *Phillips Brooks* (Boston, 1899), pp. 64–65. In *The Arena*, I, No. 1: 724–727, Thomas A. Hyde describes his voice as "free from all metallic and repulsive sounds. It has not the silvery clearness, nor penetrating quality of Wendell Phillips, nor the compass and flexibility, volume, and expressive intonation of Henry Ward Beecher, but it has a depth and grandeur of resonance and intensity of enunciation, and animated and expressive utterance, a natural and sympathetic tone. . . . "

audiences worthy of Spurgeon. He was not, in the ordinary sense of the words, either a theologian or a reformer; it is hard to discover specific evidence of his influence on the history of religious thought or the course of public events. He preached a simple gospel of the brotherhood of man and the fatherhood of God; but he preached it with such grace, such awareness of our cultural heritage, and above all with such sincerity that those most suspicious of cant and emotional oversimplification in religion heard him gladly.

When he died on January 23, 1893, less than two years after his election to the bishopric, there was an extraordinary demonstration of popular affection for him. For more than a week Boston papers devoted their columns almost exclusively to accounts of his life and work. At his funeral, Trinity overflowed into the streets, and triple banks of mourners lined the route in Harvard Yard over which the cortege passed. Churches united in memorial services at the Old South Meetinghouse, and in New York 5,000 people assembled in Carnegie Hall to hear Lyman Abbott, Joseph Choate, and Rabbi Gottheil honor the Bishop of Massachusetts. Within a few weeks nearly $100,000 had been raised for the statue by Saint-Gaudens that stands in Copley Square, and a large sum was rapidly collected to build and endow Phillips Brooks House as a center of religious and philanthropic activities at Harvard. A memorial window with an inscription written by the Archbishop of Canterbury was dedicated at St. Margaret's, Westminster. Ministers of all denominations preached hundreds of memorial sermons throughout the world; scores were published. As the years have passed, the torrent of tribute has merely abated; it has never ended. Theses are written about him;[1] homileticians quote him; new evidences of his personal influence appear as the biographies and memoirs of his contemporaries are given to the world.

That "the roots of his influence were in his personal character" cannot be doubted. He led men because he was a good man, exhibiting in visible form the serenity and happiness that are the best products of the best Christianity. He was superbly endowed physically, intellectually, and temperamentally; but the most careful examination of these qualities and the most detailed analysis of his sermons force agreement with the testimony of his contemporaries: personality was the decisive factor. The total man is something more than the sum of his analyzable parts, Phillips Brooks was fond of observing, and it was the totality of Phillips Brooks to which his disciples yielded.

[1] Hance, *op. cit.;* Orvin P. Larson, Phillips Brooks' Theory and Practice of Preaching (Master's Thesis, University of Iowa, 1937).

To the appreciation of Brooks as a person must be added an understanding of his fitness for the time and place of his greatest work. Van Wyck Brooks has spoken accurately of the happy conjunction of intellectual, emotional, and aesthetic needs with the man who could satisfy them.[1]

The dignity of man and the beauty of virtue had ceased to excite the thrills of old, and the religion of reason had starved the senses: it could not compete any longer with the rapidly rising Catholic Church and the Anglican Church that stole the Roman thunder with its choirs and illuminations, its colour and music. No use to protest that rites and forms were shallow, where the feminine mind especially had grown so strong. They appealed to the aesthetic depths, they appealed to other emotional depths which the old New England faiths had left unsounded; and it only required a preacher of genius, who appeared at once in Phillips Brooks, to establish the Episcopal Church in the heart of Boston. What Channing had once been, Phillips Brooks became, the typical divine of an epoch; for this fuller-blooded Channing, this muscular Christian, exuberant, robust and cultivated, had all the traits that made the Boston leader . . . he revived the moribund art of the orator in a world that was less concerned for social reform and more concerned for science, art and travel. He spoke for an age that was saturated with Tennyson and Browning, with the gospel of *In Memoriam* and "the larger hope."

Brooks, the disciple of Schleiermacher, Browning, Tennyson, and Ruskin, talked to a Boston that read and believed the same things, a Boston under the spell of the Victorians, a Boston less concerned with reason and more concerned with emotion, a Boston that was Hellenistic and Tennysonian, rather than Hebraic and Miltonian. Boston wanted to feel confident about something, wanted to remember her gentility, wanted to see that gentility in the flesh, a living proof of its reality. Phillips Brooks was the man that an incarnate Boston would have wished to be. He shared and expressed the emotions that agitated Boston, and he expressed them in a tradition-hallowed atmosphere that fitted the aesthetic temper of the period. The hope of Boston was restored by one who had found a way of helping her to retain her religion in a scientific age, by showing that all truth comes from God and that religion can never be shaken by science unless religion itself forgets essentials and takes a stand on the irrelevant or incidental.

Phillips Brooks throughout his life, by both precept and example, emphasized the importance of intellect and character. As a man, and as one who had that unfailing confidence in his fellow men which is the ultimate foundation of democracy, he fully merited from Oliver Wendell Holmes the honor of being described as "the ideal minister of the American gospel."[2]

[1] *New England: Indian Summer, 1865–1915*, pp. 150–151.
[2] Addison, *The Clergy in American Life and Letters* (New York, 1900), p. 341.

SELECTED BIBLIOGRAPHY
Books and Magazines

Abbott, Lyman: "Phillips Brooks, Prophet of the Spiritual Life," *Outlook*, 128 (May 18, 1921).
———: *Reminiscences*, New York and Boston, 1915.
Addison, Daniel Dulany: *The Clergy in American Life and Letters*, London and New York, Macmillan & Company, Ltd., 1900.
Allen, A. V. G.: *The Life and Letters of Phillips Brooks*, 2 vols. New York, E. P. Dutton & Company, Inc., 1900.
———: "The Theological Renaissance of the Nineteenth Century," *The Princeton Review*, November, 1882.
Ayres, Milton C.: *Five Years' Editorial Estimates*, Boston, George H. Ellis Co., 1893.
Beecher, Henry Ward: *Yale Lectures on Preaching*, Boston, Pilgrim Press, 1900–1902.
Blackwood, Andrew W.: *The Fine Art of Preaching*, New York, The Macmillan Company, 1937.
Brastow, Lewis O.: *Representative Modern Preachers*, New York, The Macmillan Company, 1904.
———: *The Work of the Preacher*, New York and Chicago, Pilgrim Press, 1914.
Brooke, Stopford A.: *Phillips Brooks: A Sermon*, Boston, Cashman, Keating and Co., 1893.
Brooks, A.: "Phillips Brooks," *Harper's Magazine*, 86 (May, 1893).
Brooks, Phillips: *The Candle of the Lord and Other Sermons*, New York, E. P. Dutton & Company, Inc., 1881; *Essays and Addresses*, E. P. Dutton & Company, Inc., 1894; *The Influence of Jesus*, E. P. Dutton & Company, Inc., 1879; *Law of Growth and Other Sermons*, E. P. Dutton & Company, Inc., 1902; *Lectures on Preaching*, E. P. Dutton & Company, Inc., 1877; *Letters of Travel*, E. P. Dutton & Company, Inc., 1894; *The Life and Death of Abraham Lincoln*, Philadelphia, H. B. Ashmead Co., 1865; *The Light of the World and Other Sermons*, E. P. Dutton & Company, Inc., 1890; *New Starts in Life and Other Sermons*, E. P. Dutton & Company, Inc., 1897; *Our Mercies of Re-occupation: A Thanksgiving Sermon*, Philadelphia, W. S. & A. Martien, 1863; *Sermons*, E. P. Dutton & Company, Inc., 1878; *Sermons*, 6th series, E. P. Dutton & Company, Inc., 1893; *Sermons of the Church Year*, E. P. Dutton & Company, Inc., 1901 (1895); *Sermons Preached in English Churches*, E. P. Dutton & Company, Inc., 1883; *The Spiritual Man and Other Sermons*, London, 1891; *Twenty Sermons*, 4th series, E. P. Dutton & Company, Inc., 1887.
Brooks, Van Wyck: *New England Indian Summer*, New York, E. P. Dutton & Company, Inc. 1940.
Chadwick, John W.: *Phillips Brooks: A Sermon*, Boston, George H. Ellis, 1901.
Clark, Thomas N.: *Reminiscences*, New York, Thomas Whittaker Co., 1895.
Crocker, Lionel: *Henry Ward Beechers' Speaking Art*, New York, Fleming H. Revell Company, 1937.
Davis, Ozora S.: *Principles of Preaching*, University of Chicago Press, 1924.
Deland, Margaret: "Phillips Brooks," *Atlantic Monthly*, July, 1940.
De Voto, Bernard: *Mark Twain's America*, Boston, Little, Brown & Company, 1932.
Dunbar, Newell: *Phillips Brooks: The Man, the Preacher, and the Author*, Boston, John K. Hastings, 1893.
Eliot, Charles W.: "On the Education of Ministers," *The Princeton Review*, May, 1883.
———: "What Phillips Brooks Did for the College," *The Harvard Monthly*, 15, No. 5 (February, 1893).
Farrar, Frederick William: "Phillips Brooks, Bishop of Massachusetts," *Review of the Churches*, 3, No. 17 (Feb. 15, 1893).

Fosdick, Harry Emerson: Recent Gains in Religion, *Recent Gains in American Civilization*, Kirby Page, ed., New York, Harcourt, Brace and Company, 1928. .

————: "What's the Matter with Preaching?" *Harper's Magazine*, 57 (July, 1928).

Gladden, Washington: *Recollections*, Boston, Houghton Mifflin Company, 1909.

————: *The Christian Pastor and the Working Church*, New York, Charles Scribner's Sons, 1898.

Gordon, George A.: *Phillips Brooks as the Messenger of God: A Sermon*, Boston, Damrell and Upham Co., 1893.

Hance, Kenneth G.: The Rhetorical Theory of Phillips Brooks, Ph. D. Thesis, University of Michigan, 1937.

Hapgood, Hutchins: *A Victorian in the Modern World*, New York, Harcourt, Brace and Company, 1939.

Harper, Ralph M.: "Phillips Brooks' Vocal Lessons," *The Churchman*, Mar. 14, 21, 28, 1925.

————: *The Voice Governor*, Boston, E. C. Schirmer Music Co., 1940.

Hitchcock, Henry C.: "The Broad Church Theology," *Bibliotheca Sacra*, 48 (October, 1891).

Howe, Mark A. De Wolfe: *Phillips Brooks*, Boston, Small, Maynard and Co., 1899.

Hyde, Thomas A.: "The Reverend Phillips Brooks," *Arena*, 1, No. 6 (May, 1890).

Jones, Edgar DeWitt: *Lords of Speech*, Chicago and New York, Willett, Clark and Co., 1937.

Kennard, J. Spencer: *Psychic Power in Preaching*, Philadelphia, George W. Jacobs Co., 1901.

Larson, Orvin P.: Phillips Brooks' Theory and Practice in Preaching, Master's Thesis, University of Iowa, 1937.

Lawrence, William: *Life of Phillips Brooks*, New York, Harper & Brothers, 1930.

————: "One or Two Characteristics of Phillips Brooks," *The Harvard Monthly*, 15, No. 5 (February, 1893).

Masterman, C. F. G.: *Frederick Denison Maurice*, London and Oxford, 1907.

May, Joseph: *Phillips Brooks*, Boston, George H. Ellis, 1893.

Mott, Frank Luther: *A History of American Magazines*, 1865–1885. Cambridge, Mass., Harvard University Press, 1938.

Nash, Henry S.: *The Rt. Rev. Phillips Brooks, D. D.: A Sermon*, Jan. 29, 1893, reprinted from *North Dakota Churchman*, Boston, Damrell & Upham Co., 1893.

Newton, R. H.: "Phillips Brooks: The Preacher and the Man," *The Critic*, 38 (March, 1901).

Parks, Leighton: *The Theology of Phillips Brooks*, Boston, 1894.

Pattison, T. Harwood: *The Making of a Sermon*, Philadelphia, American Baptist Publication Society, 1902.

Perry, H. F.: "The Workingman's Alienation from the Church," *American Journal of Sociology*, IV.

Potter, Henry C.: *The Life Giving Work—A Sermon Memorial of the Rt. Rev. Phillips Brooks, D. D.*, Boston, Damrell and Upham Co., 1893.

————: *The Mission and Commission of the Episcopate: A Sermon*, New York, E. P. Dutton & Company, Inc., 1892.

Prothero, Rowland E.: *The Life and Correspondence of Arthur Penrhyn Stanley, D. D.*, 2 vols., London, John Murray, 1894.

Richards, Laura E., and Maude Howe Elliott: *Julia Ward Howe*, 1819–1910, 2 vols., Boston, 1916.

Rowe, Henry K.: *The History of Religion in the United States*, New York, The Macmillan Company, 1924.

Schlesinger, A. M.: *The Rise of the City*, 1878–1898, New York, The Macmillan Company, 1933.

Thwing, C. F., and F. W. Farrar: " Phillips Brooks: Two Characterizations of the Late Bishop of Massachusetts," *American Review of Reviews*, 7, No. 38 (March, 1893).

Tiffany, Charles C.: *A History of the Protestant Episcopal Church in the United States of America*, New York, The Christian Literature Co., 1895.

Newspapers

Boston Daily Advertiser, Dec. 17, 1888; Dec. 26, 1888; Jan. 24, 1893.
Boston Evening Transcript, Feb. 7, 1893.
Boston News, Jan. 24, 1893; Jan. 30, 1893; Feb. 6, 1893.
The Philadelphia Inquirer, Feb. 16, 1865; Apr. 19, 1865.
Zion's Herold, Jan. 25, 1893.

10

Wendell Phillips

by WILLARD HAYES YEAGER

Wendell Phillips was born on November 29, 1811, a descendant of the Reverend George Phillips, who landed at Salem on the *Arbella* in June, 1630. His father, John Phillips, was the first mayor of Boston. Wendell attended Boston Latin School, 1822–1827, Harvard College 1827–1831, Harvard Law School 1831–1834. He made his first important antislavery speech at Lynn, March 28, 1837; first established his reputation as a great orator at the Lovejoy meeting, Faneuil Hall, Boston, December 8, 1837. Phillips was the most famous of all the antislavery orators; also active in reform movements concerned with woman's rights, labor, temperance, capital punishment, religion, Indians, money and banking, prison management, and education; one of the best known lecturers of the lyceum movement. He never held an elective public office but was the unsuccessful candidate of both the Labor Reform party and the State Temperance Convention for governor of Massachusetts in 1870; died February 2, 1884.

Education

Wendell Phillips, eighth of nine children born to John and Sarah Phillips, began his formal education in 1822 at the Boston Latin School; there he came under the influence of Benjamin A. Gould, who was master of the school from 1814 to 1828.

The curriculum of the Latin School, under Gould, was based almost entirely on Greek, Latin, and mathematics, with some attention given to declamation. Gould was an ardent supporter of classical learning, at a time when it was beginning to be questioned, and wrote a defense of it for the school's *Prize Book*, No. III. In part, he said: "By the common consent of the eminent statesmen and lawgivers, as well as the learned in the most polished nations of Europe, a *good education*, whether designed for an accomplished gentleman, or for him who is destined for the labour of a professional life, must be founded upon what is emphatically called *Classical Learning*."

In a later issue of *The Prize Book*, Gould described the method used in the training of students in declamation:

On Saturdays, the whole school comes together in the hall for declamation. The four upper classes speak in turn, a class on each Saturday. The youngest class attends this exercise, but does not take part in it. After a boy has spoken, and the presiding instructor has made such observations as he sees fit, any individual of the class that is speaking, has a right to correct any errors in pronunciation, or any violation of the text, that may not have been pointed out; and if none of the class does this before another boy is called out, it may be done by any boy in the school.[1]

Phillips distinguished himself in declamation, being one of six third-prize winners in 1825; and, in 1827—the year of his graduation—he was one of six Latin School students to be honored with the coveted Franklin medals.[2]

After his graduation from the Latin School, Phillips entered Harvard College, where at that time rhetoric and oratory were a highly important part of the curriculum, being, in fact, the only field in which students were required to take work through the entire four years.

In Phillips's first year, instruction in rhetoric and oratory was entirely in the form of declamations, which were given every Saturday morning, ten members of the class of sixty-one students being heard at each meeting.[3]

In the Sophomore year the class commence Lowth's Grammar in the first term, and finish it in about *nine weeks*, at the rate of ten pages an exercise. To Lowth succeed Blair's Lectures, which the class finish in about *twenty weeks*, at the rate of one lecture an exercise. The study of Hedge's Logic follows. This is finished by the end of the year, at the rate of about twelve pages the lesson.

The Class are heard in the above works every Thursday and Friday during the first Term, and every Tuesday and Thursday during the second and third Terms, for two hours, from 10 to 12 o'clock, reciting in sections, half an hour each.

Besides the above, the Professor hears this Class every other Saturday, for two hours from 9 to 11 o'clock A.M., in declamation; and every intermediate Saturday, at the same hours, he has a critical examination of their themes.

The usage in relation to declamations, . . . is, for *ten* persons to speak in each hour, and of course *twenty* every fortnight.[4]

In the *Junior Year* instruction is given in this branch wholly through the medium of themes, lectures, readings, and declamations. . . .

Twenty lectures on Rhetoric are given in the second term of this year, on Tuesdays and Thursdays, at 11 o'clock.

Dr. Barber hears this Class either in reading or declamation in sections on four days of the week, an hour being given to each section. . . . [5]

In the *Senior Year* this branch was conducted wholly through the medium of themes and declamations; each of which occupied a like time, and was conducted

[1] *The Prize Book* (Boston, Publick Latin School, 1823), No. IV p. 55.

[2] Established by Benjamin Franklin "for the encouragement of scholarship."

[3] *Third Annual Report of the President of Harvard University to the Overseers*, 1827–28, (Cambridge, Hilliard, Metcalf & Co., 1829), pp. 4, 10, 11.

[4] *Fourth Annual Report of the President*, etc., 1828–29, Appendix, p. xx.

[5] *Fifth Annual Report of the President*, etc., 1829–30, Appendix, pp. vii, viii.

in the same manner by the respective instructors, as is above specified in relation to the Junior Year.

In addition to the above Dr. Barber was engaged to deliver a public lecture to all of the classes once a week on Elocution; which he did as frequently as was found expedient.[1]

Besides all this instruction by the department of rhetoric and oratory' the department of moral philosophy, civil polity, and political economy conducted forensics for the juniors and seniors, alternately, on every Friday afternoon for three hours.[2]

To understand the nature of Phillips's instruction in public speaking at Harvard, we must also appraise the work of the teachers who were responsible for it. During all the period of Phillips's residence, Edward T. Channing was the Boylston professor of rhetoric and oratory. Shortly before accepting this position, he helped to found the *North American Review* and served as its editor for a little over a year. Although he left no record of conspicuous scholarship in his field, his influence was felt in many ways. He had excellent taste in literature and in usage and a great reputation as a teacher.[3]

Channing's "Inaugural Discourse," delivered in 1819, when he was twenty-eight years old, after reviewing the power of the orator in ancient and modern times and emphasizing the need for his services, defined the object of eloquence as follows: "The object of eloquence is always the same—to bring men, by whatever modes of address, to our way of thinking and thus to make them act according to our wishes."

At another place, he stated: "We want our orators now, first of all, to think powerfully and speak earnestly."

Again, he asserted:

We want then the orator who feels and acts with us—in whom we can confide even better than in ourselves, who is filled with our cause and looks at it with solemnity and wisdom. We want then the orator who is unmoved by the reproaches or threats that alarm us, who walks over the injurious as over the dust, unconscious even that he tramples on them, who fears nothing on earth but a bad action, and regards no considerations but those of good principle.[4]

For the most part, Phillips followed Channing's definition of the object of eloquence, and this may help to explain his lack of scrupulousness at times. Also, that Phillips was an orator who could "think powerfully and

[1] *Sixth Annual Report of the President,* etc., 1830–31, Appendix, p. viii.

[2] *Fifth Annual Report of the President,* etc., 1829–30, Appendix, p. ii; 1830–31, Appendix, p. ii.

[3] Sidney Willard, *Memories of Youth and Manhood* (Cambridge, J. Bartlett, 1855), II, 215.

[4] Edward T. Channing, "Inaugural Discourse," delivered in the chapel of the University in Cambridge, Dec. 8, 1819 (Cambridge, Hilliard and Metcalf, 1819).

speak earnestly" there is no doubt; and it is probable that no orator sur-passed him in fearing "nothing on earth but a bad action" and in regarding "no considerations but those of good principle."

In Phillips's last two years, Professor Channing was assisted by Jonathan Barber, M.D. Barber was appointed to the staff after the recom-mendation of President Quincy, in his *Report* of 1828–29, that more attention be given to the teaching of elocution. He was the author of a number of books on elocution, in which he developed his theories in con-siderable detail.

It is difficult to estimate the influence of Dr. Barber on Phillips. It is probable that he had some influence, but it is plainly apparent that Phillips did not swallow his instruction hook, line, and sinker. Phillips's mode of delivery was so uniquely his own and so different from that of others who were subjected to the same instruction that it does not seem possible that it could have come out of the narrow mold of Barber's voice and gesture mechanics. Analyses of Phillips' delivery by those who heard him and were competent to judge indicates that he was little influenced by this aspect of his training. This view is supported, also, by one of his classmates: "It was a great treat to hear him declaim as a college exercise. He was always studying remarkable passages, as an exercise in elocution, to give language its greatest possible effect. In this he did not accept the aid of his teachers. His method was his own."[1]

At his graduation from Harvard College, Phillips had a place on the commencement program. John Quincy Adams recorded his impressions of the performances in his diary on August 31, 1831: "The merit of the per-formances was beyond the usual average. Of the undergraduate perform-ances, the two orations of Eames and Simmons were most remarked, with one part of a conference by Wendell Phillips, the youngest son of my old friend and associate, John Phillips."[2]

In the fall of 1831 Phillips entered the Harvard Law School, where he had the opportunity to continue his training in speechmaking in the Moot Court. Meetings were conducted every week by one of the professors, four of the students, in rotation, appearing as counsel. "They begin to take their turn at the commencement of the second year. There are extempore disputations and debates on legal and miscellaneous questions, as voluntary exercises."[3] That Phillips took advantage of this opportunity was attested by Charles Sumner. In February, 1833, they were on opposing sides of

[1] The Reverend Dr. John Hopkins Morison, in a letter to Theodore D. Weld, reported in Weld's *Lessons from the Life of Wendell Phillips*, Nov. 29, 1885 (Boston, J. Cooper, 1886).

[2] Charles Francis Adams, *Memoirs of John Quincy Adams* (Philadelphia, J. B. Lippincott Company, 1874–1877), VIII, 405–406.

[3] *Annual Report of the President*, etc., 1831–32, 1832–33, 1833–34.

the subject, "Whether a Scotch bond, assignable by the law of Scotland, can be sued by the assignee in his own name in our courts."[1]

This brief review of Phillips's education shows that he had a thorough training in rhetoric, oratory, and declamation in Harvard College. Not only did he study outstanding books on the theory of public address and of writing (such as Hugh Blair, *Lectures on Rhetoric and Belles Lettres*) and listen to lectures on rhetoric by Professor Channing, but throughout the four-year course he was required to engage in very frequent practice. We must remember, also, that a considerable part of the study of Latin and Greek was really a study of oratory and theories of public address; numerous speeches are parts of ancient epics and histories. During his three years in the law school, he continued to practice the art of speechmaking in the Moot Court. In all this experience, he had excellent training, which was the foundation of his later success as a public speaker.

Antislavery—The Major Issue of Reform

Although Wendell Phillips was identified closely with the reform movements for women's rights, labor, temperance, and others, it was in the antislavery cause that he first won a place for himself as a great speaker.

Three influences were chiefly responsible for bringing him to accept the antislavery views of William Lloyd Garrison and the abolitionists. These were (1) his conversion in a religious revival conducted by Lyman Beecher (probably in 1826), which made a deep and lasting impression upon him; (2) the mobbing of Garrison in 1835, which he witnessed; and (3) his acquaintance early in 1836 and growing friendship with Ann Terry Greene, who became his wife in October, 1837.

His conversion was an intense religious experience and laid the foundation for the later development of a fierce and burning hatred of everything that seemed to him to be wrong. However, from the time of his conversion to 1835, there is no evidence that he had anything more than a general interest in the slavery question.[2] It took the mobbing of Garrison and the persuasive power of Miss Greene to bring him into the fold of the abolitionists.

[1] Edward L. Pierce, ed., *Memoir and Letters of Charles Sumner* (Boston, Roberts Brothers, 1877-1893), I, 94.

[2] The report of the meeting of the New England Anti-Slavery Society, held May 25, 1835, contains no mention of Wendell Phillips, either among the delegates or the speakers.—*The Liberator*, May 30, 1835. Charles Sumner, in a letter to the Reverend George Putnam, April, 1848, on the subject of Phillips's interest in slavery, said: "One word on the slavery question. Shortly after my admission to the bar, say in 1835, I became interested in this. The earliest newspaper that I remember to have subscribed for is the *Liberator*. This was at a time when my schoolmate and fellow student in college and the law school, Wendell Phillips, was still indifferent to the cause which has since claimed so much of his time."—Pierce, *op. cit.*, III, 69.

His earliest known speech on the slavery question was delivered on February 28, 1837, when with Charles Sumner and others he addressed the Adelphic Literary Society, an association of colored people.[1] We next find him addressing the quarterly meeting of the Massachusetts Anti-Slavery Society, at Lynn, on March 28, 1837. He made two speeches; one was on the subject, "Having a great work to do, and but comparatively feeble means wherewith to do it, our influence and effort should be devoted mainly to the cause of abolition," and the other approved the "exertions of the Hon. John Quincy Adams, and the rest of the Massachusetts delegation who sustained him, in his defense of the right of petition."

Following the Lynn meeting, Phillips addressed a number of other anti-slavery audiences before the great meeting in Faneuil Hall on December 8. On July 4 he spoke at two antislavery celebrations; one at Lynn and the other at Salem. At both places he spoke to large audiences, and the *Liberator* reported that both meetings "were deeply interesting."[2] According to the *Liberator*, also, his address at Salem "was listened to with very great attention by the audience; it was a spirited and sensible performance, and parts of it were truly eloquent."[3] On August 22 and 23, he attended and made two speeches at a Young Men's Anti-Slavery Convention, at Concord, N.H. At the quarterly meeting of the Massachusetts Anti-Slavery Society, held at Worcester on September 27, 1837, he spoke again.[4] At the meeting of the Essex County Anti-Slavery Society, at New Rowley, on October 4, 1837, he served on the resolutions committee. He introduced two resolutions, on each of which he made speeches, and he participated in the debates on other resolutions, also.[5]

The preceding brief review of speeches made by Wendell Phillips in 1837, prior to the meeting in Faneuil Hall, on December 8, together with the record of his training in speechmaking at Harvard, show—unmistakably —that the "Murder of Lovejoy Speech" was not a sudden flowering of matchless speaking ability but the outcome of both training and practice.

Attended by an audience estimated at 5,000 persons, the meeting was opened by Jonathan Phillips, who acted as chairman. He was followed by E. M. P. Wells, who offered prayer; William Ellery Channing, leader of the citizens who had requested the use of the Hall; Benjamin F. Hallett, who read a series of resolutions condemning the action of the mob at Alton, which had been prepared by Channing; and George S. Hillard, who seconded the resolutions. At this point in the proceedings, the attorney general of the

[1] Pierce, *op. cit.*, I, 154.
[2] July 7, 1837.
[3] July 14, 1837.
[4] *The Liberator*, Oct. 6, 1837.
[5] *The Liberator*, Oct. 13, 1837.

state, James T. Austin, rose to speak from the rear gallery. He attempted to justify the mob at Alton by comparing it to the Boston Tea Party of the Revolution. Of the slaves of the South, he asserted:

We have a menagerie here, with lions, tigers, hyenas, an elephant, a jackass or two, and monkeys in plenty. Suppose now, some new cosmopolite, some man of philanthropic feelings, not only towards man but animals, who believes that all are entitled to freedom as an inalienable right, should engage in the humane task of giving freedom to these wild beasts of the forest, some of whom are nobler than their keepers; or having discovered some new mode to reach their understanding, should try to induce them *to break their cages and be free?* The people of Missouri had as much reason to be afraid of their slaves, as we should have of the wild beasts of the menagerie. They had the same dread of Lovejoy that we should have of this supposed instigator, if we really believe the bars would be broken, and the caravan let loose to prowl about our streets.

Later, he asked, "What will be said to us by the citizens of Illinois and Missouri, whom it is our self-assumed prerogative to rebuke?" Then he continued:

Will they not tell you that your fathers were colonists, and as such under obligations to pay a tax levied upon them by the British Government, fatal to their liberties, their rights, their happiness—they implored, they besought its remission, and urged that their people should not be goaded to violence, and instigated to a madness which human reason could not control. And when these prayers, and entreaties, and supplications were vain, and there was no law that could protect them, and no middle path between ruin and resistance, did they not take their protection under the security of their own arms, and marching down from this Hall—*an orderly mob*—pour the disgusting instrument of their degradation into the sea? So will the people of Missouri claim to do, when their lives are threatened by the operations of these abolition conspirators. Do you suppose they will wait for the slow progress of the laws? They will tell you they will call on the God of Heaven, as your fathers did, and with his favor will defend themselves.[1]

Whether Wendell Phillips had intended, or had been scheduled, to speak at this meeting has been both affirmed and denied. In their biographies, both Austin and Martyn say that he was there as a mere listener, with no thought of speaking.[2] Weld and Sears, on the contrary, believed that he had intended to speak but had no prior knowledge that the attorney general planned to talk or knowledge of the nature of his remarks and that he,

[1] James T. Austin, *Speech at Faneuil Hall*, Dec. 8, 1837 (Boston, John H. Eastburn, 1837). It is also reported in *The Liberator*, Dec. 15, 1837.
[2] George Lowell Austin, *The Life and Times of Wendell Phillips* (Boston, B. B. Russell & Co., 1884), p. 79; Carlos Martyn, *Wendell Phillips—The Agitator* (New York, Funk & Wagnalls Company, 1890), p. 94.

therefore, could not have been prepared to answer them.[1] The view of Weld and Sears is supported by the *Liberator* and appears to be correct.[2]

It seems probable, therefore, that he had agreed to speak and was prepared to do so; of course, there can be little doubt that he was not prepared for the unscheduled attack of the attorney general. His speech, accordingly, either was impromptu or was the result of very skillful adaptation of his prepared speech to the situation facing him or (as seems most likely) partook in a measure of both.

As Phillips spoke there were many interruptions, one of which was rather violent and lasted for many minutes, requiring the intercession of a Mr. Bond and a Mr. Sturgis, before he was allowed to go on. Phillips said, in part:

We have heard it asserted here, in Faneuil Hall, that Great Britain had a right to tax the Colonies, and we have heard the mob at Alton, got up to murder Lovejoy, compared to that band of our patriot fathers who threw the tea overboard! [Great applause.] Fellow-citizens, is this true? [No, no.] The mob at Alton were met to wrest from a citizen his just rights—to resist the laws. We have been told that our fathers did the same; and the glorious mantle of Revolutionary precedent has been thrown over the mobs of our day. For to make out their title to such defense, the gentleman says that the British Parliament had a *right* to tax these colonies. It is manifest that without such an assertion, his parallel falls to the ground; for Lovejoy had stationed himself within constitutional bulwarks. The men who assailed him went against and over the laws. The *mob*, as the gentleman terms it, which assembled in the Old South to destroy the tea were met to resist, not the laws, but illegal exactions; not the King's prerogative but the King's usurpation. . . .

Sir, when I heard the gentleman lay down principles which place the rioters, incendiaries, and murderers of Mt. Benedict and Alton side by side with Otis and Hancock, with Quincy and Adams, I thought those pictured lips [pointing to the portraits in the Hall] would have broken into voice to rebuke the recreant American —the slanderer of the dead. [Great applause and counter applause.] The gentleman said that he would sink into insignificance if he dared to gainsay the principles of these resolutions. Sir, for the sentiments he has uttered, on soil consecrated by the prayers of Puritans and the blood of patriots, the earth should have yawned and swallowed him up. [It was at this point that the chief interruption took place.][3]

[1] Theodore D. Weld, *Lessons from the Life of Wendell Phillips* (Boston, J. Cooper, 1886), p. 34; Lorenzo Sears, *Wendell Phillips—Orator and Agitator* (New York, Doubleday, Page & Company, 1909), p. 55.

[2] In the issue of Dec. 8, 1837, which went to press before the meeting but in which it is announced, may be found: "Among the speakers who are to address the meeting, we have been told, are the Rev. Dr. Channing, who is also to offer the resolutions, George S. Hillard, and Wendell Phillips." In the issue of Dec. 15, 1837, containing a full report of the meeting, just after a description of the speech of the attorney general, it is reported: "Wendell Phillips, who was to follow Mr. Hillard in the arrangement, rose to reply."

[3] From the report of the speech in *The Liberator*, Dec. 15, 1837, and in *The Massachusetts Spy*, Jan. 10, 1838.

In the remainder of the speech, Phillips took up Austin's principal points and answered them.

There are a number of eye-witness accounts of this unusually stirring scene. Oliver Johnson made the following comment:

> I had heard him once before myself [in his first important antislavery speech at Lynn], as a few others in that great meeting probably had, and my expectations were high; but he transcended them all and took the audience by storm. Never before, I venture to say, did the walls of the "Old Cradle of Liberty" echo a finer strain of eloquence, or to more exalted and ennobling sentiments than those which then fell from the lips of the young orator of freedom. It was a speech to which not even the completest literal report could do justice; for such a report could not bring the scene—the occasion and the manner of the speaker—vividly before the reader.[1]

Mrs. Maria Weston Chapman wrote to Harriet Martineau in London:

> James T. Austin was there and made a diabolical speech. It was loudly cheered. I gave up all hopes of a favorable termination of the meeting then. He tried to raise a storm of indignation, but failed, baffled by the effort of a very dear young friend and connexion of ours, who from being of good family was enabled to get a hearing, though an abolitionist, and an agent of the abolition society. Wm. Sturgis and George Bond, when he was almost overpowered by the clamour, threw in their weight on the right side, and free discussion *of the subject of free discussion* prevailed.[2]

Sarah H. Southwick, many years later, wrote: "I think Mr. Phillips's power over that audience was one of the most remarkable scenes on record. I suppose he was known to some people present, but to the abolitionists generally he was a stranger."[3]

The reporter for the *Boston Daily Advocate* said: "The torrent of his eloquence, as it moved along like a mighty river in its course, brushed away the fabric which the gentleman [Austin] had erected upon a foundation of sand."[4]

Dr. Channing is said to have "frequently referred to the tone, look, gesture, with which this young man, beaming with truth, upborne by justice, strong in rectitude, careless of consequences, in the Hall consecrated by grand associations, and before a vast audience of fellow-citizens half hostile to freedom, poured forth the vial of his indignation, as 'morally sublime.'"[5]

[1] Oliver Johnson, *William Lloyd Garrison and His Times* (Boston, B. B. Russell and Co., 1880), p. 229.

[2] *Westminster Review* (London), 32 (December, 1838): 49.

[3] Wendell Phillips, "The Freedom Speech," with descriptive letters from eye witnesses (Boston, Wendell Phillips Hall Association, 1891).

[4] Quoted by *The Liberator*, Dec. 29, 1837.

[5] William Henry Channing, *Memoir of William Ellery Channing* (Boston, Crosby, Nichols, Lee & Co., 1860), III, 215–216.

George William Curtis, who did not hear the speech, in his "Eulogy of Wendell Phillips," asserted: "In the annals of American speech there had been no such scene since Patrick Henry's electrical warning to George the Third. . . . Three such scenes are illustrious in our history; that of the speech of Patrick Henry at Williamsburg, of Wendell Phillips in Faneuil Hall, of Abraham Lincoln at Gettysburg—three, and there is no fourth."[1]

Careful search has not revealed a single adverse comment about Phillips's speech on the occasion in question. Although this speech stirred the souls of abolitionists and was well publicized in antislavery and in a few general newspapers, some general newspapers did no more than publish the official report of the meeting, which was prepared by the secretaries, containing only the resolutions that were passed and the names of the speakers. The editor of the *Boston Daily Advertiser* stated: "Our reporter has furnished us a sketch of the speeches which were made, but we have not room for it. We do not deem it important, as the meeting has not excited any very deep interest."[2]

The speech situation provided the opportunity for great eloquence on this occasion. Had it not been for the exciting and inflammatory speech of the attorney general, the whole meeting would have gone off as quietly as a Sunday church service. In Boston and in Faneuil Hall, opinion on the killing of Lovejoy was divided; but it had been supposed when the meeting was arranged that only those who condemned the action would speak. As it turned out, all the speakers, with the exception of Austin, did condemn it. So it was the unexpected speech of the attorney general, and it alone, that provided the clash of issues that called forth this early example of Phillips's denunciatory speaking.

Although it is true that the resolutions, condemning the action of the mob, passed and that Phillips's speech had no small share in bringing that result, it is very probable—if not certain—that those resolutions did not represent the views of the majority of the people of Boston. The *Boston Daily Advertiser*, which was not too friendly toward the abolitionists, referring to the audience, stated: "The Hall was well filled, but it was evident that the greater part considered themselves as mere spectators, and not actors in the proceedings, and on the adoption of the resolutions, comparatively few voted."[2]

Even the *Liberator*, which was—naturally—in opposition to the views of Austin and friendly to Phillips, admitted that a considerable number of the audience did not vote at all.[3]

[1] Memorial service from the city of Boston, Apr. 18, 1884.
[2] Dec. 9, 1837.
[3] Dec. 15, 1837.

338

In a later issue, the editor of the *Boston Daily Advertiser*, in referring to the attitude of the people of Boston, generally, wrote:

. . . had the meeting been held in the evening, instead of at 10 o'clock in the morning, as had been originally proposed by Dr. Channing and his co-signers of the petition, on an invitation addressed to all citizens, but under the auspices and direction of the managers of the Anti-Slavery Society, aided by Dr. Channing, it is almost certain that the resolutions . . . would have been defeated by an immense majority.[1]

In the period from the "Murder of Lovejoy Speech" to June 6, 1839 (when he sailed for Europe with his wife, in the hope that some cure for her illness might be found there), Phillips made a number of speeches for the antislavery cause.[2]

While in London, he was a delegate of the Massachusetts Anti-Slavery Society to the World's Anti-Slavery Convention; there he carried the burden of the speaking of those who tried unsuccessfully to seat women delegates. He spoke also at the first annual meeting of the British India Society on the subject "Cotton, the Cornerstone of Slavery."

They returned from Europe on July 17, 1841, with Mrs. Phillips little if any improved. Shortly thereafter he again became active in the antislavery movement, and it was not long until he was generally recognized as the leading speaker for the abolitionists. The speech that went a long way so to label him and that earned for him the epithet "fanatic madman" was delivered at Faneuil Hall, October 30, 1842, at a meeting called to discuss the case of George Latimer, a runaway slave.

A large number of the members of the audience had come to the meeting for the purpose of breaking it up. Samuel Sewall was chairman and spoke first. He was followed by Francis Jackson, Joshua Leavitt, and Edmund Quincy. All the remarks of these gentlemen were accompanied by great disturbances, including hisses and catcalls. After the last of these speeches, a young Negro, Charles L. Remond, who had recently become active in the antislavery cause, was introduced and attempted to speak. His appearance upon the platform was greeted with a great shout of disapprobation. For several minutes he attempted to make himself heard, without success; there was continuous uproar, with hisses, groans, noise, and shouts of "Down with the damned nigger," "Turn the darkey out," "Tip him into the pit." After an attempt by George S. Hillard to gain a fair hearing for the Negro, Wendell Phillips tried. His complete speech follows:

[1] Dec. 11, 1837. It was charged that the abolitionists, knowing that there would be great opposition to any action that they officially proposed, because of the disfavor in which the antislavery societies were held, had enlisted the aid of Dr. Channing and submitted the petition for the use of the hall in such a way as to conceal their active support of the project.

[2] For reports of them see *The Liberator*.

Fellow-citizens, I will ask your attention but a single moment. I wish only to bear my testimony in favor of liberty. [Uproar.] There are husbands, brothers, and sons before me. I ask, in the name of humanity that you will hear me speak for a son and a husband. [Great confusion.] No generous man will try to drown my voice, when I plead the cause of one not allowed to speak for himself. Many will cry, "Shame," *here*, when they are told of the imprisonment of an innocent man. But where shall that shame rest? On needy attorneys, who would sell the fee simple of their souls for an attendance fee of thirty-five cents a day? On ambitious lawyers, panting to see their names blazoned in southern newspapers as counsel for slave-catchers? No. They are but *your tools. You* are the guilty ones. The swarming thousands before me, the creators of public sentiment, bolt and bar that poor man's dungeon tonight. [Great uproar.] I know I am addressing the white slaves of the North. [Hisses and shouts.] Yes, you dare to hiss me, of course. But you dare not break the chain which binds you to the car of slavery. [Uproar.] Shake your chains; you have not the courage to break them. This old hall cannot rock, as it used to, with the spirit of liberty. It is chained down by the iron links of the United States Constitution. [Great noise, hisses, and uproar.] Many of you, I doubt not, regret to have this man given up—but you cannot help it. There stands the bloody clause in the Constitution—you cannot fret the seal off the bond. The fault is in allowing such a Constitution to live an hour.

A distinguished fellow-citizen is reported to have said in this hall, that the "abolitionists were insane enough to think that the duties of religion transcended those they owed to the Constitution." Yes, silly men that we are, we presume to believe that the Bible outweighs the statute book! [Continued uproar.]

When I look upon these crowded thousands, and see them trample on their consciences and the rights of their fellow-men, at the bidding of a piece of parchment, I say, "my CURSE be on the Constitution of the United States." [Hisses and shouts.] Those who cannot bear free speech had better go home. Faneuil Hall is no place for slavish hearts. [Hisses.] Fools! You know not the inestimable value of free speech. Cowards! You dare not hear a colored man speak in these liberty-loving walls. [Great confusion.]

Fellow-citizens, no law binds our police to aid the slave-catcher, nor our jailor to keep slaves. If they act at all, they are volunteers. Shall our taxes pay men to hunt slaves? Shall we build jails to keep them? [Uproar.] If a southerner comes here to get his lost horse, he must prove title before a jury of twelve men. If he comes to catch his slave, he need only prove title to any Justice of the Peace, whom he can make his accomplice. Again, if he comes for his horse, he sues at his own expense. If he comes for his slave, it seems he is to get him at ours! I record here my testimony against this pollution of our native city. The man in the free states who helps hunt slaves is no better than a blood-hound. The attorney who aids is baser still. But any judge who would grant a certificate would be the basest of all.

> "And in the lowest deep, a lower deep
> Still threatening to devour him, opens wide."

Are you ready yet to hear a colored man speak?[1]

Most of the Boston newspapers condemned the action of the mob only and spoke of the disgrace that it brought upon the city.[2] The *Boston Daily Bee*, however, also condemned Phillips's speech, in part, as follows:

They would not listen to the darkey, so Wendell Phillips arose; and here we must digress from the general strain of our remarks to notice this speaker. We have frequently met Mr. P. in the halls of justice, and deemed him a gentleman; but, as we listened to his language last evening, we thought him anything *but* a gentleman. His remarks were of the most outrageous character, disgraceful alike to the place, the evening [Sunday], and to the speaker. Never did we hear such a volley of blackguardism and shameless abuse as came from the lips of this fanatic madman.[3]

Having once reached the point of placing his curse on the Constitution of the United States, it was a short step—in common with the Garrisonians —to the advocacy of the doctrine that abolitionists should neither vote nor hold office under that Constitution; and from that argument, another short step took him, and them, to the advocacy of disunion, as the only way the people of Massachusetts and other free states could avoid living under a Constitution that supported slavery and the only way of providing a place on American soil where the long arm of the slave catcher could not reach. In this period, also, with other Garrisonians, he took up the cudgel against the complacent attitude of the churches toward slavery. He had a certain amount of reluctance to do this, as his own ardor for the orthodox faith had in no way diminished; but he could not restrain the expression of his very deep conviction that the churches and the state together provided the front-line of defense of the slaveholders. *Until 1861, he continued to curse the Constitution of the United States, to advocate nonparticipation in holding office and in voting, to advocate disunion, and to denounce the position of the churches on the slavery question.*

Although he made many speeches, with one or more of these ideas as his theme, it is not possible to refer to more than a very few here. Those which have been selected for comment are typical.

At the anniversary meeting of the American Anti-Slavery Society, in New York, on May 9, 1843, he stated:

"Calling a slave-holding nation a Christian nation—that is the fatal error; encouraged by the pulpit, which forms the mind on which your statesmen are to

[1] *The Liberator*, Nov. 11, 1842. After Phillips's last sentence, there appeared to be some "slight disposition to listen, Mr. Remond took the platform, but an uproar immediately ensued and he was at last compelled to desist." The riot became so noisy that the proceedings were stopped.

[2] See the *Bay State Democrat*, Oct. 31, 1842; the *Boston Courier*, Oct. 31, 1842; and the *Boston Recorder*, Nov. 4, 1842.

[3] Oct. 31, 1842. See also an editorial in the issue of Nov. 2, 1842.

act. Your Constitution, sir, is in the way! Yes, sir; your boasted, free Constitution. And your churches are in the way, too, sir! And the fealty you owe to each of these must be trampled beneath your feet, sir, before you can be considered a friend to freedom."[1]

Before the same society, meeting in New York from May 7 to May 10, 1844, Phillips reported, for the business committee, and defended resolutions declaring that secession from the Federal government was an anti-slavery duty and that abolitionists should work for the dissolution of the Union.[2]

On March 20, 1848, he made one of a number of appearances, extending over a period of several years, before a committee of the Massachusetts legislature, at which he advocated the withdrawal of Massachusetts and other free states from the Union.[3]

On May 9, 1848, at the meeting of the American Anti-Slavery Society, in New York, among other resolutions, he proposed and defended the following: "Resolved, that . . . this Society deems it a duty to reiterate its convictions, that the only exodus for the slave out of his house of bondage is over *the ruins of the present American Church, and the present American Union.*"[4]

At the Disunion Convention at Worcester, January 15, 1857, he remarked: "For my part, I am for a dissolution of the Union, and I seek it as an abolitionist. I seek it, first and primarily to protect the slave. My second motive is to protect the white race."[5]

After the capture of John Brown and his men at Harper's Ferry, he asserted: "It was the covenant with death and agreement with hell, which you call the Union of the thirty states, that took the old man by the throat with a pirate hand; and it will be the disgrace of our civilization if a gallows is ever erected in Virginia that bears his body."[6]

At the Music Hall in Boston, January 20, 1861, in a speech on "Disunion," he said: "Let us not, however, too anxiously grieve over the Union of 1787. Real Unions are not made—they grow. This was made like an artificial waterfall or a Connecticut nutmeg. It was not an oak which today a tempest shatters. It was a wall hastily built, in hard times, of round boulders; the cement has crumbled, and the smooth stones, obeying the law of gravity, tumble here and there."[7]

[1] *National Anti-Slavery Standard*, May 18, 1843.
[2] *National Anti-Slavery Standard*, May 16, 1844.
[3] *The Liberator*, Mar. 24, 1848.
[4] *National Anti-Slavery Standard*, May 25, 1848.
[5] *The Liberator*, Jan. 30, 1857.
[6] From the speech on "The Lesson of the Hour," delivered at Henry Ward Beecher's church in Brooklyn. See *The Liberator*, Nov. 11, 1859.
[7] *The Liberator*, Jan. 25, 1861.

And then, on April 21, 1861, after Lincoln's call for troops and after a period of several months in which his life frequently was in danger because of popular disapproval of the disunion doctrine and the vituperation he had been showering on those who opposed his views,[1] he about-faced and, in ringing tones, announced his support of the Union and the President: "I rejoice before God today for every word that I have spoken counseling peace; but I rejoice with an especially profound gratitude, that now, the first time in my antislavery life, I speak under the stars and stripes, and welcome the tread of Massachusetts men marshalled for war."[2]

Shortly after his speech of April 21, 1861, he began to appraise the acts of the Administration in Washington to determine whether they appeared to be leading in the direction of (what for him was the purpose of the war) the emancipation of the slaves. He soon became critical of the members of

[1] In a letter to Mrs. S. B. Shaw, Mrs. Lydia Maria Child wrote an unusually vivid description of one of these occasions. The disturbance occurred at the meeting of the Massachusetts Antislavery Society, Tremont Temple, Boston, on Jan. 24, 1861. She described the meeting, in part, as follows:

"I went very early in the morning and entered the Tremont Temple by a private labyrinthine passage. There I found a company of young men, a portion of the self-constituted bodyguard of Mr. Phillips. They looked calm but resolute and stern. I knew that they were all armed, as well as hundreds of others; but their weapons were not visible. The women friends came in gradually by the same private passage. It was a solemn gathering, I assure you; for though there was a pledge not to use weapons unless Mr. Phillips or some other antislavery leader was personally in danger, still nobody could foresee what might happen. The meeting opened well. The antislavery sentiment was there in strong force; but soon the mob began to yell from the galleries. They came tumbling in by hundreds. The papers will tell you of their goings on. Such yelling, screeching, stamping, and bellowing I never heard. It was a full realization of the old phrase, 'All hell broke loose.' Mr. Phillips stood on the front of the platform for a full hour, trying to be heard whenever the storm lulled a little. They cried, 'Throw him out!' 'Throw a brick-bat at him!' . . . Then they'd sing with various bellowing and shrieking accompaniments, 'Tell John Andrew, John Brown's dead.' I should think there were four or five hundred of them. At one time they all rose up, many of them clattered downstairs, and there was a surging forward towards the platform. My heart beat so fast I could hear it; for I did not then know how Phillips' armed friends were stationed at every door and in the middle of every aisle. They formed a firm wall which the mob could not pass. At last it was announced that the police were coming. I saw and heard nothing of them but there was a lull. Mr. Phillips tried to speak, but his voice was again drowned. Then by a clever stroke of management he stooped forward and addressed his speech to the reporters stationed directly below him. This tantalized the mob, and they began to call out, 'Speak louder! We want to hear what you're saying.' Whereupon he raised his voice, and for half an hour he seemed to hold them in the hollow of his hand. But as soon as he sat down they began to yell and sing again, to prevent any more speaking."—Lydia Maria Child, *Letters of Lydia Maria Child*, with a biographical introduction by John G. Whittier and an Appendix by Wendell Phillips (Boston, Houghton Mifflin Company, 1883), pp. 147ff. See also George W. Smalley, "Memories of Wendell Phillips," *Harper's Magazine*, 89: 133–141.

[2] *The Liberator*, Apr. 26, 1861. See also his speech at Framingham, July 4, 1861, in *The Liberator*, July 12, 1861.

the cabinet and, later, of the President himself. On January 7, 1862, in a lecture in Tremont Temple, Boston, some ten months after the Republican party had come into power, he severely criticized President Lincoln and the members of his cabinet for their failure to accomplish anything toward emancipation and for the military losses and defeats that had been suffered by the north.[1] In a speech at Abington, Mass., on August 1, 1862, he asserted: "I believe that Mr. Lincoln is conducting this war, at present, with the purpose of saving slavery."[2] On November 19, 1862, in a speech at Music Hall, Boston, he mildly approved of the President but condemned the cabinet and some of the Union generals.[3] In a speech before the Sixteenth Ward Republican Association of New York, on May 11, 1863, he bitterly attacked the cabinet.[4] On January 28, 1864, at the meeting of the Massachusetts Anti-Slavery Society, he introduced and spoke at length on a resolution that began, "Resolved, that, in our opinion, the Government, in its haste, is ready to sacrifice the interest and honor of the North to secure a sham peace; . . . "[5] These and other speeches against the conduct of the war by the President and the members of his cabinet culminated in his advocacy of the defeat of the President for re-election, in a speech in Tremont Temple, Boston, on the subject "The Presidential Election," October 20, 1864. In this speech he reviewed all Lincoln's Administration, pointed to his alleged mistakes, and charged that he was unfit for the task of reconstruction.[6]

Mention must be made, also, of another well-known antislavery speech, which he delivered first in 1860 and repeated many times thereafter; this is his famous "Toussaint L'Ouverture," in which he attempted to show that the black race was capable of assuming the obligations of freemen.[7]

After the emancipation of the slaves, when Garrison decided that his life work had been accomplished and advocated the dissolution of the antislavery societies, Phillips successfully opposed him and took up the fight to obtain for the freed blacks all the rights of citizenship. In the period from the end of the war to the proclaiming of the ratification of the Fifteenth Amendment in 1870, he made many speeches in behalf of the

[1] *The Liberator,* Jan. 17, 1862

[2] *The Liberator,* Aug. 8, 1862.

[3] *The Liberator,* Nov. 28, 1862.

[4] *The Liberator,* June 5, 1863.

[5] *The Liberator,* Feb. 5, 1864.

[6] *The Liberator,* Oct. 28, 1864. See this issue also for an editorial by William Lloyd Garrison taking issue with Phillips's strictures on the President and, in opposition to the views of Phillips, advocating his re-election. This was probably the beginning of the coolness that developed between the two men, which was further intensified by their different views on the dissolution of the American Anti-Slavery Society in 1865.

[7] *The Liberator,* Apr. 3, 1863.

freedmen, because he believed that the objects of the antislavery societies would not be accomplished until they were given the same rights, as citizens, as the whites. In a large number of other speeches he was bitterly critical of Presidents, cabinets, and Congresses.

In this review of Wendell Phillips's career as an orator, agitator, and reformer in the antislavery cause, we see that, from the time of his speeches at Lynn on March 28, 1837, to the end of the Civil War, he made many speeches before meetings of the antislavery societies and before popular audiences on the issues of the slavery question. We see, also, that he early was regarded by many as a "radical" and a "fanatic" and that throughout this great controversy, he fearlessly expressed his opinions, although these were unpopular with people generally.

Minor Issues of Reform

As a reformer, Phillips was catholic in his interests. In addition to the antislavery movement, he was active in reform movements concerned with women's rights, labor, temperance, capital punishment, religion, Indians, money and banking, prison life, and education. Since he was more interested in women's rights, labor, and temperance than in the others, to judge by the number of speeches he made on them, only these three are touched upon here.

His first public expression of interest in the women's-rights movement appears to have been at the meeting of the World Anti-Slavery Convention, which was held in London, during his visit there in 1840. The British antislavery leaders, who were in control, refused to seat women delegates. Phillips took the floor to argue against the position of the British but was unsuccessful.

Later he made many speeches in favor of women's rights, many of which emphasized the necessity for giving them the suffrage with which, he thought, they could get rid of other objectionable discriminations. His first important speech in this cause was made at the Woman's Rights Convention, held at Worcester, October 15, 16, 1851. In it he reviewed the discriminations against women and the objections commonly raised against giving them the right to vote.[1]

At the Woman's Rights Convention held in New York on September 7, 1853, after quieting a boisterous mob that had collected for the purpose of breaking up the meeting, he said, in part:

I ask you now as reasonable men to consider a few facts. In Boston there are nine millions of property in the names of women, and this property is taxed as

[1] *Proceedings of the Woman's Rights Convention*, Worcester, Oct. 15, 16, 1851 (New York, Fowlers and Wells, 1852).

the property of women. I have myself paid into the treasury at Boston $1,500.00 as the taxes of two women; and on the day I did so, the illiterate Irishman who landed here five years before, who could not write his own name, had the privilege of voting on the disposition of that $1,500.00, while the women who paid it had no voice upon the subject![1]

At the Ninth National Woman's Rights Convention in New York, on May 12, 1859, he was faced again by a large group of people who came to the meeting for the purpose of interfering with the proceedings and breaking them up, if possible. He had a difficult time handling the interruptions, and a part of the speech is quoted here, not only to show the nature of his argument but to show his skill in handling a heckler:

You have no right to hang a citizen who has not a voice in the law under which he suffers. Napoleon once asked Madame de Stael, "Why will you meddle in politics?" "Sire," said she, "so long as you hang women we will ask the reason why."

A Voice—"Have we a right to hang a foreigner?"

Certainly we have; because when a man comes voluntarily into a country, he subjects himself for the time being to the laws which he knows exist in that country, and that is the evidence of his assent. But woman is born here, as we are. God gives her her place. We have no right to drive her from it. He gives her thought; He gives her moral being and responsibility to law. She has a right to them all; for our government rests on brains and thought, and not upon bayonets and power.

A Voice—"Have we a right to hang negroes?"

I will tell you just the difference between the man who asked that question and the negro who was sold yesterday in the Carolinas. The man in the Carolinas is black outside; the questioner is black inside. [Laughter and applause.] The man in the Carolinas has a black face; the questioner has a black heart. [Applause and cries of "Good, good."] The man in the Carolinas takes a box six feet by three and is nailed up within it, and, at the risk of his life, rides four hundred miles on the railway to a free state, because he values liberty like a man; and the questioner, if he had been born a slave, would have cowered like a spaniel and rotted to death like a dog, [tumultuous applause]; because, in fine, the slave of the Carolinas is a man, and the being that would insult a depressed and hated race, in a community like ours, is a brute. [Renewed applause.][2]

He continued to speak in favor of woman's rights; but from this time to 1865 he was much more concerned about the emancipation of the slaves, and, although urged to do so, he refused to tie the two issues together; and from 1865 to 1870 he was more interested in obtaining full rights of citizenship for the freedmen.

[1] *Proceedings of the Woman's Rights Convention*, New York, 1853 (New York, Fowlers and Wells, 1853).

[2] *Proceedings of the Woman's Rights Convention*, New York, 1859 (Rochester, N. Y., A. Strong & Co., 1859).

After 1870 he occasionally spoke in favor of woman's rights, and he wrote some editorials on the subject for the *National Standard*. His chief interests after 1870, however, were in the labor reform and temperance movements, with the former claiming most of his attention.

Let us now examine a few of his labor reform speeches. On April 9, 1870, in bringing to a close the last meeting of the American Anti-Slavery Society, of which he had been the president since the retirement of William Lloyd Garrison from that office in May, 1865, he announced: "And so, friends, we will not say, 'Farewell,' but, we will say, 'All hail, welcome to new duties.' We sheathe no sword. We only turn the front rank of the army against a new foe."[1] It is doubtful whether more than a handful of the members of his audience saw more than a few nicely turned phrases in this. They were soon to learn, however, that the man who had spent more than thirty years of his life working in the interest of the Negro had turned his attention to the failure of those who labor to receive just compensation and treatment at the hands of their employers.

His first important utterance on this question, however, came in 1865, when it appears to have been little noticed, because of the general interest in the slavery controversy. At a mass meeting of workingmen held in Faneuil Hall, November 2, 1865, he spoke on "The Eight-hour Movement." This was a mild speech, which merely advocated the eight-hour day, with the object of providing workingmen with more leisure time, some of which might be used to keep themselves better informed about public questions. A large part of the speech was used for pointing out how workingmen might best promote their interests.[2]

On April 6, 1869, he appeared before a Committee of the Massachusetts Legislature to advocate the appointment of a commission "to inquire into the condition of labor in the State; to acquire statistics and facts on which the movement can work; to obtain in detail the actual condition of the laboring classes—rates of wages, mortality, ages of employment, rent, prices of provisions, average hours of employment," etc.[3]

On October 18, 1870, he spoke in Music Hall, Boston, on the labor reform and temperance issues in Massachusetts politics, as the candidate for governor of both the Labor Reform party and the State Temperance Convention.[4]

He made a number of other speeches in the campaign of 1870, and he spoke before various groups in 1871. From the viewpoint of a clear statement of his principles, the most important of all of these was delivered

[1] *National Anti-Slavery Standard*, Apr. 16, 1870.
[2] *Boston Daily Advertiser*, Nov. 3, 1865.
[3] *National Anti-Slavery Standard*, Apr. 17, 1869.
[4] *Boston Daily Advertiser*, Oct. 19, 1870.

at the Convention of the Labor Reform Party, at Framingham, on October 4, 1871. The platform of this convention, drawn up by Phillips, who also was the presiding officer, makes clear why he is recognized as one of the early leaders in the socialist movement in America: "We affirm as a fundamental principle, that labor, the creator of wealth, is entitled to all it creates. Affirming this, we avow ourselves willing to accept the final results of the operation of a principle so radical; such as the overthrow of the whole profit-making system, the extinction of all monopolies, the abolition of privileged classes. . . . "[1]

In his speech on "The Foundation of the Labor Movement," October 31, 1871, he lashed out at individual owners of great wealth and at corporations, and advocated placing heavy taxes on wealth of all kinds, so that it would be unprofitable to be rich.[2]

For the remainder of his life, he continued to express these views; and, just as his extreme views on the slavery issue had made him unpopular throughout most of that long struggle, his advanced views on labor reform again brought the disapprobation of people generally. Few men have ever been as bitterly hated as Phillips was for his efforts to improve the lot of the laboring class.

Finally, let us examine a few of his temperance speeches. His first important speech on temperance was delivered before a committee of the Massachusetts legislature, February 28, 1865. The legislature had enacted a law for the stricter regulation of the liquor traffic; however, it was not being properly enforced, and Wendell Phillips appeared before the committee to speak on the subject "The Laws of the Commonwealth—Shall They Be Enforced?"

He expressed his views on the harmfulness of liquor, in part, as follows:

I contend that no man needs argument, no man needs evidence on such a subject as this; and no man has lived forty years who has not seen his pathway of life marked by the graves of some that he loved most, from whose promise he augured most, whose career was to be the brightest, who have not fallen at his side, victims to this sin. I should not dare to uncover one single roof in this city, no matter how guarded by wealth, education, or any other fence; for I should be sure to find, even in the narrowest family circle, one vacant seat which this gigantic tempter had emptied. I have only such a tale to tell as every one of your hearts bears witness to. Lawyer, merchant, divine—no matter where you take

[1] *Boston Morning Journal*, Oct. 5, 1871; *Boston Daily Advertiser*, Oct. 5, 1871. In Wendell Phillips, *Speeches, Lectures, and Letters* (2d series, Boston, Lee and Shepard, 1891), p. 152, both the place and date of the meeting are incorrectly stated.

[2] *Boston Morning Journal*, Nov. 1, 1871.

your testimony, every man's heart is full, every man's memory is the most accusing witness against this great social evil.[1]

Many of his later temperance speeches emphasized the need of breaking the close relationship that had been established between the liquor traffic and politics. At a temperance convention in Boston, May 28, 1880, he asserted: "The ballot cannot be rested upon a drunken people, for, if it is, there will soon be a despot in the saddle."[2]

Eulogies and Popular Lectures

Although Wendell Phillips's fame rests chiefly on his agitation for social reforms, he was distinguished as a eulogist and as a popular lecturer.

Probably his best, as well as best known, eulogy was on Daniel O'Connell. He spoke on him many times, and there are a number of reports of what he said, corresponding to the different occasions; in fact, there are different versions of what he said on the same occasion.[3]

Phillips had occasion to come to the defense of Charles Sumner a number of times, and he delivered several separate eulogies on him. One of the most striking of these was delivered in Boston shortly after the news arrived of the assault on Sumner in the Senate chamber. A defense of Sumner was coupled with an attack on the South, on the perpetrator of the outrage, and on all those who either aided in the plan or excused it.[4]

He was called upon also to pay tributes to a number of the dead leaders of the Abolition movement. Those to Francis Jackson and William Lloyd Garrison are particularly worthy of study.

Two of his popular lectures are especially well known. The first of these, "Street Life in Europe," was prepared shortly after his return from Europe; he delivered it many times. Even better known was his famous lecture "The Lost Arts"; he delivered it first in 1838 and is said to have repeated it more than two thousand times.

With this brief discussion of Phillips's ability as a eulogist and popular lecturer, this review of his efforts as a reformer, agitator, and distinguished speaker comes to an end. He was very active in many reform movements, the most important of which were Abolition, woman's rights, labor, and

[1] "The Laws of the Commonwealth—Shall They Be Enforced?" speech before the legislative committee, Feb. 28, 1865 (Boston, Wright & Potter, 1865).

[2] *Boston Morning Journal*, May 29, 1880.

[3] For his address on the one hundredth anniversary of the birth of O'Connell, Aug. 6, 1875, see the *Boston Morning Journal*, Aug. 7, 1875.

[4] *The Liberator*, May 30, 1856. About this speech, Sumner wrote to Phillips, July 24, 1856: "I cannot close without letting you know how joyfully and tearfully I read your most beautiful and spontaneous utterance at the first meeting in Boston."—Pierce, *op. cit.*, III, 506.

temperance, and he was outstanding as a eulogist and popular lecturer. In the preceding pages the facts about his participation in reform movements have been described. We are now ready to appraise his character, his influence on his times, the accuracy of the surviving texts of his speeches, and his style and delivery.

Character

Through Lyman Beecher, Wendell Phillips early came under the influence of the Great Revival,[1] the effect of which on his speeches is readily recognizable. Throughout all his life, he remained a deeply religious man, with a mission to perform. Under the spur of this religious impulse, he became the enemy of oppressors everywhere and the friend of the weak and downtrodden; he became the foe of every evil and wrong and the *apostle of social justice.* He is said to have once remarked, "God has not sent me into the world to abolish slavery, but to do my duty."[2]

On all matters of social reform, his religious nature made him a man of strong convictions and singleness of purpose. He was a sincere believer in every great reform for which he fought and was honest and straightforward in expressing what he thought and felt. His convictions were so deep-rooted that, for him, truth—on highly controversial topics—was absolute rather than relative; and since it was absolute, there could be no compromise. Men and measures, usually, either were all "black" or all "white"; there was no middle ground. When he had once made up his mind to support a social reform and had determined what—to him—was the best method to make it an accomplished fact, all who opposed the reform were subjected to specimens of his finest scorn and most bitter invective; and those who joined in advocating the reform but disliked his method were severely rebuked. In the main, he was faithful to his convictions and did not swerve from them for friend or foe, in victory or in defeat.

His ardent love of justice often betrayed him into great injustice toward those who differed with him, and his clear, swift insight into right and wrong frequently caused him to ignore the complexities of social action; when he found a wrong to be righted, he wanted it done immediately, by the method that he proposed. In striving for the desired end, he was careless in the use of means to accomplish it; sometimes he was careless with facts and reckless with the reputation of others. *Very little mattered to him except reaching his objective.*

[1] It is impossible to understand the Abolition movement without knowing its connection with the Great Revival, which began in the 1820's, rose to its climax in 1837 and 1838, and declined in 1839.—Gilbert Hobbs Barnes, *The Anti-Slavery Impulse* 1830–1844 (New York, D. Appleton-Century Company, Inc., 1933).

[2] Letter from William Lloyd Garrison to H. C. Wright, Aug. 26, 1846 (MS, Garrison Collection, Boston Public Library).

It is obvious from the discussion of a number of the speech situations in which he was faced by hostile audiences that Phillips was a man of courage. It took courage to face hostile audiences and to say what he knew would not be acceptable to them. It took courage also, to desert his family and friends to espouse detested and unpopular causes.[1]

Phillips, also, was kind and generous to his family and friends, while his devotion to Mrs. Phillips through over forty-six years of their married life, during most of which she was an invalid confined to her bed, is attested by Francis Jackson Garrison.[2]

Phillips inherited property from his father and made a considerable income from his lectures, but he was so generous in giving financial aid to causes in which he was interested and in helping friends that he died a poor man. For instance, he frequently came to the aid of William Lloyd Garrison, whose income often was insufficient to take care of his large family. On one of these occasions, he joined with Francis Jackson in an appeal to the friends of Garrison, with the object of raising $5,000 to be used for the purchase of a home for him, or for such other benefits as the trustees of the fund deemed best; to this fund Phillips subscribed $250.[3]

He was religious; he had strong convictions and singleness of purpose; he was courageous; he was kindly and generous; and withal he had a sense of humor. Most of his speeches were very serious expressions of his convictions, but his keen sense of humor frequently came to the surface, particularly when he was ridiculing an opponent by poking fun at him. His speech at the New England Anti-Slavery Convention, Faneuil Hall, May 30, 1850 —in which Daniel Webster is the object of his attention—is an example of this.[4]

Influence on His Times

It is very difficult, if not quite impossible, to measure Phillips's influence on his times; so great were his merits as a public figure, so closely were those merits interwoven with his faults, and so great were the controversies

[1] What this meant to him is shown in a letter that he wrote to a friend, Jan. 31, 1846. He said: "Dear Ann has spoken of my dear mother's death. My good, noble, dear, mother! We differed utterly on the matter of slavery, and she grieved a good deal over what she thought was a waste of my time, and a sad disappointment to her; but still I am always best satisfied with myself when I fancy I can see anything in me which reminds me of my mother."—MS (Garrison Collection, Boston Public Library).

[2] Francis Jackson Garrison, *Ann Phillips, Wife of Wendell Phillips* (printed for private circulation, Boston, 1886).

[3] Letter from Wendell Phillips and Francis Jackson to Thomas Davis, Dec. 13, 1847, and a record of contributions dated Nov. 27, 1847 (MS, Papers of William Lloyd Garrison, Massachusetts Historical Society).

[4] *The Liberator*, June 28, 1850.

raging around him that his contemporaries and present-day students of his influence, alike, differ very greatly.

In the first place, he represented minorities (and sometimes very small minorities) almost all his life. For a brief period of about ten months, in 1861, to January 7, 1862 (in which he had supported the President and the Union), he enjoyed the rare experience—for him—of finding himself acting with the majority; then intermittently from the end of the war to the ratification in 1870 of the Fifteenth Amendment, he enjoyed a considerable following, as one of the leading men who were working to obtain full rights of citizenship for the freedmen; and then from 1870 to his death in 1884 (in the period when his principal interest was labor reform), his views were entirely unacceptable to the majority, and he was as bitterly hated by the so-called "upper classes" as during the long antislavery struggle.

From 1838 to the early 1840's he had some, although not very great, influence on his times; he was too young and too new to the antislavery movement to build a large following. Nevertheless, he did help to arouse the people of the North to the realization that slavery was an evil. Strangely enough, this was accomplished, in large part, because the whole Abolition movement was the source of great irritation to the South and aroused intense anger toward all abolitionists; this anger was expressed in newspaper attacks, petitions to Congress and the various state legislatures, offers of rewards for the capture of abolitionists, etc.—all of which publicized the Abolition cause better than the abolitionists alone could possibly have done it.

From the early 1840's to the outbreak of the war, his extreme views on nonvoting and holding office, his cursing of the Constitution, and his advocacy of disunion never were accepted by more than a small minority, even of the abolitionists themselves; *his views in this period, therefore, had no direct influence upon the policies of the state and Federal governments.* He was merely one of the very articulate leaders of the small left, or Garrisonian, wing of the Abolition movement.

Although he had no direct influence upon governmental policies on the antislavery issues, *as an agitator—of the very first rank—he helped to keep all phases of the subject alive throughout the country.* His ability as an orator before popular audiences was so great that large crowds came to hear him on almost all occasions. Although he exhibited considerable mastery of more argumentative discourses, particularly before committees of the Massachusetts legislature, it is to his speeches before popular audiences that his chief fame is due.

Although he had very little direct influence on governmental policy throughout most of his life, nevertheless, *no other orator who was active in these reform movements—particularly in the antislavery cause—had the pub-*

licity value of Wendell Phillips. In addition to his reputation as a speaker, interest in him was greatly enhanced by the fact that his bitter attacks on men and measures and the circumstances under which he spoke—very frequently—had great news value; his speeches, therefore, were widely publicized and were used as models for declamation in the schools and colleges. His abusive attacks on friends and foes became so commonplace that his audiences expected them and were disappointed when they were sometimes omitted. Besides, he so often was the object of mob violence or intended mob violence and so often was faced by hostile audiences that *the occasions had certain interest and entertainment values beyond the subject matter itself.*

His chief service to antislavery and to the other reforms in which he was interested, therefore, was in stimulating people to think about the evils of the system he condemned and the methods of bringing t to an end; in short, his influence was principally as an *agitator.*

Accuracy of Speech Texts

Almost all Phillips's speeches from January, 1837, to December, 1872—either at the time of their delivery or shortly thereafter—were published in one (or two) of three newspapers; from January, 1837, to May, 1865 (at the time of his break with Garrison over the dissolution of the American Antislavery Society), the best single source is the *Liberator;* from May, 1865, to April, 1870 (when the publication ceased), the best single source is the *National Anti-Slavery Standard;* from July, 1870, to December, 1872 (the entire life of the publication), the best single source is the *National Standard.*[1] Of course, a large number of the speeches reported in these newspapers may be found also in general newspapers, while from 1872 to 1884 his important speeches are found in general newspapers only.

In using the *Liberator,* the *National Anti-Slavery Standard,* and the *National Standard,* students of Phillips's speeches must keep in mind that only a part of the texts published in them accurately and completely represent what he really said; a very large portion of them were revised by Phillips before publication. The accurate texts usually are identified by a line indicating either that the speeches were reported for the newspaper (the name of the reporter is sometimes given) or that they were copied from another newspaper (not one of these three). The *Liberator* frequently copied from the *National Anti-Slavery Standard,* and vice versa, and when this

---

[1] From 1865 to 1870, he was a special editorial contributor to the *National Anti-Slavery Standard* and—particularly from 1866 on—made very frequent contributions on the questions of the day. He was a special contributor to the *National Standard* throughout its life.

happened other evidence of accuracy must be found before it may be assumed that the text had not been revised before publication.[1]

In view of the fact that the *Liberator*, the *National Anti-Slavery Standard*, and the *National Standard* are available for the use of students at only a limited number of places, the common source of the texts of the speeches of Wendell Phillips is the two-volume collection, under the title *Speeches, Lectures, and Letters;* the first of these, published in 1863, is commonly designated as "first series," while the second, published in 1891, is called "second series." The publisher's advertisement, in the first volume, includes a letter from Wendell Phillips. After mentioning that four or five of the speeches were delivered in such circumstances that they were substantially prepared beforehand and that the preservation of the rest is due to phonography, Phillips said, in referring to his own revisions: "Giving them such verbal revision as the interval allowed, I left their substance and shape unchanged." In the Prefatory Note to the second volume, the editor, Theodore C. Pease, wrote: "At the time of his death he not only had a further selection in mind, but had revised certain lectures, and had promised a second volume to the present publishers."

When Phillips said that he had left the "substance and shape unchanged," he was taking some license with the meaning of words. All but a few of the speeches in this collection underwent revision; and some of them underwent such thoroughgoing revisions as to both materially add to and subtract from their "substance," in such fashion as to leave no doubt about changing their "shape."

A considerable number of the texts in both volumes of *Speeches, Lectures, and Letters* have been traced back to more accurate sources, and the conclusion is unavoidable that in a large number of cases their "substance and shape," in the collection, is very different from their "native state" when delivered.

Let us examine, first, his speech on "The Murder of Lovejoy." It was reported for the *Liberator* by B. F. Hallett and appears in the issue of December 15, 1837. It is also in the *Massachusetts Spy*, January 10, 1838, in which it appears, because of a note by the editor of the *Boston Daily Advocate* (which is appended), to have been copied from that newspaper. Since the Lovejoy meeting was on December 8, and the *Liberator* report is in the issue of December 15, and since the *Advocate* was a daily, while the *Liberator* was a weekly, it is not probable that the *Advocate* copied from the

---

[1] These three newspapers, for the periods indicated, appear to be the only ones to allow Phillips considerable license in the revision of his speeches; and *The Liberator*—particularly— permitted him frequently to revise speeches that had been especially reported for it. These usually carry the line, "Reported for *The Liberator* by _____, revised [or revised and enlarged] by Wendell Phillips."

Liberator. Therefore, either there are two reports of this speech prepared by different reporters or the same reporter reported for both newspapers. In either case, suffice it to say that the two versions differ only in a few minor and relatively unimportant details.

How do these reports compare with the text in *Speeches, Lectures, and Letters*, first series? There are very great differences. Not a single page of the text in the collection is identical with the corresponding material in the two newspapers. There are many changes in sentence content and structure; some paragraphs are completely reworded; some paragraphs are deleted and others added; in one place more than a page was added; and in another, one short paragraph in the newspapers was expanded to almost a full page. These changes are major ones of structure, and they result in somewhat different rhetorical effects.

A comparison of the structure and style of the reports in the *Liberator* and *Spy* with the text in *Speeches, Lectures, and Letters* leads to the conclusion that the latter text is more mature. The evidence points to the newspaper reports as accurate statements of what Phillips actually said and to the text in the collection as revision of the speech, which was prepared at a much later date; it is probable that Phillips revised this speech just before the publication, in 1863, of the volume in which it appears.

The same sort of major revisions are found in many other speeches. The text in the collection of his speech on "Woman's Rights," delivered at Worcester, at the meeting of the Woman's Rights Convention on October 15, 16, 1851, varies greatly from the text in the *Report of the Second General Convention of Friends of Woman's Rights*. There are many additions, deletions, and rewordings. His speech on "Harper's Ferry," delivered in Brooklyn, November 1, 1859—as reported in the *Liberator*, November 11, 1859—has similar wide variations from the text in the collection. His speech on "The War for the Union," delivered in New York on December 19, 1861 —reported in the *New York Tribune*, December 20, was revised in the same drastic manner before publication in the *Liberator*. William Lloyd Garrison, in a letter to Oliver Johnson, December 26, 1861, described Phillips's revision of this speech as follows:

You will see in the *Liberator*, this week, the speech of Mr. Phillips, delivered at New York, as revised and corrected by himself. And such revision, correction, alteration, and addition, you never saw in the way of emendation! More than two columns of the *Tribune's* report were in type before P. came into our office; and the manipulation these required was a caution to all reporters and typesetters! I proposed to P. to send his altered slips to Barnum as a remarkable curiosity, and Winchell [J. M. W. Yerrinton] suggested having them photographed! But P. desired to make his speech as complete and full as he could, and I am glad you are to receive it without being put to any trouble about it. Doubtless you will be requested to make some new alterations; for he is constantly criticizing what he has spoken, and pays no attention to literal accuracy.[1]

The version of this speech in the collection, also, is very different from the *Tribune's* report.

Not only are a large number of the texts in the collection inaccurate but this work is open to the equally serious charge of not being representative. It is quite evident that the selection of the speeches in both volumes results in presenting Phillips in a more favorable light than can be justified on the facts. Some important phases of his agitation are very inadequately represented.

In the period from his return from Europe, in 1841, to the speeches growing out of John Brown and the Harper's Ferry incident, in 1859, the included speeches do not give a fair cross section of his antislavery agitation. Speeches like the one he delivered in Faneuil Hall on October 30, 1842—in which he cursed the Constitution—are not included; the same thing is true of his most virulent attacks on the churches; and the references to disunion in the collection do not convey a correct impression of the importance of this issue to Phillips. Also, there is very little more than a hint in the collection of the bitterness that existed between the two chief groups of abolitionists—those who believed in voting, holding office, and trying to achieve their ends under the Constitution and those, like Garrison and Phillips, who opposed voting, holding office, and advocated disunion—a bitterness that Phillips helped, by many of his speeches, to intensify.

In the period from 1862 to 1884, also, his bitter assaults upon Presidents, cabinets, and Congresses, are very insufficiently represented.

Besides the omission of speeches that are necessary to give a correct impression of Phillips's services as a reformer, the collection conveys only a very meager impression of his consummate ability in handling hostile audiences.

All students of Phillips's speeches would do well to use this collection as a point of departure only; no speech text appearing in it should be accepted as accurate without corroborative evidence from original sources, and it should be remembered also that the selection of speeches in it is not faithfully representative of his public-speaking career.

Style and Delivery

A detailed study of Phillips's style is not attempted here; rather, the reader's attention is called to only a few of the more important aspects of it.

In the first place, he was a master of the art of extemporaneous speaking. It was the flexibility of this form that made it possible for him to develop

---

[1] MS, Garrison Collection, Boston Public Library.

his great power as a speaker. All the advantages of immediate adaptation to the speech situation, which have been assigned to this type by teachers of speech, are attested by the speeches of Wendell Phillips and the reactions of his audiences. Without his great skill in extemporaneous speaking, he never would have attained the heights he reached as an orator of agitation; for in no other kind of speech is rapid and skilled adaptation more necessary for success.

On subjects with which he was thoroughly familiar, he was a master of the art of impromptu speaking, also. Very often, in meetings of the anti-slavery societies, labor unions, woman's rights conventions, etc., he spoke impromptu with brilliance and effect.

In response to a compliment about his remarkable power in extemporaneous speaking, Phillips replied that "it was the result of hard work (the joint product of temperament and experience), the fruit of close self-scrutiny and study of audiences while on his feet, and *incessant* practice in public speaking." Again he said, "The chief thing I aim at is to master the subject I wish to speak about, and then earnestly try to get the audience to think and feel as I do about it."[1]

Of course, when the speech situations permitted, he frequently wrote his speeches out in full and memorized them. He was able in each case to use the method that was best suited to his purpose.

As an agitator, he studied the art of irritation and became an expert in its use. His most effective weapons in the use of this art were invective and frontal attacks on long-cherished and accepted beliefs. Both methods were so striking and so attention-compelling that his listeners were shocked into attending to what he had to say and irritated into thinking about his ideas, even though not agreeing with them.

In his use of invective, he was often charged with using violent and intemperate language. When a similar charge was made against O'Connell, Phillips defended him by saying: "The criticism is of little importance. Stupor and palsy never understand life. White-livered indifference is always disgusted and annoyed by earnest conviction."

In the same speech, he made the following reference to the attitude of the abolitionists: "It needed with us an attitude of independence that was almost insolent; it needed that we should exhaust even the Saxon vocabulary of scorn, to fitly utter the righteous and haughty contempt that honest men had for slave-stealers. Only in that way could we wake the North to self-respect, or teach the South that at length she had met her equal, if not her master."[2]

[1] Editorial, *Andover Review* 1 (March, 1884): 309–316.
[2] "Daniel O'Connell," Aug. 6, 1875; *Boston Morning Journal*, Aug. 7, 1875.

When people remonstrated with him, he was fond of quoting, also, Garrison's reply to the same sort of criticism, "Brother, I have need to be all on fire, for I have mountains of ice around me to melt."

Since irritation was the method of agitation, Phillips was not greatly concerned about the art of persuasion in his speeches on social reforms. His attitude toward his audiences usually was not conciliatory, but hostile, and sometimes even defiant. Very often his purpose was to irritate his audience into open opposition; frequently it took a few hisses to stimulate Phillips to his best effort. *He was most brilliant as a speaker when he was most bitter.*

He commonly beheads his victims with a single stroke of his blade. He wastes no words either in praise or in censure. . . . It was the same stern economy of words that labelled Abraham Lincoln, "the slave hound of Illinois. . . . " There is little in these phrases when they are read; but in the manner of their utterance, albeit calm and smooth as ice, there is a power that electrifies the listener like the sound of a trumpet. Who that heard Mr. Phillips say in his Massachusetts campaign speeches last year, "I announced that I never again would speak to William Chaflin," did not feel at the instant that William Chaflin was withered up and puffed away like a rose leaf? And yet, who, reading the remark in the faithful newspaper report next morning, could discover where lay the eloquence of the arrogant words?[1]

Finally, his speeches are replete with pointed and pleasing anecdotes, striking statements, examples, comparisons, and witticisms.

Let us now examine the methods that he used in delivery. A number of analyses of his delivery were made by persons who heard him. The best of these, by far, is in the form of an editorial, written shortly after his death, for the *Andover Review*. There were five members of the board of editors of the *Review* at the time, all of whom were professors in the Andover Theological Seminary, Andover, Mass. Among these men, the Reverend William J. Tucker was Bartlet professor of sacred rhetoric and lecturer on pastoral theology, and the Reverend J. Wesley Churchill was Jones professor of elocution. The authorship of the editorial is not indicated; however, since it quite obviously was written by a person who was thoroughly familiar with rhetorical theory, particularly with delivery, it is probable that it is the product either of Professor Tucker or of Professor Churchill. It is thorough, discriminating, and judicious:

The chief weapon of his oratory was his voice. In its natural powers it was not remarkable, either for its intensity, volume, or compass. The secret . . . lay partly in its peculiar "quality," or "*timbre.*" The musical register was a baritone, used in the upper series of the chest notes. With its absolute purity, and its density of vibratory resonance, his voice possessed a carrying power that penetrated to every

[1] Editorial, *Every Saturday*, Apr. 22, 1871.

part of any large audience-room. The *character* of the voice—the man in it—had the effect of "finding" its auditor. It had an *intimate* tone, as if it were speaking to each one as an unknown friend. . . . Another element in its magical charm was the easy method of its production. . . . The modulations were regulated by the sureness of his perfect taste. They were the flexible intonations of elevated conversation. His modulation, like his style and diction, was the perfection of talking to people. . . .

In the rate of utterance, he achieved the rare excellence of speaking deliberately without seeming slow. He was thus enabled to secure audibility and distinctness by giving sufficient time, or "quantity" to the formation of the open vowels and a clear cut stamp to the consonants. Who ever heard Wendell Phillips mar his speaking by hurry? Yet who ever heard him when he did not speak like a man *alive?*

His natural sense of perfection in his art led him to conform his pronunciation to the best standards. Occasionally, he would make a slip. In the same speech, he would say, "ēither" and "īther," "phĭlosophical" and "phīlosophical." With an indifference to the foppery of culture, he would put to frequent use the colloquialisms, "well," "can't," "wasn't," "don't," "won't," "wouldn't," "shouldn't," but from his refined lips they seemed almost to gain authority and propriety. . . . He possessed the power of investing significant words and phrases with a peculiarly impressive effect. Whenever he wished the audience to weigh any important thought he had just uttered, he made a most skillful use of the emphatic pause. Sometimes the pause would be made before the word; then the word came with the added value of an aroused curiosity. But when his voice stopped, his mind did not. The interval was always filled with some expressiveness of manner that enhanced the vividness of the thought.

The dramatic expression of emotion he almost never indulged in. There was no "start theatric" in his sincere manner. There were no tears in his beautiful voice. His was a nature full of tenderness but not of pathos. "Why cannot I make an audience cry as you do?" he once asked Anna Dickinson. "Because, Mr. Phillips, you never cry yourself," was the truthful reply. . . .

His action was characterized by a manly force, unstudied grace, significance, and just precision. His gesture was neither vehement nor redundant. . . . Nor did he enfeeble his delivery by too much action, any more than he weakened his vocal expression by over-emphasis. The effectiveness of his action resided in its significance and its comparative rarity, neither overdoing the significant nor multiplying the significant movements. And yet, it was managed with so much ease and propriety that his auditors were deceived as to its frequency. He made many more gestures than he was supposed to have made. His colloquial method governed his action; hence, there was great variety. He freely used the open palm, now with one hand, now with both. In the expression of ideas that were disagreeable to him he used the averted palm. In the more moderate emphasis of feeling he placed the index finger, or the palm, or the fist of one hand on the supine palm of the other. Imagination influenced his gesture and led to the temperate use of symbolical action suggested by his language. . . .

The difficult art of gracefully standing still before an audience he observed to perfection. The hands either hung quietly by the side, or were clasped behind or in front of him; a gesture made with one hand would sometimes be finished by allowing it to rest upon the body, or action with both hands would occasionally terminate with hands clasped and gently resting upon the body. He had no favorite mode of rest but used all modes in a self-forgetful way. His changes of position were few, and in a narrow space. He never walked the platform. . . .

Mr. Phillips' delivery in its general treatment, as has been suggested already, was colloquial in style and extemporaneous in method. His private conversation on earnest topics was simply ennobled, or idealized. His public speaking was his part of a public conversation addressed, as it were, to the farthest auditor. . . . [1]

SELECTED BIBLIOGRAPHY[2]

Manuscripts

William Lloyd Garrison Papers, Library of the Massachusetts Historical Society. William Lloyd Garrison Collection, Boston Public Library.

A. A. Lawrence Collection, Library of the Massachusetts Historical Society.

Miscellaneous MSS, Library of Congress, American Antiquarian Society, New York Public Library, Yale University Library, Brown University Library, Massachusetts Historical Society, Boston Public Library.

Elizabeth Cady Stanton Papers, Library of Congress.

Charles Sumner Collection, Harvard University Library.

Louis Tappan Papers, Library of Congress.

Eliza Wright, Jr., Papers, Library of Congress.

General Works

Adams, Charles Francis: *Memoirs of John Quincy Adams*, 12 vols., Philadelphia, J. B. Lippin-cott Company, 1874–1877.

———: *Charles Francis Adams*, Boston, Houghton Mifflin Company, 1900.

———: *Richard Henry Dana*, 2 vols., Boston, Houghton Mifflin Company, 1890.

Anti-Slavery History of the John Brown Year, New York, American Anti-Slavery Society, 1861.

Austin, George Lowell: *The Life and Times of Wendell Phillips*, Boston, B. B. Russell & Co., 1884.

Austin, James T.: "Speech at Faneuil Hall," Dec. 8, 1837, Boston, John H. Eastburn, 1838.

Barnes, Gilbert Hobbs: *The Anti-Slavery Impulse*, 1830–1844, New York, D. Appleton-Century Company, Inc., 1933.

———, and Dwight L. Dumond: *Letters of Theodore Dwight Weld, Angelina Grimké Weld and Sarah Grimké*, 1822–1844, 2 vols., New York, D. Appleton-Century Company, Inc., 1934.

Beecher, Henry Ward: "Wendell Phillips," a commemorative discourse delivered at Plymouth Church, Brooklyn, Feb. 10, 1884, and issued as *Plymouth Pulpit*, 7, New York, No. 20, Fords, Foward, & Hulbert, 1884.

Channing, William Henry: *Memoir of William Ellery Channing*, 3 vols., Boston, Nichols, Lee & Co., 1860.

Child, Lydia Maria: *Letters of Lydia Maria Child*, with a biographical introduction by John G. Whittier and an Appendix by Wendell Phillips, Boston, Houghton Mifflin Company, 1883.

---

[1] *Andover Review* (March, 1884): 309–316.

[2] This is a selective rather than a complete bibliography. Because of space limitation it includes neither a list of Phillips's speeches nor all the sources referred to in the text.

Cole, Arthur C.: *The Irrepressible Conflict*, New York, The Macmillan Company, 1934.

The Constitution, a Proslavery Compact, or *Extracts from the Madison Papers*, etc., selected by Wendell Phillips, 3d ed., New York, American Antislavery Society, 1856.

Curtis, George William: "Eulogy of Wendell Phillips," Apr. 18, 1884, in *A Memorial of Wendell Phillips from the City of Boston*, Boston, printed by order of the City Council, 1884.

Darling, Arthur B.: *Political Changes in Massachusetts*, 1824–1848, New Haven, Yale University Press, 1925.

Emerson, Ralph Waldo: *Journals of Ralph Waldo Emerson*, 10 vols., Boston, Houghton Mifflin Company, 1909–1914.

Garrison, Francis Jackson: *Ann Phillips, Wife of Wendell Phillips*, a memorial sketch, printed for private circulation, Boston, 1886.

Garrison, William Lloyd, the story of his life, by his children, 4 vols., New York, The Century Company, 1885–1889.

Holland, F. M.: *Frederick Douglass—The Colored Orator*, New York, Funk & Wagnalls Company, 1895.

Johnson, Oliver: *William Lloyd Garrison and His Times*, Boston, B. B. Russell & Co.; New York, C. Drew, 1880.

Lowell, James Russell: *Anti-Slavery Papers of James Russell Lowell*, 2 vols., Boston, Houghton Mifflin Company, 1902.

Martyn, Carlos: *Wendell Phillips—The Agitator*, New York, Funk & Wagnalls Company, 1890.

Phillips, Albert M.: *Phillips Genealogies*, Auburn, Mass., Press of C. Hamilton, Worcester, Mass., 1885.

Phillips, Wendell: "The Freedom Speech," with descriptive letters from eye witnesses, Boston, Wendell Phillips Hall Association, 1891.

———: "The Philosophy of the Abolition Movement," *Anti-Slavery Tracts*, n.s., No. 8, New York, American Anti-Slavery Society, 1860.

———: *Review of Lysander Spooner's Essay on the Unconstitutionality of Slavery*, Boston, Andrews & Prentiss, 1847.

———: *Review of Webster's Speech on Slavery*, Boston, American Antislavery Society, 1850.

———: *Speeches, Lectures, and Letters*, 2 vols., 1st series, Boston, J. Redpath, 1863; 2d series, Boston, Lee & Shepard, 1891.

Pierce, Edward L.: *Memoir and Letters of Charles Sumner*, 4 vols., Boston, Roberts Brothers, 1877–1893.

Proceedings of the Woman's Rights Convention, Worcester, Mass., Oct. 15, 16, 1851, New York, Fowlers and Wells, 1852; New York, Sept. 6, 7, 1853, New York, Fowlers and Wells, 1853; New York, May 12, 1859, Rochester, N.Y., A. Strong & Co., 1859.

Russell, Charles Edward: *The Story of Wendell Phillips: Soldier of the Common Good*, Chicago, C. H. Kerr & Co., 1914.

Sanborn, F. B.: *John Brown and His Friends*, F. B. Sanborn, 190–?

———: *Recollections of Seventy Years*, 2 vols., Boston, Richard G. Badger, 1909.

Sears, Lorenzo: *Wendell Phillips—Orator and Agitator*, New York, Doubleday-Doran & Company, Inc., 1909.

Stafford, Wendell Phillips: *Wendell Phillips*, a centennial oration delivered at Park Street Church, Boston, Nov. 28, 1911, New York, National Association for the Advancement of Colored People, 1911.

Turner, L. D.: *Antislavery Sentiment in American Literature prior to 1865*, Washington, D.C., The Association for the Study of Negro Life and History, 1929.

Villard, Oswald Garrison: *John Brown*, Boston, Houghton Mifflin Company, 1910.

361

Ware, Edith E.: *Political Opinion in Massachusetts during the Civil War and Reconstruction,* New York, Columbia University Press, 1916.

Washington, Booker T.: *Frederick Douglass,* Philadelphia and London, G. W. Jacobs & Co., 1907.

Weld, Theodore D.: "Lessons from the Life of Wendell Phillips," at the memorial services on the seventy-fourth birthday of Wendell Phillips, Nov. 29, 1885, Boston, J. Cooper, 1886.

Wentworth, Franklin Harcourt: "Wendell Phillips," an address delivered in Faneuil Hall, Boston, Dec. 4, 1906, New York, Socialist Literature Company, 1906.

Willard, Sidney: *Memories of Youth and Manhood,* 2 vols., Cambridge, J. Bartlett, 1855.

Woodberry, George E.: *Wendell Phillips: The Faith of an American,* Boston, D. B. Updike, 1912.

11

Robert G. Ingersoll

by WAYLAND MAXFIELD PARRISH

and ALFRED DWIGHT HUSTON

Robert G. Ingersoll was born in 1833 in Dresden, N. Y., the son of a Congregational and Presbyterian clergyman. His father preached the orthodox theology of the day but offended congregations by his opposition to slavery and so seldom remained long in any one church. He moved to Ohio and thence to Wisconsin and Illinois. Robert's schooling was meager. He read in his father's theological library, but without enthusiasm or approval. His later discovery of the works of Burns and Shakespeare made a deep impression on him, and he memorized long passages from both and recited them to his brother. These remained throughout life his favorite authors. His formal schooling was completed by a brief period in an academy in southern Illinois. After a year of teaching he took up the study of law, and in his twenty-first year entered practice with his brother in Shawneetown. In 1857 the brothers moved to Peoria. Here he rapidly rose to prominence in his profession. He became known as a skeptic in religion, but his personal charm and unfailing kindliness saved him from social ostracism. In 1861 he raised and commanded a volunteer cavalry regiment, with which he saw service in the campaigns of the Tennessee Valley. He was captured by General Forrest, paroled, discharged, and in 1863 returned to the practice of law in Peoria. In 1862 he had married Eva Parker, who throughout her life shared his religious skepticism. He served as attorney general of Illinois from 1867 to 1869. His power before juries and his success as a lecturer brought him local fame and a very substantial income. National fame came through his speech nominating Blaine for the Presidency in 1876. From then until his death he was much sought after as a lawyer, campaigner, and lecturer. In 1879 he moved to Washington in order to be nearer the seat of Federal litigation. In 1885 the interests of his corporation clients led him to move to New York. He died peacefully in his home at Dobbs Ferry, N. Y., in 1899.

For more than twenty years Robert G. Ingersoll stood in the top rank of American speakers as lecturer, lawyer, political campaigner, and speaker of occasional addresses. Few men in the history of American oratory addressed as many or as various audiences, and few enjoyed or earned such high esteem. We to whom he is only a name are likely to read with surprise and incredulity the extravagant praise of his eloquence from those who heard him. Contemporary of Phillips, Curtis, Beecher, Blaine, and many of lesser note, he was generally believed by competent judges to outshine them all.

During the Presidential campaign of 1880 Beecher introduced Ingersoll to a Brooklyn mass meeting as "a man who—and I say it not flatteringly—is the most brilliant speaker of the English tongue of all men on this globe." After his Cooper Union speech in 1876 Chauncey M. Depew remarked that it was the greatest speech he had ever heard. Hamlin Garland, who heard him lecture six or eight times and studied his methods carefully, referred to him as "our greatest orator." Of his toast at the Grant banquet in Chicago, 1879, Mark Twain wrote, "By George, I was never so stirred since I was born . . . Oh, it was just the supremest combination of English words that was ever put together since the world began. My soul, how handsome he looked as he stood on that table, in the midst of those 500 shouting men, and poured the molten silver from his lips." Later he wrote Ingersoll that he had "read the speech to the Saturday Club [of young girls] and told them to remember that it was doubtful if its superior existed in our language." A professor of Greek who heard his address at Bangor during the Hayes campaign is reported to have said, "If Demosthenes was as eloquent as Ingersoll, he was never properly reported." And Cameron Rogers says that after his speech nominating Blaine in 1876, "he was, in the seasoned opinion of men who had sat in congress for thirty years and more, the ranking orator of all those that they had heard, Clay, Webster, Everett, Calhoun, and the rest."[1]

An indication of his popularity and his influence is found in the number and size and enthusiasm of the audiences that heard him (in every state of the Union except four) during the 40 years of his active public life. As a campaign speaker he was in great demand.

But a better index of his drawing power is the size of the audiences that came to hear his lectures against religion. Here he had to face the strong opposition of the churches, and he was limited also in his appeal to those who were able to pay the customary admission fee of $1. Yet he was able every year, and often many times within the year, to fill the largest auditoriums in the largest cities of the country. James Redpath told a San Francisco reporter that he had arranged 138 lectures for him within a period of 2 years. Ingersoll's heterodoxy, he said, drove away the regular lecture-goers, and in the large cities, where the church was strong, his first audiences were small, but it rarely happened that he did not have a big house when he came a second time. "He was the 'best card' in America," said Redpath: "no other man could draw such audiences outside of the regular lecture courses. . . . His last house in San Francisco, I am told, had more money

---

[1] *Colonel Bob Ingersoll* (New York, 1927), p. 208.

in it than any lecture ever yielded since lecturing began. Ingersoll's share I believe was over $1200."

The testimony of the press during these years is monotonous in its reports of the size of the crowds that came to hear him. "Music Hall was filled in every part last night by a fine audience, attracted there by the lecture of Colonel Robert G. Ingersoll," reports the *Boston Evening Transcript* of April 14, 1880. Nine days later the *Boston Statesman* reports, "The Boston Theatre was crowded Sunday evening with an excellent audience of ladies and gentlemen, who expressed much satisfaction at hearing his lecture on 'The Gods.'" We read in the *Chicago Tribune* of September 20, 1880, that "McVickers Theatre was packed and crammed and jammed to overflowing yesterday afternoon with an audience drawn together to hear Col. Ingersoll in his new lecture—new to the West at least—'What Must We Do to Be Saved?'"

A further index of his popularity is found in the quantity of his oratorical production. During the year following the Hayes campaign he prepared five new lectures. And for the next 22 years, until the time of his death in 1899, he averaged better than one new lecture each year. Most of these lectures were delivered many times. Besides his lectures he delivered numerous occasional and ceremonial addresses—speeches in commemoration of Decoration Day and Independence Day, banquet toasts to living celebrities, and eulogies of the dead. His published works[1] fill twelve large volumes. And these prodigious labors he carried on while conducting one of the heaviest legal practices in the country. Only enough of his legal addresses have been preserved to fill one volume of his *Works*. The number of those that have not been preserved must run into the hundreds.

Surely, then, Ingersoll was one of the most prolific of American speakers and one of the most admired, and his influence upon his generation cannot but have been important. What were the sources of his power?

The Man

One who reads Ingersoll's speeches now, long after his voice has ceased, cannot but be impressed by their vitality, their perfect clarity, their sincerity, and at times by their beauty of expression. They reveal a man of independent mind, utter fearlessness, tender sentiment, and warm human sympathy. The testimony of the speeches is confirmed by the speaker's contemporaries.

Without doubt Ingersoll was one of the warmest and most genial personalities that ever breathed. His too rhapsodic and often uncritical biographer says[2] he was

[1] *The Works of Robert G. Ingersoll*, 12 vols., (Dresden ed., New York, 1900).
[2] Herman E. Kittredge, *Ingersoll: A Biographical Appreciation* (New York, 1911), pp. 295-296.

the physical, mental, and moral ideal—the embodiment of the highest possibilities of his race. By this I do not mean that he was wholly a god, nor a manlike god, nor even a godlike man—he was a *man*—absolutely human. He was of this world worldly, worldly in the noblest sense. Buoyant with health, prodigal of optimism and cheerfulness, which welled up to spontaneous overflow in every channel of expression, his name, to all who really knew him, was a reassurance, his hand-clasp an exaltation, his smile sunshine, his voice a caress, his presence a benediction.

Mark Twain said of him, "His was a great and beautiful spirit, he was a man—all man, from his crown to his footsoles. My reverence for him was deep and genuine; I prized his affection for me and returned it with usury."[1]

Judge Nathaniel French said:

I was impressed, of course, by his unequaled eloquence . . . but I was even more impressed by the sweetness of the disposition of the man than by the eloquence of the orator. It was my great good fortune to be admitted to the family circle, and to know him intimately in his relations to his family and his friends. I do not see how mortal could strive to do more for the happiness of others than Ingersoll. His constant thought was, "How can I make others happier?"[2]

Among the various artists, actors, writers, and musicians who were included in the circle of Ingersoll's friends, one of his most enthusiastic admirers was Walt Whitman. Some of his comments on Ingersoll's character are highly revealing: "That is a grand brow: and the face—look at the face —see the mouth; it is the head, the face, the poise, of a noble human being. America don't know how proud she ought to be of Ingersoll. . . . "[3] "He is one of the few, the very select few, who are alive and keep others alive with them. . . . "[4] "Damn if I don't think the Colonel is always magnificent. There was always something ample, sufficient, about Bob's ways and means: he always seemed big enough to go as high and as deep and as far around as anybody. He is the same man today [1888], only a little more so if anything: inevitably, tremendously, yet almost lethargically forceful, like a law of nature. . . . "[5] "The Colonel has a big air about him that discomposes his enemies. . . . he is a dangerous man to meet if you don't want to like him: he overcomes venom—he baffles quibblers."[6]

The *Boston Herald* gives us an excellent picture of the man as he appeared in 1894:

Col. Ingersoll is an inch less than six feet tall, and weighs ten more than two hundred pounds. He will be sixty-one next August, and his hair is snowy. His

[1] From a personal letter. See Rogers, *op. cit.*, p. 293.
[2] Pamphlet, "Unveiling the Statue of Robert G. Ingersoll" (Peoria, Ill., 1911), p. 28.
[3] Horace Traubel, *With Walt Whitman in Camden* (New York, 1908), I, 37.
[4] *Ibid.*, II, 46.
[5] *Ibid.*, III (1914), 54.
[6] *Ibid.*, 241.

shoulders are broad and as straight as they were eighteen years ago when he electrified a people and placed his own name upon the list of a nation's greatest orators
with his matchless "Plumed Knight" speech in nominating James G. Blaine for
the presidency. His blue eyes look straight into yours when he speaks to you, and
his sentences are punctuated by engaging little tricks of facial expression—now the
brow is criss-crossed with the lines of a frown, sometimes quizzical and sometimes
indignant—next, the smooth-shaven lips break into a curving smile, which may
grow into a broad grin if the point just made were a humorous one, and this is quite
likely to be followed by a look of such intense earnestness that you wonder if he
will ever smile again. And all the time his eyes flash, illuminating, sometimes
anticipatory, glances that add immensely to the clearness with which the thought he
is expressing is set before you. . . . His mentality seems to be duplex, quadruplex,
multiplex, if you please. . . . His handclasp is hearty and his manner and words
are the very essence of straight-forward directness. . . . [1]

Judge Andrew Wylie, who presided in the famous Star Route case, said
Ingersoll was the greatest lawyer he had ever met.[2] And Chauncey Depew
said, "I consider Colonel Ingersoll one of the greatest intellects of the
century."[3]

There is no doubt that in his legal pleas, public lectures, and political
addresses Ingersoll was perfectly sincere and terribly in earnest. What he
believed to be the truth moved him, and moved him deeply, and there is
abundant evidence that he refused to speak what he did not believe. It was
reported of him, as of many great lawyers, that he habitually rejected
clients whom he knew to be in the wrong. The *Anaconda Standard*, in
reporting his plea in the Davis Will case (Butte, 1891) said:

If Ingersoll himself is not absolutely convinced that the will is a forgery, he
certainly had the art of making people believe that he was so convinced. He said
he hoped he might never win a case he ought not to win as a matter of right and
justice. The idea which he sought to convey and which he did convey was that he
believed he was right, no matter whether he could make others believe as he did
or not. In that lies Ingersoll's power.[4]

Quite naturally his attacks upon religious dogma aroused the ire of the
clergy, and he was frequently accused of lecturing merely for money, but
the better element among the clergy freely admitted the sincerity of his
agnosticism. It is well known that his refusal to suppress or modify his
criticisms of the church cost him the governorship of Illinois. When a

[1] *Works* XI, 509–512. The editor of the Dresden edition has with apparent honesty inserted
many newspaper reports concerning Ingersoll's speeches. Since most of these could not be
checked at first hand, we are citing some of them here on the authority of the editor.

[2] Rogers, *op. cit.*, p. 239.

[3] *Works*, XI, 505.

[4] *Works*, X, 535.

Kansas City reporter asked him if he enjoyed lecturing, his rather surprising reply was, "Of course I enjoy lecturing. It is a great pleasure to drive the fiend of fear out of the hearts of men, women and children. It is a positive joy to put out the fires of hell."[1] This was in 1884.

It is more difficult to believe that Ingersoll was sincere in some of his campaign utterances, especially in his outrageous waving of the bloody shirt, as in his Indianapolis speech during the Hayes campaign: "Every man that endeavored to tear the old flag from the heaven that it enriches was a Democrat. Every man that tried to destroy this nation was a Democrat. Every enemy this nation has had for twenty years was a Democrat. Every man that shot Union soldiers was a Democrat." And so on for four solid pages. Before dismissing this as mere artificial hysterics concocted for political purposes, one must remember the bitterness that survived the war and consider, also, Ingersoll's passionate love of liberty and his hatred for the cruelty and injustice that he believed had been practiced upon the Negroes. Eight years later he told a reporter that he was in favor of reviving the bloody shirt "just as often as a citizen of the Republic is murdered on account of his politics. If the South is sick of that question, let it stop persecuting men because they are Republicans."[2]

It is significant that he campaigned for the Republican party only when he believed in its candidate and its policies. He delivered one speech for Harrison in 1888 but made it plain that he would have preferred to have the party nominate General Gresham.

His *Manner of Speaking*

It will be at once apparent that these qualities of honest frankness, bold independence, genial vitality, warm human sympathy, and keen wit were important factors in Ingersoll's effectiveness as a speaker. They conditioned his manner of speaking, his choice of ideas, his method of argument, his style, and his influence upon his audiences and upon posterity.

Perhaps the best description of Ingersoll's speaking is that which Hamlin Garland has given us:

He came on the vast stage alone, as I recall the scene, a large man in evening dress, quite bald and smoothly shaven. He began to speak almost before he left the wings, addressing himself to us with colloquial, unaffected directness. I say "to us," for that was precisely the effect he produced. He appeared to be speaking to each one of us individually. His tone was confidential, friendly, and yet authoritative. "Do you know," he began, "that every race has created all its gods and all its devils? The childhood of the race put fairies in the breeze and a kobold in the stream. Every religion began in exactly the same way."

[1] *Works*, VIII, 191.
[2] *Works*, VIII, 190.

These were not his exact words, of course, but such was the manner of his beginning. The stage was bare and he had no manuscript. Standing with his hands clasped behind his back, and speaking without effort, he made his words clear to every auditor. I was not especially concerned with his religious antagonism, but I enjoyed the beauty of his phrasing and the almost unequaled magic of his voice. He was a master of colloquial speech. Unlike Lowell, he eyed us, and laughed at us and with us. He bantered us, challenged us, electrified us. At times his eloquence held us silent as images and then some witty turn, some humorous phrase, brought roars of applause. At times we cheered almost every sentence like delegates at a political convention. At other moments we rose in our seats and yelled. There was something hypnotic in his rhythm as well as in his marvelous lines like a Saxon minstrel. His power over his auditors was absolute. His voice had no melody such as that of Booth possessed, but he had the singular power of making me oblivious of its quality. In the march of his ideas, in the pictures he drew, I forgot his bald head and his husky voice. As he spoke, all barriers between his mind and mine vanished. His effect on his hearers was magical, but the magic lay in his choice of words, rather than in beautiful enunciation.

As I studied him I came to the conclusion that a large part of his power lay in the fact that he vitalized every word, every syllable. He thought each sentence out at the moment he gave it utterance. He was alive to the tip of his tongue. He did not permit his organs of speech to proceed mechanically. He remained in control. . . .

He taught me the value of speaking as if thinking out loud. After hearing him, the harsh, monotonous cadences of other orators became a weariness.[1]

But he did not always speak without a manuscript. In this matter his practice varied. To a reporter who inquired as to his method of preparation he replied, "Sometimes, and frequently, I deliver a lecture several times before it is written. I have it taken by a shorthand writer, and afterward written out. At other times I have dictated a lecture, and delivered it from manuscript. The course pursued depends on how I happen to feel at the time. Sometimes I read a lecture, and sometimes I deliver lectures without any notes—this, again, depending much on how I happen to feel at the time."[2]

The speech at his brother's grave was read from manuscript, probably because he did not trust himself to speak extempore. His speech nominating Blaine for the Presidency was written out in the dead of night in his hotel room only a few hours before it was delivered and apparently was committed to memory.

There is, however, no indication that he ever allowed a manuscript to get in his way. The quality of direct personal communication that Garland

[1] *Roadside Meetings* (New York, 1930), p. 44.
[2] *Works*, VIII, 542.

felt was apparently noticed by all who heard Ingersoll, whether he did or did not have a manuscript before him.

Ingersoll had a remarkable memory, and quite naturally, after the third or fourth delivery of a lecture, he would need no notes to guide him. Quite naturally, also, the wording would vary considerably in successive deliveries of a speech, and newspaper reports of his lectures show many wide departures in style and arrangement from the text of his printed manuscripts.

Reporting his address to the jury in the Munn trial, the *Chicago Times* stated, "Colonel Ingersoll never troubles himself to take notes of anything. What he can not recollect he does not have any use for."[1] But in more complicated cases he did of necessity take notes and use them in speaking.

His manner before a jury is well described by the *Anaconda Standard* in reporting his address to the jury in the Davis Will case, tried in Butte, Mont.:

> Ingersoll stepped up to the jurors as near as he could get and kept slowly walking up and down before them. At times he would single out a single juryman, stop in front of him, gaze steadily into his face and direct his remarks for a minute or two to that one man alone. Again he would turn and address himself to Senator Sanders [opposing counsel], Judge Dixon or somebody else of those interested in establishing the will as genuine. At times the gravity of the jury and the audience was so completely upset that Judge McHatton had to rap for order, but presently the Colonel would change his mood and the audience would be hushed into deepest silence.[2]

There was apparently an infectious quality in Ingersoll's eloquence that tinctured even the reports of newspapermen who covered his speeches. Typical of these is the *Chicago Times* report of his speech nominating Blaine. But though somewhat poetical, it gives a good description of his eloquence and its effect. Ingersoll, we are told, "waited with unimpaired serenity" for the subsidence of the bedlam occasioned by the prospect of Blaine's nomination.[3]

> And then began an appeal, impassioned, artful, brilliant and persuasive. . . . Its effect was indescribable. The coolest-headed in the hall were stirred to the wildest expression. The adversaries of Blaine, as well as his friends, listened with unswerving, absorbed attention. [George William] Curtis sat spell-bound, his eyes and mouth wide open, his figure moving in unison to the tremendous periods that fell in a measured, exquisitely graduated flow from the Illinoisan's smiling lips. . . .
> Words can do but meagre justice to the wizard power of this extraordinary man. He swayed and moved and impelled and restrained and worked in all ways with the mass before him as if he possessed some key to the innermost mechanism that moves the human heart, and when he finished, his fine, frank face as calm as

[1] *Works*, X, 7.
[2] *Works*, X, 535.
[3] *Works*, IX, 56.

when he began, the overwrought thousands sank back in an exhaustion of unspeakable wonder and delight.

Some of this same enthusiasm must have affected the reporter for the *Chicago Inter-Ocean* twenty years later, in reporting his campaign speech for McKinley.

The old warhorse, silvered by long years of faithful service to his country, aroused the same all-pervading enthusiasm as he did in the campaigns of Grant, Hayes, and Garfield.

He has lost not one whit, not one iota of his striking physical presence, his profound reasoning, his convincing logic, his rollicking wit, grandiloquence—in fine, all the graces of the orator of old, reenforced by increased patriotism and the ardor of the call to battle for his country, are still his in the fullest measure.[1]

A more specific account of Ingersoll's delivery of this speech (delivered in both Chicago and New York) is supplied by Kittredge, who heard it in New York. The orator, he says, raised his hand to still the applause that greeted his appearance.

When, after several minutes, all ears were stopped with oppressive silence, and he felt that all eyes were centered upon him, he said: "Ladies and Gentlemen: This is *our* country. The legally expressed will of the majority is the supreme law of the land. *We* are responsible for what our government does. We cannot excuse ourselves because of the act of some king, or the opinions of nobles. *We* are the kings. *We* are the nobles. *We* are the aristocracy of America, and when our government does *right* we are honored, and when our government does *wrong* the brand of shame is on the American brow."[2]

He had spoken only a few minutes, says Kittredge, when he began to indulge his habit of walking slowly, leisurely from side to side. In almost the first of his trips he encountered the speaker's stand. Seizing it with his own hands, he carried it several paces toward the back of the stage. "This afforded the free field which was so essentially a part of his theory and practice of oratory." At one point in his address he paused suddenly and with a look of earnest appeal to his audience exclaimed, "Oh, I forgot to ask the question, 'If the government can make money why should it collect taxes?'"

It is apparent that Ingersoll had learned early in his career to capitalize the unique power of his personality. If even half the stories of his charm are true, it must have been very difficult for any audience that had fallen under the spell of his radiant geniality to disagree with him. And though he frequently warned his hearers to free themselves from their emotions and to

[1] *Works*, IX, 535.
[2] *Op. cit.*, pp. 187–189.

follow reason, he was apparently aware that the heat of his conviction and the charm of his personality were powerful engines of persuasion.

His speeches abound with passages whose effectiveness seems to lie chiefly in the powerful expression of his own magnificent ethos. In the well-known vision at the tomb of Napoleon is such a passage.[1] After brief pictures of the various steps in Napoleon's career, he says:

I thought of the orphans and widows he had made. . . . And I said I would rather have been a French peasant and worn wooden shoes. I would rather have lived in a hut with a vine growing over the door, and the grapes growing purple in the kisses of the autumn sun. . . . I would rather have been that man and gone down to the tongueless silence of the dreamless dust, than to have been that imperial impersonation of force and murder, known as "Napoleon the Great."

In another lecture he asks, "Do you tell me that God can be unpitying to the pitiful, that he can be unforgiving to the forgiving? I deny it; and from the aspersions of the pulpit I seek to rescue the reputation of the Deity."[2] A little later in reference to Christ's declaration that those who did not believe would be damned, he cried, "That passage contradicts the Sermon on the Mount; travesties the Lord's prayer; turns the splendid religion of deed and duty into the superstition of creed and cruelty. I deny it. It is infamous! Christ never said it!"

One of the most potent weapons in his attack on the clergy and their frightful creeds was this vehement assertion of his own moral superiority over them. In his "Mistakes of Moses" he says, "We are told in the Pentateuch, that God, the father of us all, gave thousands of maidens, after having killed their fathers, their mothers, and their brothers, to satisfy the brutal lusts of savage men. If there be a God, I pray him to write in his book, opposite my name, that I denied this lie for him."[3]

Less dramatically and less vehemently he capitalizes his personality in a campaign speech for Garfield: "I say to you tonight that there is not in this Nation, there is not in this Republic a man with greater brain and greater heart than James A. Garfield. I know him and I like him. I know him as well as any other public man, and I like him."[4]

He had a clear understanding of the relation of delivery to content. In this as in other matters he apparently followed a conscious method, evolved from his own experience (for he seems to have made no formal study of oratory). When asked what advice he would give to a young man who was ambitious to become a successful speaker, he replied:

[1] *Works*, I, 370.
[2] *Works*, I, 470.
[3] *Works*, II, 254-255.
[4] *Works*, IX, 397.

In the first place, I would advise him to have something to say—something worth saying—something that people will be glad to hear. This is the important thing. Back of the art of speaking must be the power to think. Without thought words are empty purses. Most people imagine that almost any words uttered in a loud voice and accompanied by appropriate gestures, constitute an oration. I would advise the young man to study his subject, to find what others had thought, to look at it from all sides. Then I would tell him to write out his thoughts or to arrange them in his mind, so that he would know exactly what he was going to say. Waste no time on the how until you are satisfied with the what. After you know what you are to say, then you can think of how it should be said. Then you can think about tone, emphasis, and gesture; but if you really understand what you say, emphasis, tone, and gesture will take care of themselves. All these should come from the inside. They should be in perfect harmony with the feelings. Voice and gesture should be governed by the emotions. They should unconsciously be in perfect agreement with the sentiments. The orator should be true to his subject, should avoid any reference to himself.

The great column of his argument should be unbroken. He can adorn it with vines and flowers, but they should not be in such profusion as to hide the column. He should give variety of episode by illustrations, but they should be used only for the purpose of adding strength to the argument. The man who wishes to become an orator should study language. He should know the deeper meaning of words. He should understand the vigor and velocity of verbs and the color of adjectives. He should know how to sketch a scene, to paint a picture, to give life and action. He should be a poet and a dramatist, a painter and an actor. He should cultivate his imagination. He should become familiar with the great poetry and fiction, with splendid and heroic deeds. He should be a student of Shakespeare. He should read and devour the great plays. From Shakespeare he could learn the art of expression, of compression, and all the secrets of the head and heart. . . .

After some comment on Beecher, Parker, Webster, Clay, Benton, Calhoun, Kossuth, and Prentiss, most of whom he had not heard, he continued:

In my judgment, Corwin was the greatest orator of them all. He had more arrows in his quiver. He had genius. He was full of humor, pathos, wit, and logic. He was an actor. His body talked. His meaning was in his eyes and lips. . . . Lincoln had reason, wonderful humor, and wit, but his presence was not good. His voice was poor, his gestures awkward—but his thoughts were profound. His speech at Gettysburg was one of the masterpieces of the world. The word "here" is used four or five times too often. Leave the "heres" out, and the speech is perfect.[1]

This interview was reported in the *New York Sun* in 1898, a year before Ingersoll's death, and so represents his mature thought, ripened by years of experience. Every statement he makes about oratorical method could be illustrated from his own practice.

[1] *Works*, VIII, 594–599.

His Ideas

In considering Ingersoll's ideas and their sources we need not pay much attention to his legal pleas, the materials for which were necessarily drawn from the case under consideration. That he was eminent and highly successful in his profession there can be no doubt. Some religious bias may have influenced the opinion of the *Outlook* (edited by the Reverend Lyman Abbott) that though he was an effective jury lawyer and popular campaign orator, "he was eminent neither as a legal nor as a political advisor."[1] When Henry W. Scott assembled a volume of studies of distinguished lawyers, he said that to omit Ingersoll from the list "would be an omission verging upon culpability" and that "his practice ranks in magnitude with the greatest in the country."[2] But while he was a keen reasoner and a powerful advocate before a jury, he probably contributed nothing of value to the interpretation of law in the broader sense. Worth noting, however, are his occasional eloquent pleas for liberty and toleration.

Ingersoll's eulogies, like elegies, are concerned chiefly with generalities and are dependent for their effect largely upon a poetic style. In his panegyric on Roscoe Conkling, for instance, he praises intelligence, integrity, and courage with little specific reference to their exemplification in his protagonist's deeds. Much of his argument is based upon pungent aphorisms of his own coining, such as, "Charity should hold the scales in which are weighed the deeds of men," "Fortunate is that nation great enough to know the great," "Nothing is more despicable than to reach fame by crawling," and, "We rise by raising others—and he who stoops above the fallen, stands erect."

In his tribute to Anton Seidl, the orchestra conductor, delivered at a banquet in his honor, he tells how he first discovered Robert Burns in the hands of a Scottish shoemaker and Shakespeare in the hands of an old man in a small Illinois hotel. He tells of the powerful effect these two poets had upon him throughout his life, owns a similar indebtedness to Rembrandt, Wagner, and the sculptor of the "Venus de Milo," and then praises Seidl as the greatest interpreter of Wagner.

Since Ingersoll was never a member of any legislative body, one must find his views on social and political questions chiefly in his occasional addresses, interviews, and campaign speeches. "I will follow my logic," he once said, "no matter where it goes, after it has consulted with my heart." But on most questions his views were apparently dictated by his heart. He opposed vivisection, favored decent hours and wages for labor, greater diffusion of wealth, reform of penal institutions, equal rights for Negroes,

[1] July 29, 1899.
[2] *Distinguished American Lawyers* (New York, 1891), p. 473.

easy divorce for women, and birth control to prevent unwanted children, but he waged no active campaign for any of these reforms. He was for annexing the Philippines "only if the Philippines want us." His political speeches supported the policies of the Republican party—resumption of specie payments, coercion of the South, sound money, and a protective tariff. And always he waved the bloody shirt. He was unable to rise above the political prejudices of his time. His argument for the tariff was merely the conventional one. His heart bleeds for the Negro, but he has no pity for the sufferings of the South under Reconstruction. He abhors war but apparently falls a ready victim to Hearst's propaganda for a war with Spain, influenced partly by a belief that Spain was a barbarous country dominated by heartless and ignorant priests. It is only fair to say that Ingersoll was not a statesman. He made no contribution to political thought.

The best of Ingersoll's thought is in his lectures. These show the breadth of his reading and the acuteness of his thinking. There are forty or more addresses that may be classified as lectures—addresses carefully prepared and intended for a general audience. Some were prepared for special occasions and delivered only once, but most of them were delivered many times, some of them in all parts of the United States. The first, on "Progress," was delivered in 1860; the last, on "What Is Religion?" in 1899. Seven have as their subjects the achievements of great men: Humboldt, Thomas Paine, Robert Burns, Shakespeare, Walt Whitman ("Liberty in Literature"), Lincoln, and Voltaire. Several others are patriotic addresses. Twenty-two or more are criticisms of orthodox Christianity, and it is for these that Ingersoll is best known.

Since in considering his lectures we shall be chiefly concerned with his antireligious thought, it will be well to give the dates and titles of the principal lectures that deal with this subject: 1872, "The Gods"; 1873, "Individuality"; 1874, "Heretics and Heresies"; 1877, "The Liberty of Man, Woman and Child"; "The Ghosts"; "My Reviewers Reviewed"; 1879, "Some Mistakes of Moses"; 1880, "What Must We Do to Be Saved?"; 1881, "Some Reasons Why"; "The Great Infidels"; 1884, "Orthodoxy"; "Which Way?"; 1885, "Myth and Miracle"; 1886, "A Lay Sermon"; 1894, "About the Holy Bible"; 1895, "The Foundations of Faith"; 1896, "Why I Am an Agnostic"; 1897, "The Truth," "A Thanksgiving Sermon"; 1898, "Superstition"; 1899, "The Devil"; "What Is Religion?"

Newspapers of the time report other lectures, under such titles as "Skulls," "Intellectual Development," "Hereafter," "Hell," and "Human Rights." These, when examined, prove to be merely duplicates, variations, or combinations of those above. Ingersoll generally spoke from memory, extemporized freely, and kept his thought constantly alive. Quite naturally he would depart from the text of his written lecture as the spirit moved him and at times mixed one lecture with another. There is, however, no ground for accepting as true the charge of some of the more violent clergy that he gave the same lecture under various titles in order to deceive his audiences and make them believe they were getting something new.

But it is true that he used more than once certain phrases, passages, and illustrations that he had found to be effective. And his lecture on Voltaire repeats verbatim some ten pages from "The Great Infidels," first delivered 13 years earlier. Considering the quantity of his work, the wonder is that there are not more such repetitions.

Harry Emerson Fosdick says that there is "a constant, consistent, and logical kinship between thoroughgoing irreligion and lowered enthusiasm about life." In Ingersoll's case nothing could be further from the truth. He radiated vitality, warmth, and joy. Indeed, it was this very warmth of his nature that made him revolt against religious dogma and practice. He found the religion of his day depressing, cruel, superstitious, intolerant, and ignorant. Even as a boy he rebelled against the barbarities of Jehovah, and this flame of indignation, nourished later by his reading of Paine and Voltaire and other infidel writers, burned steadily to the day of his death.

Ingersoll's schooling was of the most meager sort; but he had a keen, logical mind, and he repaired the defects of his schooling by deep and wide reading in literature, in philosophy, in theology, in the history of the religions of the world, and in science. Especially was he influenced by Humboldt, Darwin, Spencer, Huxley, and Haeckel.[1] And all that he read confirmed the early impulse of his heart that Christianity was a myth and all religion mere ignorant superstition.

Nothing could be wider of the mark than the charge of some of his critics that he was a wicked man who wished to destroy religion so that he could be unrestrained in his wickedness. But he preached the doctrine of good living —and practiced it, as his stout figure testified. He opposed religion because he found it immoral. Constantly he sets up a higher morality than that of the Bible and its interpreters. He is more forgiving than God—more just, more merciful. "I am told," he says, "that I must render good for evil. I am told that if smitten on one cheek I must turn the other. I am told that I must overcome evil with good, I am told that I must love my enemies; and will it do for this God who tells me to love my enemies to damn his? No, it will not do. It will not do."

At other times he is the defender of God against his orthodox detractors. "I insist" he says, "that the real God, if there is one, never commanded

---

[1] "Why I Am an Agnostic" contains the story of his education. See *Works*, Vol. IV.

man to enslave his fellow-man, never told a mother to sell her babe, never established polygamy, never urged one nation to exterminate another, and never told a husband to kill his wife because she suggested the worship of another God. From the aspersions of the pulpit, from the slanders of the church, I seek to rescue the reputation of the Deity." Though he classified himself as an infidel, he did not specifically deny the existence of God. In later life, after Huxley had invented and popularized the word *agnostic*, he described himself as an agnostic. He hoped for immortality but insisted that no one had or could have any certainty of it and vehemently denied that priests had any knowledge about it. "The clergy know," he said, "that I know that they know that they do not know."

His essential objection to the Old Testament is that its God is cruel, barbarous, petty, and evil. He is especially revolted by Jehovah's encouragement of slavery and polygamy. The account of creation he dismisses as utterly unscientific. He ridicules the miracles and narrations and shows that, judged by the record, the God of orthodox teaching is neither infinite nor good. His essential objection to the New Testament is that it teaches the doctrine of eternal punishment. "This dogma of hell is the infinite of savagery—the dream of insane revenge. It makes God a wild beast, an infinite hyena. It makes Christ as merciless as the fangs of a viper." He objects also to the doctrine that salvation depends upon credulity and belief, instead of upon goodness, and insists that the atonement is immoral in that it allows those who do wrong to escape and punishes the innocent Christ instead. In later life he came to believe that the passages in which Christ demanded belief as a condition of salvation and consigned all unbelievers to hell were interpolated by the church. In "What Must We Do to Be Saved?" he goes through the gospels one by one, reading all the statements in which Christ teaches unselfishness, good works, forgiveness, etc., and pronounces after each a hearty "Good. I accept that doctrine. That suits me." But when he finds a threat of hell-fire for those who do not believe, he exclaims, "I deny it. Christ never said it."

In several lectures he paints moving pictures of the horrors of religious persecution, all traceable to this, to him, perverted doctrine that men must believe as the church tells them to. And he insists that no man is responsible for his beliefs, that every man believes as he must, and so it is both wrong and futile to punish him for his beliefs. This psychological or metaphysical determinism he carried to absurd extremes, for it led him to admit that criminals, religious persecutors, orthodox clergymen, Southern rebels, and Northern Democrats all believed as they must and behaved as they must, and yet he went right on condemning them for their beliefs and behavior. This was one of the weakest points in his armor, though it was never successfully probed by his opponents.

377

Indeed *none* of his arguments seems to have been very effectively answered and perhaps none could be answered on purely logical grounds. Many of his views were accepted and defended by the more liberal clergy, and one finds it difficult to discover in them anything that would now be thought evil by an intelligent churchman. He vehemently denied the accusation that his teachings were merely critical and destructive. Always he preached (and practiced) the tenderest sympathy for the poor and the unfortunate. He taught the blessedness of home and fireside. He glorified love. He idolized liberty. He believed the world would be "saved," or perfected, by man's efforts through science. Surely these are generally admitted "good's." Why, then, did his lectures stir up such a torrent of hatred, vituperation, and abuse? Perhaps the answer is to be found in his method of argument.

His Method of Argument

Ingersoll was "no respecter of parsons." Neither was he a respecter of the forms, traditions, and beliefs that the church held sacred. Against the religious dogma and practice of his day he let loose a terrific blast of coarse common sense. A sympathetic critic, writing in 1882, when Ingersoll's reputation was at its height, said, "He seems to take peculiar delight in shocking the religious sensibilities of his audiences by speaking of the most solemn subjects in the rudest and coarsest language of jest and buffoonery." Is he satisfied, the critic asked, to "make the galleries ring with cheers whenever he descends to rude jest, or coarse buffoonery, or bitter vituperation? We believe his aims and his purposes are far nobler and far higher than this; but, at the same time, we believe he has adopted methods that can never lead to their accomplishment."[1]

Another critic, writing 10 years after his death, deplores the lack of judicial quality in his mind and his want of reverence. "It will always remain a ground for just criticism of Mr. Ingersoll," he says, "that in the treatment of sacred things he was irreverent and flippant."[2]

Ingersoll had three chief weapons of argument: ridicule, appeal to reason, and vehement assertion. Perhaps the greatest of these was ridicule. While his ridicule took various forms and was often keenly and wittily ironic, it must not be overlooked that at other times it took the form of withering sarcasm, intolerant invective, and vulgar abuse.

He enjoyed applause and was apparently carried away by it at times and lapsed into the coarse language of the rough-and-tumble political and legal debates of the prairie—a language seldom found in the manuscripts he

[1] William Myall, *International Review*, March, 1882, pp. 229, 230.
[2] J. T. Sunderland, *The Arena*, January, 1909, p. 298.

prepared for publication. Here, for example, is a newspaper account of his reply to a preacher who had falsely accused him of encouraging obscenity:

When Cook made that statement he wrote across his reputation the word liar. When he said that he knew he lied willfully and malignantly, and every man who repeated the slander knew that he lied, and every religious editor who put it into his paper knew that he lied. With one or two exceptions I never knew an honest editor of a religious paper. . . . Men who are trying to blacken my reputation are not fit to blacken my shoes. It is one of my arguments against a personal God that such men exist; an infinitely wise God would never have produced them.

In one of his political addresses he said, "I have been reading some Democratic papers today, and you would say that every one of their editors had a private sewer of his own (Laughter) into which had been emptied for a hundred years the slops of hell. (Laughter and applause)." Of Samuel J. Tilden he said, "He never gave birth to an elevated, noble sentiment in his life. He is a kind of legal spider, watching in a web of technicalities for victims. He is a compound of cunning and heartlessness—of beak and claw and fang." And he said of William Jennings Bryan, "When Major McKinley was fighting under the flag, Bryan was in his mother's arms, and judging from his speeches he ought to be there still. What is he? He is a populist. . . . His brain is filled with vagaries. A fiat money man. His brain is an insane asylum without a keeper."

Somewhat more refined is his satirical treatment of Genesis:

We read that our first parents were placed in a pleasant garden; that they were given the full run of the place and only forbidden to meddle with the orchard; that they were tempted as God knew they were to be tempted; that they fell as God knew they would fall, and that for this fall which he knew would happen before he made them he fixed the curse of original sin upon them, to be continued to all their children. Why didn't he stop right there? Why didn't he kill Adam and Eve and make another pair who didn't like apples? Then when he brought his flood why did he rescue eight people if their descendants were to be so totally depraved and wicked? Why didn't he have his flood first and then drown the devil? (Laughter) That would have solved the problem, and he could then have tried experiments unmolested.

Typical of his satire at its best is this treatment of predestination: "The fact is that if you believe in an infinite God, and also in eternal punishment, then you must admit that Edwards and Calvin were absolutely right. There is no escape from their conclusions if you admit their premises. They were infinitely cruel, their premises infinitely absurd, their God infinitely fiendish, and their logic perfect."

Ingersoll's appeal to reason is often very definitely an appeal. It is addressed to his hearers in the form of questions. It is based not on authority but on common sense. His premises are commonly accepted facts, beliefs, and feelings. And always he insists upon the supremacy of reason over faith, mysticism, and authority.

In many of his arguments there is apparent the method of the trial lawyer. He examines the evidence minutely, concentrates on vulnerable points, pounces upon absurdities and contradictions, and addresses his hearers as if they were a jury from whom a verdict was expected. Sometimes he uses the pattern of a dramatic narrative and cross-examines his opponents as if they were witnesses, as in this passage:

> The other day a young gentleman—a Presbyterian who had just been converted —came to convert me. (Shouts of Laughter) He gave me a tract and told me that he was perfectly happy. Humph! (Laughter) Said I, "Do you think a great many people are going to hell?" "O yes." "And you are perfectly happy?" Well, he didn't know as he was quite. (Laughter) "Wouldn't you be happier if they were all going to heaven?" "O, yes." "Well, then you are not perfectly happy?" No, he didn't think he was. (Laughter) Said I: "When you go to heaven you will be perfectly happy?" "Oh, my! yes." "Now, when we are only going to hell you are not quite happy, but when we are in hell and you are in heaven then you will be perfectly happy. You won't be as decent when you are an angel as you are now, will you?" (Laughter)

Sometimes the effectiveness of Ingersoll's argument seems to depend chiefly upon a vehement assertion of his own feelings and beliefs—assertions repeated and amplified with cumulative force. He is a master of the art of development by amplification. The units of development are short, meaty phrases or sentences, all similar in structure. He piles up particulars until they make a mountain of evidence. The amazing fertility of his mind supplies him with an endless chain of facts, reasons, examples, illustrations, and details, and when these are combined with repeated assertions of his own feelings and convictions the argument moves and grows with overwhelming power.

Ingersoll's speeches have no uniform plan of organization. Often they seem to have no plan at all but merely to follow a loose chain of association, and this is especially true in the speeches as reported by the newspapers. Gladstone noted this incoherence. He said, "Colonel Ingersoll writes with a rare and enviable brilliancy, but also with an impetus which he seems unable to control. The paper, noteworthy as it is, leaves on my mind the impression of a battle-field where every man strikes at every man, and all is noise, hurry, and confusion."[1] But this tumultuous method, or lack of method, is not characteristic of all Ingersoll's speeches. Some are strictly coherent and logically developed, with transitions clearly indicated.

[1] See *Works*, VI, 223, 224. The Ingersoll-Black-Field-Gladstone controversy, first published in the *North American Review*, is included in this volume of Ingersoll's *Works*.

There is seldom anything that might be called a formal introduction. The speaker merely begins on his subject, usually with a general statement, as, "Religion makes enemies instead of friends." "Happiness is the true end and aim of life." "For the most part we inherit our opinions." Or, "An honest God is the noblest work of man."

His perorations seemed to have received careful attention, and some of them are worked out into elaborate patterns, and rise to the heights of eloquence. "The Liberty of Man, Woman, and Child" ends with a brilliant apostrophe to liberty. "The Ghosts" concludes with the carefully designed sentence, "Let them cover their eyeless sockets with their fleshless hands and fade for ever from the imaginations of men." In "Which Way?" he closes with a highly imaginative picture of the past, ending with, "This was," then a description of the present, ending with, "This is," and finally a prophetic vision of the future, ending with, "This will be." Nearly always his conclusions are hopeful or hortatory in tone. His political speeches conclude with a prophecy of victory for his candidate and his legal pleas with faith that the jury will decide for his client.

His Style

Herman E. Kittredge well says that Ingersoll, "more perhaps than any other orator or writer that we know, put his personality into his lines. His style . . . is utterly unique. Should one of his marvellous pages, separated from its context, be found in the sands of Sahara, its author would be instantly recognizable."[1] The qualities that make his style unique are perhaps best defined as clarity and energy, and after these, what James Redpath called "an Oriental style of rhetoric," which, he said, characterized even his most familiar conversations. Hamlin Garland says that 40 years after he heard Ingersoll speak he reread his speeches and found them still "well written and vibrant. Only last summer," he continues, "I read one of them to an audience of young people of literary training, and its English, crisp and clear and vital as when I first heard it forty years ago, aroused the applause of my auditors."[2]

Ingersoll is never obscure. It is doubtful whether a person of average intelligence would find in all his writings a single sentence that required for its understanding a second reading. His is preeminently a spoken rather than a written style. He is always conscious of his audience—and of their limited intelligence, their inability to follow long chains of argument. His sentences are brief, terse, and simple. They rarely have anything like Latinized balance or Johnsonian elegance, but they do not stutter or hesitate. They pour forth as from an exhaustless fountain. The clarity of his

[1] "Ingersoll as an Idealist," *The Arena*, 31: 245.
[2] *Op. cit.*

own mind and the simple directness of his thought made him impatient with the ambiguities and circumlocutions of some of the creeds he criticized. He scolds Gladstone for his obscurity as if he had been a schoolboy: "If you knew the trouble I have had in finding out your meaning, from your words, you would pardon me for calling attention to a single line from Aristotle: 'Clearness is the virtue of style.'"[1]

He was a master of exposition, and his discussions of sound money, resumption of specie payments, and the protective tariff are classics of lucid explanation. In many instances his fluency, clarity, and vigor of expression are enhanced by repetitions of phrase patterns that run to remarkable length. In one passage twenty-three successive sentences begin with *I see*. In another, fourteen consecutive phrases begin with the word *free*. And nearly always his clarity and energy are natural and unforced, proceeding from a clear mind and strong emotions.

But though all his writings have a characteristic style, it must not be inferred that that style is uniform or in any sense monotonous. He shifts constantly from assertion to question, from narrative to argument, from humor to pathos, from indignation to tenderness, from invective to praise. Like Demosthenes he was a master of all styles and varied them consciously in the interest of liveliness.

Doubtless Ingersoll is chiefly remembered for his occasional flights of poetic imagination. Some of these, notably his soliloquy at the tomb of Napoleon and his "Vision of War," have become classics of schoolboy declamation. And while it is the fashion of the present age to scorn such flowery effusions, there is little doubt that if well spoken they are still both moving and beautiful. Such passages occur frequently in Ingersoll's speeches, sometimes seeming to be little interludes that break the continuity of his argument and sometimes firmly woven into his thought. Though his poetic imagination was capable of throwing off spontaneously the most brilliant metaphors, it is likely that these extended "purple patches" were consciously designed and carefully composed. Most of them, perhaps unintentionally, fall into poetic rhythms, some having definite runs of blank verse. Here is a picture of autumn from "The Ghosts," as arranged by Kittredge.

> The withered banners of the corn are still,
> And gathered fields are growing strangely wan,
> While death, poetic death,
> With hands that color what they touch,

[1] This may indicate that he knew Aristotle's *Rhetoric*. Thomas Huxley wrote him concerning Gladstone's reply, "Gladstone's attack on you is one of the best things he has written. I do not think there is fifty per cent more verbiage than necessary, nor any sentence with more than two meanings." See Rogers, *op. cit.*, p. 252.

Weaves in the autumn wood
Her tapestries of gold and brown.

Ingersoll deeply loved the works of Burns and Shakespeare, and the influence of the latter can be easily inferred from the passage just quoted. Much of his imagery is suggestive of Shakespeare, though it is never directly borrowed from him. But he was also a lover of Walt Whitman, and sometimes his poetic passages are suggestive of *Leaves of Grass*, for example, this one, as arranged by Hamlin Garland:

Strike with the hand of fire, O weird musician, thy harp
Strung with Apollo's golden hair;
Blow, Bugler, blow till thy exalted notes
Do touch and kiss the moonlit waves
And startle the lovers wandering amid the vine-clad hills.
Fill the vast cathedral aisles with thy sweet symphonies
Hushed and dim, deft toucher of the organ's keys;
But know, thy sweetest music
All is discord compared to childhood's happy laugh,
The laugh which fills the eyes with light
And the very heart with joy.
Oh, rippling river of laughter, thou
Art the blessed boundary line ·
Betwixt the beasts and men
And every wayward wave of thine
Doth drown some fretful fiend of care.[1]

We may, if we wish, deprecate this as mere maudlin sentimentality, but there is no doubt that to Ingersoll it was deep and sincere sentiment.

Ingersoll's metaphors are nearly always clear, fresh, true, and unhackneyed. They seem to arise spontaneously from a vivid imagination and heated passions or from a characteristic blending in him of what he would have called "heart and brain." But his style was not, of course, consistently poetic, and before an audience he frequently descended to the commonest colloquialisms.

Ingersoll's style, then, like his manner of speaking, his choice of ideas, and his method of argument, is at every point determined by his personality. Of him, more than of any other orator, perhaps, it may be said that his speeches were shaped and colored and limited by what he was—by his vibrant vitality, his keen lawyer's mind, his deep manly feeling, his unyielding honesty, his reckless irreverence, and his love of humanity, beauty, and truth.

[1] *Op. cit.* The official text varies considerably from Garland's version. Perhaps he was quoting from memory. See *Works*, I, 382.

His Influence

Professor Lionel Crocker has pointed out in some detail the influence of Ingersoll's style and delivery upon such later speakers as Beveridge, La Follette, and Darrow and has shown how that influence is continued down to the present in the quotations from his speeches included in modern textbooks on public speaking.[1] It may be well to point out that this influence, exerted directly through his speeches, or more indirectly through their publication in hundreds of newspapers, in "books for the trade," and, though generally abbreviated, in current textbooks, has reached thousands upon thousands of lawyers, preachers, politicians, teachers, and other speakers and students of speaking. Nearly always Ingersoll's style has been admired, and what men admire they are prone to imitate. Somewhat too extravagant is Kittredge's statement: "Preeminently the word wizard of his century, the whole of rhetoric was rejuvenated by his genius."[2] But certainly his style has the *power* to rejuvenate rhetoric, especially if it is studied not so much for its poetic beauty as for its remarkable vitality and perspicuity. It is well to note also Kittredge's statement, "He was preeminently the teacher of the masses. Farmers, mechanics, laborers, used to say, on hearing his explanation of a political or economic question, 'Well, I understand that *now.*'"[3]

Ingersoll's influence in politics was strong while it lasted. There is no doubt that he was a powerful influence in the election of three Republican presidents—which may, or may not, have been a contribution to the common good. His chief influence, however, must be sought in the field of religion.

Beyond question he was a thorn in the side of the orthodox church. Thousands of sermons were preached against him, and numerous books and magazine articles attempted to refute or belittle him. Upon his death enterprising newspaper editors canvassed the clergy for their opinions of him, drawing from most a sigh of relief, well expressed in the statement of one minister, "That's the last of the Infidel!" Typical of the more uncharitable comments was one that appeared in *Catholic World:* "He had a tenth-rate intellect, much inferior to that of Tom Paine or of Voltaire, whom he affected to imitate. . . . Nothing that he ever wrote or said will live a decade."[4] And the *Outlook* stated, "Probably no man of commensurate

---

[1] "Robert Green Ingersoll's Influence on American Oratory," *The Quarterly Journal of Speech*, 24 (1938): 299–312.

[2] "Ingersoll as an Idealist," *The Arena*, 31: 246.

[3] *Ingersoll: A Biographical Appreciation* (New York, 1911), p. 514.

[4] 49: 790.

power has had less real influence on the religious and ethical thought of America."[1]

More liberal and less prejudiced observers, however, pretty generally believed that he would be remembered and that he exerted a very real influence upon religious thought. They believed, as Ingersoll himself believed, that he had liberalized religious teaching, freed the church from superstition, taught it to be more tolerant, and led it to emphasize Christian morality rather than orthodox dogma. More than one minister conceded that he had been one of the church's best friends, that, as Charles Frederick Adams said, instead of being an enemy of religion, Ingersoll "was one of its greatest champions and its truest friends."

This influence is well stated by Elbert Hubbard.[2] After citing the growth in liberality, toleration, and honesty of thought during the preceding twenty-five years, he says;

Let us acknowledge that this revolution in thought . . . was brought about mainly by one individual [Ingersoll]. . . . Through his influence the tears of pity put out the fires of hell. This man, more than any other of his century, made the clergy free. He raised the standard of intelligence in both pew and pulpit, and the preachers who denounced him most, often were, and are, the most benefited by his work. . . . He shamed men into sanity. . . . The history of America's thought evolution can never be written and the name of Ingersoll left out. . . . He prepared the way for the thinkers and the doers who shall come after him, reaching spiritual heights which he, perhaps, could never attain. This earth is a better place, and life and liberty are safer, because Robert G. Ingersoll lived.

SELECTED BIBLIOGRAPHY

Complete Lectures of Col. R. G. Ingersoll, published for the trade, n. d., no place or publisher; newspaper reports of the speeches; no pagination in some editions.
Mistakes of Ingersoll, and His Answers Complete, J. B. McClure, ed., Chicago, Rhodes and McClure Publishing Co., 1892.
The Works of Robert G. Ingersoll, Dresden ed., C. P. Farrell, ed., 12 vols., New York, The Dresden Publishing Co., 1900.

Brann, Henry A.: "Robert Ingersoll," *Catholic World,* 69 (1899): 787–790.
"Death of Robert G. Ingersoll," *Public Opinion,* 27 (1899): 106.
Garland, Hamlin: *Roadside Meetings,* New York, The Macmillan Company, 1930, pp. 42–54.
Hubbard, Elbert: *Little Journeys to the Homes of Eminent Orators,* New York, G. P. Putnam's Sons, 1903, pp. 301–358.
Kittredge, Herman E.: *Ingersoll: A Biographical Appreciation,* New York, The Dresden Publishing Co., 1911.
——: "Ingersoll as an Idealist," *The Arena,* 31 (1904): 244–261.
Myall, William: "Mr. Ingersoll as a Reformer," *International Review,* 12 (1882): 225–240.

[1] 62: 697.
[2] *Little Journeys to the Homes of Eminent Orators* (New York, 1907), pp. 351–358.

The Outlook, 62 (1899): 696–698.

Rogers, Cameron: *Colonel Bob Ingersoll*, New York, Doubleday, Page & Company, 1927.

Smith, Edward G.: *The Life and Reminiscences of Robert G. Ingersoll*, New York, The National Weekly Publishing Co., 1904.

Sunderland, J. T.: "Robert Ingersoll after Nine Years: A Study," *The Arena*, 41 (1909): 295–301.

"Unveiling the Statue of Robert G. Ingersoll," pamphlet, Peoria, Ill., 1911.

Ward, William Hayes: "Colonel Ingersoll," *The American Monthly Review of Reviews*, 20 (1899): 317–320.

12

Henry W. Grady

by MARVIN G. BAUER

Henry W. Grady was born in Athens, Ga., May 24, 1850. He entered school at the age of nine; remained only two years; in 1866, at fifteen, entered the sophomore class of the University of Georgia; was graduated 1868; did one year of graduate work at the University of Virginia. Edited the *Rome Daily-Commercial;* later published the *Atlanta Herald* and the *Atlanta Courier,* both ventures ending in bankruptcy. In 1880 he bought a fourth interest in the *Atlanta Constitution;* continued as managing editor until his death. After 1886 he became the outstanding spokesman for reconciliation between the North and South; died December 23, 1889.

I

Grady was a young man of thirty-nine when he died. It was not until he was thirty-six that he made a speech that attracted more than local attention. But so complete was the success of his utterance known as "The New South" that he immediately gained a national reputation as a speaker. Many know Grady today only because of that speech, and his name is linked with that movement known as "The New South" much in the same way as is Webster's with Union, Clay's with Compromise, Garrison's with Abolition, Davis's with Secession, and Lincoln's with Emancipation. He was by no means the first or the only man who pleaded for harmony between the two sections.[1] But his utterance was by far the best, and because he spoke better than anyone else, he was more representative in the sense that he was more symbolic. As comments on the man and his speaking increased, the symbolism became more firmly established. What enabled this man to make such a lasting impression upon those who heard him, as well as upon the country at large?

The temper of the particular period in which a speaker makes his appearance must be kept in mind in order to understand those subtle

[1] Benjamin Hill had spoken about "a South of union and freedom," Greeley had proclaimed that each section was "eager to clasp hands across the bloody chasm," Schurz had deplored the "animosity and distrust" between the sections, Lamar had pleaded, "My countrymen, know one another, and you will love one another," and Watterson had proclaimed, "War or no war, we are all countrymen, fellow-citizens."

forces which influence public response. At the time Grady appeared, the movement toward reconciliation between the North and the South was well under way, but there still existed factors that militated against a complete unification, the main one being psychological. The hatreds engendered by the war could not be completely removed in one generation, nor could the social milieu of the South, a chief characteristic of which had been a contempt for trade, commerce, and industrial pursuits, be completely changed in so short a time. The need of the hour was a personality, someone who could stand as a symbol of the better feeling that was gradually growing. Somehow, the forces tending toward peace had not called forth the orators as had the forces that led toward war. The yearning for kindly feeling and good will had not yet found adequate expression. And the psychology of the situation demanded that a Southerner carry the message of harmony into the North. From the Northern point of view it was the Southerner who had been the rebel—the troublemaker. Was he now integrating within himself the social, political, and economic patterns of the nation? Lynchings did not indicate such an integration, nor did occasional shoots; and the suppression of the Negro's vote appeared as evidence to the contrary. Could capital flow into the South with safety? Could the Southern politician be trusted? Was the Southerner secretly in his heart harboring bitterness and biding his time for revenge? It is difficult to recreate these forebodings today; but lurking doubts and suspicions still existed in the Northern consciousness as late as 1886. To dispel them, the South must take the initiative in establishing a belief in Southern faith and integrity. As yet this section had produced no spokesman who could command the ear of the country at large and utter in unmistakable terms the desire of the South for harmony, for nationalism, and for a new order quite different from the old. No one had enunciated from a national platform the attitude of the *new* South.

Grady realized the need for the cultivation of this attitude and had that as his purpose when he went to New York City to deliver the address that was to make him famous and inseparably link his name with the idea of *the new South*. His success was little short of a sensation. Before he was through he had his audience on its feet and cheering. The next morning the *New York Times* reported that "No oration of any recent occasion has aroused such enthusiasm in this city,"[1] and papers in all parts of the country lavished praise on the "message."[2] It was evident that something important had been said and that a new figure had emerged in the field of American oratory.

[1] Dec. 23, 1886.

[2] For a collection of newspaper comment throughout the country see *Public Opinion*, 2 (1887): 235ff. Very few speeches of the day were judged by this periodical to be of sufficient significance to justify a presentation of public reaction.

Because this speech established Grady as the outstanding Southern orator at that time, it should be carefully examined in any evaluation of him as a speaker. It was given in response to an invitation from the New England Society, organized in 1805 and known for its distinguished membership as well as the long list of outstanding orators who had addressed its meetings. Never before had a Southern man been asked to speak before it.[1] The invitation to Grady[2] was prompted by a desire for an opinion on the progressive forces at work in the South. The movement toward harmonious relations between the sections had been arrested by a growing political tension that was due to the dissatisfaction of the Republican politicians over the election of Cleveland in 1884, a tension causing considerable uneasiness on the part of businessmen who had invested large sums of money in the South. Much might be gained if some Southern speaker could deliver a message that would tend toward better understanding and cordial relations.

The situation Grady faced was a difficult one. There were about three hundred business and professional men in the audience, among whom were J. Pierpont Morgan, Russell Sage, Seth Thomas, Elihu Root, George H. Lincoln, and John H. Inman.[3] The list of speakers included well-known men, too, such as the Reverend Dr. Thomas Dewitt Talmage, General W. T. Sherman, General J. M. Schofield, William Walter Phelps, and the Reverend Dr. Henry Van Dyke, Jr. Talmage and Sherman preceded Grady on the program, and their speeches reveal to what extent the Civil War was still discussed in public gatherings. Talmage gave a vivid description of the return of the victorious Northern armies. Sherman began by saying, "I know the Civil War is uppermost in your minds," and proceeded to relate an incident deprecating to the Southern people. That he revived a sectional consciousness is indicated by the fact that when he finished, the audience "got up and lustily sang 'Marching through Georgia.'"[4] This was the setting for the guest from the conquered state!

It is interesting to conjecture what Grady's feelings were during this demonstration. "When I found myself on my feet," he later told his friend Harris, "every nerve in my body was strung as tight as a fiddle-string, and

[1] *New York World*, Dec. 23, 1886; also, *New York Sun*, same date.

[2] The choice of Grady, then known essentially as a liberal editor of the *Atlanta Constitution*, was a logical one. Reared and educated in the South, the son of a merchant, trained in the art of molding public opinion, widely traveled, and in close contact with outstanding men in both sections of the country, he was well equipped for understanding the psychology of the times.

[3] The names of the guests and the seating arrangement, as well as a complete account of the entire affair, are given in the *New York Tribune*, Dec. 23, 1886. Another detailed description may be found in the *Proceedings* of the society, 1886.

[4] *New York World*, Dec. 23, 1886.

all tingling. I knew then that I had a message for that assemblage, and as soon as I opened my mouth it came rushing out."[1]

This drive was conditioned, however, by a well-planned rhetorical procedure that can be seen in the structure of the speech itself as well as in other evidence that will be presented later. His fine sense of audience reactions made him realize that the emotions of his hearers had been stirred in a manner unconducive to his purpose, and he therefore devoted almost half of his speech to an introduction in an effort to prepare them for an open-minded reception of his message. He expressed his appreciation of the invitation to speak, made note of "the significance of being the first Southerner to speak at this board," and asked his audience to bring their "full faith in American fairness and frankness to judgment" upon what he had to say. He introduced anecdotes in keeping with the levity of the occasion, but it is obvious that they were woven into a pattern the purpose of which was to secure an open-minded hearing of his message. And in the humor of his introduction he embedded the indirect suggestion that the stock from which the Southerners had sprung was as important as the ancestry of the New Englanders, and by virtue of that fact Southerners were entitled to as much respect and consideration as Northerners. He quickly utilized his reference to the Cavalier, however, as an opportunity to emphasize the common bond of *tradition* existing between the North and the South.

. . . both Puritan and Cavalier were lost in the storm of the first Revolution, and the American citizen, supplanting both and stronger than either, took possession of the Republic bought by their common blood and fashioned to wisdom, and charged himself with teaching men government and establishing the voice of the people as the voice of God. [Applause]

The frequent interruptions by applause indicated that Grady was winning a favorable response. But the impression left by the two previous speakers made it necessary for him to build up that response. He had been talking about traditions; it was now in order to talk about heroes. But not Southern heroes or heroes in general. He needed to mention one man in particular, someone not too far back in history to have lost his appeal or too recent for general sentiment to have been built around his name. There was only one logical choice—Abraham Lincoln. Talmage had spoken of "the typical American yet to come," and taking this as a cue, Grady utilized his opportunity to proclaim that the typical American had already come. He gave a glowing tribute to Lincoln, which, according to the *New*

[1] Joel Chandler Harris, *Henry W. Grady: His Life, Writings, and Speeches* (New York, 1890), pp. 15–16.

York Tribune[1] and other papers, "brought every man to his feet." Grady had met the situation. The crescendo of response grew from "loud and continued applause" to "loud and prolonged cheering." By identifying himself with a sentiment held dear by his audience, he had succeeded in breaking down psychological barriers and stirring his hearers so intensely that from then on they were favorably disposed toward him and his message.

Part of Grady's effect was secured by a sustained energy that he revealed in the building up of a line of thought. In this instance, he had been discussing traditions and heroes, but those essentially held in esteem by the North. The South, also, had its heroes and its traditions. Grady loved them and was proud of them. He turned now from his tribute to Lincoln to a vivid picture of "the footsore Confederate soldier." Notice that Grady did not praise Lee or Davis; he glorified the common man who had fought for the ideals of the South. Talmage's description of the return of the victorious Northern armies gave him the opportunity to portray the desolation wrought by those armies. After recalling Talmage's description, he gave utterance to what is probably the finest expression of his entire career. The suffering endured by the South was summed up in his inspired picture of the "hero in gray with a heart of gold." In that part of his speech are revealed the vitality of Grady's feeling and his sincere effort to make his audience see the other side.

The force of his utterance can be appreciated if it is compared with the remarks of Talmage. He spoke with a directness, a simplicity, and a depth of feeling not to be found in Talmage's vivid but studied description. Grady's words are those of a man inspired with a message; Talmage's are from a literary workship. No doubt Grady's marked ability to extemporize enabled him to adapt himself in this vivid and impressive manner to the demands of the situation.

He felt that his adaptation to the situation was not complete, however, until he had offset the effect of General Sherman's disparaging remarks.

I want to say to General Sherman—who is considered an able man in our parts, though some people think he is a kind of careless man about fire—that from the ashes he left us in 1864 we have raised a brave and beautiful city; that somehow or other we have caught the sunshine in the bricks and mortar of our homes, and have builded therein not one ignoble prejudice or memory. [Applause]

In this reply to Sherman there is the subtle suggestion that the real victory was to be found in the spirit of the Southern people. They had risen above

[1] Dec. 23, 1886. The *New York Times* (same date) reported: "He aroused boundless enthusiasm, bringing every man in the room to his feet with waving handkerchief and sonorous cheers."

the devastation wrought upon them. Who could deny them admiration and sympathy? The response from the audience indicated that he had established his point.[1]

Now, at last, Grady had come to the theme of his speech—the spirit of the New South. His introduction had taken almost half of the allotted time, a proportion he felt necessary in order to elicit a favorable attitude toward himself and his people. He was now faced with a choice of topics for the development of his central idea.

Grady was a good rhetorician in the sense that he chose the proper means for influencing audiences. In his introduction he amplified ideas that stirred emotions favorable to his purpose. Now that he had come to the development of his theme, he selected points that inherently demanded treatment. What should be said in demonstration of his proposition that a new spirit was permeating the South? He selected three topics that, if fixed in the minds of his audience, would establish his dominant idea.

Well might Grady ask and answer the question: "What have we accomplished?" There was not time for many details, nor were they necessary. Generalizations would cover more ground than pages of figures, and most of these businessmen were well informed on the state of industrial activity in the South. They were essentially interested in *attitudes*. He told them, "We have sowed towns and cities in the place of theories and put business above politics." They applauded. In his hasty survey of the situation he let it be known that the liberal element was gaining control and that a new spirit was stirring "in these 'piping times of peace.'" It was reassuring to hear a representative man from the South speak so confidently of its progress. He felt he had made his point, even though he offered little proof, when he summarized: "In the record of her social, industrial, and political illustration we await with confidence the verdict of the world."

But what about the Southern treatment of the Negro? That problem, with the unrest it created, had kept capital from flowing freely into the South during the decade after the war. Now that capital had entered the section, business interests were concerned over the political agitation that had broken out anew since Cleveland's election to the Presidency. The South, it was maintained, had suppressed the Negro vote and thereby made possible the election of the first Democrat since the war. As a representative of the section it was necessary for Grady to touch on this point. He therefore attempted, with more generalizations, to establish the idea that the Negro had the full protection of law and the friendship of the Southern people: "Faith has been kept with him in spite of calumnious assertions

[1] The effect of Grady's comments was not lost on his larger audience. The Chicago *Inter-Ocean*, Dec. 26, 1886, noted: "Mr. Grady made a full and complete offset to General Sherman's illustration of the planter of the old South."

to the contrary by those who assume to speak for us or by frank opponents. Faith will be kept with him in the future, if the South holds her reason and integrity." [Applause]

Grady did not deny that the Negro vote was being suppressed, nor did he enter into refutation of the charges made by Northern politicians. Speaking as a representative Southern man, he merely asserted with conviction that the fate of the Negro "must be left to those among whom his lot is cast" and that the South was making progress "in honor and equity" toward a solution of the problem.

There was yet a third idea that demanded treatment, namely, the loyalty of the South. There still existed the old Bourbons, as well as a large element that treasured its social heritage and not only resented but resisted the industrialization movement. This group often gave the impression that the South was not loyal. Furthermore, the persistent election to Congress of former Confederate officers aroused suspicion. And likewise did the occasional ceremonies in which praise was given to Confederate leaders.[1] Grady, therefore, introduced his third point that had to be developed if the idea of a new spirit in the South was to be established. "But have we kept faith with you?" he asked. "In the fullest sense, yes." In the amplification of his idea he told them that the South accepted "as final the arbitrament of the sword," that she realized her shackles were broken when the slave was freed, and that "a social system compact and closely knitted, less splendid on the surface, but stronger at the core" was taking the place of the old plantation and feudal habit. He pointed out that the South was stirring "with the breath of a new life" and that she was turning her attention from the old order to a new one interested in "a diversified industry that meets the complex needs of this complex age." This was no new point of view;[2] it was an attitude that needed repeated emphasis to convince the North that the South was playing her part in the development of the nation.

Grady did not leave the point until he added the weight of his own personal conviction. In a sense, he had previously been speaking as a representative of his section. Now for a moment he spoke as one man might to another. His father was killed on the field of battle, he told his audience. And although he revered his father as an honest and brave man,[3] he was

---

[1] For the storm of protest and indignation that swept the Northern press over the Jefferson Davis ceremonies in the spring of 1886 see *Public Opinion*, 1 (1886): 61–62.

[2] Paul H. Buck, in his excellent book *The Road to Reunion* (Boston, 1937), pp. 186–187, states: "No concept was more often transmitted to the North in the eighties than that the South had buried its resentments and had entered a new era of good feeling based upon an integration of material interests."

[3] His father was a Union Democrat and was opposed to slavery.

glad "that human slavery was swept forever from American soil [and] that the American Union was saved from the wreck of war." Here was an expression of the true spirit of the new generation of the South, an expression more persuasive than a compilation of impersonal statistics and arguments. It came as a fitting climax in the amplification of the central idea of his address and revealed to his audience the reality of what he was trying to convey.

So far as the body of the speech was concerned, these three ideas were all that needed to be presented. But there yet remained, and Grady knew it, the need for vivifying his "message." He wanted to link it with the desire generally felt for friendship and good will; he wanted to build up the favorable response he had been winning all through his speech. So in his conclusion, he returned to and amplified the idea of "the imperishable brotherhood of the American people." This brought an even greater response—"immense cheering," the newspapers reported. The time had come to drive his main point home with telling force. If any prejudice remained, it was on the part of the North, for the new South had buried the past. As a representative of his section and a guest of the society, he had brought a "message of good-will and friendship." The South had gone as far as it could go and still retain its self-respect. What would the answer be?

Now, what answer has New England to this message? Will she permit the prejudice of war to remain in the hearts of the conquerors, when it has died in the hearts of the conquered? [Cries of "No! No!"] Will she transmit this prejudice to the next generation, that in their hearts, which never felt the generous ardor of conflict, it may perpetuate itself? ["No! No!"] Will she withhold, save in strained courtesy, the hand which straight from his soldier's heart Grant offered to Lee at Appomatox? Will she make the vision of a restored and happy people, while gathered above the couch of your dying captain, filling his heart with grace, touching his lips with praise and glorifying his path to the grave; will she make this vision on which the last sigh of his expiring soul breathed a benediction, a cheat and delusion? [Tumultuous cheering and shouts of "No! No!"]

Grady, in his swelling peroration, stirred the highly emotional attitudes of his audience toward the two outstanding national heroes of the Civil War and intimated that these men would have given only one answer to his message. Would the present generation speak otherwise? To the shouts of "No! No!" Grady assured his audience that if the offer were accepted "in frankness and sincerity," then there would be a united country, in fulfillment of the prophecy Webster made "amid tremendous applause," when speaking to this very society in 1850. And he closed with Webster's own peroration—an appeal for patriotism, for a united country. Nothing more needed to be said; his theme had been adequately developed. The wild demonstrations of the audience bore eloquent testimony to the fact that his appeal had deeply stirred these men.

The plan of the speech is excellent. He was conscious of the problems involved in his introduction; he selected the necessary topics for treatment in the body of his address; and he built up in his conclusion the response he desired. All parts of the speech are knit together into an organic and vital whole. His management of ideas was such that a singleness of effect was obtained. Throughout the entire pattern was woven the idea of the common brotherhood of the American people. It is significant that Grady did not rely primarily upon proofs as the means of his persuasiveness; he essentially dealt with attitudes and emotions conducive to his purpose. There were a vitality and rich imagery that permeated the entire utterance. And behind it all was the intense sincerity of a man devoted to the welfare of his people.

In all his speeches Grady exemplified his ability to release attitudes favorable to himself and his message. He was particularly adept in recognizing the psychological factors predominant in each speech situation and in utilizing them in his treatment of theme. There is always a sense of movement in the progression of ideas, as well as a power in the building to a climax.

In the several speeches Grady gave in the South during the three years following his success in New York City, his rhetorical practice was much the same; but his shift in emphasis is worth noting. When in the North, his emphasis was on harmony between the sections and the oneness of the American people; when in the South, it was on industrial development and the necessity for a "solid South." And he did not do at all in the North what he did with much force in the South, that is, direct a sharp attack against the Republican party. His fundamental purpose was different in each section, for he sought to modify the attitude of the North toward his people, whereas he tried to hold the South together as a unit and stimulate interest in industrial progress.

Three years after his sensational success in New York Grady was asked to discuss the race problem in Boston. During the interim, the two sections of the country had been drawing closer together economically, but a new note of discord had arisen over the proposed Federal Election bill. Tension was greater than at any time since the days of Reconstruction, and once again Grady faced a trying situation that had to be handled with tact and force. Again he sought to bring to the North a better understanding of the problems facing the South, thereby hoping to create a more amicable relationship.

His method in many ways was similar to that used in his "The New South" speech. A third of the entire address was devoted to an introduction in which he endeavored to establish a common ground with his Republican audience. The topics, woven together with a deep sincerity and lightened at times by a humorous touch, strongly suggested to his hearers that all misunderstanding between North and South could eventually be removed. In a sense he again disarmed his audience of whatever antagonism it might have held. Again there was strong movement in the development of the theme, ending in an emotional climax, and a tendency toward the use of stereotypes, *e.g., frankness, fairness, traditions.* Once again he constantly held uppermost the idea of the oneness of the American people. With characteristic vividness he portrayed a people coping with a tremendous social problem, and his forceful imagination heightened his plea for sympathy. There was nothing academic about his statement. He brought his hearers face to face with the difficulties confronting the Southern people.

Yet there are certain differences between the two speeches. At Boston, Grady is bolder and more defiant. His argument is more closely knit, and the address—about twice as long as the New York one—is full of refutation. He takes care to meet objections as he proceeds from one point to another. He reasons rather than inspires and charms. There is a certain gravity not present in the earlier effort, and his preparation is more evident. There are more dignity and formality, less humor and sparkle. The speech does not seem to grow out of the occasion as did the New York address but reveals a carefully worded case directed against a political movement. It is an excellent example of a persuasive statement of a point of view contrary to that held by most of the audience; but it does not have the elements of beauty inherent in "The New South."

Grady's rhetorical skill is evident. But was his method responsible for the favorable reaction of his hearers? He stirred his audiences, sometimes to a fever pitch. Can this reaction be accounted for by his voice, his gestures, or the charm of his delivery? Everyone was impressed by his sincerity; but does this explain his success? In a sense, society was ready for his message; but were there not others also stressing the need and desirability of cordial relations between the North and the South?

One has to consider more than method or style or ideas in order to account for Grady's influence on those who heard him. One has to ponder the personality of the man himself, for Grady's effectiveness *grew out of everything that he was.* Rhetorical criticism that stresses method to the neglect of *ethos* fails to get at those subtle yet powerful forces which sway people. One can discern Grady's method, but it explains little unless considered as an inherent part of the man's personality. He possessed stylistic niceties, but they were overshadowed by the intensity of his nature. His speeches were never performances in the sense of a studied effort to produce an effect; he thought of speech as a form of power rather than as a thing of beauty. His force essentially grew out of his background, to which we now turn in more detail in order to observe the growth of this unique personality that found its full expression on the public platform.

II

Even as a youth in college, Grady had a bent toward public speaking. Perhaps this tendency had its roots in the Irish ancestry of his father and the French strain of his mother.[1] His particular interest lay in the activities of the literary societies, and he not only engaged in debating but also delivered the commencement oration of the Phi Kappa Society.[2] The defeat of his ambition to become "society orator" at the University of Virginia "was the main factor in steering him away from the public career which he associated with oratory and into journalism."[3] It is clearly evident, however, that he was interested from the very beginning in the spoken word as a medium of expression.

In addition to his early interest in speaking, Grady also evidenced an intense devotion to the languages and literature, and "by a large and extended course of reading, secured that full vocabulary which he handled so easily and fluently in after years."[4] While at the University of Virginia he continued his study of literature and rhetoric, as well as modern languages. He was an insatiable reader. "This habit of reading he kept up to the day of his death. He read all the new books as they came out, and nothing pleased him better than to discuss them with some congenial friend."[5] He had an extraordinary memory, so prodigious that, according to the testimony of his son, he could "repeat a page of print almost word for word after one reading." This remarkable memory, coupled with an intense interest in language and literature, enabled Grady to secure a mastery of words that he used as an effective tool in all his writing and speaking. His effectiveness was partly due to his command over his medium of expression.

This aptitude in the use of language aided him in his career of journalism, in which profession he gained many experiences that, indirectly at least, trained him for the public platform. As one of the editors of the *Atlanta Constitution* he was constantly discussing with various people the

[1.] Professor Raymond B. Nixon, of Emory University, who is writing the first complete and reliable biography of Grady, states: "I am convinced that his dominant traits—his genuine love for people, his sense of humor, his deeply emotional nature, his talkativeness, and his unselfishness—come, so far as inheritance goes, from the French strain of his mother rather than the Irish strain of his father."

[2] Grady was graduated from the University of Georgia in 1868 and in the fall of that year entered the University of Virginia for a year of graduate work.

[3] Raymond B. Nixon, personal correspondence.

[4] T. R. Crawford, "Early Home of Henry W. Grady," *New England Magazine*, 2 (1890): 425–436. See also Harris, *op. cit.*, p. 43.

[5] Harris, *op. cit.*, p. 43.

timely topics of the day. This long period of active discussion was undoubtedly an important factor in producing the speaker, for it enabled him to carry over to his platform appearances the experience he had gained in the give and take of alert conversation. It was necessary, also, for him to take part in an increasing number of local meetings, and often he acted as "master of ceremonies." Furthermore, as an active newspaper man, he was in more or less constant contact with speakers of the day. "I have heard every man of note in Georgia speak," he wrote in the *Constitution*, July 13, 1878. He organized the Piedmont Chautauqua, and having caught the feel of the popular lecture, went about himself giving lectures in small Georgia towns and, occasionally, in Atlanta.

This constant handling of ideas was not the only factor that aided Grady's growth in effective expression. In his wide reading he undoubtedly encountered the speeches of most of the prominent speakers of the day.[1] In his opening remarks before the New England Society he referred to his careful reading of the *Proceedings* of the organization. These records included the speeches of such prominent men as Webster, Depew, Henry Cabot Lodge, William M. Evarts, Curtis, Beecher, Clemens, Choate, Blaine, President Hayes, Eliot of Harvard, Edward Everett Hale, Emerson, Bryant, and Sumner. In his address "The Farmer and the Cities," he refers to Washington, Jefferson, Clay, Webster, Lincoln, Hill, Brown, Stephens, Toombs, Cobb, and Calhoun; and it seems reasonable to suppose that he had, at one time or another, perused the printed records of their utterances.[2] It is difficult to trace the influence of these speakers on Grady, but one can catch at times the rhythm, imagery, and concepts of Ingersoll and Webster.[3] Perhaps, also, in matters rhetorical, such as organization, climax, amplification, and proof, Grady discovered much that he incorporated in his own manner of handling ideas.

Of particular significance in Grady's development as a speaker is the fact that for years before he gave any important address he wrote in an oral style. His writing was done with a definite audience in mind and was

[1] Grady's period was that of such well-known speakers as Beecher, Brooks, Blaine, Curtis, Depew, Ingersoll, Lamar, Schurz, and Talmage. Grady knew some of these men personally and undoubtedly read the speeches of the others with more than casual interest.

[2] Grady seldom referred to English speakers, however. Once he spoke of Gladstone as "the wisest man that has lived since your Jefferson died." But English oratory apparently exerted little influence on him.

[3] Compare, for example, the passage in Grady's speech "The Farmer and the Cities," commencing with "We note the barracks of our outstanding army," etc., with the passage in Ingersoll's speech "The Liberty of Man, Woman, and Child," commencing with "A little while ago, I stood by the grave of the old Napoleon—" Compare also the closing paragraph of Grady's address in Boston on "The Race Problem in the South" with the closing paragraph of Webster's "Reply to Hayne."

therefore direct and persuasive. As an editor of the influential *Atlanta Constitution* he was personally interested in sponsoring various local and state projects. To achieve these ends it was necessary to stir enthusiasm in his readers, as well as to win converts to the various causes. This demanded a vividness and directness such as one finds in oral discourse. One might easily mistake some of his editorials for recorded conversations or speeches.[1] As a matter of fact, one frequently finds passages in his speeches that had appeared in his writings, but it is interesting to note that the imagery had become more vivid in the oral presentation of the idea.

Of especial import, however, is the fact that throughout his writings and speeches there runs one central theme—the South and its welfare—and that for years before he turned to the spoken word as a medium of expression, he had been handling the idea in all its ramifications. "I suppose I have written more about the South than any man living," Grady said as early as 1881.[2] It was this constant attention to a subject that dominated his thought which must be taken into account if we are to understand the speaker who could mount the platform and discuss with ease and effectiveness various aspects of the topic of the day.

Above all, Grady had an honesty of purpose that colored his entire life. Throughout all that he said and wrote one can detect a dominant motif that might be characterized as an intense devotion to the welfare of the South. As a young man he chose the profession of journalism in the belief that through that medium he could best serve the interests of his section. At the age of thirty-two, when urged to become a candidate for Congress in the Atlanta district, he refused, because he felt he could wield more beneficial influence through journalism than in politics. In civic and state activities he was a prominent figure, constantly endeavoring to improve conditions in his section of the country. His contacts with men of note in the North as well as in the South were numerous, and his contributions to newspapers and magazines, in an effort to stir the people and proclaim the possibilities of the South, were manifold. In all this activity there was a zeal that could not escape notice. Many differed with him in his belief that the welfare of the Southern people lay in an industrialization of the section; but few, if any, doubted his sincerity. This characteristic ardor gave Grady a strength and power that manifested themselves in everything he said or did. For the most part, journalism served as an adequate outlet for this inner drive; eventually, however, he found speech to be the more effective medium. In this latter method of

---

[1] For a collection of his writings see Russell F. Terrell, "A Study of the Early Journalistic Writings of Henry W. Grady," *George Peabody College for Teachers Contributions to Education*, No. 39 (1927), Nashville, Tenn.

[2] Clipping from *Charlotte Observer*, April, 1881, in Grady Scrapbooks.

reaching the people, his varied background focused into a dynamic personality that was tremendously effective on the public platform. Let us look briefly, therefore, at Grady, the speaker.

III

One of his outstanding characteristics as a speaker was the ability to extemporize. "Every person to whom I have talked and who ever heard Grady speak," writes his biographer, Raymond B. Nixon,[1] "has said that he never used a manuscript, and his secretary, Mr. Holliday, says that he never memorized or followed any outline that he might write out in advance. He seemed to write out something merely to fix his ideas in his mind." This testimony is corroborated by many who knew Grady intimately. But it must not be thought that he did not make careful preparation of his speeches. As a matter of fact, he prepared written drafts of all his important addresses; yet he was never bound by his manuscript. On the contrary, his preparation gave him freedom. In all his more important speeches he departed widely from his original compositions, his departures being prompted by the inspiration of the moment or the need he felt for adaptation of material to the specific set of circumstances.[2] In one notable exception, "The Race Problem," Grady rather closely followed his manuscript, written with great care and submitted for criticism—"to have it fit with the local flavor in Boston."[3] According to Clark Howell,[4] Grady dictated most of his speeches and could repeat them word for word without referring to the transcription. Nevertheless, "the preparation of a speech in cold blood (as he phrased it) was irksome to him, and failed to meet the approval of his methods, which were as responsive to the occasion as the report of the thunder-clap is to the lightning's flash."[5] All available evidence supports the conclusion that one of Grady's chief characteristics as a speaker was his ability to adapt himself to his audience and to the occasion—an ability that resulted in speeches that were the spontaneous expression of his whole personality.

[1] Personal correspondence.

[2] Harris gives several instances of the extensive changes Grady made while speaking. Shortly before he died, Clark Howell, president and editor of the *Atlanta Constitution*, stated in a letter to the author that in the case of "The New South," Grady had prepared an address covering about four columns but delivered an entirely new one, the change being prompted essentially by the remarks of Dr. Talmage. Unfortunately, the original drafts were not preserved.

[3] Jack J. Spalding, who accompanied Grady back to Atlanta, in a letter to the author, says that Grady gave his address exactly as he had prepared it except for the few suggestions made by General Pat Collins.

[4] Personal correspondence.

[5] Harris, *op. cit.*, p. 16.

His delivery reflected the depth of his active thinking and feeling. Witnesses fairly well agree[1] that on set occasions Grady spoke in an "oratorical" manner, that his voice was clear, high-pitched, pleasant, that his rate of speaking was rapid, his movement on the platform easy, his gestures frequent, expressive, appropriate to the thought, and largely suggestive rather than emphatic in nature. All were deeply impressed with the ring of sincerity and conviction in Grady's tone of voice and indicated that he abounded in animation and enthusiasm. His delivery was never monotonous, the attention of the audience was always good and often rapt, and his speech was characterized by a distinct softness but had none of the Southern drawl. He began talking in an easy, graceful manner but rose to frequent climaxes at various intervals. His intensity grew as he progressed, and he ended with what we think of as an oratorical climax. These witnesses were impressed also by the dramatic quality of his delivery and the enthusiastic response of his audiences. There was a charm as well as an earnestness about Grady's speaking that moved his hearers. His *ethos* was highly persuasive.

It has already been noted that Grady's mode of handling ideas, even in written form, was characterized by the objectivity of oral style. His speeches in particular are distinctive in their clarity, vividness, and rich imagery. His easy flow of words seemed to be an inherent gift but may have been developed through his attention to language as well as his habit of dictation. Permeating his entire utterance was a warm emotional element that clearly reflected the nature of the man.[2] This energy, coupled with a rare fluency, was probably responsible for a certain amount of ornamentation for which he was sometimes criticized. It cannot be denied that Grady lacked a definite discipline in his style. But in spite of this, his emotional energy was one of the main sources of his power.

Also characteristic of his style is a rhythm that at times resembles the movement of verse. Grady had a well-developed sense of graceful motion, the source of which probably lay deep in his physical make-up. W. T.

---

[1] The following living contemporaries corroborate the general impression one finds in books and newspaper reports: Jack J. Spalding, counsel for the law firm Spalding, Sibley, Troutman, and Brook, in Atlanta, Ga., friend and neighbor of Grady for many years; Clark Howell, former president and editor of the *Atlanta Constitution*, intimate associate of Grady and night editor of the paper when Grady was managing editor (Mr. Howell died Nov. 14, 1936); James R. Holliday, Grady's personal secretary; T. W. Reed, registrar of the University of Georgia, who heard Grady many times; and Dan G. Fisher of Dallas, Tex., who heard Grady's speech "The South and Her Problems," delivered at the Texas state fair, Dallas, Oct. 27, 1888.

[2] See Charles F. Lindsley's article "Henry W. Grady, Orator," *Quarterly Journal of Speech Education*, 6 (April, 1920): 28–42. Lindsley develops the thesis that Grady "emotionalized everything he touched."

Turnbull, former judge of the superior court in Rome, Ga., was sufficiently impressed with this element to note:

In the delivery of a speech he always tried to get what he called the "swing." He said that whenever he arose to address an audience he felt the same sensations he had felt as a child trying to "jump" in a swing. That if he could succeed in moving off easily and gracefully, gradually increasing in length and sweep the "back and forth," he always felt secure and knew the warning symptoms of a great speech.[1]

In Grady's style this "sweep" is revealed in a balanced sentence structure and a judicious repetition of words and phrases. Consider for examples the following: "Under the old regime the Negroes were slaves to the South; the South was a slave to the system." "Crushed by defeat, his very traditions are gone." " . . . that of a brave and simple man who died in brave and simple faith."

Grady's expression was never heavy; his utterance came as an overflowing of his vitality. He was remarkably alert and had an ardent and impetuous nature that manifested itself in an extrovert personality. His distinctive aliveness—a combination of vigorous mental and emotional activity—imparted to his style a fervor that elevated it above that of most of his contemporaries.

All these factors combined to make Grady an effective speaker. The importance of each one should not be underestimated. Yet no one of them, nor even the combination of all of them, fully explains his influence on people. The strength of the man cannot be adequately portrayed in the sum total of his characteristics; only in the functioning of his powers was his real force revealed. From the interplay of all the experiences that went to make up his personality came an effectiveness greater than any that can be attributed to the component parts. The testimony of all who knew Grady confirms the conclusion that it was his magnetic personality *as a whole* that impressed itself upon the minds of people.

IV

The problem of estimating the force that Grady exerted on society through the spoken word is complicated by the fact that during most of his life he was an active journalist. He rose to prominence in his section primarily through the role of editor, but even as a roving correspondent before he joined the *Atlanta Constitution*, in 1880, Grady was attracting local attention as a speaker. In 1877 he delivered his first formal lecture "Just

[1] Unpublished manuscript entitled Grady as an Orator, deposited in the Grady Collection at Emory University.

Human," an undisciplined piece of work in comparison with his later speeches. He repeated this lecture and another—"The Patchwork Palace" —several times in towns near Atlanta. After he joined the *Constitution*, his position as one of the editors of this liberal organ made it necessary for him to participate in an increasing number of local meetings. His reputation as an impromptu speaker grew steadily.

His dramatic success in New York City immediately established him as the outstanding representative of his section. The medium of journalism no longer served adequately to convey the force he was to exert. Demands to speak poured in upon him from all over the South. He turned down many invitations for addresses, one, according to a clipping in his scrapbooks,[1] being an offer for a series of fifty addresses under the auspices of lyceum system. He preferred to continue his active role as an editor. But the demands for him as a speaker could not be long ignored. In August, 1887, he made an address to the Interstate Farmers' Convention in Atlanta, in which he outlined in extemporaneous fashion his view of the agricultural and industrial possibilities of the South. It was essentially an outgrowth of his article "Cotton and Its Kingdom," which he wrote for *Harper's Magazine*, October, 1881, and foreshadowed his speech "The Farmer and the Cities," given two years later. Moved by the drive for prohibition in Atlanta, Grady entered the local campaign in November, 1887, and gave two stirring pleas that reveal his intense feeling on the subject.[2] He also appeared as a speaker at a local affair the next year, when, as vice-president of the Piedmont Chautauqua, he delivered the closing address, "Cranks, Croakers, and Creditors," a typical illustration of the style and content of the lyceum speeches of that period. But later in the year he rose to the level of his best speeches when he spoke at the state fair in Dallas, Tex., on "The South and Her Problems." With characteristic fervor, he unfolded the opportunities that the South faced in the development of diversified crops and industries. Shortly afterward, he spoke at the Augusta, Ga., Exposition on "The 'Solid South.'" Here he urged a united front in the solution of the race problem—a topic developed in all probability as an offset to the growing Republican agitation for Negro suffrage. The following year he delivered an address "Against Centralization" at the University of Virginia and another, "The Farmer and the Cities," at Elberton, Ga. His increasing number of public appearances indicated his growing importance as a speaker. He was reaching various types of audiences, and his effectiveness was heightened by the fact that he had taken on a new significance. He

[1] Deposited in the Grady Collection at Emory University.

[2] For the text of his first speech see the *Atlanta Constitution* Nov. 4, 1887. The second address is included in *The Complete Orations and Speeches of Henry W. Grady* (Edwin DuBois Shurter, ed., New York, 1910). Grady's opponents, incidentally, won the campaign.

spoke now as the outstanding representative of his section and symbolized the new spirit permeating the South.

The extent of a man's influence is always difficult, if not impossible, to determine. The difficulty is even more apparent in Grady's case, when one recalls that he was active as a prominent speaker for only three years, that he gave only two speeches in the North that attracted general interest, and that political tension between the sections was more pronounced at the end of his career than when he first delivered his message of good will in 1886. And yet it is significant that the impact of his ideas on the minds of his generation caught the attention of the entire North, as well as the South, and symbolized him as the advocate of good will as well as the representative of a new order permeating the South. No one stirred the public imagination as he did.

Grady's sectional influence lay in the impetus he gave to the industrial movement already spreading through the South when he appeared on the scene. The encroaching advance of industry on a predominantly agricultural district naturally met resistance. It was this resistance to industrialism that Grady helped break down. He constantly preached the benefits of industrial self-sufficiency as well as diversification of agricultural pursuits. All this was predicated upon the conviction that the welfare of the South lay in material prosperity and that through the development of its resources, in keeping with the industrial expansion then sweeping the North and West, lay the surest defeat of sectionalism. Furthermore, he counteracted the influence of recalcitrant journals, such as the *Southern Review*, which helped keep alive the bitterness engendered by Reconstruction; and with his vision of a new order he helped nullify the irreconcilable conservatism characteristic of a large element, represented, for example, by the churches and such die-hards as Robert Louis Dabney and Charles Colcock Jones. As a young liberal he represented a new generation that had arisen since the war.

His national significance lay in the modification he made in the Civil War psychology still dividing the American people as late as the eighties. Gradually generous impulses were supplanting a war psychosis, and Grady's fundamental contribution lay in the release he gave these impulses. He was able to put into words the desires felt in both sections, and he did this so effectively that his words were caught up and spread all over the country, In a sense he sounded the keynote of the period in which he lived and gave a new meaning to patriotism. The kind of Americanism he spoke of could not tolerate the perpetual estrangement of one section from another. He crystallized into words the concept of a united people at last emerging to form a strong and vigorous nation.

Grady will not go down in history as one of America's great thinkers but rather as one of its great personalities. He was not, in the strict sense of the word, a scholar, as can readily be seen if one compares his utterances with those of such men as Curtis, Phillips, Emerson, or Parker. But he possessed the intellectual force of an alert and inquiring mind and could catch in fine perspective the significance of an event or movement. Together with his grasp of men and affairs, as well as his practical knowledge of rhetorical devices, Grady had a nature that ideally fitted him for the task of stirring enthusiasm in the South and creating a more kindly feeling in the North. His work was cut short by his untimely death,[1] but historical perspective justifies the opinion of his contemporaries that he was an outstanding man of the difficult reconciliation period.

SELECTED BIBLIOGRAPHY

I. *Books*

Buck, Paul H.: *The Road to Reunion*, Boston, Little, Brown & Company, 1937. The best general background against which Grady and his work should be viewed.

Dyer, Oliver, ed.: *The New South*, New York, Robert Bonner's Sons, 1890. This title should not be confused with that of Grady's famous speech. The book contains a series of articles written for the *New York Ledger* shortly before his death, as well as a character sketch of Grady by Oliver Dyer of the *New York Sun*. Useful in comparing Grady's written treatment of the subject with his oral presentation.

Harris, Joel Chandler: *Henry W. Grady: His Life, Writings, and Speeches*, New York, Cassell Publishing Company, 1890. This memorial volume, although laudatory in character, contains the most comprehensive collection of material on Grady to be found. Included is a character sketch by Harris, who was a life-long friend and a coeditor of the *Atlanta Constitution*. There are several errors in such matters as date of birth and dates of various speeches; also several omissions in the text of the speech "The New South," as reported in New York papers.

Life and Labors of Henry W. Grady, His Speeches, Writings, Etc., Atlanta, H. C. Hudgins & Company, 1890.

Nixon, Raymond B.: *Henry W. Grady, Spokesman of the New South*, New York, Alfred A. Knopf, Inc., 1943. This biography is in preparation, and the title is still subject to change. The work, which is to be off the press soon, promises, however, to be the most reliable biography available. In reference to Professor Nixon and the publication, Henry Grady, the son of Henry W. Grady, stated in a letter: "I know from working with him that it is to be very full, absolutely accurate, and I believe the first really worthwhile thing that has been written. Mr. Nixon has dug up facts and history about the Grady family and my father's work that none of us knew about or had forgotten."

Shurter, Edwin DuBois: *The Complete Orations and Speeches of Henry W. Grady*, New York, Hinds, Noble and Eldredge, 1910. This is not a complete collection, but it does contain eight of Grady's most important speeches, as well as a short introduction on Grady as an Orator. The dates given for the first, second, third, and sixth speech in the collection are incorrect. The date given for Grady's birth is also incorrect.

Terrell, Russell F.: *A Study of the Early Journalistic Writings of Henry W. Grady*, Nashville, Tenn., 1927. A Ph. D. thesis, sometimes referred to as *George Peabody College for Teachers Contributions to Education*, No. 39. Part I contains a study of Grady's literary style;

---

[1] Grady died of pneumonia contracted during his trip north to deliver his address "The Race Problem."

also a consideration of him as an editor and a comparison of him with other journalists. Part II is devoted to a collection of early journalistic works. The author has taken some liberties with the text of the writings.

II. *Periodicals*

Commercial and Financial Chronicle, 43 (1886): 761–762. An editorial on Grady's speech "The New South," in which is reflected the favorable reaction of financiers.

Crawford, T. R.: "Early Home of Henry W. Grady," *New England Magazine*, new series, 2 (1890): 425–436. Contains a portrait and illustrations, as well as biographical material on Grady's boyhood.

Hadley, Dorothy Seidenburg: "Henry W. Grady as a Student Speaker," *Quarterly Journal of Speech*, 25 (1939): 205–211. This examination of the records at the University of Georgia and the University of Virginia indicates that Grady was a prominent but not an outstanding student speaker.

Howell, Clark: "Henry W. Grady," *Chautauquan*, 21 (1895): 703–706. (Portrait on p. 659.) The personal impressions of an intimate friend who was night editor of the *Atlanta Constitution* during Grady's connection with the paper.

Lee, J. W.: "Henry W. Grady: Editor, Orator, Man," *Arena*, 2 (1890): 9–23. An extravagant treatment of Grady but an interesting impression of the man from a contemporary.

Lindsley, C. F.: "Henry Woodfin Grady, Orator," *Quarterly Journal of Speech Education*, 6 (April, 1920): 28–42. A rhetorical study, with emphasis on the emotional means Grady used in his persuasive procedure.

Nation, 43 (1886): 532. A worth-while editorial on Grady's speech "The New South."

Nixon, Raymond B.: "Henry W. Grady, Reporter," *Journalism Quarterly*, 12 (1935): 341–356. A well-written article on an important phase of Grady's life.

Public Opinion, 2 (1887): 235, 278–280; 8 (1889): 258, 282. A collection of newspaper comments on Grady's speeches "The New South," "The Race Problem in the South," and comments on his death.

Reed, T. W.: *Bulletin, University of Georgia*, 35, No. 3a. An intimate description of Grady by one who knew him well.

Wade, John Donald: "Old Wine in a New Bottle," *The Virginia Quarterly Review*, 11 (1935): 239–252. A good statement of a Southern attitude with which Grady had to contend.

III. *Unpublished Sources*

Bauer, Marvin G.: Henry W. Grady: Spokesman of the New South, Ph. D. thesis, University of Wisconsin, 1936. A critical study of the man and his speeches. Also contains text of Grady's unpublished speeches.

Turnbull, W. T.: Grady as an Orator, MS in the Grady Collection at Emory University. A study of Grady's speaking by a contemporary.

Newspaper files, particularly those of the *Atlanta Constitution;* the Boston papers—*Evening Transcript, Herald,* and *Journal;* the New York papers—*Herald, Sun, Times, Tribune,* and *World.* See issues following Grady's two important speeches and his death for news reports and editorials.

Scrapbooks and MSS of unpublished speeches, in the Grady Collection at Emory University.

13

Booker T. Washington

by KARL R. WALLACE

Booker T. Washington was born a slave in Franklin County, Virginia. The exact date is uncertain, but it was probably in 1856. He worked in a salt furnace and in a coal mine and attended night school until he was able to enter Hampton Institute; was graduated from Hampton in 1875 after three years in attendance; taught school at Malden, W. Va., 1875–1878; attended Wayland Seminary, Washington, D. C., 1878–1879. He was instructor at Hampton Institute, 1879–1881; principal of Tuskegee Normal and Industrial Institute, Alabama, 1881–1915. He became the leading spokesman of the Negro cause in America; was awarded an honorary M. A. degree from Harvard in 1896 and an honorary Ph.D. degree from Dartmouth in 1901; died November 14, 1915.

Booker T. Washington once declared that he never planned to devote much of his life to public speaking,[1] yet during his career he probably delivered from two to four thousand speeches.[2] Although he preferred to

[1] *Up from Slavery: An Autobiography* (New York, 1901), p. 199.

[2] His most active years as a speaker are from 1884 to 1915. The author has the exact dates and places of 322 speeches and knows the approximate date of 62 more. Add to these at least 500 Sunday Evening Talks at the Tuskegee Chapel, the hundreds of unrecorded speeches made before lowly black audiences, and a conservative estimate as to the total number of speeches must run to 2,000. Dr. Monroe Work, head of the department of records and research at Tuskegee and close associate of Washington from 1908 to 1915, puts the figure at no less than 4,000.

The chief source materials of this study are (1) the extant texts, extracts, notes, and outlines of speeches that appear in the Booker T. Washington papers and materials at Tuskegee Institute and (2) the texts and extracts found in newspapers, in two volumes of Sunday Evening Talks delivered at Tuskegee and in the collection of *Selected Speeches of Booker T. Washington*, edited by Washington's son. So far as I know, there are only nine complete texts standing word for word as they were uttered. Of these, four are stenographically reported: "The Influence of the Negroes' Citizenship," Buffalo, N. Y., July 10, 1896, before the National Education Association; two speeches at Muchakinock, Iowa, Jan. 27, 1899, one to children, another to adult coal miners; and "The Problem of the South," Charleston, S. C., July 11, 1900, before the N.E.A. If we may accept the testimony of Washington's son, at least four were memorized: "Memorial Address on General Samuel Chapman Armstrong," Hampton Institute, Virginia, May 25, 1893; the "Atlanta Exposition Address Delivered at the Opening of the Cotton States Exposition," Atlanta, Ga., Sept. 18, 1896; the "Address Delivered at the Harvard Alumni Dinner," Cambridge, Mass., June 24, 1896; and the "Address Delivered at the Dedi-

do things rather than to talk about doing them, he won through his utterances wider respect and acclaim than any modern Negro leader. Even reluctant witnesses—Southerners and those Negroes opposed to his program of Negro advancement—spoke justly of his power. At Washington's death, the *Montgomery Advertiser* thought he had "more influence among white people than any negro that ever lived. . . . Always has he shared the respect and even the admiration of the white people of Alabama, frequently has he enjoyed the applause of this people."[1] W. E. B. Du Bois, in a critical appraisal in 1903, conceded that "he stands as the one recognized spokesman of his ten million fellows, and one of the most notable figures in a nation of seventy millions."[2]

By intelligence, tact, and hard work Booker Washington made his way from obscurity to fame; his life was a brilliant example of the success-story formula. But he was more than a product of his age; he understood his contemporaries, their desires and ambitions, their foibles and virtues. His speeches, accordingly, show that he is in tune with all classes of listeners; in line with their desires and attitudes, he selects the ideas and arguments that serve to recommend and amplify his program of Negro advancement and racial understanding; and in keeping with his own sincerity and keen sense of propriety, he presents his program simply, tactfully, and directly.

Chief Lines of Thought

Washington's program of Negro advancement and racial harmony shows a simple unity. He reasons that racial progress rests upon education and upon character. He believes that for the mass of his race education must be vocational, for in the long pull the Negro will gain prosperity and position, not by agitation and by political office but by making himself manifestly useful, even indispensable, to the community of which he is a part. Furthermore, the primary result of vocational education, carried out in the Tuskegee pattern, is not merely skill and efficiency but socially acceptable traits of character, for through training, Negro men and women

---

cation of the Robert Gould Shaw Monument," Boston, Mass., May 31, 1897. One speech was read: "Address Delivered to the Faculty and Members of the Theological Department of Vanderbilt University and Ministers of Nashville," Nashville, Tenn., Mar. 29, 1907. In addition to these, it is probable that the "Peace Jubilee Address," Chicago, Ill., Oct. 16, 1898; and the speech at Carnegie Hall, Mar. 3, 1896, were also memorized and that the two William Levi Bull lectures at the University of Pennsylvania, Philadelphia, 1907, were read. With variety of occasion and chronology in mind, the author has selected for study, besides the addresses just mentioned, forty-three of the longer extracts and press releases and forty-six sets of notes that do not duplicate the extracts and complete texts.

[1] From an editorial, Dec. 15, 1915.

[2] W. E. B. Du Bois, *The Souls of Black Folk* (New York, 1903), p. 43.

become industrious, dependable, honest, prideful, temperate, patient, even morally good. Of these qualities, perhaps the most important is industriousness:

> Our greatest danger is that in the great leap from slavery to freedom we may overlook the fact that the masses of us are to live by the productions of our hands, and fail to keep in mind that we shall prosper in proportion as we learn to dignify and glorify labor, and put brains and skill into the common occupations of life. . . . No race can prosper till it learns that there is as much dignity in tilling a field as in writing a poem.[1]

The secondary result of Negro education, the black orator asserts, is racial understanding and tolerance. If the Negro is to win the respect of the white race, he must demonstrate his own worth, both economically and morally. Deplorably, the dominant race, by denying the facilities for education, by discrimination on the common carriers, and by the substitution of mob justice for court justice, often hinders progress and tries the Negro's patience. Yet, substantial achievement—ownership of property, possession of a savings account, and work well done—is preferable to mere protest, militant agitation, and political maneuvering as means to greater civic and political privileges. This, then, is the program that both North and South received with sympathy, for instead of something radical and strange, it reflected "all that is best in the life of our republic."

Type of Address

Washington probably never made a speech that did not advance his program. His speeches, accordingly, are at bottom persuasive discourses. "Most of the addresses in the North," Washington asserts, "were made for the direct purpose of getting funds with which to support the school. Those delivered before the coloured people had for their main object the impressing upon them of the importance of industrial and technical education in addition to academic and religious training."[2] The immediate purpose of some short talks to his own kind may be expository, for he would talk to his

[1] "Atlanta Exposition Address Delivered at the Opening of the Cotton States' Exposition," Atlanta, Sept. 18, 1895, *Selected Speeches of Booker T. Washington* (E. D. Washington, ed., New York, 1932), pp. 32–33. The key phrase here, "to dignify and glorify common labor, and put brains and skill into the common occupations of life," occurs with greater or less amplification in fourteen speeches. According to the Talented Tenth, who with their followers militantly opposed the Atlanta Compromise, this doctrine condemned the Negro to be a hewer of wood and a drawer of water.

[2] *Up from Slavery*, p. 206. Dr. Emmett J. Scott reports that Washington habitually refused lucrative fees for talks "unless they carried with them some opportunity to make a direct appeal for his work."—E. J. Scott, and L. B. Stowe, *Booker T. Washington: Builder of a Civilization* (New York, 1917), p. 253. Mr. Scott was Washington's secretary for many years.

students on how to clean their teeth and to farmers on how to start a savings account and to take a bath. They are, however, but means of reaching his ultimate end. Even in the eulogies and occasional addresses he is essentially persuasive.

In promoting his ends, Washington spoke to all kinds of audiences. He talked to Northern groups, Southern groups, and mixtures of the two; he spoke to the ignorant and illiterate of both races, particularly to farmers, and to the educated of both races, especially to college students and teachers; he addressed business and professional men, religious organizations, missionary societies, and similar humanitarian groups. For the most part, however, Washington saw his hearers as three groups: Northern whites, Southern whites, and Negroes; indeed, these three general groups dictate the content and presentation of practically every speech, for beyond the immediate audience, no matter how localized or how homogeneous in interests, race, and education, lay a larger public reached by press and oral report. Like those of any public figure, his utterances are addresses to the country.

Washington was not utterly unprepared to persuade such groups. While toiling through school at Hampton Institute, he not only participated in existing debating societies but organized another to utilize the 20 minutes between supper and study. At Hampton, too, he had some private lessons in "breathing, emphasis, and articulation." After graduation, he took to the stump in West Virginia, helping materially in the establishment of the new capital at Charleston. Later, as a teacher at Hampton, he made occasional addresses. Hence, before going to Tuskegee as principal, he had acquired training and experience that was useful in pleading for Negro education and race adjustment.

Adaptation of Program to the General Audience

In addressing the country, Washington might have won a hearing by merely a clear statement of his program. His plan of racial understanding and Negro advancement is, basically, but a reflection of the economic and social values held by all regions, and its presentation constitutes approbation of the beliefs, opinion, and attitudes that made up the temper of the period 1880–1910. The industrial North, the agricultural West and South, in spite of schisms over silver, railroad rates, the tariff, and big-business monopoly, extolled the virtues of individualism, competition, hard work, and self-help. The same groups went to church in greater and greater numbers, sent more and more missionaries abroad, contributed increasingly to philanthropic enterprises, and in general revered the Christian moralities like cooperation and mutual helpfulness. To such groups Booker Washington's program probably sounded like the familiar litany of laissez-faire economics and Christian idealism.

But Booker Washington was a consummately persuasive speaker, not a teacher merely. With extraordinary skill, he amplifies and relates his topics to the temper and opinion of his hearers. He identifies his program with the desires and prejudices that, to some extent, are peculiar to the North, the South, and the Negro, irrespective of special time and period or of specific occasion.

To the North—rich, curious, and friendly to him and his cause—Washington likes to talk in terms of dollars and cents. Tuskegee's purpose is the training of a substantial citizenry—black men with property and a respect for property. Its purpose, also, is to inculcate the attitudes and habits of independence and labor so necessary for meeting the test of the American crucible, especially the attitude of self-help and self-reliance; " . . . we ask for nothing that we can do for ourselves."[1] Even the fruits of industrial education may be measured tangibly; the sharp growth in the Negroes' tax bill "from nothing to $16,000,000 in one state in forty years does not seem to prove that education is hurting the race very much."[2]

Directed especially at the receptive Northern listener, although probably equally pleasing to the Southern ear, are lines of amplification that identify his program with prevalent religious and humanitarian attitudes. Washington counsels submission, abnegation, and stoicism as means of meeting the ills that beset his race and of attaining sublimity of character:

We are a patient, humble people. We can afford to work and wait. There is plenty in this country for us to do. Away up in the atmosphere of goodness, forbearance, patience, long-suffering, and forgiveness the workers are not many or over-crowded. If others would be little we can be great. If others would be mean we can be good. If others would push us down we can help push them up. Character, not circumstances, makes the man.[3]

It is in line with this plea for forbearance and forgiveness that he often reiterates that no man can make him hate another.[4] Furthermore, in aiming unerringly at the humanitarian impulses of the North, he works out subtopics addressed to sympathy, justice, and duty. It is only just that the

[1] "The Educational Outlook in the South," Madison, Wis., July 16, 1884, *Selected Speeches*, p. 9.
[2] "Negro Education Not a Failure," New York, Feb. 12, 1904, *Selected Speeches*, p. 128. *Cf.* another speech 6 months later, *ibid.*, pp. 141–142. With the statistics brought up to date, this thought occurs in at least five other speeches.
[3] "Democracy and Education," *Selected Speeches*, p. 76.
[4] "The Problem of the South," *Addresses and Proceedings of the National Educational Association* (Chicago, 1900), p. 122. In this speech Washington states: "I propose that no race shall drag down and narrow my soul by making me hate it."

North, having brought the black man to America against his will, should extend to him sympathy and help. It is only right that the "great and prosperous" North, having impoverished the South and expecting it, alone and unaided, to turn four million slaves into citizens in two decades, should perceive her special responsibility and duty to Southern white people. In times of stress, furthermore, in order to win a fair hearing for his program and his race, he seeks to evoke religious sentiments directly. When the lynchings and unrest of the nineties had culminated in the Atlanta riot of 1906 and the Brownsville incident, he pleads that both races should view the race problem from a "high and pure atmosphere." Accordingly, to the blacks he preaches "patience, forbearance, and self-control," lest the race "descend to the level of the mob."[1] To the whites he suggests the application of the golden rule:

> If you want to know how to solve the race problem, place your hands upon your hearts and then, with a prayer to God, ask Him how you, today, were you placed in the position that the black man occupies how you would desire the white man to treat you, and whenever you have answered that question in the sight of God and man, this problem in a large degree will have been solved.[2]

Occasionally he will even make a direct plea to Christianity by name.[3]

To Southern whites, Booker Washington likewise recommends his program in the language of a competitive economy. His address is almost exclusively to the influential and substantial whites, who, at first critical of his program, gradually lent a sympathetic ear when they saw that his scheme of Negro advancement coincided with their own interests. Rarely does Washington speak to the poor white.

In speaking to white Southerners, Washington takes care to amplify those topics which, if not in every instance wholly peculiar to the South, relate to it directly. Above all, he emphasizes lines of argument that touch the critical hearer in terms of his own self-interest. To a region whose soil had been imperiled by a one-crop system, he asserts that a Negro educated in agriculture will permit crop diversification.[4] To the landlord, storekeeper, and banker who, essential to a system of tenant farming, had found the Negro lazy and unreliable, he demonstrates that vocational training will make black labor dependable and cites the testimony of white employers. Rather than raising the Negro above ordinary tasks, education fits him "for the common labors and duties of life; . . . in proportion as we get educa-

[1] "Rights and Duties of the Negro," June 2, 1903, *Selected Speeches*, pp. 95, 116–117.
[2] "Address at the Jamestown Exposition," Aug. 3, 1907; *cf. Selected Speeches*, p. 189.
[3] *Ibid.*, p. 178.
[4] "The Negro and His Relation to the Economic Progress of the South," Huntsville, Ala., Oct. 12, 1899, *Selected Speeches*, pp. 84–85.

tion we will be more useful in field and shop, in kitchen and laundry . . . and in every walk of life."[1] He shrewdly indicates to the South that education, by increasing the desires and wants of the Negro, forces him to work long and regularly.[2] To the Southern employer, whether farmer or industrialist, who had found Negro labor unstable and mobile, he advances the creed that the black man belongs in the South. Indeed, the black leader advises his people to become property owners partly because ownership brings obligations that can be met only by steady work. He frowns on emigration to the North or elsewhere, and to the employer who is tempted to import immigrant labor, he flatly asserts that it is in the South alone "by reason of the presence of the Negro, that capital is freed from tyranny and despotism that prevents you from employing whom you please and for that wage that is mutually agreeable and profitable."[3] "You should remember," he continues, "that you are in debt to the black man for furnishing you with labor that is almost a stranger to strikes, lock-outs, and labor wars; labor that is law-abiding, peaceful, teachable; labor that is one with you in language, sympathy, religion, and patriotism; labor that has never been tempted to follow the red flag of anarchy, but always the safe flag of his country and the spotless banner of the Cross."[4] Stable labor, furthermore, is secured to any community or plantation that provides good schools and metes out equal justice to black and white.

On the matter of Negro morals, a persistent subject of criticism in the South, Booker Washington proceeds along three lines. He bluntly sketches to his own race the evil consequences of whiskey and dissolute living and urges his people to cooperate with the whites in the detection and punishment of crime. To the whites he points out that criminal and immoral conduct decreases in proportion as the Negro is educated.[5] Finally, he compellingly states time and again that the South, by fostering Negro education and by granting equal civic privileges to his race, will improve the entire moral tone of the country; "no man can plan the degradation of another race without being himself degraded."[6]

On the subject of political and social equality, so crucial to the Southerner, Booker Washington took care to avoid offense. Adopting the position

---

[1] "The Southern Sociological Congress as a Factor for Social Welfare," Memphis, Tenn., May 8, 1914, *Selected Speeches*, pp. 237–238.

[2] "An Address to the Faculty and Members of the Theological Department of Vanderbilt University and Ministers of Nashville," Mar. 29, 1907, *Selected Speeches*, p. 169. *Cf. ibid.*, pp. 119–120; also, speeches at Vicksburg, Oct. 8, 1908; at Brooklyn, Nov. 12, 1908; and at London, Oct. 6, 1910.

[3] Speech at Huntsville, Ala., Oct. 12, 1899, *Selected Speeches*, p. 81.

[4] *Ibid.*, p. 82. That the Negro is not a striker is specifically stated in six other speeches.

[5] "The Education of the Southern Negro," *Selected Speeches*, pp. 142–143.

[6] *Selected Speeches*, p. 79.

that Henry Grady had earlier espoused without success, he enunciates his position on social privileges in the Atlanta Address: "In all things that are purely social we can be as separate as the fingers, yet one as the hand in all things essential to mutual progress."[1] Although reaffirming this ambiguous doctrine at intervals afterward, he rarely risks more than a short abstract statement of it. Rather, he emphasizes a solution of the race problem acceptable to the Southern mind. The Negro who through skill, intelligence, and character can make himself *indispensable* to his community will win respect and civic rights:

> Wherever I have seen a black man who was succeeding in business, who was a taxpayer, and who possessed intelligence and high character, that individual was treated with the highest respect by the members of the white race. In proportion as we can multiply these examples North and South will our problem be solved. . . . When an individual produces what the world wants, whether it is a product of hand, head, or heart, the world does not long stop to inquire what is the color of the skin of the producer.[2]

Politically and socially, in the long run, "it is important and right that all privileges of the law be ours, but it is vastly more important that we be prepared for the exercise of those privileges. The opportunity to earn a dollar in a factory just now is worth infinitely more than the opportunity to spend a dollar in an opera house."[3]

If Booker Washington thus identifies his program with the dominant attitudes of his white audience, to what extent do his utterances reflect the attitudes of the Negro? This question may be answered briefly. Apparently every Negro has at least one great desire: to be respected by his white neighbor. The measure of that respect, he feels, is the extent to which he can exercise the political, civil, and social privileges of the white man. With this desire Washington, of course, agrees. He unceasingly criticizes mob justice as an alternative to court justice. He maintains, too, that the Negro should be given opportunities for work and living quarters, for travel and entertainment, that are equal to those of the whites, although separate.

---

[1] *Selected Speeches*, p. 34.

[2] "Speech to the First Meeting of the National Negro Business League," Boston, Aug. 24, 1900, *Selected Speeches*, p. 89. This line of argument, alluded to in 1884, recurs in eighteen speeches and appears as late as 1911. Its complete amplification as delivered by Washington is best seen in a speech to the N. E. A. at Buffalo, N. Y., July 10, 1896, *Addresses and Proceedings of the National Education Association* (Chicago, 1896), p. 216.

[3] *Selected Speeches*, p. 36. *Cf.* "Speech at Vicksburg" and the "Address at Vanderbilt University." Before the Institute of Arts and Sciences in Brooklyn, Washington is more specific concerning political privileges: "It is more important that we be prepared for voting than that we vote, more important that we be prepared to hold office than that we hold office. . . . "—*Selected Speeches*, p. 76.

But beyond agreement in such respects he does not go. To urban blacks, pressed by the temptations of city life, he dwells uncompromisingly on the sins of gambling, drinking, and loose living. To the rural and urban Negroes alike, he never speaks sympathetically of their superstitions or approves of the attitude that the Negro is free to work as little as he pleases and to subsist as best he can. Nor does he countenance the belief that all Democrats are bad, all Republicans good, or that all white people are to be distrusted. Rather, he urges them to work hard, save, get property, and become taxpayers. Or, as Emmett J. Scott puts it:

Make your own little heaven right here and now. Do it by putting business methods into your farming, by growing things in your garden the year around . . . by keeping your bodies and your surroundings clean, by staying in one place, by getting a good teacher and a good preacher, by building a good school and church, . . . by keeping out of debt, by cultivating friendly relations with your neighbors both white and black.[1]

It is evident, therefore, that in the advancement of his program Booker Washington selects and exploits ideas that match, to an astonishing degree, the beliefs and attitudes of the North, the South, and the Negro.

It may be asked at this point: Did Booker Washington make such an identification deliberately? Or, as a representative product of American culture who made his own way in Horatio Alger fashion, does he make such adaptations intuitively? There is some evidence that he proceeded artistically. In his book *My Larger Education*, he relates that after some trial-and-error fumbling in the first years of his career he clearly saw his general audience as Southern, Northern, and colored. Although implying that he rejected the temptation to say to each group what it wanted to hear, he recognized that "the South was poor and the North was rich." He thought that the North believed, as the South at first did not believe, "in the power of education to inspire, to uplift, and to regenerate the masses of the people." Northern people, he believed, were willing to see the Negro free in fact and would be glad, therefore, "to give their support to any school or other agency that proposed to do this work in a *really fundamental way*." Accordingly, there is at least the hint that Washington's program of industrial education, rightly understood, would be considered "fundamental" by the prosperous and friendly North.

With respect to the economic interests of his Southern audience, the testimony is more direct. Washington perceived that "the two races needed each other and that for many years to come no other labouring class of people would be able to fill the place occupied by the Negro in the life of the Southern white man." He saw, furthermore, that the South had every

[1] Scott and Stowe, *Booker T. Washington*, pp. 141–142.

"motive of self-interest" to assist Negro progress, "since to uplift and educate the Negro would reduce the number of paupers and criminals of the race and increase the number and efficiency of its skilled labourers."

It is significant that Washington's interest in the attitudes of his listeners extended even to an individual's crotchets. When W. E. B. Du Bois and Washington were once considering ways of approaching Andrew Carnegie, the Tuskegee principal advised Du Bois to read a particular book, because, as he stated pointedly, "Carnegie likes it."

Adaptation to the Special Audience and Occasion

Booker Washington seems to have thought habitually, not only in terms of the general attitudes of his audience, but also in terms of the special interests that mark a particular occasion. His willingness to utilize the special occasion is seen in the "Address at the Peace Jubilee," at Chicago, in 1898. Appreciating that the country, jubilant over the successful termination of the Spanish-American War, felt gratitude toward the Negro soldier, Washington eloquently points out that the Negro race in crises had always chosen the loyal way. Illustrative of his practice in making topics of current interest serve his ends is the speech "Democracy and Education," delivered at Brooklyn two months before the election of 1896. Fully alive to the jittery state of mind into which Bryan and soft money had thrown the industrial North, he draws a double lesson from the topic of the hour: (1) that a democracy cannot thrive on the votes of the ignorant; and (2) that the intelligent voter who employs dishonest methods to prevent the Negro from voting destroys his own political conscience.[1] Here Washington has taken one of his commonplace themes, "You cannot degrade another without yourself being degraded," and has neatly adapted it to the current situation. Once, when asked to speak impromptu at a county fair, he picked up some cans of corn, turnips, and tomatoes on his way to the platform. Holding them up to the audience, he pointed out that each product, grown and canned in Northern states, had a profitable sale to Alabama farmers. He then drove home the moral that every farmer could, and should, grow his own corn and turnips and tomatoes.

That Booker Washington should be in the habit of adapting his ideas to a particular audience and occasion is not mere accident. He recognized that no two audiences are identical:

I always make it a rule to make especial preparation for each separate address. No two audiences are exactly alike. It is my aim to reach and talk to the heart of each individual audience, taking it into my confidence very much as I would a person. When I am speaking to an audience, I care little for how what I am saying is going to sound in the newspapers, or to another audience, or to an individual.

[1] *Selected Speeches*, p. 62.

At the time, the audience before me absorbs all my sympathy, thought, and energy.[1]

Aware of the peculiarity of audiences, he endeavored systematically to find out what a particular audience wanted to know. One of the chief sources of such knowledge, Washington states, is the newspaper reporter, for "the sort of questions the reporters . . . ask indicate pretty clearly, not only what the people in the community know about my work, but they tell me a great deal, also, about the feeling of the average man toward the members of my race in that community and toward the Negro generally."[2] On the important occasions—before audiences of mixed color especially—Booker Washington apparently always tried to get criticism from local men on what he intended to say. Before speaking in Kansas City on one occasion— so H. O. Cook, principal of the Lincoln High School in that city, writes the author—Washington consulted in some detail with a group of men in that community:

> I had the rare privilege once of hearing him discuss, with a small group of interested men, a speech he was preparing for a plea he was making on the topic of Segregation. He was anxious to have the advice and comments of each of us . . . as to what points we felt should be stressed and what phraseology employed and even what jokes he might weave in to carry his points. . . . It was interesting to see him make notes of these suggestions, his deference to the opinions of others, especially of plain, ordinary folk. . . . [3]

The Atlanta Address is, of course, the cardinal instance of such consultation. The speech not only was read aloud to Negro friends and students for the sake of criticism but copies were sent to men of both races in the North and South. Perhaps Washington made a habit of sending the manuscripts of important addresses to representative men of both races and regions. Bliss Perry suggests that Booker Washington once said as much to him.[3]

Address to the Emotions

Beyond skillful selection and amplification of lines of argument that harmonize with the temper and attitudes of his general audience and special groups, Washington stirs up his auditors emotionally. The lines of amplification already set forth, of course, are heavily charged with emotion; they are often concerned with the profit motive, self-interest, duty and responsibility, sympathy and pity. Independent of such emotional address, however,

---

[1] *Up from Slavery*, p. 214.
[2] *My Larger Education* (New York, 1911), pp. 82–83.
[3] From a letter to the author.

Washington makes a direct attack on the elemental individual by appeals to loyalty, gratitude, fear, pride, and christianity.

But of all emotional means that Washington employs of bringing the hearer and his program together, perhaps the most characteristic is humor. The singing of spirituals as a means of group control may precede a talk to farmers, but for the control of any audience—except the English group, perhaps[1]—humor is the great leavening and binding force:

> If in an audience . . . there is one person who is not in sympathy with my views, or is inclined to be doubtful, cold, or critical, I can pick him out. When I have found him I usually go straight at him, and it is a great satisfaction to watch the process of his thawing out. I find that the most effective medicine for such individuals is administered at first in the form of a story. . . . [2]

The story that thaws out is, to Washington, an anecdote, and it is the anecdote with its dialogue, with its narrative and descriptive details, that finds most favor. At least one-fifth of any speech to a general audience in advocacy of Negro advancement is devoted to such illustration, real or hypothetical.[3] Not infrequently, however, Washington in a turn of phrase or in juxtaposition of idea obtains his humor by the incongruous, through which runs sympathy so tolerant as to be almost objective. Consider, for instance, his way of saying that the Negro has some right in America:

> We are the only people . . . who ever came here by a special invitation and by a special provision. Your race came to this country against the protests of the leading citizens at that time. Having been so important to the prosperity of this country that we had to be sent for at great inconvenience and expense on the part of yourselves, do you think we are so foolish as to leave now? No, we have a mission here and part of that mission is to help lift you up; to help make you better. . . . I suspect you think we have a pretty hard job on our hands. But we are not discouraged by any means.[4]

Although functioning primarily to thaw out an audience, Washington's humor has special sharp and subtle ends. It may serve to clarify and emphasize:

> Once . . . an old colored man was very anxious to have turkey for his Christmas dinner, and he prayed for it night after night: "Lord, please send this darkey a turkey;" but no turkey came. So one night, when it got near Christmas time, he prayed: "Lord, please send this darkey *to* a turkey;" and he got it that same night.

[1] See *Up from Slavery*, p. 287.

[2] *Ibid.*, p. 243.

[3] See "The Problem of the South," *Proceedings of the National Education Association* (Chicago, 1900), pp. 114-123. The text is stenographically reported.

[4] "The Influence of the Negroes' Citizenship," *Proceedings of the National Education Association* (Chicago, 1896), p. 209.

I don't know how you white people get hold of turkeys, but, my friends, we don't get hold of very much as a race or as individuals, unless we put forth something of the kind of effort that old black man put forth.[1]

It may carry a hidden point that cannot be directly phrased to Southern whites:

> There was a white man who wanted to cross a river, and he went to a colored man near by and asked him to lend him 3 cents to pay his way across the ferry. The colored man said: "Boss, how much money have you got?" The white man replied: "I haven't got any today. I am broke and in bad circumstances, and I want to borrow 3 cents to pay my way across the ferry." "Boss," said the colored man, "I know you are a white man, and I expect you got more sense than this old 'nigger,' but I ain't going to loan you no 3 cents. The man that ain't got no money is just as well off on one side of the river as on t'other." Now, in reference to our race, I would say that a race that is without bank accounts, or property, or business standing, is just as well off on one side of the river as on the other.[2]

Beyond the literal significance, is there here the suggestion that some blacks are wiser than some whites? Finally, Washington makes humor serve as refutation where explicit counterargument might only solidify opposition. To those who believed that the race problem would be solved by the white man eventually assimilating the Negro, he replies thus:

> I do not know as you have noticed it, but the moment it is proven that a man has even 1 per cent of African blood in his veins, he becomes a Negro; he falls to our pile; in the count we claim him every time. The 99 per cent of Anglo-Saxon blood is not strong enough to overcome the 1 per cent of African blood; the 99 per cent counts for nothing and we claim the man. So you see we are a stronger race than you are; we have a greater power of attraction and absorption, and at that rate we will ultimately absorb you.[3]

One who has heard Washington many times comments on "his fine sense of humor and his happy way of using it effectively."[4] No small part of its effectiveness lies in its being in point; merely to drag a story in, Washington states truly, is "empty and hollow, and an audience soon finds it out."[5]

Impact of Character and Personality

In his own character and personality probably lies the greatest single source of Washington's persuasiveness. Whether an audience's portrait of him was based on his reputation or derived from the content and manner of

---

[1] "The Problem of the South," pp. 117–118.
[2] *Ibid.*, p. 121.
[3] "The Influence of the Negroes' Citizenship," pp. 208–209.
[4] J. H. Dillard, in his Preface to *Selected Speeches*, p. xv.
[5] *Up from Slavery*, p. 243.

utterance, his weight as a witness in his own cause was doubtless tremendous. He must have reminded his hearers of Quintilian's dictum that the great orator is a good man skilled in speaking.

As Tuskegee Institute prospered Washington stood before his white listeners as a living instance of what labor and intelligence can do under adversity. Dr. George Washington Carver has declared, with a sweeping gesture that took in the institute's buildings, that "Dr. Washington always insisted that this school was his greatest argument."[1] To the Negro farmer he stood as the only black leader who had widespread influence with whites.

But apart from the force of his reputation, his utterances amply testify to the good man. He doubtless impressed his hearers by his utter sincerity. Almost the first observation made by anyone who has heard Washington speak is this: "He meant what he said." Secured through the press, letters, and personal interview, the uniformity of that observation is convincing. The speaker's apparent forgetfulness of self, his directness of utterance, and simplicity of language made an enduring impression of sincerity. In searching for the outstanding attribute of Booker Washington's speaking, J. H. Dillard hits the essence of the matter: "An impression of his outstanding quality as a speaker . . . is the quality of sinking self. It is the quality that takes attention away from the speaker and turns it to what he is saying. It is the quality that makes you know the speaker is not thinking of his own glory but of the cause for which he pleads. . . . "[2] After hearing Booker Washington in the national capital in 1904, a Washington correspondent reported to his Des Moines paper:

As an orator he is not pretentious, but impressive and interesting because he is direct and is saying something all the time. There is none of the airs or imaginary or oratorical style which frequently marks the efforts of the negro speakers who are heard in political conventions. . . . He is in earnest, he has a message to deliver, and he goes straight to the point without any striving for effect, or any thoughts about the figure he is making.[3]

Probably Booker Washington's sincerity led him to respect his audience and to scorn mechanical rules of delivery:

[1] Interview with the author.

[2] *Selected Speeches*, pp. xiii–xiv. Perhaps Washington's habit of prayer before each speech promoted the "tone" of sincerity.—*Up from Slavery*, p. 214.

[3] *Des Moines Register and Leader*, Mar. 30, 1904, p. 4. Dr. R. R. Moton, friend of Washington and his successor as principal, writes in a personal letter: "Dr. Washington was a remarkable speaker. I wouldn't call him an orator as such, but his earnestness and his simplicity as well as his intensely practical attitude toward life made his words carry deep conviction." James Weldon Johnson writes in the same vein: "He impressed me more as a forceful speaker than as an eloquent speaker. I mean he was not at all eloquent in the Websterian sense of the term. . . . His great earnestness carried his message over to his hearers."

I do not believe that one should speak unless, deep down in his heart, he feels convinced that he has a message to deliver. When one feels, from the bottom of his feet to the top of his head, that he has something to say that is going to help some individual or some cause, then let him say it; and in delivering his message I do not believe that many of the artificial rules of elocution can, under such circumstances, help him very much. Although there are certain things, such as pauses, breathing, and pitch of voice, that are very important, none of these can take the place of *soul* in an address. When I have an address to deliver, I like to forget all about the rules for the proper use of the English language, and all about rhetoric and that sort of thing, and I like to make the audience forget all about these things, too.[1]

Moral courage is a striking attribute of Washington's character, and it is moral courage compounded with sincerity that is reflected in those ideas Washington's audience might not have wanted to hear. Although his speeches reflect the social and economic attitudes of his audiences, he says much that his audience may not have welcomed wholeheartedly. The South, for example, could not have enjoyed hearing even a tactful presentation of its sins, particularly sins of discrimination against the Negro in the courts, at the polls, in the schools, and in the common carriers. Nor could the Negro have been exactly pleased at hearing that he was slothful, improvident, immoral, and intemperate or that as a race he lacked both shame and pride. Nevertheless, the persistence of the unwelcome idea in the long run may have convinced the audience of the speaker's devotion to what he deemed just and true, and admiration of his character, therefore, may have offset the unpleasantness of the unwelcome idea, if not actually winning its acceptance.

Another trait in Washington's make-up is modesty. No text or extract of a speech refers to what *I* did in the development of Tuskegee. For generous acts on the part of both whites and blacks, he almost digresses to give due credit. In the complete texts, furthermore, phrases like *it seems to me* and *I believe* suggest that the speaker realizes he is in the realm of the probable, rather than of demonstrable fact, and that dogmatism, consequently, is out of place. The opening sentence of the "Harvard Address" is more than modest; it approaches the humble: "It would in some measure relieve my embarrassment if I could, even in a slight degree, feel myself worthy of the great honor that you do me today."[2] Washington, indeed, frequently refers to himself as "a humble representative" of his race. Not even to the lowliest audience of Negroes, so I am told, did Booker Washington assume the

---

[1] *Up from Slavery*, pp. 243–244.

[2] *Selected Speeches*, p. 51. *Cf.* the opening of a speech to the Republican Club, New York, Feb. 12, 1909: "I am not fitted by ancestry or training to be your teacher. . . . "—*Ibid.*, p. 190.

cocky, overbearing attitude sometimes present in the underdog who has made good.

A fourth trait of personality evident in Washington's speeches is good judgment and tact. If by tact is meant saying the right thing at the right time in the right way, it is clear that Washington's skill in associating his program favorably with the climate of economic, social, and religious opinions of the period and his skill in securing favorable emotional response from his hearers constitute ample evidence of good sense in the selection of ideas and their adaptation to his audiences. Striking evidence of tactfulness, also, is Washington's habit of never speaking to a mixed audience or to a white group except upon invitation. In every reliable text of his introductory remarks there is a reference to his having been invited to speak on the occasion, and almost invariably in the first few lines of the notes of his speeches, there is the entry *invited here*. It is evident, then, that Washington tried not to push himself forward. There are many instances, moreover, where the speaker prefaces advice to the white group in the audience with the phrase *were I permitted*. The Atlanta Address is again a case in point: "To those of the white race who look to the incoming of those of foreign birth and strange tongue and habits for the prosperity of the South, were I permitted, I would repeat what I say to my own race, 'Cast down your bucket where you are.'"[1]

As an indication of tact, too, it is significant that Washington never indulges in hyperbole. But doubtless the most dramatic instance of Booker Washington's exercise of tact occurred in a speech delivered in a Florida town two days after a lynching had taken place. Race feeling was so intense that those who had scheduled the address advised against his coming. Preferring to keep the engagement, however, he stepped to the platform to discover in the front row a poor white with a cocked pistol in his lap. After a gracious acknowledgment of the chairman's introduction, he began, so Dr. Work reports, somewhat in this fashion: "I am glad to see many of our white friends here. In these trying circumstances, it is gratifying to know that some of them are here to see that my friends and I are well protected." It is said that these remarks were followed by an anecdote, at the conclusion of which the pistol was no longer in evidence.

Booker Washington exhibits good judgment, furthermore, in never playing North and South against each other. This, in fact, was one of Washington's carefully considered policies of persuasion.[2] In addressing the National Education Association at Buffalo (1896) and at Charleston (1900), he employs the same lines of argument and, except for changes in illustration, the same lines of amplification. Whenever pointed criticism of one

[1] *Selected Speeches*, p. 33.
[2] See *Up from Slavery*, pp. 200–201.

region seems in order, it is addressed only to audiences in that region. Washington, for example, is at times quite willing to make the South keenly conscious of unjust race discrimination on the common carriers, but the criticism is offered to Southern groups only. In fact, the stories, anecdotes, and illustrations pertaining to race discrimination have their setting in the region to which they are addressed. Hence, by not indulging in abuse and by not playing region against region, Booker Washington gained the respect and confidence of intelligent and influential Southerners.

It may well be, then, that Booker Washington's tact, modesty, sincerity, together with an espousal of the cardinal Christian sentiments, reveal the black orator to his hearers as a man of good will, good judgment, and the right moral qualities.

Use of Evidence and Testimony

Washington does more than paint his own character favorably and stir up his hearers emotionally; when necessary he makes a powerful address to their intellects. When on the defensive and engaged in refutation before a critical and informed group, the black orator marshals his data and witnesses most convincingly. During the last decade of the nineteenth century, lynchings reached their zenith.[1] Simultaneously there was considerable discussion as to the efficiency of Negro labor.[2] Hence, to many people the unrest and discussion meant that Negro education, rather than making the Negro a tractable and law-abiding citizen, had made him criminal and antisocial. When J. K. Vardaman became governor of Mississippi in 1904, his inaugural address reflected this attitude: "As a race, they are deteriorating morally every day. Time has demonstrated that they are more criminal as free-men than as slaves; that they are increasing in criminality with frightful rapidity, being one-third more criminal in 1890 than in 1880."[3] Vardaman's views were widely reported, and after 1904 Washington proceeds to more systematic explanation and proof of the values of Negro education than formerly he thought necessary. He employs statistical evidence to show that the Negro has steadily increased his ownership of land and of business enterprises and has paid greater taxes;[4] he presents the evidence gathered from a questionnaire circulated among prominent Southern men to prove that they believe the trained Negro is superior to

[1] *Negro Year Book* (M. N. Work, ed., Tuskegee, 1912), pp. 148–149.

[2] In 1891 *The Tradesman*, a Southern publication edited by G. W. Ochs, undertook a survey of the wage, the efficiency, and the general effect of training of Negro labor. Two years later the *Manufacturers Record* of Baltimore conducted a similar investigation. W. E. B. Du Bois also made a survey for *The Tradesman* in 1902. For a more complete discussion, consult C. J. Johnson's *The Negro in American Civilization* (New York, 1930), pp. 68–69.

[3] B. Brawley, *Social History of the American Negro* (New York, 1921), pp. 325–326.

[4] *Selected Speeches*, p. 128.

the untrained as a laborer and as a citizen;[1] and to the same effect he quotes in full the testimony of men like Joel Chandler Harris.[2] He offers data derived from penal institutions to demonstrate that 90 per cent of Negro criminals have had no education.[3] Such evidence is usually followed by an attempt to place upon the audience some of the responsibility for permitting conditions that invite wrongdoing.[4] The public, so Washington demonstrates statistically, woefully neglects Negro education;[5] the failure of the cities to abolish vice districts, saloons, and slums puts undue temptation in the way of the simple-minded Negro.

To the modern reader, such tactics are impressive; they were no less impressive to Washington's hearers. In an address at Brooklyn, the Tuskegee leader, using all the resources of statistical data and authoritative testimony from Southern whites, defended education so effectively that the *New York Daily Tribune* believed the speech to be a "complete refutation" of the Vardaman view.[6]

Washington, nevertheless, is not always successful in answering critics. In a meeting at which the Talented Tenth—a group of Negro intellectuals led by Du Bois—rained unsparing criticism on his program, he replies with an exposition of education at Tuskegee, utterly ignoring the arguments of his critics. Although Washington's adherents pronounce it a brilliant reply, it seems weak and ineffective. In fact, Booker Washington's philosophy of vocational education and of racial harmony did not gain acceptance among many Negroes who held that the progress and rights of their race might be advanced chiefly through liberal education, through positive political action, and through militant agitation.[7] Washington recognized such opposition[8] but never, by speech or pen, undertook any refutation that reveals a clear understanding of the Du Bois point of view. He may have felt that a good presentation of his own case constituted the best persuasion.

In speaking to Negro farmers and laborers, Washington depends little upon logical proof; rather, to achieve an impact upon such classes comparable to the impact of reason upon educated folk, he relies upon the cumula-

---

[1] "Negro Education Not a Failure," *Selected Speeches*, pp. 126–127; "Education of the Southern Negro," *ibid.*, p. 140.

[2] *Selected Speeches*, pp. 122–126.

[3] *Ibid.*, p. 122.

[4] *Ibid.*, pp. 121–122.

[5] "Negro Education Not a Failure," *Selected Speeches*, pp. 118–134.

[6] Feb. 15, 1904, p. 6.

[7] W. E. B. Du Bois summarizes the position of these "intellectuals" who opposed Washington in *The Souls of the Black Folk* (1903), pp. 56–58, and suggests that Washington's program had little effect upon the lower classes of Southern whites. *Cf.* J. W. Johnson, *Along This Way* (New York, 1934), pp. 313–314.

[8] *My Larger Education*, pp. 112–113.

tive effect of assertion and reassertion, of direct suggestion, and of vivid illustration.[1] He employs the same technique in talking to Tuskegee students.

Ordering of Thought and Speech Composition

Skillful in adapting his lines of argument to attitudes and emotions of his listeners, masterly in sketching his self-portrait, Washington is extraordinarily felicitous in the presentation of his utterances. The pattern of his thought, although simple, appears in ingenious arrangements that gently lead his hearers into his program; and the earnestness and quiet directness of his delivery seem designed to let his ideas and his great purpose speak for themselves.

The rhetorical arrangement of his speeches for the most part shows the modern tripartite division: introduction, discussion, or body, and conclusion. The 15-minute Atlanta Address is representative of such partition. With the introduction and conclusion each about two minutes long, the speech also reflects Washington's preference for brevity in these divisions. Except in one instance, no introduction is longer than 5 minutes,[2] even though Washington usually spoke for about an hour. Perorations are invariably short.

In moving from the opening remarks to the body of a speech, Washington rarely states his governing idea completely and explicitly in sentence form. The topic, or the purpose, however, is occasionally alluded to unmistakably. To Muchakinock children, for example, he is explicit; they are "to think what you are going to school for."[3] To his own students at Tuskegee, he proceeds, almost without preliminaries, to announce that he wants "to emphasize the importance of teamwork."[4] At times, as in the Atlanta Address and in the talk to Muchakinock coal miners, he moves from introduction to body by means of a narrative illustration whose point is the governing idea of the speech.[5] Washington's practice, then, is to lead an audience to his theme, without stating it as a proposition.

Similarly, in developing the body of a speech he avoids throwing his program abruptly at a group. In effect he surrounds his hearers before they realize what is happening. Accordingly, to biracial audiences in both North and South—particularly to groups from whom he is seeking support of

[1] The only extant example is the "Speech to Muchakinock Miners."

[2] "The President's Annual Address before the Alabama State Teachers' Association," Montgomery, Ala., Apr. 11, 1888, has 8 to 10 minutes of introduction.—*Selected Speeches*, pp. 12–15.

[3] *Oskaloosa Saturday Globe* (Iowa), Feb. 4, 1899.

[4] *Selected Speeches*, p. 271.

[5] *Selected Speeches*, p. 32; *Oskaloosa Saturday Globe*, Feb. 4, 1899.

Tuskegee—Washington's favorite method of disposition in the body proper resembles an expository-inductive process. First comes a short sketch of Tuskegee's growth and an explanation of the methods and aims of manual and industrial training for Negroes, followed by a brief, general description of the poverty and ignorance of the Southern Negro. Then, in a much longer section, emerges the idea that such education will improve the Negro's lowly state and will enable him to determine his own economic status. Finally, with the ground thus laid, comes discussion of industrial education as affording the techniques and attitudes necessary for racial harmony. By such a method, therefore, Washington adduces and applies his theme.[1] Such a sequence, also, constitutes the order of climax, for it is probable that most audiences—even educational groups—were more

---

[1] Unfortunately the student of rhetoric has available in print no reasonably complete text of a speech embodying this arrangement, although 23 of the 102 speeches that form the basis of this study unmistakably reveal this order and sequence. The plan persisted throughout Washington's career; it is evident as late as Dec. 2, 1912, in an address at the Academy of Music, Philadelphia.

The best illustration of the inductive plan is an address delivered at the Carnegie Music Hall, Mar. 3, 1896. In the Booker T. Washington materials at Tuskegee the entire text exists in the author's handwriting. What Washington may have intended as a complete statement of the controlling idea occurs there after the brief history of Tuskegee's growth.

Cited below is an outline of a typical speech in support of Tuskegee. The heads, taken from sheets in Washington's handwriting, represent either the notes he took to the platform or the guide he employed in dictating the speech to his secretary, or both. The speech was delivered at the Presbyterian Church, Ithaca, N. Y., Apr. 8, 1894.

Location—
Number
History
Students:—
No. age, sex, Teachers
Earnestness
Studies:—
Mental
Moral & Rel.
Board
Ind. Skill & Value
Dignity
Moral Value
Property:—
$200,000
Land
Buildings
No debt
Trustees
$66,000

(Footnote continued on page 427.)

interested in his solution of the race problem than in a discourse merely upon education at Tuskegee. The expository-inductive plan, it should be observed, may well have been the result of Washington's belief that "the average audience . . . wants facts rather than generalities or sermonizing. Most people . . . are able to draw proper conclusions if they are given the facts in an interesting form. . . . "[1]

Besides the expository-inductive method of disposition, Washington likes to present the chief parts of the discussion topically, often in this order: material or industrial, educational, moral, religious, and social. Most of his speeches reveal all these heads, but they are not all developed to the same extent. Special heads receive extended treatment according to the group addressed. When, for example, he bids frankly for support of Tuskegee before a receptive Northern group, he devotes most time to education, although the other heads are treated adequately.[2] Or when he faces an audience, Northern or Southern, that has heard of Vardaman's denunciation of Negro education, he passes lightly over education at Tuskegee and amplifies the topic of the salutary industrial and moral results of the limited education vouchsafed his race.[3] Similarly, in his annual addresses to the National Negro Business League, he dwells primarily on the material progress made by businessmen, on the additional opportunities before them, and considers but briefly the other heads. Thus, Washington's method of classification enables him to strike the right notes for a given audience and occasion.[4]

Country:—	Remedy:—
Mortgage	Good of Slavery
Ind. Debts	Negro works
Rents—	Mt. Meigs
Cabins	Old Man
Tenn.	Conference
Educational Teachers	Hungry Man
Houses	Give up world
81 cents	Races:—
Body & Chickens	Business
Moral & Rel. Cabins	Something whites want
$55—3	Brick yard
Scattered families	Saying "Mr"
	Voting

[1] *Up from Slavery*, p. 244.

[2] See the topical outline already cited and "The Influence of the Negroes' Citizenship," *loc. cit.*

[3] "Negro Education Not a Failure," *Selected Speeches*, pp. 118–134.

[4] Some of the Sunday Evening Talks reveal such classification, although they are not made evident by captions and signpost phrases. See "Teamwork," Oct. 17, 1915, *Selected Speeches*, pp. 271–276, where the speaker counsels cooperation because it means honesty and

Such topical disposition and classification may be in part responsible for the extraordinary vigor in the movement of Washington's addresses. Since most of his speeches boil down to the same logical content,[1] the scheme, applicable to most of his audiences and yet elastic to allow easy and logical amplification of any part, manifestly encourages great variety of emphasis and subordination. The apparent inclusiveness of the scheme, furthermore, gives the impression of having revealed all the facets of the theme, until the hearer feels that he has been shown not merely the beginning of the subject but its end.[2]

The progression of ideas in Washington's speeches is distinguished, also, by movement from the less interesting to the more interesting. In most instances this does not involve a methodical building up in stair-step fashion from topic to topic until a single climactic point is attained;[3] rather, the more factual, less emotionally charged topics, placed in the first half or two-thirds of an address, are succeeded by the more emotionally charged, intenser lines of argument, and the hearer is thus carried from a lower to a higher tone. In the expository-inductive arrangement the effect is obvious.[4]

Delivery

Booker Washington chose to deliver his speeches in a direct, lively conversational mode. Probably he is the first important Negro speaker in this country to forsake stilted elocutionary methods of utterance in favor of

economy of time and money. Even in commemorative addresses, the usual categories are manifest upon careful inspection. The Shaw speech hails the freedom granted by the Civil War but suggests that freedom can be *won* only through the Negro's own industry to raise himself mentally, morally, and materially.—"Address Delivered at the Dedication of the Robert Gould Shaw Monument," Boston, May 31, 1897, *ibid.*, pp. 54–59. The Lincoln anniversary speeches contain a similar line of thought, but instead of exhorting to future action, as does the Shaw speech, they emphasize what the Negro has already done along educational, material, moral, and social lines.—"Address on Abraham Lincoln Delivered before the Republican Club," New York, Feb. 12, 1909, *ibid.*, pp. 190–199. *Cf.* "Address in Commemoration of the Birth of Abraham Lincoln," Philadelphia, Feb. 14, 1899, and "The Proclamation: Forty-eight Years Afterward," Grand Rapids, Mich., Feb. 12, 1912.

[1] Similarity in the content of speeches, extracts, and notes, of course, demonstrates this. Testimony furnishes further corroboration. Dr. Monroe Work has asserted that Washington really had but one speech, and an editor has observed that the black orator's message "does not vary, although great force and benefit attend the repetitions."—*Washington Evening Star*, Sept. 14, 1907, p. 4.

[2] Observe that Washington did not find very useful a threefold classification consisting of body-mind-spirit, for it appears only in the first half of an address at Quinn Chapel, Chicago, Aug. 13, 1909.

[3] Notable exceptions are the "Atlanta Address" and the "Harvard Address," both in *Selected Speeches*, and the "Address at the Peace Jubilee Exercises," Chicago, Oct. 16, 1898, printed in the *Chicago Times-Herald*, Oct. 18, 1898, pp. 5, 8.

[4] See the speech on the "Influence of the Negroes' Citizenship."

428

a direct conversational quality. His mode of utterance has little of the grand style and the thunder of Frederick Douglass. People who knew Washington for many years—such as Dr. Robert E. Park, of the University of Chicago, Dr. Robert Moton, who succeeded Washington as principal of Tuskegee, and James Weldon Johnson—state that "he had none of the oratorical tricks of the average Negro orator. . . . "[1] Certainly there is no striving stylistically, for his utterances contain few rhetorical figures. Fond of contrast and balance, he uses both not only in antithetical constructions[2] but in the arrangement of divisions within the speech in such a way that advice to the whites is balanced by advice to the blacks,[3] that praise is followed by condemnation, and that pleasant images are offset by unpleasant images.[4] Except in illustrations, his diction is not rich in imagery. Such imagery as does appear consists of simple, visual pictures of external reality; save for occasional synecdoche and personification, it is literal, not figurative.

Washington's conversational quality in delivery has at least two elements. There is a keen and vivid rethinking and recreation of what he prepared to say, the badge of such mental activity being an appearance of spontaneity, for which some observers have used the phrase "quite unstudied." The second element, of which Washington was ever conscious, is a keen sense or feeling of direct communication. On this element of conversational quality, George Foster Peabody's observation is representative of many others: He "was always finely reponsive to his audience which was fully responsive to him. . . . " His address to white groups was frequently interrupted by applause, and his talks to his own race, especially the farmer, were punctuated with responses of, "That's right, Booker"; "You've got him there, Mr. Washington."

Booker Washington was well aware of being in direct contact with his hearers. In *Up from Slavery*, after confessing to extreme nervousness before a speech, he records impressions that only a real speaker has:

There is great compensation, though, for this preliminary nervous suffering, that comes to me after I have been speaking for about ten minutes, and have come to feel that I have really mastered my audience, and that we have gotten into full and complete sympathy with each other. It seems to me that there is rarely such a combination of mental and physical delight in any effort as that

[1] Letters to the author.

[2] A favorite antithetical passage may be seen in the Atlanta Address, *Selected Speeches*, p. 35.

[3] The Atlanta Address is a good illustration.

[4] In the last "Business League Address," *Selected Speeches*, pp. 251–270, as H. O. Cook has suggested, Washington carefully balanced forces for good and for evil, *e.g.*, on the one hand, an improvement in Negro health, on the other, an increase in the number of lynchings. See also the last two paragraphs of the "Harvard Address," *Selected Speeches*, p. 53.

which comes to a public speaker when he feels that he has a great audience completely within his control. There is a thread of sympathy and oneness that connects a public speaker with his audience, that is just as strong as though it was something tangible and visible.[1]

Perhaps in self-defense, Washington set out early in his career to compel his audience to listen, for he reports that "nothing tends to throw me off my balance so quickly, when I am speaking, as to have some one leave the room. To prevent this, I make up my mind . . . that I will try to make my address so interesting . . . that no one can leave."[2]

Washington's habit of speaking extemporaneously—except on some of the greater occasions early in his career—may well have promoted that "thread of sympathy and oneness" between speaker and audience. In the preparation of his speeches, he studied and repeated enough to assimilate a sequence of ideas and words, whose pattern was sufficiently elastic to allow last-minute adaptation.[3] "When I first began speaking in public," he writes in 1911, "I used to follow the plan to a great extent of committing speeches to memory. This plan, however, I soon gave up. At present I do not commit speeches to memory, except on very important occasions, or when I am to speak on an entirely new subject."[4] Confronted with intensive speechmaking activity soon after the Atlanta Address, he may well have modified his method of preparation:

The plan which I now follow is this: I think out what I want to say pretty carefully. . . . I write head lines or little suggestions that will call my attention to the points that I wish to make. . . . After having thought out the general line of my speech, and then having prepared my head lines, I have for a number of years been accustomed to dictate my speech to a stenographer. By long practice, I have found that . . . I can take my headlines or memorandum sheet and follow the dictation almost exactly. . . . [5]

The dictation, he explains, not only makes possible an advance copy to the press but also "leaves me free while speaking to throw aside . . . stiffness and formality . . . and to take advantage of any local interests that would give a more lively colour to what I have to say."[6]

Concerning the physical aspects of utterance—pitch, tempo, volume, and quality—the available evidence is contradictory. Some people declare

[1] *Up from Slavery*, pp. 242–243.

[2] *Up from Slavery*, p. 244. " . . . I always suffer intensely from nervousness before speaking. More than once, just before I was to make an important address, this nervous strain has been so great that I have resolved never again to speak in public."—*Ibid.*, p. 242.

[3] Washington considers the merits of the memorized and the extemporaneous speech in *My Larger Education*, pp. 95–96.

[4] *Ibid.*, p. 95.

[5] *Ibid.*, p. 96.

[6] *Ibid.*

that Washington's voice had considerable modulation and flexibility, yet a phonograph record of part of the Atlanta Address reveals a fairly high-pitched voice in a flat reading pattern that borders on monotony. For the performance on the record, however, allowance must be made for the imperfections of reproduction of 40 years ago, for the speaker's reading from manuscript, and for the strangeness of the recording experience. Most of those who have heard Washington describe his voice as low and vibrant and fairly responsive to changes of mood.

With respect to tempo, opinion also differs sharply. In the Tuskegee Sunday Evening Talks, Washington is supposed to have talked so fast that shorthand experts had to invent special symbols to keep abreast, yet his son declares that his father *always* spoke rather slowly. Many people state that Washington spoke the introduction of a speech haltingly, as if he were feeling his way for words or seeking to establish control over himself; those who have heard him many times before Negro groups, particularly on his tours among farmers, say that he invariably commenced vigorously and swiftly. We may perhaps conclude, therefore, that the tempo of Booker Washington's utterance represents an adaptation to the occasion and the subject matter.

The cadence of his speech seems to be marked by short periods, rather than long, and always to be distinguished by a kind of explosive emphasis—some describe it as clipped—at the close of the final breath group of a sentence. Although unable to describe or to illustrate this phenomenon accurately, all observers agree that this gave to his delivery great impact and drive. Such forcefulness, however, is doubtless due in part to simple predication, relatively unencumbered by qualifying clauses and by restrictive phrases except the adverbial. The active voice, the finite verb, the simple adjective rule an utterance that is seldom interrupted by signpost devices.

Washington never gave the impression of speaking loudly or with effort. Despite this, the audience never missed a word, whether it numbered 300 people or 12,000, whether it was in an auditorium having perfect acoustics, in a tobacco warehouse, or in the open air. In reporting the Atlanta Address, George Creelman sat 75 feet from the speaker in a press box so placed that he missed half of the other speeches. Booker Washington's he heard word for word. It is probable, then, that in his early speaking days at Hampton Institute, Washington established correct habits of voice placement. After hearing him make eight speeches in a single day, one man asserts that Washington's voice did not sound tired. In his early days, also, Washington probably achieved good habits of articulation and enunciation, and these, along with proper voice placement, probably account for his distinctness of utterance.

Booker Washington's pronunciation was in the main that of the educated Southerner. His speech betrayed nothing of the Negroid, a fact often deemed worthy of remark by the educated white. An English observer seemed delighted to discover that "his accent is exactly that of the educated American. Shutting one's eyes, it would be impossible to know that a Negro was speaking."[1] Some observers, moreover, suggest an impediment in his speech, although no one has designated it exactly. Some say he experienced difficulty with the word *institution;* others intimate that the speaker showed traces of a defect that had not been entirely conquered. His utterance, as one young woman expresses it, was "clear and distinct . . . , but suggesting careful control of some slight impediment."[2]

As he faced an audience, Booker Washington's personal appearance was not striking. That he was a tall, magnificent physical specimen who dominated a group by sheer presence is a fond folk tale. Negroes who expected to see a flashily dressed man with at least one sparkling diamond were greatly disappointed.[3] Habitually dressing conservatively in a black cutaway coat with pencil-striped trousers, he probably appeared to most people as he did to a Washington journalist: "There is nothing in Dr. Washington's appearance to distinguish him from thousands of other negroes of the mulatto type. He is of medium stature, and his features are not large, but rather of the 'pug' or bull-dog type."[4] Such is the man who would stand beside the lectern, talking directly and forcefully to his hearers.

In gesture and in movement about the platform Booker Washington exercised good taste. Unlike most Negro orators, he gestured little and walked about even less. In his right hand, held in front at waist level, would be a few notes or a lead pencil, firmly clutched. His left hand, if not engaged with a watch chain, would hang at his side, its thumb often caught in the left trouser pocket. The free hand would occasionally mark an emphatic point, in sympathy with a bending forward of the body, as if to get in close touch with the audience. Occasionally, he would move from one side of the lectern to the other and at times turn momentarily to speak to those on the platform behind him. It seems, accordingly, that Booker Washington did not take care to go beyond the simple emphatic gesture and bodily movement necessary to reach the wings and extremities of an audience.

Booker T. Washington, then, appears as a speaker who is remarkably shrewd in identifying his program with those attitudes and opinions that

[1] Clipping from a London newspaper (name and date not known).

[2] From a personal letter. *Cf.* James Weldon Johnson: "It appeared to me that he always made a great effort to secure clear enunciation."

[3] Scott and Stowe, *Booker T. Washington*, pp. 223–224. The jacket of *Selected Speeches* has a good picture. The typical posture, thumb in trousers pocket and pencil gripped in hand, is seen in a photograph in the *New York Evening Mail*, Jan. 23, 1906.

[4] George Roberts, *Des Moines Register and Leader*, Mar. 30, 1904, p. 4.

were congenial to the North and South and, in some degree, to the Negro. Skillful in such adaptation and in the use of humor and emotional address to the hearer, skillful in his self-portrait as a man of good judgment and the right moral qualities, he must have seemed to an American audience as an American orator. A happy choice of ideas, coupled with good sense in the arrangement of his speeches and in their style of delivery, mark this good man skilled in speaking.

In view of Washington's qualities as a speaker, it is not surprising that Henry Watterson should have declared that "the death of Booker Washington is a national misfortune. . . . "[1] Hundreds of news reports and editorials bear witness as to the enthusiastic reception of his various speeches by North and South alike. But praise was not all, for the development of Tuskegee—and, indeed, the growth of Negro education elsewhere—is beyond doubt traceable in some part to the wisdom with which Washington used his skill in speech. Perhaps ultimately the effectiveness of his rhetoric is no better seen than in the phenomenal increase, since 1880, in the Negroes' ownership of homes, land, and business enterprises. Many forces, of course, are responsible for such growth, but the message of thrift and industry, so persistently delivered, so clearly and compellingly presented to all classes of Negroes, at least served as a powerful catalyst.

SELECTED BIBLIOGRAPHY

Of Booker T. Washington's own works, *Up from Slavery* (1901), *Working with the Hands* (1904), and *My Larger Education* (1911) are autobiographical. *Selected Speeches of Booker T. Washington* (E. D. Washington, ed., 1932) is the only readily available source of speeches and speech extracts that are addressed to the general public; *Character Building* (1902) and *Putting the Most into Life* (1906) are collections of Sunday Evening Talks to Tuskegee students, carefully edited before publication. Valuable for general information concerning Negro orators is C. G. Woodson's *Negro Orators and Their Orations* (1925). For additional biography as well as for background, consult B. F. Riley, *The Life and Times of Booker T. Washington* (1916) and E. J. Scott, and L. B. Stowe, *Booker T. Washington: Builder of a Civilization* (1917).

In W. E. B. Du Bois's *The Souls of the Black Folk* (1903) and Merle Curti's *The Social Ideals of American Educators* (1935) may be found a general statement and appraisal of Washington's educational and racial ideals. Excellent are Benjamin Brawley's *A Social History of the American Negro* (1921) and his *A Short History of the American Negro* (1931) for a general appreciation of the Negro's lot; good also are Charles S. Johnson, *The Negro in American Civilization* (1930) and James Weldon Johnson's autobiography *Along This Way* (1934). The various editions of the *Negro Year Book* (Monroe N. Work, ed.) contain statistical data.

General knowledge of the period may be derived from Louis M. Hacker and B. B. Kendrick, *The United States Since 1865* (1932), Charles A. Beard, and Mary R. Beard, *The Rise of American Civilization* (1930), Harold U. Faulkner, *American Economic History* (1931). Also very helpful are Allan Nevin's *Letters of Grover Cleveland* (1933), Henry F. Pringle's *Theodore Roosevelt: A Biography* (1931), and J. B. Bishop's *Theodore Roosevelt and His Time* (1920). Adequate studies of the South are E. G. Hawk, *Economic History of the South* (1934), F. P. Gaines, *The Southern Plantation* (1925), and Holland Thompson, *The New South* (1919).

[1] E. J. Scott, "Memorial Address," in C. G. Woodson, *Negro Orators and Their Orations* (Washington, D.C., 1925), p. 609.

14

Rufus Choate

by JOHN W. BLACK

Rufus Choate was born at Hog Island (Choate Island), Ipswich, Mass., October 1, 1799; early education under private tutors; was graduated from Dartmouth, 1819 (valedictorian); attended Cambridge Law School one year; subsequent study in private offices. He was admitted to the bar in 1823; practiced at Danvers, Mass., 1823–1828; at Salem, Mass., 1828–1834; Boston, Mass., 1834–1859. Politics, Whig. Offices, Massachusetts state legislature, 1826–1830; United States House of Representatives, 1831–1834; Senate, 1841–1845; attorney general, Massachusetts, 1854. Died at sea, July 13, 1859.

In his native Massachusetts Rufus Choate earned a speaker's fame that carried him up and down New England, to New York, and on to Washington. His vigorous delivery, seemingly limitless sentences, acute cross examination—these and "success" gave rise to a legend that with a few manuscripts of speeches remains a romantic story in American oratory. It is both legend and fact that he addressed juries and judges, legislators and the public on subjects and occasions as varied as the scope of public address. The legend yields another fact, and one often forgotten: this name, prominent among forensic, deliberative, and demonstrative speakers, denoted primarily a lawyer. Whenever another interest threatened to encroach upon his professional duties the lawyer returned to law office and court.

Certainly his offices in the upper and lower houses of both the Massachusetts General Assembly and the United States Congress were not a major interest. His colleague, Cushing, lamented Choate's irregular attendance in the assembly, and Choate himself reported his return to legal duties some time before the assembly adjourned.[1] Nor was he attached wholeheartedly to his work in Congress. He wrote to Briggs during their term in the lower house that his legal work would cause him to arrive 10 days late in Washington and added, "Let us do our duty . . . but stick chiefly to our profession of law."[2] After two terms in the House of Representatives

[1] C. M. Fuess, *Caleb Cushing* (Harcourt, Brace and Company, 1923), I, 85. Choate autographs, Harvard College Library; Choate to William Calhoun, Mar. 10, 1827.
[2] Choate to George N. Briggs, Nov. 10, 1832, Dartmouth College Library.

Choate refused to be a candidate for re-election. Later, when drafted to succeed Webster in the Senate, he found his office far from engrossing; he frequently wrote of his plans to withdraw and subsequently resigned. Meanwhile, he never withdrew from the court. For example, in preparation for the boundary case between Rhode Island and Massachusetts before the United States Supreme Court, Senator Choate, counsel for Massachusetts, wrote several letters to Sumner for pertinent information. And when, three days prior to the date set for the hearing, February 20, 1844, the counsel for Rhode Island succeeded in having the case continued, Choate immediately wrote to Sumner:

> To my horror and annoyance the court has just continued our cause to the next term! . . . I regret this result, on all accounts and especially that the constant preparatory labors of a month are for the present wholly lost. I had actually withdrawn from the Senate chamber to make up this argument. . . . Shall I ask you as a confidential and special act of friendship, to make this matter known to the public through *any of our papers*—in such manner . . . as to convey the fact that counsel of Massachusetts have somewhat *engrossingly prepared . . . the cause.* It explains *silence elsewhere;* is true, and might be kind. The honest truth is, I have spent a full month, day and night on the [this?] thing.[1]

Clearly then, regardless of the quality of his deliberative speeches, Choate's first interest was not in legislative work.[2] Likewise, demonstrative speaking was secondary. Of eight letters at hand in which he declined invitations to deliver occasional speeches, seven state or imply, as his reason for not accepting, legal engagements.[3] Although some of his demonstrative speeches may merit high rank in American oratory, they represent a superstructure built upon a reputation gained in forensic speaking.

In his first interest, law, Choate was eminently successful throughout his practice of 35 years, 1824–1859. The evidence of his early success as a pleader lies in court dockets. For example, he entered thirty-five cases in the docket for the court of common pleas, Essex County (Massachusetts),

---

[1] Choate to Sumner, Feb. 17, 1844, Harvard College Library; material collected by Samuel Gilman Brown for his biography of Choate.

[2] Further evidence that Choate held his profession of the active lawyer above what was to him the routine of office lies in his resigning the post of attorney general (Massachusetts) after he had held office scarcely a year (1854) and in his declining Governor Briggs's offer of a seat on the (Massachusetts) supreme court. (1849).

[3] Massachusetts Historical Society Library: letters decline invitations to speak before the Roxbury Lyceum, 1839, at Plymouth, 1845, and to deliver eulogy of Webster at Boston, 1852. Dartmouth: letters decline invitations to speak before South Boston Lyceum, 1834, and at Dartmouth, 1858. Boston Public Library: letters decline two invitations to speak, one invitation being from Dartmouth. Essex Institute: letter declines invitation to speak at Danvers, 1836.

March term, 1827.[1] These were civil cases and include neither his work in criminal actions nor trials before other courts—this in his third year of practice. In the same year he first appeared before the supreme judicial court in Essex County and had a part in four of the eighteen cases reported for the November term.[2] Two years later he was involved in eight of the sixteen cases reported from that court, and in 1836, as a resident of Boston, he returned to Essex County to have a part in three-fourths of the reported cases before the same court. So complete was his success during his early practice that the rumor became current that Choate never lost a case before a jury in Essex County. His place in the more competitive Suffolk County bar became equally high during his long Boston practice, where, according to his son-in-law and partner Bell, he appeared before the court in seventy cases annually. Corroboration is too abundant for one to suppose that the law reporter for the *Advertiser* (Boston) bore mere flattery to Choate in 1849 in a note of introduction written by Parsons: "As you will provide him with a large share of his work, I have taken the liberty of asking for him the pleasure of your acquaintance."[3] So it is that facts justify the laudatives of the Choate legend, *e.g.*, the great American advocate, the wizard of the law, foremost jury lawyer.

In view of his primary interests and rank in his profession, it appears appropriate to devote this study to an investigation of Choate's extant forensic oratory, more especially since this aspect of his endeavors has been largely a neglected topic.[4]

[1] Office of the clerk of court, Essex County (Massachusetts).

[2] Of the varied types of cases tried before the supreme judicial court only cases dealing with points of law were recorded in the *Massachusetts Reports*.

[3] Theophilus Parsons to Choate, Jan. 23, 1849, Dartmouth College Library; E. P. Wheeler, "Harvard Law School and the Lawyers of 1858," 2 New York Law Review, 2, No. 8: 317.

[4] It is not difficult to surmise why Choate is represented in American oratory as a deliberative and demonstrative speaker and his forensic speeches are given merely praise. This has been determined partially by the availability of speeches. The demonstrative speeches usually were written before delivery and published subsequently in pamphlet editions; likewise, his important deliberative speeches were recorded, at least partially, and often put into pamphlet editions. The courtroom speeches, however, existed only as notes and pleas, no court stenographer recording the addresses. Choate's lament on John Adams, "Of that series of spoken eloquence all is perished; not one reported sentence has come down to us," is nearly true of his own legal speeches—"The Eloquence of Revolutionary Periods." Only Parker's excerpts from pleas and a few cases reported by newspapers remain. Also, it is likely that subject matter has contributed to determining what speeches should be preserved. Brown, Choate's biographer and the most extensive collector of his speeches, was aided by members of Choate's immediate family, and it is possible that the lofty themes of the occasional speeches, *e.g.*, the eulogies on Webster, made them much easier to include than the few available forensic speeches, all scandalous in nature. Finally, the great length of the courtroom speeches prohibits extensive reprintings. Even Snyder's *Legal Masterpieces* and *American State Trials* reproduce only portions of the plea in the Dalton trial. So complete has been the dominance

Professional Training

There is little reason to assume that in Rufus's preparation for Dartmouth College his reading of Vergil, Cicero's orations, or the Greek Testament had a professional aim. Indeed, in view of his word to Washington Choate, a younger brother, during Rufus's third year at Dartmouth, that he disdained law and desired to teach, it seems apparent that for the greater part of his time in college he had at most no inflexible desire to become a lawyer.[1] By the early part of his fourth year, however, he had determined to follow law and wrote to his brother David a plan for securing the money necessary for a period of study at Cambridge Law School.[2] Meanwhile, according to Professor Foster, Choate pursued at Dartmouth a curriculum heavily weighted with Greek and Latin, both language and literature, composition and speaking, mathematics and philosophy.[3] There was also the Wednesday-afternoon "speaking," probably the device for administering the allied curricular requirement, and more speaking in the Social Friends, Choate's literary society.[4] Although he was not often on its programs, he doubtless achieved a reputation among the membership for being an effective speaker, for on April 7, preceding the commencement of August, 1819, he was selected unanimously the commencement speaker for the society and was elected to a committee to determine the subject for the commencement disputation.[5] Further, he was elected, presumably by the faculty, to deliver the valedictory. Rufus Choate's record during his five years at Dartmouth as a student and a tutor was a good one, and although he was not studying the law he was shaping the forensic speaker. Characteristics of the undergraduate that later distinguished the lawyer were a fondness for and familiarity with literature, a capacity for effective

---

of his deliberative and demonstrative speeches that today no complete forensic speech is available to the general reader.

[1] James Adams to John Wheelock, Aug. 4, 1815; Choate to Washington Choate, Nov. 8, 1817; both letters in the Dartmouth College Library.

[2] Choate to David Choate, Mar. 25, 1819, Dartmouth College Library.

[3] H. D. Foster, "Webster and Choate in College," *Dartmouth Alumni Magazine*, 19: 509–519, 605–616.

[4] S. H. Willey, MS, Dartmouth 1841–1845, Dartmouth College Library. This manuscript casts doubt upon the prominence of speaking in the Dartmouth curriculum. Although Willey describes the curriculum in effect 20 years after Choate left Dartmouth, he is writing of a teacher of rhetoric who was graduated from Dartmouth but 11 years after Choate was graduated. "But the college training in the Rhetorical department in those days was wholly with the pen. We never had a lesson from any college officer in extemporaneous speaking of any kind. . . . There were supposed to be some debates in the societies, but they were few, and awakened little interest."

[5] Minutes of the meetings of the Society of the Social Friends, 1812–1819, Dartmouth College Library.

speaking, and an eagerness for work. Throughout all he was both thorough and systematic.

After studying for a year in the Cambridge Law School, Choate completed his apprenticeship in the offices of William Wirt, Asa Andrews, and David Cummins, in Washington, D.C., Ipswich, Mass., and Salem, Mass., respectively.

A critical analysis of Choate's works and of his friends' reminiscences reveals a striking constancy in the man. It is especially pertinent that he developed a system of forensic rhetoric and never altered it materially. Similarly, Parker's accounts of his conversations with Choate show a similarity in topics year after year.[1] This, although possibly due to the biases of an editor, is in keeping with a marked constancy in habits of study and reading and the consistency between his advice for young lawyers and his own practices both early and late. He strove diligently to perfect a forensic system but never tried to change it fundamentally. If this assumption is correct, Choate did more creating as an apprentice and a beginning lawyer than in his later years as a flourishing advocate.

Although no examination of extant documents can reveal the whole of Choate's work during this early period, some indications of its nature can be gleaned. Apart from an obvious note of success in his work under Attorney General Wirt, a few lines from a letter indicate an activity of major importance, Choate's attachment to books:

> W[ebster] promised me [Sewall] that if he [Choate] could come with him he would grant him every facility in his power. While here [Washington] he made great proficiency & gained the admiration & esteem of all who knew him. Mr. Wirt told me a few days since that he never met with a young man who was his equal. . . . The only fault he had while here was too close application to books. . . . [2]

This reading was not limited to legal topics but extended to divers fields. It was while suffering from "too close application to books" that he wrote his college friend James Marsh:

> I am sadly at a loss for books here, but I sit three days every week in the large Congressional Library, and am studying our own extensive ante-revolutionary history, and reading your favorite Gibbon. The only classic I can get is Ovid; and while I am about it, let me say, too, that I read every day some chapters in an English Bible.[3]

[1] E. G. Parker, *Reminiscences of Rufus Choate* (Mason Brothers, 1860).

[2] Thomas Sewall to Mills Olcott, Apr. 10, 1822, Dartmouth College Library. Because of Choate's desire to be near his family in Ipswich he never studied in Webster's office.

[3] S. G. Brown, *The Life and Writings of Rufus Choate* (Little, Brown, & Company, 1862) I, 15. The Marsh-Choate correspondence seems to be lost.

Nor was this apparently extralegal reading purely recreational. Choate considered it a part of the study of law, an essential part, and later advised all students of law to include it in their professional preparations. Among these tasks which he outlined for students—the master lecturing the aspiring—was to read English law, the statute law, the annual reports of decisions, and—American history, general literature, and rhetoric.

Choate's study of legal works during his apprenticeship is reflected by subsequent practices and advice. Since Choate's habits were constant, it is possible to state almost categorically as some of his preparatory labors the practices that he followed throughout his professional experience. First, he studied Roman and English law in order to discover the sources of American law. Second, he read the reported arguments for a case, wrote the probable decision for that case and then compared his decision with the actual one handed down. Third, he divided legal books into topics and pursued each topic through other books. Fourth, and throughout all, he read with a pen in hand and made copious notes on the material.

Thus a large share of the training of Rufus Choate lay in his devotion to books, both legal and general. If his "fault" in 1822 was "too close application to books," it was one that he incorporated so completely that it remained his throughout his practice, and again the fact ascended into the Choate legend. About twenty years after the "fault" had been noted he made a note of his reading for a week.

I have read and digested a half-dozen pages of Greenleaf on Evidence, and as many of Story on the Dissolution of Partnership. Other studies of easier pursuit, nor wholly useless—if studies I may denominate them—I have remembered in those spaces of time which one can always command, though few employ. The pregnant pages in which Tacitus reports . . . I have read for Latin. They include pp. 14–17 in the edition of Ernesti and Oberlin. . . . In Greek I have reached the two hundred and fifty-first line of the fifth Odyssey . . . I read in French a dissertation of the Memoirs of the Academie of Inscriptions, vol. 2; on the Chronology of the Odyssey; began one on Cicero's Discovery of the Tomb of Archimedes. For English I have read Johnson's Lives to the beginning of Dryden; Alison, a little; Antony and Cleopatra, a little; Quintilian's chapters on Writing, and on Extempore Speech, I have read and re-read; but mean tomorrow to abridge and judge.[1]

A further part of Choate's legal training came from eminent lawyers. He talked with them and watched them in action. For example, during his study under Wirt he heard Pinkney and Webster before the Supreme Court. How extensive such experience was is not clear, but that he con-

---

[1] Brown, *op. cit.*, I, 67.

sidered hearing these two men to be important is implied in his frequent references to the events in his conversations with Parker. Also, he conversed with Judge Story, particularly with respect to further preparation for law, and it was Story, formerly of Salem, who advised him to enter Cummins's office in Salem.

Here is at least a part, and probably the larger part, of the training of Rufus Choate, a preparation that fitted him for the legal scene of a pre-specialization era. He made himself ready for the sundry branches of law: criminal, patent, marine, constitutional; in varied courts: city, state, Federal; and before many officials: justices of the peace, police magistrates, referees, juries, single judges, and a bench of judges. Such a prospect made the Choate legend possible.

Invention

In view of the variety that circumscribed the forensic endeavors of Rufus Choate and the success that he enjoyed, one might expect his legal speeches to reflect an extraordinary versatility. On the contrary, they abound in similarities. His methodology, although exactly applied in each instance, remains practically identical among his cases. This is especially true in the invention of his argument, and perhaps in establishing this fact and describing the typical endeavor lies whatever may be of value in an analysis of Choate's forensic oratory.

The essential characteristics of the Choate plea were detected by a news reporter and put into his account of the inconsequential Mumfords case, a trial in which Choate had a part scarcely two years after the beginning of his practice.

The Counsel [Choate] for the defendants then opened the defence in an address to the Justice of an hour's length: remarked with great emphasis upon the contradictory evidence on the other side; the character of the complainant and his family, and the fact that the Commonwealth's Counsel had, after repeated solicitation, refused to introduce him as a witness: . . .

The witnesses on both sides all underwent close and scrutinizing cross examinations, particularly by the defendants' counsel, in regard to many minute circumstances, contradictions in testimony, &c. . . . The defence occupied four hours, and we venture to say a more ingenious or plausible one could not have been made.[1]

[1] *The Salem* (Mass.) *Gazette*, Nov. 18, 1825. The Mumfords case grew out of a tavern brawl. Two Crowninshields of Danvers were refused drinks, helped themselves, and engaged in a fight with the tavern owners, the Mumfords, a colored family. The owners alleged destruction of property and riot; the Crowninshields alleged assault. Larkin Thorndike sued for the Mumfords. Choate defended the Crowninshields. The trial was before Justice Ezekiel Savage in Salem, Mass.

This prophetic passage might have been recast in terms of other dates and courts and used as a general description of Choate's defense of Helen Dalton (alleged adultery), of Albert Tirrell (alleged murder), of Devins (alleged mismanagement of ship), of ship *Timor* (to determine the value of certain towage services), of William Tuckerman (alleged embezzlement), or of his charges for the complainants John Hammond (for divorce) and the natural heirs of Oliver Smith (to break a will), the nucleus of Choate's extant law practice.

A similarity is especially evident in Choate's treatments of like cases as revealed in documents relative to two actions argued 18 years apart, both being libels for divorce. The *Hammond v. Hammond* case was brought to trial in May, 1839, with Choate representing the libelant John Hammond.[1] *Dalton v. Dalton* was tried in April, 1857, with Choate for the defendant Helen Dalton.[2] These cases have been preserved in totally different forms, Choate's manuscript brief for the former and a presumably verbatim account of the latter. Thus, in view of the intervening 18 years, the dissimilar types of extant documents, with Choate for the defendant in one instance and the libelant in the other, discernible similarities between

[1] John D. Hammond and Lucinda Eaton were married by S. Streeter, Apr. 3, 1836. Some time in 1838 Hammond sued his wife for divorce on the charge of adultery. Mrs. Hammond retaliated with a similar charge on May 16, 1839, a very short time before the original libel was tried. Mr. and Mrs. Hammond lived together less than a year, after which he went to Canton, N.Y., while she remained in Boston. The case in itself was probably of little importance. Hammond was a housewright and a painter; Mrs. Hammond was a house friend. No mention was made in the newspapers of the trial. The case becomes important in a study of Choate, however, because of its similarity to the Dalton case several years later. The brief and the examination notes for the case are divided, part of them being in the Dartmouth College Library and the remainder in the Massachusetts Historical Society Library. Just when Choate came into the case is not clear. The original libel was brought by Osgood Park, justice of the peace and counsel for the defendant. Choate either entered the case at Osgood's request or supplanted him in the case.

[2] B. Frank Dalton (twenty-four) married Helen Maria Gove (seventeen) July 12, 1855. Business forced Dalton to be away from his home and his wife spent much of her time with her sister, Mrs. Edward Coburn. Unknown to their husbands, the two women began to keep company with two young men, Sumner and Porter. Dalton happened to find a letter from Sumner to Mrs. Dalton. Both women confessed to their husbands. The husbands at once met Sumner and Porter, who confessed their relationships with the women but denied all charges of adultery. The husbands, infuriated, beat the young men. Subsequently, Sumner became critically ill and died. Dalton and Coburn, after living with their wives during the ensuing three weeks, were charged with manslaughter and placed in jail for 1 month. They were then freed on the charge of manslaughter but refused to return to their wives. They were later charged with murder, found guilty, and served a jail term of 5 months. Meantime Dalton became convinced that his wife was guilty of adultery and brought suit for divorce. Perhaps his action was based upon a miscarriage that his wife had suffered and that had been construed as an abortion. Richard Dana, Jr., represented Dalton; Choate and Henry Durant represented Mrs. Dalton. The trial was before a jury and excited much public interest.

his apparent speeches in the two actions would seem unlikely. On the other hand, any resemblances should bear correspondingly greater weight as being representative of Choate's forensic practices.

Quoted from the brief for Hammond v. Hammond (1839)	*Quoted from the defense of Helen Dalton* (1857)
[Importance of the case]	
I consider this case of vast importance to the libelant as well as important in a more general [view].	To both of these parties [libelant and libelee] it is of supreme importance that you find this young wife . . . innocent.
[History of the parties]	
My client is a young man, child of very respectable parents, an only son, brought up in extreme habits of life, who when just turned by 21 was lured into marriage with a profligate woman 12 or 15 yrs his adult.	These parties were married in June, 1855; he was very young not more than 22 or 23 and she was only a child, not yet 18. She was the child, notwithstanding the testimony of Mrs. Coburn yesterday, of respectable, Christian parents, their youngest, and they afforded her an education and a Christian example.
[The court's opportunity to aid Choate's client]	
If we have proved a case which comes justly within the rules of law the court can extricate him from this dreadful condition. He may yet be respectable, useful and happy. If we have not he is ruined.	No verdict can give her back complete happiness. But whether she can be branded with the scarlet letter, be stricken from the role of virtuous women, be cast out, the sport of libertines—this rests with you.
[Praise of the court and the court's responsibility to the evidence]	
But it is a reason his friends and counsel should very earnestly desire to give utmost loyal, fair [consideration] to the actual evidence.	If you can here and now, on this evidence, assure this husband, that a jury of Suffolk men of honor some of them his personal friends, that he has been misled. . . .
[Statement of issues]	
There are two questions: 1. Did we fix adultery on the resp[ondent] 2. If so does she [challenge his] right of divorce.	I submit she never came to love Sumner with that love that endangers virtue. I submit also that there was never a moment when the thought of criminal connection was entertained by her. [I submit also] that her husband had her heart at first and has it today.

[Proof][1]

1. I submit we find adultery and I put this under two lines.	This woman is not guilty of adultery.

[*Prime facie* case]

1. We make a perfectly clear *prima facie* case.	There is no positive evidence of proximated acts.

[Evidence]

2. That anyone in the neighborhood who saw them at all supposed [them] man and wife is not doubted.

> Mrs. Cass, Mrs. Scott, Mr. and Mrs . . . , Mrs. Emett, Miss . . . expressly all so swear.
> They were mistrusted not. . . .
> The night is small & close
> What close walls. . . .
> A life and mode of inhuman.
> Subjected to a sunny hour. . . .

3. The next question is if they or either [one] did anything . . . calculated to carry to Miss . . . the impression that they are man & wife.

> 1. Let me say first [there is nothing to show] they did not wish to pass as man and wife. [this has been shown] by evidence that ought to satisfy the judges and man.
> 2. We make a clear *pri. fa.* case. Take it first as we have it. I rest this on this piece of fact, that his woman. . . . That is definite. They were living together in the assumed character of man & wife for 2–3 months under such circumstances as taken in connection with the former station of the parties I am not [wrong in alleging that they were guilty] of adultery, of committing the crime.

All reliable witnesses believe that Mrs. Dalton is innocent.

> The cabman so swears.
> The husband so believed originally.
> The physicians show guilt improbable.
> Literature distinguishes between flirtation and adultery.
>> Dr. Johnson, Addison, Edgeworth, Scott.

Only unreliable witnesses believe that Mrs. Dalton is guilty.

> John H. Coburn [thief].
> Edward Coburn [liar].
> Mary Hunter [mother of illegitimate child]

All known events connected with this case point to the innocence of Mrs. Dalton.

> She usually met Sumner in public places.
> On other occasions proximate acts were impossible. Mrs. Dalton was pregnant before meeting Sumner.
> The birth of the premature child was not abortion.
> Her private meeting with her husband was not the scene of a confession.
> She repulsed the advances of Sumner.
> She did not open a letter from Sumner.

[1] Throughout the remainder of the Dalton case the points are summarized by the writer. The remaining excerpts from the Hammond brief contain obvious omissions of sufficient

[Conclusion]

Let me review proof	There was no abortion.
I.*ʃ*. . . together to all. . . .	There is no reliable evidence pointing
He took her arm in his arm and	to guilt.
went [to] get a house.	All reliable evidence points to innocence.
He helped furnish this. . . .	
He . . . her & his together. . . .	
He . . . out walk together	
He . . . is fault.	
2. He ate at [and] slept under the	
same roof [with her] & in this	
event [the] outcome relates . . .	
of an attached & happy couple.	

These two outlines indicate the advocate's reliance upon commonplaces and, together with the Mumfords case, imply similarity—almost an identity—among Choate's pleas, a conclusion that is corroborated by the reported defense of Tirrell.[1] In all these cases the framework of Choate's speeches was one pattern:

I consider this case of vast importance (to you, to Massachusetts, to my client). Note the parties in the case. My client is good (young, old, Christian, honest). My adversary's client is wrong (by nature, *e.g.*, profligate, or by unintentional error). My client is unfortunately oppressed. It lies in your power to give the good man the happy life. You can do this if you will only listen to the evidence.

Look at the evidence in this case. In view of most of this evidence the following story seems probable. (There follows a detailed narrative which is both a plausible explanation of the case on trial and one which favors Choate's client.) Witnesses confirm it; motives confirm it. It is the explanation. The opposition cannot prove that it is not the explanation. In view of this explanation note the dates again in detail; note the witnesses in detail; the motives in detail. Beyond a doubt this is the true explanation. The only evidence contrary to this is the evidence of *x* witnesses. Of these witnesses *A* is bad (liar, thief, inconsistent, perjurer), *B* is bad,

---

import to reduce some of the material to disconnected words. These words are included for the information they give about the nature of Choate's briefs. Bracketed materials include interpolations and uncertain interpretations of Choate's illegible writing.

[1] Albert J. Tirrell deserted his wife and child for the company of Mrs. Maria Bickford, one of the members of a house of prostitution. Early in the morning, Oct. 27, 1846, after Tirrell had spent the night with Mrs. Bickford, she was discovered dead in her room, apparently as a result of wounds inflicted by a razor. Moreover, the house was on fire. Several articles belonging to Tirrell were in the room. Tirrell had left, and it was found that he had called in haste at a livery stable early that morning and had rented a vehicle and driver. He was later discovered in New Orleans. He was returned to Boston for trial. The case received much publicity and was published in pamphlet edition by the *Boston Daily Mail*. S. D. Parker represented the state; Choate and James C. Merrill, the defendant.

and *C* is bad. Therefore there is no reason for not accepting my explanation. Let me review the case. I now appeal to your sentiments for the sake of my client.

Choate turned this skeleton into a plea of 50,000 words in defense of Helen Dalton's character, elaborated it into a full day's speaking in defense of Albert Tirrell, and into a scarcely legible twenty-eight-page brief for John Hammond. Another glance at the Mumfords case and a scrutiny of all the available examination notes from the many other cases, a thought to the span of years over which it all occurred, and there develops a universality of a single plan among Choate's pleas. Perhaps the founders of the legend saw it, but the legend has long since lost this fact.

Much like the similarity among Choate's completed cases, appears a constancy in the contributing process; for example, the sources of his material are identified easily and show no variation from plea to plea. He spoke from two sources, the examination notes for the case and relevant books, both legal and extralegal. By far the larger part of the substance of his pleas originated in the detailed examination of witnesses. And this early step in gathering material was detailed! There are 400 pages of examination notes remaining from the case *Kimbull v. Devins*, and it is obvious that more notes for this case have been lost.[1]

With the facts before him, Choate turned to editing them, a step in which he selected the evidence to be used in his plea. Many marginal notes and underscored words in the Kimbull-Devins notes depict an early stage in the editing of the available evidence and point the way to a later organization of the material under topical headings. Examples of this reorganization are in the papers for *Thomas Brown 2D. v. Ship Timor and Cargo*, in which important testimony from all the witnesses is arranged under such topics as *weather* and *current*, or in *Kimbull v. Devins*, in which all the testimony pertinent to a *master's right to dismate* is segregated.[2] The results

[1] *Kimbull v. Devins*. The *Storm King*, a clipper ship, was engaged in the trade with China and the East Indies. She left the United States for Foo Choo Foo in June, 1855. From China she sailed for England and the United States. Her master was Henry Devins; her owners, Dane, Dana and Co. Early in the voyage a mate, Kimbull, was dismated. After leaving China, Kimbull and other members of the crew became victims of scurvy; Kimbull secured the legal services of Benjamin F. Butler and sued the master of the ship for damages. It was maintained that the ship had not been stocked with proper provisions and that the expedient course had not been followed after scurvy broke out on board ship. Choate and G. A. Somerby defended Devins. Apparently the case had two hearings, both before Metcalf and both in Middlesex County, Massachusetts. Dates, Feb. 20 or 26, 1856; Dec. 22, 23, etc., 1857. *Cf. Butler's Book* A. M. Thayer & Co. (Boston, 1892); C. C. Cutler, *Greyhounds of the Sea* (G. P. Putnam's Sons, 1930); MS notes for the case, Dartmouth College Library.

[2] Ship *Timor* left New Orleans Dec. 2, 1855, for Boston. En route she struck shoals. The sea was rough, and the ship began to leak badly. The *Island Home*, a passenger ship that ran between Nantucket and Hyannis, went to her rescue and towed her into Edgartown and

of these labors in the gathering of material are plain in both his briefs and his speeches. With the steps in mind, it is possible to trace the path that led to an array of evidence in his Hammond brief, "Mrs. Cass, Mrs. Scott, Mr. & Mrs. . . . , Mrs. Emett, Miss . . . expressly all so swear," or to its culmination in the Dalton speech, "She told Mr. William Richardson, Mr. Powers, Mrs. Ware, and Mrs. Coburn on four different occasions. . . . " And the large number of disinterested captains and physicians who testified in *Kimbull v. Devins* to the practical course for the ship and the nature of the plaintiff's disease only manifest Choate's apparent respect for voluminous evidence. That his use of material gained through examinations of the witnesses did not go unnoticed by his auditors is apparent first in the reporter's version of the Mumfords trial and again—as one of many instances—in the similar account of the Tirrell plea, "He [Choate] relied upon the testimony of nine witnesses. He read his minutes of Eben Tirrell's evidence, and referred with great effect to the testimony of the medical gentlemen. He likewise read the testimony of Mr. and Mrs. Head and dwelt upon it with great force."

Other material for the Choate plea came from his reading, this being particularly true in the instances of definitive passages and rulings in parallel cases. For example, in both the Hammond brief and the Dalton plea he referred to rulings in the ecclesiastical court, decisions that covered circumstances similar to those he was discussing. In order to establish definition in the Dalton plea, Choate read to the jury the rules governing circumstantial evidence; similarly for Tirrell, "The learned counsel . . . read from authorities some of the principles of evidence"; and for the heirs of Oliver Smith, "Mr. Choate proceeded to state his views of the legal meaning of competent witness to a will.[1] On this point various authorities were cited and commented upon, particularly the opinion of Lord Camden."

---

later into Boston. The decision of the district court was appealed to the United States Circuit Court by the owners of the *Island Home*, because they were dissatisfied with valuation placed upon the services of their ship. Choate and Harvey Jewell represented ship *Timor*. Notes for the case and the printed brief are in the Boston Athenaeum.

[1] Elderly Oliver Smith, a wealthy philanthropist of Hampshire County, Massachusetts, left the larger part of his estate to charities. The will had been witnessed by Charles P. Phelps and his sons, Charles and Theophilus P. Phelps. The heirs alleged that the testator was not of sound mind when he made the will and that the will was not witnessed by three competent witnesses. The first charge was later abandoned. The argument hinged on the competency of Theophilus P. Phelps to witness a will. Previously he had left Amherst College because of mental or nervous disorder. Counsel for the heirs, Choate, R. A. Chapman, and C. P. Huntington, attempted to show that he had never recovered. The executor was represented by Daniel Webster, C. E. Forbes, and Osymn Baker. The case was published in a pamphlet edition.—James W. Boyden, *The Evidence of the Validity of the Will of Oliver Smith* (Amherst, H. B. Nims, 1847).

In the same manner Choate based his argument in the ship *Timor* case on previous verdicts in parallel cases. Plainly, then, a share of Choate's material came into his pleas as a result of his legal reading. Somewhat more individual was his use of extralegal material, a kind of testimony that made his pleas personal and that might account for his being called by some "a literary lawyer." Typical examples of this material appear in his frequent use of maxims from the Bible and from Shakespeare in the Dalton plea, in his quotation from Burton's *Anatomy of Melancholy*, in the Oliver Smith case, and in his quotation relative to capital punishment from the *North American Review* in the Terrill trial.[1] Thus Choate compounded in his pleas some of his examination notes, pertinent material from legal works, and applicable instances from his general reading. Together they made up the testimony from which he spoke. The legend may be more generous but not more praiseworthy.

In cutting across Choate's speeches in an attempt to determine his characteristic practices, it is hardly possible to establish temporal sequences among the stages of invention. For example, it cannot be clear just when in the preparation of a case he established a line on one side of which he would not defend his client. Clearly, however, his practice of determining such a line was universal among his speeches, and it is likely that it became a part of the case before he accepted it. To say pedantically that he admitted some of the issues is not enough, for he not only admitted them but condemned his client on the grounds of these issues. For example, he censured Helen Dalton for carrying on a flirtation and heaped abuse upon Albert Tirrell for committing adultery, "He needs all the time that his Maker originally allotted him for repentance." Similarly, he praised for their noble services the claimants in the ship *Timor* case. Always, however, he broke with the opposition at the critical issue: Mrs. Dalton was not guilty of *adultery*, Tirrell did not commit *murder*, and the claimants for ship *Timor* did not deserve the *sum* they were asking. Some idea of the importance

---

[1] That Choate was not always successful with this type of evidence is shown in the judge's charge to the jury in the trial of William S. Tuckerman: "The presiding judge also remarked in this connection, that he did not think an instance put by the defendent's counsel [Choate] in argument to the jury, of the treasurer of a religious society who had, while on the street, received a small sum of money for the society, and having occasion to make a necessary purchase for himself, had used the money in his desk at home from which he intended to replace the money so spent on his return to his house, at all analogous or applicable to the case on trial."

William S. Tuckerman, of Suffolk County, Massachusetts, admitted to a member of his board of directors that he had embezzled some money. An audit of the company's finances revealed a shortage of $174,418.30. Charges were brought against Tuckerman, who retained Choate for his defense. The case was heard before the municipal court in 1856 and the supreme judicial court in 1857. Printed briefs for the case are at Dartmouth.

Choate placed upon this point of departure, up to which he could condemn his client and beyond which he must defend him, is evinced in his statement that he would have nothing to do with the Professor Webster murder case because the defendants (Webster and his friends who were seeking Choate's services) would not admit homicide. An observer might say that Choate was only doing the ordinary service of a lawyer in detecting the most proper basis for an attack or defense. Perhaps this is largely true, but it must be remembered that American law had not yet established a highly uniform system of precedents and modes; rather, it approached a state of individual treatments of cases, depending upon lawyers, judges, and juries. And his apparently self-evident approaches become more praiseworthy when viewed through his advice to Parker that in patent cases the defense should deal with infringement rather than novelty or value of the plaintiff's invention. This idea is now commonly accepted, but Choate had to discover it through experiences in the court.[1] The point is simply that Choate was making astute distinctions in analyzing his cases at a time when such distinctions were not common in the American bar and when it was the lawyer and not an accepted mode that determined procedure. Moreover, he emphasized and clarified his position in a case by discussing the issues he was admitting much as though he were on the other side of the case.

A most significant part of Choate's invention, common to his forensic speeches, was a narrative of probabilities so drawn that they appeared to be a series of established facts. Such an explanation may have led the unknown reporter for the trivial Mumfords case to write, "We venture to say a more ingenius or plausible one [defense] could not have been made." The sentiment became a commonplace, became legend. The characteristic narrative was corroborated by whatever evidence was consistent with it; the remainder of the evidence was disposed of later. Two typical narratives serve to illustrate the method, those in the Tirrell and the Dalton trials. In the former instance Choate made it appear plausible that Tirrell was with Maria Bickford the night she was killed and was happy in her company. There being no motive for his killing her, it was she who awoke in the night and—believing her hold upon him to be weakening—set fire to the house and committed suicide. This, a natural death for a prostitute, was the more probable because she had made two previous attempts to kill herself and always kept in her room the instruments for suicide. Further, Choate related, Tirrell, upon awakening, found himself near a dying woman and fled, not because he had committed murder but because of fear of being indicted a second time on the charge of adultery. Lest this story leave the

---

[1] Parker, *op. cit.*, 273; *The Dartmouth*, 8: 4. "J. B." related an instance in which Choate attacked the merits of a patent in a trial and thereby played into the hands of Webster, the opposing counsel.

jury unconvinced Choate added another, that Tirrell, previously subject to somnambulism, murdered the woman while he was asleep and thus could not be held responsible for the act. Both these alternatives were plausible and consistent with the evidence, although not consistent with each other.

And for Mrs. Dalton, Choate made compatible with innocence of adultery (1) an admitted clandestine intimacy with a Mr. Sumner, (2) an alleged subsequent abortion, (3) an alleged confession of adultery by Mrs. Dalton, and (4) allegations that Mrs. Dalton's father attempted to bribe witnesses. In brief, Choate's explanation was that Helen Dalton carried on a flirtation, a harmless affair, with an exchange of trifles but with nothing improper. Through all this she loved her husband but being denied his company found the companionship of Sumner preferable to loneliness. Why? (And the facts rise to the level of the Choate legend.) A perfectly natural response to the restlessness brought about by pregnancy. The miscarriage? (More tears for the plagued.) It resulted from the excitement of the discovery of her affair with Sumner, his death, and *her dear husband's* imprisonment. Dalton's friends then poisoned him with lies to such an extent that he imagined he had heard a confession of adultery from his wife. In this unfortunate state of mind he easily imagined that the miscarriage was an abortion and that in all honesty he should sue for divorce.

Choate elaborated upon these and similar narratives in fullest detail as he presented them to the jury, citing at every step all the corroborating evidence in order to establish probability or improbability. It should be noticed, however, that not all Choate's suppositions were warranted by the testimony and that some of them scarcely became more formidable than mere guesses. For example, from the Tirrell case:

(1) This transaction took place just when the heart of this mighty city began to stir with life. The prisoner has common sense, and how easy to have committed it at another place and at another time when detection could not have followed. (2) That a man who had deserted his wife and child for this woman and whose guilty love burnt as bright till he went to sleep in her arms on that night, as it had at any time before, should in an hour or two cut her throat, dash her body upon the floor, and fire the house, in the absence of all motive, is out of the circle of anything human, and brings us to where devils would blush to live. (3) I think there is a fair probability that she took her own life. Waking sadly with her hold upon the prisoner about to give way, with no other friend to look to. . . . This is more probable than that the prisoner did the deed.

The foregoing quotations to the contrary, it must be admitted that usually Choate defended his narratives with sufficient evidence to make his possibilities appear reasonable. Perhaps he did not believe always that the events did occur just as he narrated them; it was enough that they might have followed that order. Evidence showing the latter view lies in his gener-

449

ous offering of two wholly incompatible explanations for the death of Mrs. Bickford, their only common characteristic being the innocence of Tirrell.

Choate's narrative, compatible with innocence and probabilities, was not complete in its invention until he disposed of the unfavorable testimony, a feat usually accomplished through the use of *ad hominem* and with little regard for the validity of the argument. Although he frequently discussed personalities, praising witnesses, his client, or his adversary, his treatment of the person became more conspicuous where evidence was to be attacked. Of course, there is some justification, if not complete validity, in attacking the character of a witness when the fault in question bears directly upon the value of the testimony. On the other hand, the practice becomes utterly fallacious when the condemned trait bears no relationship to the testimony. Both conditions obtain in the instance of his attacks upon witnesses in the Dalton case, where he had to destroy the testimony of the two Coburn brothers and Mary Hunter or admit that his narrative of probabilities was untrue. He achieved his end by proving one Coburn a swindler and a liar, the other a thief, and Mary Hunter a wet nurse and the mother of an illegitimate child. There is considerable validity in destroying confidence in the testimony of the Coburns, because the points at issue are closely allied to truth and it would be difficult to assume that the Coburns were testifying truthfully on the witness stand when they frequently were not truthful persons. With Mary Hunter the case is different. The probable relationship between her testimony and her being a wet nurse and the mother of an illegitimate child is almost nil, and if there is a relationship it might serve to make her more truthful quite as well as less truthful. Thus, in this instance, Choate was obviously using a convenient though illogical means of destroying evidence. Similarly, in pleading for John Hammond's divorce from "an adulterous woman some fifteen years his adult," Choate was confusing valid and invalid *ad hominem*, the "adulterous woman" being pertinent to the charge while the age was not. Again, in the incomplete reports of the Tirrell case are these remarks:

(1) The infamous characters in this house of infamy. An old man of sixty and an old woman of sixty, the parents of children, keeping a house of prostitution, with an infamous woman of the town with another witness who passes the night in her arms. . . . (2) The awful infamy of the house where the deed was done, and the reckless character of the woman herself, were eloquently given as proofs.

The obvious fact here is that regardless of the topic under discussion, Choate was neither proving nor disproving; rather he was resorting to his customary *ad hominem* in an attempt to destroy evidence and apparently was succeeding in the eyes of the reporter. This whole process is reminiscent of the penetrating reporter and the early Mumfords case: "Choate remarked with great emphasis upon . . . the character of the complainant & his family."

That Choate saw the personalities involved to be a vital part of the case is evident in the Hammond brief, wherein he wrote, "And who is Hayden, and who are his associates, male, female" and then developed a vituperative paragraph on the topic. Nor was the brief the first part of a case to lean toward personalities. Indeed, one must go to the minutes of the examination to find the purposeful planning that led to subsequent and mature *ad hominem*. For example, the minutes for his defense of ship *Timor* reveal questions obviously designed to disclose material that would permit him to denounce the complainants as scavengers who fed upon the shipwrecks among the shoals, a dishonorable business. Or in his examination in defense of Devins, Choate was questioning in order to make the complainant's alleged scurvy appear to be a venereal disease and particularly to show that the complainant's habits made a venereal disease probable. This method, the discussion of personalities, formed his most universal practice of counteracting damaging evidence but not his only method. For example, when he was confronted with detrimental evidence in the early depositions of the captain of ship *Timor*, Choate found it expedient to allege that his competitors had taken unfair advantage of his captain in the excitement just after the rescue of the ship, a degree of duress. Similarly, Mrs. Dalton's father, although not quite guilty of attempting to bribe a witness as alleged, had taken unfortunate steps because of the duress of parental love. These deviations in conjunction with the commonly used *ad hominem* indicate that Choate disposed of unfavorable evidence by an expedient method determined by the circumstances.

The aggressive portion of the typical Choate case is almost complete; perhaps it should rest. However, the spoken plea contained another item, one that he maneuvered into play at every conceivable juncture: his reliance upon the absence of evidence or proof that was contradictory to his stand. Whatever the proper distinction between negative evidence and *argumentum ad ignorantiam* may be, Choate employed both. Whether for the plaintiff or defendant he demanded proof that had not been given. He asked for facts probably discoverable if existent. He even attempted to shift the burden of proof with full knowledge that no facts existed to establish the contrary.[1]

[1] These practices are so closely related to his plausible narrative of the events of the case that they might well be discussed in conjunction with that part of his invention. On the other hand, they enter into his general plan for his case so completely that they merit isolated treatment. In referring to these practices there is no attempt made to segregate negative evidence from *ad ignorantiam.*

In the instance of Mrs. Dalton, Choate established—at least, claimed to establish—the date of the conception of Mrs. Dalton's child and contended that her husband was the father of the child because there was no evidence to show that she knew Sumner on or before that date. Upon the absence of such evidence Choate built his narrative. So it was with Tirrill. (In both instances Choate was able to rely on no evidence from a leading party, both being dead.) Because Choate could say, "No human being saw him strike the blow; no human being saw him run from that house of death— or was the ensanguined evidence upon his hands, that he had done the deed. No human being saw him take the life he loved so tenderly," because he can say that, he could go further to speculate: "Suppose him to have rushed to the closet to get something to staunch the flow of life with a light in his hand! He touches the clothes and they take fire, and then he rushes downstairs, slipping in his haste down one or two of the steps." Moreover, in the larger aspects of that defense he relied upon the inability of the state to prove anything; otherwise he could not have offered two lines of defense, one death by suicide and the other, murder at the hands of a somnambulist.

A similar and prominent use of *ad ignorantiam* by Choate was his bickering about the burden of proof with the intent of showing that the opposition must assume it. An unexpected defense of a case cited by Bell shows to what extreme Choate sometimes went in relying upon the assumptions underlying burden of proof.[1] A vessel, which was insured while within a specified body of water, was destroyed, and there was some question about the scene of the accident. When the case came to court, Choate— for the plaintiff, the owner of the ship—decided not to introduce evidence about the location but to let the defendants prove that the ship was not in the specified area. One witness was examined to establish that there had been a wreck, and Choate rested the case. The opposition, expecting him to occupy considerable time with an orthodox case, had no witnesses in court, and the judge decided for the plaintiff. Clearly, the case was won on the basis of *ad ignorantiam*. Another, although unsuccessful, attempt to rest a case upon *ad ignorantiam* appears in the Oliver Smith case. Choate, for the heirs in an attempt to break the will, tried to establish that one of the witnesses to the will was incompetent, a thing that could not be proved for the date on which the will was drawn.

Mr. Choate then went on to argue the burden of proof, as to the competency of the witness, was upon the party setting up the will; and that inasmuch as it had been shown, on the part of the heirs at law, that the witness was of unsound mind a few months before the date of attestation; it became necessary for the other party to show a restoration. This rule as to burden of proof was qualified by another

[1] Brown, *op. cit.*, I, 279.

rule, that where the insanity originated in some sudden acute, particular cause, then there was no presumption that the insanity continued, after such cause had subsided. He then argued upon the testimony that no such sudden cause had been shown in this case, the accident of his father being inadequate.

The tendency to give to the opposition the burden of proof is almost universal in the available Choate forensic speeches. Among his notes for both Devins and ship *Timor* are segregated documents developing the topic, burden of proof. Obviously Choate incorporated as a significant part of his forensic system the practice of bridging gaps in evidence with a plausible explanation and relied much upon the opposition's inability to prove the contrary.

The preceding material has stressed the case and has been limited to those aspects of invention universal among Choate's extant legal documents and to elements that are relatively free from subjectivity. To neglect the pathetic in the courtroom speeches would be to depersonalize Choate altogether. The passages quoted from the Hammond and Dalton divorce trials show that the pathetic not only was in the speech but also was incorporated in the brief for the case; moreover, since the former was tried before a judge or bench of judges and the latter before the jury, *pathos* must have been addressed to both groups. Every indication points to the assumption that Choate saw only the case and that the pathetic was intrinsically involved. Its prominence in the final speech was probably conditioned by the availability of evidence, the type of case, the kind of official audience—perhaps even by the galleries. Above all, it was used as was expedient for Choate's client. Hence, virtues and vices were confused in the different appeals to the courts. For example, age was a virtue in the instance of Mr. Gove, father of Mrs. Dalton, but a vice in the persons keeping the house in which Mrs. Bickford was killed; again, Helen Dalton, Albert Tirrill, and John Hammond, all young and weak, were to be trusted and helped, but Theophilus Phelps and Mary Hunter, also young and weak, were not to be trusted; and again, a jury should trust circumstantial evidence against the Coburns, but it was the jury's duty to distrust circumstantial evidence that would convict Tirrell.

Arrangement

As was implied in the formula for the Choate forensic speech, his plea contained (1) introductory remarks, (2) a statement of issues, (3) a running account of events that make a probable story and one that is consistent with a large share of the testimony and with the client's welfare, (4) substantiation of this account, (5) removing obstacles to the account, and (6) conclusion. Items 3, 4, and 5 did not necessarily follow the indicated temporal order. For example, Choate often referred to the fact that step 5 was to occur and sometimes dealt with it early in the speech. Furthermore, in progressing through the speech, he did not follow an order I *ABC*, II *ABC*. Rather he repeated and amplified. Thus, a more nearly correct description is given by the arrangement I *abc* ABC *ABC*, II *abc* ABC *ABC*. Such notations are deficient in describing his entire arrangement of a speech, because he had no single order for his repetitions and amplifications. Sometimes he hurriedly outlined the entire case and then developed the segments more thoroughly; again, a single argument often was repeated and amplified several times successively. Restatement and amplification were invariably a major part of the forensic address.

Whether Choate warped his theory to fit his practice or developed his practice systematically from his observations is, of course, not clear. However, it is important that he thought that juries were popular assemblies and demanded special treatment. Parker's comments on this are corroborated by Choate's conversations with him.

A speaker makes his impression . . . in the *first hour*, sometimes in the first fifteen minutes; . . . he then puts forth the outline or announces all the airs of the coming opera. All the rest is mere filling up; answering objections, giving one juryman little arguments with which to answer the objection of his fellows, etc. Indeed this may be taken as a fixed rule, that the popular mind can never be vigorously addressed . . . and fixed more than one hour in a single address. The jury address of four hours is no exception to this; for they don't, in its whole course, give more than *one hour's fixed attention*.

And he continues with this enlightening comment: "Always, in my long address to juries, *some one goes to sleep*."[1] Apparently, then, the arrangement of the plea was determined by the audience. Some slight idea of that audience may be gained by looking at a typical jury, the twelve men who found Tirrell not guilty of murder. The names, when checked with a contemporary Boston directory, show the following occupations: Samuel Aspinwall, mastmaker; Theophilus Burr, housewright; Benj. P. Bowman, not listed; Calvin Haskell, blacksmith; John Mardin, blacksmith; Calvin S. Magoon, housewright; Daniel Messinger, hatter; George W. Parmenter, not listed; Joseph Winsor, Jr., fish dealer; William Washburn, housewright. Evidently it was the men of brawn, the blacksmiths and carpenters of New England, who were responsible for the arrangement of the material in the pleas of Rufus Choate. If he was for the plaintiff he must capture all of them; if for the defendant, he must hold some of them. How much of the repetition in the speech is addressed to a single juror is beyond conjecture.

[1] Parker, *op. cit.*, p. 267.

Style

Comments on Choate's style have been confined largely to the unusual length of his sentences and to his figurative language. Neilson made an extensive study determining the number and derivation of Choate's words.[1] Such exercises, whether mere fact grubbing or not, were hardly more laborious than Choate's persistent attempt to improve his style. The use of his vocabulary of nearly twelve thousand words was of sufficient concern to him that he labored, pen in hand, to improve his expression. Moreover, he practiced translating with the same end in view. From his comments to Parker it is apparent that he considered the end of a good style to be clarity and not display, and of himself he said, "I at one time ran too much to words and phrases."[2] A letter to Winthrop discussing the merits of some college themes written by R. Choate, Jr., and R. C. Winthrop, Jr., bears some testimony on what Choate expected in a composition: "I really think both the 'ingenious' chaps make a very good first of the affair. The narratives are clear, plain, preserve and present the point. That they shortly will beat their fathers respectively is as much to be hoped as it is to be expected."[3] As for his own language, certainly the Dalton case is eminently clear. Moreover, it is florid, sufficiently ornate that his contemporaries were probably justified in saying that he "drove a substantive and six." Modern critics are inclined to say, half apologetically, that it was the vogue of the age to be florid. This does not seem to be the answer. The entire trial of Dr. Webster, a case that Choate refused and that was handled by eminent lawyers of Boston, reveals little ornate language such as Choate used in the Dalton and Tirrell trials.[4] The difference, however, lies not so much in quantity as it does in quality. Again, Daniel Webster, whose courtroom address was commonly ornate, used matter-of-fact language in opposing Choate. This change in the language of Webster was remarked on by those who listened to Choate and Webster on many occasions. When these items are viewed with the additional facts that Neilson, lawyer and chief justice of the supreme judicial court (Massachusetts), considered Choate's language of sufficient character to warrant a painstaking study of its scope and origin and that Marsh, a prominent educator, had given it sufficient attention that he was surprised to learn that Choate employed merely twelve thousand words, the language of Choate appears to have been unique even in its time. Nor is it inconsequential in this regard that among the many anecdotes that form a part of the Choate legend there are

[1] Neilson, *Memories of Rufus Choate* (Houghton Mifflin Company), 1884.
[2] Parker, *op. cit.*, p. 260.
[3] Choate to R. C. Winthrop, 1843, Massachusetts Historical Society.
[4] *The Trial of Dr. Webster* (Phillips, Sampson and Company), 1850.

several that deal with his language. Probably his ornate language, distinctive in an age characterized by ornate eloquence, was developed conscientiously through rigorous practice, listening to advocates, reading oratory, and giving speeches to the court. Such a system allowed him to establish a standard by which he could criticize the language of his contemporaries and label the speeches of at least one of them as mere raillery. Webster's deference to this style and the respect for it that led Neilson to investigate it and the universal homage that legal contemporaries paid Choate would seem to indicate that his use of language was not just different; it was rather of an order to which they aspired. Beyond opinions, however, lie two facts: (1) the thought in every recorded Choate speech is clear; and (2) the speeches phrased in Choate language won decisions. Although the language may not have been responsible for the decisions, it is self-evident that it did not cause the advocate to lose.

Some of the more prominent stylistic devices used by the advocate were hyperbole, simile, alliteration, inverted phrases, questions, direct discourse, long sentences, multiple modifiers, and, preeminently, copiousness. The major effect of the language appears to be the augmentation and diminution of ideas whereby he created innumerable degrees of vice and virtue.

The length of the Choate sentence has probably caused too much concern in proportion to its importance. However, the sentences were remarked upon by auditors and have been mentioned frequently by critics. A few statistics from the Dalton case may show why this topic has evinced so much interest.

Dalton v. Dalton

Number of words (excluding quoted matter)	48,168
Number of sentences	1,274
Average length of sentences, in words	37
Maximum length of sentence, in words	220
Sentences containing more than 80 words	95
Sentences containing fewer than 10 words	93
Number of interrogatives	193

These quantitative measurements do not describe Choate's style. The fact that 15 per cent of the sentences are interrogative is especially misleading because the questions do not appear at regular intervals throughout the plea but are bunched in those portions of the speech in which Choate discusses the credibility of witnesses. In those passages, in turn, the advocate had a minimum of evidence and had to make a maximum effect. In general, it seems that Choate was able to manipulate his language in such manner to make him the master of the forensic style in his time and place.

Summary and Appraisal

A summary of the rhetoric of Choate might rest with the reporter's description of the Mumfords case. That description was as prophetic of Choate's system of rhetoric as the Hammond case was of the Dalton case. The evidence seems to show that the advocate worked to perfect his system rather than to alter it fundamentally. His rhetoric, although not divorced from Burke and Cicero, was essentially determined by expediency. A popular audience, called a jury, a list of evidence—not decisive, a firm belief that every man deserved what protection the law offered—these were among the things that operated to make Choate's rhetoric a combination of faultless logic, probabilities, fallacies, and amplification. Nor was he necessarily evading truth in such fallacies as the attacks upon the character of the Coburns. To him such an attack was just a part of the case and the expedient method of handling the evidence. So were his style and arrangement primarily expedients. The copious treatment of the case and the elevated style tended to give to the forensic speech greater scope and·importance, but, again, this was expedient.

He who would place an estimate on Rufus Choate as a lawyer must place the man in Salem and Boston during the first half of the nineteenth century when the population of Massachusetts scarcely exceeded a half million people. In both towns he was surrounded by veterans, and in both instances he reached the top of the city's legal fraternity. It was not the time for a lawyer to indulge in a specialty. A preparation over a wide scope of subjects was necessary, and Choate, who was at once brilliant and persevering while an undergraduate at Dartmouth, continued to apply himself to achieve perfection in his profession during his 35 years of practice. The wide variety and the large number of cases in which he was involved are testimony of his success in gaining favorable verdicts. Even though he might have continued to be elected to offices in spite of the infrequent speaking he did while occupying them, it cannot be assumed that he would have attracted clients in the face of adverse decisions. The dockets in the courthouses of Salem, Boston, and Cambridge are sufficient evidence that there Choate stood first in his profession. Although he occasionally appeared in the United States Supreme Court and other Federal courts, his forensic career centered in the few courts in the vicinity of Boston.

Witnessing the fact that he was competent in handling the law are the numerous citations of legal references in his printed briefs, occasional words of praise for Choate in the decisions of the judges of the supreme judicial court—decisions on points of law—and the success he had in arguing points of law. His skill in addressing juries is attested by countless anecdotes and favorable verdicts. It is a proper distinction that the courtroom of Essex

County contains as its most conspicuous picture a portrait of Rufus Choate and that the main hall of the courthouse of Suffolk County, Boston, contains but one statue, a bronze by French of Rufus Choate.

SELECTED BIBLIOGRAPHY

Books

Brown, S. G.: *The Life and Writings of Rufus Choate*, Boston, Little, Brown & Company, 1862.

Caverno, C.: *Reminiscences of the Eulogy of Rufus Choate on Daniel Webster*, Boston, Sherman, French and Company, 1914.

Fuess, C. M.: *Rufus Choate: The Wizard of the Law*, New York, Minton, Balch and Company, 1928.

Jamesson, E. P.: *The Choates in America*, Boston, A. Mudge and Son, 1896.

Neilson, Joseph: *Memories of Rufus Choate*, Boston, Houghton Mifflin Company, 1884.

Parker, E. G.: *Reminiscences of Rufus Choate*, New York, Mason Brothers, 1860.

Stone, E. F.: *Choate-Cushing-Rantoul*, Salem, Essex Institute, 1888.

Whipple, E. P.: *Some Recollections of Rufus Choate*, Half Hour series, New York, Harper & Brothers, 1879.

————: *Recollections of Eminent Men*, Boston, Ticknor, 1886.

Collections (in order of importance)

Dartmouth College Library, Hanover, N.H.
New England Historical Society, Boston, Mass.
The Essex Institute, Salem, Mass.
Boston Athenaeum, Boston, Mass.
Boston Public Library, Boston, Mass.
Harvard College Library, Cambridge, Mass.
The American Antiquarian Society, Worcester, Mass.
Congressional Library, Washington, D.C.
New Hampshire Historical Society, Concord. N.H.

15

Jeremiah S. Black

by WILLIAM NORWOOD BRIGANCE

Jeremiah S. Black was born near Somerset, Pa., January 10, 1810. He was educated in Somerset County public schools and in the Brownsville Classical Academy, read law under Chauncey Forward, and was admitted to the bar in 1830. He was president judge of the Pennsylvania Sixteenth Judicial District, 1842–1851; associate and chief justice of the Pennsylvania Supreme Court, 1851–1857; Attorney General of the United States, 1857–1860; Secretary of State of the United States, 1860–1861; his nomination to the United States Supreme Court was rejected by the Senate, 1861; and he was reporter of the Supreme Court, 1861–1864. He became the leading defender of civil rights and the opponent of Reconstruction in cases appearing before the Supreme Court, 1866–1873. He.drafted Andrew Johnson's veto message of the Reconstruction Act, 1867, and was appointed on Johnson's counsel in the impeachment trial but resigned without serving; defended Secretary of War William K. Belknap in his impeachment trial, 1876; and was on the counsel for Samuel J. Tilden before the Hayes-Tilden Electoral Commission, 1877. He exposed the Credit Mobilier scandal, 1872. He was counsel for United States government and American settlers in the California land cases involving twelve million acres of land, the sites of San Francisco, Oakland, Berkeley, Sacramento, etc., 1861 *et seq.;* for the Choctaw nation, 1868 *et seq.;* for the settlers of Kansas in the Osage land case, 1875; for the Mormons in the Edmunds Act franchise suit, 1882. He died August 19, 1883.

I

Jeremiah S. Black's influence on legal history was primarily as a defender of the constitutional Bill of Rights against encroachment in time of stress.[1] Colorful, eloquent, eccentric—for a quarter century in the most tragic era of American history, he stood as an independent gladiator, ready to defend the cause of personal liberty, however forlorn the hope or unpopular the cause.

[1] He was also influential in defense of the people's rights against corporate interests, especially the railroads; and the last speech of his life was given in this behalf. For copies of this speech, see C. F. Black, *Essays and Speeches of Jeremiah S. Black* (New York, 1885), pp. 172–188, and D. J. Brewer, *The World's Best Orations* (Chicago, 1899), II, 470 *et seq.* But the day of the railroad was to be a long one; Black was not to live to see the end of the struggle; and he was one of many who played a part. Therefore, this phase of his life has been omitted from the present study.

To see him at the height of his power, let us consider his defense of the right of trial by jury in the historic case *ex parte Milligan*. The hearing was held March 6 to 13, 1866, in a period of intense political excitement. Passions and prejudices aroused by the Civil War were still flaming. The alleged crimes of Milligan and his associates, of aiding the Confederacy, had aimed at the nation's life. On their arrest in Indianapolis in 1864 they had been tried, not in a civil court but by a military commission, and had been sentenced to be hanged. Public temper was aroused against them; one senator and three congressmen from Indiana had protested officially against any commutation of the sentence; and the newspaper files of any historical library today will reveal how vehemently was the voice of the fourth estate raised in clamor for their lives.

The Supreme Court, of course, was beyond the direct reach of press and public temper, but the Dred Scott decision was only nine years old, and the court could not fail to hear the clamor, not wholly without menace, outside its halls of justice.

More serious, however, were the legal entanglements. The issues on which appeal had been taken to the Supreme Court were three: (1) Was Milligan entitled to a writ of habeas corpus? (2) Ought he to be discharged? (3) Had the military commission jurisdiction legally to try and sentence him?

But the President had suspended habeas corpus early in the war. Congress later had legalized the suspension; and some 38,000 imprisoned men had been denied its writ. Even the end of the war had not ended the suspension, and at the moment of Milligan's hearing, a year after the war had ended, Congress was debating whether military control should not be continued in Northern states. "Congress . . . cannot invest brigadiers with power to abolish jury trial or to suspend the privilege of *habeas corpus* in time of peace," protested that sturdy chronicler Gideon Welles, Secretary of the Navy.[1] But Congress had done so, and intended to intrench its brigadiers in control. To save Milligan, the Supreme Court must pronounce void Lincoln's whole policy of habeas corpus during the Civil War, and it must overthrow the Radical Congress's plan for continuing military control in the North.

Who were the "nine old men" on the court in 1866? Three had been members when the Dred Scott decision was rendered—James M. Wayne, of Georgia, appointed by Jackson in 1835; Samuel Nelson, of New York, appointed by Tyler in 1845; and Robert C. Grier, of Pennsylvania, appointed by Polk in 1846. One other was also a prewar appointee, Nathan Clifford, of Maine, appointed by Buchanan in 1858. The remaining five were Lincoln appointees. Chief Justice Salmon P. Chase, of Ohio, had

[1] *Diary of Gideon Welles* (Boston, 1911), Apr. 29, 1867.

openly favored the Radical Congress's policy of Reconstruction; David Davis was the former judge of Lincoln's famous court circuit in Illinois, was his closest friend and the administrator of his estate; Samuel F. Miller had been a Republican organizer in Iowa; Noah H. Swayne was an anti-slavery ex-Virginian from Ohio; and Stephen J. Field was a pro-Union Party and ex-Democrat from California.

In the opening days of the trial Henry Stanbery, James Speed, and Benjamin F. Butler had argued the case for the government, contending that Lincoln had legally suspended habeas corpus, that Congress had affirmed this suspension, and finally that the constitutional amendment guaranteeing trial by jury was suspended in time of war.[1]

For Milligan, David Dudley Field had argued chiefly the question of military jurisdiction, and James A. Garfield had examined the Constitution, acts of Congress, and precedents of law.[2]

II

Jeremiah S. Black then rose to close the case for the Milligan counsel. He was about to make the greatest argument of his life. Eulogists have hailed it as "indisputably the most remarkable forensic effort" ever made before the Supreme Court,[3] comparing him to "one of King John's angry barons who had re-appeared upon the earth to punish a violation of the Magna Charta and the Bill of Rights."[4] These represent the extreme in appreciation. Whatever justification they may have arises from the fact that Black faced the court under a cloud, a man scorned as a Copperhead, one who had openly denounced Lincoln's whole conduct of war as a violation of the Constitution, that he faced a court potentially hostile to his views,[5] yet spoke with an effect that startled those who listened.

For more than two hours he addressed the court, without a single note before him, presenting an array of law, fact, and argument; lifting the case above questions of jurisdiction, above proclamations of Presidents and acts of Congress, making Freedom his client, and compelling the great cause of constitutional liberty to hang by the slender thread of Milligan's life.

[1] 4 Wallace 10 *et seq.*

[2] *Ibid.*, pp. 22 and 42.

[3] Levi Maish, quoted in Mary Black Clayton, *Reminiscences of Jeremiah Sullivan Black* (St. Louis, 1887), p. 131.

[4] United States Senator Edgar Cowan to Chauncey Black, Black Papers, Apr. 1, 1884.

[5] Of course he was not a Copperhead, had been the most aggressive leader against secession in Buchanan's cabinet, and was opposed to Lincoln's mode of conducting the war rather than to the war itself. But these facts were not to be generally known and accepted until the publication of Black's memoirs in 1881. *Cf.* W. N. Brigance, *Jeremiah Sullivan Black* (Philadelphia, 1934), pp. 76–117, 282–283.

But before he begins to speak, let us look at the man himself. He was fifty-six years of age, just under 6 feet in height, with a "strong, compact, and active frame." He was famed for his ruddy complexion, his red-brown wig, his immense overhanging eyebrows, once reddish but now white, and a pair of glittering gray eyes that lay in ambuscade. They were eyes that drew attempted description in every portrait ever written of him; eyes that were luminous, volatile, and quizzical; stern in repose but quickly melting as they lighted up in conversation, yet capable of withering effect in anger.

His appearance and eccentricities lent themselves to easy cartooning. "When a man as wise as Jere Black wears a red-brown wig above snow-white eyebrows," wrote an observer, "we conclude he abides in that supernal sphere of mental action where the thought of anything so trivial as a wig never enters in." Wrote another:

He is a tall, grizzle-haired, big-nostriled, long-nosed man. . . . In the Supreme Court he has a spittoon set in the middle of the floor, and walks up and down as he talks with the precision of an Elizabethan dramatist, spitting as straight as a syllogism. The power of his argument is measured by the number of spittoons he fills. A small and easily surmountable case takes two spittoons; a good tough argument requires four; for a great feat of legal gymnastics he requires as many as nine successive spittoons.

Whether he actually required a spittoon in the Supreme Court chamber is uncertain, but at least his famous silver tobacco box filled with "fine cut," was much in evidence there, almost always in his hand as he spoke, and kept constantly in motion as he turned it "alternately sidewise and 'end for end,' never twice in succession the same way."[1]

In temperament, "he was a debater to the very last . . . " wrote Whitelaw Reid. "There was hardly a time in his life when he was not involved in some controversy, yet few public men had more staunch friends in both parties. With his kindly nature and his fierce rhetoric and his abundant humor, he was one of the most interesting characters in public life."[2]

"*May It Please Your Honors,*" Black's voice was lifted in the stilled courtroom. "*I am not afraid that you will underrate the importance of this case. It concerns the rights of the whole people. Such questions have generally*

---

[1] This description is summarized from W. U. Hensel, "Jeremiah Sullivan Black," *The Green Bag*, 2, (May, 1890): 196; David Paul Brown, *The Forum* (Philadelphia, 1856), II, 108; Clayton, *op. cit.*, p. 126; *Washington National Republican*, Aug. 20, 1883; and Mary Clemmer, in the *New York Independent*, (date uncertain), preserved with other Black memorabilia in Mary Black Clayton's four-volume scrapbook collection, now in the Library of Congress. These four volumes will herafter be cited as the *Clayton MSS*.

[2] *New York Tribune*, Aug. 20, 1883.

been settled by arms. But since the beginning of the world no battle has ever been lost or won upon which the liberties of a nation were so distinctly staked as they are on the result of this argument."

These were grave words, too grave for a speaker who might fail to measure his argument by their weight. But grave as they were, to Black they were insufficient. He added more of almost equal weight, in a stinging indictment of the opposing counsel, by warning judges that he must "necessarily refer to the mere rudiments of constitutional law" and "to the most commonplace topics of history." He explained, continuing his indictment of the government attorneys:

I beg your honors to believe that this is not done because I think that the court, or any member of it, is less familiar with these things than I am, or less sensible of their value; but simply and only because . . . if the fundamental principles of American liberty are attacked, and we are driven behind the inner walls of the Constitution to defend them, we can repel the assault only with those same old weapons which our ancestors used a hundred years ago. You must not think the worse of our armor because it happens to be old-fashioned, and looks a little rusty from long disuse.

He then came to the issue at law: Had the military commission jurisdiction? "We answer, No." Here he brushed away the opposing arguments on the validity of Presidential proclamations and acts of Congress. They were temporal things and petty. His concern was with the life stream of the nation. "*I take upon myself,*" he said with measured solemnity, "*the burden of showing*" that trial by jury "*is immovably fixed in the very framework of the Government, so that it is utterly impossible to detach it without destroying . . . the life of this nation as completely as you would destroy the life of an individual by cutting the heart out of his body. I proceed to the proof.*"

It was not proof adduced by "a long chain of legal argumentation, nor by the production of numerous books with the leaves dog-eared and the pages marked," although "I think I could produce as many as might be necessary." He went instead behind the acts of Congress, behind even the Constitution, to Tacitus on the Saxons of Germany, to Alfred, the *Magna Carta*, Bill of Rights, Petition of Right—until he had erected a mountain range of jurisprudence extending unbroken for twenty centuries.

Behind this range he rested the Constitution, and stood beside it.

I prove my right to a trial by jury, just as I would prove my title to an estate if I held in my hand a solemn deed conveying it to me. . . . There [pointing to it] is the charter by which we claim to hold it. It is called the Constitution of the United States. It is signed by the sacred name of George Washington, and by thirty-nine [*sic*] other names, only less illustrious than his. . . . The Attorney-General [of opposing counsel] himself became a party to the instrument when he laid his hand upon the Gospel of God and solemnly swore that he would give to me and every other citizen the full benefit of all it contains.

What does it contain? . . .

"The trial of all crimes, except in cases of impeachment, shall be by jury" . . . .

Is there any ambiguity there? . . . No; the words . . . are all-embracing.

After thus entrenching the Constitution behind twenty centuries of jurisprudence, Black turned to Butler's quasi-political argument that this provision of the Constitution was "silent amid arms." For 10 minutes he turned on it the heat of reason and legal precedent.

The learned counsel on the other side will not assert that there was war at Indianapolis in 1864, for they have read "Coke's Institute," and Judge Grier's opinion in the *prize cases* [Grier, remember, was sitting on the court]. . . . This, therefore, must be their position: That . . . if there was a war anywhere . . . the technical effect of such war was to take the jurisdiction away from the civil courts and transfer it to army officers.

General Butler at this point—seeing the lifeblood being crushed out of his case—attempted to save it. "We do not take that position," he objected. Black shot him a piercing glance and broke his lance with these words: "I do not wonder to see them recoil from their own doctrine when its nakedness is held up to their eyes. But . . . what else can they say?" Only that "the Constitution is repealed, or its operation suspended, in one State, because there is war in another. . . . This certainly puts us in a most precarious condition. . . . The President or Congress can wantonly provoke a war whenever it suits the purpose of either to do so; and they can keep it going as long as they please, even after the actual conflict of arms is over." Such an "argument, when turned into plain English, means this, and only this: that when the Constitution is attacked upon one side, its official guardians may assail it upon the other; when rebellion strikes it in the face, they may . . . sneak behind it and stab it in the back."

Next he turned to a full consideration of trial by military commissions. Here his sentences ring with the clink of steel and are attuned to the rhythm of martial music. "Come, Mr. Attorney," said he, turning invective upon his personal friend, Attorney General James Speed, "'gird up thy loins now like a man; I will demand of thee, and thou shalt declare unto me if thou hast understanding.' How is a military commission organized? . . . What offenses come within its jurisdiction? What is its code of procedure? . . . Is it perjury for a witness to swear falsely? . . . Does he [the judge advocate] tell the members how they must find, or does he only persuade them to convict?"

But the Attorney General had witnessed Butler's retirement. He made no answer. Black, turning to the court, disposed of him in one thrust. "To none of these questions can the Attorney-General make a reply, for there is no law on the subject. . . . Therefore, like Job, he can only lay his hand upon his mouth and keep silence."

He had finished the legal exposition. He now turned to a form of argument so often found in this part of his discourses, one that he always used with telling effect—a historical argument that made the ancient struggle for civil liberty live again in the present, that revealed it as a heritage won at terrific costs, delivered to his generation as a sacred trust, and to be transmitted to posterity regardless of price. The right of the executive government "to capture, imprison, and kill" whom it chooses had been an agent used by oppressors since the days of Nimrod.

"It operates in different ways. . . .

'It can change shapes with Proteus for advantages,
And set the murderous Machiavel to school.'"

The *lettre de cachet* of the French monarchy . . . the imperial ukase of Russia . . . verbal orders in Turkey . . . Nero . . . Herod were examples.

But it was not to history that he turned for the crowning example. Out of Shakespeare—his constant companion in reading—he lifted an instance well known by every member of the court. Said he:

Macbeth understood the whole philosophy of the subject. He was an unlimited monarch. His power to punish for any offense or for no offense at all was as broad as that which the Attorney-General claims for himself. . . . But he was more cautious how he used it. He had a dangerous rival. . . . The necessity to get rid of him was plain enough, but he could not afford to shock the moral sense of the world by pleading political necessity for a murder. He must—

"Mask the business from the common eye."

Accordingly he sent for two enterprising gentlemen . . . "made love to their assistance"—and got them to deal with the accused party. . . . The commission thus organized in Banquo's case sat upon him that very night . . . and they did precisely what the Attorney-General says the military officers may do in this country—they *took* and *killed* him, because their employer at the head of the government wanted it done, and paid them for doing it out of the public treasury.

At this point a spectator rushed from the room. He was from Kentucky, had come to hear his congressman address the House, but missed the way and found himself in the Supreme Court room. He saw Black's towering figure striding back and forth, heard his ringing voice, listened for a while, and sensed the approaching climax. Out of the room he rushed, across the hall into the House chamber, past the doorkeeper, down the aisle to the spot where his congressman stood addressing the House, plucked him by the coattail, and said in a voice that could be heard a dozen seats away: "Wind her up, Bill! Wind her up, and come over here and listen to old Jerry Black giving 'em hell."[1]

While this little diversion was going on in the House, the speaker in the Supreme Court room closed his argument. Swiftly he drew the threads together. Military commissions "will always be organized to convict, and the conviction will follow the accusation as surely as night follows the day. . . . Plied on as it may be by the arts of a malignant priesthood, and urged on by the madness of a raving crowd," it will be a combination of the popish plot and the French Revolution, "with Fouquier-Tinville on the bench, and Titus Oates in the witness's box. . . . You alone can 'deliver us from the body of this death.' To that fearful extent is the destiny of this nation in your hands."[2]

He had finished. "Never," said S. S. Cox, "had the question of personal liberty been so thoroughly discussed, from the time of the Magna Charta down."[3]

The Supreme Court decision was complete and unequivocal. Milligan was freed, the rule of military commissions at the North was overthrown, habeas corpus was restored; indeed, the court went even further, rendering an opinion that neither President nor Congress ever could legalize military commissions except in actual theatres of war where civil courts were not open.[4]

How much the court was influenced by Black's argument and how much by other considerations is obviously impossible to know. But courts admittedly are sensitive to argument. Washburn, in discussing witchcraft trials in his *Judicial History of Massachusetts*, presses the point that such abuses could not have occurred had there been an enlightened bar whose services could have been enlisted in favor of the accused; and John Marshall himself once reversed a decision of the Supreme Court, and apologized for the previous error by explaining that in the former case it had not been "argued by counsel"—a factor that he deemed of exceeding importance.[5]

The overthrowing of military commissions in this dangerous era, by whomsoever, was of momentous importance in legal history. The

---

[1] Clayton, *op. cit.*, pp. 132–134; *Clayton MSS.*

[2] The first printed copy of this speech, outside newspapers and pamphlets, appears in W. L. Snyder, *Great Speeches by Great Lawyers* (New York, 1881). It also appears in C. F. Black, *Essays and Speeches of Jeremiah S. Black* (New York, 1885) and in most collections of forensic speeches since that date.

[3] S. S. Cox, *Three Decades of Federal Legislation* (Providence, 1886), p. 230.

[4] 4 Wallace 107.

[5] See *Congressional Record*, Forty-fourth Congress, first session, Part 7, p. 319.

court opinion, that neither President nor Congress could restore military rule, stands today as a pillar of personal liberty. To have had this decision reversing Lincoln's policy of habeas corpus written by the hand of David Davis, "Lincoln's closest friend," his appointee to the court, and the former judge of his famous circuit in Illinois, gave a dramatic emphasis to the decision that has not quite been attained by any other in the history of Supreme Court.

This was not generally appreciated, however, in that day of postwar hysteria. Not even the Dred Scott decision was more violently assailed. Wendell Phillips impetuously proposed the abolition of the Supreme Court, for "the nation must be saved."[1] Thaddeus Stevens held it to be "far more dangerous" than the Dred Scott decision.[2] The *Independent* denounced it as "the most dangerous opinion ever pronounced" by the Court.[3] *Harper's Weekly* urged that "the Supreme Court be swamped" with enough new judges to outvote those then on the bench.[4]

III

Who was the man Jeremiah Sullivan Black? He was a former chief justice of the Pennsylvania Supreme Court and Attorney General of the United States. His schooling had been slight and ended at seventeen. His reading of law had begun in a private office in a western Pennsylvania village. But he had a classical turn of mind, reciting the poems of Dryden and Pope, Horace and Vergil, even as a boy "behind the plow and to the music of the crumbling soil." "Mental inactivity is to me a great pain," he said in late life. "I must have law or metaphysics for substantial mind food."[5]

David Paul Brown—who is rated by Dean John H. Wigmore as one of the half dozen greatest lawyers in American history—was deeply impressed by Black's style of speaking and writing. It was "unlike any other with which we are acquainted . . . fluent, sententious, argumentative, facetious and sarcastic. . . . Whether right or wrong, no man can misunderstand him." Brown summarizes with both a judgment and a query: "It is . . . a beautiful style, and the wonder is, where he should have formed it."[6]

Allowing always for the influence of thought on style, the answer to Brown's query on how Black attained his distinctive style is found in his early and intensive contact with masters of English and Latin diction. At fifteen he had committed the poems of Horace verbatim, translated them

[1] A. B. Hart, *Life of Salmon Portland Chase* (Boston, 1899), p. 346.
[2] *Congressional Globe*, Jan. 3, 1867, p. 251.
[3] The *Independent*, Jan. 10, 1867.
[4] *Harper's Weekly*, Jan. 19, 1867.
[5] F. A. Burr, *Philadelphia Press*, Aug. 20, 1883.
[6] Brown, *op. cit.*, p. 106.

into English prose and thence into English verse of his own.[1] Of Milton he said, "Paradise Lost took me like Niagara. . . . "[2] At eighteen he discovered Shakespeare, reading and rereading the plays until he was thoroughly familiar with the major characters. Throughout life he could quote at will, was never known to misquote, and it annoyed him to hear others misquote.[3] Finally, there was the Bible, which he read first for its Jewish law and later as a chart of faith, but always as a student of style.

History and philosophy he read, also, and other poets, but these four—Horace and Milton, Shakespeare and the Bible—he studied so intensely that they served as reservoirs from which he could draw, at random and at will, to "startle or thrill with a variety of apt quotation." They became direct sources of power.

In the study of law, he at first despaired of mastering its many branches of abstruse learning and finally realized that it could not be done by one man. So he began to reduce the law to a few fundamental principles, solving legal problems by the application of fundamental maxims and drawing upon his growing power of language to apply those maxims in striking and convincing language. His knowledge of the law, thus begun, was refined by nine years on the district bench and six more on the Supreme Court of Pennsylvania. On the Supreme Court alone he wrote 282 opinions, covering 117 subjects of law. This was his last formal discipline in legal education, testifying to a high legal eminence, for those opinions have been cited some three thousand times by various courts and legal authorities. Only one seems to have been ever overruled, and that was because of a change in the legislative act that had not been called to the attention of the court.[4]

When he became Attorney General of the United States in 1857, Black found the government faced with an almost unbroken string of defeats in the California land cases, involving title to twelve million acres of land, large mining claims, the islands of San Francisco Bay, and the land sites of San Francisco, Oakland, Berkeley, Sacramento, Stockton, and lesser cities. He conceived an entirely new basis of argument, uncovered new evidence, and won thereafter practically every case that came before the Supreme Court. In preparing himself to argue these cases, he studied the Spanish language and the Mexican land laws in their original text.[5]

---

[1] C. F. Black, *Essays and Speeches*, etc., p. 3.

[2] Clayton, *op. cit.*, 23.

[3] H. C. Niles, "Jeremiah Sullivan Black and His Influence on the Law of Pennsylvania," *Ninth Annual Report of the Pennsylvania Bar Association*, 1903, pp. 464–465.

[4] James L. Kennedy, *Index to Judicial Opinions of Jeremiah Sullivan Black* (Greensburg, Pa., 1935), p. 3.

[5] Francis J. Kooser to the author, Jan. 23, 1930.

"You never meet the Attorney-General at a ball or a *soirée*," commented a reporter on this stage of his life, but "you can find him all day in the Supreme Court, and nearly all night at his office, which he rarely leaves till two o'clock A.M."[1]

After retiring from public office in 1861, he was hired by the California settlers to protect their claims. Eight claims he won out of court. Sixteen he argued before the United States Supreme Court, winning thirteen, compromising another, and losing two. Each case (excepting, strangely, the two he lost, which were very small) involved enormous amounts of land, running as high as 100,000 acres. The fees were commensurate, ranging from $4,000 to $180,000 gold in each case. So by the close of the war he was financially independent and was able to give his time without fee in defense of civil rights.

The Milligan case was his opening gun. It ended military rule in the North. In the next, *ex parte McCardle*, he attempted to end military rule in the South by overthrowing the Reconstruction Acts. Other lawyers twice attempted to bring these acts before the Supreme Court for review but failed.[2] Black, however, planted the review on docket in the McCardle case in face of the ablest legal opposition in the United States Senate and argued it on the same grounds as the Milligan case. The Radicals in Congress, thoroughly alarmed, rushed through a bill without debate and passed it over Johnson's veto, forbidding jurisdiction by the courts on appeals that might be made *or had already been made!*[3] The Supreme Court backed down, declining to render its decision.

His third such case involved the Civil Rights bill and the Thirteenth Amendment. Under these, an attempt was made to transfer from state to Federal courts all crimes to which a Negro was a party or a witness. "Nine tenths of the lower class of crimes committed by negroes, and by white men under protection of negro witnesses, must go unwhipped of justice," he argued. The Supreme Court responded by an opinion that such jurisdiction could not be taken from the states.[4]

The last of these cases in which Black appeared involved the Fourteenth Amendment and were known as the Slaughter House cases. The first section of that amendment had been written "to bring the private life of every citizen directly under the eye of Congress."[5] But the court, in an

---

[1] *Harper's Weekly*, Feb. 19, 1859, p. 119.

[2] *Mississippi v. Johnson*, 4 Wallace 475; and *Georgia v. Stanton*, 6 Wallace 50.

[3] *Congressional Globe*, Fortieth Congress, second session, pp. 1859, 2115–2129, 2165–2170.

[4] The Blyew case, 13 Wallace 590–595.

[5] Charles Warren, *The Supreme Court in United States History* (Boston, 1922), III, 262; John W. Burgess, *Political Science and Comparative Constitutional Law* (Boston, Ginn and Company), I, 325; James G. Blaine, *Twenty Years in Congress* (Norwich, Conn., 1884), II, 419–420.

opinion that it regarded as the most "far-reaching and pervading" during "the official life of any of its present members,"[1] contended that no such transfer of civil rights could be made. This intent of the amendment was thus severed from the Constitution.

So Black, without public office, achieved almost the only success of any man who planted himself across the course of the Radical Congress.

The era of Reconstruction closed with his philippic ringing in the ears of the Hayes-Tilden Electoral Commission because of its partisan eight-to-seven vote on every hearing. Standing defiantly before it, Black spoke the searing words of Isaiah:

"Well may you say: . . . '*With hell are we at agreement; . . . for we have made lies our refuge, and under falsehood have we hid ourselves.*'"[2]

His life ended while he was preparing to defend the Mormons from the ex post facto application of the Edmunds Act on polygamy. To him the most sacred thing in political life was the Bill of Rights; and when he visited England his first act was to stand at Runnymede, on the ground where the *Magna Carta* was wrung from King John.

IV

We come now to the consideration of Black's qualities as a speaker. Always his greatest efforts were before a court.

He was, it is true, an effective political campaigner, sought after by all sections of the country. He was, it is also true, an effective occasional speaker; and his efforts in this direction deserve some attention. At Andrew Jackson's death in 1845 he delivered a eulogy that lifted him from the obscurity of an unknown judge in a mountain district to state-wide attention. David Paul Brown first heard of him through "one of the literati, who had a right to judge," informing him "that the best biography or memoir of General Jackson that was ever produced, was written [that is, delivered] by *one* Black, from the backwoods of Pennsylvania, whom he had never seen, but should always admire."[3]

Again, when John Bannister Gibson died in 1853, after serving 37 years on the Supreme Court of Pennsylvania, Black delivered a eulogy that Niles, himself a legal scholar and careful critic, said "has become a classic in legal literature."[4]

---

[1] 16 Wallace 61.

[2] *Proceedings of the Electoral Commission*, Forty-fourth Congress, second session, Part 4, pp. 190–191; Black, *op. cit.*, p. 620.

[3] Brown, *op. cit.*, II, 109. A copy of this speech may be found in *Essays and Speeches*, pp. 189–205.

[4] Niles, *op. cit.*, p. 403.

Upon the centenary of Grattan's declaration of Irish independence, in 1882, Black addressed a great audience in Baltimore. Although he was past seventy-two years of age, this address in its written form impresses one with its sustained power. Its immediate effect both on the audience and in the press was tremendous.[1] He was begged to address the state centenary meetings in New Jersey and Massachusetts.[2] Centenary meetings in this year were numerous, and many speeches were heard. But among them all, Black's so stood out that the *Catholic World*, four years later, pointed back to it as their epitome and one that would unite Black's memory with that of Irish champions.[3]

Nevertheless, these addresses do not reach the sustained level of George William Curtis's commemorative addresses and perhaps not even of Webster's overrated Bunker Hill addresses. Historians, to be sure, may rank the force of thought in the Grattan centenary address above Wendell Phillips's eulogy on Daniel O'Connell, which covered the same general subject, in that Black developed therein a plan for the self-government of Ireland in harmony with the integrity of the British empire, and did so years before Gladstone outlined his own similar policy of Irish home rule. This address perhaps equals Phillips's eulogy in its strength of style, but it lacks the variety of style and the positive literary touch so marked in all Phillips's efforts.

Nor do these commemorative addresses equal Black's own greatest efforts at the bar. Black was himself well aware of his limitations in this direction. "I do not perform well," said he, "in what rhetoricians call demonstrative oratory."[4]

Because of Black's admitted power as a forensic speaker, however, a minority of his contemporaries sought to disparage his legal learning and to explain his rare success at law wholly in terms of his eloquence. "That he was really a great lawyer," said one critic, "was not so universally admitted as that he was a bold pleader and an eloquent, forcible, and most interesting speaker."[5] He was "a brilliant rather than a profound lawyer," said another. "Whatever he said was invariably so happily put, or aptly illustrated, as to attract attention, be taken up, commented upon, and generally remembered."[6]

This was, of course, a minority view, even among critics. At the other extreme were those who believed "that he belonged to a giant race of

---

[1] *Baltimore Sun*, Apr. 19, 1882, carries a full copy of this speech and discusses its effect at some length. A copy appears also in *Essays and Speeches*, pp. 158–171.

[2] Black Papers, Apr. 28, May 24, 1882.

[3] *Catholic World*, September, 1886, p. 758.

[4] *Hollidaysburg* (Pa.) *Standard*, July 4, 1877.

[5] Editorial, *Philadelphia Press*, Aug. 20, 1883.

[6] Editorial, *Washington National Republican*, Aug. 20, 1883.

lawyers, now almost if not quite extinct; . . . the greatest advocate at the bar . . . since Pinkney."[1]

Black's standing as a lawyer is not here at issue, but the attempt of some critics to explain away his rare success at law in terms of eloquence may be taken as unwilling testimony to his conceded power as a pleader.

The superiority of Black's forensic speaking over his public oratory sprang from inherent causes. To begin with, he was a lawyer, and a lawyer only, in mental outlook. Law was the religion of his life, as sacred as theology. Justice was godliness, "the practical enforcement in daily affairs of the Golden Rule." His views upon the great issues that swayed the passions of the nation—slavery, secession, reconstruction—were undiluted legal views. "Black," said W. H. Trescot in his famous diary on the inside of Buchanan's administration, treated secession as a "question exclusively . . . of constitution law. . . . What is the legal wrong involved in secession, and what is the legal remedy? A question to be solved judicially, not politically."[2]

This sharp legal focus that disqualified him for the highest rank in popular oratory, however, enhanced his powers before the bar. There were, of course, other contributing qualities. He loved a fight without quarter. The courtroom satisfied that side of his nature better than popular audiences. Even out of the courtroom his speeches were purely argumentative. He was a swordsman on the attack. But a swordsman without an adversary becomes a shadow fencer. His highest skill is seen only in parrying the lunges and thrusting behind the defenses of a skilled opponent.

Likewise his mind was severely logical. The final judgment placed upon it by a contemporary critic, A. F. Faust, is not overdrawn: "Persuasive and eloquent as he may appear at times, all the links in the chain of his reasoning are carefully forged and welded together. . . . Every fact, and every argument follow in strictest sequence and when complete, exhibit both a consummate power in art and an unrivalled perfection in presentation."[3]

Logic is a more powerful weapon before judges than before the general public. If one doubts that, he may take a page at random from Phillips or Bryan—then measure its logic beside a page from Webster or Erskine.

Perhaps, also, in the matter of physical endowment, Black was better adapted to the courtroom than to the public platform, although here it is

[1] J. Hubley Ashton, quoted in *Essays and Speeches*, p. 30.
[2] Trescot MSS; quoted in S. W. Crawford, *The Genesis of the Civil War* (New York, 1887), p. 24.
[3] *Catholic World*, September, 1886, p. 759.

not possible to speak with certainty. In person, he was a man of striking appearance, physically large, imposing in manner, marked in features. The "magnetic eye," so fabled among great speakers, he possessed in unusual degree.[1] These are advantages more imposing at close range than long, in a courtroom than upon the platform. On the other hand, although both appearance and voice are high assets to a speaker under all conditions, yet before the multitude a powerful and resonant voice outweighs appearance alone.[2]

As to Black's voice, there is no extant contemporary testimony concerning it. If any conclusion can be drawn from this negative evidence it must be that his voice did not impress friends, reporters, and contemporary biographers sufficiently to produce any written record. Yet John G. Ogle, of Philadelphia and Somerset, 52 years after Black's death stated positively that it was a rich and pleasing baritone, perhaps the most pleasing to which he had ever listened.[3] Half a century is a long time to carry any memory with accuracy, yet Ogle's knowledge of Black's life from personal recollection was surprisingly accurate. On no recollection that could be checked was he in error, and he never hesitated to say "I don't remember," when he was not certain.

On a few occasions, however, Black disappointed large public audiences by not reaching them with the range of his voice. Particularly were there places in the Belknap impeachment trial,[4] and even in his Grattan centenary address,[5] where fringes of the audience missed a few parts of his speech. Whether this was due to his well-drilled habit of talking to the handful of men on the court or to sheer lack of vocal power cannot now be determined. At all events, however rich or pleasing his voice might have been, it probably was not one of extraordinary power.

On the other hand, his manner of speaking, in at least one respect, gave him an advantage over most contemporaries at the bar. He spoke wholly without notes. Many times there would be long decisions to adduce, page references to cite, yet through his long career at the bar one seeks in vain to find a time when he ever stood before a court or jury with notes to sustain his memory. Repeatedly the court, jury, and spectators marveled at his unerring memory in speaking uninterruptedly for two or three hours without a scrap of paper before him—citing decisions even to the

[1] Hensel, *op. cit.*, p. 196; Clayton, *op. cit.*, p. 46; H. C. Niles to the author, Jan. 10, 1930.
[2] No small part of Bryan's triumph in 1896 before the Chicago convention, for example, came from the singular fact that his was the only voice distinctly heard by auditors in every part of the poorly constructed Coliseum.
[3] To the author, June 19, 1935.
[4] *New York Tribune*, July 25, 1876.
[5] *Baltimore Sun*, Apr. 19, 1882.

exact page, reviewing evidence and testimony, reciting poetry, and startling with apt quotations of literature.[1]

Take as an example his argument in the Goodyear Rubber case, where, said a press correspondent, he

spoke for three hours without notes, making one of the most masterful arguments heard for years. . . . He . . . [was] never at a loss for the name of a witness, and quoting his language so accurately, that the opposing counsel in no instance corrected him. He read no law book, but from his vast stores of knowledge cited decision after decision, giving book, title and page. . . . He enriched his argument with illustrations drawn from nature, science, history, the Bible, literature, art and poetry.[2]

As to the method by which Black prepared these speeches, very little is known. His daughter recorded that "in preparing his speeches, he studied through and through upon his subject until his mind was literally saturated with it. When he came to delivery his sentences rolled off his tongue . . . without a scrap of paper to guide him."[3] The Washington, D.C., correspondent of the *Cincinnati Commercial*, after once writing that "Black is a very curious character, full of idiosyncrasies," added that "he prepares most of his arguments at home, walking up and down the floor at night, where he would walk the whole night long if his wife did not appear along toward one o'clock and lead him to bed."[4] Perhaps this correspondent knew; perhaps he was guessing, but his remark is reminiscent of the testimony of many who knew Black intimately.

These facts are scanty, yet taken together with the manner and quality of his speaking, they afford a general idea of his method. It was purely extemporaneous. That is, with all the careful preparation in organization and arrangement, the collecting of legal decisions and assembling of apt quotations from prose and poetry, which his speeches show, they were not written out and memorized. His arguments were too adaptable to the moment, the court, and the opposing counsel; and his repartee was too quick and devastating to have been hampered by frozen manuscripts. Nor is there to be found among his papers even one draft or outline of any speech he ever prepared—although there are many stenographic reports of his speeches as they were actually delivered.

Throughout life he was a prolific controversial writer, engaging at times Stephen A. Douglas, James A. Garfield, Charles Francis Adams,

[1] Hensel, *op. cit.*, p. 195; Levi Maish, *cf.* Clayton, *op. cit.*, pp. 126, 131, 171, 203; newspaper reports, *Clayton MSS.*
[2] Press clipping, *Clayton MSS.*
[3] Clayton, *op. cit.*, p. 126.
[4] Press clipping, *Clayton MSS.*

Henry Wilson, and Robert G. Ingersoll; and in these writings he gained fame as a dangerous adversary. Yet his speeches, as they come unrevised from his lips, are superior in style to his controversial articles that were carefully written and revised. Like the poet and the prophet, he thought more profoundly and phrased more eloquently when impassioned. But with him passion came not in the sequestered calm of the study but in the heat of forensic combat.

His invective was at times compared with that of Swift and repeatedly with that of Junius.[1] It is true he used invective with terrible power, but he used it cautiously in the courtroom. In controversial writing it was his commonplace weapon, for here he delighted to "have at" his victim, and that seemed to be his only goal. Not so when he spoke. Before him was the court, which he, as a former judge, held always in deep respect. He had in view a decision to be won, and he allowed no uncontrolled language to injure his efforts. True, he used invective before courts; but his sarcasm was syllogistic and was seasoned with anecdote until even the victim seldom bore malice.

Toward the court there was a fearlessness in his manner that gained him the reputation of being allowed greater freedom of utterance than any other living man at the bar.[2] Yet basically his attitude toward the court was one of deep respect. He himself was an ex-judge. He revered the judiciary; and he repeatedly made it clear—to use his words in the Milligan argument—that

the highest compliment that has ever been paid to the American bench is embodied in this simple fact: that if the Executive officers of this Government have ever desired to take away the life or the liberty of a citizen contrary to law, they have not come into the courts to get it done; they have gone outside of the courts, and stepped over the Constitution, and created their own tribunals.[3]

Let us come to the qualities that mark Black's style of speech. Consider first his motivation of ideas. He never appealed to mere passions, yet there was always a powerful emotional drive behind his arguments. Indeed, one of his great sources of power sprang from a rare ability to unite argument with the springs of action in human beings. He could premise logic upon impelling motives—self-preservation, progress, honor—things that men live for and at times are willing to die for. When he had finished, not only had he impelled the mind to accept his logic as true but he had aroused emotions to *want* what the mind proclaimed as true. But this was not *argumentum ad populum*. It was logic surcharged. "I make no appeal

[1] *Cf. Albany Law Journal*, 28: 259, for one of these discussions.
[2] *Cf. New York Tribune*, Aug. 20, 1883.
[3] *Essays and Speeches*, pp. 516–517.

to the passions," he said scornfully to the Supreme Court in the Civil Rights argument after they had listened to an address of this sort. "Let the stump and the newspaper do that."[1]

The argument that followed in this case will illustrate the motivation behind his logic. The issue was whether Kentucky or the Federal government had the right to try a murder case in which a Negro was witness to the crime. Black's propositions were simple: (1) The effect of the Civil Rights bill, passed by Congress in 1866, was to abolish the autonomy of the states. (2) Such an act was a "sheer, naked, flat breach of the Constitution." The treatment of these propositions clicks with logical precision, but behind the logic were powerful turbines of emotional drive. He was arguing before the Supreme Court. They were judges, learned in the law; they were high in cultural level, well-versed in history; they were human beings, proud of their country and of its form of government. All these attributes and attitudes he used in applying motivation to his argument. Consider in brief the motivation of argument on the first proposition, that of abolishing the autonomy of states:

The state of Kentucky—and therefore every state of the Union—would be stripped by this law of the power to administer justice, even "to the smallest and the lowest cases." State lines would fade into dark shadows, and Federal prosecutors, like the proconsuls of Rome, would rule with a heavy hand. But the prosecutors went further than proconsuls, for the Empire of the Seven Hills in her most vicious days had never interfered with the local tribunals to the degree that the Civil Rights bill empowered Federal courts. Justice, removed to these distant courts, would leave nine-tenths of the lower class of crimes "unwhipped of justice," until people "graduate in crime from the lowest to the highest, and society is altogether broken up." "The autonomy of a free State is not a thing to be trifled with," and out of Megara and Corinth, Thebes and Athens, he lifted examples of disaster that flowed from such triflings; and fitted them in outline to the disaster that hung over Kentucky, and through her, over all states of the union. But one must read the full score to test the logic and sense the full drive behind it.

It was of this address that Augustus H. Garland, Supreme Court attorney and later Attorney General of the United States, hearing Black for the first time since the Civil War, said: "He not only became his client, but his client's cause; he was wrapped up and lost in it; he moved and acted in it. So great were his earnestness and power of assertion, I . . . fancied I could see the convictions of judges giving away reluctantly before him and surrendering to him as he spoke."[2]

[1] *Essays and Speeches,* p. 541.
[2] *Essays and Speeches,* p. 26.

476

Jeremiah S. Black

Interwoven with this powerful motive drive was a severe and sustained logical structure, described by the correspondent of an unfriendly newspaper as Black's *"surgical ability"* in argument,

> reviewing and analyzing the testimony with searching precision, exposing its weakness, tearing aside the flimsy covering of false pretense, and with scorching sarcasm cauterizing the wounds so mercilessly opened.
>
> The legal propositions seemed uttered with an abrupt consciousness of assured authority, and the points were presented in forcible, jerking, and sinewy sentences, that almost startled from their freshness of style, and absence of accustomed prosy formality.
>
> What appeared most to fix the attention of the court and audience, was the continuous and consistent logic, in which the argument was sustained in all its parts, holding the mind of both with eager and excited interest from the premises to the conclusion.[1]

He also knew well the art of condensation, as comparison of the full court evidence with his arguments will show. "He could," said Senator Edgar Cowan, "pack up the conclusion of a hundred pages of argument in a little bundle no larger than a greenback; and yet the whole was there, every light and shade of meaning."[2]

From this fleeting picture, one may grasp some idea of the broader aspects of Black's style. Cicero lays stress upon two things a forensic speaker should be able to do—delight his audience by wit and move them to tears. The first of these Black could do in a rare degree, but the second was wholly alien to his temperament. He did not, and could not, do it. Yet he could move his audience in a way more effective in modern annals than excitement to tears. He could rouse them to "fight Philip." He did so through a peculiar surcharging of logic with passion and through attaching his arguments to broad and sweeping maxims of law.

We now come to the lesser strokes of style—the management of words, the coining of phrases. He was, said Augustus H. Garland, "A rhetorician without a superior—the best phrase-maker I ever heard—he used the English language after the style of Shakespeare."[3]

Black indeed compounded much of Shakespeare into his language, yet the finished product was not "after the style" of that writer. It more nearly approached the forensic style of Macaulay. Yet it is not Macaulay's. It is Black's own, his personality itself. If any one word can be found to express its quality, that word is *strength*. True, it has beauty of a kind, but it is the rugged beauty of Romanesque architecture; not the slender

---

[1] Washington, D.C., correspondent, *Philadelphia North American*, Jan. 8, 1858, referring to Black's first argument in the California land cases.

[2] Black Papers, Apr. 11, 1884.

[3] Quoted in *Essays and Speeches*, p. 26.

lines or the fine carvings of a Gothic structure. It has a music, too, but it is not the music of the flute that one hears in Burke or yet of the trumpet that resounds from Webster. It is the raw clang of steel on shield, echoing with grim purpose, but it is tempered steel of which Damascus might be proud, and both clang and echo are music of a kind.

As to "phrase-making," Garland was right. Black was indeed a phrase-maker, seldom content with the common currency that serves the purpose of placid men. His phrases were of special mintage, coined with precision, and marked with distinctive hues. This quality, above all others, was the trade mark of his style. In part it sprang from his choice of colorful words and striking figures and in part from the apt and telling quotations of Shakespeare and the Bible that were always at his tongue's tip. They served him even in private conversation, and once, when he had given unwitting offense to a lawyer named Chambers, the apology was instant on his tongue, taken from Othello:

> Haply, for I am *black*
> And have not those soft parts of conversation
> That *chamberers* have.

A sustained example better illustrates his method. During the course of the Goodyear Rubber argument, Black had occasion to disagree with an *obiter dictum*, clung to by the opposing counsel, once made by Judge Grier, who just three days prior had resigned from the Supreme Court bench. Grier, in effect, had said that "we could know nothing of matter, except by its qualities" and that "the matter was new if its quality was changed." Therefore if rubber be changed in its sensitivity to weather, though it still be rubber, yet it was new "matter." Not until one has read the heavy philosophy of Locke, Berkeley, and Hume in the original can he appreciate Black's brilliant phrasemaking summary of this philosophy and his attack upon its soundness.

This [he countered] is specious enough to have received the assent of some great thinkers long before Judge Grier uttered it. The metaphysical philosophy of the last century was full of it. Locke [asserted that] color existed in the eye, the odor of a violet in the nose, and the temperature of a hot iron in the nerves that shrunk from its contact; or, as Butler put it,

> "There's no more heat in the fire that heats you,
> Than there is pain in the stick that beats you."

Berkeley, by the same reasoning, showed the unreality of the primary qualities, and removed the seat of their ideal existence to the mind. . . . It was a dismal theory. It abolished the created universe without restoring the reign of Chaos and old Night. It dissolved all human relations, for the bodies of men were merely "*such stuff as dreams are made of.*" It did not "*strike flat the thick rotundity of the globe,*" but it did worse, for it made it a nonentity. "*This brave o'erhanging firmament, this gorgeous canopy, fretted with golden stars,*" was not even what Hamlet called it, "*a pestilent congregation of vapors*"; it was a huge phantasm, hung on high to cheat and delude us. . . . If you adopt it, you will craze the law, and make it as mad as the metaphysics of Berkeley and Hume.[1]

He did not weary the listener, however, by overuse of quotation and allusion. His description could also be lucid from severe plainness, and always it was within range of the listener's experience. In describing the disputed land grant involved in the New Almaden Quicksilver suit, he remembered that judges on the court knew Latin but not Spanish:

Somewhere in the valley . . . lies a league of land which the government of Mexico granted to Justo Larios. . . . The grant itself describes the location of the land granted. On the south it is "*colindante con la Sierra.*" This word *colindante* has as clear and plain a signification in the Spanish language as any word in any language can have. It is translated by the two Latin words *adjacens* and *contiguus*, which signify *lying next to, touching with.* The etymology of the Spanish word itself shows very clearly what it means. *Linde, lindano, lindero*, are synonymous terms, and mean always a landmark, a boundary. *Co* is the Latin *cum* and the English "with." *Colindante* signifies *coterminous, adjoining.* . . . If Justo Larios had a league of land *colindante* with the mountain, then his land begins where the mountain ceases, and the mountain ceases where his land begins.[2]

In one sense, however, Black's speeches are not the literature claimed for Burke or Webster. There are redundancies on occasion and, more rarely, digressions in the midst of argument. But the digressions flow from interruptions of the opposing counsel or questions from the court. They break the unity of the discourse, yet they add immensely to the immediate effect of the argument. They reveal a speaker ready, on the instant, to meet all obstacles and to turn his argument into whatever channels the moment demands.[3] The redundancies flowed from the inherent nature of extempore speaking. They are the price paid by every speaker who phrases thoughts before an audience. Comparison in this regard with Burke or Webster is impossible, for Burke's masterpieces were perfected upon manuscript; and Webster's were revised *afterward* until slovenly sentences—"caught," as he said, "in the hurry of the moment"—were replaced by smooth and stately periods.[4] Black, upon the other hand, never prepared a manuscript and left to posterity his speeches exactly as uttered. The copies of them are

[1] *Essays and Speeches*, pp. 501–502.

[2] *Ibid.*, pp. 437–438.

[3] *Cf.* New Almaden Quicksilver argument, *ibid.*, p. 456; Goodyear Rubber argument, *ibid.*, p. 503; Milligan argument, *ibid.*, p. 528.

[4] E. P. Whipple, *Great Speeches and Orations of Daniel Webster* (Boston, 1879), p. xxiv.

479

stenographic reports, and among his papers there is not one alteration made to polish the style. The reporting of the McCardle speech was so defective that he repudiated it and undertook to dictate a revised report of what he actually said, but he lost interest before the task was completed and gave up the undertaking.[1] Style with him was not a matter of glitter, grace, and beauty. It was a weapon to win decisions, and when the speech was over, the purpose was served. There was no polishing for the plaudits of posteriority.

Nevertheless, taken as a whole, it was a style always lucid and forceful, and at times brilliant. A discriminating editorial critic commented:

We confess in reading him to a sort of editorial pang, such as Kent avows, with professional pride, in regard to Blackstone's chapter on Contingent Remainders: We read "with mingled emotions of admiration and despair." He makes the most difficult question plain to a child's comprehension. He gives to each familiar topic a novel grace of expression. . . . It is all done, too, with an ease that gives the highest impression of strength and power. He never seems toiling and "spreading himself." . . . It is, to our mind, the perfection of the "*proprie communia dicre.*" Horace might well say "*difficile est.*"[2]

The effect of Black's speaking cannot be passed without comment. Court decisions speak their own language, but there are also other significant indexes. Whenever great cases were pending and famous lawyers had gathered for argument, it was not Evarts, Curtis, Cushing, or even that brilliant and witty Irish American Charles O'Conor, who drew the greatest crowds to the courtroom. It was Black.[3] We "had a crowded court room nearly all day yesterday in anticipation of the argument of Judge Black," noted a Philadelphia reporter; and again, "as though by magic the usually empty court room filled up with listeners" when it was learned that Black was to speak. "Judge Black began his argument about a quarter before one o'clock," noted a reporter before the Pennsylvania Supreme Court, "and when it became known that he was speaking the little room that was left was rapidly filled up."[4]

When he appeared before the Supreme Court of New Jersey, in an attempt to break up the interstate operations of the Pennsylvania railroad ring, an outstate newspaper correspondent wrote:

His argument was listened to throughout with the greatest interest both by the court and the large audience which had collected in the court room. It is ad-

[1] This defective copy, the only copy of the speech now extant, is found in the *Washington National Intelligencer*, Mar. 3 and 4, 1868.

[2] Editorial, *Upper Marlborough* (Md.) *Prince Georgian*, Sept. 4, 1868.

[3] *Cf.* McCardle case, *National Intelligencer*, Mar. 3, 1868, and the Belknap impeachment trial, *New York Tribune*, July 25, 1876.

[4] *Clayton MSS.*

mitted by all who heard him that he gave the death-blow to the case. . . . The great force of his argument lies in the plain and homely way in which he goes to the very pith of the subject, and clears away all the flimsy, sophistical cobwebs which his opponents may have thrown around it. He has a great fund of wit and genuine humor also, and his sallies invariably brought down the house and forced a broad grin and sometimes a hearty laugh from the sedate Chancellor. There is no other subject spoken of in Trenton this afternoon but "Black's great argument." You hear it on the street, in the hotels, and on the fairgrounds, and it is held by all to have settled every phase of this great case.[1]

Justice David Davis's statement that "Judge Black is the most magnificant orator at the American bar"[2] was made in a moment of enthusiasm after Black had completed an argument before the United States Supreme Court. But the statement of Justice David J. Brewer was deliberately weighed and made 16 years after Black's death:

He stood for one of the great forces of minority opinion, seldom strong enough to control by mere weight of impact, but always liable to assert itself in every emergency as a controlling balance of power. . . . As a man and as a lawyer he showed an individuality so marked, and in certain ways so representative, that men of all parties listened to him with an attention they seldom give the official utterance of any public man.[3]

SELECTED BIBLIOGRAPHY

Life

The leading manuscript sources on Black's life are The Papers of Jeremiah S. Black (73 vols., Library of Congress); the Black file of The Papers of James Buchanan (Philadelphia Historical Society of Pennsylvania); and The Papers of Andrew Johnson, for the years 1865–1868 (Library of Congress).

The four-volume collection by Black's daughter, Mary Black Clayton, of newspaper clippings, speeches, and miscellaneous information (Library of Congress) contains invaluable, information. It has been cited above as *Clayton MSS*. Mary Black Clayton, *Reminiscences of Jeremiah Sullivan Black* (St. Louis, 1887) is an appreciation but contains valuable data. Black's so-called memoirs were published in the *Philadelphia Press*, Aug. 7, 14, 21, 28, 1881; and in the *Weekly Press*, Aug. 11, 18, 25; Sept. 8, 1881. These deal chiefly with his part as a Buchanan cabinet member in opposing secession; but supplementary articles in the *Press* on Mar. 16, 1882, Aug. 20, Sept. 10 and 17, 1883, contain more general information.

Valuable short portraits by men who knew Black well are those of David Paul Brown, in *The Forum*, Vol. 2 (Philadelphia, 1856); W. U. Hensel, "Jeremiah Sullivan Black," *The Green Bag*, May, 1890; and Henry C. Niles, "Jeremiah Sullivan Black and His Influence on the Law of Pennsylvania," *Ninth Annual Report of the Pennsylvania Bar Association*, 1903.

Black's decisions as a member of the Pennsylvania Supreme Court are contained in the *Pennsylvania State Reports*, Vols., 17–27; and the summations of cases he argued before the United States Supreme Court are found in *United States Reports*, Vols., 62–109.

[1] A.M.G., *Clayton MSS.*
[2] Hensel, *op. cit.*, p. 194; *Clayton MSS.*
[3] *World's Best Orations* (Chicago, 1899), II, 470.

Secondary material regarding his life is found in every history of the Buchanan and Johnson administrations and in all histories of the Supreme Court covering 1857–1883. W. N. Brigance, *Jeremiah Sullivan Black* (Philadelphia, 1934), is the only full-length biography.

Speeches

The official collection of speeches is *Essays and Speeches of Jeremiah S. Black* (C. F. Black, ed., New York, 1885). Many pamphlet and newspaper copies of speeches also appear in the *Clayton MSS* (Library of Congress, see above). The only copy of the famous McCardle argument before the Supreme Court seems to be in the *Washington National Intelligencer*, Mar. 3 and 4, 1868. This speech was omitted from the official collection of speeches because Black held the stenographer's copy of it to be defective.

The argument in the Belknap impeachment trial is found with its full setting in *Proceedings of the Senate Sitting upon the Trial of William W. Belknap*, Forty-fourth Congress, first session, Part 7, 1876. Those before the Hayes-Tilden Electoral Commission are found in *Proceedings of the Electoral Commission*, Forty-fourth Congress, second session, Part 4, 1877. The many speeches that Black gave in the Pennsylvania Constitutional Convention, 1872–1873, are reported in *Debates of the Convention to Amend the Constitution of Pennsylvania* (Harrisburg, 1873).

The setting and the audience response of the Grattan centenary address, along with the full copy of the speech, are throroughly reported in the *Baltimore Sun*, Apr. 19, 1882.

The most noteworthy speeches are the Milligan argument and the Civil Rights (Blyew) argument, both in defense of constitutional liberty; the Fossatt (or New Almaden Quicksilver) argument involving a civil suit; the eulogy on John Bannister Gibson; and the Grattan centenary address. All are found in C. F. Black, *Essays and Speeches of Jeremiah S. Black*.

16

William M. Evarts

by LESTER THONSSEN

William Maxwell Evarts was born in Boston, February 6, 1818. He was educated in the Boston public schools, Boston Latin School, Yale College, 1833–1837, and Dane Law School, 1838–1839; admitted to the New York bar in 1841; formed law firm following year. He was assistant United States attorney for the southern district of New York, 1849–1853; chairman of New York delegation at Republican convention that nominated Lincoln for the Presidency; candidate for United States Senate in 1861; counsel for the government in privateering cases; American agent in England during crisis when ships were being fitted out for the Confederacy; defense counsel in Johnson Impeachment trial, 1868; United States Attorney General, 1868–1869; helped to organize the Bar Association of the City of New York in 1869; counsel member for United States before Arbitration Tribunal in Geneva, 1872; counsel for Republican party before Electoral Commission in election dispute of 1877; Secretary of State of the United States, 1877–1881; United States Senator, 1885–1891; died in New York City, February 28, 1901.

I

Edward A. Parry once remarked that the great lawyer is like the great actor who for a brief moment occupies the stage, wins applause, then makes his last bow before the curtain falls. "Nothing is so elusive," Parry went on to say, "as the art of acting, unless indeed it be the sister art of advocacy."[1] Perhaps that will explain why the long and at times outstanding public service of William Maxwell Evarts is dismissed today with a few passing remarks in our history textbooks. Not until 1933, when Brainerd Dyer published his excellent work,[2] did the public career of Evarts receive any measure of popular recognition. Since the record of Evarts's life, like that of John Bright, to whom Evarts's son alludes in this connection,[3] is found in his speeches, it will be of interest to examine the addresses and to

---

[1] *The Seven Lamps of Advocacy* (London, 1923), p. 11.

[2] *The Public Career of William M. Evarts* (Berkeley, Calif., 1933). Subsequent quotations from this work are used with the permission of the University of California Press.

[3] *The Arguments and Speeches of William M. Evarts* (Sherman Evarts, ed., New York, 1919), I, ix. Subsequent quotations from this three-volume edition are used with the permission of The Macmillan Company, publishers.

determine what place Evarts should occupy in the records of American oratory.

The nineteenth century produced a full measure of notable public address. The problems growing out of the slavery issue and subsequent Reconstruction measures provided full opportunity for sharp clashes of opinion in the popular assembly and before courts of law. Although Evarts was more actively interested in the law, as a profession, than in politics, the pressure of events forced him to assume an important role in the affairs of the nation. Perhaps his most enduring contributions to the public welfare, apart from his private work as a lawyer, are associated with the issues that gave rise to or grew out of the Civil War.

II

Like many prominent figures, Evarts was the product of a good family background, a severely disciplined education, and an almost unbelievable capacity for hard work. On his father's side he was descended from a family that had come to Connecticut from England during the early part of the seventeenth century. His mother was a daughter of Roger Sherman, a public figure of some renown in Connecticut. Although Jeremiah Evarts, William's father, died when William was but thirteen years of age, he exercised a powerful influence over the boy. Jeremiah Evarts was a religious leader to whom Professor Leonard Woods, of Andover Theological Seminary, ascribed a "*scrupulous and inflexible* integrity."[1] "To that paternal influence," says Brainerd Dyer, "may be attributed in large measure the unquestioned integrity, the respect for religion, the sense of public responsibility, and the world-range of his thinking which marked William M. Evarts' whole life."[2]

That William learned some lessons in speaking from his father is a reasonable conjecture. While not professing to oratorical greatness, his father possessed an eloquence that "was often impressive, and sometimes powerful."[3] Gardiner Spring, one-time pastor of the Brick Presbyterian Church in New York City, said that as a speaker Jeremiah Evarts was "manly and energetic. In deliberative assemblies and in extemporaneous discussion, he was justly celebrated."[4]

"From the time that I was five years old at the primary school," said William Evarts in his speech at the Boston Latin School in 1870, "and then from seven to ten at the ward school, and then onward till I went to

[1] *A Sermon on the Death of Jeremiah Evarts, Esq.* (Andover, 1831), p. 8.
[2] *Op. cit.*, p. 2.
[3] Woods, *op. cit.*, p. 5.
[4] *A Tribute to the Memory of the Late Jeremiah Evarts, Esq.* (New York, 1831), p. 19.

college, I was a schoolboy of Boston."[1] Unrevealing as those words are, they represent about all that is known regarding his early years. However, it is known that from 1828 until 1832 he was a pupil at the Boston Latin School; that in 1832 he studied for a short period under Frederic P. Leverett, a former headmaster of the Latin School; and that in 1833 he entered Yale College.

An examination of the college catalogues of the period reveals the intensive character of the course of study to which Evarts set himself. Each of the college years was divided into three terms. Studies in Greek and Latin figured prominently in all the instruction schedules. Repeated reference is made to Livy, Horace, Homer, Juvenal, Demosthenes, Cicero, Tacitus, and Plato. Chief among the other subjects listed in the instruction schemes were algebra, geometry, trigonometry, history, philosophy, theology, logic, and rhetoric.[2]

Thoroughly classical in character, the schedules of instruction included courses upon which Evarts drew freely throughout his public career. That his respect for the spoken word grew out of this rich college experience can hardly be doubted. Here was a direct contact with some of the better treatises on rhetoric, not to mention the contact with distinguished teachers. Alexander Jamieson's *Rhetoric*, which was used during the second and third decades of the nineteenth century, contains a sentence that might well have been accepted by Evarts as his guiding standard. Jamieson, in commenting on the need for careful training during the formative years, observed: "It is then that he should be taught, that a minute and trifling study of words alone, and an ostentatious and deceitful display of ornament and pomp of expression, must be exploded from his compositions, if he would value substance rather than show, and good sense as the foundation of all good writing."[3] On May 27, 1875, in a speech in defense of Beecher in the celebrated *Tilton v. Beecher* case, Evarts made a remark of a similar nature: "All exhibitory or ostentatious speech has always been foreign to forensic art."[4]

Other direct contacts with rhetorical theory, not to mention the tremendous sweep of the classical studies generally, include Cicero's *De oratore*, to which Evarts referred frequently in later life, and Blair's *Rhetoric*. It is of interest to note the important place that Blair's *Rhetoric* occupied in the curriculum. Introduced about 1785, it remained in use at Yale until the Civil War. In fact, it was accepted for "a longer time than any other

[1] *The Arguments and Speeches of William M. Evarts*, III, 265.
[2] *Cf. Catalogue of the Officers and Students in Yale College*, 1832–1833 (New Haven), p. 24; *Catalogue . . . 1834–1835* (New Haven), p. 24.
[3] *A Grammar of Rhetoric and Polite Literature* (New Haven, 1826), p. iii.
[4] *The Arguments and Speeches of William M. Evarts*, II, 6.

text-book, barring Ames's *Medulla*, the New Testament, and particular editions of Greek and Latin authors."[1]

Perhaps the most important factor in Evarts's rhetorical training was the influence of Chauncey A. Goodrich, who at that time was professor of rhetoric and oratory. The members of the several classes were asked to attend the "private exercises and lectures" under Professor Goodrich, while in addition a formal course of lectures on the "Oration of Demosthenes on the Crown" was given especially for the members of the Senior class. Goodrich made the "Oration on the Crown" the basis of his lectures on the principles of oratory. He also offered a course in modern eloquence, in which, by the method of examples, he attempted "to awaken in the minds of the class that love of genuine eloquence which is the surest pledge of success."[2] Furthermore, his object was to assist the students

in catching the spirit of the authors read, and, by analyzing passages selected for the purpose, to initiate the pupil in those higher principles which . . . have always guided the great masters of the art, till he should learn the *unwritten* rules of oratory which operate by a kind of instinct upon the mind, and are far more important than any that are found in the books.[3]

One other important influence upon Evarts's training in speaking should be mentioned. He had an opportunity to deliver many speeches during his college days. The junior and senior classes engaged in forensic disputations once or twice a week.[4] These speaking activities were conducted before the instructors. Declamations were also delivered frequently before "the Tutors, before the Professor of Oratory, and before the Faculty and students in the Chapel."[5]

Perhaps of greater importance than the regular speaking exercises were the activities into which Evarts entered in the Linonian Literary Society. In this society, which "rests on the love of letters, the cultivation of the imagination, and of the social sympathies, to which literature so truly ministers," Evarts learned much about debate and public speaking. On the one hundredth anniversary in 1853 of the founding of the Linonian Society, Evarts delivered an address in which he paid tribute to its importance: "The valuable benefits which its discipline afforded him (the member of the Society), the full treasury of moral, intellectual and social influences there gathered and ever since attending him, attract his love and gratitude to the scene and the means of these instructions and these delights."[6]

[1] John C. Schwab, "The Yale College Curriculum," *Educational Review*, 22: 7.
[2] *Select British Eloquence* (New York, 1854), p. iii.
[3] *Ibid.*
[4] *Catalogue of the Officers and Students in Yale College*, 1834–1835 (New Haven), p. 25.
[5] *Ibid.*
[6] *The Arguments and Speeches of William M. Evarts*, III, 3.

Evarts closed his college years at Yale by delivering a commencement oration, an honor conferred upon him by virtue of his high scholastic standing. This oration, entitled "Intellectual Independence," contained an appeal for intellectual freedom in political activities—an appeal for a political leadership that would hold fast to high principles and not vacillate with every shift in public opinion. Brainerd Dyer remarks that "through most of his life . . . [Evarts] followed with more than ordinary fidelity the course charted in his commencement oration."[1]

Following his graduation from Yale, Evarts accepted a position to teach Latin in a private school in Windsor, Vt. He also studied law in the office of Horace Everett and in 1838 entered Dane Law School, now the Harvard Law School. After a year of study he left for New York, where, in 1841, he was admitted to the bar. The active career of William M. Evarts was now to begin.

III

It is necessary to bear in mind that the "chief reminders of Mr. Evarts to day are his speeches."[2] Hence it is advisable to turn to such selected addresses as will bring out the chief characteristics of the man's thought and action. From the time Evarts was admitted to the bar until his death in 1901 his primary interest was in the law, but the application of law to politics became an absorbing ambition. Like Daniel Webster, whom he admired, Evarts came soon to command a position of such prominence in public life that his name was frequently mentioned as a Presidential possibility. Brainerd Dyer remarks that the careers of Webster and Evarts "well illustrate the American tendency to ignore the ablest men when awarding the highest political honors."[3]

The earliest speeches of Evarts reveal the close interaction of legal and political aspirations. In 1850, when Evarts was only thirty-two years of age, the compromise measures brought forth a full round of spirited controversy. Among the measures was a provision that made more effective the functioning of the Fugitive Slave Law of 1793. This provision had aroused many people in the North, because it gave virtually "summary remedy" for the return of runaway slaves.

On October 30, 1850, a mass meeting was held at Castle Garden, now the Aquarium, in New York, to offer support to the compromise measures. According to the newspaper report[4] the hall was appropriately draped with mottoes from Jackson and Webster, such as "The Union, it must and shall

---

[1] *Op. cit.,* p. 7.
[2] *The Arguments and Speeches of William M. Evarts,* I, ix.
[3] *Op. cit.,* p. 28.
[4] *New York Herald,* Oct. 31, 1850.

be preserved" and "Liberty and Union, now and forever, one and inseparable." A large audience was in attendance to hear the speeches of James W. Gerard, Edward Sanford, James T. Brady, Charles O'Conor, Ogden Hoffman, and William M. Evarts.

Evarts's speech is of interest, not because it evoked an unusual response at the time, but because it was his "first recorded public utterance."[1] In it he enunciated a principle that in some measure characterized all his subsequent addresses. With regard to the immediate response of his hearers this speech was far from successful. Coming as he did at the end of a long program, Evarts confronted a restless audience. The *New York Herald* reports that he did not finish the speech.[2] At one point in his address a "large portion of the audience, not being able to hear the speaker, here became impatient, and kept up whistling and various noises, so that he was obliged to withdraw."

As a specimen of effective argument, however, this speech merits notice. In the main it is a refutation of the many objections that had been leveled against the Fugitive Slave Law. According to Evarts, nothing that could properly be called an *argument* had as yet been brought against "the validity of the law or the propriety of its enactments." He then proceeded to show that the provisions of the compromise measures affecting slave status were consistent with constitutional obligations in the Act of 1793 and that the argument that the new law abolished trial by jury was of no force because the Act of 1793 had never granted it under such conditions. After elaborating thus upon the theory of the Fugitive Slave Act, Evarts developed the analogy between that law and the one affecting, through treaty agreements between nations, the surrender of deserting seamen. He indicated that although there was no criticism of the operation of the latter, should such objections arise the proper point of attack should be "not upon the law, but upon the treaty stipulation which has made the law necessary. . . ." "So, too, the Fugitive Slave Act finds its place in our statute book, not from any present motive of complacency in its purpose and effect in themselves considered, but as a necessary fulfillment of the antecedent obligation imposed by the Constitution. . . ."

Evarts reduced to the absurd the contention that the act was ex post facto:

It is true that the procedure of the new act is intended to be more efficient towards its object than the previous law has been, but an objection to it as *ex post facto* on that ground would be as reasonable as the complaint of a criminal that a law was *ex post facto* which after the commission of his crime should increase the number of the police, thus diminishing his chances of escape, or enlarge the judicial

[1] *The Arguments and Speeches of William M. Evarts*, Introduction, I, xvii.
[2] Oct. 31, 1850.

force of the tribunals having cognizance of the case, thus accelerating the approach of his trial.

The concluding sections of the address contain the summarizing declarations that reveal not only the guiding principle for this address but also the determining thought for many later presentations. In condemning all types of "forcible resistance" to the proper execution of the act, Evarts remarked that the

supremacy, absolute and universal, of the law, is an essential notion of every organized community, and he who doubts this supremacy strikes at the foundation of society. . . .

Let us, then, be misled from the plain path of duty by no idle clamor, by no specious sophistry; let us know and feel that he who strikes at a law, strikes at *the* law; that he who violates or avoids the obligation of one clause of the Constitution, is faithless to that great charter of our national government, and to the Union of these States, which exists by and under it, and by and under it alone; above all, let no one who loves his country—who reveres the memory of his fathers—who hopes for the happiness of his children—ever doubt or ever forget that as we the citizens of this great republic, acknowledge no superior, and bow to no master but the law, so have we no guardian of our rights, no protector of our liberties, but the law, and that every wound to its *authority*, as surely enfeebles its *protection*.

As a final appeal he outlined the duty of all good citizens:

Let the line be fairly drawn between the foes of public order, the laws and the Constitution—and whatever others may do, let us see to it, that in our breasts the love of country shall reign predominant, and that neither the cold selfishness of politics shall quench, nor the fickle flame of fanaticism shall supplant, its sacred fire.

These citations are important in setting forth Evarts's position, for the Castle Garden speech was used in later years to suggest that Evarts favored slavery. Evarts's son indicated that it was fortunate for an ultimate evaluation of his father's position that this speech came "at the beginning and not at the end of a career."[1] Subsequent speeches dispelled all possible doubt that might have arisen from the first.

The high civic principle to which Evarts appeals in the Castle Garden address is indicative of the man's character. He disliked slavery. But much as that fact might mean emotionally, he suppressed its influence and dwelt mainly upon the logical issues in the case. As a firm proponent of the Union he urgently requested the support of the citizenry in upholding the compromise measures. "His speech," says Brainerd Dyer, "was not a defense of slavery but a defense of the constitutionality of the fugitive slave law."[2]

[1] *The Arguments and Speeches of William M. Evarts*, I, xvii.
[2] *Op. cit.*, p. 25.

Two other speeches, one purely political and the other legal-political, demonstrated unmistakably that Evarts was no friend of the slave system. On April 29, 1856, at the Broadway Tabernacle, in New York, a public meeting was held to hear reports on the activities of the New York State delegates to the Pittsburgh convention of the newly formed Republican party. Although Evarts had not expected to give a formal speech, the inability of several political figures to appear required him to take an important part in the meeting.

His speech dealt mainly with the changes in the status of the slavery question from the Ordinance of 1787 to the Missouri Compromise to the Kansas-Nebraska Act. "We gave once all to Freedom. We gave next half to Slavery. We take away next the half given to Freedom, and there is nothing left for us." While denying that the Republican party maintained sectional ties, Evarts branded the slave system so that no one could in the future honestly accuse him of leaning toward it.

I have no stone to cast at the slaveholder, upon any accusation of a sinful exercise of mastery over the abject population that crouches at his feet, for though each slave owner may have a gyve and a manacle upon the person of each slave, the *system of slavery*, by a terrible retribution, is a gyve and a manacle upon the *whole body* of the society in which it exists. How urgent, then, the obligation upon us to see to it that neither by us, nor through us, nor *over* us, this gyve and manacle are fastened upon any nascent State, any new community.

Another matter of interest, rhetorically, is the introduction of emotional details into the body of the speech. Evarts used logical proof primarily; excursions into the realm of the emotional were not particularly numerous. This passage, growing out of a consideration of whether the statesmen in the South regarded slavery as a domestic or a national institution, is therefore of interest:

Allow me, by way of illustration, to revert for a moment to an incident of the last winter. The unwonted rigor of the season had spanned the Ohio with a *free* bridge. A poor slave-mother, with all the treasure that she had in the world—her children, from a growing boy and playful girl to an infant upon her breast—had passed over that free bridge without let or hindrance, and was on the free soil of Ohio.

The power of the Federal government, under a law of which I have here no complaint to make, pursued that slave-mother to send her back to servitude; and, not able to release herself, she let out the spirit of her child into the free light of heaven, even through the dark portal of death. If it was noble and brave in the stern Sempronius to taunt the Roman Senate with their long debate which of the two they would choose, slavery or death, who shall say it was ignominious in that poor slave-mother, by a quick decision and flashing execution, to determine that question for her posterity. Ah! gentlemen, "one touch of nature makes the whole world kin." And there are many of us who feel a greater pride in sharing the bright red blood that ran through a heart bounding for freedom, under the dark bosom of that poor slave-mother, far greater than in what we have in common with the pale faces of some of the statesmen of the North.

The legal-political speech that further demonstrated Evarts's hatred of slavery dealt with the Lemmon case. In 1852 Mr. and Mrs. Jonathan Lemmon, of Virginia, came to New York on their way to Texas. With them were eight Negroes, slaves under the laws of Virginia. During the temporary stay in New York a writ of habeas corpus was issued inquiring into the causes for detaining the Negroes. In reply to the writ claim was made that the Negroes belonged to Lemmon under Virginia law and that their stay in New York was simply for passage. In the lower court the writ was sustained. The slaves were freed, and through private subscription the former owners were reimbursed. However, the case was appealed. The Supreme Court of New York sustained the lower court's decision, whereupon in 1860 the case was taken to the Court of Appeals. Here Evarts, appearing for the respondent, engaged in a legal battle with O'Conor and won his case.

Evarts's argument in the Lemmon slave case is a model of clarity. Speaking of Evarts's intellectual mastery at the bar, Chauncey M. Depew said that the "mysteries of the most complicated cases seemed simple, the legal difficulties plain, and the solution comprehensible to everybody under his analysis."[1] This speech illustrates admirably well the truth of Depew's remark.

After discussing the importance of habeas corpus proceedings, Evarts set forth the matter before the court:

The only question, then, was, and is, whether the relation of slavery (as described in terms in the return), existing in Virginia, and existing conformably to the laws of Virginia, is a cause for the restraint by our law, of these persons under the dominion of their owners as slaves in New York, during a brief or other stay, under the circumstances detailed in the return, and so as to compel the authority of our State to be actively exerted to maintain and continue such restraint of liberty.

He then went on to show, with abundant legal documentation, that neither state legislation, nor the Federal government nor the "principles of comity" show "legal cause of restraint." In fact, he even demonstrated that statute law of New York specifically declared that "every person *brought* into this State as a slave . . . shall be *free*." In the end the Court of Appeals affirmed the decision of the Supreme Court. Evarts had won a bitter battle

[1] *My Memories of Eighty Years* (New York, 1924), p. 105.

from O'Conor and, incidentally, had established himself as one of the great lawyers of the period.

Because of his legal acumen and speaking ability Evarts was called upon often during the next few years to serve his country in an advisory and professional capacity. But with the possible exception of his work in England during the time when ships were being built for the Confederacy, no contribution of a public nature stands out quite so prominently as his defense of Andrew Johnson in the Impeachment trial. One of few Republicans among the defense counsel, he distinguished himself by presenting the most brilliant and luminous exposition of the entire proceedings.

Evarts's speech on this occasion is of such tremendous length that it can not conveniently be considered here in detail. Extending over parts of four days, it includes a scope of material almost encyclopedic in nature. However, an examination of the argument in Johnson's behalf reveals in bold form three characteristics of Evarts's oratory. The first feature to attract notice is the sweep of the man's learning and the remarkable grasp of details. Perhaps this speech is a particularly suitable specimen in which to examine these items, for, as G. L. Rives indicated, Evarts's oratory "seemed always to gain in dignity and power in proportion to the importance of the cause and the intellectual quality of the tribunal."[1] His was essentially an intellectual appeal. Although he is reported to have had a clear, resonant voice, most observers are agreed that it was the "intellectual qualities he displayed in his forensic career that made him eminent. . . . "[2]

In the speech in defense of Johnson, Evarts reveals a thorough mastery of his subject. Even more, he articulates the subject with broad philosophic principles derived from an intensive study of both ancient and modern literature. The speech abounds in literary allusions aptly drawn from the classics. In fact, it is the literary quality of the production that attracts first notice. While the trial was in progress a reporter for the *New York Times* remarked that "there was a noticeable absence of argument or logic especially adapted to Mr. Johnson's case" but all were agreed that "Mr. Evarts is a brilliant, polished, cultivated, fascinating orator."[3] Brainerd Dyer also concludes that in "concentrated logic Evarts' argument was not the equal of Curtis', but as a literary and philosophic production it was superior."[4]

Another distinguishing characteristic of this address—as well as of others that Evarts delivered—is its extreme length. That the speech in Johnson's behalf was too long seems to be the almost unanimous opinion

[1] *New York Evening Post*, Feb. 28, 1901.
[2] *New York Times*, Mar. 1, 1901.
[3] Apr. 30, 1868.
[4] *Op. cit.*, p. 96.

of the observers. Whereas Evarts had received a full measure of attention during the opening parts of the address, he began to lose the interest when the end seemed to the listeners never to be in sight. Bingham, one of the managers of the prosecution, aptly commented on this point by saying that Evarts's speech presented one lesson, namely, "that the right way and the effectual way by which a man may make his speech immortal is to make it eternal."[1]

Even more significant because it reveals a definite rhetorical characteristic is the fact that Evarts's sentences were, in the main, very long. It was no extension of the truth to call him "the long sentence champion. . . . "[2] Evarts was often reminded of this distinction. When he came to the Senate, Hoar told him "that we should have to amend the rules so that a motion to adjourn would be in order in the middle of a sentence. . . . "[3] Timothy Dwight, in introducing Evarts at a Yale commencement dinner, said simply that "Mr. Evarts will now give us a single sentence." And Evarts immediately replied, "It will be a life sentence."[4]

Although Evarts's sentences were what Thomas Wentworth Higginson called "prolonged and cumulative,"[5] they were not dull. "If, like certain machinery, they were intricate," said Albert Shaw, "there was system rather than confusion in it all, and every word or qualifying phrase had its use and meaning."[6] However, there can be no doubt that the extremely long sentences militated to some extent against the effectiveness of the oral presentation. Because of their elaborate construction many of the sentences are not adapted to the oral medium. While they may read well, they cannot but impress the hearer as being heavy and involved.

One other characteristic deserves mention before closing this reference to the speech in Johnson's defense. That is the wit and humor for which Evarts was deservedly popular. It is freely acknowledged that he "forged the light blades of wit and humor as successfully as he did the weightier weapons of analytical argument and sustained eloquence."[7] Two excerpts from the Johnson defense speech will illustrate the point. From Evarts's speech of the second day, April 29, 1868, comes this section:

It has usually been supposed that, upon actual trials involving serious consequences, forensic discussion was the true method of dealing with the subject, and we lawyers, appearing for the President, being, as Mr. Manager Boutwell has been

[1] Quoted from Dyer, *op. cit.*, p. 92.
[2] "William Maxwell Evarts," *Albany Law Journal*, March, 1901, p. 111.
[3] George F. Hoar, *Autobiography of Seventy Years* (New York, 1903), II, 349.
[4] *Memories of Yale Life and Men* (New York, 1903), pp. 443ff.
[5] *Contemporaries* (Boston, 1899), p. 267.
[6] "The Career of William M. Evarts," *American Monthly Review of Reviews*, 23 (1901): 436.
[7] "William Maxwell Evarts," *Albany Law Journal*, March, 1901, p. 110.

polite enough to say, "attorneys whose practice of the law has sharpened but not enlarged their intellects," have confined ourselves to that method of forensic discussion. But we have learned here that there is another method of forensic controversy which may be called the method of concussion. I understand the method of concussion to be to make a violent, noisy, and explosive demonstration in the vicinity of the object of attack, whereas the method of discussion is to penetrate the position, and if successful to capture it. The Chinese method of warfare is the method of concussion, and consists of a great braying of trumpets, sounding of gongs, shouts, and shrieks in the neighborhood of the opposing force which rolled away and the air clear and calm again, the effect is to be watched for. But it has been reserved for us in our modern warfare, as illustrated during the rebellion, to present a more singular and notable instance of the method of warfare by concussion than has ever been known before. A fort impregnable by the method of discussion, that is, penetrating and capturing it, has been on the largest scale attempted by the method of concussion, and some two hundred and fifty tons of gunpowder in a hulk moored near the stone walls of the fort has been made the means and the occasion of this vast experiment. Unsatisfied with that trial and its result, the honorable manager who opened this case (Mr. Butler) seems to have repeated the experiment in the vicinity of the Senate. The air was filled with epithets, the dome shook with invective. Wretchedness and misery and suffering and blood, not included within the record, were made the means of this explosive mixture. And here we are, surviving the concussion, and after all reduced to the humble and homely method of discussion, which belongs to "attorneys whose intellects have been sharpened but not enlarged by the practice of law."

The second passage is well known to all. Boutwell, in a moment of rhetorical extravagance, had charged that Johnson's crime was so serious that if the "earth were capable of the sentiments and emotions of justice and virtue," it would heave "this enemy of two races of men" into that space "in the southern heavens, near the southern cross . . . which the uneducated call the hole in the sky." "The hole-in-the-sky" allusion has become almost a part of our historical tradition. During the course of his argument on April 29, Evarts made his equally well-known reply:

I may as conveniently at this point of the argument as at any other pay some attention to the astronomical punishment which the learned and honorable manager, Mr. Boutwell, thinks should be applied to this novel case of impeachment of the President. Cicero, I think it is, who says that a lawyer should know everything, for sooner or later there is no fact in history, in science, or of human knowledge that will not come into play in his arguments. Painfully sensible of my ignorance, being devoted to a profession which "sharpens and does not enlarge the mind" I yet can admire without envy the superior knowledge evinced by the honorable manager. Indeed, upon my soul, I believe he is aware of an astronomical fact which many professors of that science are wholly ignorant of. But nevertheless, while some of his honorable colleagues were paying attention to an unoccupied and unappropriated island on the surface of the seas, Mr. Manager Boutwell, more ambitious, had discovered an untenanted and unappropriated region in the skies, reserved, he would have us think, in the final councils of the Almighty, as the place of punishment for convicted and deposed American Presidents.

At first I thought that his mind had become so "enlarged" that it was not "sharp" enough to discover the Constitution had limited the punishment; but on reflection I saw that he was as legal and logical as he was ambitious and astronomical, for the Constitution has said "removal from office," and has put no limit to the distance of the removal so that it may be, without shedding a drop of his blood, or taking a penny of his property, or confining his limbs, instant removal from office and transportation to the skies. Truly, this is a great undertaking; and if the learned manager can only get over the obstacles of the laws of nature the Constitution will not stand in his way. He can contrive no method but that of a convulsion of the earth that shall project the deposed President to this infinitely distant space; but a shock of nature of so vast an energy and for so great a result on him might unsettle even the footing of the firm members of Congress. We certainly need not resort to so perilous a method as that. How shall we accomplish it? Why, in the first place, nobody knows where that space is but the learned manager himself, and he is the necessary deputy to execute the judgment of the Court.

Let it then be provided that in case of your sentence of deposition and removal from office the honorable and astronomical manager shall take into his own hands the execution of the sentence. With the President made fast to his broad and strong shoulders, and, having already essayed the flight by imagination, better prepared than anybody else to execute it in form, taking the advantage of ladders as far as ladders will go to the top of this great Capitol, and spurning then with his foot the crest of Liberty, let him set out upon his flight while the two houses of Congress and all the people of the United States shall shout, "*Sic itur ad astra.*"

But here a distressing doubt strikes me; how will the manager get back. He will have got far beyond the reach of gravitation to restore him, and so ambitious a wing as his could never stoop to a downward flight. Indeed, as he passes through the constellations, that famous question of Carlyle by which he derides the littleness of human affairs upon the scale of the measure of the heavens, "What thinks Boötes as he leads his hunting dogs up the zenith in their leash of sidereal fire?" will force itself on his notice. What, indeed, would Boötes think of this new constellation?

Besides, reaching this space, beyond the power of Congress even " to send for persons and papers" how shall he return, and how decide in the contest, there become personal and perpetual, the struggle of strength between him and the President? In this new revolution, thus established forever, who shall decide which is the sun and which is the moon? Who determine the only scientific test—which reflects the hardest upon the other?

Little wonder that J. Hampden Dougherty, in a speech before the law department of Brooklyn Institute on October 28, 1901, commented on the "solidity and massiveness of . . . [Evarts's] intellect in argumentation and . . . the ease and readiness with which he could draw from the armory of debate the lighter weapons of wit and sarcasm."[1]

Before arriving at any definite conclusions regarding Evarts's speaking skill it will be necessary to examine a specimen of his commemorative oratory. And it is of interest to note that Evarts did a great deal of occasional speaking. Perhaps the most important work in this field was the delivery of the "Centennial Oration" in Philadelphia, on July 4, 1876. To be chosen the principal orator was a signal honor. It indicated the esteem in which the man was held.

Evarts considered this assignment both important and difficult. His son speaks of a conversation with Joseph H. Choate, Evarts's partner in the law firm, in which Choate remarked: "I never understood why your father was so nervous about his centennial oration. I remember well how he said to me in all seriousness 'You must come down to Philadelphia and sit near me on the platform, and if I should break down in the delivery, you can finish from the manuscript.'"[2] The speech, as has just been indicated, was written in full and delivered from manuscript. This was not Evarts's usual practice. Sherman Evarts says it was his father's habit to prepare a speech by "making brief notes of headings and topics" and then using those references as speaking guides.[3] It is reported that shortly before the oration was delivered an anxious inquirer asked how long the speech would be. Evarts replied: "I spoke for four days in the Johnson Impeachment Trial, two days before the Geneva Tribunal and for eight days in the Beecher trial; no limit of time has been set for my centennial oration, but there is an implied understanding that I shall get through before the next centennial."[4]

The conditions under which Evarts spoke at the celebration were not favorable. It was hot, and the program was long. Furthermore, the physical setup for the event was faulty. A platform large enough to accommodate 4,000 guests had been built in front of Independence Hall. Other thousands assembled in the square. Without benefit of the amplifying systems that today make such performances relatively easy, Evarts was called upon to address this large group. That he had some difficulty in making himself heard in all parts of the assembly is evident from the reports.

Evarts's speech, entitled "What the Age Owes to America," opens with a reference to the occasion and the subject. The first part of the discussion bestows praise upon the Revolutionary fathers for having established a new kind of state. " . . . at one breath, 'independence and union' were declared

[1] Pamphlet, "William M. Evarts, Lawyer and Statesman," pp. 31ff.
[2] *The Arguments and Speeches of William M. Evarts*, III, 95.
[3] *Ibid.*, III, 264.
[4] *Ibid.*, III, 95.

and established. The confirmation of the first by war and of the second by civil wisdom was but the execution of the single design which is the glory of this great instrument of our national existence to have framed and announced." In comparing the American Revolution with the Puritan revolution in England and the French Revolution, he remarked:

A glance at the fate of the English essay at a commonwealth, which preceded, and to the French experiment at a republic, which followed our own institution "of a new State of a new species," will show the marvelous wisdom of our ancestors, which struck the line between too little and too much; which walked by faith indeed for things invisible, but yet by sight for things visible; which dared to appropriate everything to the people which had belonged to Caesar, but to assume for mortals nothing that belonged to God.

The second section of the oration deals with a comparison of "our age with that of our fathers, our structure with their foundation, our inter-vening history and present condition with their faith and prophecy." An examination of the social, political, economic, and spiritual forces in the nation leads him to conclude "that the original principles of equal society and popular government still inspire the laws, live in the habits of the people, and animate their purposes and their hopes." "Unity, liberty, power, prosperity—these are our possessions today."

Evarts then concluded the address with this peroration:

Time makes no pauses in his march. Even while I speak the last hour of the receding is replaced by the first hour of the coming century, and reverence for the past gives way to the joys and hopes, the activities and the responsibilities of the future. A hundred years hence the piety of that generation will recall the ancestral glory which we celebrate to-day, and crown it with the plaudits of a vast population which no man can number. By the mere circumstance of this periodicity our generation will be in the minds, in the hearts, on the lips of our countrymen at the next centennial commemoration, in comparison with their own character and condition and with the great founders of the nation. What shall they say of us? How shall they estimate the part we bear in the unbroken line of the nation's progress? And so on, in the long reach of time, forever and forever, our place in the secular roll of the ages must always bring us into observation and criticism. Under this double trust, then, from the past and for the future, let us take heed to our ways, and while it is called to-day, resolve that the great heritage we have received shall be handed down through the long line of the advancing generations, the home of liberty, the abode of justice, the stronghold of faith among men, "which holds the moral elements of the world together," and of faith in God,which binds that world to His throne.

This oration is severe in its organization. It contains four distinct parts: an introduction by reference to the occasion and the subject, an appraisal of the work and wisdom of the Revolutionary fathers, a comparison of the conditions in America in 1776 and 1876, and a peroration. Each part is introduced by clear-purpose statements; each section is closed with appropriate summarizing declarations. Although the speech is in no sense of the forensic type, the structure is as sharply defined and logically continuous as might be found in the most methodically prepared brief. The clarity in structure marks not this speech alone; it is an unmistakable characteristic of all of Evarts's recorded utterances. While the development of topical leads may in many cases become involved and perhaps too much extended, there is no evidence to suggest even a trace of confusion in thought.

The "Centennial Oration" reveals what Burke would no doubt have called a respect for the ancestors. Relatively free from anything that partakes of criticism, the discourse is distinguished by its note of reverence for the public figures who made possible our governmental structure. Its character is essentially intellectual. Direct appeals to the emotions are rare, as they were in most of Evarts's speeches. However, the sentences, characterized as they are by considerable length and by a free sprinkling of adjectives, have a flowing quality and rhythmic movement that in themselves have emotional value. But those are indirect and, perhaps for that reason, very effective motivating instruments. However, the philosophic nature of the speech with its appeal to authority and order—principles upon which Evarts's life was grounded—places it on a high intellectual plane. It is a speech characterized more by brilliance of thought and nobility of conception than by nonrational appeal or pictorial effect.

IV

The foregoing sections have outlined briefly the more important facts dealing with the development of the speaking ability of William Maxwell Evarts and have surveyed a number of speeches that representatively embody the principal characteristics of his oratory. It has been seen that much of his public performance as well as some of his private work in the law dealt with the issues giving rise to or growing out of the Civil War. A lawyer by profession and interest, thoroughly trained in classical literature, calm and self-possessed, even to the point of egotism, brilliantly lucid in his thinking, lacking in the popular appeal that brings many public figures to the top, Evarts presents to the student of oratory a fine example of the intellectual, philosophic speaker.

He respected the art of oratory. Eloquence, he said in his Linonian Society oration, "is a weapon, and its effect depends chiefly on the force and skill to use it. In public life, this force is character, this skill is civil prudence, and when the bright weapon of oratory is thus wielded, we may limit neither our admiration nor its power."[1] But when oratory

is used for exhibition, or lent to the service of mere dexterous cunning, or, double-tongued, pleads in public controversies for the private fee of office or emolument, or . . . stoops to the tricks of acting and buffoonery, or feeds the unholy fires of faction and sedition, we may yield an unwilling tribute to perverted talents, but no such homage as gives power over will and action. Such orators, in ever-changing shapes, are all varieties of the Homeric type, Thersites, who embodies talent without character; and in every scene of epic action, they will effect no more than their great original.[2]

Evarts's speeches testify eloquently to a close union of talent and character. They give intelligent dignity to the spoken word.

SELECTED BIBLIOGRAPHY

Addresses Delivered February 17, 1920, *and Historical Sketch Prepared to Commemorate the Semi-centenary of the Association of the Bar of the City of New York.*

Annual Reports of the Association of the Bar of the City of New York.

The Arguments and Speeches of William M. Evarts, Sherman Evarts, ed., 3 vols., New York, The Macmillan Company, 1919. The most valuable contribution to the study of Evarts's speaking activities. Contains the most accurate texts of addresses, in addition to personal observations and notes by Evarts's son. In this paper all quotations from speeches are made from these texts.

Autobiography of Andrew Dickson White, 2 vols., New York, The Century Company, 1905.

Autobiography of Thurlow Weed, Harriet A. Weed, ed., 2 vols., Boston, Houghton Mifflin Company, 1883.

Barrows, Chester L.: *William M. Evarts—Lawyer, Diplomat, Statesman,* Chapel Hill, University of North Carolina Press, 1941.

Bigelow, John: *Retrospections of an Active Life,* 5 vols., New York, Baker & Taylor Co., 1909.

Catalogue of the Linonian Society of Yale College, New Haven, Hitchcock and Stafford, 1841.

Catalogue of the Officers and Students in Yale College, 1832–1833; 1834–1835; 1836–1837.

Depew, Chauncey M.: *My Memories of Eighty Years,* New York, Charles Scribner's Sons, 1922.

Dougherty, J. Hampden: "William M. Evarts, Lawyer and Statesman," *pamphlet,* New York, Evening Post Job Printing Company, 1901.

Dwight, Timothy: *Memories of Yale Life and Men,* New York, Dodd, Mead & Company, Inc., 1903.

Dyer, Brainerd: *The Public Career of William M. Evarts,* Berkeley, University of California Press, 1933. A thorough study. Places considerable emphasis upon the rhetorical aspects of Evarts's public work. Contains excellent bibliography.

Goodrich, Chauncey A.: *Select British Eloquence,* New York, Harper & Brothers, 1852.

Hale, Edward Everett: *Memories of a Hundred Years,* 2 vols., New York, The Macmillan Company, 1902.

Higginson, Thomas Wentworth: *Contemporaries,* Boston, Houghton Mifflin Company, 1899.

Hoar, George F.: *Autobiography of Seventy Years,* 2 vols., New York, Charles Scribner's Sons, 1903.

[1] *The Arguments and Speeches of William M. Evarts,* III, 27.
[2] *Ibid.,* III, 27f.

Jamieson, Alexander: *A Grammar of Rhetoric and Polite Literature*, 4th ed., New Haven, A. H. Maltby and Company, 1826.

Lodge, Henry Cabot: *Early Memories*, New York, Charles Scribner's Sons, 1913.

Martin, Edward Sandford: *The Life of Joseph Hodges Choate*, 2 vols., London, Constable & Company, Ltd., 1920.

Proceedings of the Centennial Anniversary of the Linonian Society.

Reminiscences of Carl Schurz, 2 vols., New York, McClure Company, 1907.

Scott, Henry W.: *Distinguished American Lawyers*, New York, Charles L. Webster and Company, 1891, pp. 341–350.

Shaw, Albert: "The Career of William M. Evarts," *The American Monthly Review of Reviews*, April, 1901, pp. 435–440.

Sherman, John: *Recollections of Forty Years*, 2 vols., Chicago, Werner and Company, 1895.

Sketches of Yale College, by a member of that institution, New York, Saxton and Miles, 1843.

Spring, Gardiner: *A Tribute to the Memory of the Late Jeremiah Evarts, Esq.*, New York, Sleight and Robinson, 1831.

Stoddard, Henry L.: *As I Knew Them*, New York, Harper & Brothers, 1927.

Stokes, Anson Phelps: *Memorials of Eminent Yale Men*, 2 vols., New Haven, Yale University Press, 1914.

Tracy, E. C.: *Memoir of the Life of Jeremiah Evarts, Esq.*, Boston, Crocker and Brewster, 1845.

Watterson, Henry: "*Marse Henry*," 2 vols., New York, Doubleday, Doran & Company, Inc., 1919.

"William Maxwell Evarts," *The Albany Law Journal*, March, 1901, pp. 107–112.

Woods, Leonard: *A Sermon on the Death of Jeremiah Evarts, Esq.*, Andover, Flagg and Gould, 1831.

Index

Volume I includes pages 1 to 500;
Volume II includes pages 501 to 992

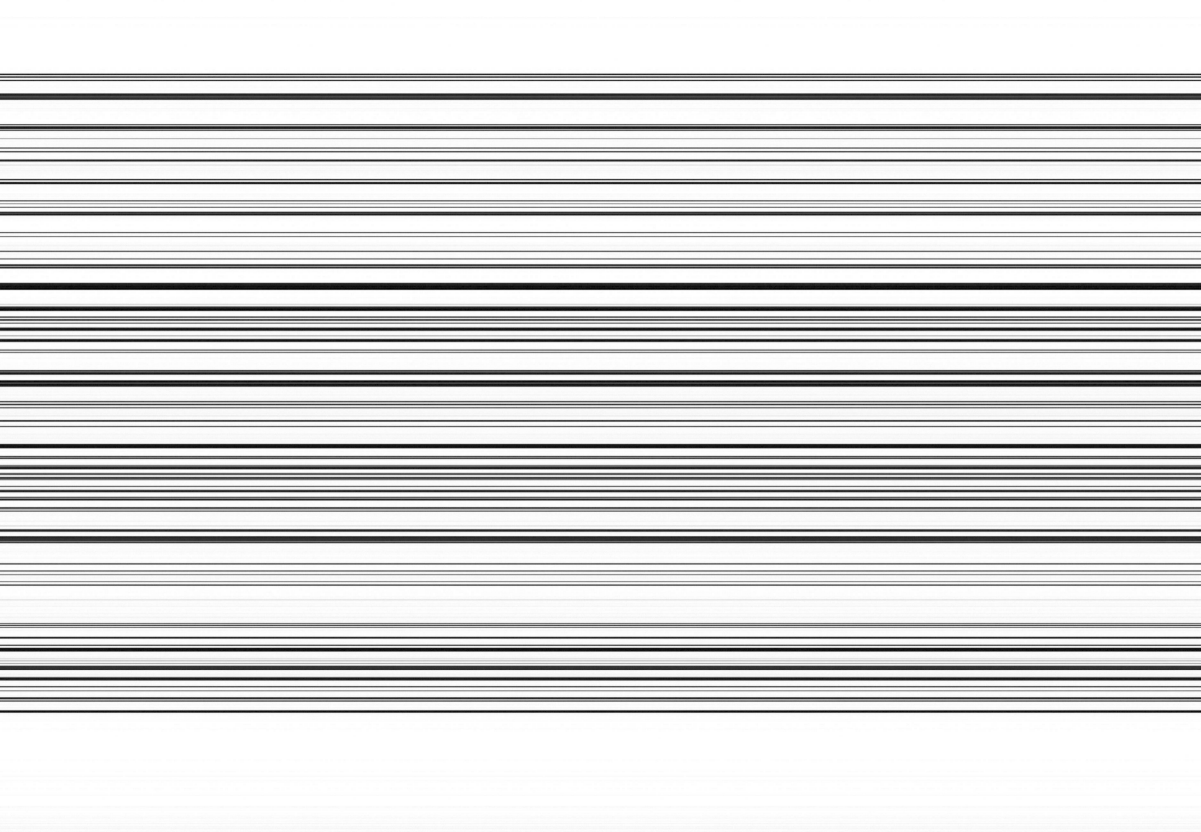

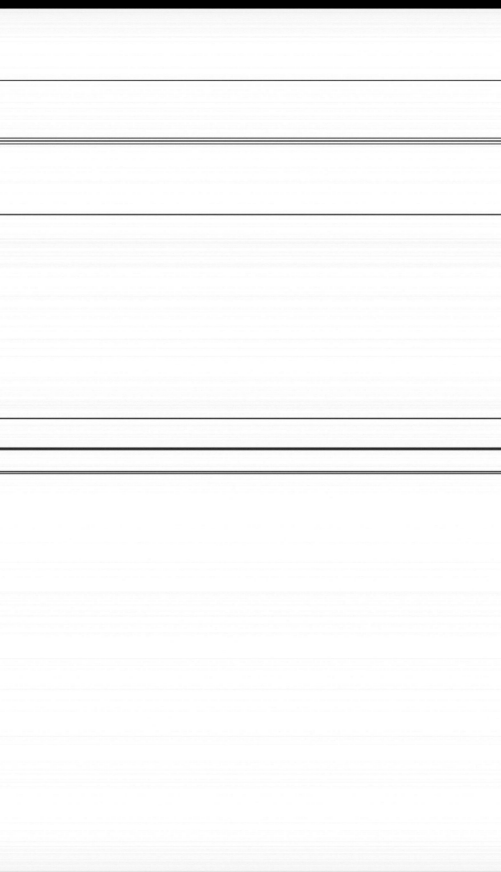

Y

Z